Divide and Perish

Second Edition

By

Curtis F. Jones

authorHOUSE®

AuthorHouse™
1663 Liberty Drive
Bloomington, IN 47403
www.authorhouse.com
Phone: 1-800-839-8640

First published by AuthorHouse   05/19/2011

ISBN: 978-1-4634-1013-1 (sc)
ISBN: 978-1-4634-1012-4 (ebk)

Printed in the United States of America

To Fallen Colleagues

Preface to the Second Edition

Americans have incontrovertible reason to be patriotic, but those who carry patriotism to the extreme of my-country-right-or-wrong seem incapable of recognizing that some American actions are partial enough to provoke retaliation in any form the infuriated victims can devise.

On September 11, 2001, over 3000 Americans died in a clandestine strike by a Middle Eastern cabal, mostly Saudi, operating independently of any government. In a historical blink of an eye, Washington overescalated the episode into simultaneous wars against two states that had little to do with each other, and nothing to do with the attack. One of them is not even in the Middle East.

For this unnatural turn of events, we can blame three patriotic folk-narratives: 1) After years of painstaking effort by the benevolent superpower to save the developing world from stultification, brutality, and misery, America was the last country to deserve such barbaric conduct; 2) No one should misconstrue America's campaign for world peace as diffidence in fighting for its rights — above all, the sacrosanct security of the homeland; 3) America cannot be held responsible for the collateral consequences of its self-defense.

The double standard embodied in these sophistic mindsets is apparent to informed observers, undoubtedly including Barack Obama. A totally objective calendar of remedial action was inevitably inhibited by the political restrictions on his office. The unwieldy ship of state cannot make nimble course adjustments. Consensus holds that his determination to accelerate withdrawal from the Iraqi quagmire, without activating the "liberal wimp" chorus from the war hawks, led him to make a snap commitment to escalation in the Afghan quagmire – a commitment that may come back to haunt him.

While the Europeans, the Chinese, and even the Russians are focusing most of their energies on the sensible enterprise of political and economic consolidation at home, America had lost itself in the anachronistic practice of imperialism and its obsession with the impossible exercise of determining the political realities in other countries (George Kennan's warning), and suppressing opposition, particularly in the Middle East. Washington is making in Afghanistan the same mistake it made in Iraq – fighting a "preventive" war against a hypothetical threat (resurgence of Al Qaʻidah).

Washington is pursuing the archaic alchemy of divide and rule, which would condemn our adversaries to the opposite path of divide and perish. We reject that destiny for ourselves; how can we recommend it to any of our neighbors on the planet?

Thesis

Comprehensive review of 5000 years of the history of the peoples that have inhabited southwest Asia and the adjoining corner of Africa indicates that these areas comprise a discrete segment of the planet that is irrevocably conjoined by valleys, plateaus, routes, and rivers, while separated from neighboring lands by deserts, seas, and mountain ranges.

The geographic coherence of the region thus delineated has imparted to its inhabitants an overlay of cultural and political commonality. It has a geopolitical identity that has received conventional recognition in the appellation, the Middle East.

Any foreign policy formulated in disregard of this identity is doomed to fail. In the opinion of the author, since World War II American policymakers have fallen deep into this geopolitical trap, costing the United States a high price in frustration, wealth, and lives.

Transliteration

Most foreign words and names are spelled as they appear in the *Encyclopaedia Britannica,* Fifteenth Edition, 1995. Aside from established spellings of place and author names, Arabic words and names are spelled in accordance with the system established by the United States Board of Geographic Names, wherein the guide is printed text, not pronunciation (which is subject to dialectal variation). Some Iraqi names contain a borrowed (from Turkish?) ch – as in much – which is customarily represented in Arabic text as a triple-dotted jim; the borrowed p may be represented by two dots under a ba'.

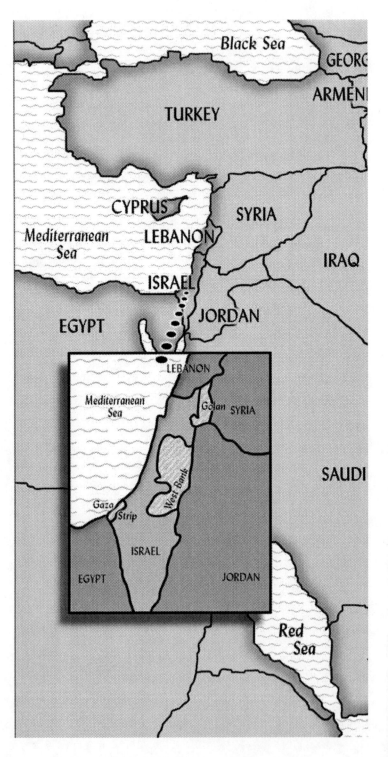

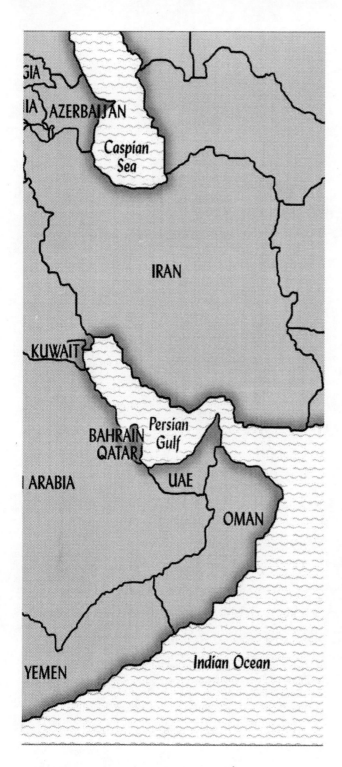

Table of Contents

Chapter 1
The Dictates of Geopolitics

Humanity lives in tension. That tension is summed up in the term geopolitics. "Geo" – the Earth – has a fixed surface area. "Politics" – the interaction of the people who live on it – is never fixed, and their number is generally on the increase. The resultant competition for living space takes place in four interactive arenas: political, economic, military, and cultural.

Since the focus of this book is the Middle East, not the science of geopolitics, this chapter has a limited objective: To present a summary plausible enough to serve as a conceptual matrix into which Middle Eastern events can be instructively integrated. Since this text lays no claim to legal or ethical expertise, it avoids judgmental terms like "aggression" in favor of neutral ones like activism or expansionism. It does cite legal opinions from authoritative sources.

The Environment

As human society has evolved, the operative unit of competition has escalated from family to tribe to nation to state to continental power. In this discussion, nation is used to mean a community unified by one or more common elements, such as origin, lineage, history, sect, or language. State is used for a community whose affairs are directed by a government accorded official recognition by other governments. A state may comprise one nation (Japan) or several (Russia).

Relations among states are herein termed international, in deference to convention, and to avoid the ambiguous connotation of "interstate". The parallel between international competition and the vastly greater

1

complexity of inter-species competition was noted by German geographer Friedrich Ratzel. The term geopolitics was coined, in a narrow sense, by Swedish political scientist Rudolph Kjellen during World War I.

Of a global surface approximating 197 million square miles, one-fourth is land, and one-fifth of that is virtually uninhabitable. For practical purposes, the units of human society are in competition for access to some 40 million square miles, distributed among six "continents" and countless islands, large and small.

The Societal Trade-off

Scholars from Aristotle to Toynbee have recognized that man is a social animal. Affiliation with a group is the best guarantee of survival. However, it imposes a trade-off between the security provided by the group, and the price in freedom of action paid by the individual.

As the operative unit of society has risen in size and complexity on the evolutionary ladder, some participants have become preoccupied with maximizing their freedom, others their security. American history features a memorable example of each sentiment: George Washington is revered as the liberator; Abraham Lincoln commands equal veneration as the unifier.

In each case, geography may have dictated the outcome. Monarchist England, much stronger than the Thirteen Colonies, was handicapped by the logistic complications posed by 3,000 miles of ocean. The cost of sending more and more troops across the Atlantic was reportedly driving the country into intolerable debt. In the American Civil War, the juxtaposition of unionists and secessionists on the same accessible landmass militated in favor of unionist victory.

Anarchy at the Top

In the year 2010, the evolution of political systems stops well short of world government. The operative unit in global politics is the state. International relations are inherently anarchic. There is a global economy and a global society, but no global polity. In its absence, the security of any state tends to equal the insecurity of its rivals.

Security is a function of power. In international affairs, power is a state's ability to influence the activities of other states. Politics – local, state, and international – is a struggle for power. Power is always limited; no actor is omnipotent. But nations are compelled by their very existence to a relentless drive to acquire it. Power is an essential ingredient at every level of human organization. The struggle for power is universal in time and space.

The truism "nature abhors a vacuum" applies no less to society than to physics. A vacuum of power will inevitably be filled. Any locus of vacuum is doomed to turmoil. Subsequent chapters will demonstrate that this principle is currently operative in the Middle East, which has been the site of a power vacuum since the collapse of the Ottoman Empire in the 1800's.

The Urge to Expand

In the global contest for survival, every major competitor is instinctively expansionist, since expansion is the best insurance against the encroachment of rivals. The fuel of expansion is power. (As if the science of international relations is not complex enough, English semantics imposes two different political uses of the word power: 1) the competitive potential of any protagonist; 2) any state that stands high in the roster of competitors.)

Shifting to the second usage of the word, we see that the immediate objective of any great power is to establish hegemony (control) over its own neighborhood. The broader the area of control, the better. When the United States annexed the Hawaiian Islands in 1900, the action seemed like a blatant case of usurpation, but forty years later, it seems to have benefited both parties by facilitating the American military campaign against Japan – notably the crucial victory in the battle of Midway, June 3-6, 1942.

So far, no great power has achieved the putative ultimate guarantee of its security – hegemony over the entire globe. In issuing in September 2002 a policy statement entitled "The National Security Strategy of the United States", the administration of George W. Bush seemed to adopt that hubristic objective.

Expansion commonly takes either of two basic forms: imperialism or colonialism. The paradigm of imperialism in modern times was established by Britain, which brought enough countries into its sphere to create an empire on which "the sun never set." It had lasting effects on both rulers and subjects. The demography of England was transformed by immigration from onetime dependencies. Conversely, the dependent societies acquired British attributes; the multilingual peoples of India have found English an invaluable lingua franca.

In essence, however, the two parties to empire remained separate. There was no determined initiative to incorporate any of the dependencies into the British polity – not even those largely populated by migration from the British Isles (like the Thirteen Colonies). Imperial ties were severed worldwide after World War II without intrinsic repercussions to Britain.

History tells us that imperialism is not a viable long-term policy. Sooner or later, the occupied country will expel the occupiers. Colonialism, however, is usually permanent. Its most momentous example was accomplished by the United States. Operating under the gospel of Manifest Destiny, and facilitated by demographic and technological advantage over the Native Americans and the Mexicans, the thirteen founder states needed less than a century to annex and assimilate nearly four million square miles of North America.

In the communalist cauldron of the Middle East, assimilation is a challenge that continues to bedevil the politics of the region. The most intractable problem of all is posed by the two segments of Palestine occupied by Israel in 1967. The West Bank is presently divided between areas appropriated for Jewish settlement (colonialism), and areas in which the preponderance of Arab residents is so great that Israel can maintain its hegemony only by outright imperialism – the control of one country, or society, by another.

From Expansionism to War

In an anarchic world, conflict is inevitable. It takes many forms, but if conciliation or nonviolent coercion fails, the parties turn to violence. Archaeologists have unearthed evidence that mankind has always engaged in war, often brutal, in prehistoric times even cannibalistic.

In the internal affairs of a state, whoever holds the baton of power calls the tune. At the national level, governments survive by the "legitimate" use of violence. International violence always risks crossing the threshold of war. As political entities have evolved in size and complexity, the scope, intensity, and duration of armed conflict have escalated. According to Robert Pinsky, the world has been "entirely at peace" for only eight percent of its recorded history.

Most analysts dismiss the thesis that mankind goes to war because it is innately evil; war is a natural consequence of the struggle for survival. "The state makes war, and war makes the state" : (Charles Tilly). No war goes on forever. Sooner or later, one side will prevail, or both will desist from exhaustion. Meanwhile, war feeds on itself. In the words of Desmond Morris, "Nothing ties tighter the in-group bonds than an out-group threat." The line between self-defense and expansionism is so indistinct that no international organization has achieved a consensus on the definition of aggression (an operative term in Article 39 of the UN Charter).

In any given era, some parts of the world are politically stable – relatively violence-free – but where hegemony is in dispute, turbulence rules until one or more parties to the power struggle prevails. The ideal would be to complete the progression from turbulence to stability with a minimum of violence. The reality is generally centuries of recurrent war, as in Europe until recent times, and in the Middle East still.

The Evolution of International Organization

There is no apparent *deus ex machina* to mediate human affairs. Humans are hard-pressed to marshal conclusive evidence of the existence of the overarching moral law in which most people devoutly believe. Traditionalist devotees of the three "religions of the book" share a belief in a God who plays favorites, but they disagree on which faith enjoys that favor. Geopolitics draws no such distinction. The only ostensible criterion of performance is survival. To this end, combatants are tempted to jettison all empathy for the adversary – to lose themselves in a mindless battle between "good and evil".

Nevertheless, with or without extra-human help, humanity has made demonstrable progress in lifting itself up by its own ethical bootstraps. According to Konrad Lorenz, writing in *On Aggression,* evolution is not irrevocably red in tooth and claw; it engenders instincts that control intraspecific aggressions. Humanity has made some progress in mitigating its own predestination to violence – in moderating, in the resonant words of Alexander Pope, "Man's inhumanity to man."

James Q. Wilson postulates that four innate sentiments dispose people to a universal moral sense: sympathy, fairness, self-control, and duty. In training soldiers to kill, the American military has to override an ingrained reluctance. Moreover, *homo sapiens* may be the only creature that is not "locked into its environment." Humanity has learned to refine the machinery of its own society. It may not be the only species to practice altruism at the level of the family (as when a parent risks death in the defense of its offspring), but it may be unique in its voluntary acceptance of the same risk for the sake of the community. The survival of a state seems to require a fine calibration between self-interest and altruism.

Montesquieu discerned a basic principle "that the various nations should do to one another in times of peace the most good possible, and in times of war the least ill possible, without harming their true interests."

In appreciation of the adverse consequences of brute force, rival factions have long groped for common agreement on universal limitations. The last war of total destruction, in the view of Theodore Draper, was the Third

Punic War of 146 B.C. between Rome and Carthage. Humanity shares a compelling interest in the avoidance of war altogether or, failing this, in agreement on limitations on military action, like guarantees of humane treatment of prisoners. In fact, savagery embodies its own retribution. By singling out the Jewish people for extinction, Nazi Germany set a deadly precedent for equivalent condemnation of the German people. Israel is paying a price for its obdurate refusal to set Gaza free: See "Israel Confronts Deeper Isolation in Gaza's Wake" on page one of the 3/19/09 *Times.* If survival must have an altruistic component, that altruism must be grounded in a single standard.

This is not to contend that every dispute has one right answer. The ongoing battle for Palestine is a tragic case of two rights in conflict: the right of the Jews to sanctuary from persecution, and the right of the Palestinians to live in their ancestral homeland. Perhaps Reinhold Niebuhr is correct in his judgment that the only choices given us in life are between the immoral and the less immoral.

In any event, humanity soldiers on toward some form of world order. The authoritative statement on the sources of International Law is Article 38 of the statute of the International Court of Justice. The global machinery to enforce its decisions remains to be set up. Meanwhile, national government is the ultimate authority, and self-defense the ultimate motivation.

Keeping the Peace

Violence has been endemic to human interaction. The enlightened effort to restrain its agonizing effects has been frustrated by innovation in military technology, and by the evolution of nationalism, with its grim talent for mass mobilization. The American Civil War reportedly inflicted unprecedented carnage. On its heels came the Twentieth Century – assessed by Niall Ferguson as the bloodiest era in history. In the 5/14/09 *New York Review of Books,* Avishai Margolit and Michael Walzer reported that civilians constituted fifteen percent of the casualties in World War I, fifty percent in World War II.

Over recent centuries, philosophers and governments have cooperated in devising an elaborate structure to moderate the incidence and ferocity of war:

1625 - *On the Law of War and Peace,* Hugo Grotius's monumental contribution to the evolution of international law.

1859 - Jean-Henri Dumont foreshadowed the evolution of today's International Movements of the Red Cross and Red Crescent.

1899 - Establishment at The Hague of the progenitor of the International Court of Justice (World Court), the judicial arm of the UN system.

1945 - The Charter of the United Nations came into force on October 24. As principal organs, it specified a General Assembly, a Security Council, an Economic and Social Council, a Trusteeship Council, an International Court of Justice, and a Secretariat. The UN Charter's restrictions on the use of armed force were adopted from the Atlantic Charter, proclaimed by President Roosevelt and Prime Minister Churchill August 14, 1941. The UN Security Council viewed the UN Charter as an instrument to protect international peace and security by peaceful means (Chapter VI) or forceful (Chapter VII): Samar El Masri, *Middle East Policy,* Fall 2008. Article 103 of the Charter asserts its primacy over any other international agreement.

1949 - The Geneva Conventions of 1864, 1906, and 1929, and the Hague Conventions of 1899 and 1907, were capped by the four Geneva Conventions of 1949. The Fourth Convention of 1949 reaffirmed the rights of civilians in time of war, and outlawed deportation, torture, hostage-taking, collective punishment, and ethnic and political discrimination.

1951 - The UNGA approved the Convention Relating to the Status of Refugees.

1952 - A UN High Commissioner for Refugees was appointed to act under the 1951 convention.

1966 - The American Congress adopted the War Crimes Act, which designated violation of the Geneva Conventions a war crime.

1977 - Adoption of two protocols extending protection under the Hague and Geneva Conventions to guerrillas fighting for self-determination.

2000 - The International Criminal Court, designed to deal with war crimes and crimes against humanity, came into force. El Masri reports that it does not apply to crimes versus peace, because of the absence of a consensus on the definition of aggression. Its statute had been adopted in Rome in 1998 by a conference convened by the UN General Assembly. The United States and Israel are among the many countries that oppose the existence of the Court and insist on exemption from its jurisdiction.

2006 - By a vote of 170-4 (Palau, Marshall Islands, Israel, and the United States), the UN General Assembly created the UN Human Rights Council.

2007 - The International Committee of the Red Cross reported that US CIA interrogation methods on a high-level prisoner had constituted torture (which is prohibited by US criminal law, by the Geneva Conventions, and by the International Convention Against Torture).

The Power to Exterminate

As physical science has raced ahead of political science, a growing number of states have acquired weapons that, if misused, could wipe out the species. The destructive capacity of nuclear weapons was utilized by the United States to end the war with Japan. The full potential of all weapons of mass destruction – nuclear, chemical, and biological – will never be inflicted, if sanity prevails.

In the Middle East, Israel is the only state known to possess nuclear weapons; there is a widespread assumption that it would use them as a last resort from an imminent threat of being overrun. As Israel's patron, the United States would bear the awesome responsibility for their use. Its interdiction has to be an imperative of United States policy. Hanging over Washington's head like the sword of Damocles, this contingency spotlights the dilemma America has inflicted on itself by embracing the Israeli cause as its own. In 1981, it ritually condemned Israel's preemptive destruction, by aerial bombing, of the Osirak nuclear installation near Baghdad. In 2002, an American administration that espoused preemption retrospectively endorsed the Osirak action.

There are arguable grounds for this endorsement: Granted that the attack was an act of war, it could be held that Iraq has been in a state of war with Israel since 1948, and consequently that the Osirak operation was a legitimate act of self-defense. However, insofar as the United States is committed to preserving Israel's nuclear monopoly in the region, it is open to challenge on two counts: From the standpoint of principle, monopoly contravenes the rule against a double standard; from the standpoint of pragmatism, no technological monopoly is likely to endure; the historic record of arms control initiatives is overwhelmingly negative. The use of nuclear weapons to interdict a rival's acquisition of nuclear weapons would be self-defeating.

The consequences of confrontation between two nuclear powers are unpredictable. Between the United States and the Soviet Union, it produced a stalemate with arguable benefits: greater care on both sides to avoid limited conflict, and Soviet abandonment of the Marxist thesis that war between communism and capitalism was inevitable. Nevertheless, many analysts believe the Cuban missile crisis of 1962 brought the two states close to a nuclear exchange. The nuclear standoff between India and Pakistan has aroused similar apprehension.

The emergence of systems of mass destruction has intensified the pressure on world powers to collaborate in converting Earth – to borrow words from Herbert Spencer – from <u>arena</u> to <u>community</u>.

Grounds for Military Attack

The UN Charter authorizes a member state's resort to force in two circumstances: 1) under Article 51, self-defense against armed attack; 2) under Article 42, authorization by the Security Council.

In March 2003, the United States and the United Kingdom took drastic action outside the Charter by invading and occupying Iraq. Their motives, still obscure, are explored farther on in the book. Their justification was nebulous. They adduced no evidence of hostile Iraqi action, actual or imminent. They were reduced to the speculative contention that Iraq was developing weapons of mass destruction for eventual use against America and Britain.

Writing before the invasion, David Hendrickson drew a distinction between preemptive war (resort to force against an antagonist demonstrably on the verge of striking) and preventive war (force inflicted on an antagonist suspected of contemplating a strike at some opportunistic date). In this lexicon, the invasion of Iraq was preventive. As such, it set a tendentious precedent – one that demands rigorous examination in UN councils. On its face, preventive war is illegal and indefensible.

A common consequence of military victory is imperialism – retention of territory of the loser by the forces of the winner. Like war, an imperialist action can be justifiable or unjustifiable. Over time, the distinction is easily drawn. As in every evolutionary process, the criterion is success. If the peoples that inhabit the conquered territory are ultimately reconciled to the conquest, it is justified.

Britain's absorption of its Norman conquerors meets that criterion. So does America's fulfillment of its "Manifest Destiny" – even though its genocidal aspects have to be condemned. Territorial acquisition by consensus (the formation of the United Arab Republic in 1958; the putative unification of western Europe in the late 1900's) is vastly preferable.

Any conquest that is aborted is *ipso facto* unjustifiable. The American intrusions into the Philippines a hundred years ago and Vietnam fifty years ago have to be relegated to this category. In the short term, no definitive assessment is possible. America's occupation of Iraq (Chapter 15) can evoke nothing but inconclusive debate until American intentions and Iraqi reactions crystallize.

The Elements of National Power

Politics is the art of the possible. In an intricate world, the optimal falls far short of the ideal. Total security is not attainable. The American

9

superpower, bent on managing the affairs of the globe, is notoriously derelict at controlling infiltration of its own territory. The following catalog must be evaluated in this light.

Area - All the requisites of great-power status start from a territorial base large enough to support them. In time of war, a crucial factor is defense-in-depth. It enabled Russia to repel the French invasion of 1812 and the German invasion of 1941. The Soviets' phenomenal transfer of arms factories from Europe to Siberia under enemy fire maintained production of the T-34 tanks that drove the Germans back from Stalingrad.

Population - Technology can counter demographic advantage, but can never eliminate it. Every great power needs the people to work the farms, run the factories, staff the institutions, serve in the government and armed forces, and – in the worst case – occupy the territory of an adversary. The Arab-Israeli conflict has been stalemated for over fifty years because the Arabs lack the cooperation and technology to defeat Israel, but Israel lacks the manpower to subdue the Arabs – let alone assimilate them.

Military - When states are attacked, most governments choose to defend the national security (which they customarily identify with their own tenure) by responding in kind. "There has been a constant acquisition of military strength by man" [because] "the strongest nation has always been conquering the weak;" those words are from K. J. Holsti.

Although the UN Charter devotes Chapter VI to "Pacific Settlement of Disputes", it bows to reality in Chapter VII, whose Article 51 endorses "the inherent right" of self-defense against armed attack. The bellicose premise that underlies international politics is exemplified by the magnitude of the global arms trade, in which the United States is the leading supplier. In 2003, the Department of Defense reportedly awarded a contract for the design of a "shore-hugging combat ship". Washington seems intent on exploiting its naval preeminence in implementation of the National Security Strategy proclaimed in September 2002. 2008 witnessed intense competition for the global arms market among several European states and the United States, which in that year sold 38 billion dollars' worth out of a global total of 55 billion dollars: *Times*, 9/7/09.

In 1983, countries devoting over ten percent of their gross national product to military spending included five in the Middle East – Israel (a startling thirty-one percent), Syria, Saudi Arabia, Egypt, and Iraq.

In isolation, military proficiency is not enough to win a war. Analysts have evaluated German "fighting power", unit for unit, as superior to that of its adversaries in the two world wars (presumably because German forces were more experienced), but Germany lost both for lack of physical assets.

Technology - Military prowess has several components, but technological ascendancy leads the list. In accordance with "the law of progressive simplification", technology has made all human activities easier – including killing. Subject to the other variables, advances in weaponry – stone axe, sword, lance, longbow, crossbow, musket, rifle, cannon, machine gun, tank, aircraft, missile, unmanned aircraft – have determined the fates of nations.

Some centuries behind in the technological race, the states of the Third World have been easy pickings. The first *Arab Human Development Report,* issued in 2002, cited in *The Economist* of 7/25/09, was a grave indictment of Arab cultural achievement. In 2009 the *Times* carried an article assessing elementary education in Arab countries as among the worst in the world. The technological gap seems to have widened with the rise of the American superpower, which is deploying the latest advances in wireless communication, night vision, overhead surveillance, aerial drones, laser-guided missiles, deep-penetration ordnance, and electronic surveillance in the contemporary effort to expunge anti-American subversion – an effort pompously mischaracterized as a "global war on terror".

Industry - Technological advance requires massive diversion of the national product to industry. According to Jared Diamond, industry evolved in the Middle East some 11,000 years ago, when society's transition from hunting/gathering to agriculture led to the emergence of towns, denser population, occupational specialization, and the storage of surpluses that provisioned government and the forces to maintain it.

Eleven millennia passed, and Britain became the cradle of the Industrial Revolution. Within 200 years, at least six states – Britain, France, Germany, Japan, the Soviet Union, and the United States – had built the industrial base on which conventional military prowess depends. The Soviets demonstrated that industrial might is not a capitalist monopoly; John Mearsheimer has cited evidence that in World War II the Soviet and American economies were better organized than the German to channel production to the armed forces.

Finance - Commerce, industry, and finance are intimately linked. Britain's industrial head start resulted from a combination of technological innovation and its status as the largest free-trade area in the Western world. Niall Ferguson contends that Britain beat out bullion-rich Spain in the 1700's because it had a more sophisticated banking system. In the 1800's the United States surpassed the UK in the economic realm. In 1956 American financial pressure alone aborted the Anglo-French invasion of Egypt. The geopolitical consequences of America's current budget and foreign exchange deficits remain to be determined. Candidates for future world leadership are the European Union and China.

At this writing, the United States dominates global finance, in consequence of its own wealth and its preeminent control over the resources of the International Monetary Fund and the World Bank. The economies of many underdeveloped countries are dependent on loans from those two organizations. George Soros has stressed that the US enjoys veto rights in the IMF. American financial assistance to western Europe under the Marshall Plan is generally regarded as the paradigm of enlightened economic policy. Washington's efforts to exploit its financial leadership for political advantage in the Middle East have been less successful – as will be elaborated in Chapters 9 and 15.

The solidity of America's finances has been challenged by some economists who decry the persistent deficits in its balance of trade. Even if government financiers could chart a course that satisfied every economist, America would remain vulnerable to the inflationary/deflationary vicissitudes of the interlocked global economy.

Natural Resources - No state has ever been self-sufficient in all the products required to maintain a modern economy. Roderick Peattie points out that Babylonia was particularly bereft: no wood, no minerals, no stone. Its building and even its writing were based on clay. Babylonian farmers made do with sickles made of clay.

Germany, cut off by Allied blockade from natural rubber supplies in two world wars, responded to dire necessity by developing and refining the production of synthetic rubber from petroleum. As the United States evolved from net exporter of petroleum products to net importer, its foreign policy shifted accordingly, with special reference to the Middle East, site of half the world's known crude and natural gas reserves. America's attention to oil supply was galvanized in 1974, when its "sovereignty" was severely degraded by the embargo imposed by some Arab oil states on the sale of oil to two states allied with Israel – the Netherlands and the United States.

Economic power has been defined as the capability to provide or deny access to essential commodities or services. It was wielded with some effect in both world wars by both sides; in general, however, economic sanctions have not achieved dramatic shifts in the policies of target states.

Geographic Situation - Fernand Braudel wrote "To discuss civilization is to discuss space, land and its contours, climate, vegetation, animal species and natural or other advantages ... and what humanity has made of these basic conditions." Jared Diamond carries the geographic argument a step further. In his view, Eurasia was the only landmass that offered humanity the variety of edible plants and domesticable animals essential to the development of civilization.

Political System - Evolution thrives on diversity: Presented with a broad spectrum of options, nature has a better chance of hitting on a viable cast of the genetic dice.

In the arena of human society, Toynbee identified five major contenders for cultural preeminence – Western Christianity, Orthodox Christianity, Islam, Hinduism, and the culture of East Asia. At the time he was writing, he should probably have identified two rival ideologies in eastern Europe and added Communism to his list. Perhaps an identifiable ideology of Humanism is evolving in the West.

Under each of these cultural umbrellas, hundreds of political systems have emerged – each one *sui generis*. History points up the characteristics most likely to prolong survival. Six seem to warrant special mention:

Social Equity - Maldistribution of a state's resources, to the advantage of one class or coterie, has always been the fuel of insurrection. In the United States, the gap between rich and poor has so far been alleviated by the lure of upward mobility. Soviet Communism spawned a rigidity and an entrenched bureaucracy that failed the equity test. Both systems have their defects. "Everything the Communists told us about Communism was a ... lie. Unfortunately, everything (they) told us about capitalism turned out to be true."

Honesty - Politicians habitually traffic in equivocation, prevarication, and platitude. Media and electorate tend to follow their lead. In the arsenal of the statesman, dishonesty has its constructive uses, but only in the interest of the state – not of the faction. The abiding strength of the American system lies in the (restrained) right of dissenters to speak their minds. Thomas Paine said, "My own mind is my own church." America's eventual disengagement from disaster in Vietnam demonstrated that, in our system, truth still ultimately prevails. The search for truth calls for constant upgrading of the educational system. In a democracy, ignorance is a crime.

Culture - The blend of equal opportunity, business enterprise, freedom of expression, and secular government has produced, in the coinage of Joseph Nye, an American brand of "soft power" whose worldwide appeal has helped to counteract the myriad enormities of American foreign policy.

Adaptability - The insidious effect of money on America's political campaigns raises the question whether its political system is more accurately termed democracy or plutocracy. Either way, the system has achieved a redeeming balance between stability and flexibility.

Stability has enabled it to ride out the ineptitude, venality, and mental aberrations of wondrously incompetent administrations. Flexibility served to meet the abrupt challenges of the Civil War, the Great Depression, and Twentieth-Century totalitarianism.

No government has learned how to accelerate the glacial pace of cultural change, but the American government, so far, has managed to deal with crisis. As early as 1869 Walter Bagehot recognized that crisis properly gives the leader of a democracy dictatorial power. Perhaps if we had not elected a Lincoln in 1860, or a Roosevelt in 1932, or a Kennedy in 1960, we would be telling a sadder story.

Morale - In terms of hardships endured and lives lost in battle (300,000 Americans, 400,000 British, 28 million Russians: *The New York Review,* 8/13/09, Max Hastings review of *Masters and Commanders* by Andrew Roberts), the Russians won World War II. Communism could not sell itself, but it never dimmed the devotion to Mother Russia. In 1990, the Russians gave way to ethnic separatism, but in the 1930's and 40's, they presented an illustrious example of "a civic rather than an ethnic definition of nationality".

Weaker states have defeated stronger, out of a more resolute will to win – or readiness to die. The concept of political solidarity ('*asabiyyah*) was stressed in the *Muqaddimah* of Ibn Khaldun, the Tunisian phenomenon whose writings and storybook career made him the confidant of Arab, Tatar, and Ottoman rulers, manifested the sweep of Islam in the 1300's, and made him known to the ages as the greatest Arab historian.

Arab military efforts have been habitually undercut by the Middle-Eastern subjugation to communalism – loyalty to tribe, sect, or language group rather than to the state (Chapter 6). Country of birth or citizenship is devalued. Ethnic affiliation is overriding. A crucial element of American power is the facility for assimilation of immigrants from all ethnic origins. The advantage of inclusivity is the lesson most Middle Easterners have yet to learn.

Policy - Since many aspects of the environment are beyond human comprehension, national policy for dealing with its ups and downs is bound to be flawed. The very formulation of foreign policy is likely to involve mindsets imperceptible to the policymakers themselves. The consequences can be devastating. Napoleon capped a string of dazzling military successes with a disastrous foray into Russia. David Fromkin notes that Britain's sudden embroilment in a world war in 1914 was unforeseen by any member of the British Cabinet. Many analysts (notably John Maynard Keynes) condemned the draconian terms of the Treaty of Versailles and linked them to the rise of Adolph Hitler.

British Prime Minister Neville Chamberlain has been generally reviled as an appeaser for accepting German annexation of the Czech Sudetenland in 1938. In retrospect, many commentators (reportedly including Winston Churchill and, in Gerhard Weinberg's judgment, Hitler himself) concluded that the Munich Accord was an Allied triumph, because Germany was readier than the Allies for war. Hitler went on to replicate Napoleon's ill-starred invasion of Russia.

The parade of policy errors is long and all-inclusive: 1914 - The expectation of the British leadership that World War I would last only a few months; 1956 - British, French, and Israeli failure to anticipate American quashing of their invasion of Egypt; 1965 - American invasion of Vietnam; 1967 - Egyptian closure of the Strait of Tiran, bringing on the Six-Day War; 1980 - Iraqi invasion of Iran; 1982 - Israeli invasion of Lebanon; 1990 - Iraqi invasion of Kuwait; 2003 - (in the opinion of most Middle-East watchers) American invasion of Iraq.

Policy choices vary hugely among individuals, and among societies. William J. McNeill has noted a cosmic contrast in the utilization of the printing press: In introverted China, it was focused on the propagation of classical texts; in Europe, it produced an explosion of scientific innovation. Hence the "European miracle" that brought much of the world under Western domination. (There is no intent here to argue that the world was better off for it.)

Sound policy sometimes resorts to dishonesty. When Nazi submarines attacked the USS Greer in September 1941, Roosevelt issued an inaccurate version of the incident, in order to promote American entry into World War II. More often, falsity can have disastrous consequences, as when Lyndon Johnson relied on erroneous intelligence to claim a Vietnamese attack on US warships in the Gulf of Tonkin.

In any conflict between autocracy and democracy, the former has the advantage of instantaneous reaction, but the latter has the more fundamental advantage of adaptability; the electoral process tends to correct mistakes.

Temporal Constraint on Power

"Nothing endures but change." We owe this terse axiom to Heraclitus, who dispensed his insights in Greece 2500 years ago. Its application in the realm of geopolitics was encapsulated by Paul Kennedy: "… the relative strengths of the leading nations … never remain constant, principally because of the uneven rate of growth among different societies and of the technological and organizational breakthroughs which bring greater advantage to one society than to another."

In this universe, change is subject to a relentless corollary: At the elemental level, it is governed by sheer happenstance. In this respect, the consequences of human action are impenetrable to human insight – let alone human control.

Incumbents cannot be faulted for resisting these realities. Regimes try to prolong their reigns. States try to expand their hegemonies. According to Michael Doyle, much of history has been written in terms of the quest for world domination.

James Ray tabulates the recent cycle of world leadership:

1516-1540: Portugal
1580-1688: Netherlands (Should he have included Spain?)
1688-1914: Great Britain
1914 - ? : United States

The Nineteenth Century added three states to the roster of great powers – Germany, Japan, and the United States. By 2002, the US had come closer than any previous world power to achieving global preeminence. In the Victorian era, the British Empire had ringed the globe with colonies, "protectorates", dominions, and annexations – including large sections of India. Britain was the primary beneficiary of the "mandates" handed out to the Allies by the League of Nations after World War I. Its garrisons were supplied and supported by the maritime supremacy of the British Navy, whose original purpose was to repel invasion of the British Isles, but which was an essential pillar of world empire.

In the more politically correct environment that prevailed after World War II, America tended to take a more nuanced route to global primacy. After the occupations of Germany and Japan wound down, America cloaked its occupations under cover of regional defense compacts like NATO and SEATO, or UN authorizations like the Security Council Resolution of June 26, 1950, under which American forces entered South Korea. In the Middle East, bilateral agreements have allowed the United States to station forces at specified bases – notably Air Force units at Incirlik in Turkey, Prince Sultan in Saudi Arabia, and al 'Udayd in Qatar, and the command center of the Fifth Fleet in Bahrain.

These deployments have been backed up by the new ruler of the seas – the United States Navy, by a growing penchant for unilateral intervention (Lebanon in 1958 and 1982-84, Vietnam in 1965, Panama in 1980, Grenada in 1983, Iraqi "No-Fly Zones" in 1992-2003, and Iraqi invasion in 2003), and by the ubiquitous sweep of American economic and cultural influence. The American dollar is presently the principal international medium of exchange. English is becoming a universal lingua franca. American styles in clothing, food, music, sports icons, turn up where least expected. America's rivals – Russia, China, the European Union – are not only far behind in the running, they are themselves so beholden to Washington's political, economic, and military support that they tacitly defer to American overlordship in the UN Security Council.

In this heady era of American dominance, Washington would do well to remember the lesson of history. Every aspirant to world domination has eventually succumbed to "political entropy" (William Pfaff's coinage). The individual circumstances of decline differ, but in most cases, if not all, the causes are internal. Toynbee advises that "…great empires do not die by murder, but by suicide." Paul Kennedy is the most recent to warn that a common policy error is overextension – of military expenditures at home or expansionist objectives abroad.

In the American political system, foreign policy is often driven off the track by the undue influence of special-interest groups. The "China Lobby" helped push America into the Vietnam debacle, from which the country took ten years to extricate itself. The Zionist and Evangelical lobbies provided impetus for the illegal and probably ill-advised occupation of Iraq.

The ephemerality of nations was articulated by Rudyard Kipling, the gifted exponent/critic of British imperialism, in "Recessional" (1897):

> Far-called, our navies melt away,
> On dune and headland sinks the fire,
> Lo, all our pomp of yesterday
> Is one with Nineveh and Tyre.

Spatial Constraint on Power

The interaction between geography and politics is a two-way street. In one direction, people revise geography – by canalizing isthmuses (Panama, Suez), tunneling under mountains (Alps, Caucasus), reclaiming land from the sea (Netherlands), and transforming regional economies by creating microclimates in homes, cars, businesses, factories, and shopping malls. Technological advances enhance a society's ability to escape environmental constraints.

But on an immensely larger scale, geography dominates society. Hear Napoleon: "The policy of a state lies in its geography." Twenty-five miles of ocean were enough to accord England nine centuries of freedom from invasion and to engender a sense of separateness strong enough to delay its entry into the European Union. On the other side of the globe, Japan reaped the same benefit of insularity.

In the analysis of Braudel, the most significant historical agents are shaped by the economics and institutions in which they operate, and those are shaped by geography and climate. "...[C]ultural thoughtways...are very much the product of geography..." In *Wealth of Nations,* Adam Smith noted that lands near navigable waterways are far richer and more densely settled than interior regions.

William McNeill perceives four evolutionary advantages afforded the inhabitants of Europe: 1) a host of navigable rivers; 2) expanses of fertile soil; 3) an abundance of minerals; 4) a climate moist enough for agriculture but inclement enough to promote physical activity. Result: easier access to goods and markets, and an early start in the development of modern technology. Another climatic benefit: Winter is the world's best public-health intervention; tropical climates inflict a higher incidence of disease – and inhibit the production of many field crops. Robert Kaplan cites Brandel's thesis that the poor soils of Mediterranean Europe favor the evolution of large holdings, which tend to freeze a social order dominated by rich landholders – to the disadvantage of the economies of southern Europe relative to those of the north.

Terrain is also consequential. Mountain ranges tend to insulate their inhabitants from conquest, thereby fostering independence of spirit. The Swiss lived for centuries unscathed by Europe's enduring civil war. Conversely, plains invite invasion. The level topography of central China, interrupted only by two great east-west rivers (Yellow and Yangtze), enabled the Chin Dynasty to meld it into a political and cultural unit by 221 B.C. On an even broader scale, the latitudinal expanse of Eurasia gave rise to great inland empires. The Macedonian and Roman Empires (Chapter 10) stretched 3000 miles, the Mongol Empire 6000.

Continental configuration imposes a dichotomy of strategy between inland states – which place primary reliance on land power – and coastal states – which lean on sea power. Which approach provides greater military advantage? During World War I, geopolitical pioneer Halford Mackinder of Britain advised the Allies to aim for control of eastern Europe – the "Heartland" of Eurasia – as the key to world domination. Two successive victories by the Allies, led by maritime powers Britain and the United States, whose troops never reached the Heartland in either war, undermined Mackinder's thesis in favor of the argument advanced in 1890 by American naval historian Alfred Thayer Mahan, in his classic *The Influence of Sea Power Upon History.* Mahan contended that the land power of an inland state could be offset by the combined maritime power of the "single community of nations" that comprised the democracies of western Europe and North America.

But this formulation is also open to question. First, the Heartland state (Russia) bore the brunt of the Nazi war machine. Second, Mahan conflated two separate elements of power – geographic location and governmental system. Third, man is a land animal. When war is fought *a outrance,* ground troops always deliver the *coup de grace.* Alexander's greatest military achievement, conquest of the island city of Tyre, was accomplished only after a seven-month siege from the landward side. The British siege of Gallipoli in 1915 was repelled by superior Ottoman tactics.

Nevertheless, on this watery planet, maritime deployment is valuable for defense and essential for offense. On defense, the Atlantic helped the American colonists throw off British rule, it has spared the United States from any invasion more onerous than the mini-war of 1812, and it exempted the country from direct involvement in Europe's endemic civil war for over a hundred years. On offense, America's warm-water coastline – 5000 crow-flight miles along the lower forty-eight states – facilitated the projection of power in several ways. It made the country a world leader in shipbuilding. It accelerated economic development by promoting America's participation in world trade; bulk commodities are cheaper to move by water than by land. It helped build the naval power that took control of the sea-lanes required for the transport of the supplies and troops that sealed the Allied victories over Germany and Japan.

In the late 1700's, British maritime power and French continental power deadlocked. Neither could eliminate the other. The conclusion seems clear: Land power wins wars, but not without coordinated deployment of forces at sea, in the air – and now in space.

The Evolution of Political Entities

For the vast majority of people, the life of a hermit is not a valid option. As population rises and civilization ramifies, people's opportunities to evade the strictures of society are ever more remote. Under the social contract identified by Hobbes, Locke, and Rousseau, every social group exacts allegiance and compliance in return for the protection and amenities it promises its adherents. It has been the misfortune of most humans to be consigned by blind fate to groups that failed to carry out their side of the bargain.

Communalism - Beyond the family, the earliest affiliation was the tribe. Tribes learned to enhance their chances of survival by merging into ethnic groups, distinguished from each other by appearance, dress, language, custom, and ritual. Graham Fuller tells us there is no algorithm for defining an ethnic group; it defines itself.

The ethnic approach to political organization seems to have been the rule in all undeveloped societies, and it persists in many parts of the Third World, including the Middle East. Since the Europeans blazed the global trail to the modern state, European history may well provide some indication of how other parts of the world are likely to change – if, as the writer contends, communalism is not the last word in the political evolution of the Middle East, or anywhere else.

From the collapse of the Roman Empire in the 400's until the conclusion of the Peace of Westphalia in 1648, communalism prevailed in western Europe. A congeries of tribes, sects, principalities, and city-states interacted under the nominal secular leadership of the Holy Roman Emperor and spiritual leadership of the Roman Catholic Pope.

Although the Middle East today is nominally divided into states, many of their frontiers are relics of European imperialism, and extensive areas are under dispute. There are consequent grounds for arguing that the region has not had its own Westphalia. Certainly the savagery of rampant communalism still holds sway: the genocide visited on the Armenians by the Ottoman Turks and Kurdish irregulars during World War I, the Jewish expulsions of Arabs from Palestine in 1948 and 1967, the reciprocal massacres of Christians and Muslims in the Lebanese civil war of 1975-90, Palestinian suicide bombings of Israeli gatherings, and on and on.

The State - In Europe, over the course of the second millennium, the diffuse authority of empire gave way to the more precise control of the state. Urbanization facilitated the change by expanding the production of the resources rulers needed to establish political control. The milestone Peace of Westphalia ended a century of religious war, along with the primacy of emperor and pope. The new operative unit of global power was the "sovereign" state. States professed to respect each other's territorial inviolability, although violations have abounded up to the present day. Few countries have deserved the rubric of nation-state (where ethnicity and citizenship are congruent), but monarchs maintained that their rule by "divine right" entitled them to determine the state religion.

For almost three centuries, European states continued to be cloaked in the mystique of empire. When the world was being sucked into the maelstrom of World War I, its affairs were being handled in the main by thirteen emperors. The scope of British influence and the interlocking nature of European royalty were captured at a later time by British official Tony Benn's observation that in 1901, three descendants of Queen Victoria "ruled the world." He presumably had reference to Victoria's son, King

Edward VII of England, her grandson, Kaiser Wilhelm II of Germany, and her grandson-in-law, Czar Nicholas II (married to her granddaughter, Alexandria of Denmark).

Nationalism - The French Revolution has been characterized as the first war of nationalism. Not to be confused with nation, the common term for an ethnic community, nationalism is allegiance to a state. In the view of George Kennan, it has become the strongest motivational force of the age, at least in the developed world. The relative influence of ethnicity, nationalism, and ideology in the Middle East will be considered in Chapter 6. Note that professed loyalty to Communism did not prevent the rift between China and the Soviet Union in 1959, nor did sectarian affiliation stop Shiite Iraqis from following their Sunni leadership into war against Shiite Iran in 1980-88.

Democracy - Toynbee anointed democracy as the political expression of humanitarianism. The French Revolution is regarded by many as the threshold from the era of divine right to that of majority rule. A crucial date in the transition was 1791, when France instituted conscription – to the military benefit of Napoleon, still styled Emperor. Drew Gilpin Faust has flagged the American civil war as the first "war of peoples".

The Continental Power - The United States combines an aptitude and an appetite for expansionism in both its forms. It displaced Native American tribes and the governments of Mexico and Hawaii to clear the way for American colonialism; it has often resorted to imperialism elsewhere, notably in the Philippines, Central America, the Caribbean, and lately in Afghanistan and Iraq.

If the means and motives were questionable, the general result was a step forward on the path of political evolution: The United States was the original continental power, given its direct hegemony over the heartland of North America, and its indirect hegemony over the rest of the continent. By exertion of its influence in ways implicit and explicit, it has drawn Canada, Mexico, and the states of Central America into its political/economic sphere. In the Caribbean, American overlordship is attenuated by the island effect, which has left various small territories under the anachronistic control of allies France and Britain, and enabled Cuba to follow a quasi-independent line. France also retains two small islands off eastern Canada.

If we assume that the expanse and geography of Eurasia allow for the existence of more than one continental power within its confines, we are led in 2009 to recognize two extant examples – the United States and China – and three putative candidates – Europe, Russia, and India.

Globalization

In a spontaneous and haphazard manner, the process of globalization is well underway. No state has ever wielded absolute power within its borders, and advances in communications technology are further eroding state power. The concept of absolute sovereignty is a useful legal construct, on the analogy of the imaginary number in mathematics, but it does not reflect the real world. In blatant violation of national and international law, states have taken it on themselves to abduct criminal suspects from foreign soil, to assassinate adversaries abroad, and to conduct preemptive and retaliatory attacks on foreign installations without any conventional legal formality.

This way, it seems, lies anarchy; it is reassuring that the planet-wide access facilitated by modern communications and transportation is also altering international relations in a more orderly way. Countless institutions – government, supragovernment, and non-government – have materialized to meet the demands of global travel, communication, commerce, finance, arms control, crime control, humanitarian intervention, and protection of the ecosystem. By the same token, economic mishap in one state can have instantaneous repercussions worldwide – as exemplified by the fall of foreign stock markets in reaction to the September 29, 2008, collapse of the New York market.

No one state is up to these challenges. A state, says Daniel Bell, is "too small for the big problems and too big for the small problems." "Nationalism is a phase in political evolution, not an end product," writes William McNeill. With the evolution of language and society, humanity has learned to collaborate in ever-larger aggregations; every region finds itself deeply influenced by the global political, economic, military, and cultural currents of the age.

The vanguard of globalization is the United Nations, whose Charter lays down three basic principles: The sovereignty of every state; its right to defend itself from attack; collective security against such attack. The first two principles are deeply ingrained in the international system of the Twenty-first Century. The third remains in the realm of theory – except insofar as UN member states have conducted military operations under the UN flag. The United Nations is a pallid reflection of the global distribution of power. Still, the Charter of the United Nations is widely regarded as the supreme law of every signatory, even though most of them – including the United States – have often violated it. The Charter is reinforced by various UN criminal tribunals, by the International Criminal Court in The Hague, and by the International Court of Justice.

Political segmentation feeds on itself. Every state, however insignificant, and every regime, however unrepresentative, has a vested interest in its own survival. At last count, there were 192 of each in the roster of the United Nations. More may be on the way. It will take generations of negotiation and violence to reduce them to a more manageable number.

But reduction is bound to come, and greater global centralization in its wake. An imminent threat of universal catastrophe (global pollution, nuclear war, climatic convulsion, approaching asteroid) might concentrate humanity's parochial mind, but one hopes for a less stressful transition to global unification – the only convincing promise of reconciling humanity's needs with Earth's limitations.

The Ineluctable Geopolity

There is a high correlation between geographic barrier and political frontier. This principle applies at every organizational level – principality, state, and continental power. The last four hundred years of European history centered on the efforts of regimes to match their domains to topographic configuration.

One of the first statesmen to appreciate this desideratum was Cardinal de Richelieu who, as chief minister to Louis XIII from 1624 to 1642, masterminded the campaign to unify France under the monarch. Richelieu and his successors saw the Pyrenees, the Alps, the Rhine, and the Atlantic as their state's natural borders. All such geographic provinces (Roderick Peattie's term) tend to crystallize into states. The most clear-cut cases are islands (Great Britain, Japan, Australia) and peninsulas (Italy). Until they unify, they are likely to live with tension (Cyprus, Korea).

The same political force is at work at the next level up, the region. Dante wrote that "…in a multitude of rulers there is evil." Inside a region, a frontier between two states invites instability: Toynbee. The dynamic of the "turbulent frontier" (John S. Galbraith) explains the frequency of alliance between two states separated by a common neighbor. In regions whose hegemony is still under dispute, frontiers tend to respond to circumstance like elastic membranes – expanding or contracting in reflection of the relative power of the states they separate. When the states in a region merge, they reduce the risk of regional tension, and they enhance their ability to confront challenges from outside the region. American students learn the maxim of Benjamin Franklin: "We must … all hang together, or … we shall all hang separately." Winston Churchill reportedly predicted "eternal war" with the Muslim world if the treaty-makers at Versailles cut up the Ottoman Empire. That Empire's partition into a bevy of states was the latest swing in the Middle East's age-old pattern of oscillation between the poles of unity and segmentation.

Segmentation serves the parochial interests of communal groups, ministates, and the authorities that govern them. The price their constituents pay is greater regional instability, backwardness, weakness, and vulnerability to intrusion from outside.

Unification affords the profound advantages of size: suppression of communal rivalries; economies of scale; cultural interchange; more rational development of resources; greater power. These benefits are most apparent in the case of the United States. Americans are not the only beneficiaries. Perhaps Canada and Mexico find the pressure from Washington overweening at times, but it has compensated them with military protection and a start toward a common market in goods and labor. The Europeans must have the American precedent in mind as they blaze the trail toward the pacific unification of their own continent. Any region geographically and culturally coherent enough to aspire to political unity deserves inclusion in a special geopolitical category – say geopolity. The intent of the following pages is to examine events in the Middle East to determine to what extent it warrants this designation.

The record of the past hundred years is negative. As the site of extreme fragmentation, the region seems more deserving of inclusion under the heading of shatterbelt – a term devised by Saul Cohen to represent any strategically located region occupied by a number of contesting states and disputed by outside powers. The Middle East has been a zone of contention among its component states and several foreign powers, notably Britain, France, Germany, Italy, Russia, and the United States. If shatterbelt is the region's permanent status, it may be condemned to endemic violence as long as the era of nationalism endures. But if it meets the criteria for a geopolity, we must appraise its segmentation as a passing phase, and anticipate the rise of a new hegemon or hegemons that will achieve the same degree of stability and security America and Europe have lately attained.

Chapter 2
The Middle Eastern Geopolity

Delineation

Comprehensive review of events over the past five millennia in southwest Asia and northeast Africa reveals a <u>region</u> with its own particular history. That particularity has been imposed by geography.

Internally, it is lashed together by rivers, age-old trade routes, oil fields, pipelines, a common history, a kindred culture, and four major languages (Arabic, Turkish, Persian, and Kurdish). Externally, it is separated from adjacent geopolities by five seas (Mediterranean, Black, Caspian, Arabian, Red), two deserts (Iranian, Libyan), and one formidable mountain range (the Caucasus).

These barriers form a roughly circular periphery of some 9,000 miles. It is porous enough to admit the more keenly motivated intruder, but forbidding enough to constitute a barrier to ordinary traffic. As Hannibal demonstrated 2,200 years ago by leading a Carthaginian army of some 40,000 men and a troop of elephants across the Rhone River and over Alpine passes into Italy, barriers can be penetrated by dint of special means of transit and the requisite ingenuity and determination; the Middle Easterners know this to their repeated misfortune. However, to the extent that the bounds of the Middle East have spared it from intrusion, they have crystallized into political and cultural frontiers, and the region has found respite to evolve its own geopolitical identity.

The land thus circumscribed can be visualized as a pinwheel centering on the Fertile Crescent (Mesopotamia and the Levant) and branching into five vanes: Egypt, Anatolia, the southern Caucasus, Persia, and Arabia.

These seven <u>sectors</u> (Peattie used <u>province</u>) comprise the geopolitical entity conventionally identified as the Middle East.

The Libyan Desert

Egypt would be little more than an extension of the Sahara, except that it is dramatically punctuated by one of the world's great rivers. The Nile is the gift of annual rains in the Ethiopian highlands, 1,500 miles to the south, and Egypt is the gift of the Nile – valley, delta, oases, and (since the completion of the Aswan High Dam in 1970) Lake Nasir. The lower Nile is a major transportation route for Egypt, but river travel between Egypt and the upper Nile (Sudan and beyond) is blocked by six cataracts: one in Egypt, at Aswan, and five in northern Sudan.

Egypt is separated from Libya by the Libyan Desert, whose forbidding terrain is slightly alleviated by the semi-maritime climate of a narrow strip along the Mediterranean coast. That strip has been the infrequent route of military expeditions – notably, Libyan invasions in the age of the pharaohs, the westward surge of the Islamic forces in the 600's, the eastward invasion in 969 by the forces of the future Fatimid rulers of Egypt, and the gigantic tank battles between Axis and British forces in the early years of World War II. The British defense line at Al 'Alamayn in 1942 was crucially enhanced by the Qattarah Depression, whose northern edge is thirty miles from the Mediterranean. Descending over 400 feet below sea level, the marshy depression was impassable to tank traffic.

The Mediterranean

The western coast of the Middle East has invited countless maritime invaders, including the mysterious "Sea Peoples" around 1200 B.C, the Crusaders between 1100 and 1300, the French in Egypt 1798-1801, and the British to expel the French. The British and French came back again and again. In 1827, hostilities between the Ottoman Empire and an alliance of Britain, France, and Russia culminated off the southwestern coast of Greece in the naval battle of Navarino – the last major engagement of wooden sailing ships. Most of the warships of Turkey and Egypt went to the bottom, and Greece won its independence.

A subsequent challenge to the Ottoman Sultan's dominion by his nominal vassal, Muhammad 'Ali, brought Egyptian troops north to southern Anatolia. David Fromkin describes how Britain, France, Russia, Austria, and Prussia combined to pose an interventionist threat sufficient to induce Muhammad 'Ali to bring his forces home.

An Anglo-Egyptian treaty of 1838 gave foreign enterprises in Egypt special rights, which – according to Reader Bullard – destroyed state industries on which Egyptian military power had been based. In 1878, Britain and France took over two key Egyptian ministries. Four years later, Egyptian resistance under Commander-in-Chief Ahmad 'Urabi and concurrent anti-foreign riots brought British troops back. Britain exiled 'Urabi and imposed an occupation which was to last in one form or another for seventy-four years.

Ottoman acceptance of an armistice in 1918 enabled the forces of Britain and France to implement their secret wartime agreement to divide the Fertile Crescent into de facto possessions – with Syria and Lebanon going to France, and Palestine, Jordan, and Iraq going to Britain. In 1954, Britain contracted to evacuate its last foothold in Egypt – the Suez Canal Zone. Two years later, British and French forces, acting in secret compact with Israel, briefly reoccupied the northern terminus of the Canal. They left within months under the irresistible American financial pressure cited in Chapter 1.

The more recent interventions from the Mediterranean have been mounted by the United States, which staged deployments – of no strategic consequence – into the Beirut area of Lebanon in 1958 and 1982-84 (Chapter 10).

With one exception, none of the past penetrations of the Middle East – from the Mediterranean or anywhere else – resulted in extended foreign control that has survived uninterrupted up to the present day. The exception is a momentous one. Israel has emerged as a fully independent state, a full-fledged member of the Middle Eastern community; but as the product of British and American initiative, beginning at the time of World War I and continuing to this writing, it poses special questions for the future of the region – questions that continue to defy resolution (Chapter 8).

Zionism's unique colony began with autonomous settlements which subsequently became an independent state. Its unique relationship with the United States (Chapter 13) does not alter the status of the Middle East as a region that holds its own against the other regions of the world, and will work out its own problems in its own way. Britain and America have impacted its future, but they cannot determine it. In this basic sense, the Mediterranean Sea remains the age-old divider between the political systems of the Middle East and those of the West.

This generality holds good for the Mediterranean's northeastern basin, the Aegean Sea, whose multifarious archipelago facilitated an ancient function as a corridor for east-west trade; naval power was wielded there at least as far back as the Greek victory over Persia at Salamis in 480 B.C.

27

Nevertheless, land power has always determined the outcome of every extended Western venture into the Middle East, and every extended Middle Eastern venture into Europe or Africa.

Marmara and the Straits

As empirical support for this last assertion, consider the recourse taken by land armies to the Sea of Marmara's western and eastern straits – the Dardanelles and the Bosporus (elaborated on in Chapter 7):

516 B.C. - Persian Emperor Darius I crossed the Dardanelles (or the Bosporus) on a bridge of ships to challenge the Scythians and the Greeks.

480 B.C.- Abortive invasion of Greece by Persian Emperor Xerxes I.

334 B.C. - Invasion and subsequent lightning conquest of the Middle East and beyond by the Graeco-Macedonian forces of Alexander.

133 B.C. - Roman entry into Anatolia via the Dardanelles, culminating in four centuries of Roman rule over the western half of the Middle East.

1097 - The First Crusade, which introduced a two-century period during which European armies on their way to liberate the Christian Holy Places in Palestine exploited or despoiled Christian Byzantium.

1354 - The Ottoman Turks landed at Gallipoli, on the European side of the Dardanelles, establishing a foothold for their eventual conquest of the Balkans.

1920 - Five years after the British effort to establish a beachhead at Gallipoli had been repelled by the Ottomans, an alliance of French, Italian, and Greek forces occupied parts of Anatolia under the abortive Treaty of Sèvres.

1922 - The occupation of Anatolia was reversed by the military genius of Mustafa Kemal, who in two years built the army of the new Turkey, dispersed the remnants of the Ottoman army, convinced France and Italy to evacuate their forces, and drove the Greek forces out of Turkey.

The boundaries of geopolitical regions are generally dictated by geography, but when the geography is ambiguous, history can prevail. The Straits provide a dramatic example. Throughout recorded history, their European shore has been the political center of gravity for the Anatolian Peninsula – which is an indisputable sector of the Middle East.

The explanation lies in the uninterrupted primacy of the city founded as Byzantium by Greek colonists around 660 B.C., dedicated by Roman Emperor Constantine as the "New Rome" around 330 A.D., converted by Emperor Justinian to the capital of the Byzantine Empire after 550, and designated by the Ottoman Sultan as the capital of the empire in

1453. It came to be called Istanbul, and to remain the preeminent city in the Turkish Republic, even after Ankara was made the capital. Today, Istanbul is a bicontinental city. Overcrowded suspension bridges seem to have converted the Bosporus to a Turkish Canal. A railway tunnel is under construction.

The Black Sea

There is no record of major naval action in this eastern extension of the Mediterranean, although it did facilitate Czarist Russia's imposition of military pressure on the Ottoman Empire. In 1774, Russia exacted a treaty according it a voice in the internal affairs of the Empire. In 1833, the Ottomans signed a treaty granting Russia the right of military intervention. This right was never exercised.

The Caucasus

This isthmus between the Black Sea and the Caspian comprises a European and an Asian segment. They are divided by the Caucasus Range, which extends 750 miles from sea to sea and rises to a height of 18,500 feet at Mt. Elbrus. With one exception, the high Caucasus has been the historic point of farthest advance for forces attacking from north or south. In the 600's it enabled the Khazars to stop the forces of Islam. In modern times, it enabled Russia to block the Turks in 1914, the Georgians to block the Russians in 1921, and the Allies to block the Germans in 1942.

From the early 1800's on, Russia took advantage of negotiable passes to conquer the southern Caucasus. The Soviet Union achieved its southernmost advances in the form of two secessionist movements in Iran. The Russian revolution of 1917 left most of Iran's Caspian coast under control of Bolshevik troops, who participated in the proclamation of the "Soviet Socialist Republic of Gilan"; the Soviet Union handed the territory back to Iran in 1921. In 1946 the Soviet Union backed a Kurdish effort to establish the "Republic of Mahabad" in Iranian Azerbaijan. American intervention, including sending a carrier force to the Dardanelles, enabled Iran to reestablish control of the province.

The people of the southern Caucasus itself regained independence in 1991 when the Soviet Union disbanded – although two Georgian enclaves have lately accepted the status of Russian protectorates (Chapter 11). During the Russian-Georgian clash of 2008, the new Roki Tunnel provided Russian troops immediate access to south Ossetia.

Looking at this territory from the west, recent Turkish governments have considered it a vital link with the Turkic states of Central Asia, but there have been no noteworthy economic or political developments to validate this thesis.

The Caspian Sea

With an approximate area of 152,000 square miles, the Caspian is important to the transportation networks of the five littoral states, but it has not served as a major invasion route. The abortive Russian attempt to set up the Republic of Gilan was supported by a naval attack on a White Russian flotilla off Bandar-e Anzali, northwest of Tehran.

Persia

The deserts of eastern Persia provided a natural frontier for the pre-Islamic Persian Empire of the Achaemenians, for the Islamic Empire, and for later manifestations of Persian power. As William McNeill has noted, forays of Central Asian cavalry into the Middle East could not be sustained in areas of forest, mountain, or desert that were deficient in grassland. The Arabian camel was used in southern Persia, but rarely if ever for military purposes; the Bactrian camel of Central Asia was too slow.

To skirt the desert, armies on foot or horseback, eastbound or westbound, took the northeast corridor between the arid Dasht-e Kavir and the lofty Elburz Range, which rises to 18,000 feet but offers the Caspian Gates as passage to the Caspian Sea, twenty-five miles to the north. The Mongol forces of Genghis Khan transited the northeast corridor to the Middle East and back. The corridor provided entry to successive waves of Turks, including the Seljuqs in the 1000's and the Ottomans in the 1200's. After a century or so of service under Muslim rulers, both Persian and Arab, a majority of the Ottomans settled in Anatolia, where they established the base for one of the Middle East's largest and most enduring empires.

The one modern power with a vital strategic interest in this sector has been the USSR/Russia. With restricted access to ice-free waters (St. Petersburg is on the Baltic, Vladivostok on the Sea of Japan; the Black Sea is bottled up by Turkish control of the straits), Russia's strategic situation would be greatly enhanced by guaranteed passage through Iran. This objective has never been realized; the Anglo-Russian occupation of Iran in 1941, with its division into a Russian sphere of influence in the north and a British sphere of influence in the south, was a temporary arrangement that expired at the end of World War II.

The Indian Ocean

In historic times, the Middle East has been invaded four times from the south. First on the scene were the Portuguese. Impelled by the vision of Prince Henry the Navigator, they initiated the first great enterprise of the Age of Discovery – the search for a sea route to Asia. In 1487, Bartolomeu Dias rounded the Cape of Good Hope. Ten years later Vasco da Gama reached India. Portugal controlled the coast of Oman from 1507 until the 1600's and also built a fort in what is now Ra's al Khaymah, in the UAE.

By the late 1700's, British naval forces based in India had become the preeminent power in the Indian Ocean, the Arabian Sea, and its northern extension, the Persian Gulf. In those days, the eastern shore of the Arabian Peninsula was politically fragmented among shifting tribal confederations that welcomed foreign protection from the hegemonic aspirations of the Saudis and the Ottomans. This gilt-edged invitation was readily accepted by Britain, whose primary interest was not to move in, but to keep its European rivals out. The result was a series of alliances of convenience with factions flanking the "Lifeline" to India (Chapter 10). In 1793, Britain concluded an alliance with the ruler of Muscat. In 1813, those areas of India under British control were proclaimed British territory. The resultant "Government of India" concluded on Britain's behalf diplomatic agreements such as the peace treaty of 1820 with the cluster of shaykhdoms on what came to be known as the Trucial Coast.

In 1825, Britain and Persia signed a treaty replacing Russia with Britain as the privileged power in Persia. By 1830, British shipping enterprises had instituted regular steamship sailings between Bombay and Suez. This maritime segment of the Lifeline was anchored in 1839 by British acquisition from Yemen of the strategically sited port of Aden, which Britain was to hold for 128 years. From 1937 until it was granted independence in 1967, Aden was a British colony – the only segment of the mainland Middle East ever to be so designated. (Cyprus was a crown colony, 1924-60.)

Britain continued to dominate the foreign affairs of the tribes along the western shore of the Persian Gulf until 1971.

1800's - From the middle of the nineteenth century it shored up a faltering regime in Oman.

1861 - It established a protectorate over Bahrain.

1868 - By concluding a treaty with Britain, Qatar insured its independence from Bahrain and Saudi Arabia.

1892 - The Trucial Coast accorded Britain a monopoly over its foreign relations.

1899 - To bolster its autonomy within the Ottoman Empire, the Emirate of Kuwait accorded Britain the same privilege.

1916 - Qatar ceded to Britain foreign policy control, which lapsed with Qatar's declaration of independence in 1971.

During World War I, all these arrangements facilitated the British campaigns to minimize German infiltration into Persia and roll back the Ottomans from Iraq and the Levant. By 1920, Britain had established in Oman a proprietary role, which is still operative, with American military help, at this writing (Chapter 10). By 1972, all seven shaykhdoms on the Trucial Coast had joined the new federation, the United Arab Emirates (Chapter 11).

America's two momentous invasions of Iraq are dealt with in Chapters 9 and 15.

The Red Sea

The sixth century featured a bizarre episode in the history of Yemen. Having reputedly converted to Judaism, a Yemeni ruler committed massacres of Christian inhabitants of the country. The Byzantine emperor came to their rescue by prevailing on his coreligionists in Ethiopia to occupy Yemen and kill the offender. Within a few decades, the Ethiopians were expelled, at the request of the Yemenis, by forces from Persia.

Placing the Middle East in the Global Context

The region delineated in this chapter has an approximate land area of 2,800,000 square miles and a population of some 360,000,000 (Table A), which is 4.5% of the land area of the planet and 5% of its population.

"Middle East" is a Eurocentric misnomer – meaningless except from the viewpoint of Westerners, who attached matching labels to the Balkans (the Near East) and East Asia (the Far East). Nevertheless, the rubric is here to stay. Even the Arabs have adopted it (*Al Sharq al Awsat*). Nomenclature aside, the region commands global preoccupation as the crossroads of three continents that comprise 57% of the world's land area and 81% of its population. The unique strategic importance of the Middle East is uncontested. For western Europe, it is the direct route to South Asia and points east – and a potential base for attack on eastern Europe. For Russia, it holds the coveted promise of access to open ocean. For the states of Central Asia, it (and Pakistan) is the optimal commercial avenue to the outside world. For the planet as a whole, it is the cheapest source of petroleum, the indispensable fuel. For the United States, it incorporates the eternal homeland of the Jewish people.

Of the four aspects of power – political, economic, military, and cultural – the military packs the hardest punch (Chapter 1). The global incidence of military supremacy is highly variable. From the 700's to the 1000's, it was the Saracens who bore the banner of invasion. From the 1000's to the 1200's, it was intermittently the Crusaders and the Mongols. In the 1500's and 1600's, it was the Ottomans. In the 1700's and 1800's, it was the Europeans. Since World War II it has been the Americans. The final convulsions of Europe's ancient civil war, one hopes, were World Wars I and II. As a side door to Europe, the Middle East was an obligatory participant in both.

In the twenty-first century, there is a whole new global array: two actual powers – the United States and China; four potential powers – Japan, India, Russia, and the European Union. In the summer of 2003, the Union was beginning to consider setting up a GHQ independent of US-dominated NATO. This unprecedented hint of assertiveness may have been a reaction to the new unilateralism Washington displayed when it picked up the tattered old flag of imperialism and invaded Iraq, even though its motives were as obscure as its prospects (Chapter 15).

Any agency responsible for formulating policy for the Middle East may have to accept the validity of the following propositions:

1- The strategic importance of McNeill's "world bridge" constantly inspires importunate foreign interest.

2- The collapse of Ottoman hegemony left a power vacuum that foreign powers – notably Britain, France, Russia, and America – have variously exploited but never managed to fill.

3- The dictates of geopolitics condemn the region to a violent power struggle until the emergence of one or more new indigenous hegemons able to fill the vacuum.

4- This process will require a massive advance in regional modernization and cooperation.

5- The current segmentation of the region into nineteen states and seven disputed territories, as enumerated in Table A, is antithetical to the achievement of the two objectives specified in Proposition 4.

Table A. POLITICAL DIVISIONS OF THE MIDDLE EAST

State	Area (sq. miles)	Pop. (mil.)	Major Ethnic Groups
Armenia	11,500	3.3	Armenian Orthodox – 94%
Azerbaijan	33,400	7.8	Azeri (Muslim) – 90%: Shia majority
Bahrain	250	0.7	Shia – 40%; Sunni – 35%; Iranian – 8%
Cyprus (Gr.)	2,300	0.7	Greek (Orthodox) – 99%
Egypt	384,000	80.3	Sunni – 94%; Copt – 6%
Georgia	26,900	5.0	Georgian – 70%; Armenian – 8%; Russian – 6%
Iran	631,700	66.6	Persian – 51%; Azeri – 24%; Kurd – 7%; Arab – 3%; Baluchi
Iraq	167,600	27.5	Arab Shia – 56%; Arab Sunni – 19%; Kurd – 19%; Turkmen – 4%; Christian – 2%
Israel	8,000	7.0	Jewish – 76%; Arab – 20%
Jordan	35,300	6.1	Arab – 98% (over half Palestinian origin)
Kuwait	6,900	2.5	Sunni – 24%; Shia – 16%; noncitizens – 60%
Lebanon	3,900	3.9	Shia – 55%; Sunni – 20%; Christian – 25%
Oman	82,000	3.2	'Ibadi – 75%; other Arab – 15%; Asian – 10%
Qatar	4,200	.9	Arab – 40%; South Asian – 36%; Irani – 10%; expatriates – 750,000
Saudi Arabia*	757,000	27.6	Sunni – 72%; Shia – 4%; expatriates – 24%

Syria	71,100	19.3	Sunni – 56%; 'Alawi – 14%; Christian – 10%; Kurd – 10%
Turkey	301,400	71.2	Turk – 70%; Kurd – 15%; Alevi – 15%
UAE	32,300	4.4	Citizens – 20% (majority Sunni, minority Shia); expats (S. Asians, Iranians) – 80%
Yemen	203,800	18.7	Sunni – 59%; Shia – 40%
Disputed Territories			
Abkhazia	(3300)	(.45)	Abkhazian
Cyprus (Tur)	1,300	.1	Turk – 99%
Golan	480	.04	Arab Druze – 50%; Jewish – 50%
Gaza Strip	140	1.5	Arab – 100% (over half originate from what is now Israeli territory)
Nagorno-Karabakh	(1700)	(.15)	Armenian
South Ossetia	(1500)	(.07)	Ossetian
West Bank (inc. E. Jerusalem)	2,300	3.0	Arab – 84%; Jewish – 16%
Total	**2,767,770**	**361.4**	

*According to *The New Yorker* of 1/15/04, population figures for Saudi Arabia are a state secret.

Chapter 3
Demography

In 2007 there were 6.6 billion people in the world, by estimate of the United States Census Bureau. Of this total, the 360 million in the Middle East (Table A) comprised slightly over five percent. The region ranks well behind China's 1.4 billion, India's 1.1 billion, and Europe's 730 million, but ahead of the 300 million in the United States.

Population is only one of many components of the power equation (Chapter 1). In the current Middle Eastern power struggle, inadequacies in some of the other components have lately prevented the most populous contenders – Iran, Turkey, and Egypt – from translating demographic advantage into political or territorial aggrandizement. The eight-year war between Iran and Iraq ended in stalemate. Turkey turned its back on the Muslim World after World War I. Only American intervention has enabled Egypt to hold the line against Israeli expansion.

No Open Frontier

Most states in the region have more inhabitants than they can cope with. Looking at all the open space on the map of the Middle East, uninformed observers have criticized Arab states for denying sanctuary to the millions of dispossessed Palestinian refugees (Chapter 8). The Arab political argument – that taking in the Palestinians would constitute unconscionable capitulation to Western imperialism – may be open to debate. The demographic actuality, however, is beyond question: At its present stage of development, perhaps even in absolute terms, the Arab World is severely overpopulated.

American attitudes may be subliminally influenced by the tradition of the open frontier. The Native Americans were inundated by the tide of European settlement. Tribes that subsisted on hunting and gathering needed as much as a square mile per person to survive. In the early years of the European influx, the aboriginal population of North America north of Mexico has been estimated at 1.2 million – less than half of one percent of that area's population today.

Population Explosion

Although drought, pestilence, earthquake, and war have taken terrible tolls in the Middle East, in quieter periods population density in arable areas has been high for millennia. By early historic times, the Nile and Tigris-Euphrates valleys probably supported millions of inhabitants. Albert Hourani estimated the population of the Asian and African sectors of the Ottoman Empire in 1600 at 20 million – as compared with some 35 million in the Romance countries of Europe at the time.

The Twenty-first Century has dawned on a region that is straining at its demographic seams. Underdeveloped societies favor large families – in part as a defense against high rates of infant mortality. In 1990 Yemen, for example, life expectancy at birth was 46, far below the 75 in the United States and Israel. The introduction of modern medical standards will ultimately reduce family size, but in the short run it has produced a welcome but problematic flood of children. The Arab countries have the youngest population in the world.

The consequences for Middle Eastern governments are overwhelming. On top of a population density in the Nile valley of 2700 persons per square mile, Egypt's population has been rising at the rate of a million every nine months. The population of Iran has doubled since the Islamist revolution of 1979, despite the heavy casualties from the war with Iraq. Population increase in Saudi Arabia, from six million in 1981 to fourteen million in 1995, caused a decline in the country's per capita GNP.

In Israel and Occupied Palestine, the interaction between population and politics is particularly critical. In the 1990's, already crowded Israel undertook to assimilate a sudden influx of a million immigrants from Russia. On the other side of the "Green Line", the constricted, impoverished Arab residents of the Gaza Strip have achieved in recent years the highest recorded birth rate in the world.

At this writing, the territories under Israeli hegemony (Israel, the West Bank, East Jerusalem, the Gaza Strip, and the Syrian Golan) have a total area of 10,900 square miles and a population over 11,000,000 – over 1000 per square mile, in a country running short of arable land and water. In the face of these statistics, discussion of prospective repatriation of Palestinian refugees challenges reality. A UN survey estimates that the population of these lands and Jordan – now 17,000,000 – will reach 23 million by 2025. All are dependent on substantial financial assistance from foreign governments and international organizations.

Flight to the Cities

If the Sumerians created the earliest civilization, they must have built the first cities. The linkage between city and government was automatic: Rulers surrounded themselves with soldiers, retainers, and public officials; citizens found social, economic, and security advantages in clinging close to the ruler.

As dynasties rose and fell, some urban centers went the way of Nineveh and Tyre, and some survived the centuries – perpetuated by proximity to natural harbors (Beirut, Alexandria), shipping lanes (Constantinople), oases (Damascus), or caravan routes (Aleppo, Mecca). Gibbon noted the flourishing of cities in Roman times. He estimated the population of Antioch around 400 A.D. at over 500,000. (Today it is a modest Turkish community of 150,000.) Islam was a civilization of crowded, tumultuous metropolises, each centered around a Great Mosque. By 900 A.D., Baghdad had a population approaching a million, and drew traders from as far away as Scandinavia. In Christian Byzantium, Constantinople was soon to attain comparable size.

In the Middle Ages (defined by *The American Heritage Dictionary* as the period from 476 to 1453), the depredations from west (Crusaders) and east (Mongols and Turks) decimated the cities of the Middle East. In 1099 forces of the First Crusade slaughtered the Muslim and Jewish inhabitants of Jerusalem. In 1258 a Mongol army largely destroyed Baghdad, killed 800,000 of its citizens, and laid waste irrigation works that had survived from the time of the Sumerians.

The advance of urbanization resumed with the spread of Ottoman rule. After World War I, socioeconomic forces accelerated the trend. Population increase, mechanization of agriculture, and expansion of an absentee-landlord class reduced opportunity for independent farmers, driving them and their families into the cities. As for the storied nomads of the desert, they have lost their onetime status as a key element of Arab society.

In the Middle East of the Twenty-first Century, urbanization is the norm: Turkey- over 50%; Iran- approaching 65%; Iraq- 75%; Saudi Arabia- 83%. According to recent sources, four of the twenty-one biggest cities in the world were in the Middle East: At 12,000,000 (?), Istanbul may be the biggest city in Europe; *The Guardian*'s current estimate for Tehran is 14,000,000; *The New York Times's* figure for the Cairo area is 18,000,000. Baghdad's millions have been depleted by the ethnic cleansing precipitated by the American invasion. Some projections of the U.S. Census Bureau for the population of Middle Eastern countries in the year 2050 have the flavor of science fiction: Egypt - 128 million; Saudi Arabia - 50 million.

Family Planning

Now for the good news. In the battle against tradition, the techniques of population control are beginning to gain ground. Tradition is still strongly entrenched. While Islam does not prohibit birth control, conservative clerics infer that interpretation. When a UN agency sponsored a conference on population in Cairo in 1994, Mufti 'Abd al 'Aziz bin 'Aziz of Saudi Arabia denounced the proposal to discuss family planning as part of a plot to spread Western immorality. Deep-seated social forces are also at work. For women who are denied careers outside the home, the best guarantee of societal status is production of offspring, especially sons.

According to a report of 1998, the only Middle Eastern states to have legalized abortion were Turkey, the three states of the Caucasus, Iraq, and Israel – the last two only in cases of rape or incest. In 1979 Iran, the newly installed theocracy banned contraception. More recently, however, population pressures have induced Tehran to take the regional lead in family planning – setting up clinics, providing free contraceptives, and – according to Robin Wright – cutting off health benefits and food coupons after the third child. Iran's success in reducing its fertility rate (from 6.5 in 1980 to 2.1 in 2008, according to Martin Rees) has won it a citation from the UN. In Oman, a family-planning program has begun to reduce the birth rate. In Gaza, the Palestine Authority, an advocate of large families, has allowed UN and private agencies to reduce infant mortality by propagating modern methods of birth control.

Variegations of Citizenship

The American blend of democracy and free enterprise is justifiably admired worldwide. One of its noteworthy achievements is a high correlation between residence and opportunity. The day an immigrant arrives, he/she acquires certain constitutional rights, and is encouraged to pursue naturalization. Once the applicant acquires citizenship, the rights thus won are essentially the same as those of a citizen by birth.

In the Middle East, citizenship is jealously restricted. The multiple afflictions of Middle East society – overpopulation, communalism, economic underdevelopment, geopolitical fragmentation, power vacuum, Israeli-American imperialism, and violence – have combined to create a category of unfortunates who have been forced out of their ancient homelands and converted to the wretched status of political refugee.

So it was for millions of Palestinians strewn across the Occupied Territories, Jordan, Syria, and Lebanon after the wars of 1948 and 1967 (Chapter 8), and millions of Iraqis uprooted by the American invasion of 2003 and now struggling to survive in alien areas of Iraq, Syria, and Jordan. The Palestinians have been assigned impecunious but caring protection from UNRWA, a UN organization created for that specific purpose. After the 1967 war, many Palestinians found refuge in Kuwait, but no room in Kuwaiti schools. Their only alternative was "PLO school" in Kuwaiti school buildings at night. In Lebanon, as reported by *The Economist* in June 2007, they are barred from owning property or receiving state schooling or medical care.

In the Middle East, insidious communalism has even driven a wedge between East-Bank and West-Bank Jordanians. The *Times* of 3/14/10 reported anecdotal evidence of discrimination in the award of citizenship— allengedly stemming from the monarchy's apprehension about Israeli hints that Jordan may become "the new Palestine".

The Iraqis have no sponsorship at all aside from the minuscule resources of the Office of the UN High Commissioner for Refugees, and no hint from Washington of any recognition of its responsibility for their misfortune. Jordan, reluctant host of over half a million Iraqi refugees, placed restrictions on new admissions in 2006. Syria, contending with the social dislocations caused by the sudden appearance of a million and a half Iraqis, enacted legislation in 2007 intended to close the border to new arrivals and require the previous arrivals to leave Syria. In weighing the damage attendant on the invasion of Iraq, Washington should not forget respectable Iraqi women driven to prostitution to feed their homeless children: *Times* of 5/29/07. In 2009 Delinda Hanley reported that many Iraqi refugees in Syria and Jordan were denying their children schooling and medical treatment for fear of being sent back to Iraq.

A fortuitous exception benefited the Kurdish refugees from Iraqi Government harassment after Gulf War I (Chapter 9). Too embarrassed to duck this responsibility, Washington set up in northern Iraq a safehaven zone that has evolved into the Kurdish Autonomous Region.

Even the few who have managed to acquire a new nationality find that in the Middle East citizenship is a slippery concept, often adulterated by elaborate systems of gradation. Lebanon has naturalized a favored few Palestinians, most of them Christian, but most of their community have been denied not only citizenship but also the residence rights that Lebanon customarily extends to the thousands of guest workers imported from South Asia. Lebanon bans non-citizen Palestinians from most professions. Syria routinely denies Palestinian refugees citizenship, but allows them the same access as citizens to government services, education, and jobs. In Jordan, the only state to have granted citizenship to Palestinians en masse, there are at least three categories: full citizens; holders of Jordanian passports valid for two years; and "transients" who carry travel documents issued by Palestinian authorities in the Occupied Territories. In the Arabian Peninsula, foreign workers rarely if ever acquire citizenship by birth or long service in their country of employment.

In Israel, complexity is carried to the ultimate. The founders felt compelled to grant resident non-Jews the citizenship (*ezrahut* in Hebrew) of the new state, but to distinguish Jews from non-Jews by instituting the concept of nationality (*le'um*). The result of relevant legislation (Israel has no formal constitution) is the following intricate hierarchy of status (outlined by Oren Yiftachel in *Middle East Report* of Summer 2002):

1- Torah scholars, who receive a government stipend and are exempted from military service.

2- Mainstream Jewish nationals.

3- Non-Jews granted citizenship as relatives of Jewish immigrants; denied some health benefits accorded Jewish nationals.

4- Citizens of Druze and Circassian nationality, who are eligible to serve in the military and to receive the benefits that accrue from such service.

5- Citizens of Arab nationality, who are generally barred from military service.

6- Citizens of Bedouin nationality.

7- Citizens of Occupied East Jerusalem. On June 28, 1967, Israel formally extended the municipal frontiers of Jerusalem to include East Jerusalem and adjoining segments of the West Bank totaling thirty square miles. Israel did not call the action annexation, and it has not been recognized by any other state, but it has had consequences: a determined effort to Judaize the area, and conversion of its original 70,000 Arab inhabitants to permanent residents of Israel. Arabs in this category can move freely in Israel, but those who move out of the area or obtain residence rights elsewhere are likely to lose their Israeli residence status. Israel has ruled that Arabs born in East Jerusalem are aliens.

8- Non-Jewish residents of the Syrian Golan, to which Israel extended its administration and jurisdiction on December 14, 1981. The district's few thousand holdout Syrian residents, mostly Druze, were offered Israeli citizenship but few if any accepted.

9- Non-Jewish residents of Occupied Palestine outside the expanded Jerusalem. The Arab residents of the West Bank and the Gaza Strip have no rights of Israeli citizenship and few if any rights of residency. Dissidents can be unilaterally deported to a neighboring state.

Categories (1) and (2) in the table above apply to Jewish residents of all territories under Israeli hegemony: Israel, Occupied Palestine, and Occupied Syria. According to the late Israel Shahak, the State of Israel officially discriminates against non-Jews in three primary domains: right of residency, right to work, and right to equality before the law.

Over ninety percent of the land in Israel and substantial areas in the Occupied Territories are owned by the state. Palestinians cannot buy state land, and cannot buy or lease state land held by the Jewish National Fund. In reaction to a Supreme Court ruling of March 2000 that this prohibition was inconsistent with more basic law, the Israeli cabinet endorsed on July 8, 2002, a bill intended to override the Court's ruling (Chapter 8).

The preferential status of all Jews over all non-Jews was laid down in three basic laws (Chapter 8):

May 14, 1948 - Simultaneously with the proclamation of independence, the Provisional State Council abolished all restrictions on Jewish immigration and purchase of land.

1950 - The Knesset adopted the Law of the Return, which accords anyone, anywhere in the world, who is officially recognized as "Jewish" the right to enter Israel and settle there.

1952 - The Knesset adopted the Citizenship Law, which entitles any Jew the right to Israeli citizenship upon arrival in Israel.

The "Jewish" category includes anyone who can establish he or she had a Jewish mother, or is a legitimate convert. Judgment in these cases is left to the Rabbinate, presumably under the unwritten alliance concluded between the Rabbinate and Israel's secular leadership in 1948. (In its dedication to the Zionist doctrine, the Rabbinate would undoubtedly disallow any mass professions of conversion by communities suspect in their fidelity to Zionism.)

Unlike Jewish citizenship, Arab citizenship can be revoked, and has been in some cases. Israeli telephone directories single out Arabs by assigning them an introductory digit of identification. Israel delineates vehicle ownership by the color of the registration plate: All citizens of Israel, including all Jews in the Occupied Territories - yellow; Palestinian residents of East Jerusalem - yellow; Arabs from the West Bank - blue. In 2003, the Knesset passed a law barring Palestinians who marry Israeli citizens from acquiring citizenship or permanent residence status from the marriage. In 2008, Israel placed restrictions on marriage between Palestinians from the Occupied Territories and Palestinians from Israel: *Middle East Report*, Winter 2009, Oren Yiftachel.

Imbalances in the Labor Force

In the realm of economics, the countries of the Middle East fall into two categories: haves and have-nots. The haves include Israel (the only modern economy in the region) and the major oil producers – since the extraction and refining of petroleum products is the only consistently lucrative industry in the underdeveloped countries of the region.

Overpopulation, economic mismanagement, societal distortion, and political discord have combined to inflict endemic unemployment on all the countries of the region. Some illustrative estimates:

Egypt - 26% : *London Review of Books,* 5/27/2010, Adam Shatz.

Iran - Over 30 %: *Current History*, December 2009.

Iraq - 2002 estimate: 25%. Unemployment skyrocketed after the American invasion of March 2003 and the subsequent demobilization of the armed forces. In October 2003 the American administrator estimated unemployment at 60%. 2009 estimate, including underemployed: 38%.

Israel - 2006: over 8%.

Jordan - 2006: 30%.

Saudi Arabia - In the Arab oil states, discretionary unemployment is a prominent phenomenon (see below). By 1996, Saudi unemployment was high enough to fuel political unrest. In 2006, thirty percent of Saudi males and 90% of Saudi females were idle.

Syria - 2005: 20-30%.

Turkey - 2008: 10%.

Unemployment: Imposed and Discretionary

In an orderly Middle East, there would be a natural symbiosis between the haves – as manufacturers, investors, and employers – and the have-nots, as suppliers of raw materials, markets for products, and – above all – as labor pools. Opportunity for unskilled employment in the have states is particularly enhanced by the multitudes of citizens who, by virtue of generous welfare programs, can afford to choose unemployment over menial jobs. The ranks of the inactive are also swelled, in Saudi Arabia at least, by the women hobbled by a social system that educates them as well or better than men, but denies them appropriate jobs.

It is the misfortune of citizens of the <u>have-not</u> states that, in the Middle East, economic logic is nullified by political caprice:

Arabian oil states - In the 1970's, the Arabian oil states began to import Asian laborers. In 1990-91, the governments of Yemen, Jordan, and the Palestinian territories stayed out of the anti-Iraqi coalition assembled to expel Iraq from Kuwait (Chapters 9 and 10). The oil states of the Arabian Peninsula retaliated by expelling most of the guest workers who had come from these countries.

In the Kuwait of 1990, a resident population of 1.9 million comprised 800,000 citizens and 1.1 million expatriate workers and families – who could not own Kuwaiti property and had no political rights under Kuwaiti law. The Arab expellees were replaced by South Asian contract workers who, by 1997, held most of the jobs in Kuwait's private sector and nearly half the jobs in the public sector.

In 1990, the maintenance of the equipment of the Saudi military establishment was mainly done by Yemenis. War-related expulsion sent 350,000 people back to Jordan and Occupied Palestine, 100,000 back to Syria (despite its participation in the anti-Iraqi coalition), and 800,000 back to Yemen.

This demographic upheaval created sudden strains on the economies of the home countries – notably the termination of the remittances the expellees had been sending back to their families. In 1999, two-thirds of government jobs in Saudi Arabia and 95 percent of jobs in private corporations were reportedly held by South Asians or non-Saudi Arabs. In 2006, Saudi Arabia employed 8.5 million foreign workers, most of them from South Asia, 35,000 from the United States. In 1999, only one-eighth of the 2.4 million residents of the UAE were citizens. In Oman in 1998, Omanis expected cushy government jobs; 600,000 expatriates held most of the jobs in the private sector.

More recently, the Arab monarchies along the Gulf have embarked on programs to hire and train more of their citizens, but as of 2006 guest workers still did most of the hard labor along the Gulf: Oman - 600,000; Qatar - 660,000; UAE - over 3,000,000.

Israel and the Territories - On September 13, 1993, Israeli Prime Minister Yitzhak Rabin and PLO Chairman Yasir 'Arafat signed in Washington, in the presence of President Clinton and former Presidents Carter and Ford, a Declaration of Principles which was intended to implement the Oslo Accord, under which Israel finally recognized a Palestinian leadership (Chapter 8). Although the Declaration avoided all the hard issues, it was hyped as a historic breakthrough in the fifty-year-old Arab-Israeli dispute. In its afterglow, Palestinian investors began to repatriate funds to the Territories, and the signatories set out to lay plans for economic cooperation – which was grievously overdue, given the geographic interlinkage of their two domains. In August 1994, Israel was issuing work permits to 27,400 day workers from Gaza and 56,000 from the West Bank, as compared with 180,000 from both territories in 1987, before the outbreak of the first intifadah.

Meanwhile, however, as insurance against the continuing threat of Palestinian Islamist violence (Chapter 12), Israel had begun to import guest workers from Romania and Thailand. This process was stepped up in late 1994 in reaction to further attacks by Hamas. In May 1995, 16,000 Gazans and 29,000 West Bankers had permits for day-jobs in Israel. Increasingly, employment in Israel for Palestinians from the Territories was being held hostage to the activities of the Islamists, who did not recognize Israel, let alone the Oslo Accords. Security tensions fluctuated with the incidence of bombings, but the overall trend was negative.

In early 1996, Israeli imposition of tighter border and work-permit controls had elevated unemployment in Gaza to 50%. Toward the end of 1996, of a total labor force in the Occupied Territories of 433,000, 18,000 had Israeli work permits. Unemployment in the Territories was up to 60%, while hundreds of thousands of male temps from Asia, Africa, and eastern Europe were reportedly causing serious social problems in Israel. As of 1998, unemployment in all three domains was high: Israel (in recession) over 9%; the West Bank - approaching 50%; the Gaza Strip - 70%.

In 2003, after a suicide bombing on October 4, Palestinian day-workers in Israel numbered no more than a few thousand. This total included those resourceful illegals who still managed to slip across the border without getting shot by the Israeli guards. (Two years earlier, it had been estimated that up to 20,000 desperate Palestinians were taking this daily route to work.) Separate from the statistics cited above are the West Bankers employed by Jewish settlements in the West Bank and East Jerusalem. They may include as many as one fourth of the West Bank labor force, but they receive no benefits beyond their wages. There were 260,000 foreign workers in Israel, but government officials estimated that 180,000 of them were in the country illegally.

Chapter 4
Too Much Oil

By accident of geography, the Middle East is the richest region of the world in known reserves of crude oil. With Russia, it is one of the two richest in natural gas. Although these two commodities have different uses and pose different problems of exploitation, taken together they will be crucial to the global economy for the foreseeable future. For the major producing countries in the Middle East, oil and gas are the primary source of foreign exchange, but a painful cause of economic, social, and political stress.

Global Distribution of Reserves

Although calculation of oil and gas reserves is an inexact science, authorities were in general agreement on the following approximations as of 2006:

	Crude Oil Reserves (billion barrels)	Natural Gas Reserves (trillion cubic feet)
World	1200	6200
Middle East	730	2550
Saudi Arabia	265	242
Iran	132	970
Iraq	115	100
Kuwait	103	56
UAE	90	210
Qatar	20	900
US	22	204

Over the years, estimates of commercially viable petroleum reserves have varied widely, along with fluctuation in price, the vagaries of exploration, and technological advances in extraction from difficult formations like oil shale (which is prevalent in North America but not in the Middle East). In some countries, possibly including the United States, production may already have peaked. In others, notably Iraq and Azerbaijan, geologists suspect important fields remain to be discovered.

Natural gas, which burns more cleanly than oil, may eventually eclipse oil as the world's primary source of energy. In 1997, the ten biggest known gas fields in the world included six in Russia, one in Iran, and one – the biggest of all – in tiny Qatar; by one estimate, this one field holds 900 trillion cubic feet. Jean-Francois Seznec reported in the summer 2008 issue of *Middle East Policy* that Qatar and Iran share the North Dome gas field. Iraqi gas fields are also of particular interest, because of their situation in the Iraqi northeast – convenient for shipment to Turkey and the Balkans.

Middle East Production and Pricing

The modern petroleum industry was born in North America in the 1850's with the refining and sale of kerosene. In the Middle East, the industry took off in the 1870's in Baku, Azerbaijan, then part of the Russian Empire. In 1901, Russia's arch-rival in Asia, Great Britain, obtained through the initiative of William Knox D'Arcy a concession from the Shah of Persia to exploit oil fields countrywide except in the five provinces closest to Russia. In 1906, D'Arcy's Anglo-Persian Oil Company went public. Two years later, it struck oil.

In 1927, a consortium of British, French, and American companies and Armenian-Turkish entrepreneur Calouste Gulbenkian struck oil near Kirkuk in northeastern Iraq, then under British control. In 1933, in return for badly needed cash payments, King 'Abd al 'Aziz Al Sa'ud awarded the American company Socal a concession over a large area of eastern Saudi Arabia. A year later, Texaco went into partnership with Socal, under the name Aramco; commercial production began along the Gulf in the late 1930's. Oil in commercial quantities was found in Kuwait in 1938 by a British-American combine called the Kuwait Oil Company.

In the ensuing sixty-five years, skyrocketing petroleum exports from the Middle East to Europe, America, and East Asia have had global economic and political repercussions, and overriding significance for the Middle East. Production and price have fluctuated wildly. The oil states were alternately energized and buffeted. James Fallows has identified three "oil shocks" that had adverse consequences for the United States: 1973 -

The *Yom Kippur* War (Chapter 8) damaged the American economy and empowered OPEC; 1979 - the price rise sparked by the Iranian revolution caused inflation that helped cost Carter reelection; 1990 - economic stresses from the Iraqi occupation of Kuwait helped Clinton defeat Bush 41.

In 1960, in an effort to get a better grip on the petroleum market, the major Third-World producers founded OPEC – the Organization of Petroleum Exporting Countries. (The more politically oriented Organization of Arab Petroleum Exporting Countries materialized some years later.) Of OPEC's eleven members in 2005, six were in the Middle East: Iran, Iraq, Kuwait, Qatar, Saudi Arabia, and the UAE.

OPEC has had only mixed success in controlling prices; indigent members have often exceeded its production ceilings. In 1986, Saudi Arabia sharply increased production by way of reprimand, and the price of crude declined to twelve dollars a barrel. Under the budgetary gun, Iran dropped its demand for a ceiling double that assigned Iraq (those two states were locked in an exceptionally lethal war), and all OPEC members agreed on production levels calculated to bring the price back up to eighteen dollars a barrel.

In 1994, a Saudi decision to raise its production of crude to eight million barrels a day dropped the price back toward fifteen dollars and put budgetary pressure on Saudi Arabia itself; over the next two years, OPEC engineered a rise to around twenty-one dollars, only to see it fall again to fifteen dollars.

In 1998, an OPEC effort to raise the price to twenty-five dollars failed, in part because of an economic crisis in Asia. Threatened with loss of the American market to South American producers, Saudi Arabia let the price of crude fall below ten dollars. In 1999, Saudi Arabia perceived an interest in bolstering Iran's moderate President Khatami against his radical adversary, Supreme Leader Ali Khamenei, and patched up a dispute over production ceilings; the price moved up to the thirty-five dollar range.

In 2000, OPEC relieved the pressure on the importers by agreeing to set production ceilings aimed at bringing the price of crude down to the mid-20's. In late 2003, this range was still OPEC's declared objective, although the actual price – affected by a decline in Iraqi supply caused by the American invasion – was hovering at or above thirty dollars a barrel.

For the first half of 2005, the top fifteen producers of crude oil were: Saudi Arabia (9.5 million barrels per day), Russia, United States, Iran (4.1 million), China, Mexico, Norway, Venezuela, Nigeria, UAE (2.5 million), Kuwait (2.5 million), Canada, Iraq (1.9 million), Algeria, and Britain.

In 2004, a constellation of political complications combined to elevate the benchmark price of crude to 50 dollars a barrel and higher – far above the 22-28 dollars OPEC had projected as the ideal from the collective points of view of producers and consumers. World demand had exceeded 80 million barrels a day, and most exporting countries were producing close to capacity. World production was being reduced by resistance sabotage in Iraq, and by Islamist sabotage worldwide. By 2005, domestic economic pressures had led Saudi Arabia to support an elevated reference price of 40 dollars a barrel.

In 2007, according to *The Washington Post Weekly,* the leading exporters of crude, in millions of barrels per day, were: Saudi Arabia - 7.9; Russia - 7; UAE - 2.5; Norway - 2.3; Iran - 2.3. By this time, as reported by Michael Klare in *The London Review of Books,* the proliferation of SUV's in the US and passenger cars in China had inflated world oil consumption to 85 million barrels a day. In 2008, economic boom in India and China, combined with political unrest in some producer countries and repercussions of the American invasion of Iraq, had inflated the price of a barrel of crude to the all-time high of 150 dollars – before the global financial crash torpedoed the demand for energy. By March 2009 OPEC had managed to slash its oil production by three million barrels a day, but the price was still hovering in the range of 40-45 dollars a barrel – as the oil giants fell into deficit along with the rest of the world. In January 2010 it was back over 70 dollars a barrel, close to OPEC's target of 75 dollars.

Middle East Revenues from Petroleum

For fifty years or more, petroleum has been the primary revenue source for the Middle East, but the distribution of petroleum deposits and revenues has been vastly uneven – or, as an Arab nationalist would say, grossly inequitable. Arab oil states make periodic donations of conscience to their less privileged neighbors – notably Egypt, Jordan, and the "moderate" Palestinian faction led by Mahmud 'Abbas – but most unsquandered oil revenue has gone into building astronomical, but secret, "sovereign wealth funds" (SWF's). In late 2008 Rami Khouri reported that Sven Behrendt of The Carnegie Foundation had estimated the total value of SWF's in the Arab World at 1.5 trillion dollars – an amount far too large to be instantly invested in primitive Arab economies. Seznec's 2008 estimate for the major holders (before the sharp decline in world financial markets): Abu Dhabi - 350 billion dollars; Saudi Arabia - 289 billion; Kuwait - 213 billion; Qatar - 60 billion.

Following is an overview of the fortunes of selected producers:

Bahrain - In 1997, oil was contributing 60 percent of government revenue, but production seemed to be approaching the point of decline.

Iran - In 1998, with crude down to 12-13 dollars a barrel, sales were still 12 billion dollars a year – 80 percent of export income. By 2006, export revenues were estimated at 83 billion dollars a year, but then – because of a deteriorating infrastructure – they had fallen to 65 billion. Iran had been compelled by a gasoline shortage (caused by inefficient state management and illegal exportation to exploit government price fixing) to spend four billion dollars a year on imported gasoline. According to Seznec, Iran lacked the funds and the expertise to compete with Qatar for exploitation of the North Dome gas field.

Iraq - In the banner year of 2007, Iraq earned 37 billion dollars from oil exports, but the *Times* of 2/26/09 reported that the collapse of the price of oil had seriously undermined Iraqi plans to stabilize and rebuild the ravaged country.

Kuwait - In 1998, at 9 billion dollars per year, oil revenues were financing 70 percent of government expenditures. In 2007, crude export revenue had risen to 60 billion dollars a year.

Oman - In 1996, oil sales were 40 percent of GDP, but by 1999, production looked to be close to peaking.

Qatar - Oil and gas revenues were assessed at 3.5 billion dollars in 1998, at 40 billion dollars in 2008. Qatar has huge expectations from eventual LNG revenue.

Saudi Arabia - In 1999, oil revenues financed 90 percent of government spending. In 2007 they exceeded 206 billion dollars. In 2009 David Ottaway reported in *Foreign Affairs* that by 2004 Saudi Arabia had lost its ability to manage the global price of oil.

Syria - By 1995, Syria's modest crude production of 600,000 barrels a day had become the country's main source of income. The pipelines from Iraq to the Mediterranean, until their closure, had also been an important source of revenue. They were reopened for limited use by 2002.

UAE - In 1999, oil revenues were 86 percent of government expenditure. *Middle East Policy* reported in 2006 that Abu Dhabi, the only major producer among the seven emirates, shares its revenues with the other six. In 2007 the UAE earned close to 75 billion dollars.

Remittances

In October 2008 Michael Slackman reported in the *Times* that the resurgence of Arab expatriate workers in the Gulf had produced significant remittance income for their countries of origin: Egypt - three billion dollars; Jordan - two billion dollars; Syria - one billion. Lebanon's impressive remittance income of five and a half billion dollars in 2007 was presumably due to the loyalty of its farflung emigrant communities.

Processing

The Middle East oil states have had considerable success in augmenting their revenue by expanding petroleum operations to include refining and downstream marketing. Ultimately, they have an interest in using petroleum less as an energy source than as feedstock for plastics and other more lucrative end products.

As of 1991, there were twenty-four major (capacity of at least 70,000 barrels per day) refineries in the region: Egypt - 2; Iran - 4; Iraq - 3; Israel-2; Jordan - 1; Oman - 1; Saudi Arabia - 4; Syria - 2; Turkey - 4; Yemen - 1. In 2009, Iran was an importer of gasoline, and Oman and the UAE importers of gas to fuel their industries.

In 2008, *Middle East Policy* reported that the Gulf oil states were importing LNG to fuel booming chemical industries. According to Seznec, Saudi Arabia had become a ranking producer of chemicals and aluminum.

Expanding Web of Pipelines

When law and order prevail, the underground pipeline is the cheapest and safest means of overland transport of liquid petroleum products. Even in the picture-puzzle Middle East, where pipelines are subject to arbitrary closure by any one of the concessionary governments, and – as the United States has experienced in Iraq – pipeline sabotage is almost impossible to prevent, the lines have proved their long-term utility.

As of early 2009, the region was striated with oil and gas pipelines, some of which had particular economic importance and political sensitivity:

From Kirkuk, Iraq, to Turkey's Gulf of Iskenderun, with an extension to central Turkey (closed in 1991 by the anti-Iraq coalition, reopened in 1998 for exports permitted under the UN's Oil-For-Food Program, intermittently sabotaged after the American invasion).

A network of lines from fields in southwestern Iran to Gulf ports, and north to Tehran and Tabriz.

Across Egypt from the Gulf of Suez to Alexandria – bypassing the Suez Canal, which is too narrow for supertankers.

From fields in southern Iraq through Saudi Arabia to the Red Sea.

From fields in northern Iraq, through Syria, to the Mediterranean coast (inactivated for years by Syrian-Iraqi political disputes, but reopened for limited use by 2002).

The Trans-Arabian Pipeline (Tapline), from fields in northeastern Saudi Arabia across Jordan and Syria to Sidon on the Lebanese coast; completed in 1950, it was a major carrier for Aramco, and fuelled the recovery of Europe; closed in Syria and Lebanon in 1983, it has since been used only to supply a refinery in Jordan.

Georgia - In *TomDispatch* of 9/2/08, Michael Klare told a complex story of American-Russian intrigue, which has made pipelines Georgia's primary area of foreign investment. In the 1990's, Clinton conceived a plan to break the Russian monopoly over the transport of Caspian oil by converting pro-American Georgia into an energy corridor. By 2008, three lines from Baku in Azerbaijan crossed Georgia: to Supsa on Georgia's Black Sea coast; the BTC, to Ceyhan on Turkey's Mediterranean coast; to Novorossiysk (operated by British Petroleum) on Russia's Black Sea coast. *Current History* cited construction of the BTC line as a political victory for Clinton.

CNN reported in August 2008 that the BTC line had been shut down by Kurdish sabotage in Turkey, and that a second Georgian line (to Novorossiysk?) had been inoperative during Russia's intervention in northern Georgia in 2008 (Chapter 11). *The Wall Street Journal* of 9/4/08 reported that the intervention had damaged the prospects for additional pipelines across Georgia.

A natural gas pipeline across the floor of the Black Sea from Russia to Turkey opened in 2005.

In 2007 a proposed natural gas pipeline from Azerbaijan via Turkey to Greece would be the first non-Russian route from the Caspian to Europe. Western interests contemplated a Nabucco pipeline (from Azerbaijan via Georgia, Turkey, Bulgaria, and Romania to Hungary) as a major route to Europe for Caspian gas – but not Iranian! *Foreign Policy* of September 2009 noted that the project would require full access to Azerbaijani gas, which Russia had been trying to buy up.

The Battle for Control of Middle East Oil Fields

In the corporate rivalry for access to Middle East oil, the companies of America and western Europe once had telling advantages: 1) Western technology blazed the trail in the discovery and exploitation of oil and gas fields; 2) every state in the region has been swayed on occasion, by one means or another, in favor of Western interests; 3) the Atlantic basin is one of the two primary markets for Middle East exports (the other is East Asia); 4) Western companies have been more efficient, and in many cases better financed, than Middle East governments – let alone Middle East entrepreneurs.

In resisting the Western onslaught, the states of the region have had the one crucial advantage that they own the oil – although some of the policies of America and Britain suggest a conviction that their dependence on Middle East oil gives them an equal claim. Negotiations are generally tough, with both sides exploiting the standard strategy of playing rival bidders off against each other. In every auction the West profits from the political fragmentation of the area – another element in the rationale of those Westerners who contend that regional unification can never be tolerated.

Over the acrimonious decades, the owners of the Middle East fields have made fitful progress toward local control of the industry. The following chronology hits the high points in a process steeped in rancor, high policy, and war:

1886 - As characterized in Daniel Yergin's *The Prize,* the basic text on the global oil industry, outbreak of a "fierce, thirty-year struggle for the oil markets of the world" occurred among the Rothschilds of Europe, the Nobels of Sweden, and John D. Rockefeller's Standard Oil. The main objective was the oil fields of Baku, in Azerbaijan, then part of the Russian Empire.

1901 - William D'Arcy (British) won a sixty-year oil concession from the Shah of Iran. D'Arcy received crucial political support from Britain against the rival efforts of Russia.

1914 - Britain and Germany agreed to take over Gulbenkian's Turkish Petroleum Company (TPC), to be divided among the Anglo-Persian Group (50 percent), the German Deutsche Bank (25 percent), and Royal Dutch/ Shell (25 percent). Gulbenkian was to receive 5 percent of the revenues, to be contributed equally by Anglo-Persian and Royal Dutch/Shell. The Ottoman "concession" was never clarified, although the TPC had begun prospecting in Iraq in 1912 (per *Middle East Report,* Summer 2007).

1920 - In return for abandoning its territorial claim to Mawsil (Chapter 10), France acquired the German share of the TPC.

1920 - At San Remo, Britain and France concluded a secret deal to monopolize Middle East oil. They later relented under American pressure.

1920's - Oil concessions in Bahrain and Saudi Arabia were acquired by the American Socal.

1922 - Since the US, not at war with the Ottoman Empire, had not been represented at San Remo in 1920, the UK conceded the transfer of roughly half of Anglo-Persian's half of the TPC to an American consortium.

1925 - Major oil companies concluded the "Red Line Agreement", awarding control in the Arabian Peninsula to the US, and control in Iran and Iraq to the UK.

1925 - Faysal I, installed by the UK as the new King of Iraq, legitimated the operations of the TPC by awarding it an exploration monopoly, just in time for the 1927 discovery.

1928 - Wrangling among British, Dutch, French, and American interests over control of the TPC was resolved. In 1929, the TPC was renamed the Iraq Petroleum Company (IPC).

1933 - A year after the founding of the Kingdom of Saudi Arabia, Ibn Sa'ud granted an exclusive oil concession to Socal.

1934 - The Amir of Kuwait granted a concession to the Kuwait Oil Company. The United States and Britain agreed on an equal division of its petroleum operations.

1946-47 - A joint venture of Socal and Texaco in Saudi Arabia brought in Standard Oil of New Jersey (now Exxon Mobil) and Standard Oil of New York (later Mobil) under the corporate name of Aramco. French overtures to participate were rejected.

1947 - Aminoil, a consortium of American independent companies, won a concession for the Kuwaiti half of the onshore Neutral Zone (established in 1922 as part of the Saudi-Kuwaiti boundary settlement imposed by the British High Commissioner). The Getty Oil Company (American) acquired the concession for the Saudi half.

1948 - The Anglo-Iranian Corporation brought Standard Oil of New Jersey and Standard Oil of New York into its operations.

1951 - Pressed by new Prime Minister Mohammad Mosaddeq, the Shah signed a bill nationalizing the Anglo-Iranian Oil Company. Having owned 51 percent of the company, Britain was sufficiently exercised by the loss of revenue to impose an embargo on the export of Iranian oil – to the consternation of the United States, dependent on aviation fuel from Iran's Abadan refinery in its prosecution of the Korean War.

1953 - Perceiving rapprochement between Mosaddeq and the USSR, the United States and Britain concluded that drastic action was required to avert a Soviet takeover of Iran. In collusion with the Shah, the CIA headed an operation that, after initial reverses, including the temporary flight of the Shah, ousted Prime Minister Mosaddeq (Chapter 10).

1954 - The United States oversaw the formation of a British-French-American consortium that obtained from the Shah a concession dividing profits equally between Iran and the eight constituent companies.

1954 - The global petroleum industry was now dominated by the "Seven Sisters" – five American companies (Esso, Mobil, Chevron, Texaco, and

Gulf) and two British (Royal Dutch Shell and British Petroleum – formerly the Anglo-Iranian Oil Company).

1955 - An Anglo-French-American consortium took over control of the Iranian oil industry.

1956 - Alienated by American favoritism for the Israeli position in the Arab-Israeli dispute, Egypt refused American efforts to recruit it to the Allied side in the Cold War. The deadlock (Chapter 8) culminated in President 'Abd al Nasir's nationalization of the Suez Canal, whose several uses to the West included that of a transit route for petroleum tankers. Nasir seemed overmatched by a determined combine of America, Britain, and France, until the latter two overreached by colluding with Israel in a bizarre scheme intended to consummate British control of the Canal Zone, French control of the Canal Company, and Israeli control of the Gaza Strip and Sinai. The enterprise far exceeded the more conventional expectations of the Eisenhower Administration, which summarily scotched it, in a sobering display of America's postwar economic power. As an unintended byproduct, Nasir won a major political victory.

1957 - The Government of Japan cantered into the lists by winning concessions from Kuwait and Saudi Arabia for the offshore rights of the two Neutral Zones.

1960 - In reaction to an ill-advised price cut initiated by Standard Oil of New Jersey, several oil states created the Organization of Petroleum Exporting Countries (OPEC), a cartel designed to maintain price in the face of oversupply. In later years, OPEC would accelerate the gradual shift of control of the oil industry from the Western multinational companies to the governments of the producing states.

1961 - Iraq nationalized most of the IPC concession, although it lacked the technology to fully exploit the recovered fields.

1967 - The day after the outbreak of the Six-Day War (Chapter 8), major Arab oil states declared an oil embargo against the United States and Britain because of their support for Israel, which had just invaded Egypt. Production shutdowns, closure of the Suez Canal and the pipelines from Iraq and Saudi Arabia to the Mediterranean, and closure of Iran's Abadan refinery (because traffic through the Shatt al 'Arab was blocked by a strike of Iraqi pilots) drastically reduced the flow of Middle East oil. Within a month, however, deployment of new supertankers around Cape Horn and activation of surplus capacity in the United States and elsewhere had neutralized the "Arab oil weapon". The embargo was lifted within three months.

1971 - UAE President Zayid bin Sultan Al Nahyan nationalized the UAE oil industry. (Oil had been discovered in Zayid's emirate, Abu Dhabi, in 1958.)

1971 - Nixon instituted price controls and severed the linkage between the dollar and gold. As reported by *The Wilson Quarterly* in 2007, OPEC was discomfited by its consequent loss of income and took advantage of the 1973 war to raise its prices.

1972 - Iraq nationalized the rest of the IPC concession, including the Iraqi segment of the pipeline to the Mediterranean. Syria nationalized its end of the line.

1973 - A price dispute between OPEC and the multinationals was suddenly exacerbated by the outbreak of the Yom Kippur War (Chapter 8) between Egypt/Syria and Israel. When the fighting turned against the Arabs, the Arab oil states imposed a graduated embargo against the United States and the Netherlands. 1973 was a different story than 1967. The supply-demand equation had shifted in favor of the Arabs, and the new embargo was given teeth by production cuts. The consequences included a sharp increase in price, gas queues in the United States over the winter of 1973-74, and acrimony among the members of the North Atlantic Alliance. By spring of 1974, the inevitable leaks had begun to appear in the embargo, and the United States was exploiting differences in military and political strategy between the two Yom Kippur allies, Egypt and Syria. On March 18, a majority of the Arab oil ministers agreed to end the embargo. Meanwhile, however, the new posted price of crude was $11.65.

1973-80 - By incremental buy-outs from Aramco, Saudi Arabia nationalized its petroleum industry.

1980 - Iran reacted to the Iraqi invasion (Chapter 9) by blocking export of Iraqi oil via the Persian Gulf. Iranian ally Syria closed the pipeline from Kirkuk. Iraqi exports of crude fell from three million barrels a day to half that amount.

1981 - Kuwait took an initial step toward reversing the balance of control of the world petroleum industry between East and West by buying an American company, Santa Fe International.

1987 - Having turned itself into an integrated oil company by acquiring refineries and service stations in Europe, Kuwait bought ten percent of British Petroleum from the British government.

1988 - A number of Western companies had entered into participation with the government of Oman, and others with the government of Qatar, in projects for the production of liquefied natural gas and petroleum byproducts such as ammonia, urea, and plastics.

1990's - In its issue of Fall 2009, *Middle East Report* noted that Qatar was developing LNG exportation in partnership with Exxon, and Saudi Arabia had concluded massive petrochemical production deals with Dow and Sumitomo.

1995 - By executive order, Clinton voided a one-billion-dollar production deal between Iran and Conoco: *Foreign Affairs,* July 2009, Mohsen Milani.

1996 - The ban on dealing with Iran was expanded by the ILSA law (Chapter 10).

1997 - Iran concluded a two-billion-dollar deal with TOTAL.

1998 - A consortium of American firms began to export oil from Azerbaijan by pipeline across Russia. Azerbaijan had awarded Russian companies shares in the development of its Caspian Sea reserves.

1999 - ENI (Italian) and ELF-Aquitaine (French) signed a joint contract for oil exploration in Iran.

2001 - Saudi Arabia awarded nine development contracts to foreign companies, the first awards since the 1975 nationalization. By this time, the Saudis had invested heavily in refining and marketing in the United States.

2003 - Many Middle Easterners concluded that oil was Washington's prime motive in invading Iraq (Chapter 15). They were probably wrong; even the fantasists in the hawk camp had the means to realize the repercussions on the price of oil. In 2007 *McClatchy* reported that the 6000 aircraft of the USAF were burning seven million gallons of fuel a day – over half of total US Government consumption.

2003 - Exxon signed with Qatar an agreement to build a 10-billion-dollar liquid natural gas (LNG) facility. Royal Dutch Shell was to produce diesel fuel from Qatar's natural gas.

2004 - China signed production-sharing contracts with Oman and Iran.

2004 - According to the Summer 2009 issue of *Middle East Policy,* Iran and China signed an agreement for Chinese development of a major Iranian oil field, and planned construction of a pipeline via Kazakhstan to China.

2005 - Dow Chemical completed construction of a petrochemical plant in Oman.

2005 - Report Qatar had promoted formation of a Gas-Exporting Countries Forum, with eleven other participants. The media styled it – inaccurately – as the OPEC for natural gas (which is more expensive to ship than oil and more vulnerable to political vagary). (See 12/08 entry.)

2005 - *Foreign Affairs* reported Iran had agreed to supply oil and gas to India in return for development assistance.

2006 - Writing in *Harper's,* George McGovern and Bill Polk argued that the US should reimburse Iraq for the nearly 200 billion dollars the CPA had overcharged Iraq in oil-concession negotiations.

2007 - According to *Middle East Report,* Iraqi labor unions were blocking the CPA's effort to impose an inequitable oil law on the Maliki Government.

2007 - *Foreign Affairs* reported Turkey had granted Iran oil and gas exploration rights in return for construction of a pipeline to carry Iranian product to Europe. The US was opposed to the arrangement. According to *The Guardian Weekly,* the US persuaded Turkey to back out of an agreement to buy natural gas from Iran.

2008 - Iran concluded a petroleum development contract with China. After thirty years, Iran's principal petroleum market had switched from Europe to Asia.

2008 - *The New York Times Magazine* reported that Saudi Arabia had contracted to invest a billion dollars in Chinese oil refineries, and to accord China a multibillion dollar development/supply contract for natural gas.

2008 - Iraq signed a twenty-year 3.5 billion dollar contract with China to develop oil and gas production in Wasit Province, and a partnership with Royal Dutch Shell to recover natural gas.

2008 - Pepe Escobar took the position that Iraq's conclusion of oil production-sharing agreements with several Western oil companies proved that oil had been the primary British and American motive for invading Iraq. Michael Klare shared that view.

5/08 - Egyptian courts were hearing a case against Egypt's piping of natural gas to Israel under a fifteen-year agreement signed in 2005.

9/08 - Iraq's Southern Oil Company signed a 51-49 deal with Royal Dutch Shell to recover natural gas.

12/08 - Russia led the founding of The Forum of Gas-Exporting Countries, which could not be considered a cartel because gas is not sold on the spot market like oil, but by long-term contract. The fourteen members included Egypt, Iran, Qatar, and the UAE.

2/09 - The French oil company TOTAL would soon be shipping LNG from Yemen.

2/12/09 - The *Times* reported that Iraq had sold development rights on two southern oil fields to a combine of Royal Dutch Shell and Petronas (Malaysia), and a consortium headed by the China National Petroleum Company.

6/29/09 - Iraq put up for bids twenty-year service contracts on six oil fields – four in the south and two near Kirkuk. Iraq needed advances from contracting companies to finance reparation of infrastructure and restaffing of management, in hopes of achieving a radical rise in the annual production rate – now averaging only 2.4 million barrels a day, most of it produced by the government's South Oil Company. Most of the countries expelled by the nationalization of Iraq's oil industry in 1972 were expected to bid, despite Iraq's unsettled security situation. The thirty contracts awarded by the Kurdish Regional Government were not recognized by the central government.

6/30/09 - The response to Iraq's service-contract auction was disappointing – one deal with a joint venture of BP and the China National Petroleum Corporation. Most foreign companies preferred the more lucrative production-sharing agreements, and guessed that Iraq's production capacity had been so badly depleted by sanctions, mismanagement, and deterioration of infrastructure that its need for foreign financial and technical assistance would force it to capitulate on the issue.

June 2009 - Iraq signed a development contract for the vast Rumaylah field with British Petroleum: *Times,* 9/6/09.

12/1/09 - The *Times* reported that Iraq was shunning production-sharing agreements (more lucrative to the concessionaire) in favor of fee-per-barrel service contracts – including the Rumaylah deal with the British and Chinese.

12/12/09 - According to the *Times,* Iraq's prize contract – development of the West Qurna field – had gone to Russia's Lukoil.

The Battle for Control – Recap

As of 1975, the producer states of the Middle East had essentially nullified the original Western control of the oil fields. Once national interest had been insured, however, pragmatism asserted itself. The pendulum swung back toward reliance on Western financing and technology. This trend was enhanced by the new focus on the complex and costly process of producing and shipping LNG. In 2003, among foreign oil companies operating in the region, American companies were still the most active.

It has been said that, as the Twenty-First Century dawned, six Arabian families controlled a third of the world's oil. While most of the major oil states were at full production, Kuwait, UAE, Venezuela, and above all Saudi Arabia long had the strategic advantage of regularly pumping below full capacity. In sixty-five years, as reported by Ambassador Pete Hart, Saudi Arabia had been transformed from a desert principality with foreign-exchange receipts of six million dollars a year (mainly from taxes on the *Hajj*) to an affluent society with the trappings, though not the institutions, of a modern state.

No longer the quintessential swing producer, Saudi Arabia has lost the unique degree of control it once had over oil supply, and the consequent interest in exploiting this control to calibrate the world price of oil – high enough to pay Saudi bills, but low enough to preserve petroleum as the world's basic fuel. In 1998, Saudi Arabia flexed its productive muscles to drive the price down toward ten dollars a barrel, inflicting budgetary pain on itself, but teaching a hard lesson to states that had been violating the production ceilings assigned them by OPEC.

By 2004, 85 percent of the employees of Saudi Aramco – largest oil company in the world – were Saudi nationals. The company still employed 2000 Americans, most of whom lived in an Americanized compound in Dhahran. The company's official language was English.

Patterns of Trade in Petroleum Products

1914 - Large-scale export of Middle East oil began with shipment from Iran to Europe through the Suez Canal.

1939 - Direct tanker shipment to Europe was augmented by transit of Iraqi oil via the IPC pipelines to Tripoli in Lebanon and Haifa in Palestine.

1948 - Arab refusal to ship via Israel led to the closure of the IPC line to Haifa.

1950 - Tapline, built by the Trans-Arabian Pipeline Company from Saudi fields a thousand miles across Jordan and Syria to Sidon in Lebanon, went into operation. Its throughput equaled that of sixty tankers making a constant run between the Gulf and the Mediterranean via the Suez Canal.

1956 - Sabotage of the IPC pipeline in Syria to protest the tripartite invasion of Egypt penalized European importers at an annual rate of twenty-five million tons. From the late sixties on, shipment through the line was largely interrupted by political friction between the rival Baathist regimes in Syria and Iraq (Chapter 14).

1997 - As production in the North Sea and South America came closer to meeting the needs of Atlantic-basin importers, exports from the Gulf were increasingly directed to eastern Europe and East Asia.

1998 - Deprived of Iranian shipments since the 1979 revolution, and still denied Arab oil or gas (except from Egypt) despite the burst of Oslo-Accord euphoria in the mid-nineties, Israel was importing mainly from Norway and Mexico.

1998 - Russia was buying forty percent of the oil exported by Iraq under the UN's Oil-for-Food Program.

1998 - The biggest buyer of Omani crude was Japan.

1998 - LNG had become competitive in price with oil.

2000 - Although the states of East Asia were importing most of the oil they consumed, they were cushioned from price rises by their development of nuclear power and by their shift from heavy industry to the less energy-dependent electronics industry.

2000 - The United States was consuming one-fourth of world output of petroleum products; half its consumption was imported, half of that from OPEC states, primarily Saudi Arabia.

2000 - Total world consumption of oil was 76 million barrels per day. Europe was importing over half the oil it consumed, Japan most of the oil it consumed. In September 21 million barrels per day were being produced by six states along the Persian Gulf (Saudi Arabia, Iran, Iraq, UAE, Kuwait, and Qatar).

2001 - Thirteen percent of world exports of LNG were coming from Qatar and the UAE.

2002 - A looming factor in the global petroleum trade was China, which already imported 60 percent of its consumption from the Gulf, and may exhaust its own reserves by 2025. China was cultivating producers on bad terms with the United States, like Iraq and Iran. India's importation was also significant.

2002 - Saudi Arabia reclaimed its position as the principal oil supplier to the United States.

2003 - America's imports of natural gas were expected to continue to rise. Its major supplier was Canada, but the biggest potential suppliers were Russia, Iran, Qatar, and Saudi Arabia.

2003 - America was importing over half its daily consumption of 20 million barrels of oil. A country with 5 percent of the world's population was consuming 25 percent of the world's production.

2004 - It was predicted that, by 2010, China would be Saudi Arabia's biggest trading partner. China had signed a massive oil deal with Iran.

2004 - Much of world traffic in oil and gas was transiting four chokepoints vulnerable to terrorist attack: the Straits of Bab al Mandab, the Bosporus, Hormuz, and Malacca.

2006 - Since Iraq had no gas pipelines, it was burning off gas in the production of oil.

2008 - Michael Klare: The rise in world oil consumption to 85 million barrels a day was due primarily to China's 1994 decision to make private car ownership a pillar of the economy.

Economic Costs of Over-Reliance on the Oil Industry

The oil states of the Middle East have provided an unhappy example of the sometime paradox that more is less. The benefits of sudden wealth are apparent in the abrupt Twentieth-Century transition from the life-style of the cadaverous nomad to that of the well-fed recipient of government subsidy from cradle to grave. Not so apparent are the punitive costs that this transition inflicts on society:

Revenue Shocks - Just as one-crop agriculture lives in the shadow of intermittent famine, the oil state is dogged by the specter of price collapse. The most recent instance was in 1997, when economic crisis in East Asia contributed to the fall of crude below 14 dollars a barrel, imposing drastic cuts on the budgets of Middle East producing states – and on the foreign-exchange positions of Middle East remittance states (Egypt, Yemen, Jordan, Syria, and Lebanon). Saudi Arabia's 2003 budget surplus of 12 billion dollars was its first in three years. (The country has no income tax.)

Economic Mismanagement - Affluence engenders careless budgeting. The economic literature contains copious documentation of the financial ills contracted by Middle East oil states: overvaluation of their currencies, flooding of local markets with cheap imports – to the disadvantage of indigenous industry and agriculture; investment in grand projects devoid of economic rationale; disproportionate enrichment of the mercantile class; underinvestment in human capital; erosion of financial discipline; over-concentration on the petroleum industry; efflorescence of corrupt and bloated bureaucracies; and steep rises in population (as detailed in Chapter 3).

Inflation - In July 2008 Patrick Seale reported via *Agence Globale* that unmanageable income from oil sales pegged to the dollar had been an endemic cause of inflation. He cited five Arab states (Kuwait, Saudi Arabia, UAE, Oman, and Qatar) with inflation rates ranging from ten to fifteen percent.

The Corrosive Politics of Middle East Oil

The petroleum bonanza burst on a Middle East that was not ready for prime time. After four hundred years of uneven Ottoman and Safavid rule, more recently adulterated by haphazard intrusions from the West, the burden of government had fallen on an aggregation of tribal principalities, dilettante dynasties, and "accidental states" (Chapter 11). Absorbed in the simultaneous processes of building the institutions of government and wriggling free of foreign control, neophyte regimes lacked the managerial and technological resources required for orderly development of the petroleum industry. Instead, it emerged as the adventitious product of domestic ineptitude and great-power importunity. Miraculously enriched, the hoary structure of tribal and sectarian hierarchies was propelled into the leadership of communities whose sovereignty was brand-new but whose mindsets were, as John William Burgon said of the storied Jordanian city of Petra, "half as old as time."

In the countries more exposed to the outside world, the mold of tradition has been cracked. Turkey, Iran, Syria, Egypt, Iraq, and Yemen have already had their military coups. Iran seems to be embarked on the next developmental phase – social revolution. But in the Arabian Peninsula beyond Yemen, the tribal-clerical alliance has managed to hang on (Chapter 11).

Oil money has been the medium of survival. Continuity is the watchword. Change is doubly suspect: 1) It challenges the precepts of the *Qur'an* – the cornerstone of the Muslim hierarchy; 2) It threatens the survival of the ruling families. Bolstered by the American Fifth Fleet (based on Bahrain), the Gulf rulers have felt secure enough to experiment with innovation such as consultative assemblies, women voters, and satellite television, but they subsist in the shadow of the preeminent oil state:

Saudi Arabia is the paradigm of Jill Crystal's observation that oil may be the one export that accords its controllers structural autonomy from other power centers. The ruling family does not depend so much on other power elites inside the country as on multinational oil companies. Oil wealth and repression go hand in hand. Governmental and civic institutions are fragile. Democratic initiatives are stifled. Money better used for education and technology is diverted to recruiting and equipping an army to defend the monarch and a national guard to keep an eye on the army, and – in extremis – to compensating foreign rescuers. Rewarding the United States for expelling the Iraqis from Kuwait in 1991 occasioned Saudi Arabia and Kuwait major budgetary trauma.

Oil wealth has also eroded Saudi security in a more visceral way. Tribalism evolved as an early system of defense of the community against the rigors of the primitive geopolitical environment. Amidst the inhospitable sands of Arabia, it stood the test of centuries. Now the tide of oil money is pushing tribalism toward reductio ad absurdum. Preferential treatment for every member of the burgeoning royal family, plus less generous perquisites for citizens not so well connected, have deteriorated into a nationwide case of featherbedding.

The Saudi power structure grows increasingly top-heavy with the expansion of the royal family, which is split over an existential dilemma: Continue the subsidies and break the budget, or reduce the subsidies and fuel dissent – already smoldering among cohorts of young males denied the prestige of a government sinecure but unequipped to hold down a real job, and of young females barred from rewarding careers of any kind.

Special Problems

The broad field of Middle East oil politics is complicated by issues unique to the region and sufficiently intractable to demand separate attention. The following were uppermost at the time of writing:

Arab-Israeli Politics - Under constant pressure from Congress, Washington is unable to meet Arab demands for objectivity in the Arab-Israeli dispute (Chapter 8), or for sales of arms as sophisticated as those provided Israel. China has offered to consider Arab arms demands in return for greater access to Saudi oil.

Oil Supply for Israel - Although there are hints of gas reserves off the coast of the Gaza Strip, Israel remains totally dependent on imported gas and oil. The Shah of Iran had reportedly been negotiating supply arrangements. The regime that succeeded him in 1979 has been hostile to Israel. Prospects for access to Arab oil have not materialized. Discussions with Qatar in 1995 and Egypt in 1999 came to no known consequence. They were probably casualties of Intifadah II (Chapter 8). Washington has promised to insure Israel's oil supply. Israel began receiving gas from Egypt in 2008.

OPEC Infighting - Although the immediate provocation that sparked the founding of OPEC was a price reduction sprung on the producers by Standard Oil of New Jersey, the cartel had deeper significance as a declaration of independence from the West. Even at this formative stage, it also reflected the endemic rivalry among Middle East regimes. In promoting the founding of OPEC, the government of 'Abd al Karim Qasim in Iraq hoped to undercut the influence then wielded by Egypt's 'Abd al Nasir over the Middle East oil industry.

In the 1970's, OPEC was the arena of a feud between Iran, which wanted higher crude prices, and Saudi Arabia, which wanted lower. As Sheikh Ali noted in 1986, Iran was under much greater population pressure than Saudi Arabia. *Times* columnist William Safire speculated in April 1986 that the Saudis perceived three advantages in keeping the oil price low: 1) Destroy the competitive position of coal and nuclear power; 2) Reduce Iran's capacity for war; 3) Try to lure Britain into OPEC.

In 2000, the Arabian oil states perceived a special interest in maintaining oil prices in the upper range in order to enhance the likelihood that moderates would win the Parliamentary elections in Iran.

The Division of Caspian Oil - With the discovery of significant reserves under the Caspian Sea, offshore ownership became a pressing issue. The ongoing dispute engages one European state (Russia), two Central Asian states (Kazakhstan and Turkmenistan), and two Middle East states (Azerbaijan and Iran). Since most known offshore reserves lie in the zones plausibly claimed by Azerbaijan, Kazakhstan, and Turkmenistan, Russia and Iran are advocating joint exploitation of all Caspian petroleum resources.

Economic Sanctions Against Iraq - After the Iraqi invasion of Kuwait in 1990, the American animus against Saddam, its recent ally, expressed itself in the maintenance, under UN auspices, of punitive economic sanctions against Iraq (Chapter 9). The effect on the Iraqi petroleum industry was severe. Although the Iraq National Oil Company, founded in 1968, was considered one of the world's better-run state companies, production plummeted as Turkey stopped loading at its end of the pipeline and the sanctions blocked the importation of replacement parts. The huge Kirkuk field gradually became a "wasteland". Production fell from 3.8 million barrels a day before Gulf War I to a low of 850,000. Aside from appreciable quantities smuggled out by truck and barge with the cooperation of neighboring countries, exportation ceased except to Jordan, which was allowed to import Iraqi oil for its own needs.

In 1996, affected by the damage done by the sanctions to the health and quality of life of the Iraqi people, the UN initiated the Oil-for-Food program, under which Iraq was allowed to resume pumping at specified levels through the pipeline to Turkey. By 1998, Iraq was allowed to export crude worth some 10 billion dollars a year, although one-third of the proceeds went to Kuwait as war reparations. Iraqi production was limited to 2.2 million barrels a day by the degradation of its oil-field infrastructure.

In 2000, Syria unilaterally reopened the pipeline from Iraq; the action did not have UN approval, but the United States chose not to challenge it because France had threatened to raise the counterissue of Iraqi smuggling to Turkey, America's ally. Iraq signed development contracts with Russia and China, subject to abrogation of the sanctions. Support for the sanctions was beginning to fray under pressure from interested states, particularly Turkey, which had lost billions of dollars in pipeline fees and sales of commodities to traditional markets in Iraq.

In 2002, Daniel Yergin calculated that Iraq had brought its crude production back up to 2.8 million barrels a day. But by May of 2003, the

Iraqi oil industry had been so devastated by the American invasion and subsequent looting that it was producing only 300,000 barrels a day. Later in the year, in the face of intermittent sabotage, the American occupation authorities had brought production back up to approximately two million barrels a day. In 2003, France was concerned that the American occupiers of Iraq would freeze out French companies – notably Total Fina Elf, which had development rights to approximately one-fourth of Iraq's reserves. In 2004, Iraqi oil exports were in the range of a million and a half barrels a day.

Invasion of Iraq - According to *Foreign Policy* of March 2007, the invasion of 2003 caused a rise in the price of oil from 30 dollars a barrel to 80.

Pipeline Politics - In the mid-seventies, the pipeline from north Iraq to the Mediterranean was carrying one-third of Iraq's total production. However, the line has been a perennial victim of Middle East instability. Closed by Syria in 1976, it was reopened in 1981, then closed again under Iranian pressure in 1982, then reopened by Syria in 2000.

Since the freeze in American-Iranian relations that followed the Iranian revolution of 1979, Washington has pursued a punitive economic policy toward Iran. A law adopted in 1995 denied American financial services to any foreign corporation or bank investing 40 million dollars or more in the Iranian petroleum industry. Integral to this policy has been opposition to any pipeline from the Caucasus or Central Asia through Iran, even though that may well be the cheapest and most practicable route to the outside world, and its denial does a strategic service to Russia, which controls one of the two alternative routes.

Washington favors routing oil from the Caucasus and Central Asia through the political and geographic obstacles of the Caucasus, either on through Turkey to the Mediterranean, or to the Black Sea and on through the increasingly constricted Dardanelles-Bosporus seaway. In 1998, Washington prevailed on the consortium developing Azerbaijan oil to start a pipeline to Turkey's Mediterranean port of Ceyhan – a route that had scant economic rationale but would promote American and Turkish ties with Azerbaijan. American oil companies favored the more economical route through Iran or, failing that, expanding the line to the Georgian port of Supsa on the Black Sea – although Turkey had announced its intention to ease the ecological threat to the straits by reducing the flow of tankers from its current rate of 4500 a year.

Clinton's plan to promote a Georgian corridor (see above) faces political uncertainties (Georgian instability, Armenian-Azeri hostilities), and this route transits a seismic area. The plan took shape in the form of the Baku-Supsa line and the Baku-Ceyhan line (completed in 2006).

The Misfortunes of War - Since the end of World War II, the Middle East has been infested by sixty-three years of endemic warfare:

1920's-30's - Jews and Arabs repeatedly clashed in Palestine.

1940's-50's - Tribal warfare in Yemen.

1948 - Israelis won a war of independence against Britain, the Palestinians, and adjoining Arab states.

1950's - Civil war in Oman between 'Ibadi tribes and the Sultanate.

1956 - Israel, Britain, and France invaded Egypt. Eisenhower forced their evacuation in 1957.

1960's - South Yemeni insurrection against British rule.

1961 - Syrian secession from union with Egypt.

1962-70 - Civil war in Yemen between the monarchy (backed by Saudi Arabia and Yemen) and revolutionaries (backed by an Egyptian expeditionary force).

1967 - Israel conquered Sinai and Gaza from Egypt, the West Bank from Jordan/Palestine, and the Golan from Syria.

1970 - Civil war in Jordan between the monarchy and the Palestinian resistance (backed by Syria).

1970-82 - Civil war in Syria between Islamists and the Baathist regime.

1970-73 - War of attrition between Israel and Egypt.

1973 - War between Egypt/Syria and Israel.

1974 - Turkish occupation of northern Cyprus.

1975-90 - Civil war in Lebanon between pro-Western and pro-Arab factions.

1978 - Israeli incursion into south Lebanon, followed by twenty-two years of Lebanese resistance.

1980-88 - War between Iran and Iraq (backed by the US and the Arab oil states). The US engaged Iranian naval forces in the Persian Gulf. Iraqi Kurds backed Iran.

1982-2000 - Israeli occupation of southern Lebanon. US intervened briefly on the Israeli side. Syria and the Palestinian resistance backed Lebanon.

1987-93 - Palestinian Intifadah I versus Israel.

1990 - Iraq occupied Kuwait.

1990's - Georgia fought two insurgencies backed by Russia.

1991 - The US expelled Iraqi forces from Kuwait and conducted punitive military action against Iraq.

1991 - Iraq put down a Shiite insurgency in the south.

1991-3 - War between Armenia (backed by Iran and Russia) and Azerbaijan (backed by Turkey). (Armenia still holds Azerbaijani territory.)

1992-2004 - Kurdish insurrection in Turkey.

1994 - Civil war in Yemen between north and south.

2003-200? - US occupation of Iraq – against protean resistance.

2006 - The withdrawal of Israeli forces from The Gaza Strip was followed by an electoral victory of Hamas over The Palestinian Authority, and a military takeover of the Strip by Hamas.

2006 - Hostilities between Israel and the forces of Hamas in The Gaza Strip.

2006 - Hizballah held its own against invasion of south Lebanon by Israel, which conducted massive air action against diverse targets in south Lebanon and west Beirut.

2007-8 - Turkey and Iran attacked bases of Kurdish insurgent organizations (PKK in Turkey, PEJAK in Iran) located in the Kandil Mountains of the Kurdish Autonomous Region of Iraq.

2008 - Russian intervention in support of Ossetian and Abkhazian secession from Georgia dealt a serious blow to American planning on Georgia as a major pipeline route.

2008 - Second round between Israel and Hamas.

Many of the military actions catalogued above obstructed the petroleum industries in the region. The tripartite invasion of Egypt in 1956 caused the temporary closure of the Suez Canal and the pipelines from Iraq to Syria's Mediterranean coast. The Yom Kippur War closed the Suez Canal from 1973 to 1975. The ongoing Arab-Israeli conflict finally shut down the northern sector of Tapline in 1983.

The Iran-Iraq War severely disrupted the petroleum industry along the Persian Gulf. Iraq damaged the Iranian refinery at Abadan. Iran blocked shipments from Iraq and carried out air strikes on Saudi tankers. Saudi Arabia, which was providing financial support for the Iraqi war effort, encouraged Iraqi attack on the Iranian oil port on Khark Island – in part to boost oil prices. Syria shut down the Iraqi pipeline to the Mediterranean. The US Navy intervened in force to protect oil shipments, but Iraq's oil exports fell from 3.3 million to 750,000 barrels a day.

In 1991, Iraq retaliated for US expulsion operations by devastating the infrastructure of the Kuwait oil industry and burning two billion barrels of Kuwaiti oil.

By 2000, having failed to gain control of the Shatt al 'Arab from Iran or the Khawr 'Abdallah from Kuwait, Iraq was reduced to exporting by truck, barge, and pipeline via Jordan, Syria, and Turkey.

Turkey's lucrative receipts from pipeline fees were interrupted from 1991 to 1996 by UN sanctions against Iraq, alleviated from 1996 to 2003 by the Oil-for-Food program, reinterrupted in March 2003 by the American invasion, resumed that summer, but intermittently sabotaged thereafter.

Wanted: A Better Energy Strategy

America's oil imports far exceed those of any other country. The world's top ten exporting countries include four in the Middle East – Saudi Arabia, UAE, Iran, and Kuwait – plus a fifth once Iraq is stabilized.

The attendant transfer of wealth from the United States to foreign suppliers (970 billion dollars in 2006, according to Michael Klare) is unsustainable. In the long term, America will have to reduce its dependence on fossil fuel. In the short term, it will have to do a better job of promoting affordable access to foreign sources.

The current American effort to dictate policy to key exporting states is failing. Blandishing autocratic regimes is ultimately self-defeating. Military operations bog down in regional politics, escalate the cost of oil, and squander fuel in the process. Granted, the region is fated to endure decades of turmoil, but foreign intervention only makes matters worse. To keep oil prices down, and above all to guard against political confrontation with rival buyers (China), Washington should abandon its predilection for trying to housebreak oil-state regimes, and wielding the Fifth Fleet as a bulldozer against threats to maritime chokepoints: the Strait of Hormuz (17 million barrels per day), the Suez Canal (4.2 million with the SUMED Pipeline), the Turkish straits (3.1 million), and the Bab al Mandab (3.0). The Hormuz bottleneck is so narrow that supertankers have to transit it single file.

Washington is undoubtedly resolved to maintain American dominion of the seas and Israeli-American preeminence in the air, but the case for permanent deployment of ground troops in the Middle East (or central Asia) will be increasingly awkward to defend. The indicated policy is reliance on astute negotiation and low-key diplomacy – avoiding partisan engagement in regional disputes, and efforts to repeal geography by trying to dictate pipeline routes in accordance with political caprice.

The Future of Non-Renewable Energy

A study by Jan Kalicki in *Middle East Policy* of Spring 2007 estimated that, of total annual energy consumption, 24 percent was obtained from coal and 63 percent from oil and gas. Half the oil was coming from the Middle East. The equivalent cost of alternative fuels was still prohibitive:

American oil shale - 80 dollars; Venezuelan tar sands - 60 dollars; Albertan tar sands - 40 dollars, plus massive damage to the environment.

In his definitive study of the petroleum industry, *The Prize,* Daniel Yergin highlighted the geopolitical centrality of oil as the world's most essential commodity in this "era of hydrocarbon man". His analysis is incontrovertible. Modern machinery runs on oil. Oil won World War I. In World War II, Allied reliance on oil-fuelled vehicles, ships, and planes altered the character of war. Someday, perhaps, natural gas will emerge as the fuel of choice. Gas already meets one-fourth of United States energy requirements, but for now, oil runs the world. In 2003, world consumption of crude oil approximated 78 million barrels per day. The International Energy Agency estimated that world consumption of oil would reach 120 million barrels a day by 2030, and that most of it would come from the Middle East.

As the primary source of oil, and a major source of gas, the Middle East has mesmerized every great power since the British Navy went from coal to oil in 1914. Access to the oil fields of Azerbaijan was central to Hitler's invasion of southern USSR in the summer of 1941. In the ultimate irony, the enterprise expired on the northern slopes of the Caucasus Range in August 1943 when German tanks ran out of diesel fuel. By 1997, when the United States had managed to diversify its sources by turning to West Africa and South America (Venezuela was then its leading foreign supplier), Japan and China had become heavily dependent on imports from the Middle East – under the tacit protection of the United States Navy. Some analysts speculate that turmoil in the Middle East – such as an Arab civil war or the emergence of an Islamic theocracy in Saudi Arabia – could precipitate a global recession.

In the dialect of the oil industry, the Persian Gulf and the lands around it are the "surge pot" – the area that will dominate the global price of oil. In the contest for markets and revenue, the leaders will be Saudi Arabia and Iran – two neighbors divided by language, sect, and ancient political rivalry. Middle East producers have a huge price advantage over the rest of the world. The cost of producing a barrel of crude in the Middle East in 2003 averaged 20 cents – as against 80 cents in Venezuela and 90 cents in Texas. The challenge for Middle East producers is to set the price high enough to meet their escalating budgetary demands, but not so high as to depress the economies of the consumers, or to drive them toward developing alternative sources of energy.

Oil is widely traded on the <u>spot market</u>, where immediately deliverable shipments are sold for immediate payment. In the view of some analysts, oil has become so fungible (exchangeable) that no producer is likely to find a way to wield it as a strategic weapon – as Arab producers did for a few months in the winter of 1973-74.

On the crucial issue of how best to guarantee supply, the powers seem to have split into two camps. Japan, China, and continental Europe rely on conventional means of access to Middle East oil – negotiation, economic maneuver, and financial incentive. Only the United States and Britain have gravitated toward a neoimperialist stance, which culminated in March 2003 in the illegal and unprovoked occupation of Iraq. The genuine motivation for this action is a mystery shrouded in a nebula of incoherent assertions out of Washington and London, but oil clearly figured in their strategic equation (Chapter 15). Despite the suspicions of many Arabs and Iranians, oil seems unlikely to have been the only objective of invasion, or even the primary one: Intuition suggests that the United States has spent billions more on armed intervention than it would have had to pay to insure adequate commercial supply – barring political conflagration, which would be beyond the control of any foreign entity.

In the long run, parochial concerns will be overshadowed by macroeconomic imponderables. Petroleum is a finite resource. How long will the oil supply hold out? Some predict world production will peak between 2004 and 2008. Others estimate that the world has proven resources good for another ninety years. On this latter side of the debate are those who fear that, before the world runs out of oil, it will run out of the ecological capacity to absorb the products of its combustion. This school of thought recommends urgent conversion to renewable sources of energy, whatever the cost. In this event, the Middle East seems well positioned to move to the forefront in the production of solar power.

Prospects of Phosphorus Production

Scientific American reported in 2009 that the world's known reserves of phosphorus, an essential component of fertilizer, approximated 15 billion metric tons – enough for ninety years at current consumption rates. Although the major known reserves were in Morocco, China, South Africa, and America, Middle East planners looking for export income to supplement oil shipments could focus on development of Levantine and Egyptian phosphorus reserves totaling 1.3 billion metric tons.

Chapter 5
Not Enough Water

Since the rise of civilization 6000 years ago, its most populous centers have emerged in river valleys. Even those favored locations have suffered crushing periods of drought, but it was not until the Twentieth Century that society began to run out of water. The average daily consumption of water in developed countries (North America and Japan) is 158 gallons per capita. As populations increase and standards of living rise, demand inexorably escalates. So far, the shortfall between consumption and annual precipitation has been met from subterranean aquifers, but many around the world are close to depletion. Water consumption is widely subsidized, but Lester Brown has noted that since it takes a thousand tons of water to grow a ton of wheat, the price of wheat is a reliable gauge of the true price of water.

Worldwide, the primary demand on the water supply is for irrigation – 80 percent in the Middle East though only 20 percent in the United States. In the short term, irrigation produces handsome results, but in the long run – failing adequate drainage – it salinizes and destroys the land it waters. Sandra Postel contends that "most irrigation-based civilizations fail." Middle Easterners have practiced irrigation for at least 6000 years, with unhappy result. Vast areas of Iraqi desert were fertile farmland in ancient times. Israel, inventor of the highly economical technique of drip irrigation, is now phasing out irrigated wheat production.

The West is beginning to realize that the benefits of mammoth dams are equally ephemeral, although dams continue to fascinate the Middle East. Egypt completed the Aswan High Dam in 1970, Syria the Euphrates Dam in 1973. Turkey is intently building a massive array of dams on the

73

upper Tigris and Euphrates. The utility of all these projects will expire in a century or so when their reservoirs silt up.

The ultimate resort is desalination, but current technology is prohibitively expensive for most countries and – like dams and canals – highly vulnerable to military attack in an unstable area like the Middle East.

Most of the Middle East would be an eastern extension of the Sahara Desert, but for the sparse rainfall trapped by the mountains of Yemen, Oman, western Iran, Turkey, and the Levant, by the watersheds their runoff supplies, and by two major river systems. The Tigris-Euphrates system rises in the region, but the Nile – the only world-class river in the Middle East – rises outside the region, in eastern Africa, 2000 miles south of the Mediterranean.

The Middle East water story has one central theme – the relentless decline of per capita supply. Records of punishing droughts go back as far as 2200-2100 B.C., when a cluster of dry years imposed famine on Egypt and collapsed the vibrant society of city-states in Mesopotamia, Syria, and the Akkadian Empire. It was only in recent times that Middle Easterners woke up to the reality that river flow was being fully exploited and aquifers laid down over millennia were beginning to salt up or even run dry.

Chapter 3 noted a sharp disparity in the economic fortunes of the region's have and have-not states. There is a comparable disparity in the distribution of rainfall. It is apparent from meteorological maps that in Egypt, the Arabian Peninsula, and much of Jordan, Syria, Iraq, and Iran, average annual precipitation falls below ten inches a year. Areas receiving the agriculturally significant average of thirty inches or more are restricted to the Black Sea coast of the Caucasus, the Mediterranean coast of Turkey, and the mountains of Iran, Iraq, Lebanon, Syria, Turkey, and Yemen. Of the nineteen countries in the Middle East, only three receive enough precipitation to meet anticipated needs: Turkey, Armenia, and Georgia.

Water is increasingly the subject of bitter dispute. If oil was the bone of contention in the Twentieth Century, water may commandeer a similar role in the Twenty-First. In the Middle East, four situations invite special attention:

Crisis in Arabia?

In the Middle East, some 1700 plants convert 5.5 billion gallons of seawater to fresh water every day. About half the water consumed in Saudi Arabia is pumped from deep aquifers, but the rest comes from desalination plants along the Persian Gulf. Desalination provides two-thirds of the

UAE's water supply, much of which has been diverted to uneconomical agricultural projects. The Arabian aquifers are primarily fossil water, the product of centuries of capricious rainfall. Hydrologists are concerned that they may be close to exhaustion from overpumping and pollution. (Most Saudi cities have no sewerage system.) In the words of Lester Brown, Saudi Arabia is a country where the "water bubble" is about to burst.

Yemenis have a national addiction to *qat,* a native plant which according to Kristian Ulrichsen (*Middle East Policy*) depletes the soil and consumes over two-thirds of the country's annual water consumption.

Cheap oil has naturally inclined Arabian governments toward reliance on desalination. However, the production of one nonrenewable resource by the burning of another does not look like a sound policy for the long run. There is no technology in sight to relieve the rulers from their responsibility to defuse the bomb of skyrocketing population.

Allocation of the Flow of the Nile

The flow of the Nile, some 90 cubic kilometers per year, is about one-sixth that of the Mississippi, but it is the lifeblood of Egypt. In 1929, a British-orchestrated treaty guaranteed Egypt 55.5 billion cubic meters of the average annual discharge, plus veto power over diversion projects of upriver states: *Middle East Policy,* Winter 2009, Harald Frederiksen. In 2009, the major users of Nile water were Ethiopia (population 83 million), Egypt (82 million), and Sudan (40 million).

At considerable expense, including sharp reduction in the annual deposit of nutrients on the fishing grounds adjoining the Nile delta, Egypt has deferred its water crisis by building a dam and a reservoir big enough to cushion the variation in the annual flow of the Nile – and even to pipe water under the Suez Canal into Sinai. Even so, severe drought in the 1980's almost emptied the reservoir: Frederiksen.

In 1959 Egypt and the Sudan achieved temporary resolution of an ongoing water dispute by agreeing to divide the flow at a ratio of 87 percent for Egypt and 13 percent for the Sudan. The other upriver states, including Ethiopia, where most of the flow originates, did not participate. Sudan has not yet drawn its entire quota, but it has plans to construct a reservoir 106 miles long at Marawi, near the Fourth Cataract.

According to the 5/28/10 *Guardian Weekly,* five upriver states have signed a treaty that bids for greater access to Nile water. Egypt and Sudan oppose it.

Preempting the Waters of Babylon

From the dawn of civilization to the present day, the societies of Mesopotamia and eastern Syria have been largely dependent on two rivers that rise in Anatolia and Persia, now join in southern Mesopotamia, and flow into the Persian Gulf. In current political terms, the Euphrates flows from Turkey through northeast Syria and Iraq, the Tigris and its tributaries flow into Iraq from Turkey and Iran, and their product, the Shatt al 'Arab (the Seashore of the Arabs), marks the Iraqi-Iranian frontier from their confluence to the Gulf. The primary source of the entire system is the 40plus inches of rain that normally falls in the Taurus Mountains of Turkey and the Zagros Mountains of Iran.

In 1920, the Ottoman Empire expired, and Britain and France separated Turkey from its former dependencies by drawing a portentous frontier that approximated the 37th parallel. Politically, it fixed the northern frontier of two new states, Syria and Iraq. Hydrologically, it awarded Turkey potential control over the water supply of Iraq and eastern Syria. Fifty years later, Turkey began to exercise that potential. The Southeastern Anatolian Project, at a projected cost of 32 billion dollars, is scheduled to link the upper Tigris and Euphrates in a network of 22 dams, 19 hydroelectric plants, and irrigation canals that will serve 2500 square miles. Since the completion of the Keban Dam on the Euphrates in 1974, Turkey has gradually reduced the flow into Syria. By 1997, in accordance with a Turkish-Syrian agreement of 1987 (in which Iraq did not participate), Turkey was generally limiting the flow at the border to 500 million cubic meters per second.

In April 1990, Iraq and Syria agreed on a 58-42 division of whatever Euphrates flow Turkey released across the Syrian border. The two downstream states have been increasingly concerned by Turkish designs on the Euphrates and the upper Tigris. (More than half the flow of the lower Tigris comes from tributaries that rise in the mountains of western Iran.)

In 1999, *The Nation* alleged that Turkish diversion of water from the Euphrates had violated several treaties. Turkey has declined to sign the UN convention of 1997 on the equitable division of international rivers. The political implications of the Southeastern Anatolian Project are further complicated by its location in an area largely populated by members of Turkey's restive Kurdish minority. At latest report, Turkey, Syria, and Iraq were all basing their economic planning on presumed off-takes of Euphrates water that would exceed its total flow, even though the discharge across the frontier into Syria had already fallen below the minimum prescribed under the agreement of 1987.

As the last of three off-takers of Euphrates water, Iraq is in the most precarious situation. If Turkey and Syria were to carry out all their diversion plans, the annual flow into Iraq would be reduced to 5-8 billion cubic meters. Already, Iraq has suffered a decline in the quantity and quality of its water supply – despite its receipt of 20 billion cubic meters a year from sources independent of the Tigris and the Euphrates.

The most sensitive indicator of Iraq's hydrological situation is the marsh area where the Tigris and Euphrates meet. From time immemorial, the Iraqi marshes were one of the largest wetland ecosystems in the world. Covering an area between 'Amarah and Basrah of some 4,000 square miles, the area was the home of the legendary Marsh Arabs, who lived a unique life among the reeds. This life-style was brutally assaulted in the 1990's by the Baathist regime. During the Iran-Iraq war (Chapter 9), the marshes were a major element of the Iraqi defense, but during the Shiite insurrection of 1991, they suddenly became an insurgent hideout, and Saddam set out to drain them. By 1997, drainage was 80 percent complete. After Saddam's overthrow in 2003, the Iraqi interim authorities complied with the request of the locals to re-flood the region, but it will never be restored to pristine productivity. Some of the residents have already converted to dry-land farming, but the main obstacle is water supply. Upriver, in Turkey, Syria, Iran, and Iraq (Iraq has built eight hydroelectric dams on the Euphrates), the construction of dams goes on. Downriver, water flow declines and salinity rises.

In the summer of 2009, crisis struck Iraq's water supply. The causes were wasteful management, drought, and the reduction in the flow of the Euphrates at the Syrian-Iraq border to 300 million cubic meters per second – as Turkey (five dams) and Syria (three dams) increased their off-take. Turkey obliged by a temporary increase in the flow.

According to *TomDispatch* of 12/13/09, Turkish and Syrian diversions of the Euphrates, Iranian diversion of the Karun (a tributary of the Tigris), dilapidation of Iraq's irrigation system, and three years of drought had caused calamity in Iraq – river levels down sharply, the southern "marshes" dry, and agriculture ravaged. The *Times* of 6/13/10 characterized pollution of the Shatt as an environmental disaster for south Iraq.

The Hydrological Aspect of the Arab-Israeli Dispute

The chief source of fresh water for Israel, Palestine, and western Jordan is the watershed of the Jordan River, which rises in the mountains of southern Lebanon and southwestern Syria and flows south through Lake Tiberias (the Biblical Sea of Galilee) to the Dead Sea.

As elsewhere in the Middle East, the correlation between watershed and political frontier is low. Long before the independence of Israel in 1948, the Zionists had focused on insuring maximum control over the water supply of the land they envisaged as their national home. When the Allies divided up the Ottoman Empire by the Agreement of San Remo in 1920, Britain complied with Zionist concerns by drawing the northern frontier of their new Palestinian Mandate to include as much of the headwaters of the Jordan as France, the prospective mandatory authority in Syria and Lebanon, would accept. Zionist forefather Chaim Weizmann made an unsuccessful appeal to Prime Minister Lloyd George to set the frontier even farther north to include the lower Litani, one of the two principal rivers of Lebanon. (The other, the Orontes, flows from northern Lebanon to the Mediterranean via Syria and southern Turkey.)

Israel has managed to preempt most of the flow of the Jordan – and of the aquifers that derive from the modest mountain range that parallels the 1948 frontier between Israel and the West Bank. In 1953 Israel launched an ambitious project to pipe water from the upper Jordan around the West Bank (which was then a highly vexatious enclave in the center of Israel) and on to the Negev Desert. Aside from watering its arid south, Israel had the basic political objective of preempting UN plans to set up international supervision of the development of the Jordan watershed. At that point President Eisenhower intervened. By suspending American aid to Israel (and reportedly threatening to cancel the tax-deductible status of private American contributions to Israeli charities), he prevailed on Israel to defer the diversion project. This intervention, plus Eisenhower's pressure on Israel to evacuate Gaza and Sinai in 1957 (Chapter 8), exemplified the thesis, now conventional wisdom, that the Arab-Israel conflict will never be peacefully resolved without massive American participation.

The United States followed up this minor diplomatic success by sending out a succession of representatives in a vain effort to negotiate resolution of the Jordan water dispute. By 1956, Israel had resumed the diversion project, which eventually made the flow of the lower reaches of the river too saline to serve the needs of the Kingdom of Jordan, which was the sovereign power on both banks until Israel occupied the West Bank in the Six-Day War of 1967.

The Jordan has four major tributaries: the Hasbani, which rises in Lebanon; the Dan, which rises in northern Israel; the Baniyas, which rises in the Golan; and the Yarmuk, which rises in southern Syria. For most of its course, the Yarmuk is the boundary between Syria and Lebanon. Israel controls its last fourteen miles by virtue of the 1967 conquest of the Golan.

In 1958, in an effort to rectify the imbalance caused by the Israeli diversion, the United States financed construction of the East Ghor Canal, which runs from the Yarmuk south on the Jordanian side of the Jordan River. Jordanian usage of the East Ghor has been repeatedly impeded by Israeli military action.

In 1964, Egyptian President 'Abd al Nasir convened an Arab "summit" (meeting of heads of state) to concert an Arab strategy to abort Israel's plan to divert the Jordan. That effort failed, but the Summit did have other consequences – the creation of a pro forma joint Arab military command, a Syrian-Jordanian plan for counter-diversion of the Jordan's tributaries on the east side, the establishment of the Palestine Liberation Organization (the PLO), initially under the leadership of a Palestinian protégé of Egypt, and a campaign of "fedayeen" (guerrilla) raids into Israel. These activities contributed materially to the situation that erupted into the Six-Day War (Chapter 8).

In 1964, Israel formally designated the diversion project the National Water Carrier. President Johnson acquiesced in its operation.

The occupations of 1967 brought Israel immense strategic advantages, both hydrological and military. 'Abd al Nasir had bestowed valuable political cover on the action by his illegal and unaccountable closure of the Strait of Tiran, the narrow passage between Sinai and Saudi Arabia that connects the Gulf of 'Aqabah to the Red Sea and is Israel's only maritime access to the south. The principal victims of the war were the residents of the Golan and the West Bank. Most Golanis fled to Syria. Residents of the West Bank found their access to water sharply reduced. Israel nationalized the water supply of both territories, declared all data on water resources state secrets, and essentially banned the drilling or repair of wells by non-Israelis.

In 1980, a commission established by UN Security Council Resolution 446 of 1979 concluded that Israel's water policies had violated Security Council decisions and the Fourth Geneva Convention of 1949. In 1982, Israel transferred management of the West Bank water system from the military government to Mekorot, the national water company. Under Israeli law, all water belongs to the state. The state has uniformly administered water distribution to favor Jewish Israelis over its Arab subjects – citizens or not. The Oslo Accord of 1993 between Israel and the PLO (Chapter 8) deferred the most sensitive issues between the two parties, including the ultimate disposition of water. The water-related provisions of the Israel-Jordan peace treaty of October 26, 1994, have not been implemented.

In 1998, of the total water supply of the West Bank, 56 percent was flowing west for consumption by Israel proper, leaving 24 percent for some 200,000 settlers, and 20 percent for over 2,000,000 Arabs. Two years later, in the grip of a severe drought, Israel's water replenishment was running below its annual requirement of 528 billion gallons per year, and the level of Lake Tiberias was falling sharply.

At this writing, the status of the countries interested in the Jordan watershed is as follows:

Syria - Most of the flow of the Yarmuk is consumed in Syria. Aside from the water consumed by the residents of the Golan (18,000 Jewish settlers, 20,000 Syrians), the balance of its annual runoff goes into the upper Jordan and thence into Israel's National Water Carrier or to Jordan.

Jordan - Divides with Israel whatever Yarmuk flow leaves Syria. The lower end of the Jordan River has become a sewer for upstream urban and industrial waste. In 2008 *The Guardian Weekly* predicted that The Dead Sea is due to dry up in thirty years. Chronic shortage restricts the water supply of 'Amman, Jordan's capital, which lies 25 miles east of the Jordan River.

The West Bank - Per capita consumption of water by the Palestinian residents of the West Bank has been estimated at 70 liters a day – as against the acceptable minimum of 100 liters a day (in the judgment of the World Health Organization) and the estimated per capita consumption by Israeli citizens in Israel and the West Bank settlements of 348 liters a day. To add insult to injury, water supplied to the settlers is subsidized by the Israeli government. Although the Palestinian "mountain aquifer" rises primarily in the West Bank, 80 percent of its supply is consumed in Israel. Water consumed by Arab residents of the West Bank is controlled by the West Bank Water Department, which nominally reports to the Palestine Authority set up under the Oslo Agreement, but which is still financed by the Israeli Government and also controls water supply to the Jewish settlements. Whereas Israel irrigates most of its irrigable land, Arabs in the Occupied Territories irrigate less than one fourth of the irrigable land they control. The area of that land is now being reduced by expropriation for construction of a "Security Barrier" east of the 1948 frontier (Chapter 8).

Expropriation of Palestinians' land for construction of the Barrier has already cost them over 50 wells – exacerbating a situation in which Jewish settlers intercept the Palestinians' water supply and sell it back at scalpers' prices (*The Washington Post Weekly,* 2/9/04).

In 1999, the Israeli Water Commission asserted that international law does not apply to the water claims of Arab West Bankers "because they have no state." Two prime ministers of Israel, Ehud Barak and Ariel Sharon, have held that Palestinian statehood should be conditioned on continued Israeli control of the water supply. A former head of the Water Resources Unit of the World Bank has reportedly contended that this position violates the Oslo Accord and international law. According to Sharif Elmusa, Israel has retaliated for acts of anti-Israeli insurgency by suspending the water supply to the communities of the suspects.

The Gaza Strip - In 1996, the World Bank assessed Gazan water consumption at 15 gallons a day per capita, the lowest in the world. The Gazan aquifer has been severely depleted. Water supply and sewerage service have been further impaired by Israel's so-called withdrawal from the Strip and its punitive policies since the ouster of the Palestine Authority by Hamas (Chapter 8).

Israel - By monopolizing the output of the Jordan and drawing on the four Palestine/Israel aquifers and on desalination projects, Israel supplies its citizens somewhere between 1½ and 2 billion cubic meters of water a year. For guaranteed maintenance of this level, hegemony over the West Bank and the Golan is essential. In the minds of some Israelis, this consideration alone rules out Israeli acceptance of a two-state solution to the Palestinian dispute.

Middle East Policy reported in 2003 that drought and population increase had combined to plunge Israel's water problem into crisis. In 2002 Israel had signed a twenty-year deal with Turkey for eventual delivery by sea of water from the Manavgat River, a stream in south central Turkey. Ten percent of Israel's water budget comes from the Wazzani-Hasbani system, which flows from south Lebanon into the upper Jordan. Beirut has considered basing an irrigation project on this system, but Israel has informed Lebanon that any attempt to reduce its flow into Israel would be *casus belli*. Thomas Stauffer took the gloomy view that the only permanent solution of the Arab-Israeli dispute lies in military action.

The plan to pipe sea water from the Gulf of Aqaba to the Dead Sea, in order to reverse its gradual desiccation and exploit the net fall of 1300 feet to power a desalination plant, will presumably await quieter political times. Meanwhile Israel is building another desalination plant on the Mediterranean coast.

Chapter 6
The Curse of Communalism

As the "world bridge", the Middle East has been an arena for two concomitant but antithetical processes: 1) the blending of countless blood lines into a population of immense genetic diversity; 2) the fragmentation of this population into myriad ethnic groups.

The most effective government (Chapter 1) is the one that best mobilizes its population in allegiance to the national interest. The indicated policy is <u>inclusivism,</u> which welcomes ethnic diversity and profits from it. In the geopolitical evolution of the Middle East, <u>exclusivist</u> policies have prevailed. Most of its inhabitants are afflicted by a communalist syndrome that inclines them to pay ultimate loyalty – not to class, political party, or state – but to their own ethnic in-group. When government is not the citizen's friend, prudence requires him – while paying it lip service – to look to his own community for ultimate security. This affliction has exacted a dreadful toll in political discord, in vulnerability to foreign exploitation, in ethnic cleansing, and in a dreary concatenation of inconclusive wars. It is an evolutionary dead end.

Examined in visible wavelengths, the region seems to consist of twenty-six states and territories (Table A). In the infrared optic of communalism, it breaks down into a kaleidoscopic mosaic. Before the evolution of states, the ethnic group offered the best assurance of individual survival. Under the exclusivist policies still pursued by all Middle Eastern regimes, it still does.

Civilization was born in the Tigris-Euphrates Valley. As towns evolved, communal groups tended to settle in separate clusters. As towns grew larger, the rulers retreated to the outskirts, farther from the flash point of urban riots. For greater security, alien residents sought to live close

83

to the rulers. Thus it was, in the year 2005, that old Jerusalem was still partitioned into Muslim, Christian, Jewish, and Armenian "quarters", and each community continued to draw an invisible curtain around itself.

The American Constitution, as amended, has gone far toward the abolition of explicit ethnic discrimination at home. America's foreign policy is a different story. Insofar as it focuses on the survival of Israel (Chapter 13), it sits in the exclusivist camp. The exclusivist character of the Israeli political system was starkly exposed by the late Israel Shahak in *Jewish History, Jewish Religion.*

Since the occupation of Iraq, Washington's professions of intent to democratize that state have rung hollow, given the discrepancy between its abbreviated program for political modernization, and the generations Iraq's ethnicity-ridden society will likely require to bridge the chasm between communalism and democracy.

Ethnicity operates in three basic forms: tribe, sect (which generally overrides tribe), and language group (which generally overrides tribe and sect).

The Obstinacy of Tribalism

Fourteen hundred years have passed since Arab tribesmen from the Arabian Peninsula sparked the Islamic conquest of the Middle East and the Mediterranean world, and over seven hundred since Turk and Mongol tribesmen began their sweeps across the Middle East. Tribes no longer win wars, but in the Middle East, tribal ties still matter. In a sense, Middle Eastern society is still stuck where European society was in 1215, when King John codified the rights of the barons in the Magna Carta, but left it up to them to look after the rights of the peasants. That relationship between peasant and baron is still mirrored in the Middle East in the relationship between tribesman and shaykh: the exchange of the tribesman's service for the shaykh's protection.

The age-old Middle Eastern contest for hegemony has always had a tribal dimension:

1500's - Tariq Ali has noted that rival Kurdish factions, unable to coalesce within their language family, fought each other across the Ottoman-Safavid divide.

1900's - The Kurdish fight for statehood has been crippled by bitter tribal divisions. Even under ruthless Turkish repression, ancient blood feuds led some Kurdish tribes to collaborate with Ankara against their kinsmen.

1920-58 - Whereas the Ottomans had worked to undermine Iraqi tribalism in favor of feudalistic landowners (Chapter 11), British rulers tried to revitalize and exploit tribal ties.

1960's - Although Baathist doctrine professed allegiance to secular nationalism, Iraq's Baathist leadership (Chapter 9) was headed by two cousins, Ahmad al Bakr and Saddam Husayn, and Saddam's 35-year rule relied on a power structure dominated by his relatives. His campaign to disempower the old-regime landlords was intensified after Gulf War I by an effort to integrate tribal lineages into his power structure.

1991 - Tribal vendettas kept many Iraqi Shia from joining the anti-Baath insurrection after Gulf War I.

1995 - The elections to Egypt's People's Assembly precipitated considerable violence, much of it intertribal.

1996 - Hostility between the Barzani and Talabani Kurds enabled Baghdad to crush a CIA project to build a unified Kurdish insurgency.

2003-08 - *Foreign Affairs* reported that Washington, replicating the standard strategy of its conservative Arab allies, was trying to retribalize Iraq. American administrators in Baghdad had to grapple with a startling tribal statistic: Nearly half the marriages in Iraq are between first or second cousins.

2004 - Voting in municipal elections in the Palestinian Occupied Territories was largely along tribal lines. In 2007, *The Economist* took note of parochial alienation among the various accidental Palestinian communities (Israel, East Jerusalem, the West Bank, the Gaza Strip, and the diaspora).

2008 - The head of al Bu Nasir (Saddam's tribe) was killed, presumably for advocating reconciliation with Maliki's Shiite regime (Chapter 15).

2008 - Forces of the Palestine authority had to restore order in Hebron, site of an ancient feud, between the 'Ajnuni and Rajabi tribes, that had lately taken nine lives.

2008 - Tribal ties were influential in the outcome of December Student Council elections at Jordan University.

2008 - The last bastion of tribal government may be the Arabian Peninsula, home of six tribal monarchies (Chapter 11). The only Arabian state to have had a military takeover is Yemen, where the regime is still wrestling with tribal confederations that trace their histories back 2000 years. As a nominal member of the Hashid confederation, President 'Ali 'Abdallah Salih is presumably a member of the Zaydi sect, but he leads a secularist faction that is trying to subdue Hashid insurgency in northern Yemen.

The Mythology of Race

By piecing together fragments of data from stone inscriptions, moldering documents, archeological clues, and Holy Writ, scholars have acquired a rough idea of the confluence of migration, invasion, expulsion, and exile that produced today's ethnic mosaic. The "races" that activated the process are conventionally designated thus:

Indo-European (including Armenians, Circassians, Greeks, Hittites, Kurds, Medes, Parthians, Persians, Philistines, and Romans).

Semitic (including Akkadians, Amorites, Arameans, Arabs, Assyrians, Berbers, Canaanites, Chaldeans, Egyptians, Hyksos, Jews, and Phoenicians).

Altaic (including Azerbaijanis, Mongols, Turkmens, and Turks).

Unknown origin (including Cimmerians, Elamites, Hurrians, Kassites, Scythians, Sumerians, and Ubaidians).

The concept of race is less genetic than folkloric. It has been brutally perverted by deranged politicians, but it has minimal relevance for geopolitical analysis. *Scientific American* has noted that individual genomes differ only by geographic gradients. Many Arabs treasure impressive family trees that go back centuries, in many cases to the Prophet Muhammad, but few can show proof. The distortion of genealogy was typified on May 6, 1952, when Egypt's King Faruq (descendant of Muhammad 'Ali, who entered Ottoman service as an Albanian conscript) reacted to political unrest in his country by declaring that he was a descendant of the Prophet.

A recent Y-chromosome study suggests that most of the inhabitants of the Levant who call themselves Arabs or Jews are descended from common ancestors who lived there four thousand years ago. The Jewish people have had a tradition of ethnic purity, but this tradition has been contravened from earliest times. David, the "ideal" Jewish king, followed the traditional tribal practice of consolidating political ties by taking wives from many various tribes. David's successor, King Solomon, was the son of Bathsheba, who may well have been Indo-European (see Marriage below).

According to Steve Olson, "It makes no sense to talk about 'races' when we are all complex mixtures of many different peoples."

Fractious Sectarianism

"Freedom of the will" is a subject for endless debate. As long as people differ on the relative influence of nature, nurture, and circumstance on individual decision, there is no hope of agreement on the extent to which sectarian affiliation is motivated by ideology, opportunism, or divine revelation. The geopolitician must confine his analysis to the social forces that seem to influence a specific choice, and the consequences that seem to ensue from it.

Analysis is complicated in that belief is not a given, like fingerprints or skin color. It can be altered or feigned. The *Qur'an* allows Muslims to deny their faith for self-protection. For Shiites, often a persecuted minority, *taqiyyah* (religious dissimulation under duress) is a fundamental article of faith. For *'Ibadi* Shiites, it is a requirement. Religious affiliation is clearly an insubstantial foundation for a state, but states in the Westphalian sense did not reach the Middle East until the Twentieth Century, whereas sectarianism has operated since history began. For adherents, affiliation with a sect offered the protection of the in-group. For governments, it was an invaluable instrument of authority. In time of peace, a devout population was predisposed to ascribe its misfortunes to divine will rather than to human misconduct. In time of war, troops fought more fiercely when convinced of the virtue of their cause. The forces of Islam were spurred on by religious zeal – as are many Islamist suicides today.

Hence the traditional linkage between ruler and sect. It went through stages. Early on, rulers claimed divinity. When this approach lost plausibility, they claimed divine guidance (and in some unaccountable cases still do). The final stage is alliance of convenience between secular and sectarian leaders, who can adjure their flocks to endure the aggravations of this world in anticipation of reward in the next. Such an alliance exists in Saudi Arabia, between the royal family and the clerisy of the Wahhabi sect, and in Israel, between the government and the Rabbinate. In both cases, the sectarian leadership supports the regime in return for an annual subsidy and a monopoly in the promulgation of religious decisions. Neither Saudi Arabia nor Israel is a theocracy: They might be called <u>theophilies</u> (Chapter 11).

Just as Henry VIII bent religion to his own political purposes by accepting the leadership of the new Church of England, and Protestantism came to symbolize rejection of papal domination, the Middle East has experienced theological metamorphoses that had political overtones:

700's - The pagan Khazars of southern Russia, bent on espousing book monotheism, chose Judaism, thus affirming their independence from the Christian Byzantines to the west and the Muslim Arabs to the south.

1000's - The Seljuqs' conquest of the eastern lands of the Caliphate led to their adoption of Sunni Islam, symbolizing confrontation with Christianity in Byzantine Anatolia and Shiism in Fatimid Egypt.

1295 - Hulegu's Mongols, the next wave to overrun the Abbasid Caliphate, converted to Sunni Islam.

1300's - The Ottoman Turks, already converts to Islam, conquered most of Anatolia, fell back under attack by the forces of Timur, a Mongolized Turk, then resiled to build the greatest Muslim empire since the Islamic conquest. A basic responsibility of the Ottoman sultan was defense of the *Shari'ah* (Islamic law) – particularly against the Shiites in Persia. Tolerant of their many non-Muslim subjects, the Ottomans came to place more political importance on the religious communities (*millet's*) than on the provinces (*vilayet's*). In later centuries the European states reinforced the millet system by asserting a right to insure the welfare of the empire's Christian subjects. Sectarian functionaries took over administrative responsibilities that in a more secular society would have fallen on the state. William McNeill observed that this arrangement facilitated the mobility of the members of these "portable in-groups".

1502 - The advent to power of the Shiite Safavids set Persia apart from the Sunni Caliphate – without rejecting Islam.

Since faith is a personal choice, or revelation, and attitudes are diverse, the great religions have inevitably broken up into variant sects. To establish political union out of sectarian discord, evolved states have learned to erect a wall of separation between church and state, based on the objective premise that every citizen has a right to his own convictions, but not to the point that they trespass on the rights of those who hold differing convictions.

In this rationale, the only moral absolute is equality – as stated in Christianity's Golden Rule, and in equivalent terms by other religions. No Middle Eastern state has reached this level of political enlightenment.

It is compelling for theologians, and perhaps for geopoliticians, that the three dominant faiths in the Middle East share a common tradition of monotheism, but evolved along different doctrinal paths. Judaism's adherence to the concept of the Chosen People seems to reflect tribalistic origins. In Christianity's emphasis on peace and humility, as enunciated in the Beatitudes, humanitarianism emerges as a universal value. Islam (submission) combines the elements of surrender to God's will with unrelenting opposition to those who challenge it – as exemplified by the warrior Prophet who led his followers to victory in the Battle of Badr (in 624 by the Christian calendar).

However well the dominant sects have met the theological needs of Middle Easterners, they have had a divisive effect on its politics. The founders of Islam established a tradition, honored by their Ottoman successors, of tolerance for the practice of other forms of worship, but extra taxes for non-Muslims. The Ottomans reinforced sectarian difference by dealing separately with the leadership of each sect, foreshadowing the political system of present-day Israel.

The Sunni-Shia fault line has been a recurrent source of conflict – as in Iraq in the aftermath of the 1991 Gulf War and under the American occupation. Sectarian differentiation is carried to the ultimate in Lebanon, which has not dared to take a census since 1932. Its political system meticulously apportions seats in parliament among seventeen Muslim and Christian sects, but failed to avert a civil war which raged from 1975 to 1990, and might well have gone on another fifteen years if Syria had not intervened in force.

In four Middle Eastern countries, stability is under constant pressure from a sectarian disconnect between government and people. Bahrain and Iraq have had Sunni regimes but Shia majorities. In Syria and Lebanon, Sunni and Christian or Shia pluralities, respectively, have been intermittently dominated by an Alawite Shia regime in Damascus. Alawite rule of Syria has become so entrenched that, in dealing with the police, Sunnis sometimes try for more lenient treatment by affecting an Alawite accent.

The Capricious Fortunes of the Jews

Tradition counts the Hebrews among the earliest inhabitants of Mesopotamia and the Levant. Around 1250 B.C. Hebrews in Israel/Palestine adopted the worship of Yahweh as a martial desert god who ruled mankind. Their faith evolved into the radical monotheism known as Judaism, which claimed universality but singled out Jews as God's chosen people and perpetuated the Mosaic tradition of a covenant between Yahweh and Israel. It prophesied an eventual Day of Judgment, the second coming of a Messiah, and the establishment of a heavenly kingdom on earth. A proud people, the Jews repeatedly paid for their resistance to invasion by massacre, exile, and enslavement. Whereas most sectarian communities acquired a sense of interconnection with the region's Greco-Roman culture, Fergus Miller concluded that the Jews were differentiated from the rest by their centuries-old corpus of sacred writings.

The culmination of Israeli political history was the reign of King Solomon, whose achievements included building the First Temple around 950 B.C. In 721 B.C., the Assyrians destroyed the Kingdom of Israel and deported thousands of survivors to Mesopotamia, where they lost their communal identity, and presumably gave birth to the legend of the ten lost tribes. Around 587 B.C., after two sieges by the Chaldeans from Mesopotamia, Jerusalem was destroyed and many of its inhabitants exiled to Babylon. Around 538 B.C. the Persians conquered Mesopotamia and Palestine and freed the exiles, and construction of the Second Temple began. Jerusalem fell to the Romans in 20 A.D.; the city, including the Second Temple, was destroyed in 70 A.D., in retaliation for a Jewish revolt.

In the opinion of Edward Gibbon, Judaism was never designed for conversion or conquest. However, Jews were inveterate travelers. Whether displaced by invaders or attracted abroad by commerce, by the dawn of the Christian era they had established communities in many cities around the Middle East. It is estimated that, when Rome razed Jerusalem in 70 A.D., there were two and a half million Jews in Judaea (Palestine), and four million or more elsewhere. They may have constituted as many as a tenth of the population of the empire. Although Jews were intolerant of other religions, Rome allowed them to practice their own, but not to serve in the military.

In 525, when the Ethiopians made their major foray into Yemen (Chapter 2), they found an active Jewish community. Under the rule of the Caliphate, non-Muslims were required to wear distinguishing attire and pay a poll tax, but Jews and Arabs lived together in relative harmony. Under Arab rule, Mesopotamia was the storied center of Jewish learning. Ottoman censuses indicate a decline in the numbers of Jewish citizens of Mesopotamia from 256,000 in 1906 to 87,000 in 1920, although Edwin Black reports that Jews made up a third of the population of Baghdad as late as 1922. Evidence of long Jewish residence in the Caucasus and Central Asia turned up in Russian studies of the 1800's.

Under Crusader rule, 1099-1187, Muslims and Jews were barred from living in Jerusalem, but in 1190 the Muslim ruler Salah al Din (Saladin) invited the Jews to come back. In 1492, the Catholic rulers of Spain expelled their Jewish subjects, who returned to North Africa and the Middle East as the nucleus of the Sephardic Jews. ("Sephardic" derives from a Hebrew term for Spanish Jew.) Many Jews played important roles in the economy of the Ottoman Empire until the 1600's, when Greek and Armenian Christians began to replace them. In that era, half the residents of Salonika were Jews or descendants of Jews.

The honored concept of *aliyah* has two meanings in Jewish lore: 1) the Sabbath reading of the Torah (the first five books of the Bible), preferably by a *cohen* (a direct descendant of Aaron, the first Jewish priest) for the first reading and a Levite (a member of the priestly tribe of Levi) for the second; 2) moving back to the Holy Land, which after 1948 was the state of Israel. In the 1800's, the flow of Jewish returnees to Palestine was amplified by persecution of Ashkenazi (from the name of one of Noah's grandsons)

Jews in eastern Europe, tolerated by the Russian czars, and culminating in the Final Solution ordained for Jews at the secret Wannsee Conference of Nazi officials on January 20, 1942. The initial plan was to impose lethal attrition on the Jewish community by assigning them to brutal labor camps, but within months Germany was building the gas chambers that were to exterminate six million Jews and people of many other categories condemned by the demented Nazi racism.

The creation of Israel in 1948 intensified Jewish fervor for *aliyah* and impaired the traditional Muslim hospitality for their Jewish neighbors. Sephardis joined Ashkenazis in flocking to the Holy Land, and the number of Jews living elsewhere in the Middle East fell sharply. Thereafter, Jewish participation in the politics of Middle Eastern states other than Israel has been negligible except for a tangential effort by the Palestine Liberation Organization (PLO) to project an inclusivist image, in support of its campaign to resolve the Palestine dispute by the formation of a multiethnic secular state. In 1978, Israel reported the arrest of a Fatah guerrilla cell that had Jewish members. In 1983, the PLO named Ilan Halevi, a Jew of Yemeni origin, as its representative to the Socialist International. In 1991, the Palestinian delegation at the Madrid Conference on the Palestine problem included Samih Kan'an, son of an Arab father and a Jewish mother.

In 1985, the *Times* reported that most of the five or six million Americans of Jewish lineage were affiliated with one of three Judaic denominations: Orthodox Jews, who consider the Torah divine and immutable; Conservative Jews, who accept interpretation of the Torah to comport with a changing environment; and Reform Jews, who view the Torah as a guide only, and who accept as Jews the children of a Jewish father or a Jewish mother. It seems that almost all Jews consider their faith hereditary. Orthodox and Conservative rabbis are disinclined to marry a Jew to a gentile spouse, or to recognize the progeny of such a union as Jews.

Rise and Fall of the Christian Community

Jesus Christ is believed to have been born a Jew in Judaea in 6 B.C. and crucified by order of the Roman Governor, Pontius Pilate, at the age of thirty-six in 30 A.D. He began his mission as a Jewish priest, and it was from the Jewish communities of the Levant and Anatolia that his followers made most of their initial conversions.

In Gibbon's account, Rome's policy toward Christians vacillated between tolerance and persecution. By amalgamating the countries of the Mediterranean in a political union, Rome facilitated Christian proselytization. However, Christianity was quick to break up into sects, many of which mirrored pre-Christian beliefs.

Over the first two centuries, the Christian hierarchy evolved into a system of provincial synods (councils) headed by bishops, who were regarded as the successors of Christ's apostles. The Bishop of Rome, distinguished by the fact that two of the most eminent apostles (Peter and Paul) had been martyred there, gradually assumed preeminence. In 300 Armenia became the first nation to adopt Christianity as its state religion. Georgia followed in 337.

In 312, Roman Emperor Constantine, having perceived some sort of portent of his subsequent victory over the rival forces of his brother-in-law, became the Emperor of the Roman Empire of the West. In 324, he became the Emperor of the Roman Empire of the East as well. Ascribing his success to his conversion to Christianity, he issued the Edict of Milan, which extended religious toleration to Christians. In 391, Emperor Theodosius I proclaimed Christianity the official religion of the empire. The empire reportedly saw political advantage in supporting Christianity as a unifying force against barbarian invaders.

In 451, Christian leaders convened in the Council of Chalcedon confirmed the Archbishop of Byzantium as equal in authority to the Bishop of Rome. A century later the Archbishop was elevated to the title of Patriarch. Also in 451, the Council condemned the Monophysites, who held that Christ is totally divine. The Coptic and Syriac denominations still adhere to that doctrine. In 500, the Coptic Patriarch was the most influential figure in Egypt.

The Shiite Fatimid rulers of Egypt were hostile to Christianity. In 1009, they sacked the Holy Sepulcher (a church built in Jerusalem on the reputed site of Jesus' tomb). In 1010, Fatimid Caliph Al Hakim ordered the destruction of the Sepulcher and all other Christian shrines in Jerusalem.

The defeat of the Byzantines by the Seljuq Turks in 1071 sparked the Crusades (Chapter 7). Jerusalem was in Christian hands 1099-1187, 1229-39, and 1240-44.

In the 1400's, Roman Catholic missionaries began to infiltrate Greek Orthodox territory. The Papacy eventually set up seminaries in Rome for Middle Eastern Catholics. In 1454, a year after conquering Constantinople, Ottoman Sultan Mehmed II restored the office of the Greek Orthodox Patriarch.

In 1536, Ottoman Sultan Suleiman signed a treaty of "capitulation" according religious freedom to French residents of the empire, and granting France custody of the Holy Places in Palestine.

By 1700, Christians in the Middle East had undergone a bitter split between the Orthodox adherents of the Patriarchate in Constantinople and the Catholic adherents of the Papacy in Rome – notably including the militant Maronite sect in Lebanon.

In modern times, a sharp cultural division has arisen between Christians and Muslims in the Middle East. Looking toward the West for support against inundation by the Muslim majority, Christians prized education at schools and universities established by Western churches. While they were acquiring marketable fluency in French and English, Muslims tended to gravitate to schools which taught in Arabic, even if the education they received was narrower in scope. Result: a vicious circle, with Christians looking to the West for protection against Islamism, and Muslims suspicious of Christians as a potential fifth column. Their suspicions had to be reinforced by the 1966 defection of a Christian Iraqi who flew his Mig-21 to Israel for a cash award (reported by the preeminent chronicler of the Arab-Israeli wars, Donald Neff).

In Egypt, the brief French occupation in the 1790's (Chapter 7) produced a Coptic revival which was encouraged in the 1800's by the British overlords. Their bold choice of a Copt, Butrus Ghali, as Prime Minister led to his assassination. With the evacuation of the British forces from the Canal Zone in the 1950's (Chapter 10) and Egypt's advent to full independence, Coptic influence went into decline. Coptic emigration has reduced their numbers to less than ten percent of Egypt's population. In 1980, as a sop to the Islamists, President Sadat had Coptic Pope Shenuda III placed under temporary house arrest.

At the beginning of the Twenty-First Century, various estimates numbered Christian residents of certain non-Christian states and territories as follows: Iraq - 500,000, mostly Chaldean Catholics; Israel - 50,000; Jordan - 120,000; Lebanon - 1.5 million; Syria - over a million; Turkey - several thousand; West Bank - 45,000. Of the nineteen states in the Middle East, three have Christian governments (Armenia, Cyprus, and Georgia). Elsewhere, Christian communities are suffering increasing harassment:

Egypt - The dwindling Coptic community has negligible voice in the government. Coptic villages generally have to answer to Sunni authorities, civil and police, even at the local level. Cairo tries to suppress Islamist subversion, not always successfully. Periodic violence, notably the antiregime rioting in January 1958 and the atrocities of the 1990's (Chapter 12), was directed in part against Copts and Westerners. In 2007 *McClatchy* reported that Egyptian officials had been known to force converts to Christianity to send their children to schools teaching Islam.

Saudi Arabia - Despite the de facto alliance with the United States, the Wahhabi connection requires the regime to ban Christian worship in the kingdom.

Iraq - Locked in combat with Shiite and Kurdish insurgents, dictator Saddam had an interest in cultivating the inoffensive and talented Christian community. For a time, the most prominent Christian in the Arab world was his foreign minister, Tariq 'Aziz, a Chaldean Catholic who had been a long-time Baathist. He served the regime by projecting a reassuring image of erudition, urbanity, and secularism (although the Maliki Government put him on trial in 2008). Among the penalties of the American invasion of Iraq was a grisly sectarian conflict, which had abated by 2009, but had sharply reduced the number of Christian residents of Iraq. At this writing, lethal attacks on the community in Mawsil were driving Christians out of the city.

The Vicissitudes of the Sunnis

In the vast history of the dominant sect of Islam, the following events stand out:

610-32 - The Prophet Muhammad deduced the Islamic faith from intuition informed in part by pagan, Jewish, and Christian doctrine. The *Ka'bah,* holiest site in Islam, had been the object of pagan veneration. An urban religion, Islam reaffirmed many of the attitudes and customs of the ancient Middle East.

622 - *Al Hijrah:* Muhammad's flight from Mecca to Medina.

628 - The last Persian satrap of Yemen converted to Islam.

632 - The death of Muhammad. A letter in the 8/2/07 *London Review of Books* stated that the tomb of the Prophet and the graves of most of his wives are in Madinah. His father-in-law, Abu Bakr, established the Caliphate (*al Khalifah:* the Succession) and became the first Caliph.

692 - Caliph 'Abd al Malik completed construction of the Dome of the Rock on the site of the two former Jewish Temples, regarded by Sunni Muslims as the Prophet's destination during his miraculous "night journey". Later known as *Al Haram al Sharif* (The Noble Sanctuary), it is, after Mecca and Medina, the third holiest place in Islam. Successor Caliphs built Al Aqsa Mosque in Jerusalem and the Umayyad Mosque in Damascus.

c. 1000 - The Oguz Turks (Seljuq tribe included), newly arrived in the Middle East from Central Asia, accepted Islam.

1038 - With the endorsement of the Caliph, Seljuq leader Toghril proclaimed himself Sultan of a kingdom that included most of Persia and Mesopotamia.

1171 - Salah al Din abolished the Fatimid Caliphate and returned Egypt to Sunni rule.

1300's - The Ottoman Turks, also migrants from Central Asia, proceeded to conquer most of Anatolia and the Balkans. To distinguish themselves from the Shiites of Persia, they adopted Sunni Islam, thus gaining the support of Arab Sunnis, who were a majority in the Arab World. The Ottomans welcomed Jewish refugees from Spain, and accorded citizenship to non-Muslims, who paid a head tax, were exempt from military service, and were answerable to their own sectarian leaders.

1453 - Ottoman conquest of Constantinople.

1517 - According to Ottoman claims, Sultan Selim I was awarded custody of Mecca and Medina by the last Abbasid Caliph.

c. 1750 - The Wahhabis, a puritanical sect of Sunni Islam, emerged in eastern Arabia and formed an alliance with the Saudi tribe.

c. 1800 - The Ottoman ruler claimed the title of Sultan, by analogy with the Persian tradition of king, and the title of Caliph, not in the sense of successor to Muhammad but as guardian of the Holy Places.

c. 1875 - Emergence of the *Salafi* school of Sunni Islam, more tolerant of Muslim diversity and innovation but adamant that Shiites are not Muslims.

1922 - The Turkish National Assembly abolished the Caliphate. Sharif Husayn of the Hijaz made an abortive claim to it before his ouster by 'Abd al 'Aziz Al Sa'ud.

1926 - The first major Islamic Congress, convoked in Mecca by Saudi King 'Abd al 'Aziz, recognized him as Custodian of the Holy Places.

1969 - Arson at Al Aqsa Mosque precipitated calls (unanswered) across the Arab World for *jihad* (holy war).

1979 - Under Islamist pressure, the government of Egypt proclaimed Islam the state religion. The resultant legal system is torn between a secular code and the precepts of Islamic law *(Al Shari'ah).*

2004 - The Sunni community in Iraq was reportedly divided among three main factions: Salafis and Sufis, whose contention has sparked armed conflict at times over the centuries, and the Muslim Brotherhood, lately resurfaced after repression by the Baathist regime.

Three terms in current use require definition: Muslim (Moslem) - an adherent of Islam; Islamic - pertaining to Islam; Islamist - a political term, designating those Muslims who subscribe to fundamentalist beliefs, such as the inerrancy of the *Qur'an*. Many Islamists advocate militant action to advance the cause. Al Qa'idah has been the most active such organization in recent years (Chapter 12).

In the judgment of William McNeill, Islam was the first truly universal civilization. It blended Arab, Turkish, Persian, and Indian cultures into a single overarching society which continues to proselytize, and brings multitudes of believers to Mecca at least once in their lives.

So far, no Middle Eastern agency, spiritual or temporal, has established lasting regional unity. Each successive hegemonic system has disintegrated into the hyperfactionalism that prevails today.

The Travails of Shiism

In 661, the death of 'Ali, fourth Caliph and the son-in-law of the Prophet, precipitated a power struggle between his followers and those of Mu'awiyah, then governor of Syria. Mu'awiyah won and established the Umayyad Dynasty, based in Damascus. The *Shi'at 'Ali* (Party of 'Ali) persisted in their claim to the Caliphate. Over the years, the Shia (or Shiites) acquired their own theology, which may have elements reminiscent of Christianity. Mainstream Shiites (Alawites and Zaydis apart) believe in the legitimacy of the Twelve Imams. Jon Lee Anderson cited in *The New Yorker* of 4/13/09 the doctrine that the twelfth Imam, who disappeared, has been concealed by God and will return as the *Mahdi* in the company of the Prophet Jesus Christ.

At the battle of Karbala' (in present-day Iraq) in 680, the Umayyads defeated the Shiites and killed 'Ali's son, Husayn. Sunnis condemn Shiite veneration of 'Ali and Husayn as elevating them to the heretical status of saint-like intermediaries between man and God. In the Twenty-First Century, the Salafi Islamist Al Qa'idah condemned Shiites as "the most evil creatures under the heavens".

In 1502, followers of the Sufi order of Safaviya in Ardabil, Persia, who had converted from Sunni to Shia around 1400, established the Safavid Dynasty in Persia. Welcomed by the populace, who had suffered oppression under their previous Turkmen rulers, the Safavids declared Shiism the state religion.

The prolonged power struggle between the Ottoman and Safavid empires was paralleled by the sectarian hostility between Sunnis and Shiites, who were repressed by the governments of the opposing sect (Chapter 7). In 2004, the population of empowered Middle Eastern Shia communities (excluding Syria's Alawites and Yemen's Zaydis) was estimated as follows: Iran - 60 million; Iraq - 15 million; Lebanon - one million. Vali Nasr has noted (*The Shia Revival*) that in countries where Shia communities have been politically marginalized (including Iraq, Lebanon, and Bahrain), they have tended to be secularist or Arab nationalist, and socially disadvantaged.

In Nasr's assessment, Sunni jurists have historically dismissed Shiism, and its concept of the Imam, as heresy (Chapter 12). Wahhabis and Salafis still hold this view. In the mid-1900's, the temporary rise of Arab secularism sparked a phase of Sunni-Shia reconciliation, exemplified by Al Azhar's authorization of courses in Shiite jurisprudence.

Sectarianism in Arab Politics of the Twenty-First Century

Bahrain - The number of Shia inhabitants has been estimated at 400,000 – seventy percent of all citizens of the country. High unemployment among them is a serious problem for the ruling family, the Al Khalifas, who are Sunni.

Iran - In 1925, the Shiite clerisy supported the military coup staged by Reza Shah. He stifled their political ambitions, but he did not follow the recent lead of Mustafa Kemal, who had disestablished the Islamic faith in Turkey. Iran remained the center of the *Ja'fari* (Twelver) branch of Shiism. In the early years of the Twentieth Century, the educational level of Iranian Shiites was reduced by their suspicion of secular schools, but in recent decades they have leaped ahead of most of the neighboring Sunni countries in the fields of education and the arts.

Iran is the only theocracy in the region, and probably in the world (Chapter 12). Under the clerical rule established by Ayatollah Khomeini in 1979, Iran's estimated seven million Sunnis have not been restive, even though there are no Sunni mosques in the country. The current battle for the soul of Iran between traditionalists and reformers is being fought primarily within the Shia community (Chapter 11).

Iraq - The leaders of the Iraqi Communist Party have traditionally been Shia. Nasr notes that Saddam periodically purged the Iraqi Baath of Shiite members, and blamed Shiite "traitors" for the fall of Iraq to the Americans. Almost all the members of his Republican Guard were Sunnis. The contemporary American effort to reconcile the rival aspirations of Iraq's ethnic communities is considered in Chapters 9 and 15.

Israel/Palestine - The Palestine problem is reviewed in Chapter 8. As the quintessential communalist state, Israel has encouraged sectarian division in the Occupied Territories. Glenn Bowman reports that, as of 1983, Boy Scout processions were permitted because their flags and uniforms identified them, not as Palestinians, but as members of specific sects.

Kuwait - Shiites are estimated to comprise one-fourth of Kuwait's citizens. The Sunni ruling family allows its Shiite subjects freedom of worship, their own mosques and courts, and assured representation in parliament. Kuwait's Shia resented their government's support for the Iraqi side in the Iraq-Iran war, but have not generated political unrest.

Oman - Around 657 A.D., dissenters from the Shiite faction formed a third branch of Islam whose successors finally settled as *'Ibadi* Muslims in North Africa, Zanzibar, and Oman. In the 1950's, Oman's Ibadi majority rose against their rulers. Their rebellion was suppressed in 1959. The rebellion of the Dhufar tribes, who are distinguished by the South Arabic languages they speak, was suppressed (with Iranian help : *Middle East Policy,* Jeffrey Lefebvre) in 1975.

As a descendant of the founding Imam, Sultan Qabus is presumably an 'Ibadi. According to the Omani Embassy in Washington, Sultan Qabus is a "Muslim". The *Times* of 5/16/09 reported that Saudi laborers are banned by the Omani authorities, who resent Saudi proselytization for Wahhabiism.

Saudi Arabia - Estimates of the number of Shiite citizens in Saudi Arabia range from several hundred thousand to two million (per Vali Nasr), most of them living along the Persian Gulf. Some in the Province of Al Hasa have hinted at secession. Over 100,000 Isma'ilis live along the Saudi-Yemen border.

In keeping with the ancient compact with the Wahhabis, the government holds that Shiites are not Muslims, and it bans Shia mosques. Saudi Shiites are treated as second-class citizens, and are often publicly denounced by clerics and schoolteachers as heretics or even apostates. The Saudi government proscribes Christian worship in the kingdom, and regards apostasy from Islam as a capital offense, but has not stressed its presumed obligation under the order of Caliph 'Umar in 641 that all Christians and Jews should be removed from Arabia. Saudi Arabia has abstained from the 1948 Universal Declaration of Human Rights.

Nasr reports that in 1988 some Saudi Shia were executed on a charge of bombing oil pipelines, and that the Saudi Hizballah and The Islamic Reform Movement were Shia organizations. In local elections of 2005, Shiites won seats on the city council of Qatif, where Shia are in the majority.

Syria and Lebanon - In Syria, minority parties and newspapers in minority languages are illegal. In the sister states of Syria and Lebanon, six sectarian communities have major political relevance:

Shiites - The traditional underclass in Lebanon, they have emerged from obscurity with major assistance from their coreligionists in Iraq and Iran. In 1959, according to Vali Nasr, Iraqi Ayatallah Muhsin al Hakim sent a charismatic Iranian cleric, Musa al Sadr, to Lebanon as his resident representative. Sadr formed a Shiite party with its own militia; in 1975 it acquired the name Amal (Hope). Following the ayatallah's lead, the Lebanese Shia espoused the Palestinian cause, but in 1970 the PLO forces, expelled from Jordan, converted south Lebanon to an armed camp. Many Lebanese Shia, dispossessed of their lands or apprehensive of Israeli retaliation, fled north. Resentful of the Palestinian intrusion, and deprived of guidance by the mysterious disappearance of Musa Sadr during a 1978 visit to Libya (Nasr cites a suggestion that Sadr was killed by Sunni champion Mu'ammar al Qadhafi), they mounted no initial resistance to the Israeli invasion of 1982. Instead, according to Vali Nasr, the embittered forces of Amal fought their own short but bitter war against the Palestinian refugee camps in south Beirut.

But then the IDF began to perpetrate the standard blunders of military occupations (Chapter 8), and the new regime in Iran sent military advisers and logistic support to inspire the radical wing of the Lebanese Shiites to form *Hizballah* (Party of God), an anti-Amal, anti-Israel militia which gained in effectiveness over the years, to the point that with the final Israeli withdrawal from Lebanese territory in 2000, it could claim to be the only Arab force that had ever won a war against Israel. Unlike other Shiite parties in Lebanon, Hizballah regards Iran's Supreme Leader as its *Marji' al Taqlid* (source of emulation), but Hizballah is not an agent of the Iranian government.

In 2004, the Shia were devoting more attention to cultivating their political base in a quadripartite Lebanon, where Maronites still dominated the northern end of the high Lebanon, Druze its southern end, Sunnis the coastal cities, and the Shiites the south and the *Biqa'* – the fertile plain between the Lebanon and Anti-Lebanon Ranges. All of them were still subject to Syrian supervision based on a force of 20,000 or more in the Biqa'. In 2005, the Syrian force was removed (Chapter 14).

The Shia communities of Lebanon, Iran, and Iraq have been linked by centuries of intermarriage, and by Lebanese study at the seminaries of Najaf (Iraq) and Qom (Iran).

Maronites - Long affiliated with the Church of Rome, they have held back from cooperation with their Muslim neighbors, to the extent that a rightist party colluded with Israel before and during the Israeli invasion. However, as Maronites emigrate, Muslims proliferate, and Christian Orthodox maintain better relations with the Muslims, Maronite political influence is on the decline – despite their continued hold on the Presidency and command of the sectarianism-hobbled Lebanese army.

In Syria, a dwindling Christian minority is divided among eleven main denominations: Catholic (Melkite, Syrian, Maronite, Armenian, Chaldean), Orthodox (several sects), and Protestant.

Isma'ili's, Druze, and Alawites - In 765, following the death of the man regarded by Shiites as the Sixth Imam, an Islamic schism led to the formation of a new Shiite faction, the *Isma'ili*'s – known as the Seveners because they recognize only the first six Imams and the sixth Imam's son, Isma'il. This sect produced the Fatimid Dynasty, which in 969 conquered Egypt from the Abbasids by leading a Berber army from North Africa (Chapter 2), and the dreaded band of the Assassins, who terrorized Iran, Iraq, and Syria in the Eleventh and Twelfth centuries from a mountain base in Iran. Today Isma'ilis live in Syria and South Asia. Their Imam, the Aga Khan, lives in Paris.

Their sect gave rise to two offshoots: the *Nusayri*'s (Alawites), who were active in Persia and Syria until the 1200's, and still survive in moderate numbers in Syria and large numbers in South Asia; and the Druze, mountaineers from southeast Lebanon, southwest Syria, and Palestine who imbibed a unique theology from the Fatimid regime in Egypt in the 1000's.

In 1590, the Druze became the dominant sect in Lebanon. In 1841, the Ottoman rulers reacted to fighting between Christians and Druze by dividing Lebanon into two administrative districts – one under a Christian governor, the other under a Druze.

The pervasive Druze sense of independence from other Arabs has prompted those in Israel to accept service in the armed forces, although there was evidence that some Israeli soldiers of Druze nationality sided with their Lebanese coreligionists during the invasion of Lebanon. When Israel took the Golan from Syria in 1967, most of its residents fled to Syria. The remainder have rejected an Israeli offer of citizenship. Since Druze doctrine forbids marriage outside the faith, and the Druze of the Golan shun association with the accommodationist Druze community of Israel, intermarriage among the 15,000 or so in the Golan has had some undesirable congenital consequences.

Of an estimated million and a half Druze worldwide, half a million live in southwest Syria.

Alawites - The mountainous area just east of Syria's Mediterranean coast is the historic home of the Alawite sect of Isma'ili Shiism. Their tradition holds that they migrated to Syria from Arabia in early Islamic times. Alawites share the Shiite veneration for the Prophet's son-in-law, 'Ali, but they are not universally recognized as Muslims. In 1971, the Alawite ruler of Syria, Hafiz al Asad, prevailed on Musa al Sadr, head of the Higher Shiite Council in Lebanon, to issue a fatwa (religious ruling) that Alawites are genuine Shiites (and in consequence that Asad was qualified to rule Muslim Syria).

The Alawites do not number more than fifteen percent of the population of Syria. Their rise to power is a classic example of the unintended consequence. For centuries they were an underclass, demeaned by Umayyads, Abbasids, Crusaders, Ottomans, and Egyptians. After Syrian independence, young Alawites found escape from the poverty of their hill country by flocking to the military academy at Homs, where the education was free. In the rash of military coups that rocked Syria in the aftermath of the debacle of 1948, each new ruling clique of Sunni officers cashiered or killed its predecessors, until the forgotten Alawite contingent suddenly found itself in a position to take over.

The abortive union of Egypt and Syria was sparked by the mystique of Egypt's new Arab Nationalist ruler, Jamal 'Abd al Nasir, a Sunni, and orchestrated by the founders of the Syrian *Ba'th* – Michel 'Aflaq (Greek Orthodox) and Salah Baytar (Sunni). In 1960, as Syrian disillusionment with Egyptian officiousness was coalescing, three Alawite officers, including Asad, and two Isma'ili officers began the multifactional plotting that led to Syrian secession in 1961. In 1970, after further years of infighting, exacerbated by the second debacle (the 1967 round in the ongoing Arab-Israeli war) and the subsequent civil war in Jordan between the government and the PLO, Hafiz al Asad took power.

Sunnis - Of Syria's nineteen million people, thirteen million or more belong to the mainstream sect of Islam. Their predictable uprising against Alawite rule took the form of violent subversion by Islamists in the 1970's. Asad managed to stamp out the insurrection by ruthless reprisal, which culminated in 1982 in a major military operation against Hamah, the main power base of Syrian Islamists. Upwards of 10,000 Syrian civilians died under withering fire from Syrian tanks and cannons.

Thereafter, Asad faced no critical opposition from the Sunnis, and his power structure of Alawites and co-opted Sunnis was solid enough to engineer after his death a peaceful transition to his son Bashar, an unassuming ophthalmologist who was elevated to the succession by the untimely death of his brother, and did not seem cut out for dictatorship.

Logic would call for political alliance between the Sunni majority in Syria and the harried Sunni minority next door in Iraq, but parochial jealousies made Asad and Saddam bitter rivals. Toward the end of their tenures, there were signs of reconciliation, but Asad's inclination to caution and Saddam's reckless strategy were essentially incompatible. Asad's approach got better results: By aligning Syria with the anti-Iraqi coalition in 1991, he achieved in Lebanon the dominance that Saddam failed to achieve in Kuwait.

Yemen - This lately united country is a bisectarian state. Most of the people of the southern component, formerly South Yemen, are adherents of the *Shafi'i* school of Sunni Islam. The southern part of north Yemen is also dominated by Shafi'is, while the majority in the north belong to the *Zaydi* sect of Shiite Islam. Like the 'Ibadi sect in Oman, the Zaydi doctrine has Isma'ili elements. "Zaydi" is supposed to indicate veneration of Zayd bin 'Ali, great grandson of the Imam 'Ali.

The Preeminent Influence of Language

In prehistoric times, human society was immensely diverse, and the paradigm of that diversity was language. Language is central to human interaction. Linguistic facility is the most immediate criterion in the evaluation of an individual's gravitas. Among its speakers, a language is an overriding force for cooperation; between communities whose dialects are mutually unintelligible, language is a powerful force for discord. Accent is almost impossible to dissimulate. True bilingualism is a rare talent. The classic test for validating a person's origin – *sibboleth,* Hebrew for torrent – comes down to us from the Book of Judges; the closest the impostor could get was *shibboleth.* In World War II, the test word for Japanese claiming to be Chinese was "lallapalooza".

The history of the Middle East is replete with situations in which commonality of language has unified variant tribal or religious communities. Conquest is never complete until the new subjects adopt the language of the conqueror, as Anatolian Greeks adopted Seljuq Turkish.

Conversely, the absence of a common language has nullified ethnic correlation. The Sunni Ottomans assigned many influential positions to Sunni Arabs, particularly in the armed forces, but the linguistic disconnect persisted as the ultimate barrier between Arab and Turk – regardless of the fact that the Turkish vocabulary is studded with Arabic words. The Ottoman commander-in-chief gave an Arab division the grim assignment of repelling the British landing at Gallipoli in World War I. The last Ottoman Sultan proclaimed a jihad against the Allies, but the Arab majority backed the Arab Revolt.

The Persians converted to Islam en masse, and adopted Arabic script and many Arabic terms, but they clung to their own language (except during the interim of 1502-1736, as noted by *Middle East Policy,* when a Turkic dialect was the language of the Safavid court). During the Iran-Iraq war, most Persian-speakers – including many of Arab lineage – fought for Iran, while most Arabic-speakers, whether Sunni or Shia, fought for Iraq. Even though Iraqi Shiites revere Iranian-born clerics (including their spiritual leader under American occupation, Grand Ayatallah 'Ali al Sistani), there is an abiding suspicion of Iranian designs on Iraq.

Middle Easterners have been multilingual for millennia. Trade has an ancient pedigree, and language follows trade. Nevertheless, mastery of a foreign language falls short of understanding an alien culture. "Every language constitutes a particular mode of thought:" Friedrich Schleiermacher.

Lingua Francas

For better or worse, neighbors have to communicate. There is a natural tendency for a favored language to become a region-wide medium of communication. There has been a long succession of them in the Middle East:

Sumerian - The language of the founders of civilization (and the first known written language) was widely used from 3100 B.C. until it was replaced by Akkadian.

Akkadian - With the rise of the Akkadian Empire (first in the world?) around 2000 B.C. (Chapter 10), its language eclipsed Sumerian. Progenitor of Assyrian and Chaldean, Akkadian was a Semitic language, very different from Sumerian.

Aramaic - This Semitic language, originating in Syria, was used by the Assyrian and Achaemenian (Persian) empires, and was the regional lingua franca from 600 B.C. It is believed to have become the first language of Jews, including Christ. It is the language of the Talmud, Rabbinic writings which are the basis of Orthodox Judaic doctrine. (The Palestinian Talmud was completed about 400 A.D., the Babylonian Talmud about 500 A.D.) Jews still sing a *Yom Kippur* prayer with an Aramaic title *("Kol Nidre")*. Aramaic survived as a colloquial tongue until the introduction of Arabic around 650. According to *The Washington Post Weekly,* many members of the Jewish community in Iraqi Kurdistan used Aramaic as late as 1938. It was still spoken by a few non-Jewish Syrians in 2008.

Greek - The brief reign of Alexander the Great (supplemented by two major successor regimes) mysteriously implanted his language across the Middle East and into Central Asia as the vehicle of officialdom. By 150 B.C. the Roman bureacracy in the East was bilingual in Latin and Greek. In 1 A.D., Greek vied with Latin, Egyptian, and Aramaic as the language of choice. Greek was the first language of Christianity's greatest missionary, the Apostle Paul. After the partition of the Roman Empire by Diocletian in 285, the Eastern Empire gradually abandoned Latin, although in 550 it was Emperor Justinian's native tongue. Greek became the official language of the Eastern Roman Empire in the 600's.

Arabic - In the late 600's, under the Umayyads, the Persian and Greek officials of the Caliphate were replaced, Arabic became the state language, and the official use of Greek was proscribed (as noted by G. W. Bowersock). The Turks, the Persians, and the clans of the Caucasus continued to speak their own languages. The Abbasids moved the Islamic capital to Baghdad, essentially a Persian city, but retained Arabic as their primary language. During the later Middle Ages, Arabic was the language most widely spoken by Middle Easterners of all faiths. Under the Ottomans, the use of Arabic in schools and literature was reinforced. In the 1300's the Afro-Asian sweep of the language of the *Qur'an* enabled Ibn Battutah to roam the lands from Morocco to Indonesia without major linguistic impediment.

French - In the 1800's, French reigned briefly as the preferred language of traders and the urban elite.

English - Since the late 1800's, higher education in the Middle East has been actively sponsored or supported by the West, notably by American Protestants and Jesuits. Colleges in Turkey, Syria, Lebanon, Egypt, Iraq, and elsewhere have combined with the emergence of English as the world language of commerce, science, and diplomacy to produce a class of Middle Eastern professionals with considerable facility in that language. In Qatar, English vies with Arabic as the language of job application. Georgia's President Saakashvili speaks Georgian, English, French, and Russian. In Jordan, King 'Abdallah II and Queen Ranya seem to be bilingual in Arabic and English. Iran's recent presidential candidate, Mir Hossein Moussavi, speaks Persian, English, Arabic, and Turkish.

Modern Arabic - Just as vernacular offshoots of Latin have replaced it in Europe, several mutually unintelligible dialects of Arabic have mirrored political divisions across the Arab world. Even Syrian and Egyptian Arabic differed enough to cause daily administrative problems for the short-lived United Arab Republic. In 2001, official interpreters for the United States Government were stumped by some of the obscure tribal expressions in the text of a statement by Usamah bin Ladin, the Saudi leader of the Saudi-Egyptian Al Qa'idah.

The regional popularity of Egyptian films has broadened familiarity with Egyptian Arabic, but audiences in neighboring countries still prefer the products of their own fledgling film industries. The modern ubiquity of radio, satellite television, and the Internet, backed by the appearance of Arabic-language periodicals published in Europe, out of range of Middle Eastern censors, is fostering the evolution of a standard Arabic, blended from the Levantine vernacular and the classical (Lawrence Pintak in *The Middle East Journal*), currently accessible to educated clientele, and presumably in time to all Arabic-speakers.

Special attention is due to Al Jazeera, the television station founded by Prince Hamad bin Khalifah of Qatar in 1996. It is making a dual contribution – disseminating the new universal dialect, and pushing the broadcasting envelope against the stultifying Middle Eastern tradition of oppressive censorship.

Other Middle Eastern Language Groups of Note

Kurdish - By the most generous estimate, there are over 25 million Kurds, who originated in 75,000 mountainous square miles in the adjoining corners of four countries: 15 million in Turkey, 5 million in Iraq, 5 million in Iran, and a million or more in Syria. The Kurdish language is akin to Persian; the Kurds may be descendants of the Medes. Most Kurds are Sunni Muslims, but there are Shia, Alawite, and Yazidi Kurds as well. (Yazidis are a small sect with obscure Zoroastrian, Christian, and Islamic antecedents. They believe in reincarnation, and that they did not descend from Adam. Their sacred texts are in Arabic, but in northern Iraq they speak Kurdish.)

Hebrew - The dialects of ancient Canaanite included Phoenician, spoken on the coast of Lebanon, and Hebrew, spoken in Palestine. Hebrew, the original language of much of the Old Testament, has been remarkably reactivated since 1875 as the spoken language of the National Home and now of Israel. As of 1914, Jewish schools in Palestine began to teach only in Hebrew. Arabic is also an official language of the Israeli state, but Dilip Hiro has reported that Arabic is largely disregarded by the government and Israeli Jews.

Persian - The national language of Iran is also spoken in parts of Afghanistan. It is of Indo-European origin, but it is written in the script of Arabic, a member of the Semitic family.

Turkish - Between 1000 and 1300, floods of nomadic tribesmen from central Asia overran the Middle East. They are customarily identified by the languages they spoke – components of two language families of the Altaic group: Mongolian and Turkic. The Mongols ruled Persia for a time (Chapter 7), but only the Turkic peoples stayed in force: Azerbaijanis, Turkmens, Seljuqs, and Ottomans. Strong in war and administration, the Turkic speakers arrived with no literary tradition, so they deferred to the cultures of their new subjects. Persia's Seljuq rulers used their Turkic dialect (which persisted as the language of the Safavid court), but the Seljuqs promoted Persian literature. Their Ottoman successors in Anatolia seem to have followed this example by according cultural autonomy to their non-Turkic subjects. Three Turkic dialects prevail in the Middle East today: Ottoman in Turkey, Azeri in Azerbaijan, and Turkmen in northern Iraq.

Mustafa Kemal's orchestration of the reincarnation from Ottoman Empire to Turkish state was epitomized by the promotion of the Turkish language. The modern Turks feel a special sense of kinship with the speakers of other Turkic dialects – like the Turkmens of Iraq and the Azerbaijanis of Azerbaijan and northwest Iran – while they feel compelled to suppress every minority language, including Kurdish and even the study of Aramaic in Syrian Orthodox monasteries.

In the 1990's, Armenia went to war with Azerbaijan over control of Nagorno-Karabakh, an Armenian enclave in Azerbaijan, which looked to Turkey for help. An Azerbaijani official said "We are Turks . . . one nation divided into two states." The Shiite majority in Azerbaijan does not seem to have created any political problems for its secularist government.

In Iraq, Turkey takes a patronal interest in the welfare of the Turkmens, a generic Turkish minority. The main Turkmen center is Tall 'Afar, near the Syrian border.

Chaos in the Caucasus - The break-up of the Soviet Union in 1991 left the people of the multilingual south Caucasus free to make their own way in the world. They reacted by setting up three states based on the three predominant languages: Armenian (Indo-European), Azerbaijani (Turkic), and Georgian (South Caucasian, a small and idiosyncratic language family).

All three have been inundated in ethnic conflict: Armenia and Azerbaijan over Nagorno-Karabakh, Georgia over the agitation of three smaller linguistic communities for political autonomy.

The mountainous terrain of the south Caucasus has given birth to a vast array of unrelated languages. Pliny the Elder reported that Rome needed interpreters of eighty languages to do its business there. An Arab historian counted over 300 languages. By more recent count, the 150,000 square miles of the entire Caucasus – the three independent states south of the range and the Russian segment north of the range (which includes obstreperous Chechnya) – contain fifty ethnic groups.

Costs of Communalism

In the fluctuation of the Middle East between political unity and political division, communalist violence has waxed and waned in parallel. Under the aegis of empire, stability was enhanced. When empire collapsed, turmoil surged. As one set of empirical evidence for this thesis, consider the "orgy of ethnic violence" that erupted from the disintegration of the Ottoman Empire.

Armenian Genocide - In the days of Ottoman ascendancy, Armenians benefited from their familiarity with Western languages and practices to assume an important financial and commercial function in the empire. In the 1890's, they nullified this advantage by agitating for greater political freedom. The Sultan reacted by sanctioning pogroms in which some 200,000 Armenians died.

In the early days of World War I, Armenians further enraged the Turks by forming militias that fought alongside the Russians. In retaliation, the Young Turks, a military junta which in 1913 had set up a reformist government that entered the war on the side of the Central Powers, imposed mass expulsion of Armenians and Nestorians from the eastern frontier. Pro-government Kurds participated in a brutal campaign that caused a million Armenian deaths from massacre and deprivation. Turkish officials continue to deny that this clear case of genocide ever happened.

A U.S. Senate resolution accusing the Ottomans of genocide against the Armenians in World War I has repeatedly been shelved for fear of Turkish termination of American base rights at Incirlik.

Muslim Versus Christian - Gibbon concluded that, over the first millennium of the Christian era, many more Christians were killed by other Christians than by "infidels". However, centuries of hostility between Islam and Byzantium complicated the lives of people living on both sides of the shifting frontier. Byzantium lost the crucial battle of Manzikert in 1071 when Turkmen mercenaries defected to the Seljuqs. In 1258, Georgian Christians joined the Mongols in the massacre of 800,000 Muslims in Baghdad. The Abbasid Caliphate's resistance to the Mongols was undermined by Muslim factionalism. Kitbuga, the commander of the Mongol army in the epic battle of 'Ayn Jallut in 1260, was a Christian Turk. The mass conversion of the Mongols to Islam contributed to persecution and forced conversion that gradually reduced the Christian population of the Middle East to pockets in Anatolia, Iraq, the Caucasus, Syria/Lebanon, and Egypt.

In the 1800's, the growing European presence in the Levant, based on French ties with the Maronites and British ties with the Druze, exacerbated friction between Christian and Muslim Arabs. Sectarian affiliation was hard to hide when it was specified on every citizen's ID card, and each urban dweller lived in his own community's quarter of a city. In 1860, the ancient collaboration between Maronites and Druze broke down. Under the observation of passive Ottoman soldiers, Muslims and Druze massacred Christians in Damascus and Beirut. In 1864, under pressure from the

European powers, the Ottoman Sultan reorganized Lebanon once again, this time as an autonomous sanjaq under a Christian governor – but with large Muslim and Druze minorities.

In 1933, Iraqi officer Bakr Sidqi was lionized for burning twenty "Assyrian" (Nestorian Christian) villages and killing a party who had taken refuge in Iraq from Muslim persecution in Syria, then under French rule.

In 1958, the government of newly independent Lebanon suffered a temporary loss of control when conflict flared between Muslims enthused by the proclamation of Syrian-Egyptian union, and Christians alarmed by it. The Christian commander-in-chief of the army, which was neutralized by its Muslim-Christian composition, wisely kept it out of the fighting and eventually managed to restore order.

In 1975, beset by smoldering Muslim-Christian animosity, infiltration of Israel from Lebanon by Palestinian "fedayeen", and Israeli counterattacks, Lebanon finally erupted in the inevitable civil war, which degenerated into grisly atrocities like the hurling of "enemy" babies from top-floor balconies. This time, the Lebanese army split along sectarian lines. In 1978 Israel occupied a "security zone" in south Lebanon, mobilized a force of Maronite and Shia mercenaries to defend it, and stepped up its military cooperation with the *Phalange,* a right-wing Maronite party. In 1982, General Ariel Sharon hustled his country into a full-scale invasion which was to involve the Americans and cost the Israelis heavy loss of prestige and lives (Chapter 8). The Shiites of Lebanon, like the Shiites of Iraq in 2003, welcomed invasion insofar as it depleted the forces of rival sects, but eventually became its bitter adversaries. The civil war lasted fifteen years, and would have gone on longer but for intervention by a superior Syrian force. The Israeli forces, having gradually retreated from Beirut to the Security Zone, left Lebanon altogether in 2000.

Since 1980, Iraq and Turkey have been accused of practicing ethnic cleansing against Iraqi Christians, driving them to refuge in northern Turkey or Jordan. Since 1998, sectarian disorder has broken out again in Egypt, as Islamist factions carried out sporadic atrocities against the Coptic community.

Sunni Versus Shiite - The ancient fracture of the Muslim community is still occasion for internecine violence. In the 1800's, Sunnis from Arabia launched tribal raids against Shiites in Mesopotamia. In modern Iraq, mainstream Sunnis have been more inclined toward secularism, though respectful of Islamic law; Shiites have been more deferential toward their sectarian leaders. Shiite intellectuals were the backbone of the Iraqi Communist Party: Vali Nasr.

In the late 1900's, Sunni-Shiism divisions were kept at bay by Baathist draconianism. In 1980 (Chapter 9), *Al Da'wah,* a Shiite militia, carried out bombings and assassination attempts against the Baathist regime. Saddam retaliated by mass arrests, torture, deportations to Iran, and hanging Grand Ayatallah Muhammad Baqir al Sadr (cousin of the Lebanese Shiite leader Musa al Sadr).

In 2003, the American elimination of the Sunni power structure (Chapter 15) reopened the Sunni-Shiite wound. Subsequent sectarian atrocities drove five million Iraqis from their homes. Vali Nasr expressed concern that the Iraqi split could escalate into inter-Islamic conflict across the Middle East.

Forgotten Palestinians - Of all the victims of Middle Eastern lawlessness, Arab ineptitude, and Western self-interest, the Palestinians head the list. When the British and French carved the region up after World War I, the Palestinians – as Ottoman subjects – had no responsible leadership of their own, and other Arab leaders swallowed the Europeans' lies. The Palestinians had no way of knowing that the 1947 Partition Resolution, pushed through the UN General Assembly by the United States, would eventuate in mass expulsion from most of Palestine in 1948, a second expulsion from the remainder in 1967, and ultimate Jewish hegemony over the entire territory of the Mandate.

Most of the dispossessed had no alternative to taking refuge in bleak, futureless camps administered on a shoestring by the UN. Two million survivors and their offspring are still in those camps sixty years later. In Jordan and the Occupied Territories, organization of resistance to Hashemite and Israeli rule has been inhibited by sectarian, tribal, and partisan divisions. In Jordan, the Palestinians were granted citizenship, but little freedom of political organization. In Syria, over 300,000 live in camps, closely monitored by the government. In hypersectarian Lebanon, over 300,000 endure onerous discrimination; the government has naturalized thousands of Christian Palestinians, but denied most of the Muslims social services, the unrestricted right to work, and the right to own land. Aside from Jordan, Arab states have kept their doors closed to the Palestinian refugees on the theoretical grounds that they should be allowed to return to their homes (few still exist); the real reason is that no regime is inclined to take the political risk or the economic responsibility. In 1970, the threat posed to the monarchy by the PLO led King Husayn to expel its 5000 insurgents to Lebanon.

Under rising budgetary pressure, the United Nations Relief and Works Agency for Palestinian Refugees in the Middle East (UNRWA) still manages to provide 4 million individuals food and basic education on less than a dollar a day per person (Chapter 8).

Population Exchange Between Greece and Turkey - Mustafa Kemal's greatest military triumph was routing the Greek occupation force in 1922. Undisposed to challenge resurgent Turkey, the Allies scratched the humiliating Treaty of Sèvres (1920) in favor of the Treaty of Lausanne (1923). In the unceremonious exchange of populations that ensued from Lausanne, 350,000 Turks left Greece for Turkey, and – with some loss of life – a million and a half Greeks left Turkey for Greece. Many of the transferees did not even speak the language of their obligatory new country of residence, although until World War I Greek had been commonly spoken in the European quarter of Istanbul. In 1955, anti-Greek rioting in Istanbul over the Cyprus issue led to the departure of many of the 100,000 Greeks still living in Turkey. The partition of Cyprus between an ethnically Greek state and an ethnically Turkish enclave remains as another example of the ravages of communalism.

Nagorno-Karabakh - The Armenian claim to this enclave in Azerbaijan led in 1992 to war between the two states. The conflict was temporarily resolved in 1994 by a ceasefire that left Armenia in military control of the enclave (Chapter 11).

Kurdish Nationalism - The Kurds are the largest ethnic group in the Middle East that has never had a state of its own. This misfortune derives in part from geography – they are surrounded by rival linguistic communities – and in part from their own tribal disunity. The result was four separate and largely uncoordinated movements for greater Kurdish autonomy:

In northwestern **Iran,** 1979 featured a Kurdish (and an Azeri) challenge to governmental authority: *Middle East Report,* Summer 2008. The Iraqi invasion of 1980 enabled Iran to mobilize Iranian and Iraqi Kurds on its side of the conflict. Since the turn of the century, the newly formed PEJAK (The Kurdistan Free Life Party) has been conducting sporadic resistance operations.

In northeastern **Syria,** Kurds have clashed with the authorities, notably in an incident in 2004 that took nine lives. Syria has denied citizenship to some 300,000 of its Kurdish residents: *Middle East Policy,* May 2008.

In **Iraq,** the Pesh Merga, uniformed and well armed, have become the strongest militia in the country.

The Kurds of **Turkey** have staged bitter resistance against a pathologically nationalistic regime and a constitution (1982) that specifically denies Kurds a separate entity. Law 2932 of 1983 criminalized the Kurdish language (as well as Communism and theocracy). In 1991 Turkish law was moderated to allow speaking and writing in Kurdish, but no teaching or broadcasting.

Kurdish Dissidence in Turkey - In the eyes of the Turkish authorities, the Kurds are "mountain Turks" who have no right to a non-Turkish language or culture. Since the first Kurdish revolt in 1925, relations between Ankara and the insurgency have been poisonous. In 1932, the government set out to break the rebellion by mass resettlement of Kurds from their ancestral homeland in the southeast. Imposition of martial law in 1978 coincided with assumption of leadership of the insurgency by the Kurdish Workers Party (PKK), a Marxist organization of male and female militants (Robert Pape, *Middle East Policy,* Winter 2008) which has built a formidable militia.

In 1979, the Iranian revolution sparked the founding in Turkey of a Kurdish *Hizballah,* which honors Egyptian Sayyid Qutb and is a bitter rival of the PKK.

1978 introduced two decades of mass arrests, torture, killing, deportation, destruction of Kurdish villages by the forces of both sides, and dispersal of hordes of Kurds to the cities – over a million to Istanbul.

In the 1980's, Ankara imposed a state of emergency in ten southeastern provinces. This action stirred the PKK, but induced many Kurds to migrate to western Turkey or Europe. In 1993, under Prime Minister Tansu Ciller, tough prison sentences were meted out for harmless speech, villages that supplied the PKK were burned, and Kurdish activists were killed.

In the 1990's, hostilities by both sides razed over 3000 Kurdish villages. In 1992, PKK leader Abdallah Ocalan, an egocentric who has had rivals killed, was in Syria operating a boot camp and orchestrating infiltration into Turkey. Ankara was trying to balance its conflicting interests by restricting the flow of Euphrates water into Syria, but allowing US flights from Incirlik to defend the sanctuary being set up by Iraqi Kurds in northeastern Iraq, even though Ankara detested the northern No-Fly Zone because it reduced Turkish revenue from trade with Iraq, afforded sanctuary for Turkish Kurds, and was beginning to take on the attributes of an independent state.

In 1996, Turkey made history by allowing the election to Parliament of Kurds who implicitly represented the insurgency, even though the killings of insurgents continued.

US policy was equally schizoid. Anxious to keep its base rights at Incirlik and preserve its alliance with Turkey against Islamist fundamentalism in the Middle East and Central Asia, Washington tolerated Turkish repression of the Kurdish media, schools, and language, and refrained from protesting the brutality of Turkey's military operations against the Kurds, but it was promoting the emergence of a Kurdish quasi-state in Iraq (Chapter 9).

In 1999, Washington mitigated this offense. With significant help from the CIA, Turkish agents captured PKK leader Abdallah Ocalan, then a fugitive in Kenya after his expulsion from Syria under Turkish threat of invasion. Ocalan went to prison, the PKK declared a five-year cease-fire, and Parliament lifted the ban on teaching and broadcasting in Kurdish.

In 2000, Huseyin Velioglu, founder of the Kurdish Hizballah, was killed by the police. His replacement, Isa Altsay, shifted his headquarters to Europe, residence of four million Turkish expatriates, many of whom were Kurds.

By 2004, the Kurdish resistance had been subdued by Ocalan's imprisonment, and the intensity of Turkish repression had been moderated by Prime Minister Erdogan, who was under pressure from the European Union, which the Turkish establishment hoped to join. Under Erdogan, torture of Kurds was banned, many PKK prisoners were released, private schools began teaching in Kurdish, and state TV aired its first Kurdish-language program. Nevertheless, since 2005 the PKK, operating from the KAR under the leadership of Murat Karayilan, had been killing Turkish soldiers, using new tactics learned from the Iraqi insurgency.

In March 2006 the killing of fourteen PKK militants precipitated violent Kurdish protests, especially in Diyarbakir, a largely Kurdish city of a million with 70 percent unemployment. The US and the European Union were urging a receptive Erdogan to proclaim a general amnesty for the PKK. Since the American invasion of Iraq, the PKK and the KDP had built close ties, but Ankara was cultivating President Talabani of the PUK. In Turkey, the anti-tribal PKK had had lethal clashes with the pro-tribal Kurdish Hizballah: *Middle East Policy,* Spring 2006 and 2007. Although thousands of the fundamentalist faction had been jailed, some 20,000 were still active. In August, a group thought to be the urban wing of the PKK claimed responsibility for a string of lethal bombings.

In the fall of 2006, while Ocalan's PKK was calling for a cease-fire, a new Kurdish resistance force, The Freedom Falcons (TAK), was carrying out lethal bombings of tourism sites in Turkish cities. The PKK condemned these operations. In 2007 de Bellaigue noted that Turkey's new Chief of Staff opposed amnesty for the PKK, but that over time the Kurdish problem would solve itself; half of Turkey's Kurds (including Ocalan) still spoke Kurmanji at home, but millions had been assimilated into Turkish society, and the conciliatory strategy of Erdogan's Justice and Development Party (AKP) was having good effect.

In December 2007, in *The Wall Street Journal,* Michael Rubin reported that Ocalan was directing PKK operations from prison. In September 2008 *The London Review of Books* reported that the AKP had switched to sterner action against Kurdish dissidents.

Avenues of Assimilation

The story of Middle Eastern communalism is such a dreary one that it is refreshing to end on a positive note. Even though the people of the region are ethnically fractionated, they have achieved an encouraging degree of genetic integration. This phenomenon has come about in several timeless ways: Trade, employment, slavery, migration, military service, conversion, and marriage.

Trade - Archaeological evidence of intercontinental commerce goes back to the dawn of history. The evolution of caravan routes lured the adventurous, inquisitive, and acquisitive to lives of travel. A colony of Indian merchants was noted in Memphis, Egypt, around 500 B.C. Resourceful Jews turned adversity to their advantage when, expelled from Judaea by Rome, they created an international financial network. At the time of Muhammad, the Jews of Medina were a merchant community. By 900, the Islamic Empire had a banking system operated by Jews. In 1600, a European visitor to Yemen found San'a' a large city with Armenian, Greek, Russian, Indian, and Jewish communities. Jews were leaders in the economy of Iraq until the environment turned hostile after the founding of Israel in 1948.

Employment - Conquerors often turned to their new subjects for expert assistance in government and the professions – Seljuqs to Persians, Caliphs to Christians and Jews, and Mamluks to Egyptians. Under Islamic rule, Arabic was the first language of most Jews, and their expertise was valued in finance and medicine. Musa Ibn Maymun (Maimonides), court physician to Salah al Din in Cairo, the greatest of the Jewish philosophers, had a profound influence on successors from all communities. The Ottomans also employed Jews, many of them refugees from Spain, in the fields of medicine and finance. There were Christians in the cabinets of Sultans Suleiman I and Selim III.

Slavery - Enslavement of prisoners of war was a Middle Eastern practice as early as 2340 B.C., in the time of Sargon, ruler of the Akkadian Empire, first known empire in the region, if not the world. By the time of the Islamic conquest, slaves were readily obtainable by capture or purchase. The empire's need for manpower contributed to the tolerance of a society that afforded slaves broad opportunities for advancement. A slave's conversion to Islam meant automatic liberation, since the Sharia barred enslavement of Muslims by Muslims. After emancipation, a slave could even marry into the family of the former owner. Slaves who declined conversion were still allowed to own land; their children could not be born into slavery. The civil administration and armed forces of the Ottoman Empire were copiously staffed with slaves. Between 1500 and 1900, millions of Africans were imported to the Middle East. In the egalitarian environment of Islam, skin color has not been a major social impediment. Because of Ottoman Sultans' penchant for stocking their harems with captives, many of their successors were the sons of a mother who had been a slave. As reported by Pete Hart, the institution of slavery in the Middle East expired in theory, if not in fact, when Saudi Arabia banned the practice in 1962.

Migration - Table B catalogues some of the better known manifestations:

Table B: Major Known Migratory Movements into the Middle East

Akkadians - First recorded in north central Mesopotamia around 3000 B.C.

Amorites - Possibly from Arabia, they dominated the history of Mesopotamia, Syria, and Palestine 2000-1600 B.C.

Arabs - Spread across the Middle East from Arabia from early times, and notably during the Islamic conquest in the 600's.

Aramaeans - First reported in northern Syria and Mesopotamia about 1500 B.C.

Assyrians - Reported in northern Mesopotamia and southeastern Anatolia by 1500 B.C.

Canaanites - Entered Palestine and Lebanon (as Phoenicians?) around 3000 B.C.

Celts - One of their roving bands settled in Anatolia around 250 B.C.

Chaldeans - Entered southern Mesopotamia around 1000 B.C.

Cimmerians- Driven out of Russia by the Scythians, settled in Anatolia about 725 B.C.

Circassians - Refugees from Russian penetration of the Caucasus in the 1800's.

Crusaders - Ruled the Levantine coast in the 1100's and briefly in the 1200's.

Elamites - Appeared in western Persia around 3000 B.C. Assyria deported some of them to Palestine.

Hittites - An Indo-European people who appeared in Anatolia around 2000 B.C. and by 1340 B.C. had become one of the dominant powers in the Middle East.

Hurrians - Appeared in western Persia and Mesopotamia around 2000 B.C. as rulers of the Mitanni state, which dominated northern Mesopotamia 1700-1350 B.C.

Jews - Also known as Hebrews or Israelites. By Biblical account they moved from Mesopotamia to Palestine around 1900 B.C., and some went on to Egypt with the Hyksos around 1800 B.C. and did not return until 1150 B.C. Nebuchadrezzar II took many to Babylon around 597 B.C. Liberated by Cyrus around 550 B.C., many returned to Palestine. In the Middle Ages, multitudes in eastern Europe considered themselves Jews, although their origin was indeterminate. Many of them went to Palestine and Israel in the 1800's and 1900's, as did most Jewish residents of the Arab World after 1948. Upwards of a million Jews and families migrated from Russia in the late 1900's.

Kassites - Appeared in Mesopotamia, possibly from Persia, around 2800 B.C., were conquered around 950 B.C., and moved to Persia.

Medes - Dominant in northwest Persia, 750-550 B.C.

Ottomans - A faction of Oguz Turks who migrated from Central Asia via Persia to Anatolia in the 1200's. In the early 1300's, tribal chief Osman founded the Ottoman Dynasty, which eventually established preeminence over Turkish rivals, including the Seljuqs.

Parthians - Reported in northeastern Iran from about 500 B.C.

Persians - Entered Persia, possibly from the Caucasus, around 2000 B.C.

Philistines - From the Balkans via Greece and Egypt, settled on the Palestinian coast by 1200 B.C. Gave their name to Palestine.

Phoenicians - Semites who settled on the Lebanese coast around 3000 B.C.

Scythians - Nomads of Iranian stock who migrated from central Asia to the northern coast of the Black Sea around 800 B.C., conquered the Caucasus, northwest Persia, and much of the Levant from the Cimmerians, and ruled those lands until the Medes, rulers of Persia, drove them back to southern Russia.

Seljuqs - Migrated from Central Asia to Persia, Mesopotamia, and Anatolia 1000-1100. By defeating the Byzantines at Manzikert in 1071, they opened Anatolia to settlement by several million Oguz Turks, including the Ottomans. Most present-day Turks are descendants of the Oguz.

Sumerians - Established the world's earliest village culture in southern Mesopotamia around 4000 B.C.

Ubaidians - Predated the Sumerians in Mesopotamia.

Military Service - Military service in general has had a profound assimilationist effect. Many Americans who served in World War II have personal experience of being uprooted from ancestral surroundings, being sent to far corners of the United States and the world, and in many cases marrying people they would otherwise never have met. So it has always been in the Middle East. Greek mercenaries fought in the Babylonian army that conquered Judah around 604 B.C. Persians, Indians, Syrians, Central Asians, and Greek mercenaries fought side by side for Persia against the Greek city-states, and undoubtedly broadcast their DNA along the way. Alexander found that his most formidable adversaries were Greek mercenaries. The Seleucids, one of the three successor dynasties to Alexander, billeted their Greek soldiers in colonies, some of which evolved into Hellenistic cities. The recruitment of infidel youths into military training was a common route to honored service, and often to high position, for Turkic slaves from Central Asia (mamluks) in Islamic Egypt and Syria, and for Christian slaves from the Balkans (janissaries) in the Ottoman Empire.

The Roman Empire was precocious in its practice of recruiting soldiers from all over its domain, blending them into interethnic units, and stationing them – and often retiring them – far from their countries of origin. Ethnic intermarriage was a common result.

There is evidence that, in a retreat from the Roman precedent, the armies of the Caliphate were organized along tribal lines. In the early 800's, however, the Caliphs began to augment their troops with slaves and recruits from Central Asia. From the 900's on, Turkic mercenaries from Central Asia were the mainstay of the Islamic empire. During the same period, the Fatimids conquered Egypt with Berber troops from North Africa. In 1169, Egypt was conquered for the Seljuqs by a Kurdish general, Salah al Din, who later expelled his overlords from Egypt and Syria. He imported mamluks from Anatolia and the Caucasus to serve as bodyguards. After the mamluks had risen to suzerainty in Egypt, they recruited Circassians to perform the function they had previously performed themselves. The Mongol army that devastated Baghdad in 1258 included Chinese artillerymen, Christian foot soldiers from the Caucasus, and Turks – who eventually seized control from the Mongols. The Ottomans manned their armies with janissaries. The core of the rival Safavid army in Persia was Azerbaijanis. In the late 1500's, Shah Abbas created Persia's first standing army from Georgian, Armenian, and Circassian converts to Shia Islam.

In modern times, the revolt led by Ahmad 'Urabi against British domination of Egypt was motivated in part by Egyptian resentment of the Turkish and Circassian occupancy of most high military positions. In Syria of the 1940's, dictator Husni Za'im was overthrown after he had lost the support of his Arab troops because of his heavy reliance on Kurdish and Circassian units.

Conversion - Historians may never determine the relative effects of theology, conquest, and military service on the distribution of sectarian affiliation. It can only be affirmed that paganism gave way to the "religions of the book" – Judaism, Christianity, and Islam – and that these three have ebbed and flowed like tides across the human sea that populates the region. Judaism came first and, at the time of Christ, gave evidence of becoming a world religion. However, Christianity out-proselytized Judaism, and Islam out-proselytized Christianity. Muslim overlords had less incentive to win converts, since the poll tax paid by non-Muslims was an important source of revenue, but it was a good reason for a pragmatic taxpayer to embrace Islam. Moreover, the forces of Islam needed manpower. They won many of their battles with Berber and Persian converts. Aided by the rise of Sufiism (a Muslim movement that believed in saints), Islam eventually won over most of the Christians in the Middle East.

The end product of these countervailing forces is a congeries of sects to which millions pay fervent allegiance, and a genetic medley in which few can discern their heritage. In Iraq and Turkey, Sunnis and Shiites can live side by side in the same tribe; there is no congruence between tribe and sect, let alone between language group and sect. Iraq's palace coup of 1936, the first military coup in the Arab world, was mounted by Bakr Sidqi, a Kurd. The mother of Iraq's dictator in 1963, 'Abd al Karim Qasim, was a Shiite Kurd. The lineage of members of the Jewish faith is at least as obscure as all the rest, given the evidence that many Ashkenazis could have Khazar antecedents (a theory advanced by Arthur Koestler) and the fact that many Sephardis trace their lineages back to centuries of living side by side with Spaniards, Berbers, Arabs, and other diverse peoples. Most present-day Palestinian Muslims are believed to be descendants of Christians who were descendants of Jews.

When Mongol chieftain Hulegu conquered Baghdad, he spared its Christian residents because his mother was a Nestorian Christian. In 1260, it was a Nestorian commander, Kitbuga, who led the Mongol forces in the epic battle of 'Ayn Jallut, which saved the Islamic Empire, and helped persuade the Mongols in the Middle East to espouse Islam.

In the 1500's, the conquests of the Safavids in Persia and the Ottomans in Anatolia, Egypt, and the Levant led to parallel mass conversions to Shiism and Sunniism in the two rival empires. In 1749, the Shihab family, Sunnis based in the Lebanon mountains, captured Beirut (within the context of continued Ottoman suzerainty), and formed an alliance with the Maronites that led to their conversion to the Maronite faith.

Recently in the news are the Alevis, a classification that includes various residents of Turkey who became Shiites at an unknown point in history, speak Turkish, Kurdish, or rarely Arabic, and have an adversarial history with Sunnis. They fought on the side of the government against the Kurdish rebellion of 1925. Persecuted by the Ottomans, they revere Mustafa Kemal, but rioted in 1995 against Ankara's pro-Sunni policies.

Marriage - The derogatory connotation of the English word "miscegenation" may suggest a subliminal tinge of racism in Western society. In any event, interbreeding has always been the universal solvent for ethnic bondage, and it has been occurring even in ceremonial circumstances for at least 3350 years. Around 1350 B.C., it was the practice of the Mitanni (Hurrian) kings in Mesopotamia to assign their daughters to the harems of Egyptian pharaohs. A hundred years later, Pharaoh Ramses II consolidated a treaty with the Hittites by taking a Hittite princess as one of his many wives. Israeli King David's bevy of wives and concubines included the daughters of a pharaoh and other neighboring rulers. David's wife Bathsheba, as the former wife of Uriah the Hittite, may have been Hittite herself – thereby conveying Aryan blood to her son Solomon. About 875 B.C., Israel's King Ahab married Jezebel, daughter of a Phoenician king of Tyre. In 328 B.C., Alexander of Macedonia married Roxana, a Bactrian princess, and arranged for 10,000 of his soldiers to marry Persians. The two principal empires that succeeded the empire of Alexander, the Seleucid and the Ptolemaic, were ruled by Greeks until Roman times. Mark Antony's inamorata, Cleopatra of Egypt, was of Greek origin.

According to *The National Geographic,* King Herod of Judaea, who ruled 37-4 B.C., had been raised as a Jew, but his father had been an Edomite and his mother an Arab.

In the Christian era, Byzantine emperors were known to take Khazar wives. The Umayyad rulers were of Arabian origin, but their Abbasid successors were multiethnic. Timur, who conquered the Middle East (except for Arabia) in the 1300's (and occupied Moscow for a year), shunned his grand capital of Samarkand for life in the field, but he still found time for nine wives and concubines. He was a member of a Turkicized Mongol tribe. In 1470, the ruler of Iran, a Turkmen, had a Byzantine wife. Permissive Ottoman society encouraged intermarriage. Colin Thubron (*The New York Review,* 4/9/09) noted that some Ottoman sultans, born to mothers from the harem, had "scarcely a drop of Turkish blood."

In modern Turkey, many citizens of prominence have Kurdish, Greek, or Georgian antecedents. In the Caucasus, the Soviet Union encouraged ethnic intermarriage. The collapse of the Union in 1991 led to the formation of three communalist states in which ethnic hostility has hardened.

Of the myriad ethnic groups in the Middle East, the Jews seem to set greatest store on racial purity. Many rabbis frown on marriage outside the faith. The claim to unadulterated lineage is reinforced by the prevalence of the honored names Levy and Cohen and their variants, which signify descent from hereditary priesthoods. However, there is a body of evidence to the contrary; in addition to the marital records cited above, the issue is clouded in that, in ancient times, Jews customarily traced their heredity from their fathers, whereas after Islamic conquest, custom shifted to stress matrilineal descent. Some scholars speculate that the physical resemblance of many Jews to non-Jews from their country of origin suggests considerable intermarriage of Jewish males with non-Jewish females. According to one hypothesis, around 1200 B.C. the Canaanites (the indigenous population of Palestine) split into two clans – Arabs and Jews. It would be geopolitically irrelevant, but supremely ironic, if the two factions that cite lineage to justify the lives they are taking in Palestine should turn out to be essentially one people.

Chapter 7
Frontiers of Conquest

The political map of the Middle East is dotted with supersensitive departures from elemental geography – arguably including European Turkey, partition of Cyprus, Turkish control of Alexandretta, Israeli-Arab division of Palestine, separation of Iraq and Kuwait, Armenian control of Nagorno-Karabakh, and the two autonomous enclaves between Georgia and Russia. Viewed from space, however, topographic features would seem to subdivide the region into seven <u>sectors</u>: Anatolia; Persia; Mesopotamia; the Levant; Egypt; Arabia; and the southern Caucasus.

Buffeted by the immutable geopolitical forces surveyed in Chapter 1, these seven sectors have been caught up in an endless series of power struggles. For the weaker contenders, the objective is maximum independence from their rivals. For the stronger (whose base of power may be in the region or outside it), the objective is security – which usually translates into control over the largest manageable block of territory, regardless of who inhabits it: That is to say, <u>empire</u>.

Most power struggles start small, inside a sector. With the possible exception of the Caucasus, each of these sectors has been brought under centralized indigenous rule at one or more periods in its history. Egypt, first in line, was initially unified by a mysterious ruler about 3100 B.C. Fast-forwarding to 2010 A.D., we find four sectors essentially unified: Anatolia, Persia, Mesopotamia, and Egypt.

Whenever a dynasty establishes a significant power base in its own sector, competition from adjoining sectors automatically inclines it to look for opportunities for expansion. Over the past five millennia, various aspirants to empire have had varying degrees of success. Some conquered large parts of the region; one (the Islamic Caliphate) conquered almost all of it. Some were indigenous; some were based abroad (Chapter 10). But all shared a common fate: Sooner or later, they collapsed. In this cyclical universe, every rise seems destined to end in a fall. For the Middle East, the consequence has been five thousand years of oscillation between the opposite poles of unification and fragmentation.

The Five-Millennium Story

Whereas Mesopotamia was the cradle of civilization (failing contradictory data from China or India), Egypt may have been the cradle of centralized government. First Middle Eastern sector to unite, it was conducting military expeditions into Palestine as early as 3000 B.C.

The first clear case of Middle Eastern empire occurred in the 2300's B.C., when an Akkadian dynasty unified Mesopotamia and went on to extend its rule from the Persian Gulf to the Mediterranean coast of northwestern Syria and southern Anatolia. Around 2200 B.C., the Middle East fell into political disarray, possibly as a consequence of a devastating drought that may have lasted three centuries. From the 1900's to 1600 B.C., Mesopotamia, southwestern Persia, and northeastern Syria were dominated by the Amorites, who maintained in the 1700's and 1600's B.C. what has been termed, perhaps generously, the first Babylonian Empire. It was distinguished by Hammurabi, the Lawgiver, who ruled from 1792 to 1750 B.C. For much of this period, control of Palestine was contested among the Amorites, the Egyptians, and the indigenous Canaanites. Amorite rule in Mesopotamia seems to have been subjected to serious vicissitudes. There are reports of intrusions by Hittites from Anatolia, Hurrians from northern Mesopotamia, and Kassites from Persia. Egypt was ruled from about 1630 to the 1500's B.C. by the Hyksos, who had immigrated from Asia in the 1700's B.C. and may have been of Amorite or Canaanite stock. There is evidence that over the five centuries between 1700 and 1200 B.C. the region was divided among six major power structures: Egypt, the Hittites in Anatolia, the Kassites in southwestern Persia, the Hurrians (succeeded by the Assyrians) in northern Mesopotamia, the Amorites in southern Mesopotamia, and the Aramaeans in Arabia. Mesopotamia endured three centuries of political stagnation. The Levant was contested among its inhabitants and their neighbors from 1550 to 1200 B.C. Egypt finally established some degree of control over the Levant around 1350 B.C. and held on there until 1075 B.C.

The first major battle known to history was the siege of Megiddo (near the site of present-day Haifa) around 1478 B.C., when Egypt inflicted a decisive defeat on the Hurrians, who had been ruling the Levant from

Mesopotamia. Megiddo may have given its name to the Final-Days Battle of Armageddon predicted in the Book of Revelations.

The Hittites conquered northern Mesopotamia from the Hurrians around 1325 B.C., but soon lost it to the resurgent Assyrians, while the Elamites from Persia recaptured southern Mesopotamia around 1275 B.C. Around 1193 B.C., the "Sea Peoples" from the Aegean (including the Philistines), exploiting their monopoly of steel weapons, briefly took the Levant from Egypt, the Hittites, and the resident Canaanites, but lost it around 1182 B.C. to the Egyptians, who lost it in turn around 1175 B.C. to unknown invaders from Anatolia and Europe. The years from 1100 to 900 B.C. were "dark ages" for the Middle East in general, but they marked the reign of the Babylonian King Nebuchadrezzar I, conqueror of Elam (southwestern Persia). There was a brief period of triumph for the Hebrews, who set up a principality based on Jerusalem around 1000 B.C. Within fifty years it split into the kingdoms of Israel and Judah (Chapter 8).

In 911 B.C., the Assyrians in northern Mesopotamia launched an expansion which was to establish the first enduring Middle Eastern empire since the Akkadian, 1300 years before. The Assyrian sway reached its zenith in the 800's and 700's B.C., when from its base in Mesopotamia it ruled western Persia, the Levant, southern Anatolia, and – intermittently – Egypt. From the late 700's B.C. through the early 600's, Nubian (Sudanese) rulers held sway in Egypt. In the late 600's B.C., the Assyrian Empire was crushed by an alliance of the Chaldeans from Babylon (Mesopotamia) and the Medes from Persia. The alliance is known to many as the Second Babylonian Empire. Nebuchadrezzar II went on to conquer most of the Levant and expel the Egyptians from most of Palestine. In 573 B.C., he conquered the ancient Phoenician city of Tyre.

Around 585 B.C., Persia was dominated by Medes, Anatolia by Lydians, Mesopotamia by Babylonians, and Egypt by Egyptians. In the 500's B.C., the Achaemenid clan defeated the Medes and established the first truly Persian dynasty. The Achaemenids went on to create the greatest empire in history until the rise of Rome. The objective of Emperor Xerxes was to rule the world. By 539 B.C., Cyrus II had conquered southern Anatolia, Cyprus, Armenia, and the Levant, and consigned the Second Babylonian Empire to history. In 525 B.C., the Persians conquered Egypt. Anatolia fell by 522 B.C. Persia went on to conquer large expanses of Thrace, North Africa, and Central Asia.

In 490 B.C. at Marathon – in the most famous battle in the history of ancient Greece – the heavily outnumbered Greeks defeated the Persian invaders. In 480 B.C. Greeks won a decisive victory off the island of Salamis (near Athens) in history's first great naval battle, killing 40,000

Persian soldiers (most of whom were mercenaries or slaves). In 479 B.C. Greeks won a land battle over the Persians at Plataea and executed the leaders of a Theban force that fought for Xerxes. By 466 B.C. Persia had abandoned the effort to conquer Greece. In 403 B.C., Egypt seceded from the Persian Empire.

In 333 B.C., the geopolitical tide turned with a vengeance, as Alexander led the first imperial invasion of Asia from Europe. At the Battle of Issus (in Anatolia), his 50,000 Macedonians defeated a Persian force of 70,000 – including some Greek mercenaries. It took Alexander's military genius seven months to break down the defenses of the island on which the city of Tyre was located, but only two years to accomplish the conquest of the entire Persian Empire. In Egypt he was welcomed and crowned Pharaoh. At Gaugamela (in northern Mesopotamia) in 331 B.C., his 47,000 Macedonians routed a Persian army of 200,000, and the Persian Empire expired. In 326 B.C., he reached the Indus, where his generals finally persuaded him he had conquered enough. Three years later he died, and his do-it-yourself empire broke into pieces – two of which would survive much longer than their progenitor: One of his generals established the dynasty of the Ptolemies in Egypt, Palestine, and Cyprus; another, the dynasty of the Seleucids in Mesopotamia, Syria, and southern Persia. Northern Persia came under the rule of a former general of the Persian Empire. Antigonus I succeeded Alexander as Emperor of Macedon. Anatolia disintegrated into rival principalities.

Aside from having implanted foreign dynastic rule over the heart of the Middle East, Alexander's conquests had immense cultural impact. The Hellenization of the region was epitomized by the long-term use of Greek as the lingua franca of the ruling classes (Chapter 6).

The wars among the Ptolemies, the Seleucids, and indigenous contestants for control of Anatolia and the Levant were fated to be resolved by the emergence of a second European force – one much stronger and better organized than that of Alexander. In 190 B.C., the expanding Roman Empire won a battle against Seleucid forces in Syria. In 133 B.C., Rome took over western Anatolia as a province of the empire. In eastern Persia, the Parthians had emerged to challenge Seleucid rule and finally, in 129 B.C., to deal Hellenic rule in Asia a mortal blow. Victory over Carthage in 146 B.C. in the third Punic War had given Rome a substantial empire in southern Europe and North Africa, an unemployed army and navy, ambitious commanders, and an open imperial agenda. The Middle East was destined to experience the consequences.

Anatolia was the first challenge on the way east. The remnants of the Seleucid Empire were brushed aside in 64 B.C. The Parthians were a different story; they inflicted a crushing defeat on Roman forces in Carrhae (in southern Anatolia) in 53 B.C., thereby preserving Persian independence from Rome, and establishing the Euphrates as their recurrent frontier. By 40 B.C., Rome had subdued most of Anatolia, the Levant, and Egypt. At the Battle of Actium (on the western coast of Greece), Octavian's army of 80,000 defeated Mark Antony's army of 70,000, and the empire of Rome formally acquired an emperor. Cleopatra, the last of the Ptolemies, committed suicide, and Egypt became a personal possession of the Emperor. By 1 A.D., Rome had established a permanent military base at Zeugma in Anatolia on the Upper Euphrates. At that time, as depicted in McNeill's *The Rise of the West,* the Eurasian continent was dominated by a chain of four empires that centered on the 40th parallel from Iberia to China: the Roman, the Parthian, the Kushan, and the Han. The border between Rome and Parthia, in almost constant flux, ran through hapless Mesopotamia. The Caucasus was intermittently independent.

Roman rule in Asia was repeatedly challenged, notably by the Judaeans, first in 66-74 A.D. Gibbon described the relatively quiet period under the Antonine emperors, 96-180 A.D., as a golden age in history. During the suppression of the second Jewish revolt, 122-135 A.D., Rome barred Jews from Jerusalem, destroyed the Second Temple (in 132), and symbolized its actions by renaming Judaea as Palestine. In 138, overextended Rome abandoned some of Mesopotamia to the Parthians, but it reconquered the northern section later in the century. In 224, a new Persian dynasty, the Sasanians, replaced the Parthians. They established Zoroastrianism as the state religion, and held the line against Rome at the Euphrates. In 260, they expanded their hegemony by conquering Oman, on the Gulf coast of southern Arabia.

Expansion of the Roman Empire ceased under Trajan, who died in 117. When Diocletian became Emperor in 284, he found his domain shaken by internal weakness and external attack. His administrative reorganization reflected a shift of the Roman center of power to the east – a shift that was institutionalized in 330 by the Emperor Constantine, who made the Christian city of Byzantium the new imperial capital. It was later renamed Constantinople. By the 400's, the western half of the empire had succumbed to invasion by various tribes from northern Europe. The eastern half – by then the Byzantine Empire – was to survive attacks from south and east for another thousand years.

The culture of "the new Rome" was Hellenistic, its mindsets were oriental, and its military preoccupations were primarily directed to the east, although there was a calamitous invasion of Anatolia by Visigoths from eastern Europe in 378. The Sasanian Empire reached its greatest extent in the 500's, when it ruled Persia and Mesopotamia and was knocking at the doors of the Caucasus and eastern Anatolia. Byzantium held on to Anatolia proper, the Levant, and Egypt (except for a Sasanian foray in the early 600's) – and in the 600's ruled the southern Balkans and North Africa.

There were two Ethiopian occupations of Yemen – in the 300's and in the 500's (Chapter 2). At the Yemenis' request, the Persians (then under Sasanian rule) intervened in Yemen to terminate the second Ethiopian occupation, and they remained in control there until 628, when the last Persian governor accepted the inevitable and converted to Islam.

In the 600's, the warriors of Islam unified most of the Middle East for the first time since the death of Alexander in 323 B.C. Between 624 and 648, they won five decisive battles: Badr in 624, Yarmuk and Qadisiyyah in 636, Nahavand in 642, and Persepolis in 648. By 657, they had conquered the entire region except western Anatolia and the Caucasus, and were on their way into Central Asia and North Africa. This spectacular accomplishment was facilitated by a constellation of circumstances: 1) The Arabs had lived for centuries on their proficiency in lightning raids on camelback; in effect, Muhammad united them into one big raiding party. 2) Incessant war between the Sasanians and the Byzantines had weakened them both; the Sasanians had had to confront civil war as well. 3) The Middle East had been habituated to political union under only two dynasties. 4) The Monophysite Christians of Egypt and the Levant had been persecuted under Byzantine rule; most Middle Easterners resented sectarian pressure from Christian Byzantium and Zoroastrian Persia. 5) Both regimes maintained onerous taxation. 6) Muslims saw death in battle as a direct route to paradise. 7) The probity of early Islam contrasted with Byzantine and Sasanian corruption.

Islam projected an image of invincibility until the 700's. At the crest of the Caucasus, its advance was checked by the Khazars. In Anatolia, Byzantium survived a seven-year siege, thanks to staunch defenses, cunning strategy, and a competent navy – even though a fleet of the Caliphate had destroyed a Byzantine fleet off the coast of Lycia (southern Anatolia) in 655. In 717, the Byzantine army inflicted on the Caliphate its first major defeat. The Taurus Mountains became an enduring boundary between the two empires. Islamic conquest in western Europe crested in 732; weakened by internal dissension and a Berber rebellion, the Muslim forces were turned back at Poitiers in west-central France by Charles Martel, leader of the Franks.

In 661, the first Umayyad Caliph moved his capital from Arabia to Damascus (in Syria). In 750, the Umayyads lost the Caliphate to the Abbasids, who moved the capital to Baghdad (in Mesopotamia), closer to their base of power. The point in central Mesopotamia where the two rivers came closest had been the site of previous capitals.

In 868, under the Tulunid Dynasty, Egypt won autonomy under the nominal rule of the Caliphate. In 877, the Tulunids conquered Syria. Egypt and Syria reverted to Abbasid rule in 905. The Arabs were beginning to lose their grip on the empire. The sitting Caliph remained the nominal ruler, but he was to cede actual control to his former vassals, first the Buyids, later the Seljuq Turks. Byzantium conquered northern Syria in 968, northern Mesopotamia in 975, and Armenia in 1020.

The story of Persia under the Abbasids is an epic in itself. After the move to Baghdad, the *Britannica* tells us, "The Iranian intellect played . . . a conspicuous part in what was still an Arab milieu." The empire saw its mission as defense against encroachment from Christian infidels from Anatolia, Turks from Central Asia, and pagans from India. Inside the empire, there was a series of movements for Persian independence – notably from the southeastern province of Sistan, birthplace of 'Ali al Sistani, the Shiite notable who was to checkmate elaborate American plans for Iraq over 1200 years later (Chapter 15).

In the 900's, the amalgam of Arabic and Persian produced a new Persian language, with its own imagery but written in the Arabic script (Chapter 6). The Persian struggle for independence culminated in the rise of the Shiite Buyid Dynasty, which took Baghdad in 945 but, instead of ousting the Caliphate, it co-opted it, while allowing it to remain Sunni. In an arrangement suggestive of the religious-temporal division of authority between the Pope and the Holy Roman Emperor, the Abbasid Caliph retained the leadership of Islam, while the first Buyid ruler in Baghdad assumed the old Achaemenian title of Shahanshah – King of Kings.

In 1040, Iran was conquered by a more portentous force from Central Asia, the Seljuq Turks, who were to claim dominion from Arabia and Anatolia to Central Asia until 1225. They had adopted the Sunni faith just before they took Persia and replaced the Buyids in Baghdad. Military successes on the western front earned the first Seljuq the even more expansive title of King of the East and the West. Perhaps the most significant Seljuq achievement was the annihilation of the Byzantine army at Manzikert (in southern Anatolia) in 1071. This victory opened Anatolia to settlement by another Turkish tribe, then subordinate to the Seljuqs, who later built the Ottoman Empire.

In 969, the Fatimids invaded Egypt from North Africa (Chapter 2) and ruled it until 1171. Devotees of the Isma'ili branch of Shiism, they strongly opposed the Sunni Caliphate in Baghdad. In the mid-900's, they won most of the Levant and western Arabia to their standard. However, it was the

Seljuq conquest of Jerusalem, after the Byzantine defeat at Manzikert, that sparked the Crusades. Whereas the Umayyads and the Abbasids had pursued liberal policies toward Christians and Jews, and the Fatimids had confined themselves to ordering (in 1010) the destruction of Jerusalem, the First Crusade celebrated its capture of the Holy City by exterminating its Muslim residents and burning the Jews alive in the main synagogue. The First Crusade also introduced the recurrent Western practice of misrepresentation of motives. Although Pope Urban II's real objectives were to reform his corrupt priesthoods and strengthen the Papacy, he sold the enterprise to Europe as an opportunity to "liberate" the Holy City and win absolution for past sins by killing "infidels". In the analysis of Zachary Karabell, the Crusades were not so much a war between Christianity and Islam as they were a facet of the international power struggle.

The Christian Kingdoms of Jerusalem and three adjoining coastal states survived from 1099 until the conquest of Jerusalem by Salah al Din in 1182. (Christian control of the city had a brief and turbulent revival after 1229.) Salah al Din, a Kurdish general under the orders of the Seljuq ruler in Damascus, had set the stage for victory over the Crusaders by ousting the Fatimids from Cairo in 1169. From the Egyptian base he also took over Syria, Iraq, and Yemen. He founded the Ayyubid Dynasty, which ruled his conquests until the early 1200's. Although he had beheaded Jerusalem's Christian commander for violating a truce, he practiced restraint toward its other non-Muslim residents. He consolidated his control of Palestine by defeating the Crusaders at Hattin in 1187.

From 1095 to 1270, there were eight crusades, not all of them organized by the papacy. Most of them were reprehensible failures. In 1202-04, the French leadership of the Fourth Crusade sacked Constantinople and set up a minuscule "Latin Empire" that survived until 1261, and was disavowed by the Papacy.

In the early 1200's, the forces of Genghis Khan, founder of what is conventionally called the Mongol Empire, although at least half its troops were Turks, invaded China and the Middle East. They followed up the capture of Peking in 1214 with the conquest of northern Persia in 1219 and Anatolia in 1243. The Abbasid Caliphate expired in 1258, when a Mongol army took Baghdad and killed 800,000 of its residents. As William McNeill pointed out, the Mongols always moved on as soon as grazing for their horses had been exhausted – but they stayed on long enough to set up Mongol regimes in Persia, Anatolia, and Mesopotamia.

The Mongol march on Egypt was set back by General Hulegu's recall to Karakorum, the ancient capital in Mongolia. As detailed in *Saudi Aramco World,* with Crusader help the Egyptians defeated the depleted Mongol force and killed their leader, Kitbuga. By the mid-1200's, a new Turkish force, the Ottomans, had begun to assert itself in Anatolia. Simultaneously, Egypt came under the rule of the Mamluks, who had arrived as Turkish slaves of the Ayyubids and ended by deposing them. The Mamluks were to establish in Egypt, Syria, Mesopotamia, and the Hijaz (on the western coast of Arabia) a domain that survived until the Ottoman conquest in 1517. In the 1300's, the Seljuq Dynasty disappeared for all time, and its Ottoman cousins moved with alacrity to fill the void. Late in the century, Timur, Genghis Khan's most noted successor, presented another display of the mobility of Central Asian cavalry by overrunning Persia, the Caucasus, Mesopotamia, Syria, Delhi, and Moscow.

By 1400, the Ottomans had conquered all of Anatolia except the Byzantine enclave around Constantinople, although they suffered a temporary setback by the armies of Timur in 1402. By 1453, the Ottomans had resiled sufficiently to conquer Constantinople and put an end to the last vestige of the European imperialism that had come to the Middle East with Alexander 1800 years earlier. The Byzantines were substantially weakened by their rejection of a common front with Catholic forces from the west. The truncated Byzantine Empire had held out against Islam for 800 years. The Black Sea became an Ottoman lake.

The Christian conquest of Jerusalem in 1099 had led to the founding of two militant orders, the Templars and the Hospitalers. In 1291, when the Muslims completed their reconquest of Palestine, the Hospitalers moved to Cyprus and Rhodes. They were to rule Rhodes as an independent state. Both islands were conquered by Sultan Suleiman the Magnificent in 1522. In 1529, the Hospitalers acquired the Maltese archipelago from Holy Roman Emperor Charles V, and came to be known as the Knights of Malta. Having lost Malta in the 1800's, they transferred their headquarters to Rome. Their abstract sovereignty is still recognized by the Holy See and several Roman Catholic states.

Control of the Mediterranean was resolved in 1571 by the European naval victory over the Ottoman navy and Algerian corsairs in a giant battle of open galleys off Lepanto, Greece. As narrated in Roger Crawley's *Empires of the Sea,* reviewed by *The New York Review of Books,* the victory did not alter the maritime balance of power (it confirmed European control of the the sea west of Italy, while the Ottomans remained dominant over the eastern half), but it gave a great boost to the morale of the Europeans, who had held Ottoman military power in awe. The Ottomans continued to dominate the Arabian coast of the Persian Gulf, denying bases to Portugal (Chapter 10).

The Ottomans were never able to replicate the Caliphate's conquest of Persia, which in 1502 had come under the rule of its third indigenous dynasty, the Safavids. Having evolved from a faction of fanatical Shiites about 1500, they made Shiism the state religion. In the 1600's, advised by Englishman Robert Sherley, Abbas I created for the Safavids a standing army. The Safavids ruled Persia until 1732, and also Baghdad in the early 1500's, and again in the 1600's.

In 1515-16, Ottoman gunpowder won out over Mamluk cavalry, and the Ottomans went on to conquer the Levant, Egypt, Mesopotamia, and the Gulf and Red Sea coasts of Arabia. In the 1630's, Yemen's Zaydi Dynasty expelled the Ottomans. Ottoman conquest of Mesopotamia in the 1500's was reversed by their inveterate enemies, the Safavids, in the early 1600's. In 1638, the pendulum swung back again, as the Ottomans expelled the Safavids and placed Mesopotamia under Sunni rule that was to endure until the reckless American invasion of 2003 (Chapter 15).

Today's frontier between Iraq and Iran was essentially established by treaty between the Ottomans and the Safavids in 1639, although it was violated by both sides in the war of 1980-88 (Chapter 9).

In 1727, the Safavids took the southern Caucasus from the Ottomans, but nine years later a Turkmen tribesman deposed the Safavid ruler in his own favor and waged an impressive military effort against the Ottomans in Mesopotamia, and against the Mughal Empire, which had been founded in India by a descendant of both Genghis Khan and Timur, long after their empires had crumbled. In 1733, Ottoman forces, aided by Mesopotamian Kurds, raised a Safavid siege of Baghdad, which had lost 100,000 residents to starvation. In 1747, Persia disintegrated into a melee of warring factions.

In the 1700's, in eastern Arabia, the House of Sa'ud formed an alliance with the leadership of the Wahhabi (Sunni) sect. It was a turbulent century, even for the Middle East. The Saudis conducted raids into Mesopotamia, Syria, and the Hijaz. In 1756, the Sabah Dynasty was founded in semi-autonomous Kuwait. Re-emergent Mamluks won autonomy in Egypt, under nominal Ottoman authority, and held on until France invaded in 1798. In 1771, Mamluk troops from Egypt took Damascus. In 1773, the Saudis captured their future capital, Riyadh. In 1779, the Qajars, Persian tribesmen of Turkmen stock, installed a new dynasty which was to rule an independent Persia until 1924 – subject to a fair amount of British, French, and Russian fishing in its troubled waters (Chapter 10).

The last crusade to get European soldiers as far as the Middle East had been the seventh, which sputtered out in Egypt in 1250 with the capture of its leader, Louis IX of France, whose reputation as the most popular of the

Capetian kings could not have been based on his foreign policy: He died in Tunisia in 1270 on his way to one last effort to liberate Jerusalem from Islam. Five centuries passed before the next invasion from Europe. Perhaps it was fitting that its leader should be another French ruler, Napoleon Bonaparte, who landed in Egypt in 1798, in an unsuccessful attempt to isolate Britain by cutting its Lifeline to India. His successes on land were nullified by an expeditionary force sent by the Ottomans and by Admiral Nelson's annihilation of the French fleet at Abu Qir. Nelson's historic victories of Abu Qir and Trafalgar were to consolidate British domination of the Seven Seas for the next one hundred years.

A major unexpected consequence of these events was their Macchiavellian exploitation by Muhammad 'Ali, an Albanian officer in the Ottoman army who emerged as the new ruler of Egypt, which had already won considerable autonomy in the Ottoman system under the rule of the Mamluk Dynasty. Having persuaded Britain to withdraw the force it had sent to confront the French, he quickly set out to provide the Middle East the leadership no longer forthcoming from the declining Ottoman Empire. He wiped out the Mamluk leadership in Cairo, expelled the Saudis from the Hijaz, put a stop to Arabian raids into Mesopotamia, sent troops to occupy Syria, and would have imposed Egyptian rule on these sectors and perhaps others but for intervention by the European powers, who responded to the Ottoman appeal by forcing the Egyptian troops to go back to Egypt in 1841. George Antonius wrote that British Foreign Secretary Palmerston suspected that Egyptian subjugation of the Ottoman Sultanate would benefit Russia at Britain's expense.

The brief encounter between Napoleon and the Middle East was a portent of rising Western interest in the region. The British led the way. In Arabia, pressure from the Saudis on the various tribes dispersed along the Persian Gulf afforded Britain a golden opportunity to win control of their foreign affairs (Chapter 2) in return for protection from Saudi, Ottoman, and Persian encroachment – a service performed at modest cost by naval units based in India. Since Britain's primary concern in the region was defense of the seaways via Egypt to India, it reacted to the French foray into Egypt by stationing a garrison in Aden under a treaty of 1802 with a local potentate who was enjoying an interim of independence from both the rulers of north Yemen and the Ottomans. Impelled by the advent of steam navigation, in 1839 Britain seized Aden outright and made it a coaling station which acquired even greater strategic significance after the opening of the Suez Canal in 1869. Designated as a crown colony in 1937, Aden and the rest of south Yemen won independence in 1967, and merged with north Yemen in 1990 (Chapter 11).

Concurrently – as laid out in George Lenczowski's classic text on the Middle East – Russia was vying for territorial advantage along its Middle Eastern frontier. During the 1800's it won control of most of the southern Caucasus.

Michael Doyle tells us that European rivalry for primacy in the Middle East subjected both regions to extensive and gratuitous violence. An early example was the Crimean War (1853-56), whose proximate cause was the Russian demand to become the acknowledged protector of the Greek Orthodox subjects of the Ottoman Empire. In the messy Crimean conflict, Britain, France, and the Ottomans managed to extend the empire's lease on life. Later in the century, Russia won control of the Black Sea from the Ottomans and of the southern Caucasus from Persia. In the 1870's, Ottoman expeditions to Arabia repressed Saudi ambitions for some decades, but British influence over the Gulf Coast was not affected.

As described by Perry Anderson in *The London Review of Books,* the Ottoman collapse was precipitous: 1875 - bankruptcy; 1877 - military defeat by Russia; 1878 - The Congress of Berlin confirmed a cluster of secessions in the Balkans and the Russian acquisition of Batum and Kars along the Anatolia-Caucasus border; 1881 - formation of a European-run organization to collect Ottoman debts; 1908 - seizure of power by a faction of young military officers known as The Young Turks; 1912-13 - the two Balkan wars resulted in the empire's loss of 83 percent of its European territories; 1914 - the empire's rash entry into World War I on the side of the Central Powers; 1916 - the empire reacted to advances by the Russians, abetted by Armenian volunteers, by ordering Armenian deportation to the deserts of Syria, and tolerating or colluding in the attendant massacre of a million Armenians by Kurds and Turks; in Damascus, it executed a number of Arab nationalists; 1920 - The Treaty of Sèvres deprived the empire of its Arab provinces, and professed to allocate much of its territory in Anatolia and the Caucasus to a newly created Armenian state; 1921 - a Kemalist parliament in Ankara proclaimed a Turkish state, which received early European recognition; 1922 - the parliament abolished the sultanate; 1923 - the assembly declared Turkey a republic, with Mustafa Kemal its first president.

In 1882, Egypt became a British "protectorate" and the site of a British garrison to protect the Suez Canal. A few years later, two more countries in southern Arabia – Oman and the Hadramawt – came under British "protection". A key element of Germany's Middle East strategy was a plan to build its Ottoman allies a railway from Istanbul via Baghdad to Kuwait. The project was never completed, but it motivated Britain to take over control of Kuwait's foreign affairs in 1899. (During World War I, Kuwait became a British protectorate.) European rivalry penetrated even the desert depths of Arabia, where Britain and Germany had taken opposite sides in the ancient tribal war between the Saudis and the Rashidis. In 1891, the Saudis were temporarily eclipsed, and their leaders took refuge under the British umbrella in Kuwait. In 1901, with Kuwaiti help, the Saudis entered their third (and present) incarnation by carrying out a lightning recapture of Riyadh, which became the capital of Saudi Arabia. By 1914, under their dynamic leader – known to the West as Ibn Sa'ud – they had retaken central Arabia and Al Hasa, the oil-rich area along the Gulf coast south of Kuwait.

On the Red Sea coast of Arabia, the Hashemite dynasty had ruled the Hijaz (land of the holy cities of Mecca and Medina) under the nominal suzerainty of the Ottomans and the protection of Britain. By 1925, Ibn Sa'ud had confounded British policy by conquering the Hijaz. All his conquests were united in 1932 as the Kingdom of Saudi Arabia. In 1933, 'Asir, on the Red Sea coast north of Yemen, was incorporated into the kingdom.

In the early 1900's, Britain and Russia found common cause in checking the "rising might of Germany". Putting behind them their ancient contest for preeminence, waged across the Himalayan marches between Russia and British India, they concluded in 1907 an agreement that in essence divided Persia into Russian and British zones of influence. Persia had strategic importance for both – for the Russians as a potential outlet to ice-free seas, for the British as a newly discovered source of oil and as a base for defense of the Suez Canal. Meanwhile, Germany had secretly built a close alliance with the Ottoman Emperor, who feared Russian expansion.

The Middle East was a major theater of military operation in World War I. Beginning in 1914, Britain annexed Cyprus, landed troops at Basrah in Mesopotamia, moved slowly north against Ottoman resistance (directed by a German officer), helped the Hashemite ruler of the Hijaz, Sharif Husayn, take Mecca and Ta'if from the Ottomans in 1916, took Baghdad in 1917, and eventually linked up in northern Mesopotamia with Russian forces from northern Persia.

Arab forces, inspirited by the Sharif's 1914 proclamation of jihad against the Ottomans, supported the British effort. The Ottoman rulers had traditionally sought to integrate their Arab subjects into the empire. Common allegiance to Sunni Islam was an advantage in Egypt, the Levant, and central Mesopotamia, but the Empire did not carry integration all the way. The population of the Empire was more or less equally divided between 10 million Turks and 10 million Arabs, but by 1913 the Young Turks were practicing discrimination against their Arab subjects. Troop units generally retained their ethnic identity, and the Arabs never absorbed the Ottoman mystique. "The Arab Revolt" was not difficult to organize.

In 1916, Britain invaded Palestine from Egypt. Germany sent a brigade to help the Ottomans, but British forces were bolstered by the Hashemites' expulsion of the Ottomans from the Hijaz, by the Revolt, by mass Arab defections from the Ottoman army, and by an allied blockade (which led to the starvation of 100,000 Syrians and Lebanese). The Ottomans crushed the first British foray into Mesopotamia, but by 1918, Britain and its Arab allies had taken over most Ottoman territory outside Turkey. The Rashidis and Yemenis in Arabia, like the Kurdish tribes in Anatolia and Mesopotamia, remained loyal to the Empire.

The October Revolution of 1917 took Russia out of the war. Britain reacted by proclaiming Persia a British protectorate. Ottoman capitulation in 1918 gave the Allies a free hand in its former territories. World War I ended with Britain and France in momentary control of the entire Middle East outside the Caucasus. The moment was rudely interrupted by Turkish officer Mustafa Kemal, one of the few figures in history who combined military and political genius. He rose to prominence in an empire laid prostrate by Allied occupation, including Greek forces that took Izmir and environs in 1919 with British encouragement.

For the intensely nationalistic Turks, occupation by their former subjects was intolerable. Fortuitously assigned to an undefeated Ottoman Army in eastern Anatolia, Kemal (later renamed Ataturk – Father of the Turks) resigned his commission, chaired an impromptu congress of like-minded Turks, and rallied the country against the occupation, the Treaty of Versailles, and the humiliating Treaty of Sèvres, which the Sultan had signed in August 1920. With unexpected political and material assistance from the new Soviet Union, which abandoned the Armenian Soviet Republic it had lately promoted (possibly in return for Turkish cession of the Georgian port of Batum to the Soviets), Ataturk turned his attention to his six adversaries: the Sultan in Istanbul, the Armenians in the east, the French in Cilicia, the Italians in Adalia, the British in Istanbul, and the Greeks in Izmir. By late 1921, by a combination of political manipulation and military maneuver, he had achieved the withdrawal of all the Armenian and Allied forces except the Greeks. In 1922, after hard fighting, now C-in-C Ataturk expelled the Greeks and orchestrated the abolition of the Sultanate. In 1923, he extracted from the Allies a favorable replacement for the Treaty of Sèvres – the Treaty of Lausanne – and he was elected President of the new Republic of Turkey.

In the former Arab domains of the Empire, the Allies' elaborate plans portended eventual grief for all parties, but in the short term they seemed to work.

In Mesopotamia, as early as 1918, Britain had prevailed over French designs on Mawsil by converting three of the empire's provinces into a whole new country, with its classic Arabic name – *'Iraq*. At one point, the Allies had promised the Kurds a state, but that fit of altruism, opposed by Turkey, was abandoned by Britain after oil was suspected in the area. In 1922, Britain drew the new borders of Kuwait, Saudi Arabia, and Iraq. British control of Iraq was established only after the deployment of ground and air power to put down a tribal revolt, with heavy Iraqi casualties.

In Arabia, Sharif Husayn, who had been led by devious British diplomacy to expect to come out of the war as ruler of a united Arab nation, had been compelled to settle for the kingship of the Hijaz, and even that had been snatched away when Ibn Sa'ud refused to go along with the program. The best Britain could do by way of compensation was to provide employment for two of the Sharif's sons in the Levant. A Saudi advance into Transjordan in 1922 was blocked by Britain, which placated Ibn Sa'ud by awarding him a piece of Kuwait. Yemen emerged from the rubble as an independent state. In 1934, Saudi Arabia and north Yemen signed a treaty that resolved temporarily their border disputes and allowed Yemenis to work in Saudi Arabia without visas.

In the Levant, France took immediate possession of coastal Syria, including Lebanon. The rest of Syria was to have been a monarchy under Sharif Husayn's son Faysal, but France reneged, instituting a French administration. Faysal's consolation prize was the throne in Baghdad. Britain took over Palestine, along with the Mandatory obligation to implement Balfour's 1917 promise of a Jewish National Home. To prevent Faysal's brother 'Abdallah from sending troops against the French in Syria, Britain split its Levantine Mandate into two parts – Palestine and Transjordan – and made 'Abdallah King of Transjordan.

In the Caucasus, declarations of independence by Armenia, Azerbaijan, and Georgia were aborted in 1921 by the entry of the Red Army.

World War II left the territorial consequences of World War I largely intact, but it had important repercussions on the region.

In 1939 France continued the European practice of cavalier disposition of Arab territory by transferring to Turkey a piece of Syria as an incentive to side with the Allies. Alexandretta (Iskandariyyah to the Arabs, Iskenderun to the Turks) had been the ancient access to the Mediterranean for Syria's second city, Aleppo. (The bribe didn't work; Turkey stayed neutral, although late in the war it accorded the Allies some cautious support, including allowing transit of supply ships to the Soviet Union.)

In 1940, the Nazi occupation of northern France left Syria and Lebanon under the control of the Vichy regime. In 1941, British and Soviet forces occupied southern and northern Iran, respectively. Iran became a crucial route for shipment of Lend-Lease supplies from the United States, even before America entered the war. British, Soviet, and American forces controlled Iran until 1943.

Egypt was the base for British forces confronting the Axis invasion of North Africa; in the summer of 1942, with the Suez Canal as its primary objective, General Rommel's army penetrated Egyptian territory up to the coastal community of Al 'Alamayn, close to Alexandria and only 200 miles from Cairo. Concurrently, British, Free French, and *Haganah* forces invaded Vichy Syria from Palestine, Transjordan, and Iraq, and quickly routed the Vichy holdouts. At the nadir of the Allied cause, the territory under its control along the front was reduced to Great Britain, eastern Russia, and Egypt. The Asian component of the Middle East was separated from the Axis lines by neutral Turkey.

In late 1942, the tide of battle turned. The Soviet Union (which, at a cost of 20 million Russian lives, inflicted 80 percent of Germany's casualties in the war: *Times*, 2/21/04) repelled the Nazis from Stalingrad, American forces landed in North Africa, and the British drove the Germans back from Al 'Alamayn. For the Middle East, the effective end of the war was May 1943, when Germany evacuated Tunisia. In November, a summit of American, British, and Chinese leaders met in Cairo. Also in 1943 the US sent a military mission to neutral Saudi Arabia and began construction of an air base at Dhahran.

The Cold War was foreshadowed by an abortive Soviet venture in northwestern Iran. Having occupied that area during the war, and having been denied oil concessions there, the Soviet Union supported the proclamation in Mahabad of a Kurdish Republic and in Tabriz of an Azerbaijani Republic. In 1946, the Soviets yielded to American and UN pressure and abandoned both enterprises.

In 1946, Britain and America required France to evacuate its troops from the Levant, and Syria and Lebanon became independent states. European imperialism emitted one last gasp in 1956, when Britain and France colluded with Israel in a wild scheme to reestablish their control over the Suez Canal. Their simultaneous occupations of Port Said, the Gaza Strip, and Sinai were reversed by an irate President Eisenhower, who threatened to pull the rug out from under the Pound Sterling (Chapters 1 and 10), and put unrevealed but effective pressure on Israel to evacuate

Sinai and the Gaza Strip. Eisenhower was the only President ever to coerce Israel into a major concession.

Egyptian President 'Abd al Nasir's successful defiance of the invaders, after his nationalization of the Canal, ignited a flare of Arab Nationalist zeal across the eastern Arab World. It culminated in 1958 in the agreement by the regime in Damascus – in which the pro-Arab-union Baath Party was influential – to bring Syria into political union with Egypt under Nasir's presidency. Arab political institutions were not ready for so bold a step, and a conservative faction mutinied against the tiny Egyptian-Palestinian garrison in 1961 (Chapter 14). In such circumstances, the conventional Middle Eastern response would have been to put down the insurgency by armed force – as north Yemen did when South Yemen tried to reverse their union in 1994 – but Egypt and Syria were separated by Israel, an immensely superior military power which recognized Arab Nationalism as the most lethal long-term threat to its existence (Chapter 16). 'Abd al Nasir considered sending an expeditionary force by sea but decided to acquiesce in the secession – a sounder judgment than he was to make when he invited the June War of 1967 (Chapter 8).

The initial motivation behind the perennial Iraqi claim to Kuwait was Iraqi nationalism. Unappreciative of the fact that, but for British machinations, the state of Iraq might never have come into existence, the Iraqis focused on Ottoman precedent (their state had been patched together from three Ottoman provinces – Mawsil, Baghdad, and Basrah) and on the Ottoman view that the Province of Basrah had included Kuwait. Some observers thought the Iraqi claim had merit. In 1937, Iraq's King Ghazi massed troops in support of annexation of Kuwait, but Britain squelched the initiative. In 1961, Iraq's new military dictator, 'Abd al Karim Qasim, revived the claim, but desisted when Britain rushed troops into Kuwait. Egypt and Syria also sent troops.

In the 1950's, the 'Ibadi Imam of Buraymi agitated for independence, with Egyptian and Saudi support. His effort was suppressed by 1959 by forces from Oman and Abu Dhabi, with help from British forces. In 1967, stubborn resistance to British rule over South Yemen induced London to withdraw from the land it had moved in on 138 years earlier. India was long independent, and if any Western force was to defend the Lifeline, it would be the United States Navy. South Yemen was independent until 1990, when it formed a political union with north Yemen. In 1968-72, Britain shepherded seven emirates along the Trucial Coast into a federation – The United Arab Emirates (UAE). British garrisons left the Gulf in 1971 (Chapter 10).

In 1974, Turkey reacted to a Greek-inspired coup in Nicosia by invading northern Cyprus and setting up a Turkish Cypriot "state" recognized by no government other than Ankara.

In 1979, the ruler of Dubai mediated preliminary resolution of a Ra's al Khaymah/Oman border dispute, and Oman and the UAE went on to achieve a détente based on mutual suspicion of Saudi Arabia. In 1983, Sultan Qabus of Oman helped resolve a border dispute between Dubai and Sharjah (*Al Shariqah*).

From 1980 to 1988, Iraq and Iran fought a highly lethal but inconclusive war over the southern end of their border and other issues (Chapter 9). Both sides were culpable of provocation. By one account, Grand *Ayatollah* Khomeini's sectarian regime had been trying to engineer the overthrow of secularist dictator Saddam Husayn. By another, Saddam made the reckless calculation that Iran was too convulsed by the clerical revolution to mount an effective defense, and he was secretly egged on by Washington, which had no use for the Khomeini government. The war might have ended in victory for Iran, which had three times the population and a citizen army that fought with the same fervor as the warriors of Islam 1300 years before, whereas the professionalism of Iraqi soldiers, manifested from Ottoman times, had been undermined by Baathist politics. Iraq was saved by its natural defenses (the Zagros foothills and the southern marshlands), by American military assistance, by missile attack on Tehran, and possibly by its cold-blooded use of chemical ordnance against Iranian troops and Iraqi civilians that collaborated with them. The war left Iraq in a state of destitution which goaded Saddam into an even more reckless enterprise – the invasion of Kuwait (Chapter 9).

While the Iraqis were beating their heads against the walls of Iranian resistance in the east and American omnipotence in the south, Syrian dictator Hafiz al Asad was conducting his own expansionist campaign in a subtler and more effective manner. Sectarian war broke out in Lebanon in 1975, and in 1976 the Palestinians threatened to overrun Lebanon. According to one report the Palestinians were responsible for the abduction and murder of American Ambassador Frank Meloy and Counselor Robert Waring. In these circumstances, America and Israel conditionally endorsed the entry of Syrian forces to rescue the Christian side. Later on Asad switched his support to the Muslim side – thus insuring that neither faction dominated the country.

In 1990, Asad reinforced his position in Lebanon by joining the coalition against his fellow (but rival) Baathist ruler in Baghdad. This attestation of dedication to the cause of Middle Eastern law and order under American leadership won him Washington's grudging acquiescence in the treaty of cooperation that Syria and Lebanon signed in 1991 – even though it was regarded by Israel and its Lebanese Christian allies as tantamount to Syrian annexation of Lebanon. It probably was. In 1997, *The Boston Globe* reported that all important political decisions for Lebanon were being made in Damascus.

In 1990-91, the dissolution of the Soviet Union gave the three states of the southern Caucasus a second chance. Armenia, Azerbaijan, and Georgia regained the independence they had momentarily tasted in the aftermath of World War I. In none of the three is future tranquility assured. The territorial dispute between Armenia and Azerbaijan over Nagorno-Karabakh (Chapter 6) is unresolved. Armenia receives significant Russian and Iranian support. Russia has backed the de facto secession of two former districts of Georgia – Abkhazia and South Ossetia.

Border issues between Saudi Arabia and Yemen were settled by a treaty of 2000. The major unresolved border dispute in the Gulf is between Iran and the UAE over three tiny islands – Abu Musa and the Tunbs.

The imponderable fates of Palestine and Iraq are the subjects of Chapters 8, 9, and 15. The empires that emerged from the Middle East's 5000 years of violence are examined in greater detail in Chapter 10.

The Straits Question

The passage between the Aegean and Black Seas (Chapter 2), under Turkish control for over 500 years, commands international attention as a threshold between Europe and Asia, and as a crucial doorway to the west for Russia and the southern Caucasus. Roderick Peattie's *Geography in Human Destiny* (1940) hypothesizes that centuries of conflict between Greek mariners, bent on trade with communities along the shores of the Black Sea, and piratic Anatolians gave rise to the legend of the Trojan War immortalized in the *Iliad*.

The Bosporus accommodates deep-draft ships, but it narrows at one point to half a mile – a dimension that poses military and ecological (oil tanker) problems. In the 1800's, passage became a major issue between Russia and the Ottomans – one of the issues that erupted into the Crimean War of 1853-56 (Chapter 10).

In 1914, Britain blockaded the Straits, with costly results for its Russian ally. The Ottomans' counteraction – mining the Straits – deprived Russia of the only ice-free route for its exports of wheat. A badly executed British landing at Gallipoli in 1915 was repelled by the Turkish/Arab forces of the Ottomans. The 1923 Treaty of Lausanne stipulated free passage through the Straits for ships of any country not at war with Turkey. The Montreux

Convention of 1936 recognized Turkey's right to fortify the Straits, and restricted access to them by the navies of non-Black Sea states. As a neutral in World War II, Turkey denied passage to both Allied and Axis shipping, until late in the war.

In the 1990's, as the volume of oil shipment from the Caucasus increased, Turkey began to impose restrictions on tanker traffic. The Straits had become the busiest waterway in the world, with traffic three times that of the Suez Canal and four times that of the Panama Canal. Navigation there was complicated by treacherous currents, twists in the channel, and the awkward fact that it runs through a city of 10 million people.

Chapter 8
Who Owns Palestine?

Over one hundred governments have recognized the figurative state of Palestine, even though no such state has ever existed. Around 150 B.C., the Romans had given a name to the southern Mediterranean coast of the Levant: **Palestine** – from the Hebrew *Pleshet* (Land of the Philistines) via the Greek *Palaistina.* Under late Ottoman rule, the Levant was administered by five provincial governments – the vilayets of Aleppo, Beirut, and Syria, and the autonomous sanjaqs of Lebanon and Jerusalem.

For Zionist Jews, Palestine is *Eretz Yisra'el* – the Land of Israel. The creation of the Israeli state introduced one more contender to fill the vacuum left by the dissolution of the Ottoman Empire (Chapter 7). The Arab-Israeli conflict is the most intractable facet of a multi-faceted power struggle.

That conflict is being waged at two levels. At the **regional** level, Britain abandoned the field in 1956, leaving eight major contenders: Turkey, Iran, Iraq, Syria, Egypt, Saudi Arabia, Israel, and the United States. The United States had been an indirect contender through its alliances with Britain and Israel; during the Israeli invasion of Lebanon in the 1980's, American forces became briefly involved. In 1991, America suddenly materialized on the scene as a direct contender when it expelled Iraq from Kuwait. The administration of George W. Bush confirmed the new role by the issuance in 2002 of a National Security Strategy that appeared to map out American hegemony over the planet – the Middle East incidentally included. The invasion of Iraq in 2003 took American participation to a new level.

So far, Israel has been central to five regional wars: 1948, 1956, 1967, 1970, and 1973. If Iraqi hostility to Israel was a primary consideration in the formulation of America's Middle East policy – as seems likely – the Gulf Wars of 1991 and 2003 should be added to the list as Arab-Israeli wars by proxy. Although Israel has become the preeminent indigenous military power in the region, that preeminence is largely due to American political, financial, and material support. The US-Israeli alliance is so solid that it might more accurately be termed a diarchy (Chapter 13).

At the **sectorial** level, hegemony has been contested between two unrelenting coalitions: Pro-Israel - the 5.7 million Jewish citizens of Israel and the settlements, subtly supported by the Jordanian monarchy and undefined elements in Lebanon; Anti-Israel - Syria, Hizballah, and the 4.3 million Arab subjects in the Occupied Territories. This coalition has the warm but insubstantial support of the 1.4 million Arab citizens of Israel (Table C) and the three or four million Palestinian refugees in Syria, Lebanon, and Jordan. The sectorial conflict has repeatedly erupted into extended hostilities: 1970 - the Jordanian civil war between the monarchy and the PLO; 1982-2000 - the Israeli invasion and occupation of southern Lebanon; 1987-93 - *Intifadah* I; 2000-? - *Intifadah* II; 2006 - Israel-*Hamas* war, round one; 2006 - Israel-*Hizballah* war; 2008 - Israel-*Hamas* war, round two.

The intricacy of Arab-Israeli politics is best illustrated by the recent history of Jordan. In 1970 the PLO took advantage of its control of the refugee camps to challenge the monarchy. Husayn's deployment of the Jordanian armed forces against 'Arafat's irregulars was countered by the entry of Syrian ground troops into north Jordan. Husayn unleashed his diminutive air force against the Syrian salient and secretly appealed for Western help against the contingency that Asad would activate the Syrian air force. As soon as Israel put its own air force on alert, the Syrian forces were withdrawn from Jordan. At the risk of publicizing the Hashemite monarchy's embarrassing status as a de facto Israeli protectorate, Husayn had achieved the expulsion of the PLO forces to Lebanon.

In 1997, a typical intelligence-service blunder enabled Husayn to demonstrate that the convoluted relationship between Jordan and Israel works both ways. Two men posing as Canadian tourists assaulted an Arab on a street in Amman. Their object was to surreptitiously expose the victim to an anesthetic (levofentanyl) in a concentration sufficient to kill him, but not for a couple of days, by which time the fracas on the street could have been forgotten. However, as described in Paul McGeough's *Kill Khalid* (reviewed in *The London Review of Books)*, the inclination of the Jordanian police to dismiss the incident was dispelled by the furtive entry of two other individuals into the Israeli Embassy. Further investigation revealed that the two attackers were agents of Mossad, and their victim was Khalid Mish'al, a major official of *Hamas*.

King Husayn was enraged by an action that could be interpreted as Jordanian collusion with Israel's assassination campaign, and had presumably been authorized by Prime Minister Netanyahu, who had never taken the trouble to conceal his contempt for the King of Jordan. By enlisting the support of President Clinton, Husayn managed to get back at Netanyahu, and also play the Arab solidarity card, by compelling Israel not only to supply an antidote that saved Mish'al's life, but also to release Hamas founder Shaykh Ahmad Yasin from jail.

In both the regional and sectorial conflicts, Israel has been blocked from full exploitation of its military superiority by politics and demography:

Political Restraint on Israel

In 1948, Israel conquered 80 percent of Palestine from its Arab inhabitants. It could have taken the rest, if it had not been held back on all three fronts. On the Jordan front, Israel desisted for fear of British intervention under a defense treaty with Transjordan. On the Egyptian front, the United States required Israel to pull back from its forward positions in Sinai and leave a Palestinian enclave (The Gaza Strip) in Egyptian hands. On the Lebanese front, Israel was not allowed to keep positions along the south bank of the Litani River.

In 1957, President Eisenhower forced Israel to abandon its 1956 conquests of the Gaza Strip and Sinai.

Whereas Israel's nuclear monopoly in the region currently affords it a last-ditch defense against military attack, political pressure from the international community would presumably preclude any Israeli attempt to exploit that monopoly to expand its hegemony – or to preempt against Iran's nuclear installations (?).

Demographic Restraint on Israel

The immense disparity between the Jewish population of Israel and the non-Jewish populations of the Middle East presents an insuperable barrier to Israeli hegemony over the region. In 1982, Israel drove to Beirut, but even in that narrow ambit, it was overextended. Lebanese, Syrian, and Palestinian attrition forced its gradual retreat and finally, in 2000, inglorious evacuation.

Even in Palestine, demography is a looming problem. In 1967, Israel captured the 20 percent it had been denied in 1948, but it has been blocked from consolidating its control over the West Bank (known to Zionists as Judaea and Samaria) and the Gaza Strip by their dense Arab populations. So far, Palestinian prolificacy has outstripped Israel's best efforts at ethnic cleansing. Many Israelis oppose annexation of these territories as a mortal threat to the Jewish character of the state.

Palestine: Casualty of British Imperialism

Around 1840, London urged the Ottoman Sultan to attract Jews to Palestine (as an obstacle to Egyptian expansionism). Later on, a Jewish presence on the eastern coast of the Mediterranean was seen by some British planners as an asset to the defense of the Suez Canal.

Amidst the carnage of World War I, a desperate Britain was driven to extremes of opportunism. To mobilize Arabs against the Ottomans, it promised Sharif Husayn of the Hijaz an Arab state in the Levant. To win over Jews in Germany and America, Foreign Secretary Balfour promised Jewish leaders an ambiguously defined National Home in postwar Palestine. In the view of Christopher Sykes, the British leadership secretly favored a Jewish state. In the words of Arthur Koestler, one country promised a second country to a third. Behind the scenes, Britain and France cavalierly concluded the Sykes-Picot Agreement: After the war, they would divide the Arab East between them.

The Anglo-French takeover and the Jewish National Home were realized; the promise of an Arab state was not. In 1919, the Treaty of Versailles discarded Woodrow Wilson's high-flown Fourteen Points and, inter alia, awarded the Palestinian/Jordanian Mandate (dependency) to Britain.

From 1919 until the late 1930's, British policy for Palestine was generally pro-Zionist. One element of this policy was encouragement of Jewish migration from Europe. In 1936, to win Arab neutrality in the impending conflict with Germany, and assure access to Arab oil, Britain abruptly changed course: After the Palestinians rejected partition, Britain issued in 1939 a "white paper" that proposed creation of a binational Arab-Jewish state, and limitation on Jewish immigration to Palestine. This ploy facilitated British use of Egypt and Palestine as bases in World War II.

Washington Rides Out of the West

The United States has four vital interests in the Middle East: 1) peace; 2) access to oil and gas on reasonable terms; 3) participation in the investment of oil and gas revenues; 4) interdiction of any immediate threat to American security. Washington used to rely on Britain to defend these interests. In 1945, when Franklin Roosevelt gave Ibn Sa'ud a security guarantee, and promised to take no action in favor of the Jews over the Arabs, America began to assume direct responsibility. This effort is complicated by four unwieldy circumstances:

Until the Middle Eastern power vacuum is filled, peace will be in short supply. *Foreign Policy* of July 2009 cited the following approximations of annual military expenditures of four states of this impoverished region: Israel - 13.4 billion dollars; Iran - 7.2 billion; Iraq - 3.6 billion; Egypt - 3 billion. *(Foreign Policy* did not specify whether the totals for Israel and Egypt include the billions they receive in American military aid.)

The peoples of the Middle East are no more receptive to foreign interference than those of Vietnam, America, or anywhere else.

Israel has a nuclear arsenal, and the odds are that other states of the region – and perhaps nongovernmental factions – will acquire an elementary nuclear capability in coming years (Chapter 16).

Since World War II, America's strategic interests in the region have been subordinated to a domestic political interest:

The Power of the Zionist Lobby

America's Evangelical community is said to number at least 50 million. Many of them support Israel's restoration as an omen that the End of Days is near. The Jewish Zionist lobby is much smaller, but more focused. Amira Hass writes that most American supporters of Israel have morphed into supporters of the Israeli Likud. Empirical evidence of Zionist influence on American Middle East policy is profuse:

- Woodrow Wilson's endorsement of the 1917 Balfour Declaration was the product of his own Zionist beliefs and the strong advocacy of Supreme Court Justice Louis Brandeis and legal adviser Felix Frankfurter.
- Misinformed that Arab immigration to Palestine was exceeding Jewish, Roosevelt opposed the British White Paper of 1939.
- Harry Truman's hasty recognition of Israel in 1948 was calculated, at least in part, to help him win New York State in the fall election. Secretary of State Marshall characterized the action as a "transparent dodge to win votes."
- American Zionists created The American Israel Public Affairs Committee (AIPAC) as a political lens designed to focus their views more sharply on Congress.
- When in 1957 Israel declared its intention to keep its territorial gains from the 1956 war, Eisenhower felt compelled to explain his denial in a nationwide speech. His Secretary of State (Dulles) told Senator Knowland it was almost impossible to carry out a Middle

East policy "not approved by the Jews," but he intended to try. Dulles believed the Israeli Embassy was "practically dictating to congress through influential Jewish people in the country."

- John Kennedy's 1962 decision to sell Hawk missiles to Israel was mainly driven by partisan political considerations.
- Humiliated by Washington's failure to honor its promise to oblige Israel to withdraw to the borders of 1967, King Faysal warned America and Aramco that Saudi Arabia might embargo oil shipments. Aramco told Faysal it had been overwhelmed by the Zionist lobby.
- Senator William Fulbright lost in the election of 1974, largely because he had defied the pro-Israel lobby. Fulbright estimated that at least 80 senators were "completely in support of anything Israel wants ..."
- In 1977, Jimmy Carter approved signature of a Soviet-American communiqué on behalf of resolution of the Palestine dispute. Threatened by Moshe Dayan with publication of Carter's secret promise to oppose a Palestinian state, Carter repudiated the communiqué.
- In 1982, Ronald Reagan told Israeli Prime Minister Begin the invasion of Lebanon was causing problems in Congress. Begin replied, "I'll handle Congress." According to a *Times* article by Bernard Gwertzman, the Reagan administration "never made a move in the Middle East without consulting with AIPAC." Under AIPAC pressure, Reagan cancelled the sale of AWACS surveillance aircraft to Jordan. (In 1997, *Fortune* reported that AIPAC ranked second in influence among American special-interest groups – just behind the AARP but ahead of the AFL/CIO.)
- In 1983, new Secretary of State George Shultz, under a "drumbeat of criticism" for being too harsh on Israel, switched to positions more congenial to the lobby.
- In 1984, the lobby accomplished the electoral defeat of Senator Charles Percy for having taken such neutral positions as voting to sell AWACS to Saudi Arabia and advocating that Washington open talks with the PLO (Palestine Liberation Organization).
- By 1987, AIPAC had become a major force in shaping America's Middle East policy. Three years later, approximately half the membership of the Senate and a quarter of the membership of the House attended its 32nd convention.
- The 1992 Presidential election went to William Clinton, who was the first incumbent President to address an AIPAC convention, and

whose foreign policy team was packed with advocates for Israel. (To identify officials in this category, look closely at their premises. For example, in January 2009 Martin Indyk argued in the *Times* that the Israeli-US alliance benefits the Palestinian cause because it enhances American leverage in Jerusalem. The holes in this logic are the false premises that Israel is open to compromise on Zionist articles of faith, and that Washington is intervening on behalf of such basic compromise.)

— In 1994, Norman Finkelstein wrote that most Americans regarded Palestinians as aboriginals destined to give way to (Israeli) progress.

— In 1996, annual United States Government aid to Israel, per capita, exceeded the per capita GNP of several Arab states.

— While Clinton's three top officials dealing with the Middle East had been pro-Israel, in 2000 his Republican successor went him one better: The foreign policy team of George W. Bush was allegedly staffed with dual American-Israeli loyalists at all levels. Bush made a conscious decision not to press Israel to curb the expansion of the settlements for fear of losing the Republican majority in the House.

— In 2006 noted academics John Mearsheimer and Stephen Walt wrote a hard-hitting but objective article on the damage done the national interest by the Zionist lobby. Rejected by timorous American publications, the article went to *The London Review of Books*.

— In 2009, over half the members of both houses of Congress attended AIPAC's annual meeting, and AIPAC got over 300 members of Congress to sign on to its resolution in favor of keeping private all disagreements between the US and Israel. John Newhouse wrote in *Foreign Affairs* that AIPAC's ability to influence US policy was probably without precedent; defying AIPAC could complicate one's reelection to Congress. The influence of ethnic lobbies on opportunistic members of Congress had contributed to the erosion of the credibility of the US government.

The sharp contrast between the neutrality of the Eisenhower administration and the all-out support of the George W. Bush administration, not just for Israel, but for the policies of Prime Minister Ariel Sharon, epitomized a fifty-year trend of growing Israeli influence over Washington. In the formulation of Middle East policy, the welfare of Israel comes first. Explanations for this phenomenon vary, but the one that has survived the test of history is the political influence of the Zionist hard-liners, enhanced by the following realities:

- America's 5.3 million Jews largely vote in key states.
- The Jewish community donates generously to political campaigns, generally to the Democrats.
- Ardent Zionists are well represented in the Washington power structure.
- In their understandable apprehension about the future of Zionism, its well-placed American adherents can be implacable electoral opponents.
- The mainstream media tend to slant their Middle East coverage in favor of Israel. *The New York Times* ignored an advisory from this writer that its editorial claim of an Arab "attack on Israeli territory" in the war of 1973 was fallacious. (The territories penetrated by Egyptian and Syrian forces had been seized by Israel six years earlier.) An article in *Foreign Affairs,* organ of the prestigious Council on Foreign Relations, repeated the persistent canard that communalist Israel is a "liberal democracy". Charles Krauthammer's widely syndicated column has lately advanced the following tendentious allegations:
    - The Oslo Agreement of 1993 assigned Yasir 'Arafat control over the West Bank and Gaza. (Fact: The IDF retained control over those two territories. 'Arafat spent his last days under house arrest.)
    - Israel would not reject a Palestinian state that offered genuine peace. (Fact: No Zionist government has made such an offer, and none is likely to do so. See Chapter 16, "Belling the Cat".)
    - After Ehud Barak made such an offer, 'Arafat unleashed a savage terror war. (Fact: Barak imposed conditions that made his offer a nonstarter. The Intifadah that flared up in 2000 was a spontaneous reaction to Sharon's visit to the Temple Mount.)
    - The Palestinians already have an independent state – Gaza. (Fact: This claim is too ludicrous to require refutation.)

In recent days this formidable constellation of factors has reinforced the pro-Zionist trend: In the Presidential campaign of 2004, Bush and Kerry competed all-out for the pro-Israel vote without visible attention to the policy issues involved. In 2008, as Israeli analyst Uri Avnery noted, McCain and Obama followed suit. In 2009, two of the best qualified but most forthright candidates for policy-level appointment, Anthony Zinni and Chas Freeman, were rejected in storms of pro-Zionist protest. In *The London Review of Books* of 3/26/09, Mearsheimer cited the lobby's smear campaign against Freeman, and Obama's pattern of avoidance of confrontation with the Zionists.

The special Israeli-American relationship was a probable factor in the US Supreme Court's ruling in favor of dual citizenship for Americans (WRMEA citation of 2/19/10 posting by Justin Raimondo).

Diarchy in the White House

In 1945 – three years before there was an Israel – Franklin Roosevelt assured Ibn Sa'ud the United States would not help the Jews against the Arabs. He then took a leaf from Britain's capricious playbook by allowing Rabbi Stephen Wise to announce that the President supported the formation of a Jewish state.

In late 1945, as noted by Pete Hart, Truman's call for mass transfer of Jews from Europe to Palestine broke FDR's promise to Ibn Sa'ud that the US would take no unilateral initiative on the Palestine question. In 1947, Truman mobilized all America's leverage in the capitals of UN members to push through the General Assembly Resolution 181, which proposed to partition Palestine into three segments: an international City of Jerusalem under UN administration; for Palestine's 600,000 Jews, a state of almost 6000 square miles containing the most fertile areas of the Mandate; for Palestine's 1.3 million Arabs, a state incorporating the remaining 4200 square miles. Donald Neff reminds us that Truman ignored the State Department's warning that, by overriding the Palestinian Arab majority's right of self-determination, the General Assembly was riding roughshod over its own charter.

From 1948 on, the welfare of Israel was the central plank in America's Middle East policy, and the President was the usual desk officer. Truman insured that the United States was the first state to recognize Israel. During the 1948 war, America and Britain reached a secret agreement to work for the inclusion of the principal Arab remnant of Palestine in the Transjordanian state.

The only President ever to stand up to Israel was Eisenhower, who derived special political immunity from his contribution to Allied victory in World War II. Determined to uphold the Tripartite Declaration of 1950 (see below) and the UN Charter, he used that immunity in 1956-57 to force Britain and France to abandon their invasion of Egypt, and Israel to give up its conquests of Egyptian territory in Sinai and Palestinian territory in the Gaza Strip. To break Israeli resistance, he reportedly threatened an economic boycott and cancellation of the tax-exempt status of the United Jewish Appeal (although as a carrot, he may have granted secret shipment of uranium to Israel).

Kennedy was not in office long enough to fulfill his honest effort to maintain an impartial position between Israel and the Arabs. Johnson's shift to a pro-Israeli stance was so sudden and so clandestine that several months passed after his swearing-in before this writer, a midlevel official in the State Department's Office of Near Eastern Affairs, realized the turnabout. Johnson's partisanship was so visceral that he not only stepped up financial and military aid to Israel (including offensive weapons), he entertained the illusory vision of Israel as America's agent in the Middle East, he welcomed the disruptive Israeli victory of 1967 over Egypt and Syria, and he even orchestrated a successful cover-up of Israel's apparently deliberate attempt (for reasons never revealed) to sink a US Navy surveillance ship, the USS Liberty, with all hands on board.

As watered down by the Johnson administration, UN Security Council Resolution 242 of November 1967 called for "withdrawal of Israeli armed forces from territories occupied in the recent conflict." By not specifying borders, the resolution left the diplomatic track open for interminable debate while Israel created "facts on the ground". It affirmed the necessity of "a just settlement of the refugee problem," but the word "Palestinian" did not appear in the text.

There is no evidence that Nixon shared Johnson's affection for Israel, but he turned actively pro-Israel before the 1972 election. We learn from Walter Isaacson's *Kissinger* that, as Nixon's political and psychological problems escalated, he fell increasingly under the influence of National Security Adviser/Secretary of State Henry Kissinger, who seemed more warmly disposed toward Israel and saw Arab-Israeli stalemate as advantageous in the context of the Soviet-American Cold War. When in 1973 that stalemate degenerated into war, an American emergency airlift helped rescue Israel from a surprise attack mounted by Egypt and Syria.

In early 1973, when the PLO had turned against the United States and seized two American diplomats in Khartoum, Nixon went on the air with a gratuitous reiteration of Washington's stock refusal to deal with terrorists; diplomats G. Curtis Moore and Cleo A. Noel, Jr. were killed. By that fall, however, pragmatism had prevailed; the CIA initiated secret contacts that induced the PLO to terminate attacks on American officials and help insure the security of American personnel in Lebanon – until Israeli agents killed the Agency's principal PLO contact.

Nixon and Kissinger deserve credit for arranging a series of disengagement agreements which resulted over ensuing years in Israel's withdrawal from some of the Egyptian and Syrian territories it had occupied during the 1973 war – even though the Syrian city of Al Qunaytirah received scorched-earth treatment before the Israelis left. One ambiguous but often-cited consequence of the 1973 war was Security Council Resolution 338, which reaffirmed Resolution 242, but rejected the Arab demand for implementation of 242 before conclusion of the 1973 cease-fire.

In the mid-1970's, under Nixon and Ford (and Kissinger), the United States blocked Security Council efforts to work toward a balanced Israel/ Palestine settlement, and allowed Israel to continue the fateful enterprise of settlement construction in Occupied Palestine.

In 1977, Congress legislated a ban on the provision of American aid to any state that developed nuclear weapons. To get around this prohibition in Israel's case, Washington has carefully avoided official admission of the common knowledge that the top recipient of American aid has had a nuclear capability since 1968.

Carter called for resolution of the Israel-Palestine dispute roughly along the prewar border, and was the first President to endorse the concept of a Palestinian homeland (but not a state). He took a public position that the settlements in Occupied Palestine were illegal, but his administration abstained on a General Assembly resolution to that effect. He reportedly clouded the diplomatic picture with the incongruous assertion to Prime Minister Begin that the establishment of Israel was the fulfillment of Biblical prophecy.

Carter's crowning achievement was the murky Camp David Agreement of 1978 between Begin and Egyptian President Sadat. Although Carter deserves credit for the initiative and diplomatic skill he contributed to the Agreement, he was the beneficiary of formidable serendipity. He was able to climb on a bandwagon which Sadat had set rolling, and all the elements of a deal were waiting to be assembled: Sadat's objective was to regain Sinai; for Egypt, the fate of Occupied Palestine was a secondary issue. For Israel, a free hand in Palestine was well worth the sacrifice of the Sinai desert. Hence the Egyptian-Israeli win-win peace treaty that appalled Arab bystanders and left the Palestinians out in the cold.

After the signing, when Begin did not just resume settlement construction, in variance from Carter's understanding of their agreement at Camp David, but stepped up the pace, he ignored Carter's objections.

Backed by a foreign-policy team oriented toward Zionism, Reagan took a stand that was more decisive and more pro-Israel. Under his avuncular patronage, Israel moved to the right, and Defense Minister Sharon perpetrated one of Israel's biggest blunders – the invasion of Lebanon – which briefly involved the United States in a war that carpet-bombed West Beirut and generated, in violation of an American commitment to protect the families left behind by departing PLO forces, a massacre of civilian residents of two refugee camps by the Lebanese Phalange. Joseph Harsch of *The Christian Science Monitor* contended that the atrocity had been "made possible because America [had] made Israel the dominant power in the Middle East."

Under Reagan, the United States was one of four members to vote against the General Assembly's 1980 condemnation of racism, "including Zionism," it vetoed the Security Council's condemnation of Israel's de facto annexation of the Golan and the Council's call on Israel to suspend building settlements in the Occupied Territories, and it joined Israel (and no one else) in voting against the Assembly's endorsement of the Palestinians' right of self-determination.

George H. W. Bush made one stab at projecting the even-handedness Washington had habitually professed. When Israel requested a 10 billion dollar loan guarantee, he held out over the settlement issue for eight months, but then caved before the 1992 election. According to one report, he had elicited from Israeli Prime Minister Yitzhak Shamir a promise to urge American Jews to vote Republican in the election. According to another version, he deferred to new Prime Minister Yitzhak Rabin, since his Democratic opponent, Clinton, was close to Shamir.

Clinton followed Carter's example in jumping on someone else's bandwagon. In Clinton's case, it was the Oslo Accord, an Israel-PLO product which was launched in Washington at a hyperbolic summit attended by a wincing Rabin, a resuscitated PLO leader Yasir 'Arafat, and one sitting and two retired Presidents (Clinton, Ford, and Carter). In the opinion of Norman Finkelstein, Clinton had endorsed an Israeli scheme intended to elicit Palestinian agreement to illegal Israeli demands.

It was on Clinton's watch that Washington engineered the shelving of General Assembly Resolutions 181 of 1947 on partition and 194 of 1948 on Palestinian refugees. His administration vetoed a Security Council draft condemning Israeli confiscation of land in East Jerusalem, which under 181 was to have been internationalized, and whose de facto annexation had never been recognized by any state. Clinton faithfully joined Israel in opposing the vast majority of General Assembly members that supported declarations of the Palestinians' right of self-determination. In 1994, he attended the signature of a peace treaty between Israel and Jordan, which was rewarded by an annual American subsidy and Congressional forgiveness of 900 million dollars in foreign debt. Clinton's top Middle East negotiator, Dennis Ross, was a quintessential Israel-firster.

Over the years, United States censure of the Jewish settlements had depreciated from "illegal" (Carter) to "obstacles to peace" (Reagan) to "complicating factors" (Clinton). The Palestinian territories had been euphemized from "occupied" to "disputed." No high American official has been known to articulate the simple fact that, once support for the settlements had attained critical political mass in the Israeli Knesset (sometime in the '90's?), all prospects of a negotiated Palestine state vanished – while Washington has continued to pay lip service to the defunct two-state solution.

In 2001, the Arab-Israeli conflict was intensified by the election of two devout hawks: President George W. Bush, who regarded the American-Israeli alliance as the keystone of American domination of the Middle East, and Prime Minister Ariel Sharon, who had specialized in retaliation against Arabs since he led reprisal raids into Jordan in his early twenties. Tacitly rejecting a plan advanced by American conciliator George Mitchell for a freeze on building settlements, Bush acquiesced in Sharon's campaign to torpedo the Oslo scheme by sending Israeli troops into areas marked for local Palestinian administration, assassinating Hamas leader Ahmad Yasin, and demanding 'Arafat's removal from the Presidency of the Palestine Authority on the specious grounds of his "refusal" to pacify the armed resistance (a myth propagated by America's mainstream media). The hardships of military repression and economic deprivation had keyed Palestinian desperation to such a level that no leader could have restrained it – least of all one under house arrest. Bush does appear to deserve credit for preventing Sharon from deposing 'Arafat.

Occasional conciliatory murmurs from Washington, such as support for Security Council Resolution 1397 of March 2002 for a Palestinian state, and association with Jordan King 'Abdallah II's proposal for a "road map" to peaceful partition, were not followed up; they may have been intended as sops to British Prime Minister Blair, whose electorate was more balanced on the Palestine issue than Bush's.

The Bush administration seemed averse to any resolution that mentioned the settlements, the Fourth Geneva Convention, or the land-for-peace formula of Resolution 242 of 1967. The ritual Israeli-American call for total cessation of violence, followed by direct negotiations, seemed to have no practical effect except to enable any activist on either side to block a bilateral solution, and let Israel deploy its military advantage to pursue a unilateral solution. In late 2003, the United States and Israel took their lonely stand in the General Assembly once more – this time to vote against a resolution calling on Israel to stop building the Security Barrier whose ostensible purpose was to wall out suicide bombers but whose more telling consequence was the attachment of another piece of the West Bank to Israel, at huge cost in lifestyle and expense to the Arab residents.

Bush's endorsement of Sharon's master plan for unilateral withdrawal from the seething center of the Gaza Strip, and retention of most of the settlements in the West Bank, was a historic shift in American policy. In 2003, Prime Minister Sharon gave his "personal endorsement" to Congress's draft Syrian Accountability Act. Although George W. Bush gave no evidence of matching Clinton's mastery of the details of the Arab-Israeli dispute, his policy statements were couched in terms of faith-based certainty. This approach, taken with his choice of ideologues for his foreign-policy team, suggests that his policy choices were grounded less in strategic analysis than in religious conviction. The motives of his top officials were more focused. Vice President Cheney and Defense Secretary Rumsfeld saw alliance with Israel as a key element in America's global hegemony. According to his critics, Deputy Defense Secretary Wolfowitz was obsessive in matters affecting the security of Israel.

In 2008, Bush sensibly rejected an Israeli request for authorization to overfly Iraq to bomb Iran, but he atoned by supplying Israel with state-of-the-art antimissile radar.

In recent years, the evolution of America's policy in Israel's favor has been paralleled in the staffing in the White House and the Department of State. For some decades after World War II, positions dealing with the Middle East were generally reserved for officers who, having no ethnic ties with either the Arab or the Jewish communities, were presumed to be free from bias. With the surge of the Zionist lobby came mounting pressure on the White House to exclude Arabists, on the grounds that their special training in the language and culture of the Arab World had turned them into special pleaders for the Palestinian cause. The most conspicuous statement of this position was an article in *The New York Times Magazine* of 11/7/71 by the late Joseph Kraft, who reported that all Arabists tilted in a pro-Arab direction, but the electorate could rest easy because they had lost their access to policy-making jobs. This last assessment was more accurate than even Kraft could have anticipated. It would be fatuous to issue any blanket characterizations of collective bias; the relevant fact is that, since the Reagan administration, Middle East policy has been increasingly monopolized by Americans with records of unflagging support for Israel.

The investiture of Barack Obama in 2009 returned the White House to a liberal approach on most issues, but not on the Middle East. Having assured AIPAC's policy conference of 6/4/08 that the security of Israel was sacrosanct, Obama took two devout Zionists, David Axelrod and Rahm Emanuel, to the White House, and entrusted Middle East and Afghan affairs to a uniformly pro-Israel team: Secretary of State Hillary Clinton, State Department officers James Steinberg, Jacob Lew, Michael Posner, and Jeffrey Feltman, UN Representative Susan Rice, White House advisers Dennis Ross, Richard Holbrooke, and George Mitchell, and NSC Director for Middle East Affairs Daniel Shapiro.

Counterpunch of August 2008 alleged that Obama picked Joe Biden for Vice President out of deference to the Zionist lobby, and ascribed policy relevance to the thesis that Chicago's Crown/Pritzker/Emanuel political combine jump-started Obama's Presidential campaign. In June 2009, Obama's call for a total freeze on the expansion of Jewish settlements in the West Bank seemed like a classic case of locking the barn after the horse had been stolen. Obama's expression of willingness to deal with a coalition government of Fatah and Hamas – provided that it abides by previous agreements between Israel and Fatah's Palestine Authority, renounces violence, and recognizes Israel in advance of new talks – corresponds with Israel's position. It also eliminates any possibility of a negotiated settlement. Adam Schatz reminds us in *The London Review of Books* of 5/4/09 that no such conditions have been imposed on any state that is still in a technical state of war with Israel – not even on the client regime in Iraq.

Israel's Strategy of Desperation

The Zionist aspiration is to restore the Kingdom of David, which expired almost 3000 years ago. This endeavor entails two monumental challenges: 1) to win regional acceptance of a Jewish state; 2) to insure against an Arab majority in that state. If the geopolitical principles enunciated in Chapter 1 are valid, Israel will never be able to achieve regional acceptance on its own; acceptance will have to be imposed by the United States. The occupation of Iraq in 2003 (Chapter 15) was misconstrued in Washington and Jerusalem as a step in that direction.

Optimists have made much of Israel's two peace treaties. That of 1979 with Egypt was the price Sadat paid for the return of Sinai; it has not been embraced by the Egyptian public, and its longevity may be tied to America's aid commitment to Egypt of over two billion dollars a year. A smaller annual subsidy to Jordan and its ruler produced the hat trick of the treaty of 1994 between Israel and a state whose regime is a protectorate of Israel, but whose population is well over half Palestinian in origin.

To de-Arabize its territory, Israel has applied every tactic it could get away with – economic discrimination; restrictions on movement;

land confiscation; legalistic harassment; obliteration of inconvenient villages; derogation of water rights; injection of typhoid bacteria into Arab water supply (1948); checkpoints; detentions; school closures; border closures; demolition of residences; unremitting harassment; deportation; deployment of tanks, aircraft, and artillery against residential districts; torture; assassination; and mass expulsion by intimidation and force. In 1948, the first mass expulsion drove 700,000 Arabs out of Israel; in 1967, the second drove 300,000 out of the Occupied Territories.

All these devices are failing. In Greater Israel – if the statistics in Ali Abunimah's *One Country* are accurate – by 2005 the 5.26 million Jewish residents were outnumbered by 5.62 million non-Jews. The evacuation of Jewish residents from the Gaza Strip – foreshadowed years ago in an article by the writer in *The Washington Report on Middle East Affairs* – is geopolitically irrelevant, since the territory and its 1.5 million Palestinians are still under Israeli hegemony.

If the Gaza Strip were given its freedom, Israel would still face the high reproduction rate of its other Arab citizens and subjects. There is a history of recommendations that Israel promote emigration of its Arab citizens by instituting a program to make their life more unpleasant. There is no evidence that any such statute was ever adopted. In the 1980's, the late Meir Kahane, founder of the Kach Party, campaigned for a third mass transfer of Arabs. Kach was banned as racist in 1988, but the Moledet Party, founded in 1986 and a participant in the Sharon Government of 2004, has survived by resorting to euphemism – "Transfer by Agreement". Moledet campaigns on the slogan that "Jordan is the Palestinian State." Meanwhile, as American media spin their wheels in pointless analysis of the sterile "peace process," assimilation of the West Bank marches on, with the establishment of military zones (closed to Palestinian villagers and Israeli peace activists: *New York Review*, 12/17/09, David Shulman), Jewish settlements, restricted-access roads, and the Security Barrier.

Israel's three main political factions, Labor, Likud, and Qadima for short, are fierce competitors for office, and they often differ on tactics, but on basic strategy there is no daylight among them. All three have pursued expansion of settlements. None has evinced concurrence with the counsel of Israeli doves to evacuate the West Bank. Israel was created and sustained by military action. The shock of the 1973 war drove home the defensive value of strategic depth. Without the West Bank, Israel's waist would be less than ten miles wide – an intolerable situation for any soldier charged with the national defense.

The political equation alone seems to render cession of the West Bank academic. The current number of Jewish settlers – 200,000 in East

Jerusalem and 280,000 on the rest of the West Bank – under Israel's system of proportional representation could probably keep any advocate of cession out of electoral office. The proposed "population exchange" is Israel's code for a scheme that would annex Jewish settlements in the West Bank, exclude Palestinian border towns from Israel, and strip unwanted Palestinian Israelis of their citizenship: *Middle East Report*, Winter 2009, Oren Yiftachel.

Obsessed by these sobering circumstances, Israel's leadership has periodically resorted to extremist tactics. Noteworthy cases:

1940-41 - Representatives of the Stern Gang asked Nazi representatives in Beirut for help against the British authorities in Palestine. (Shamir was in a British jail.)

1947 - According to Ze'ev Schiff, the Haganah ordered its elite strike force, the Palmach, to assassinate specified Palestinian leaders.

1948 - Expulsion of 700,000 Palestinians.

1967 - Expulsion of 300,000 Palestinians. Finkelstein writes that, after the June War, Israel set out to impose a form of apartheid on occupied Palestine.

2003 - Sharon began construction of a barrier just east of the 1967 frontier. Its presumed purpose was to inhibit suicide bombing in Israel, but it would have the ancillary effect of attaching another 2-300 square miles of the West Bank to Israel proper. In 2004, the International Court of Justice issued an advisory opinion, 14-1(US), that East Jerusalem, the West Bank, and the Gaza Strip were occupied territory, and that Jewish settlements therein violated Article 49 of the Geneva Convention – as did the Security Barrier, which should be dismantled. America and Israel do not recognize the findings of the court.

2003 - In recent years, Israel has stepped up the demolition of inconvenient Palestinian homes in the 60 percent of the West Bank assigned by the Oslo Accord (see below) to full Israeli control. Volunteers have organized The International Solidarity Movement (ISM) to block demolitions. In March 2003, as reported by Joel Kovel and by *The Washington Report on Middle East Affairs,* Rachel Corrie, a 23-year-old American member of the ISM, was crushed to death by an Israeli bulldozer.

For all such acts of desperation, the government of Israel has a rationale. Overt initiatives, like the Security Barrier, are peremptorily justified on the sacrosanct grounds of self-defense. Incidents of disputed causation, like the attack on the Liberty and the death of Rachel Corrie, are relegated to the category of tragic mistakes. Both these cases have to be evaluated from the viewpoint of a historically persecuted community that emerged out of European holocaust, and sees reason to fear a Middle Eastern holocaust.

Desperation breeds fanaticism. Teammates who saw Rachel Corrie, wearing an ISM security vest, run down in broad daylight are disinclined to accept the inadvertence defense. As Adina Hoffman wrote in *The Nation* of 2/18/08, in the implacable Zionist ethos, the moralistic adversary is the most dreaded of all.

The Chronology of Zionism

Incarnation

1800's B.C.	Egyptian texts mentioned a city known in a Semitic dialect as Urusalim (Foundation of God).
1200 B.C.	A Jewish community was taking shape in central Palestine.
1021 B.C. (?)	Saul founded the first Jewish kingdom.
1000 B.C. (?)	David succeeded Saul, made Jerusalem his capital, and established an enduring dynasty.
922 B.C. (?)	The Egyptians sacked Jerusalem. The kingdom split into rival states: Israel in the north and Judah in the south. David's successors ruled Judah, centered on Jerusalem.
900's B.C.	Solomon built the (First) Temple of Jerusalem.
721 B.C.	The ten tribes of Israel, conquered by Assyria, were dispersed, assimilated, and "lost."
586 B.C.	The Kingdom of Judah, where monotheism had lately evolved, was conquered by Nebuchadrezzar II, who destroyed the First Temple and deported many of Judah's leaders to Babylonia.
538 B.C.	The Persians, conquerors of Babylonia, allowed the Jews there to return to Palestine, under the leadership of a descendant of David.
515 B.C.	Solomon's Temple was restored.
445 B.C.	Nehemiah, Jewish confidant of the Persian Emperor, was allowed to rebuild the walls of Jerusalem and consolidate the practice of Judaism.
320 B.C.	Jerusalem came under Egyptian control.

200 B.C.	By this time, in the analysis of William McNeill, Jewry had been transformed from a nation to a caste, under non-Jewish rule.
200 B.C. to 500 A.D.	During this period, the priestly function was transferred from Levites and Cohanim (who traced descent from the father) to rabbis (who traced descent from the mother).
170–164 B.C.	Judas Maccabeus led the resistance of devout Jews to the campaign by the Seleucid king, Antiochus Epiphanes, to destroy Jerusalem and stamp out Jewish worship, in the interest of Hellenizing the empire.
134 B.C.	Antiochus VII razed the walls of Jerusalem.
40 B.C.	The Roman Senate named Herod, raised as a Jew, King of Judaea. Herod oversaw the construction of a splendid new (Second) Temple.
66 A.D.	Rome put down a Jewish revolt, devastated Jerusalem, and destroyed Herod's Temple.
135 A.D.	Rome crushed the second Jewish revolt against its rule in Judaea and excluded Jews from Jerusalem. Hadrian later rebuilt Jerusalem as a Roman city.
637 A.D.	Muslims conquered Jerusalem.
638 A.D.	Muslims built a shrine (The Dome of the Rock) on the site where the Temple had stood.
900's	Muslims built Al Aqsa mosque inside the Dome of the Rock.

Reincarnation

The remarkable preservation of the Jewish identity over the centuries of diaspora has been ascribed by Joel Kovel to the magnitude and profundity of the sacred Hebrew texts. Through the Middle Ages, the Jewish people survived primarily in isolated communities in foreign capitals. In the Middle East, site of many of their larger centers, they spoke Arabic except for worship. Dissemination afforded one advantage: the evolution of far-flung Jewish communities as a global commercial and financial network.

In the late 1700's, Meyer Rothschild founded in Germany a "royal family" of international finance. Niall Ferguson has written how the House of Rothschild, excelling in one of the few professions open to Jews, helped finance European governments through the French Revolution, the Industrial

Revolution, and Europe's internecine wars. The Rothschilds' one strategic mistake was their failure to establish a branch in the United States.

By the 1800's, the Jewish community in western Europe was largely assimilated. The sudden evolution of the new Israel from a gleam in Theodore Herzl's eye to the most powerful state in the Middle East was the product of a rare constellation of circumstances:

1830's - Britain forced Egypt to withdraw its forces from Palestine, and pressed the nominal Ottoman rulers to admit Jewish immigrants.

1850's - The Ottoman Empire's "closure of the commons" facilitated clearance of tenant farmers (notably Palestinians) from land bought by new owners.

1869 - The opening of the Suez Canal (whose purchase by the British exchequer was financed by the Rothschilds) led Britain to look on Palestine as a convenient base for the Canal's defense.

1882 - After 2000 years of deathless dedication to The Return ("next year in Jerusalem"), Jews began to establish colonies in Palestine. Their immigration was banned by Ottoman law, but it happened, spurred on by pogroms in Russia. Estimated population of Palestine at the time: 400,000 Arabs and 25,000 Jews.

1885 - The Central Conference of American Rabbis drew up the "Pittsburgh Platform", which reflected the prevailing reformist view among American Jews that Judaism was a religion, not a nationality.

1897 - Theodore Herzl, author of *Der Judenstaat,* chaired the First Zionist Congress. A majority of world Jewry were unreceptive.

1900 - Of 8.7 million Jews in Europe, 5.2 million lived in the Russian empire, largely in the Pale of Settlement along the western frontier. They were forbidden to own land, enter the civil service, or serve as officers in the army.

1901 - The fifth meeting of the Zionist Congress founded the Jewish National Fund to acquire land in Palestine and Syria.

1909 - Founding of the first Jewish *kibbutz* (collective farm) in Palestine.

1915 - Estimated population of Palestine: 690,000 Arabs, 85,000 Jews. Perhaps one percent of world Jewry were Zionists.

1916 - Britain conned the Sharif Husayn of the Hijaz into accepting the rise of Jewish immigration to Palestine.

1917 - Britain issued the Balfour Declaration, which favored the establishment in Palestine of "a national home for the Jewish people" without prejudice to non-Jewish rights. Many British leaders favored a Jewish state in Palestine.

160

1920 - To the victors belong the spoils: The post-World War I Agreement of San Remo awarded the southern Levant, including Palestine/ Jordan, to Britain, which proceeded with the implementation of the Balfour Declaration.

1921 - After the Cairo Conference of British policymakers and Middle East experts, Secretary of State for the Colonies Winston Churchill sold London on dividing its pending Levantine mandate into Palestine, site of the Jewish National Home, and Transjordan, whose throne was awarded to Hashemite Prince 'Abdallah to insure against his leading an expedition against the French in Syria.

1922 - The Council of the League of Nations approved a mandate instrument for Palestine that incorporated the Jewish National Home and allowed for the establishment of a Jewish Agency to represent Palestine's Jewish community. The Mandate came into force in 1923. The Mandatory authority adopted a policy of parity between the Arab majority and the Jewish minority, and allowed the Zionists to start forming a Jewish enclave in Palestine: Ilan Pappe, *The Ethnic Cleansing of Palestine.*

1929 - The British trend toward favoritism for the Jews led to the first Palestinian uprising: Pappe.

1932-33 - Denied immediate arms equality at the Geneva Disarmament Conference, Nazi-dominated Germany torpedoed the Conference by withdrawing, and then used the collapse of the Conference as a pretext for unilateral rearmament.

1933 - Having exploited the theme of international discrimination against Germany to take control of the Reichstag, the Nazis induced President Hindenburg to award the chancellery to Adolf Hitler, who in the next two years licked the unemployment problem, winning enough public approval to convert Germany to a totalitarian state. There ensued a rapid increase in Jewish migration from Europe to Palestine.

1936 - London transferred to Palestine a pro-Zionist officer, Orde Wingate, who provided crucial direction to the Zionist effort to create an independent military force, which became the Haganah.

1937 - Zionists took control of the Jewish Agency. Two underground Zionist bands emerged: Irgun Z'vai Leumi, which had split from the Haganah in 1931, and became the paramilitary wing of the Zionist Revisionist Movement; and the Stern Gang, which was to split from the Irgun in 1940. They began bombing Palestinian Arab assemblages.

1937 - The Peel Commission recommended partition of Palestine. The Zionist leadership accepted partition in principle.

1937 - Affected by the intensification of persecution of Jews in eastern Europe, American rabbis abandoned the Pittsburgh Platform and adopted the Columbus platform, which reintroduced the concept of the Jewish people.

1938 - The Evian Conference failed to enlist nations willing to accept Jewish refugees from Germany. World Jewry was still divided into two communities: in Europe, Ashkenazis, confronted by Naziism; in Africa and the Middle East (notably Baghdad), Sephardis, living in relative peace with Muslim communities. There was little contact between them.

1942 - Germany secretly adopted the *Endlosung,* the Final Solution, which was to lead to the death of some six million Jews and the conversion of a majority of world Jewry to Zionism.

1942 - The World Zionist Organization (still unaware of Nazi plans for the Jews?) called for the establishment of a "Jewish commonwealth" in Palestine.

1944 - Yitzhaq Shamir (who was to become Prime Minister of Israel 42 years later) directed the Stern Gang's assassination of British envoy Lord Moyne in Cairo.

1946 - Menachem Begin (Prime Minister of Israel 31 years later) directed the Irgun's dynamiting of the King David Hotel, killing 88 Arabs, Britons, and Jews.

1947 - Four years of Jewish violence against the British authorities in Palestine had caused some 500 deaths, and accelerated the British decision to pull out of Palestine. In the opinion of Donald Neff, the British High Commissioner had come to realize that the Jewish resistance movement had brought Irgun and the Stern Gang under the discipline of the Haganah.

1947 - Pappe: The Haganah was compiling an exhaustive file of data on the Arab villages in Palestine. It was to prove invaluable in the military campaign of 1947-48.

1947 - The Zionists, then owners of six percent of the land of Palestine, accepted pro tem UNGA Partition Resolution 181. Although rejected by the Arabs, devoid of any mechanism for enforcement of its ludicrous terms, and never implemented, 181 stands as the legal basis of the Israeli state.

1947 - Pappe: In return for Israeli acceptance of Jordanian acquisition of the West Bank, King 'Abdallah agreed not to join any Arab military operations versus the Jews. The Arab League Council appointed a Syrian general to lead the "Arab Salvation Army".

12/31/47 - The Zionist forces executed their first massive attack – on the village of Balad al Shaykh, burial place of the anti-Mandate hero, Shaykh 'Izz al Din al Qassam.

March 1948 - Under the direction of Ben Gurion, as detailed in *The Ethnic Cleansing of Palestine,* Zionist forces adopted and carried out Plan Dalet, which erased the Arabs' two-to-one majority in Palestine by expulsion or massacre of over 700,000 people. Some of these actions took place under passive British observation. (The treaty of 2000 that set up the International Criminal Court designated ethnic cleansing a crime against humanity.) A sniper killed Jerusalem Consul General Tom Wasson 5/22/1948.

5/15/48 - The British forces completed evacuation from Palestine. The Jewish Agency proclaimed Israel an independent state. It had 286 Jewish settlements, and hegemony over 8000 square miles of the former Mandate. In its Declaration of Independence, Israel accepted the 1947 Partition Resolution as a condition of UN membership. To conceal the glaring inconsistency between the Declaration's proclamation of equality of "race, sex, and religion", and the exclusivist Jewish state contemplated by the agnostic founders of Israel, the founders drafted no constitution. The more devout Jews were appeased by the phrase in the Declaration "Rock of Israel", which they interpret to mean God. The language on equality has not been held as "binding" by the Israeli courts. Discriminatory legislation is camouflaged by circumlocution, such as using "those entitled to come to Israel under the Law of the Return" wherever "Jews" is meant. The Israeli constitutional system is a transparent tautology, but it is all the mainstream American media need to describe Israel as a "democracy".

Re UNGA Resolution 3379 of 1975, dictionaries define racism as: 1) Belief that some races are superior to some others; 2) Discrimination based on race. Although the first definition presumably does not apply to the Israeli political system, the second one explicitly does.

From the outset, Prime Minister Ben-Gurion pursued a strategy designed to block emergence of the Palestinian state authorized in UNGA 181. He also concluded a landmark deal whereby the Rabbinate (Ashkenazi and Sephardi) promised its enduring support for the (secular) government in return for annual subsidy and a monopoly over religious matters like marriage, divorce, burial, and validation of Jewish nationality. Only Orthodox rabbis can perform weddings or funerals: Allan Brownfeld, *WRMEA,* May 2010.

For pragmatic insurance of the enduring Jewish character of their own state, the Israeli authorities have habitually assigned newly acquired land to the state or its alter ego, the Jewish National Fund. By 1999, between 92 and 95 percent of the territory of Israel fell into this category – and was off-limits to non-Jewish residence. (See below the 'Adil Kan'an case of 1998.)

1948 - Shamir directed the assassination of UN mediator Count Bernadotte, who had advocated the return of Palestinian refugees to their homes in what was now Israel.

1949 - UNGA Resolution 273 (III) admitted Israel to membership in the UN, which induced the parties to sign a protocol providing for repatriation of the Arab refugees and the internationalization of Jerusalem. Israel signed in order to win admission to the UN.

1950 - Israel's parliament, the Knesset, adopted the Law of the Return, which accorded any Jew in the world the automatic right to entry and to citizenship. Jewish credentials were to be validated by the Israeli Council of Rabbis. The law was amended in 1970 to define a Jew as a person who is born of a Jewish mother, or is a convert.

1950 - Israel enacted the Development Authority Law, assigning over 92 percent of its land, under a Land Covenant, to the authority of the Jewish National Fund, as the "inalienable property" of the Jewish people.

1950 - By the Law on the Acquisition of Absentee Property, Israel declared that land belonging to Arabs who had been absent from Israel between November 29, 1947, and September 1, 1948, was subject to confiscation.

1950 - Estimated population of Israel: 1.2 million Jews, .2 million Arabs. Most Jewish residents of Arab states were moving to Israel.

1952 - The Knesset adopted the Law of Citizenship, defining Israeli citizenship so stringently that many Arabs who had been living in that part of Palestine that became Israel in 1948 were ineligible for it.

1952 - The Knesset adopted the World Zionist Organization-Jewish Agency (Status) Law, which accorded special social, economic, and political privileges to Israelis of "Jewish nationality" (Chapter 6), and prohibited the sale of state land to non-Jews. Some 97 percent of the land of Israel was owned by the state.

1953 - Under command of young officer Ariel Sharon, who had proved his mettle as a teenager, Israeli forces carried out the first of a series of disproportionate "retaliations" for Palestinian infiltration from Jordan; 69 Jordanian civilians died in an attack on the village of Qibya. Prime Minister Ben-Gurion had approved the attack, but publicly denied government involvement.

1954 - In an effort to abort the British-Egyptian Suez agreement (Chapter 10), and/or to undermine Egyptian-American cooperation, and/ or to block a peace initiative by new Prime Minister Moshe Sharett, Israeli intelligence staged a bombing hoax against American properties in Egypt.

1955 - To short-circuit US-Egyptian détente, Prime Minister Ben-Gurion ordered an unprovoked raid that killed 37 Egyptian policemen in Gaza, and compelled Nasir (denied American arms) to look for arms from the USSR.

1967 - Israel captured the remaining 2400 square miles of Palestine (plus the 480 square miles of the Syrian Golan). Many international lawyers believe that continued occupation of these territories violates Security Council Resolutions 242 and 338, General Assembly Resolution 194, and the Fourth Geneva Convention. The UN has consistently affirmed that the Occupied Territories are governed by the 1907 Hague Regulations, the Fourth Geneva Convention, and Protocol 1 of the Geneva Convention of 1977. Israel contends that the Territories, being "disputed", are not covered by these instruments. Israel appears to follow the lead of its patron, the United States, in recognizing only those UN provisions and instruments that suit its purposes. Israel applies two separate legal systems in the Occupied Territories – one for Jews, one for Palestinians.

1967 - Labor Prime Minister Eshkol approved the colonization of the West Bank. According to Gershom Gorenberg (*The Accidental Empire*), Israel's decision to settle the West Bank was activated within seven months after the June War. In the ensuing years Israel has paid financial inducements to Jews to settle on the West Bank, while withholding from most Palestinian exiles permits to live on the West Bank.

1967 - Israel enacted the Agricultural Settlement Law, which bans non-Jewish citizens of Israel from working on lands owned by the Jewish National Fund (over 80 percent of Israeli territory).

1967-81 - Whereas Israel had expanded its presence in the West Bank at a moderate pace, it set out on a rapid program of assimilation of the Golan, expulsion of most of its residents to Syria, and annexation in 1981.

1975 - UNGA Resolution 3379 equated Zionism with racism.

1976 - Secret talks between Israel and Lebanese Maronites (the Phalange and Camille Sham'un's "Tigers") led to Israeli supply of arms and military training.

1977 - Menachim Begin, pre-independence leader of the Irgun, was elected first Likudist Prime Minister on a platform proclaiming the West Bank and the Gaza Strip as parts of *Eretz Yisrael.*

1978 - Camp David I tacitly gave Israel a free hand in the Occupied Territories, and an opportunity to deal with the PLO forces in Lebanon.

1979 - Israel lifted the prohibition against private Jewish ownership of land in the Occupied Territories.

1984 - Israel extended Israeli law over the settlements, replacing Jordanian law.

1991 - In *The London Review of Books* of 2/26/09, Amira Hass asserted that Israel began to obstruct Palestinian travel between the West Bank and Gaza, in order to block any foundation for a future Palestinian state.

1992 - Israeli Foreign Minister Peres authorized secret talks with PLO representatives in Oslo, under the patronage of the Norwegian Government. At some undisclosed point, Prime Minister Rabin came on board.

1993 - After six years of Palestinian insurrection (Intifadah I), Rabin was under pressure to find an alternative strategy to Jewish teenagers' shooting Arab teenagers down in the street – which was corrosive of national morale. He reluctantly recognized the PLO, which his predecessors had dismissed out of hand as a terrorist organization.

1993 - Under the belated aegis of Clinton, Rabin and 'Arafat concluded the Oslo Accord: Israel recognized the PLO as the representative of the Palestinian people; the PLO renounced violence and the Palestinian Covenant and recognized Resolutions 242 and 338 and Israel's right to exist in peace and security. Rabin hoped the Accord would boost Labor over Likud (which opposed it) and put down the Palestinian Islamists, whom Israel had once cultivated as a counterweight to the PLO, but were now becoming a threat in their own right. Intifadah I expired. While world attention was focused on the inconsequential details of the Accord, Israel gained a clear field for the main strategic issue: expansion and consolidation of the settlements.

1995 - Sixty percent of the West Bank and forty percent of the Gaza Strip were owned by the State of Israel.

1995 - Rabin was assassinated by a hard-line opponent of the Oslo Accord. The succession of Benjamin Netanyahu of the Likud as Prime Minister foreshadowed the collapse of the Oslo process – insofar as there actually was a process. Netanyahu ended a four-year freeze on building settlements. By 1997, the Israeli Labor Party estimated that government subsidies to West-Bank settlers totaled 300 million dollars a year.

1998 - 'Adil Kan'an, an Arab Israeli, sued to be allowed to live on land being advertised by a Jewish cooperative in Katsir, Israel. By 2004, the Supreme Court had ruled in his favor, but the Knesset was wrestling with the language of a law that would continue to exclude Arabs without contradicting too blatantly the equality provision of the Declaration of Independence. Americans may see a parallel in their own history, in that the assertion in their own Declaration of Independence that all men are created equal was violated, even in law, until the issuance of the Emancipation Proclamation in 1863 and the ratification of the Thirteenth Amendment to the Constitution in 1865.

1999 - New Prime Minister Barak (Labor) escalated settlement building.

2000 - A spokesman for Americans for Peace Now estimated there were 150-200,000 settlers on the West Bank (aside from East Jerusalem). Israel suspended immigration to the Occupied Territories.

2001 - Days before leaving office, Clinton brought 'Arafat and Israeli Prime Minister Ehud Barak to Camp David for one last effort to revive the diplomatic track. Unrealistic observers accused 'Arafat of capricious rejection of Barak's "generous offer" of "a state of some sort". There was no evidence that Barak had offered anything more than a pig in a poke – a few Arab enclaves isolated from Syria, Jordan, Egypt, and each other by "temporary" corridors under absolute Israeli dominion. Their inhabitants would still have had no control over their water supply, electric power supply, or their own borders. Their economy would have remained hostage to Israeli caprice. If Barak had genuinely come around to the two-state formula, he would have frozen expansion of the Israeli presence in the West Bank; he did not.

2001 - New Prime Minister Ariel Sharon (Likud) reacted to continued Palestinian violence by deploying greater firepower and striking deeper into areas assigned to Palestinian control by the Oslo Plan. His immediate objectives appeared to be the elimination of the Palestine Authority, and the "parcelization" of the West Bank.

2002 - According to *The Washington Report on Middle East Affairs,* Israel's Civil Torts Liability Act was amended to rescind the ability of Palestinians to bring suits in Israeli courts

2003 - Sharon began construction of a Security Barrier east of the 1967 frontier and around key settlement blocks circling Jerusalem. Its ostensible purpose was to keep out suicide bombers. Its effect was to confiscate large areas of Arab farmland and accomplish the de facto annexation of another 7-10 percent of the West Bank. Even Washington objected. Some analysts suspect the Barrier has a secret purpose: To preempt any initiative for a one-state solution to the Israeli-Palestinian deadlock.

2004 - The Knesset adopted a law denying citizenship and residency rights to the non-Jewish spouses and children of non-Jewish citizens of Israel. No Israeli agency would marry a Jew to a non-Jew.

2004 - The International Court of Justice designated East Jerusalem, the West Bank, and the Gaza Strip as "occupied territories", rejecting their Israeli classification as "disputed territories". The court issued an advisory opinion that those segments of the Security Barrier east of the 1967 border violated International Law: *TomDispatch,* 12/8/09.

2006 - Israel has designated "seam zones" (areas between the Security Barrier and the 1967 frontier) as off limits to Arab nonresidents.

2006 - Israel denies Gazans entry to the West Bank, and most West Bankers entry to the strip of territory that Israeli forces control along the western shore of the Jordan River. (Its civilian residents consist of 47,000 Palestinians and the occupants of 31 Jewish camps and settlements.)

2006 - Former Likudist Ehud Olmert's new party, Kadima, won an election over Likud and Labor. Under the Israeli system of proportional representation (threshold: two percent), every government is a diverse coalition. Olmert's government included representatives from left, right, and Arab parties.

2007 - Having apparently reached the inevitable conclusion that the national security of Israel dictates permanent hegemony over the Occupied Territories, Israeli leaders had to devise a system that facilitates passage of Jews while obstructing passage of Palestinians – like the membrane process for desalting water. The result is complex – and contrary to international law:

- the Security Barrier (wall, fence, and ditch) just east of the obsolete 1967 frontier;
- progressive confiscation of Palestinian land for siting communally dedicated roads, settlements, and army camps;
- an elaborate system of military checkpoints – some of them ostensibly operated by officials of the Palestine Authority but controlled by Israeli officials acting behind the scenes via one-way mirrors, sliding drawers, and closed-circuit TV.

2008 - Saree Makdisi wrote that Israeli expropriation of 40 percent of the West Bank for military bases, Jewish settlements, and government roads, consolidated by fragmentation of the Arab 60 percent by means of checkpoints and road blocks, had accomplished the Zionist goal of sufficient "facts on the ground" to preempt any basis for a viable Palestinian state. Yisrael Beiteinu, the party of Avigdor Lieberman, a member of the Olmert government, advocated "mutual transfer" of land as a device for excluding Arabs from the Jewish state.

2008 - Peace Now reported that in the preceding year Israel had nearly doubled settlement construction on the West Bank.

2008 - According to *Counterpunch* of September 27, Israeli information technology companies had cornered the world market in electronic interception – even of US government traffic. The FBI has reported an Israeli intelligence program aimed at US military systems: Philip Giraldi, April 2010.

2009 - Rachelle Marshall reported that in January the Israeli Supreme Court had overturned the Central Election Committee's ban on two

Arab parties, Balad and the United Arab List, from running in Israeli elections.

2009 - The Israeli Housing Ministry was still providing subsidized mortgages for homes in settlements beyond the Security Barrier: Gershom Gorenberg.

2009 - February elections swung the Knesset to the right. According to Neve Gordon, of the 33 parties that ran candidates, 12 won seats. The leaders: Kadima (Tzipi Livni) - 28; Likud (Benjamin Netanyahu) - 27; Yisrael Beiteinu (Avigdor Lieberman) - 15; Labor (Ehud Barak) - 13; Shas - 11. Awatef Sheikh reported in *The Washington Report on Middle East Affairs* that three Arab parties won 11 seats (including a Jewish candidate on the Communist Hadash list).

2009 - On March 27, Likud, Shas, the smaller rightist parties, and Labor formed a cabinet of 30 representing 69 seats in an assembly of 120. Netanyahu, who continued to resist endorsing Washington's two-state solution, was Prime Minister. Superhawk Lieberman was Foreign Minister.

December 2009 - *TomDispatch* reported that the Barrier, 58% complete, was enclosing 9.5% of the West Bank/East Jerusalem.

Palestinians Under the Wheels of the Juggernaut

Every Palestinian political suicide says something about the intensity of the human urge for liberty – particularly since the Palestinians, as a community, have never known it:

Late 1800's - Ottoman land laws, designed to encourage agriculture, operated to the advantage of tribal leaders and the disadvantage of their followers. The result was the rise of a class of absentee landlords no longer sensitive to any custodial obligation. Thousands of Palestinian sharecroppers were evicted when callous landlords, many of them absentees, sold out to Zionist organizations. Even Palestinian delegates to London had sold land to Jews. Since the Jewish settlers were socialists, they hired only a few of the dispossessed Arab laborers.

1919 - The Palestinians' pickup leadership had no effective voice at Versailles, but rejected the mandate system it promulgated.

1923 - Instead of the independence the British had promised, the imposition of the Mandate clapped the Palestinian Arabs (who still thought of themselves as Syrians) into an elaborate prison.

1929 - Beginning to sense that the Jewish arrivals might some day become Jewish overlords, Palestinians rioted, setting off violence between Arab and Jew, Arab and Briton, and Jew and Briton.

1936 - In belated reaction to the establishment of the Jewish Agency, the Palestinians formed their own approximation of a government, the Arab High Committee, under the leadership of the Grand Mufti of Jerusalem, Amin al Husayni.

1936-39 - A Palestinian revolt against Jewish settlers (the *Yishuv*) and the British authorities was put down by the British forces, with loss of 5-10,000 Palestinian lives, exile of the Palestinian leadership, and – as reported by Rashid Khalidi – the Palestinian movement gravely weakened.

1937 - The Mandate authorities outlawed the Arab High Committee. The Mufti fled to Damascus, where he sought to continue his operations. He later contacted Nazi Germany (as did the Jewish Stern Gang).

1947 - As Britain prepared to abandon Palestine to its fate, Zionist paramilitary forces launched a campaign to take territory and expel Palestinians. In World War II, the Haganah had become an effective military force, while the Palestinians had been looking for salvation to a disinterested Arab World.

1948 - A Palestinian National Assembly chaired by the Mufti proclaimed the Democratic State of Palestine, which came to nothing as Arab resistance dissolved under Israeli attack. With no history of political unity, the Palestinians were unable to overcome neighborhood, tribal, and sectarian feuding. Those who presumed to speak for the Palestinian cause made bad or pointless choices, like boycotting UN bodies, rejecting the Partition Resolution, and killing King 'Abdallah, rather than making the best of a dismal situation. Their military champion, 'Abd al Qadir al Husayni, was courageous but overmatched and died early in the war. Eighty percent of Palestine became a Jewish state.

1949 - UNGA Resolution 302(IV) established the UN Refugee and Works Agency for Palestinian Refugees in the Near East (UNRWA).

1956 - Visiting Gaza, Nasir reportedly said his government considered the Strip Egyptian territory.

1959 - Fatah took shape in the diaspora, as an offshoot of the Muslim Brotherhood.

1961 - When Syria seceded from the UAR (the United Arab Republic of Syria and Egypt), the only casualties were the Palestinian guards on the Damascus residence of Egyptian proconsul 'Abd al Hakim 'Amir. Their deaths were symbolic of the fate of the Palestinian community throughout the Twentieth Century.

1963 - King Husayn held the first of a long series of secret meetings with Israeli officials.

1964 - In reaction to rising tension between Israel and its neighbors, Egyptian President Nasir convened the first Arab Summit, which announced inter alia the formation of the PLO (Palestine Liberation Organization). The first Palestinian National Council (PNC), convened under Egyptian auspices, set up a PLO Executive Council and promulgated the Palestinian Covenant, which proclaimed a Palestinian state in all of Palestine.

1965 - Fatah, a Palestinian resistance organization formed by Yasir 'Arafat independently of Egyptian guidance, carried out its first (symbolic) raid into Israel.

1967 - The Syrian-Egyptian debacle in the Six-Day War (see below) convinced the Palestinians that if their country was ever recovered, it would be by their own devices. Egypt's puppet leadership of the resistance was eventually replaced by the 'Arafat faction, the only Arabs to benefit from the war.

1967 - In Khartoum, the fourth Arab Summit promulgated "the three noes": no talks, diplomatic relations, or peace treaties with Israel.

1967 - George Habash (Greek Orthodox) founded the secularist Popular Front for the Liberation of Palestine (PFLP).

1968 - The PFLP hijacked an El Al aircraft.

1968 - The fourth PNC rejected UN Resolution 242 and endorsed armed struggle.

1968 - Israel's Labor government began to allow Jewish squatters to settle on land in the territories confiscated from Palestinians.

1968 - PLO and Jordanian forces held out against a major Israeli reprisal raid on Karamah in Jordan. 'Arafat's prestige skyrocketed.

1969 - Under its new Chairman, Yasir 'Arafat, the PNC called for the establishment of a democratic secular state of Arabs and (some) Jews in Palestine. Dissenters (Arab Nationalists and Islamists) formed the Rejection Front.

1969 - Hostilities in Lebanon between the establishment (Maronites and conservative Muslims) and the opposition (radical Muslims and the PLO) culminated in the Cairo Agreement, which left the Palestinians virtually sovereign in the refugee camps.

1970 - Members of the Rejection Front hijacked three Western airliners to Jordan, precipitating a showdown between the monarchy and the PLO, which considered Jordan its primary base. The Jordan army, largely manned by East-Bank tribesmen loyal to King Husayn, expelled the PLO forces, which took refuge in south Lebanon.

1973 - The Melkart Agreement, recognizing the Palestinians' right to control security in the camps, facilitated a massive increase in their military strength in Lebanon.

1973 - To concentrate American attention on the Palestinian cause, the PLO killed American diplomats George C. (Curt) Moore and Cleo Noel in the Saudi Embassy in Khartoum.

1973 - CIA Deputy Director Vernon Walters met secretly in Rabat with a top aide to Arafat; there were no more PLO killings of American officials (until the Meloy/Waring killings?).

1974 - The twelfth PNC revised the Covenant, suggesting willingness to accept partition. An Arab Summit (minus Jordan) designated the PLO "the sole legitimate representative of the Palestinian People." UNGA Resolution 3236 endorsed the concept of a Palestinian state and accorded the PLO permanent observer status. 'Arafat addressed the Assembly, with the honors of a chief of state.

1976 - The Arab League granted the PLO full voting membership.

1976 - Washington received midlevel PLO representatives.

1976 - The PFLP hijacked to Entebbe an Air France plane that was recovered with few casualties by bold action by Israeli special forces. Jonathan Netanyahu, brother of Benjamin and leader of the operation, lost his life in it.

1977 - The PLO voted to accept a Palestinian state on any liberated part of Palestine, and negotiations with Israel – although not on the basis of Resolution 242 (which makes no mention of Palestine).

1977 - The Likud government stepped up settlement in the Territories.

1978 - After the Camp David Summit, Palestinians still in the Occupied Territories formed the Committee for National Guidance, independent of the PLO.

1979 - On the strength of tactical successes in the Yom Kippur War of 1973, and great-power support for the Camp David accord, Egypt concluded peace with Israel, thus recovering Sinai, signing up for annual American financial aid, and opting out of the lethal Arab-Israeli conflict.

1982 - The Israeli invasion of Lebanon failed in its central objectives – to install a puppet regime and dispose of the PLO once and for all – but it did accomplish the transfer of the PLO leadership and some of its forces to Tunis. In violation of an agreement brokered by Washington, Israel colluded in the Phalangist massacre of a thousand or more Palestinian and Lebanese residents of two refugee camps in Beirut.

1983 - An Islamist organizational meeting in Amman was a direct challenge to the 'Arafat faction.

1985 - In retaliation for a PLO killing of three Israeli intelligence officers in Cyprus, Israeli F-16's attacked the PLO compound in Tunis, killing 59 Palestinians and 15 Tunisians.

1987 - Hamas emerged, like Fatah, as an offshoot of the Muslim Brotherhood.

1987 - Intifadah I erupted against the Israeli occupation of the West Bank and the Gaza Strip.

1987 - In Tunis, Israeli agents killed 'Arafat's deputy, Khalil al Wazir.

1987 - The Unified National Leadership of the Uprising (UNLU) took shape in the Territories as a potential rival to the absent PLO leadership.

1988 - Belatedly endorsing UNGA Resolution 181 and UNSC Resolutions 242 and 338, the PLO specified 181 as the legal basis for a Palestinian state, accepted the frontier of 1967 as permanent, and proclaimed Palestinian independence in the Occupied Territories. The United States recognized the PLO. The Palestinian state was recognized by over 100 states, including India, the People's Republic of China, and the Soviet Union.

1988 - 'Arafat told a special meeting of the UNGA (held in Geneva to bypass American objections) the PLO accepted the right of all parties to the Arab-Israeli conflict to exist in peace and security, "including Israel." Hamas dissented.

1988 - Armed clashes between Hamas and the PLO.

1989 - In its first attack on Israel, Hamas abducted and killed two IDF soldiers. Israel outlawed Hamas. Its founder, Ahmad Yasin, pleaded guilty of planning the death of four Palestinians suspected of collaboration and was sentenced to life for the action. Hamas continued to operate underground, publishing a covenant calling for jihad to liberate all of Palestine. (The Hamas brand of Islamism has differed sharply from that of Al Qa'idah in that its aims are Palestinian, not regional, and it seems to concentrate its operations against Israel – not against the United States.)

1991 - Washington arranged an Arab-Israeli peace conference in Madrid. It was a failure, but it was the first in which the PLO was allowed to participate and it had one operative consequence: 'Arafat, shocked by the emergence of a rival secular Palestinian leadership, was softened up for the Oslo initiative.

1992 - Israel concluded that 'Arafat, on the ropes, would be receptive to a deal that would end the Intifadah.

1993 - Isolated in Tunis, 'Arafat was an easy mark for the Israeli offer to recognize the PLO as the representative of the Palestinian people – but not to recognize a Palestinian state. In return for Palestinian "autonomy", which 'Arafat misrepresented as the first step toward statehood, he accorded Israel unspecified rights in the Occupied Territories and the continued jurisdiction of Israeli law, while he accepted for the proposed

Palestine Authority (PA) the responsibility to suppress the rejectionists, and extracted no commitment to stop expanding the settlements – let alone to define final status. Edward Said viewed the Palestine Authority as another Vichy regime. Some observers felt the Oslo Accord violated Article 49 of the Fourth Geneva Convention and Security Council Resolution 242. While the Accord gave the Palestinians a false sense of progress, it steadily undermined their position. The Israeli presence in the Territories expanded, and spasms of violence by hard-line Palestinian factions afforded Israel the pretext to stifle the Palestinians' access to their natural labor and commodity markets in Israel. Day-laborers were replaced with expatriate workers from eastern Europe and Asia. 'Arafat won one short-term gain: The UNLU disbanded. End of Intifadah I.

1993 - Hamas rejection of Oslo and the two-state solution was a direct challenge to the PLO and its ward, the Palestine Authority. As Israel continued to expand its presence on the West Bank in blatant violation of its Oslo commitments, Hamas and the more radical Islamic Jihad began to gain adherents at the PLO's expense.

1993 - In reaction to a series of suicide bombings by Hamas, Israel picked up 413 members of the organization and deposited them in a desolate area of southern Lebanon, where they were forced by the Lebanese to make camp. (After several years they were allowed back to Palestine, but in the interim they made valuable contacts with their putative adversaries, the Shiite Hizballah.)

1993 - In Tunis, the PLO authorized the formation of a Palestine Authority, under Yasir 'Arafat, to take over land and responsibilities ceded to it by Israel.

1994 - On February 25, American-born settler Barukh Goldstein carried out a one-man massacre in a small mosque on the West Bank. He died on the scene, but the event further radicalized Palestinian attitudes.

1994 - 'Arafat's de facto recognition of Israel was all the cover King Husayn needed to sign a peace treaty with the Jewish state.

1994 - 'Arafat returned to Gaza and set out to rebuild his power base. Foreign contributions and repatriation of private funds sparked a building boom in the Territories.

1995 - Ramadan Shallah left a professional post in Florida to replace the assassinated Fathi Shiqaqi as leader, from Damascus, of Islamic Jihad in the Territories.

1996 - Assassination of Yahya 'Ayyash on January 5.

1996 - Elections confirming 'Arafat as leader of the Palestine Authority were followed within weeks by suicide bombings directed against Israeli targets by Palestinian Islamists. Prime Minister Peres closed the frontier against passage by day-laborers from the Territories.

1996 - The election of Likudist Netanyahu as Prime Minister rang the death knell for the Oslo process.

1996 - Hamas named Khalid Mish'al head of its politbureau.

1997 - Mossad's bungled attempt to poison Hamas leader Khalid Mish'al enabled King Husayn to do the Palestinians two favors: saving Mish'al's life and releasing two Israeli agents in exchange for Ahmad Yasin's release from the life sentence imposed on him in 1989.

1999 - Deported from Jordan by King 'Abdallah II, Khalid Mish'al took refuge in Damascus.

2000 - Continual expansion of the Israeli presence and stifling of the Palestinians had turned the Territories into a tinderbox. In September, cabinet minister Sharon provided the spark by making a gratuitous, in-your-face visit to the Temple Mount (which shares a site with the Muslim Dome of the Rock) in the company of several hundred soldiers, whose presence revealed collaboration from Prime Minister Barak. Palestinian demonstrations were met with gunfire, and Intifadah II began. Oslo had been torpedoed, and the rejectionism of the Palestinian Islamists vindicated.

2000 - By precipitating Intifada II, Sharon set in motion a chain of events that led to his own election as Prime Minister. Under his administration of military forays, economic repression, and assassinations, the situation of the Palestine Authority and its constituents became increasingly desperate. Oslo was a dead letter. Fatah formed Al Aqsa Martyrs' Brigade, directed by Marwan Barghuti until his imprisonment by Israel.

2001 - Bush 43 chastised Palestine Authority President 'Arafat for his failure to terminate anti-Israel violence (a feat utterly beyond the powers of 'Arafat or any other official).

2002 - First suicide bombings by Fatah (Al Aqsa Martyrs' Brigade), in reprisal for Israeli "targeted killings".

2004 - In retaliation for three Israeli deaths caused by home-made rockets fired from the Gaza Strip, Israel launched a major foray into the Jabaliyah Refugee Camp.

2004 - Sharon signaled the possibility of unilateral evacuation of the Gaza Strip (whose settler population had been restricted to a few thousand, perhaps in long-term consideration of that contingency). Meanwhile, Israel stepped up operations against Hamas, including the assassination of the revered founder, Shaykh Ahmad Yasin, if only to enable it to contend that any withdrawal from the Strip (unlike that from Lebanon) was not a sign of weakness. Israel may also have been concerned that Yasin's offer to accept an interim two-state solution would weaken its case for continuing military repression. The ungovernability of an impoverished enclave of 140 square miles, populated by 1.3 million people largely dependent on UNRWA rations, was highlighted by a story related by Christopher Hitchens: When an Israeli negotiator offered to give up the Gaza Strip, his Palestinian opposite number said, "Fine. What do we get in return?"

2004 - After the decease of Yasir 'Arafat, grand old man of the Palestinian resistance, factions of the movement, including rival wings of Fatah, maneuvered to replace him. The Palestine Authority was disintegrating. It had survived for ten years on subsidies from Arab governments and the European Union.

2004 - Khalid Mish'al replaced Ahmad Yasin as leader of Hamas.

2005 - Hamas was gaining on the PLO, in part because of tighter organization, in part because it had bet against the failed Oslo process.

2005 - Sharon evacuated all 9,000 settlers and the Israeli garrison from the Gaza Strip. Henry Siegman wrote that this action extinguished the peace process.

1/25/06 - Despite the two million dollars Washington spent to help Fatah in the elections for the PA's parliament, Hamas won 76 of its 132 seats. Writing in *The Journal of Palestine Studies,* Graham Usher cited circumstances working in Hamas's favor: 1) Fatah misrule; 2) factional split of Fatah between Mahmud 'Abbas and Marwan Barghuti; 3) Hamas's social-service system; 4) the collapse of the Oslo initiative.

2/06 - The electoral victory of a "terrorist" organization dimmed Western enthusiasm for Middle Eastern democracy. The US and Western European governments suspended direct aid to the Palestine Authority.

4/06 - Isma'il Haniyyah became Prime Minister of the Gazan government formed by Hamas.

4/06 - Jordan intercepted an arms shipment from Syria intended for Gaza, and barred Hamas officials from its territory.

6/06 - Armed clashes between forces of Fatah and Hamas in the Gaza Strip resulted in takeover of the territory by Hamas.

6/24/06 - The IDF abducted two Palestinians from the Gaza Strip.

6/25/06 - A Hamas operation on the Gaza-Israel border led to the death of two Israeli soldiers and the abduction of a third.

2006-07 - Prolonged IDF ground and air assault on the Gaza Strip led to the destruction of several government offices, heavy casualties, and the arrest of 87 Palestinian ministers and MP's.

7/12/06 - A Hizballah unit infiltrated northern Israel, killed eight Israeli soldiers, and abducted two. Presumed objectives: To negotiate the release of some of the few Lebanese and 9,000 Palestinians long under Israeli detention, and enhance Hizballah's image as the defender of Lebanon and Palestine.

7/12/06 - Israel activated a longstanding plan intended to obliterate Hizballah as a paramilitary force and delete it from Lebanese politics. During 34 days of combat, Hizballah rockets inflicted casualties and considerable damage on towns in northern Israel. Israeli bombs, including precision-guided versions rushed from the United States, precipitated mass flight from south Lebanon, inflicted massive destruction on southern and coastal Lebanon as far north as Beirut, and killed hundreds of Lebanese and four UN Observers. The House of Representatives acclaimed the Israeli offensive. The White House, supportive of Israel's objectives, held off calling for a cease-fire.

2007 - According to *The New York Review of Books* of 6/14/07, The UN World Food Program had found that, by blocking food supply and denying access to essential medical services, the Israeli occupation of the Palestinian territories was choking the life out of Palestinian communities.

2007 - *The Financial Times* reported that The UN Office for the Coordination of Humanitarian Affairs had compiled a map of the West Bank showing how Israeli roads, fences, settlements, roadblocks, checkpoints, and military zones had confined the territory's 2.5 million Arabs to sixty percent of its land area.

2007 - Mysterious death in London of Nasir's son-in-law, Ashraf Marwan. On 5/10/09, "Sixty Minutes" reported that both Egypt and Israel claimed him as a key intelligence asset who had sold Israel information – fabricated or invaluable – depending on his real loyalty. The mystery may be solved if his killers are ever identified.

2007 - After Hamas took over Gaza (see below), President Mahmud 'Abbas of the rump Palestine Authority in the West Bank named Salam Fayyad Prime Minister.

2007-2009 - Two years of hostilities between Hamas and Fatah, and Hamas and Israel, are discussed in separate sections below.

2009 - *Times*: Israeli contractors had been taking rock and sand from the West Bank to Israel in violation of the Fourth Hague Convention of 1907.

Forever Refugees

One of the many doleful aspects of the Palestine problem was the enforced resolution of a tragic Jewish refugee problem by the creation of a tragic Arab refugee problem. Of the million or more Palestinians forced or terrorized into leaving their homes, many failed to make the transition to conventional residence abroad. These unfortunates and their descendants have been consigned to Arab slums and ramshackle refugee camps – even in Jordan, the only state to confer citizenship on Palestinians en masse (Chapter 3).

To become a member of the United Nations, Israel nominally accepted General Assembly Resolution 194 of 1948, which purported to provide for the return of the Palestinian refugees, or for financial compensation. To fill the traumatic vacuum left by nugatory 194, the UN Relief and Works Agency was set up to meet the basic needs of the refugees. According to recent UN reports, UNRWA rolls included over four million registrants, most of them living in 59 camps:

Jordan - 1,700,000 registrants in 10 camps; Gaza Strip - 900,000 in 8 camps; West Bank - 650,000 in 19 camps; Syria - 400,000 in 10 camps; Lebanon - 390,000 in 12 camps.

With an annual budget of 340 million dollars (90 million from the US, nothing from Israel), UNRWA's funding per refugee was minuscule ($70 per year per refugee), and its survival was open to question In 2004, UNRWA had 25,000 employees, almost all Palestinian, and served over four million refugees in Jordan, Syria, Lebanon, and the Occupied Territories, including 900,000 of the 1.3 million Arabs in the Gaza Strip. For these victims of the implacable international power structure, the future is bleak. There is no prospect of return to the homes whose pictures many still keep, nor of the compensation that GA Resolution 194 dangles as an alternative. In these days of population explosion, no country wants them. They remain as an unhealed wound on the Arab body politic.

In December 2009, the head of UNRWA was Commissioner General Karen Abu Zayd, a longtime specialist in refugee problems: *Washington Report on Middle East Affairs*, December 2009.

While the involved parties continue to juggle the Palestinian hot potato, they evade their responsibility for supporting the millions of jobless refugees their policies have created. Until the Fatah-Hamas split, the Palestine Authority was the refugees' major employer, with a payroll in 2004 of 130,000. Twenty-five thousand had permits to work in Israel or at the new industrial park on the border.

The Ultimate Incongruity: Arabs in a Jewish State

Israel is the exclusive property of its Jewish citizens. To preserve the Jewish character of the state, the government bans intermarriage between Jews and Arabs, and scrupulously excludes the growing Arab minority from the power structure. Arabs vote, hold Knesset seats, and are sometimes accorded nominal participation in left-wing governments (Olmert), but all public institutions, including the civil service, are virtually closed to Arab applicants. The Israeli equivalent of America's military-industrial complex has no Arab member. In 2006, Scott Wilson reported in *The Washington Post Weekly* that Arab citizens of Israel faced discrimination in land ownership, education, public employment, and immigration policy. *The Link* reported in 2008 that the Israeli state arranged for Arab and Jewish citizens to live apart. Public services for Jewish communities were far superior to those for Arab communities.

The Arab voice in state policy is sharply restricted by Arab disunity and government manipulation. Anti-Zionist parties are banned. There have been no influential Arabs in the cabinet; under the existing political structure, an Arab prime minister is inconceivable.

Soon after independence, the Jewish leadership set out to prevent the coalescence of the Arabs into one political bloc by documenting them along sectarian and tribal lines. Identity cards no longer categorize their holders by "nationality", but Jews and Arabs are distinguished by entries in Hebrew or Arabic, respectively : Jonathan Cook, *WRMEA,* July 2010.

Although Arabs constitute 20 percent of the population of Israel, they generally hold 10-15 seats in the 120-seat Knesset. There are four main Arab parties: The United Arab List (Islamicist), whose leader has spent time in jail on a charge of ties with Hamas; Balad (National Democratic Alliance), whose leader, Azmi Bishara, is in exile to avoid imprisonment on a charge of selling military secrets to Hizballah; Hadash (Communist); and another influential Islamist faction which runs candidates in local council elections only, but operates an efficient social-service network.

State policy has kept the two communities separated physically and culturally. According to *The London Review of Books* of 6/25/09, the educational systems of Israeli Jews and Israeli Arabs, from kindergarden through the senior year of high school, are totally separate. In 2008 *The Journal of Palestine Studies* reported that residents of Arab neighborhoods lived at the bottom of the socioeconomic ladder. Arab high-crime areas were walled off.

In 1983, David Shipler reported in *The New York Times* that, after centuries of having lived together in harmony, the two communities now lived apart, "steeped in mutual aversion." Twenty-five years later, communal mistrust was greater than ever: *The Wall Street Journal,* February 2007. Still, there is no visible trend toward Arab emigration. As compensation for their status as second-class citizens, Israeli Arabs participate in the only modern economy in the Middle East, and they nurse the hope of Israel's evolution from Judocracy to democracy. Instances of activism against the

Zionist regime are infrequent. The most serious occurred in 2000, when police fired on Arabs demonstrating in support of Intifadah II. Three years later a judicial commission blamed overreaction by the administration of Ehud Barak for the fourteen deaths in that incident.

In Israel's earlier years, its Arab citizens supported the two-state solution. More recently, as the obstacles to genuine partition have become apparent, Israeli Arabs have begun to look toward Israel's becoming a single state.

The Failure of Armed Resistance

The disparity between the Israeli and Palestinian military establishments forced the resistance to resort to the classic strategy of the weak: underground political violence. (The media call it "terrorism" – a term too loaded to have scientific validity.) Jews used the same strategy against the British and the UN in the 1940's. The outcome of any conflict between regular and irregular forces – <u>asymmetric warfare</u> (not to be confused with "collateral damage" inflicted by regular forces on civilian targets) – is generally determined by country of origin. If a regular force is injected into a foreign country, the odds are that it will eventually be expelled – like the British from Palestine in 1948 and South Yemen in 1967; the French from North Vietnam in 1954 and Algeria in 1962; the Americans from South Vietnam in 1975, Lebanon in 1984, and Somalia in 1993; the Russians from Afghanistan in 1989; and the Israelis from Lebanon in 2000.

Conversely, irregulars are unlikely to prevail over a regular force that is defending its perceived homeland – like the American army against the Native Americans, and the Israeli army against the Palestinians. There is no evidence that Palestinian courage – including the number willing to lay down their lives – has diminished the Israeli government's resolve to hold Palestine from the Mediterranean to the Jordan River. (Nominal withdrawal from the Gazan enclave was a concession to demography, not to Palestinian valor.)

The Assassination Syndrome

The surreptitious battle of assassination has been running sharply in Israel's favor. The Palestinians have reached only one highly placed Israeli (Minister of Tourism Rehavam Ze'evi in 2001). His death was claimed by the PFLP. Israel has managed to rub out all the principals in the hostage operation at the Munich Olympics of 1972 (which led to the deaths of eleven Israeli athletes), and a long succession of Palestinian and Lebanese activists, including more than 400 Palestinians. The life expectancy of leaders of Hizballah and Hamas is particularly attenuated:

1972 - Ghassan Kanafani (PFLP spokesman, acclaimed writer, resident in Beirut), killed in apparent retaliation for a PFLP attack on the international airport at Lod: *New Yorker*, 1/18/10.

1985 - Failed Saudi-American attempt to kill Hizballah cleric Fadlallah.

1987 - Khalil al Wazir ('Arafat's deputy), resident in Tunis.

1992 - Hizballah leader 'Abbas Musawi and family.

1993 - 'Imad 'Aqil, head of the military wing of Hamas.

1995 - Fathi Shiqaqi, founder of Islamic Jihad, resident in Damascus.

1996 - Yahya 'Ayyash, Hamas explosives expert in Gaza, known as "the Engineer". According to the media, his elimination was a subtle operation in which a double agent inveigled him into using a cell phone that was rigged to explode by radio signal.

1997 - Elaborate attempt on the life of Hamas official Khalid Mish'al (discussed above).

2004 – Hamas finance officer 'Izz al Din Khalil killed in Damascus: *WRMEA* citation from *Al Ahram Weekly*, 2/4/10.

3/22/04 - Hamas founder Shaykh Ahmad Yasin, killed in Gaza.

4/17/04 - Yasin's successor, 'Abd al 'Aziz al Rantisi, killed in Gaza.

2/12/08 - Hizballah military leader 'Imad Mughniyah, killed by a bomb in Damascus. (Israeli complicity not established, though implied in a 5/21/09 citation from *Yedioth Ahronoth* by *Wall Street Journal Online*.)

1/2010 – Hamas operator Mahmud al Mabhuh killed in Dubai by large Mossad (?) team: *WRMEA*, April 2010.

In the 1980's Hizballah adopted the martyrdom mystique of its Iranian Shiite founders, carrying out suicide bombings against Americans (see below), French, and Israelis – thereby contributing to Israel's ultimate decision to abandon Lebanon.

Hamas conducted a wave of wholesale suicide bombings against Israeli targets in the 1990's. According to one theory, this campaign was seen as retaliation for the indiscriminate massacre in a West Bank mosque by American-Israeli settler Barukh Goldstein. An alternative assessment: By torpedoing Arab-Israeli peace talks, Hamas sought to leave the ultimate demise of Israel as the only outcome of the battle for Palestine.

The strategic validity of assassination, whether targeted or not, is open to serious question. Palestinian suicide operations have backfired in costly ways: They served as grounds for Israeli border closures that have rocked the Palestinians' society and devastated their economy; the bombings of 1996 helped super-hawk Benjamin Netanyahu defeat dovish

Shimon Peres for the Premiership. Nevertheless, all major Palestinian factions still defend the suicide strategy. A bombing in Dimona in February 2008 (one death) was variously claimed by Hamas, by the PFLP, and by Fatah's Al Aqsa Martyrs' Brigade. The condemnation of the assassination strategy by Palestinian Authority head Mahmud 'Abbas is perhaps to be expected from a leader who relies on Western financial assistance and Israeli security assistance, but aside from unique cases (Adolph Hitler?), automatic elimination of every successive leader of a given faction would seem to be self-defeating – particularly if that faction is on history's side.

Palestinian Rebellion

Intifadah I (1987-93) was an exercise in civil unrest: strikes, demonstrations, riots, stone-throwing, tire-burning. It arose spontaneously out of clashes between Palestinian crowds and Israeli security personnel. The leaders of the resistance took over with the apparent strategy of goading Israel into killing enough Palestinians to arouse worldwide demand for international intervention.

The world at large had problems of its own. In Washington, the one capital with leverage over Israel, Israeli political influence swamped American concern for Palestinian "terrorists". The only Israeli concession to the resistance was the Oslo Accord, which turned out to be a Trojan horse: It appeased the Palestinians with cosmetics like the creation of the impotent Palestine Authority, while Israel kept on with the business of building settlements into a geopolitical wall against cession of the West Bank. By 2000, closure of the Israeli job market had inflicted intolerable distress on the Palestinian economy, while continued expansion of Jewish settlements dispelled all hope of alleviation.

It remains to be determined whether the provocative character of Sharon's September 2000 visit in force to the Western Wall had a domestic political motivation, or was specifically intended to spark an insurrection that could be cited as justification for Israeli reentry into areas under the jurisdiction of the Palestine Authority, with the ultimate objective of wiping out the apparatuses responsible for the suicide bombings. Intensified by Hamas from 1994 on, the bombings had sharply increased the ratio of Israeli to Palestinian deaths.

Israeli strategy in Intifadah II (2000-200?) was more violent than in Intifadah I; practitioners of the Powell Doctrine (Noam Chomsky's imagery) deployed tanks, jets, and helicopters against targets in residential areas. Israel controlled the hinterland and the skies. Vastly outgunned, the resistance was driven into the shadows. Resisters learned to avoid confrontation, where they put themselves in line of fire from Israeli security personnel, armed to cripple, sharpshooters, armed to kill, and helicopter gunships.

The initial Israeli tactic was to maximize control, while minimizing adverse publicity, by putting the demonstrators out of action but killing only their leaders. It was not very successful. Excessive use of force was explicitly charged by Amnesty International and implicitly by Israeli moderates, and by a Security Council resolution of October 7, 2000. The Israeli press carried accusations that the aerial gunship is not an acceptable means of crowd control, and that "targeted killing" of Palestinian leaders is illegal, immoral, and bad strategy. Nevertheless, the Israeli government's concern for international opinion seemed to evaporate in consequence of three mutually reinforcing events: America's election of Bush 43 in November 2000; Israel's election of Prime Minister Ariel Sharon in March 2001; Al Qa'idah's lethal attacks on key American targets in New York and Washington on September 11, 2001.

Nine/eleven intensified the hawkish instincts of the Bush administration and bolstered Sharon's specious claim that the Palestinian resistance is part and parcel of America's campaign against Islamist "terrorism". (The issue in the Israeli-Palestinian conflict is land; in the US-Al Qa'idah conflict, it is hegemony.) Washington concurred in 'Arafat's house arrest in Ramallah. 'Arafat died in 2004, by which time total deaths from Intifadah II were estimated at 900 Israelis and 3000 Palestinians. The Palestine Authority was tottering, Israel was accused of neglecting its responsibility for the public health of Palestinian areas it had taken over, and the Palestinian rank and file were enervated.

Repercussions on Palestine of the Regional Power Struggle

Palestinians have periodically reverted to the hope of eventual salvation by their Arab "brothers", no matter what the impetus – kinship, Islamic solidarity, or Arab Nationalism. Circumstances have intervened:

Arab Naivete

Sharif Husayn acquiesced in the Balfour Declaration and Jewish immigration to Palestine, distracted by Britain's promises that after centuries of Turkish rule, the Arabs were to come back into their own.

The Political Rat Race

Governments have a higher priority than governing. First, they have to hold office – no small feat in the Middle East, whose 19 states have experienced an inordinate number of sudden regime changes, many of them violent. In their myopic views, Palestine is either an opportunity to advance their parochial interests, or a dangerous nuisance. These preoccupations relegate the Palestinian cause to the realm of pious hope, even in the pro-Palestinian environment of Jordan. The compliant governments of Jordan and Egypt rely on annual American subsidies – plus extra perks (like the US-Jordan free-trade agreement of 2004). As of 2006, Israel's El Al was serving the airport in Amman.

The tribal regimes in the Arabian Peninsula depend on the American military to keep the Iraqis and Iranians out; their economies are under periodic strain (Chapter 3); and the Arab Nationalist component of the Palestine resistance movement is way too revolutionary for their reactionary taste. This same sentiment activates Jordan's Hashemite monarchy, whose antecedents are Hijazi, and whose tacit relationship with Israel has always been based on a common fear of Palestinian revolution. Their relationship began with their secret partition accord of 1948. In 1977, Israeli official Moshe Dayan revealed that the two governments were still in direct communication. In 1994, Jordan and Israel agreed to prevent the Palestinians from acquiring sovereignty over East Jerusalem.

In 2002, the surge of Arab sympathy for the Palestinian side in Intifadah II forced Egypt to declare suspension of all but emergency contacts with Israel, but neither Egypt nor Jordan broke diplomatic relations. Egyptian professional associations had been shunning contacts with Israel for years. Husni Mubarak's continued closure of the border with the Gaza Strip, in agreement with Israel, if not collusion, was deeply resented by many of his constituents. Israel deeply resented Egypt's failure to shut down the labyrinth of secret supply tunnels.

Baathist Iraq provided the most direct support to the Palestinian resistance (symbolic missile attacks on Israel in Gulf War I; subsidies to the families of suicide bombers in Intifadah II; shipments of food and medicine in 2000, plus treatment of Palestinian wounded in Iraqi hospitals.) The United States disposed of the Iraqi regime in 2003 (Chapter 15).

Arabian governments provide significant subsidies to the Palestine Authority and to Hamas.

Military Imbalance

Arab states have fought eight conventional wars against the Israeli-American diarchy. In every case, the context was the Middle East power struggle – not the Palestinian cause – and the short-term result was decisive Arab defeat. The longer-term result was strong Arab disinclination to fight another conventional war. Asymmetric warfare, however, is a different story. In Lebanon, it nullified Israel's conventional victory of 1982-83 with Israel's ultimate capitulation in 2000. In Iraq, it has cast doubt on the durability of America's conventional victory of 2003. In the Levant it produced surprising results for Hamas and Hizballah (see below).

1948 - The War for Israeli Independence

The UNGA's Palestine partition resolution of November 27, 1947, precipitated civil war between Jews and Arabs in Palestine. The Zionist combatants were centered around the Haganah, a formidable fighting force of 50,000 at the start of the war, increased to 80,000 toward the end of 1948 (Pappe's statistics). They received heavy weapons from the Soviet Bloc in May 1948. As documented by Israeli historian Benny Morris, the Haganah and its commando unit, the Palmach, collaborated with the Irgun and the Stern Gang in an unavowed but highly effective operation of ethnic cleansing.

The disorganized Palestinian force of 7000 started out with no allies except a makeshift volunteer force from Syria, Lebanon, and Jordan that for reasons of its own colluded with the Haganah. The "regular" troops from the Egyptian, Syrian, Lebanese, and Iraqi military establishments, numbering fewer than 50,000, which arrived after the Israeli declaration of statehood, were undercut by the termination of weapons shipments from their main supplier, the UK. They had negligible competence and no military objective except to grab pieces of Palestine. The only combatant to achieve this objective was Egypt, whose forces (which included a vastly disillusioned Jamal 'Abd al Nasir) came out of the war in control of 140 square miles which were to acquire disproportionate political criticality and the inelegant name of the Gaza Strip. The Arab "invasion" was more helpful to the Israelis than to the Palestinians, in that it lent legitimacy to Israel's conquest of much more territory than it was to have received under the partition resolution. Awarded 54 percent, it conquered 77 percent.

The second biggest chunk of Palestine went to Transjordan, which had no plans to be a combatant. Shortly before the GA voted partition, with London's blessing King 'Abdallah had sold out his Palestinian "brothers". Under a secret deal with Israel (reminiscent of the great-power dissection of Poland in the 1700's), 'Abdallah was promised an area of adjoining Palestine in return for not interfering with Israeli seizure of the rest.

During the war, Israeli forces went over the secret line, and 'Abdallah's British masters allowed his British-officered army to resist. When Israeli forces advanced into East Jerusalem (whose residents were Arab), Jordanian and Iraqi forces blocked the advance and shelled West Jerusalem (Jewish).

Apprehensive that Britain might intervene on its own account, the Israelis stayed back from the Jordan River, and Transjordan became Jordan by temporarily acquiring 2250 square miles of central Palestine that became known as the West Bank. 'Abdallah annexed it in 1950 (and Husayn lost it in 1967).

In 1949, Israel's four neighbors signed armistice agreements. The 1948 defeat had traumatic consequences for all of them: military coup in Syria in 1949; the assassination of 'Abdallah in 1951; military coup in Egypt in 1952; and an indigestible community of stateless Palestinians in Lebanon.

1956 - The Suez Canal Crisis

The Arab-Israeli wars were periodic eruptions of a political volcano that has never been quiescent. In the years leading up to the eruption over the Suez Canal, the volcano was particularly turbulent. In 1954, Israeli agents in Egypt assailed American institutions with incendiary devices that Washington was supposed to blame on the untested new leader – Nasir. Instead, his intelligence services penetrated the plot and hanged the plotters. In retaliation, Israel raided the Gaza Strip in February 1955, killing 39 Egyptian soldiers. (Up to that point, the relative tranquility along the frontier under Nasir's cautious strategy had inconvenienced Israeli plans to escalate tensions in the interest of taking more territory in the Strip, Sinai, and the West Bank.)

Under domestic political pressure, Nasir responded to the raid on Gaza by sponsoring a flurry of Palestinian guerrilla raids into Israel. By 1956, tension among the parties had intensified. Alarmed by Israeli receipt of offensive arms from France and Canada, denied American arms for Egypt, Nasir tightened the blockade of Israeli shipping through the Strait of Tiran and looked for a supplement to arms supply from the unpredictable Soviet Union by recognizing Communist China on May 16, 1956.

Incensed by this diplomatic victory for their Communist bete noire, President Eisenhower and Secretary of State Dulles abruptly withdrew the American promise of financial aid for the construction of the High Dam on the upper Nile. The withdrawal announcement was couched in terms so insulting to the Egyptian government that Nasir felt honor bound to hit on some dramatic response. The nationalization of the Suez Canal was sprung on the world July 26, 1956. It came as a shock to the Western powers, which had swallowed their own propaganda that Egypt lacked the expertise to run the canal on its own. Before announcing the withdrawal of High Dam aid, the secretariat of the State Department had solicited the views of at least two bureaus about Nasir's political situation. The Bureau of Intelligence and Research was not given all the relevant facts: The writer (who, despite recent service in Port Said, had failed to foresee the nationalization) was charged with producing a rush assessment of the political significance of the High Dam project to the Nasir regime. His conclusion – that the regime would not stand or fall on the completion of the project – was probably accurate in isolation, but it had no relevance to the actual circumstances.

By this point, Nasir's policies had infuriated three major adversaries other than the United States: Britain was unreconciled to the recent negotiated closure of its massive base in the Suez Canal Zone; France resented Egyptian support for the Algerian rebellion; Israel was determined to abort Egypt's recent claim to sovereignty over the Gaza Strip and its obstruction of Israeli access to the Red Sea. On October 29, 1956, secret planning among this ill-matched trio produced an initiative so ludicrously devious that Washington saw through it at once.

Step one – Israeli invasion – was a multiple victory: humiliation of the Egyptian armed forces, capture of the Strip and Sinai, and eradication of the Tiran blockade. No other Arab state came to Egypt's aid. Step two – British and French invasion of the Canal Zone "to separate the combatants" – was a fiasco. Eisenhower's anger at Nasir had been blotted out by the deception practiced on him by his European allies. By threatening to pull the IMF rug out from under the British Pound, he forced Britain and France to withdraw their forces in disgrace.

In 1957, Eisenhower compelled a contumacious Israel to withdraw from Sinai and the Strip and mute its territorial claims thereto. The nationalization of the canal was confirmed. By converting military defeat into political victory, Nasir had reached the zenith of his prestige in the Arab World. His version of Arab Nationalism gained millions of adherents, and Syria threw itself into political union with Egypt (Chapter 14).

The war had one momentous consequence: Israel's reward for participation was French help in building a secret nuclear reactor at Dimona.

1967 - The Six-Day War

Israel remained determined to oust Nasir, control the headwaters of the Jordan River, and expand its defensive perimeter. In early 1965, the writer had occasion to review Israel's strategic concerns with the country teams of Embassies Cairo, Baghdad, and Damascus. The consensus of all three was that Israel would take the first political opportunity to occupy the West Bank, the Gaza Strip, and the Syrian Golan. Opportunity knocked in 1967, by which time violent border clashes between Israel and Syria, Jordan, and Egypt had led Nasir into the mystifying position of having sent troops into Sinai, dismissed the UN force stationed along the border after the 1956 war, and declared the crucial Strait of Tiran closed to Israeli shipping – while 50,000 Egyptian soldiers were engaged on the rebel side in a civil war in Yemen.

Nasir knew the Strait was casus belli for Israel. He had been misled by his generals. Perhaps he also had illusions that Washington would come to his rescue, as it had in 1957. If so, he had to induce Israel to attack first. (Under the Tripartite Declaration of 1950, America, Britain, and France had made a quixotic commitment to counter any aggression from either side or both across the armistice lines of 1949: Shlaim, *The Iron Wall.*) Nasir may not have realized that Lyndon Johnson had scrapped Kennedy's evenhanded policy of trying to "do business with Nasir."

Under pressure from the Jordanian public, King Husayn felt compelled to fly to Cairo in late May and sign a mutual defense pact with Egypt.

Israel exploited Nasir's misjudgment with alacrity. It devastated the Egyptian and Syrian air forces in a few hours, and its ground forces followed up the advantage at warp speed: four days to retake the Strip and Sinai, another two to take the Golan. Syria and Jordan paid a high price for joining Nasir's gamble. Israel's razing of Palestinian villages that obstructed its advance into East Jerusalem, taken with its rapid postwar incorporation of an expanded Old City into Israel proper, suggested that the objectives of the war had been meticulously worked out in advance. The only major miscalculation was the failure to expel the West Bankers – most of whom remained to constitute a demographic obstacle to annexation.

The annexation of East Jerusalem, in fact if not in law, remains in effect in contradiction of Security Council resolutions. In 1981, Israel extended its full jurisdiction to the Golan; the timing may have been meant to protest a contemporary rapprochement between the United States and Saudi Arabia, and/or to take advantage of Soviet and American preoccupation with a crisis in Poland, and/or to impede Arab-Israeli peace talks. As for the motivation, the Golan has strategic value: It encompasses some of the

Jordan River's headwaters, and it affords Israel a commanding optical and radar view of Damascus, 30 miles distant, and control of the escarpment from which Syrian artillery had inhibited the Israel practice of encroaching into the demilitarized zones established after the 1948 war.

1967-70 - The War of Attrition

The juxtaposition of Israeli and Egyptian forces on opposite banks of the Suez Canal meant continuation of artillery and air action. In 1969, Israel began to send air raids deep into Egypt, driving over a million people from their homes. In 1970, by threatening to turn to Washington for relief, Nasir prevailed on the Soviet Union to take over Egypt's air defense. Soviet pilots began flying operational missions over the Canal Zone. On June 30, the combination of Western aircraft and Israeli pilots reaffirmed Israel's traditional domination of Middle Eastern skies by shooting down five Mig's piloted by Soviet airmen. Simultaneously, the Israeli air force was shooting down Syrian jets on the northern front. However, by advancing surface-to-air missiles to the Canal, the Soviets had begun to bring down Israeli jets, thus stalemating the conflict.

On the crucial day of July 23, 1970, Soviet and American negotiators managed to dispel the emerging specter of Soviet-American confrontation: Nasir accepted their cease-fire proposal; Israel went along; Azmi Bishara speculated that it had a low tolerance for casualties at that time. The War of Attrition had ended in stalemate – with one momentous exception: It left on the west bank of the Canal the missiles that were to tip the scales in Egypt's favor at the outset of the Yom Kippur War.

1973 - The Yom Kippur War

After the debacle of 1967, the Egyptian commander-in-chief had committed suicide. Nasir died of a heart attack after the War of Attrition. No one had great expectations for Nasir's chosen successor, but Anwar Sadat was the improbable liberator of lost Egyptian territory and vindicator of Egyptian honor. Having seen Brezhnev tolerate Kissinger's policy of stalemate, Sadat expelled most Soviet military advisors. In the spring of 1973, Roger Merrick, Egyptian analyst in the State Department's intelligence bureau, sensing the likelihood of early Egyptian military action, initiated a warning which, after massaging by several superiors, reached the desk of Secretary Kissinger. By that fall many of us had been inclined by a CIA report of a pending Saudi oil embargo to regard Merrick's warning as premature, but in October, on the strength of unprecedented Arab military organization and political coordination (described by Patrick Seale), Egypt and Syria launched simultaneous attacks against Israeli forces based in Arab territory. Egyptians carried out an ingenious crossing of the Canal, routed the complacent defenders on the east bank, and by effective use of hand-held Soviet missiles began to inflict heavy casualties on the Israelis. For the first time, Israel felt its back against the wall.

In retrospect, America and Israel should have seen it coming – and probably did if King Husayn actually made a secret trip to warn Prime Minister Golda Meir. In any case, alerted only hours before the attack, Israel decided not to preempt, for fear of angering Washington. Less than 24 hours after the initial attack, Sadat let America (and Israel) know that he was prepared to stop firing if the great powers would intervene in the Arabs' favor. For Egypt, this delimited strategy was destined to succeed, but it left Syria far out on a limb. By focusing all its attention on the northern front, where it had total air superiority, Israel was able to pummel the Syrian forces that had just broken through the Israeli defenses.

Eight days after the initial attack, in belated response to Asad's appeals, but against the advice of his generals, Sadat suddenly abandoned his hedgehog crouch and ordered an advance into Sinai beyond his missile cover. His timing was disastrous. The pause had enabled Israel to repel the Syrian salient, regroup, and take the offensive against the Egyptians.

With Nixon mired in the Watergate controversy, American foreign policy was the province of Secretary of State Kissinger, who was allegedly partial to the Israeli side. He and Israel were one in their dedication to preserving Israel's military preeminence over any possible combination of Arab states, and to opposing the creation of a Palestinian state. His immediate contribution to the war effort was two billion dollars to finance emergency air and sealifts of state-of-the-art arms.

American aerial or satellite photography enabled the intelligence community to assure him that, by virtue of Israel's control of the air, Sharon's surprise foray by pontoon bridge to the western side of the Canal entailed no danger of an Egyptian pincers defense. Ignoring Security Council calls for a cease-fire, Israeli forces could have gone on to Cairo, but Kissinger, pressed by Moscow, finally put his foot down. However, sensing the rift between Egypt and Syria, he worked to widen it. Soon after the war, Kissinger met with Sadat in Cairo, arranged resumption of diplomatic relations, and consummated Egypt's shift from Soviet to American patronage. Success came in 1979, when Sadat bolted from the Arab camp by signing a peace treaty with Israel. Sadat's reward was the recovery of Sinai, and the knowledge that he had commanded the most impressive Arab military effort in a hundred years. (Donald Neff reported that forces from Jordan, Kuwait, and Saudi Arabia arrived late in the fighting and had no significant bearing on the outcome.) The price Sadat paid for alignment with the West was his life; he was assassinated by Islamists in 1981.

Kissinger eventually negotiated a disengagement agreement for Syria, which recovered a sliver of land, including the city of Al Qunaytirah – after Israel had razed it (Chapter 13). For the American public, the Yom Kippur war was a baptism of Middle East fire. During the winter of 1973-74, they were plagued by gas lines caused by oil embargoes imposed by Arab oil states (Chapter 4).

1982 - The Invasion of Lebanon

With both Egypt and Syria removed from the Arab-Israeli conflict, Israel's focus shifted to Lebanon, where the PLO faced Israeli and pro-Israel Lebanese troops operating in the "Security Zone" Israel had established in the south. In 1981, as exchanges between Palestinian artillery and Israeli aircraft intensified, President Reagan sent out a special representative, Philip Habib. He arranged a three-way understanding that called for a cease-fire, brought Syria back into the realm of international diplomacy after four years in the wilderness, and gave political status to the PLO – even though Habib was prohibited from direct contact with 'Arafat by a blanket commitment Kissinger had made to Israel in the aftermath of the Yom Kippur War.

The understanding left no room for Israel to pursue its fundamental goal: elimination of the Palestinian resistance in the West Bank. In August 1981, new Defense Minister Ariel Sharon, the life-long Arab-fighter, began looking for an opportunity to resume hostilities. He found his pretext in June 1982, when a Palestinian splinter group attacked the Israeli ambassador to Britain. Three days later, Israeli forces moved out of the Security Zone in force. Prime Minister Begin sought to bolster the Maronites (with whom Israel was in secret contact) and undermine the PLO. Sharon seemed to have more ambitious objectives: 1) annihilation of the PLO, which had discomfited Israel by accepting the principle of a two-state solution, per a Security Council resolution of January 26, 1976; 2) establishment of a puppet government in Lebanon; 3) destruction of the Syrian armed forces; 4) demonstration for Reagan that Israel was a strategic asset in the Cold War; 5) expulsion of Palestinians from Lebanon to Jordan, in the interest of conversion of the Hashemite monarchy into a Palestinian state; 6) expulsion from Lebanon of the Syrian forces (which had come in during the 1970's to end the civil war, in Syria's favor).

Sharon elicited perfunctory objection from Washington; the President was sympathetic to Israel's concerns, and Secretary of State Haig, Israel's foremost champion in the administration, reportedly gave the invasion a green light. Advancing against stiff Palestinian and Syrian resistance, advantaged by their total mastery of the air, Israel's forces disregarded Begin's pledge to stop 40 kilometers north of the cease-fire line. On June 13, they reached Beirut, where they linked up with Phalangist forces. The 70-day siege of Beirut had begun.

Two weeks of air attack on the Muslim quarter of Beirut, repeated Israeli violations of cease-fire agreements, and a Soviet demarche on Syria's behalf were too much for Reagan, who favored the expulsion of the PLO from Lebanon but not the erection of a pro-Israel regime in Beirut. On June 25, he dumped Haig, who had gotten too close to Sharon, and named George Shultz to replace him.

Before the war ended, Israel had carried out the devastation of west Beirut, graphically reported by Thomas Friedman to *The New York Times,* a Syrian(?) agent had assassinated Bashir Jumayyil, Israel's choice for President, appalling destruction had been visited on Beirut and Sidon, 17,500 Arabs had lost their lives, and the PLO forces had left Lebanon for Syria, Iraq, Yemen, and Tunisia. (Egypt, Saudi Arabia, and the Gulf Shaykhdoms had denied them entry.)

Shultz's own mistake was to force Lebanon on May 17, 1983, to sign with Israel an agreement that was tantamount to a peace treaty, in blatant disregard of the fact that the dominant power in Lebanon was Syria. In the process of expelling the PLO, the Israelis had alienated an even deadlier adversary, the Shia of south Lebanon. Major irritants were Israel's imposition of a tax on Lebanese villagers and the gratuitous devastation of neutral Shiite villages.

Shiites, Sunnis, Druze, Syrians, and remaining Palestinians combined to harry Israeli forces back toward the border. In February 1984, Muslim and Druze forces overran the Muslim sector of Beirut. On May 5, the Lebanese President who had signed the Shultz Agreement went to Damascus, his personal Canossa, and scrapped the Agreement. In the Syrian-Israeli contest for primacy in Lebanon, Syria had won.

As the Israelis reluctantly retreated to the Security Zone, bloody fighting among the sundry factions in Lebanon was ended in 1989 by an accord, brokered by Saudi Arabia, which in effect legitimated Syrian dominion in Lebanon. Israel evacuated Lebanon entirely in 2000. It had won the conventional war, but in the subsequent asymmetric war it had been defeated.

American miscalculation added a tragic footnote. In 1982, at 'Arafat's request, Washington sent in a contingent of Marines. Prematurely withdrawn, they returned in penitence after Sharon's forces colluded in the Maronite massacre of a thousand or two Palestinian and Lebanese noncombatants. In contravention of standing American policy never to be seen fighting side by side with Israel, in disregard of political reality in Lebanon, and over the vehement objections of the Marine commander on the scene, American forces were ordered to enter the action in the Beirut area on the Israeli side.

On October 23, 1983, suicide bombings of the French and American military compounds in Beirut caused heavy casualties. Reagan issued the standard pronouncement that America never bows to terrorism, and then withdrew the Marines a few months later. In 1996, Secretary of State Christopher secured unwritten Syrian, Lebanese, and Israeli acceptance of a cease-fire which took belated effect in June 2000, when the Security Council endorsed the Secretary General's certification that the withdrawal of Israeli forces from south Lebanon had fulfilled its conditions.

1982 - The Birth of Hizballah

For Ayatollah Khomeini, the dedicated pan-Islamist, Israeli challenge to any Muslim – Sunni or Shia – was intolerable. Under his determined leadership, Iran's newly created Revolutionary Guard Corps reacted to the invasion of Lebanon by creating and training in the Lebanese Biqa' a radical militia which was to revolutionize the balance of power in the Middle East. The anti-Palestinian Amal was supplanted by the anti-Israel Party of God. Lebanese Ayatallah Muhammad Husayn Fadlallah became its spiritual mentor.

America's expeditionary force left Lebanon in 1984. Israel withdrew its forces in 2000. Hizballah had solid grounds for claiming credit for both events.

1991 - Gulf War I

In January 1991, American forces expelled the Iraqi force that had overrun Kuwait in 1990. The administration of Bush 41 wisely resisted the temptation to go on to Baghdad and take on the challenge of nation-building. Bush prevailed on Israel not to take action on its own account, which was considerable: Under Saddam, Iraq was the first Arab state to take Israeli life (from Scud missile launches) without Israeli retaliation; more critically, Saddam's bid for Kuwait had conjured up the nightmare specter of Arab unification. In this respect, the war was round seven in the Arab-Israeli conflict (Chapter 9).

2003 - Gulf War II

By injecting a coercive military presence into the Middle East, Bush 43 took the fateful step his predecessors had ruled out. The dangerous implications are reviewed in Chapter 15.

Palestinian Power Struggle

The Palestinian resistance movement includes ten or more factions with conflicting aims and strategies. They fall roughly into three doctrinal camps: secularists, Islamists, and pragmatists. The secularists and Islamists insist on a single Arab-Jewish state of all Palestine. The pragmatists cling to the hope that Oslo will ultimately produce the visionary Palestinian state of the West Bank and Gaza. It is the pragmatists' misfortune that the one-sided posture of the Israeli and American governments has left them no negotiating room; in this case, pragmatism equals collaboration.

From the 1960's until his death in 2004, pragmatist Yasir 'Arafat was leader of the umbrella structure, the Palestine Liberation Organization (PLO). His own faction, founded in the 1950's, was Fatah *(Al Fath,* "conquest", an inverted acronym: *Harakat al Tahrir al Watani al Filastini,* "Palestinian National Liberation Movement".)

The PLO's history of superficial success (award of permanent-observer status by the UNGA in 1974, Washington summit of 'Arafat, Rabin, and Clinton in 1993, Oslo's tinsel promise of autonomy, 'Arafat's return from Tunis to Palestine in 1993) was nullified by strategic failure (expulsion from Jordan in 1970, from Lebanon in 1982, Arafat's house arrest in Ramallah until his death, relentless expansion of the Jewish settlements), and ultimately buried in perceptions of corruption, ineffectuality, dependence on Arab dictatorships, and capitulation to baleful Israeli-American influence symbolized by the insidious Oslo Accord.

Each of the major Palestinian organizations has its own militia. For Fatah, it is Al Aqsa Martyrs Brigade; for Hamas, the 'Izz al Din al Qassam Brigade. The chronology of inter-Palestinian contention reveals that the recent surge of Islamist influence across the Middle East (Chapter 12) has been paralleled by the rise of Palestinian Islamists, notably *Hamas* ("ardor" or "dedication", an acronym for *Harakat al Muqawamah al Islamiyyah,* "The Islamic Resistance Movement"). The Hamas charter of 1988 designates Palestine as a perpetual *waqf* (sacred endowment), but in practice the organization has been less doctrinaire. In the regional spectrum of Islamist factions, as noted by Henry Siegman, Hamas has taken the path of moderation: collaboration with Lebanon's Shiite Hizballah; concentration on Palestinian nationalism, not on the new Caliphate envisioned by Al Qa'idah; and tolerance of the temporary existence of Israel. A tangible benefit of this moderate policy is political and financial support from Iran and the Arab oil states.

In 1990, the Arab oil states expressed their fury at PLO support for the Iraqi claim to Kuwait by expelling Palestinian guest workers and suspending financial backing for the PLO, in favor of donations to the Palestinian Islamists.

In 1994, Hamas fell into line under the leadership of Yasir 'Arafat, Chairman of the Palestine Authority (PA), but continued to follow its own path through the jungle of Arab regimes. Ever since 1999, when King 'Abdallah II expelled Hamas leader Khalid Mish'al, its relations with Jordan have been rancorous. By 2006, Jordan blocked arms shipments to Hamas and barred Hamas officials from its territory. Syria is a different story: Flynt Leverett reported that three Palestinian factions (Hamas, the Islamic Jihad, and the PFLP/General Command) were allowed to maintain their headquarters in Damascus, on condition they not attack Western targets from Syria.

The shell of Palestinian teamwork began to crack in 2005 when 'Arafat's successor, Mahmud 'Abbas – also from Fatah – reaffirmed the PA's commitment to nonviolence in tacit appreciation for the major contributions by the US and European governments to the PA's 1.6-billion dollar budget.

In early 2006, the Palestinians in the Occupied Territories held elections for the Palestinian Legislative Council. The surprise winner was Hamas, on a platform of a Palestinian state based on the sharia, and membership in the "Arab and Muslim nation". The victory was due to Hamas's superior organization, plus widespread recognition that the Oslo process was a fraud. It came as a shock to Washington, which immediately launched a campaign against Hamas: *Vanity Fair,* April 2008.

With Khalid Mish'al exiled in Damascus, Isma'il Haniyyah was sworn in as Prime Minister of the Palestine Authority – in direct opposition to Chairman Mahmud 'Abbas, since Intifadah II, muted but not extinct, still had Hamas endorsement.

By June 2006, the Palestinian power struggle had escalated into armed clashes between Fatah and Hamas militias. In June 2007, as reported in *The Nation* of 5/25/09 by Helena Cobban, an effort by Fatah's Muhammad Dahlan to deploy his CIA-armed and CIA-trained forces for the takeover of the Gaza Strip was overwhelmed by the forces of Hamas. On the West

Bank, the forces of Mahmud 'Abbas and Salam Fayyad continued to hold out. If Washington had not sent arms to Fatah (paid for by America and Saudi Arabia), and Israel had not carried out mass imprisonment of Hamas principals, Hamas might have taken over Arab conurbations in the West Bank as well.

King 'Abdallah of Saudi Arabia took a position between the US and Hamas by sponsoring the Mecca Agreement, aimed at reconciliation between the two Palestinian factions: David Ottaway, *Foreign Affairs*, May 2009.

The ideological disunity of the resistance was manifest at Palestinian funerals in the simultaneous display of the yellow flag of Fatah, the green flag of Hamas, the black flag of Islamic Jihad, and the red flag of the PFLP – but no Palestinian flag.

By early 2008, Jackson Diehl reported to *The Washington Post* that the 'Abbas administration was little more than a shell kept in place by the IDF; one of 'Abbas's officials went so far as to hint that an Israeli raid into the Gaza Strip might help. *The New York Times* reported that the 'Abbas faction of the Palestine Authority was paying salaries to its employees in the Gaza Strip, but that territory was under the stricter and more decisive control of Hamas – despite occasional clashes with pro-Fatah hold-outs. By summer, Hamas was arresting and abusing Fatah activists in Gaza, and Fatah was reciprocating on the West Bank. In Jerusalem an American military mission was trying to solidify 'Abbas's regime by training a presidential guard.

In February 2009 'Abbas's Presidency was due to expire, but in 2010 he was still in office. His position was highly precarious: The members of the PLO Central Committee who had elected him were his appointees. He was still committed to the moribund two-state solution; observers were wondering how long he could survive the blatant kiss-of-death compliments being showered on him from Washington.

Hamas Against the Diarchy

Although the mounting demographic threat had led Israel to bite the bullet in 2005 by withdrawing its several thousand settlers from the Gaza Strip, it considered that tiny piece of real estate too close to Tel Aviv and Jerusalem to be cut loose. The only immediate alternative was the grueling assignment of trying to cage in the 1.5 million Gazans (40 percent indigenous families, 60 percent refugee families from the 1948 war). As Rashid Khalidi pointed out in the *Times,* Israel's two-pronged campaign to neutralize them by military reprisal and economic deprivation was doubly felonious under the Fourth Geneva Convention, as collective punishment and dereliction of the obligations of an occupying power. In *Counterpunch* Kathleen and Bill Christison quoted Sara Roy that Israel seemed bent on denying the people of the Strip a solid economic base.

Having chosen American subsidy over facing Egyptian indigence alone, the Mubarak regime was condemned to following Israel's lead in sealing the border, with one crucial exception: It would probably have been political suicide to shut down the Gazans' shifty network of tunnels under the border – their only independent access to the outside world.

In early 2005, Mahmud 'Abbas had concluded with Sharon a *tahdi'ah* (truce) that would have marked the end of Intifadah II but for the subsequent split between Fatah and Hamas, the Hamas takeover in Gaza, and the refusal of Acting Prime Minister Olmert to negotiate with a government that would not recognize Israel. Washington, suddenly disenchanted with Arab democracy, backed Israel's intention to expunge Hamas.

The Israeli strategy, by closing the border crossings to the Gaza Strip from Israel and Egypt, was to starve the Islamists out of office. Overlooking their historic responsibility for the subsistence of the Palestinian refugees, Washington and its submissive Europe allies went along. By mid-2006 they had cut off financial aid and public and private loans to the PA, while Israel was blocking Gazan exports and had suspended transfer of the Gazan tax and customs receipts it had been importunately collecting on behalf of the PA. The suspension prevented the PA from meeting the payrolls of its 138,000 employees. UN Human Rights investigator Richard Falk was barred from entry to the territory.

On June 25, 2006, under intolerable pressure from unpaid civil servants, Hamas staged an attack along the Gaza-Israel border, abducting an Israeli soldier, Gilad Shalit, whose whereabouts was still unknown at this writing. The immediate objective was to retaliate for Israel's recent seizure of two Gazans, and to swap the Israeli abductee for some of the thousands of Palestinian prisoners in Israeli jails. Hamas succeeded in its more fundamental interest in getting world attention; Iran and Qatar pledged compensatory aid.

In late June of 2006 Israel stepped up the pressure on the Hamas regime: ground action in northern Gaza, air strikes that damaged bridges and knocked out Gaza's only power station, and putting 64 Hamas members of the PA cabinet and legislative council in jail. Washington vetoed the UNSC's call on Israel to withdraw its troops from the Strip.

In 2007, Israel released 100 million dollars in tax receipts to the Fatah faction of the PA. On the Gazan front, hostilities continued. Islamic Jihad, responsible for most of the recent suicide bombings in Israel, claimed a

January 29 action that killed three Israelis. In April, southern Israel was under fairly steady fire from Hamas rockets and mortars, while Israel had set aside the Oslo guarantees by blocking travel between Gaza and the West Bank.

In June 2007, according to *The Wall Street Journal,* Hamas's takeover of Fatah's offices in the strip led to the discovery of documentary confirmation of Fatah collaboration with the CIA, including the targeting of Palestinian Islamists for assassination. *The London Review of Books* reported that, from 2000 through 2006, Israeli forces had killed 339 Gazans, most of them from helicopters. The Israeli offensive had failed; Hamas was more firmly entrenched than before the attack: *New Yorker,* January 2008, Lawrence Wright.

Meanwhile, borders remained closed, supplies of electricity and fuel had been cut back, bank transactions halted, imports reduced, exports shut down, water and sewerage services impaired, schools and hospitals crippled, employment negligible, building materials embargoed, and Gazans condemned to living with destitution and a moldering infrastructure. An Israeli buffer zone blocked access to thirty percent of arable land. The sea front was fouled with sewage. With Gazan export crops rotting in the fields, UNRWA was feeding 825,000 refugees, and the World Food Program was feeding 250,000 non-refugees. *Counterpunch* of 2/1/08 accused Egypt of halting NGO shipments of food and medicine to the Gazans.

In January 2008 Hamas blew holes in Egypt's security fences, and Gazans had eleven days of riotous access to shops across the Egyptian border.

Hizballah Against the Diarchy

Although Hizballah was a Lebanese Shiite organization, it proclaimed a broader mission: the defense of Lebanon, and the promotion of an independent Palestine. The withdrawal of Israeli forces from Lebanon in 2000 did not alter the Israeli view of Hizballah as a deadly enemy. Four issues were uppermost:

Prisoners - Hizballah had negotiated the release of over 400 Lebanese and Palestinian detainees in 2004, but Israeli prisons still held a few Lebanese (perhaps including Shaykh Mustafa Dirani, abducted in 1994 from a Hizballah training center in the Biqaʿ) and 9,000 Palestinians.

Shabʿah Farms - Under UNSC Resolution 425, Israel was to evacuate Lebanese territory. However, Israel held on to a ten-square-mile enclave on the claim that it had been part of the Syrian Golan, hence subject to UNSC Resolution 242. The UN concurred, but Lebanon claims the territory (with Syrian approval) on the grounds that most of the land therein is owned by

Lebanese citizens. Most of them are residents of the village of Shab'ah, which is on the Lebanese side of the cease-fire line. Habib Battah pointed out in *The Washington Report on Middle East Affairs* that they are Sunnis, so adherents of the pro-Hariri faction.

War of Assassination - In 1992 Israel used a helicopter (US-made) to kill Hizballah leader 'Abbas al Musawi. Hizballah retaliated by widening the scope of its spasmodic Katyusha rocket attacks from Shab'ah Farms to include Israel proper, and it was the suspected perpetrator of deadly bombings of the Israeli Embassy in Buenos Aires in 1992 and 1994. In May 2006 two reputed officials of Islamic Jihad died in Sidon. A Lebanese confessed to having killed them under orders from Israeli intelligence (Mossad).

Armament - Since its founding by the Iranian Revolutionary Guard in 1982 (Chapter 12), Hizballah's militia had obtained most of its weapons from the Guard, by way of Syria. The camps of its soldiers and trainees (including teenagers known as Boy Scouts, although not internationally affiliated) prominently feature portraits of the late Iranian Supreme Guide, Ayatollah Khomeini.

On July 12, 2006, seventeen days after the Hamas action on the Gazan border, Hizballah forces, under standing instructions to exploit any opportunity to take Israeli prisoners, happened on an IDF patrol that had wandered out of range of its security cover. In the ensuing clash, eight Israeli soldiers were killed and two were abducted. The incident followed a long-time pattern of friction along the frontier, except that this time the Lebanese party went into Israeli territory. It seems Hizballah had no inkling that the attack was to trigger a pending Israeli reaction plan.

On the following day Israel launched an air and ground campaign intended to eliminate Hizballah as a military threat. The assault had the full support of the Bush administration, which according to a *New Yorker* article by Seymour Hersh regarded Hizballah's missiles as a Damoclesian threat to Israel in the event of an American attack on Iran's nuclear sites. The Israeli offensive met punishing resistance from militiamen armed with Iranian-made rockets and Russian-made antitank and antihelicopter weapons, operating from well-concealed bunkers carved into the mountainous terrain. Israel then supplemented its operations in south Lebanon with a massive air attack on diverse targets in the cities of Tyre, Sidon, and Beirut, in an effort to depopulate south Lebanon, destroy Shiite communities, and turn non-Shiite communities against Hizballah. Hizballah responded with a constant rain of primitive Katyusha rocket fire on northern Israel, plus firing at least one Iranian C-802 cruise missile that damaged an Israeli warship and killed four crewmen.

By July 22, Israel's frustrated command had added schools and mosques to its air targets, called up the reserves (who arrived at the front poorly equipped for combat), opened a second air front against Gaza, and asked for replacement munitions from Washington, which readily complied. On July 18 House of Representatives Resolution 921 condemned the Hamas and Hizballah abductions and endorsed the Israeli offensive 410-8, despite the indiscriminate damage the Israeli air force was doing to the whole Lebanese coastal area as far north as Beirut.

Washington resisted pressure from its European allies for a cease-fire until August 13, when it gave in and accepted UNSC Resolution 1701, which made no reference to disarming the forces of Hizballah but called on Israeli forces to withdraw as Lebanese and UN forces moved in to the area of combat. The UN Interim Force in Lebanon (UNIFIL), which had maintained a contingent of 2,000 in south Lebanon since 1978, was statutorily committed to neutrality, but some Israelis suspected it of leaking intelligence to Hizballah. (Since 1967 a neutral strip along the quiet Syria-Golan frontier has been policed by the UN Disengagement Observation Force – UNDOP. *Asia Times Online* reports that Al Qunaytirah, razed in the June War of 1967, has never been rebuilt; Syria keeps the city in ruins as incontestable evidence in the event of future negotiations with Israel.)

Israel lifted its air and sea blockade of Lebanon in early September 2006, and completed troop withdrawal in October. The bodies of the two abducted soldiers were exchanged for five prisoners of the Israelis on July 16, 2008, a day proclaimed as a Lebanese national holiday. One of the five was Samir Quntar, a Druze operative of the PFLP who was reviled in Israel as having caused the deaths of three Israeli civilians, including an infant inadvertently smothered by its terrified mother.

Implications of the Hizballah War

The Israeli campaign of 2006 was intended to free the two hostages, expel Hizballah's forces from south Lebanon, disarm them, and cut off their resupply from Iran and Syria. A later addition to the list was termination of the missile barrage against northern Israel.

Despite the deaths of 1200 Lebanese and the temporary displacement of a million Shiites from the south, none of the basic objectives was accomplished. Hizballah emerged with its command and control systems intact – even its TV station, Al Manar (The Minaret). In contrast with previous anti-Israel campaigns by the Palestinians, who tried to build a conventional army, Hizballah conducted a skilled guerrilla operation. The Israeli offensive was poorly conceived and executed. Result: Military defeat for Israel, political defeat for the United States.

In the analyses of Augustus Richard Norton and Abbas William Samii, Hasan Nasrallah demonstrated after the Israeli evacuations of 2000 and 2006 the leadership to rein in retaliation against Christian collaborators, to show respect for the Lebanese Army, and to direct reconstruction with probity and intersectarian harmony.

Overreach

Israel is the ranking military power in the Middle East, with technological superiority on the ground and total mastery of the air. It has established this preeminence in five conventional wars: 1948, 1956, 1967, 1970, and 1982. It has always had the capacity to occupy territory outside Palestine – as demonstrated in Sinai in the winter of 1956-57, and again from 1967 to 1979, and in southern Lebanon from 1978 to 2000.

Israel could have resorted to the same strategy to expel the forces of Hizballah from south Lebanon in 2006. However, given the incidental nature of the provocation, full mobilization would have been controversial, and the abortive conclusion of the three previous expansions gave warning that expansion beyond the de facto Israel-Lebanon frontier, which aside from the Golan coincides with the frontier of mandatory Palestine, is either politically or militarily infeasible.

This consideration presumably militated in favor of the decision of the Olmert government in 2006 to deal with Hizballah by remote control – a combination of calibrated forays by ground troops and selective strikes by the air force. In so doing, Israel committed itself to an asymmetric war, in which air action is usually counterproductive, and guerrillas have the key advantage of operating on their home ground. Unified by the leadership of Shaykh Hasan Nasrallah, and fighting from defenses reportedly constructed under the competent direction of 'Imad Mughniyah, Hizballah managed to keep its own casualties on an approximate par with those of the IDF. If Syria has lately supplied Hizballah with late-model Scud SSM's (*Times*, 4/15/10), Israel will have to rethink any future action against Hizballah.

Americans are likely to look back on Iraq and Afghanistan as theaters where their own forces paid a high price to learn the same lesson of overreach.

Shock and Awe

The tenacity of the opposition goaded Israel into reactions whose military value was nullified by their political cost. The destruction visited on the Shiite quarter of Beirut (the Dahiyah) was condemned by Amnesty International. Human Rights Watch deplored attacks on civilians as violations of the laws of war. UNIFIL personnel deplored relentless air strikes on an observation post, whose four officers were killed. Air strikes on hospitals, a refugee convoy, and infrastructural targets, including a power station and the oil depot at Jiyyah, were widely viewed as unjustified, since in sectarian Lebanon most of Israel's victims had no responsibility for the actions of Hizballah (even if they were ready to celebrate any successful consequences). Israel's decision, late in the conflict, to sow south Lebanon with single-fused cluster bombs of lasting lethality was ascribed to sheer vindictiveness.

Backlash Against the US

Robotic endorsement of Israel's objectives forces America to share in Israel's successes and failures. The Hizballah War was Israel's worst setback in its 60-year history. By Washington's obstinate support for the ill-conceived initiative, its position in the Arab and Muslim worlds was undermined and its pose as a valid mediator in the Arab-Israeli dispute was further discredited.

Broader US objectives also took a hit. As Middle East authority Juan Cole emphasized, instead of weakening the Shiite alliance of Hizballah, Syria, and Iran, the war brought Shias and Sunnis closer together. Hizballah's stubborn resistance reinforced its stance as defender of Lebanon, gave it an opportunity to be the first non-Palestinian force to dedicate a military operation to the Palestinian cause, and made Shaykh Hasan Nasrallah a folk hero across the region.

Pro-American regimes lost face. Whereas Seymour Hersh had reported a long-term clandestine American effort to unite Jordan, Egypt, and Saudi Arabia against Iran, Washington's blatant favoritism for the Israeli effort to destroy Hizballah compelled the Saudi foreign minister to make a trip to Washington to plead against the administration's opposition to an early cease-fire in Lebanon.

Hamas Against the Diarchy: Round Two

On June 19, 2008, Hamas and Israel agreed on a six-month cease-fire, under which Israel eased border-crossing controls, and Hamas suspended rocket fire into Israel. In the assessment of Uri Avnery, the cease-fire amounted to de facto Israeli recognition of Hamas, and evidence that the level of conflict between them was a draw – even though the Gazans were encased in a carapace perforated only by some 200 tunnels.

On November 4, as reported by Roger Cohen in *The New York Review of Books* and Henry Siegman in *The London Review of Books,* Israel broke the truce by a lethal raid against one of the tunnels. Hamas resumed rocket attacks on southern Israel, now supplementing its home-made Qassams with longer-range Katyushas. Israel resumed the embargo on the supply of all but a trickle of essential food and medicine, and intercepted welfare payments from Fatah's PA to its personnel in the Strip. On December 27, Israel unleashed a ground offensive and an air campaign that destroyed almost every public building in Gaza – even the American International School and the science lab at Islamic University. On its own border, Egypt set up machine gun posts to deter Gazan flight from the combat zone.

On January 4, 2009, the Bush administration blocked a UNSC call for a cease-fire. On the West Bank, America's Fatah protégés were repelling pro-Hamas demonstrators with tear gas. In a radio address, Bush 43 had unhelpfully identified Mahmud 'Abbas as the legitimate leader of the Palestinian people. A cease-fire finally took effect January 19. Israel had lost 13 dead. Gaza had lost 1300. On February 10 UN Secretary General Ban Ki-Moon demanded that Israel end its restraints on the passage of relief supplies. On the Egyptian border, the business of tunnel repair was already under way.

Once again, an Israeli military offensive had failed in its objectives. Once again, the aftermath of Israeli-Palestinian hostilities had featured damaging backlash against the lethality of Israeli tactics: the 100-1 ratio of Palestinian to Israeli deaths; collateral casualties from phosphorus smoke shells and Dense Inert Metal Explosives (DIME); the "denial of access to medical personnel" (Amira Hass, *London Review of Books,* 2/26/09); firing on rescue vehicles and personnel; gunning down of bewildered bystanders; allowing extremist rabbis to preach vindictive doctrine to the soldiers.

All this was summed up in an unusually critical article in the 3/19/09 *Times* under the grave headline "Israel Confronts Deeper Isolation In Gaza's Wake".

In March 2009 Israel was allowing the entry of 70 supply trucks a day, probably in deference to Washington's efforts to resuscitate the "peace process". *The London Review of Books* reported that Western and Arab governments at a donors conference had pledged some three billion dollars for Fatah's PA.

On July 2, 2009, Amnesty International accused both Hamas and Israel of war crimes: Hamas for rocketing Israeli civilians, Israel for mounting an onslaught of unwarranted scale and intensity. Human Rights Watch had reported evidence that Israeli drone aircraft had launched six missile strikes that killed 29 Gazan civilians. Israel and Hamas agreed that over a thousand Gazans had died in the three-week conflict, but disagreed on the number of noncombatant deaths.

On October 16, 2009, The UN Human Rights Council endorsed the Goldstone Report of September 2009, which charged Hamas with rocketing Israeli civilians, and Israel with executing civilians and attempting to cripple Gaza's economy and sow desperation among its people. Russia and China concurred. The UNGA endorsed the report in November.

More disciplined than Fatah, Hamas continued to maintain law and order, and license traffic to Egypt through hundreds of tunnels; Gaza's Bank of Palestine was electronically linked with the Nablus, Cairo, and Dubai stock markets: *Times*, 10/22/09; *London Review of Books*, 10/22/09, Nicholas Pelham; *New York Review of Books*, 11/5/09, Max Rodenbeck. Washington continued to parrot the Israeli position that dialogue with Hamas was rejected until Hamas renounced violence and recognized Israel. In other words, Washington endorsed Israeli violence in violation of international law, but denounced violence on the part of the victims.

The Blockade of Gaza

Since the takeover of the Gaza Strip by Hamas in June 2007, Israel has blockaded the territory by land, sea, and air. The professed objective is to cut off arms supply to the "terrorists", but implementation has been so ruthless that it suggests Israeli intent to tear down the Gazan entity piece by piece until the Hamas leadership is forced out — regardless of the consequences for its million and a half wretched residents.

While authorities in Washington and European capitals seemed unconcerned by this medieval performance, Muslim exasperation mounted. The tipping point was when well-placed Turkish elements reinforced, with money and personnel, the feeble flotillas that altruistic Western volunteers had been launching against the maritime component of the blockade. History was made, it seems, by the coincidence of two otherwise unrelated events — the Israeli blockade of Gaza, and the seismic redirection of Turkish foreign policy from cultivating new ties with the West to renewing old ties with the Arab East.

On May 31, 2010, the rightist administration in Jerusalem characteristically overreacted against the latest foray, "Gaza Freedom Flotilla", by staging a boarding operation by commandos who, in the process of detaining the six ships and their several hundred passengers (most of them unarmed), managed to kill nine Turks on the lead ship.

The resultant outburst has achieved official relaxation of the Israeli position, and it focused unprecedented condemnation on the blockade. The UN High Commissioner for Human Rights, Navi Pillay, asserted an "almost unanimous international view that the Gaza blockade is illegal."

Russia charged Israel with "violation of the norms of international law." In response to public outrage, the Arab League, lowest common denominator of Arab audacity, boldly sent Secretary General Amr Moussa to Gaza to visit Hamas Prime Minister Haniyyah (at his home, not his office) with a call for an end to the Israeli siege. Turkish Prime Minister Erdogan charged Israel with state terrorism, and sent Foreign Minister Davutoglu to New York to demand action from the Security Council.

UNSC Resolution 1860, even as watered down by the Obama administration, called for an end to the blockage of Gaza. International opinion seemed to be coalescing behind the thesis that the blockade, legal or not, is politically unsustainable.

In the center of the firestorm was the Mubarak regime, whose antipathy to Arab Islamism and reliance on American money had made it a de facto collaborator in the blockade — reportedly even to the extent of planning to block Gaza's tunnel system by installing a US-designed steel barrier sixty feet deep along Egypt's nine-mile border with Gaza. Shaken by the impact of the May 31 episode, Cairo not only deferred the underground barrier project, but also cracked the border blockade to allow easier passage by selected Gazans.

The Survival of Israel

Israel is vibrant, affluent, and powerful – and yet it has had to be on perpetual guard against the resentment of its Arab subjects and the rivalry of its neighbors (Chapter 16). Although Israel's oppression of its stateless vassals seems morally indefensible and, in the long term, politically unsustainable, the prospects of a near-term resolution of the Israeli-Palestinian conflict, either by force or negotiation, are minuscule. In contrast with the circumstances that facilitated the Camp David Agreement, Israel and the Palestinians are locked in a zero-sum confrontation. Israel's adamant grip on the West Bank has been demonstrated by its draconian restrictions on Palestinian movement between the West Bank and the Gaza Strip, and by Netanyahu's rejection of Obama's minimalist request that Israel suspend its claim to the right to add housing units in East Jerusalem and to meet the natural population growth of the settlements.

In the *Times* of 6/22/09, Tony Judt estimated the number of settlements on the West Bank at 200-220. Under Israeli regulations, 120 were "official", but in Judt's opinion all violate Article 47 of the Fourth Geneva Convention prohibiting territorial annexation consequent to the use of force. The Israelis counter that there has been no annexation (except East Jerusalem), and no country in the sense specified in Article 47. This debate is probably academic, since the ownership of Palestine is likely to be resolved, not by international compact, but by the slow grind of the mills of the geopolitical gods.

Against the Palestinian challenge, Israel has five optional defenses:

Military Rule - East Jerusalem and the West Bank are heavily garrisoned. The Gaza Strip is enclosed by a cordon of Israeli ground, air, and naval forces. Before these forces moved out to the periphery, they systematically destroyed roads, wells, water tanks, power lines, homes, and synagogues.

Under military cover, Iraeli has steadily expanded the Jewish settlements in the West Bank. The *Times* of 6/2/09 reported that over the previous forty years they had been growing at a rate of 1500-2000 housing units per year. Some 59,000 units had been built, and building permits for another 46,500 had been approved.

Since the eruption of Intifadah II in 2000, Israel has imprisoned thousands of Palestinian dissidents and assassinated over 400 leaders of the resistance. Checkpoints, dedicated roads, and barriers have made Greater Israel the world's biggest gated community. Few Zionists advocate this way of life as permanent.

Attrition - Another central element of Israeli strategy has been a climate of harassment and repression intended to goad Arabs into emigrating. It has failed. According to Abunimah's statistics, non-Jews already outnumber Jews in Greater Israel. However many resistance leaders Israel kills, resistance to Zionist discipline seems irrepressible.

Ethnic Cleansing - Israel's two mass expulsions of 1948 and 1967 intensified Arab hatred, without reversing the demographic tide. A third such operation appears infeasible except in the context of a regional war – which Washington tells us will not happen.

Partition - Ever since 1947, most outside observers have advocated the two-state solution prescribed in UNGA Resolution 181 – as professors Mearsheimer and Walt did until recently, and Carter and Obama still did at this writing. It is the official goal of the Middle East Peace Quartet (US, European Union, Russia, and the UN). As of February 2009, Israel's friends in Congress were willingly funding the program of US Lt. General Keith Dayton to train Fatah's National Security Force, which is intended to suppress Hamas, and has already been used to inhibit pro-Hamas demonstrators in the West Bank from clashing with Israeli forces.

Israel's professions of support for the two-state solution seem to be window-dressing – a strategy that appeases Washington, while imposing conditions the Palestinians could never accept. With the Middle East in the throes of a 300-year power struggle, the future of any of its components is beyond prediction. For a Zionist regime, cession of the heart of Palestine to an imponderable foreign entity would be foolhardy. It is hard to visualize the tiny Gaza Strip as a mortal threat, but even here Israel has clung to hegemony (including control of ID's, passports, health care, movement, trade, and tax system). Zionism seems to be a recipe for endless war.

In December 2008, Jonathan Cook reported a talk by Kadima's Tzipi Livni that cast new insight on the Israeli concept of partition: When a Palestine state is created, the national solution for Israeli Arabs will be "in another place." This language seems to blend two time-honored Zionist goals: apartheid, and conversion of Jordan to the Palestinian state.

Assimilation - Elimination of the unpromising strategies cited above reduces the options to one: the process that smelted Britons, Danes, Saxons, and Normans into Englishmen, and countless blood streams into Americans. How can we expect Jews and Arabs, living side by side, to stem the irresistible forces of genetic and cultural amalgamation? Granted, these forces operate at a glacial pace, but they can be accelerated by open minds – as America dramatically showed the world in the Presidential election of 2008.

The path to assimilation in Palestine is being illuminated by a few long-range thinkers – like Abunimah (*One Country*), Bernard Avishai (*The Hebrew Republic*), Meron Benveniste, Avraham Burg, Tony Judt, Joel Kovel (*Overcoming Zionism*), Saree Makdisi (*Palestine Inside Out*), and Virginia Tilley (*The One-State Solution*) – and by pioneer institutions like Adalah and the Hand in Hand School.

With the Jews of Israel still in the thrall of the Zionist mystique, and Jews and Arabs separated by a cultural abyss, assimilation will take decades, if not centuries, but the detention of stateless victims in wretched holding pens in Occupied Palestine and ghettos in Jordan, Lebanon, and Syria is not a permanent solution.

Table C summarizes the demographics of Greater Israel. Three conclusions emerge:

With a population density over 1000 per square mile, the arid land of Palestine is already at or near its carrying capacity.

Although a majority of the Palestinian diaspora in the region (300,000 in Lebanon, 340,000 in Syria, 450,000 in Arabia, 2,200,000 in Jordan) have not been assimilated, prospects for return to Palestine are invisible.

Jews may already be a minority in Greater Israel, and face the contingency of becoming a minority in Israel proper.

Orthodoxy in the IDF

The unwritten alliance between Israel's government and Rabbinate has been exemplified by the IDF, which keeps its mess halls kosher, and equips every base with a synagogue: Stuart Cohen, *Israel and Its Army.* Eyal Press reports that over a quarter of young officers now wear skull caps: *New York Review,* 4/29/10.

Table C: Area and Demography of Greater Israel (2009)

Political Unit	Area	Jews	Arabs	Total Pop'n
Israel	8,000	5,400,000	1,400,000	6,800,000
East Jerusalem	25	200,000	250,000	450,000
West Bank (Jewish lands)	1,350	280,000		280,000
West Bank (Arab lands)	900		2,500,000	2,500,000
Gaza Strip	140		1,500,000	1,500,000
Golan	480	18,000	20,000	38,000
Total	**10,895**	**5,898,000**	**5,670,000**	**11,568,000**

(These estimates will not coincide with those in Table A.)

Chapter 9
Iraq: The Most Difficult State

Mesopotamia (Greek for "the Land Between the Rivers") has the three requisites of human habitation: arable land, a dependable supply of water, and a livable climate. It was the natural cradle of civilization, and should have evolved into a tranquil, prosperous state. What happened? In 2000 Sandra Mackey summed up Iraq as a rural tribal society ravaged by war and sanctions and governed by a tyrant. Analysis of the unhappy country we see today has to start with a dismal catalogue of afflictions. Remediation will take a century or more – and will not be accomplished by a foreign occupier.

Affliction #1: Living on a Frontier

The Middle Eastern geopolity is subdivided by prominent features of its topography. One such is the Zagros Range, long enough (550 miles) and high enough (up to 12,000 feet) to have generated a rarely overridden frontier. For the ancient regional empires (Persian, Alexandrine, Islamic: Chapter 10), it posed no problem; in more recent centuries, Iraq evolved into a *march* – an area of separation between rival cultures. As the eastern flank of the Arab World, it was the arena of recurrent wars – in the early Christian era, between Byzantium and Persia; in later times, between the Ottomans and the Safavids; in the early 1900's, between the Turks and the British; in the 1980's, between Iraq and Iran.

Affliction #2: Periodic Ruination

Iraq is an unfortunate example of the battered-country syndrome. Out of sheer vindictiveness, it seems, Hulegu's Turk armies laid waste

209

to Iraq (and Persia) in 1258. They killed the last Abbasid Caliph, burned Baghdad – including the priceless contents of its library, killed 800,000 residents, and destroyed the irrigation system. It took the country 700 years to recover.

In 1733, 100,000 Baghdadis starved to death during a siege by the Qajar Dynasty of Persia.

In the 1990's and early 2000's, Iraq's infrastructure was devastated, and its records and antiquities ravaged, by the sequence of two American ground actions, "surgical" air strikes, punitive economic sanctions, and America's post-invasion failure to honor the security obligations of an occupying power (Chapter 15). The expulsion of the Iraqi forces from Kuwait in 1991 precipitated a Shiite uprising which dictator Saddam put down by military force and environmental atrocity – draining most of the marshland where hundreds of thousands of "Marsh Arabs" had pursued a unique life style for centuries.

Affliction #3: Communalism

The tribulations enumerated in Chapter 6 apply quintessentially to Iraq, which sits on two major geopolitical faults – the sectarian division between Shia and Sunni Muslims, and the deeper linguistic divisions among Arabs, Turkmens, and Kurds. Most Kurds live in the uplands of the north. Most of the southerners are Shia. The Sunnis, the traditional ruling class, are most numerous in the region around Baghdad. Underneath these generalizations lie numerous complexities: There were two million Shia and a million or two Arabized Kurds in pre-occupation Baghdad, and one million Sunnis in Mawsil. Although there is a predilection among Iraqis to marry first or second cousins, intermarriage across ethnic lines is not uncommon. Prominent offspring of such unions included dictator 'Abd al Karim Qasim, politician Ahmad Chalabi, and some relatives of Saddam Husayn. Intertribal relations are complicated by the fact that a tribe may combine members of the Sunni, Shia, or Christian faiths.

The communal picture is clouded further by the presence of smaller minorities, including Christians (Tariq 'Aziz, Saddam's Foreign Minister, was a Chaldean Catholic), Turkmens (Muslims whose linguistic affiliation with the Turks has led Ankara to take a special interest in their welfare), and Yazidis.

A thousand years ago, Baghdad was the intellectual capital of oriental Judaism. Jews felt at home in the land where Abraham was born, Jewish law was codified, and the Talmud was written down. As recently as 1920, 15 percent of the residents of Baghdad were Jews, and they dominated banking. From 1939 on, their security was undermined by German machinations, the decision of Palestinian Hajj Amin al Husayni to take refuge in Baghdad, and the emergence of a Zionist entity in Palestine. In 1941, British troops invaded Iraq to put down the pro-Nazi Rashid 'Ali coup, but according to Adam Shatz took no action to save the Iraqi Jews killed in the ensuing rioting. In 1948 even fully assimilated Jews were compelled by Arab hostility and by bombings (ascribed by some Jews to the Zionist Mossad) to emigrate. Most of the holdouts gave in after the Israeli triumph of 1967 and Saddam's hanging of seven Jewish "spies" in 1969.

Communalism is inseparable from Iraqi politics. In the words of King Faysal I, "There is no Iraqi people." The Ottoman rulers had consolidated ethnic division by dealing with the traditional leaders of millets. In making governmental appointments in their Mesopotamian provinces, they favored their Sunni coreligionists; the downtrodden Shiite community refused to learn Turkish. British rulers perpetuated that pattern. In the natural course of events, Iraq's first enduring dictator, Saddam Husayn, was a Sunni, who ruled through a Sunni power structure. Some analysts blame British misrule for allowing the Sunni elite to reinforce their political preeminence by acquiring title to over half Iraq's usable land. Iraq's Sunni center missed out on the major oil fields, which lie in the south and the north. To rectify this geographic mischance, Saddam instituted a ruthless program to Arabize Kurdish areas by expelling Kurds and resettling Arabs. This enterprise was facilitated by the requirement that every Iraqi carry an ID card that specified ethnic origin. Kurds who refused designation as Arab were relocated.

Ever since the late 1800's, when Shiites became convinced they were a majority in Mesopotamia, they have agitated for a commensurate share of wealth and power. As loyal Iraqis, they could not applaud the American invasion of 2003, but they and the Kurds had to be vastly relieved by the instantaneous obliteration of the Sunni power structure. The consequent dilemma for the American occupiers is examined in Chapter 15.

Affliction #4: Alien Rule

Over 900 years have passed since the subjugation of the Abbasid Empire (Chapter 7), when Mesopotamia was last ruled by Mesopotamians. After a string of Persian, Seljuq, Mongol, and Turkmen rulers, Baghdad fell under Persian (Safavid) rule in 1508, but in 1534 was taken by the Ottomans, who massacred most of the city's Shiites and – excepting a brief interim under the Persians in the 1600's – were to rule the country for the next five centuries.

Having transformed themselves from central Asian barbarians to Middle Eastern Muslims, the Ottomans gave their Arab subjects a respectable degree of autonomy and some career opportunities in the service of the empire: Iraqis were the largest Arab component in the Ottoman army. However, the Ottomans trod on the rights of the Shia, colluded in the rise of absentee Sunni landlords, and in their final impotence, lost the whole country to the British in World War I.

Like the Americans ninety years later, the British came as "liberators". Acting on the imperialist strategy of breaking up the eastern Arab World into fragments small enough to control but big enough to exploit, they assembled the country out of three Ottoman provinces (Mawsil, Baghdad, and Basrah), expanded in the north to include the oil fields, truncated in the south to minimize the risk that some future Iraqi government would control too much oil, or throw its weight around in the Persian Gulf. The Arabists resurrected its elegant classic name – *'Iraq* ("noble lineage"). The Iraqi Arabs resisted en masse. Colonial Secretary Winston Churchill advocated the use of chemical weapons. Whether mustard gas was actually used is a subject of debate. The prolific use of artillery and air power is documented. After several months, the deployment of 200,000 British troops, and the loss of 10,000 Arab lives, the revolt was snuffed out.

Under British High Commissioner Sir Percy Cox, Faysal I established a Hashemite monarchy alongside that of his brother 'Abdallah in Jordan. The Iraqi "Mandate" ended in 1932, when Iraq joined the League of Nations. Iraq was a founding member of the United Nations in 1945, even though it could not be classified as independent until 1958, when Britain's puppet regime was overthrown. British imperialism left Iraq two legacies: control of the Kirkuk oil fields, and restricted access to the Gulf. The first was meant to enrich Britain; the second was meant to inhibit the emergence of a troublesome Iraq. Neither succeeded in its purpose.

As of this writing, Iraq had fallen under the domination of still another alien regime, the United States.

Affliction #5: A Violent Society

Violence and political evolution generally go together, but Patrick Cockburn has observed that Iraq seems unique in its exposure to rioting, looting, and killing. For Elaine Sciolino, its politics are "unusually murderous". In the assessment of Egyptian writer Muhammad Haykal,

"Violence has become ingrained in the Iraqi character." A thumbnail chronology tells the recent story:

1800's - Under the corrupt rule of Da'ud Basha, cities of Iraq were immersed in lawlessness (as recounted by Edwin Black).

1930's - The government and armed forces were riddled with corruption.

1933 - The armed forces committed a massacre of Nestorian Christians, suspected of colluding with the British overlords in the persecution of Iraqi Muslims.

1936 - The first in a series of Iraqi coups – first in the Arab East in the Twentieth Century. Encouraged by King Ghazi, acting Chief of Staff Bakr Sidqi (Kurd) killed Prime Minister Ja'far al 'Askari, and ruled until his own assassination. Anglophile Nuri al Sa'id (al 'Askari's brother-in-law) succeeded him as the effective leader of Iraq.

1939 - King Ghazi died in a car crash whose circumstances were never satisfactorily explained to the public. An irate mob lynched a British Consul. Prince 'Abd al Ilah (another Hashemite) became regent.

1941 - Pro-German officer Rashid 'Ali al Kaylani ousted Nuri, 'Abd al Ilah, and young Faysal II. British and Transjordanian forces expelled Kaylani from Iraq (and the Mufti from Palestine) and reinstated the three leaders. These events precipitated anti-Jewish riots in which some 500 Iraqi Jews died.

1948 - Iraqi Shia rebelled against British-Iraqi reaffirmation of their treaty of 1930. The government fell and the new treaty was abandoned.

1954 - Nuri arranged for Faysal II, crowned in 1953 when he reached eighteen, to dissolve parliament, so Nuri could take over as Prime Minister, rig an election, ban political parties, and drive opposition factions underground.

1958 - Brigadier General 'Abd al Karim Qasim led a faction of nationalist officers who overthrew the monarchy and appointed Qasim Prime Minister. Nuri, 'Abd al Ilah, and Faysal II were killed. Although the coup was a sympathetic reaction to the recent unification of Egypt and Syria under Egyptian leader Jamal 'Abd al Nasir, many Iraqis – particularly Shiites – were opposed to the unionist pact concluded in Damascus between Nasir and Qasim's Arab Nationalist Deputy Prime Minister, 'Abd al Salam 'Arif. Within weeks a coalition of Iraqi nationalists and Communists under Qasim ousted 'Arif, and a radio war ensued between Egypt and Iraq.

1959 - The Communist faction overreached, slaughtered opponents in Mawsil, and alienated their ally, Qasim.

1963 - After a four-year power struggle, Baathist and Nasirist officers killed Qasim, appointed 'Abd al Salam 'Arif (Nasirist) as transitional

President and Ahmad Bakr (Baathist) as Prime Minister. The killing of thousands of Communists, in retaliation for the 1959 Mawsil massacre, eliminated what had been the strongest Communist Party in the Arab World.

1963 - A subsequent split in the Iraqi Baath enabled 'Arif to oust its radical faction from the regime.

1966 - Killed in a helicopter crash, 'Abd al Salam 'Arif was succeeded by his brother, 'Abd al Rahman.

1968 - Under Saddam Husayn, the radical wing of the Baath regained power, instituted a brutal purge of Communists and other adversaries, repressed Iraqi Jews, and in 1969 executed some Shiites and deported 20,000 Shiites to Iran. Baathist doctrine called for a secular state. Ethnic groups were to stay out of politics. The ethnic groups refused to comply. The Kurds, who had been resisting Iraqi rule since 1951, disregarded official restraint short of punitive action – which in Iraq went as far, by Elaine Sciolino's account, as torturing children to death.

1969 - Twelve Iraqis, including seven Jews, were hanged on a charge of treason.

1978 - To impress Washington, Saddam arbitrarily executed some more Communists. (According to Tariq Ali, no American newspapers condemned this barbarity.)

1979 - Carter reportedly encouraged Saddam to attack Iran (?).

1980-88 - The long, bloody war with Iran ended in a stalemate.

1991 - The expulsion of Iraqi forces from Kuwait sparked in South Iraq an uprising of Shiites who set out to kill every Baathist official. Saddam's Republican Guard (Sunni) instituted a reign of terror in which over 50,000 Shia died.

2008 - Two citations from Dexter Filkins's *The Forever War* reflected the emotional climate in post-invasion Iraq: a proclamation at a hanging, "In revenge there is life"; episode of a widow drinking the blood of the Al Qa'idah operatives who killed her husband.

Affliction #6: Despotism

Iraq has always been ruled by autocrats: kings, emperors, sultans, dictators, and high commissioners. The institutions that are prerequisites for the evolution of democracy are nonexistent.

Affliction #7: Tribalism

Iraq has not escaped the global trend toward congregation of indigent masses in urban slums. Nevertheless, tribal ties continue to play a major role in Iraqi politics. Tribal leaders benefited from the Ottomans' illiberal laws on ownership of agricultural land, and they used their political influence to extract subsidies from the central government. The bloody revolt against the British in 1920 was waged by the tribes in the hinterland; the urbanites were much more passive, although by the end of the century many had formed ideological ties with the Communist, Nasirist, or Baath parties.

Every post-Ottoman regime – including the American occupation structure – has subsidized the tribal shaykhs. Saddam's campaign to put down the Shiite and Kurdish insurrections of 1991 combined brute force with enhancement of the tribal subsidies. Tribes and tribal courts were restored as legal entities. In return for cash and land, 586 tribal chiefs met with Saddam and swore an oath of fealty. In Sandra Mackey's analysis, the Iraqi Baath had evolved into a tribal confederation. By 2001, many of Iraq's top positions were held by poorly educated tribal leaders.

As Iraq's social structure deteriorated under eight years of war with Iran and twelve years of war with America, an increasing number of its citizens turned to the tribes (and the sectarian organizations) for the means of survival. Saddam relied less and less on the Iraqi Baath, more and more on his power base of relatives and proteges. Iraqi nationalism replaced Arab Nationalism; Islamism replaced secularism. So it is that in the Iraq of the Twenty-First Century, most Iraqis in rural areas and many in the cities pay allegiance to the tribe they came from, and there is a sociological disconnect between the village-dwellers who look first to the tribe, and Westernized urbanites who look first to the central government. One side effect of Iraq's autocratic/tribalistic society is a huge income gap between the impoverished multitude and the privileged few with access to governmental bounty – notably from clandestine licenses to smuggle.

In 2004, the "Sunni Triangle" northwest of Baghdad was a focal point of resistance to the American occupation. The impetus was tribal; Patrick Graham wrote of "an honor-based tribal society where revenge killings are integral to the culture ...." The Sunni clerics played a leadership role.

In 2008, Prime Minister Maliki got into tribal politics on his own account by assembling tribal leaders into "support councils" as backup for his Shiite Da'wah Party.

The Two Faces of Saddam Husayn

In Iraq, as in Egypt and Syria, the military academy has been the route to power for young men from low-income families. In the reign of Faysal I, a well-connected Takriti official steered a disproportionate number of Bu Nasir tribesmen into the Iraqi academy. Hundreds of Sunnis rode this conveyor belt to prosperity and influence.

Saddam didn't make it into the academy, but he was a member of one of the Bu Nasir cells of the Baath; a year later, he served a short prison term for killing a brother-in-law who had joined the Communist Party. In 1959, after having been wounded in a failed conspiracy to kill Qasim, he fled to Egypt, where he studied law, presumably under the patronage of the Nasir regime. After the coup of 1963, he returned to Iraq, only to find that Nasirist 'Abd al Salam 'Arif was jailing Baathists, and Saddam became one of that number. After his release, he was appointed Assistant Secretary General of the Iraqi Baath, with the sensitive clandestine task of rebuilding its party.

In 1968, in a nearly bloodless coup, the Baath ousted 'Abd al Rahman 'Arif and set up a Revolutionary Command Council (RCC) under Saddam's kinsman, Ahmad Hasan Bakr. Wiser and better organized, the new Baath set out under the ruthless direction of Saddam to purge the army of anti-Baathists and build it into an ideological force commanded by officers, many of them from the Takriti tribe, chosen more for political reliability than military expertise. Over the next twenty years, as Saddam consolidated his personal control of Iraq, he did the country valuable service, and serious damage.

On the constructive side, he used oil revenues to institute significant improvement in public services and create an impressive cadre of engineers, doctors, and scientists. By 1990, wrote Michael Massing, the Baath had built Iraq into a powerful nation-state. Education was free, health care was widely available, and the government was providing a monthly ration of inexpensive staples to all applicants, who numbered at least 60% of the population. In 2003 the *Washington Post Weekly* assessed Iraq's food distribution system as the most efficient in the world.

In 1971, the regime had broken up farms larger than 250 hectares, although Dilip Hiro reported a later drive for agricultural self-sufficiency led the regime to reverse that decision. By 2000, *Middle East Policy* reported, Iraq still lacked a modern economy. Political reform was more advanced. The resolutely secular Baath had the support of the Christian community, female illiteracy had been largely eliminated, and women's employment opportunities had been greatly expanded. Saddam enforced religious freedom and promulgated laws to equalize the status of women and men. Iraqis enjoyed better public services and a larger share of government revenue than the ordinary citizens of wealthier neighbors like Iran and Saudi Arabia.

On the negative side, Saddam's personality – undoubtedly scarred by his hard life and Iraq's inherently traumatic environment – evolved from ruthlessness to brutality, if not megalomania. In 1979 he convened a thousand party leaders to a chilling assembly which heard allegations of an anti-regime plot and them watched as 66 suspects were led out of the hall. Executing 21 of them, Saddam instituted a purge of the state hierarchy, sent his mentor Ahmad al Bakr into retirement, had himself appointed Field Marshal and President, and became absolute ruler of Iraq.

In the mid-90's he was Secretary General of the Arab Baath Socialist Party, Chairman of the RCC, Prime Minister, and Commander-in-Chief of the Armed Forces. As the sole candidate for President, he arranged to be elected by nearly 100% of the voters. On the home front, he pushed a personality cult, and relied on intimidation, torture, kidnapping, extortion, and murder to aggrandize his status, repress opposition, and build a police state. He excluded Shia from top government positions and made membership in the Shiite Al Da'wah a capital crime.

With 1.8 million members, Saddam's Baath Party honeycombed the country, Stalin-style, with secret cells that reported to the Regional Committee, which was run by the party. Baathists occupied every key military and civilian position. As a civilian, Saddam schemed to keep the army out of political activism, but primed to intervene on his behalf in emergency – as when the Kurds and Shia rose in 1991. Elaine Sciolino noted that Army officers who became too popular, like Major General Mahir 'Abd al Rashid, hero of the war with Iran, were likely to disappear.

In tribalist Iraq, Saddam's initial entrée to power was his family relationship to top Baathist Ahmad al Bakr. As he built up the party, he consigned crucial positions to relatives from his own Bayjat tribe, and coopted others of Iraq's 150-odd clans by subsidy and license to smuggle. He awarded his two sons responsibilities grossly incommensurate with their abilities and their judgment. As opposition mounted, the admirable tenets of Michel 'Aflaq's Baath were compromised. Foreign affairs were the party's downfall. Saddam's insular outlook and reckless nature led Iraq into three disastrous wars: Debts incurred in the war with Iran goaded him into Kuwait; his attempt to annex Kuwait precipitated the first American invasion; his defiance of post-invasion sanctions and his hostility to Israel brought on the second American invasion – from which Iraq will need decades to recover.

The Iraqi Sunnis

Beneficiaries of hidebound Ottoman and British rule, Sunnis have dominated Mesopotamian/Iraqi politics since 1638. In the Saddam era, the stories of the regime and the Sunnis were essentially congruent. Saddam's trusted (or least suspect) associates in the Iraqi Baath were Sunnis –

including high-ranking military officers and leaders in professions. The personnel of his Republican Guard were almost all Sunnis: Vali Nasr. Over the perilous years, he placed increasing reliance on Sunni tribes like the Bu Nasir in Takrit and the Dulaym in Fallujah and Ramadi. Conversely, there was no need for the Sunnis to organize; their lobby was the regime itself.

By destroying Saddam's power structure, the United States cut the Sunnis adrift. Under the direction of Sunni clerics, tribal leaders, and Baathists, they have taken preliminary steps to organize against the unforeseen Shiite threat to their traditional preeminence. The summer of 2003 witnessed the formation of a Sunni "Patriotic Front" and the resurgence of the Iraqi wing of the Muslim Brotherhood. In January 2004, the press reported the formation of a Sunni Council of State with 160 members.

Of the 25 members of the US-appointed Iraq Governing Council (IGC: Original membership listed in the *Times* of July 14, 2003), there were five Sunnis. The two with Islamist ties chose to take an anti-occupation stance by joining the Sunni Council of State (without resigning from the IGC?). In February 2004, the influential Association of Muslim Scholars announced its opposition to any national election.

The Iraqi Shia

Mesopotamia was the birthplace of Shiism; their histories are intermingled. The fourth Caliph, 'Ali ibn Abi Talib, was killed and buried in Kufah. His son Husayn bin 'Ali was killed in the Battle of Karbala' in 680. Both are revered by Shiites, for whom Husayn's death date is the holiest day in the Muslim calendar (lunar) and his tomb in Karbala' is one of the two holiest sites. Long exclusion from temporal rule has intensified the Shiite mystique of victimization (manifested by the common practice of self-flagellation on the holiest day) and their allegiance to their religious institutions – notably the revered mosques in Karbala', Kufah, and Najaf, the shrine in Samarra', and the Seminary System (*Al Hawzah al 'Ilmiyyah*) in Najaf (Iraq) and Qom (Iran). The Iraqi Hawzah, established around 1000, is the oldest in the world.

In Iraq in 2008 there were five ayatallahs, whose status derives from their reputations for deep learning and sound judgment. Each is a *marji' al taqlid* (source of emulation). The most revered is 'Ali al Sistani, characterized in 2003 in *The New York Review of Books* as the preeminent Shiite cleric in the world. In Iraq, his political handicap is suspicion that he is too responsive to pressure from Tehran.

Major Shiite Factions in Iraq

In post-Saddam Iraq, the dominant problem will be transferring power from the Sunni minority, via the US occupation authority, to the Shiite majority – without breaking up Iraq. This enterprise will be complicated by the deep factionalism within the Shia community itself – as illustrated in May 2004, when a delegation of Sunni clerics paid a courtesy call on Shaykh Muqtada al Sadr, who has implicitly challenged the traditional leadership of the ayatallahs – notably 'Ali al Sistani.

SCIRI/ISCI - In 1982, with official Iranian sponsorship, Shiite exiles from Iraq founded in Iran the Supreme Council of the Islamic Revolution in Iraq (SCIRI – lately changed to ISCI). Since the death of Grand *Mujtahid* (religious authority) Abu al Qasim al Khu'i in 1992, and the assassination of Muhammad Baqir al Hakim in 2003, a key ally of SCIRI is the reclusive Ayatallah Sistani. He has avoided contact with American officials, but his theological associate, 'Abd al 'Aziz al Hakim (successor to his late brother, Muhammad Baqir al Hakim as leader of ISCI) was a member of the IGC.

Sistani is a "quietist" – an advocate of some degree of separation between the clerisy and the government, and consequently an adversary of Ruhollah Khomeini when they both lived in Najaf, and an opponent of theocracy, as instituted by Khomeini in Iran in 1979 and continued by Khomeini's successor, Ali Khamenei. Born in Iran's eastern province of Sistan, Sistani speaks Arabic with an Iranian accent which has been disparaged by his adversaries in Iraq. His wife is Iranian, but his two sons have been raised as Iraqis; Muhammad Rida, the older, is his confidant.

ISCI is anchored in the Iraqi middle class and seems to be the most affluent Shiite faction in the country. Donations from adherents finance the social services which in turn swell the ranks of its followers. It is believed to maintain a liberal position on social issues like the role of women.

The Sadr Faction - In 1957, Muhammad Baqir al Sadr founded *Al Da'wah al Islamiyyah* (The Islamic Call) to promote a unified effort by Sunni and Shia Iraqis to combat secularism, particularly as exemplified by the Baath and the Communist Party. Galvanized by Ruhollah Khomeini's establishment of a theocratic state in Iran in 1979, The Islamic Call agitated for creation of an independent theocracy in Iraq, in opportunistic alliance with rival organizations that favored a universal Islamic state under Khomeini. Suppressed by Saddam in 1980, the party later gave birth to various Shiite factions. Contemporary Prime Minister Maliki's *Da'wah* Party is a smaller secularist offshoot of the organization founded in Iran.

After the failure of Saddam's effort to co-opt the Shia (he awarded them generous subsidies, claimed descent from the Imam 'Ali, and added

Allahu Akbar – God is Great – to the Iraqi flag), he turned to violence, expelling over 15,000 Iraqis of Iranian lineage, torturing and killing Shiite leaders, and finally, in September 1980, invading Iran. Al Da'wah al Islamiyyah reacted with bombings and assassination attempts against the Baathist regime. Saddam retaliated by arrests, torture, deportations, and the hanging of Grand Ayatallah Muhammad Baqir al Sadr (cousin and brother-in-law of the Lebanese Shiite leader, Musa al Sadr, and father-in-law of Muqtada al Sadr.)

In 1999, Saddam's Shiite victims included Muhammad Baqir al Sadr's cousin, Grand Ayatallah Muhammad Sadiq al Sadr, and two of his sons – but not another son, Muqtada al Sadr, who was only in his twenties. Muqtada was still too young and unschooled to compete for leadership on the traditional grounds of religious learning; in the Shiite hierarchy, he was a *Hujjat al Islam,* "authority on Islam". (The author is indebted to Professors Juan Cole and 'Abd al Sattar Jawad for help in determining the honorific.)

Vali Nasr reports that at the seminary Muqtada's obsession with video games earned him the nickname of Mulla Atari; in maturity, he derives enough political respect as a descendant of the Prophet Muhammad, and as the son of one revered martyr and the son-in-law of another, to have attracted a massive cult following in "Sadr City", the teeming Shiite quarter of Baghdad, and several other cities in the south. Samir Dawisha and Adeed Shehata write that Sadr's following is the marginalized lower class. He has the support of Lebanon's Hizballah. In the judgment of Patrick Cockburn, he is a skilled and judicious politician.

There are no current reports of affiliation between Muqtada and any other claimant to Shiite leadership. Muqtada's appeal is to the impoverished masses, who make up in zeal for what they lack in political discipline or military skill. He has organized an ill-trained but impassioned militia (*Jaysh al Mahdi* – JAM: Army of the Divinely Inspired One). Insofar as the Sadr faction has an ideology, it is thought to lean away from Shiite fundamentalism and toward Iraqi nationalism. Ancient enmity between the family of Muqtada Sadr and that of 'Abd al 'Aziz al Hakim of ISCI frustrated Sistani's campaign to form a united Shia front (Chapter 15).

The Struggle for Leadership of the Shiite Community in Iraq

Southern Iraq (ancient Babylonia) centers on the fertile delta created by the two rivers. In the late 1700's, the Shiite government of Ayodhya (now in the Indian state of Uttar Pradesh) financed construction at Hindiyyah of a barrage which enabled a major diversion of the flow of the Euphrates to the sacred but parched city of Najaf, sitting in the desert west of the river. As reported in *The National Geographic,* proximity to a major Shiite pilgrimage site led the new settlers to convert to Shiism, thus swelling Shia ranks in Mesopotamia.

Whereas Sunnis accepted their secularist regime, devout Shiites look for guidance from their religious hierarchy, whose primary responsibility is to interpret the wishes of the reigning Imam. However, as explained by Yitzhaq Nakash in a 2003 issue of *Foreign Affairs,* the twelfth and last Imam is believed to have disappeared centuries ago and to be out of mortal sight until he returns as the Mahdi. In his absence there is broad disagreement on policy.

In their organizational weakness vis-à-vis the Sunnis, and their ambivalence between sectarian loyalty to Iran and national loyalty to Iraq, the Shiites of Iraq have never been able to present a united front to the world. In 1920, the Shiite tribes were in the forefront of the resistance to the British occupation. As the Anglophile king, Faysal I, established control, he marginalized the Shiite community by deporting activist leaders and buying off the compliant ones. In 1935, a Shiite rebellion was brutally suppressed.

In 1974, the Baathist regime secretly executed a number of Shiite leaders; there were more executions in 1980. During the war against Iran, Saddam made a special effort to give recognition to the noteworthy Shiite participation, and to compensate the families of the hundreds of thousands who fell in the service of Iraq. However, the undercurrent of resentment of Sunni domination persisted, and it flared up during Gulf War I of 1991. Chanting slogans against Saddam and Iraq's occupation of Kuwait, Shiite rioters rose against the regime. Disaffected citizens and soldiers, backed by incoming units of SCIRI's Badr Brigade, occupied Basrah, slaughtered numbers of Baathist officials, and proclaimed an Iraqi Islamic Republic.

The insurrection ended almost as soon as it had begun. SCIRI leader Muhammad Baqir al Hakim had returned from Iran to lead it, but as noted in *Middle East Report* his narrow sectarian focus alienated Sunnis, Kurds, and anti-Iranian Shiites – who dominated "Sadr City" in Baghdad. Denied the support of the rural Shia, whose tribal leaders held to their compacts with Saddam, and inhibited by the specter of Iranian expansionism, the rebels were highly vulnerable to Saddam's tanks and helicopters. Tank forces of Saddam's militia of Iranian dissidents (MEK: Chapter 15), helped suppress the Shiite rebels in the south and the Kurdish rebels in the north.

In 2003, the second American invasion created a power vacuum which the Shiites have moved to fill. Early on, misguided American strategy advanced two longtime Washington favorites: Ahmad Chalabi (the Pentagon candidate) and Iyad 'Allawi (the CIA candidate). Neither was able to mobilize any influential following. As if their known defection to Washington was not enough, Christopher de Bellaigue assessed them as too secularist for present-day Iraq.

Under the cautious patronage of Sistani, SCIRI staged huge liberation demonstrations, but it did not join the resistance – perhaps choosing to wait out American obliteration of the Sunni power structure, while making the occupiers' lives difficult by a series of Sistani pronouncements that stymied their elaborate plans for erection of a compliant regime in Baghdad.

Outgunned in the theological arena, Muqtada al Sadr had to preempt in the realm of activism. He was suspected of implication in the post-invasion assassinations of SCIRI notables 'Abd al Majid al Khu'i and Muhammad Baqir al Hakim. (Vali Nasr suspects Sunnis in Hakim's death; Patrick Cockburn agrees, placing responsibility on Al Qa'idah: Chapter 15.) By August of 2003, elements loyal to Muqtada had set up their own system of courts to fill the judicial void left by the collapse of the Sunni regime, and issued a call for the ouster of the Americans and the establishment of an Iraqi theocracy. The funeral of 'Aqilah al Hashimi (who had been a member of the IGC, and was another mysterious victim of the post-invasion violence) was guarded by men from Sadr's JAM.

By early 2004, two Shiite militias confronted each other – JAM and SCIRI's Badr Brigade. The story of Sadr's calculated (?) strategy of backing off in the face of the superior forces of the Americans and their protégés, the army of Maliki's "Iraqi" regime, is told in Chapter 15. In 2009, after six years of turmoil under a frustrated occupation, the intra-Shia power struggle was unresolved.

A Kurdish State: So Near, and Yet So Far

Seventy-five thousand square miles of Turkey, Iran, Syria, and Iraq are a mountain fastness which has been the traditional home of the Kurds – the largest Middle Eastern community that has never had a state of its own.

Two huge obstacles stand in their way: 1) The four post-Ottoman states are dead set against the emergence of a fifth, which would have to make territorial demands on the other four; Ataturk personally opposed the Kurdish homeland provision in the abortive Treaty of Sèvres; 2) Kurdish tribalism has been exacerbated by the same rugged terrain that helped them resist assimilation by Turks, Persians, or Arabs. Since the early 1900's, Kurdish leadership has been contested between two confederations – one led by the Barzani clan, the other by the Talabanis – that speak different dialects (Kurmanji and Sorani) of their Indo-European language.

In the mid-1800's, Ottoman armies dismantled a series of Kurdish principalities. In 1926, the Iraqi monarchy accorded the Kurds certain special rights, but no hint of autonomy. During World War II, Mustafa Barzani's effort to establish a Kurdish state was crushed, and he fled to the Soviet Union. After the fall of the Iraqi monarchy in 1958, he returned with 800 tribesmen and concluded with 'Abd al Karim Qasim an agreement under which Qasim legalized Barzani's Kurdish Democratic Party (KDP) as a counterweight to Qasim's Arab Nationalist rivals. The deal paid off for Baghdad in 1959, when the Barzani Kurds crushed a mutiny by Iraqi army units in Mawsil. At this point, the leadership of Barzani, whose following was largely based in the countryside of the northwestern half of Iraqi Kurdistan, was challenged by Jalal Talabani, who commanded more support among the urban Kurds in the cities of the southeastern half.

The 1960's were disrupted by intermittent Barzani violence against the Iraqi regime, and several abortive efforts by Baghdad to negotiate a compromise between Arab hegemony and Kurdish autonomy. In 1970, the Saddam regime mollified the Iraqi Kurds by promulgating a constitution that described Iraq as a country of two nationalities – Arab and Kurd. This formula failed to resolve the issue of the division of oil revenues. In 1974, the Barzanis, emboldened by clandestine support from Iran and Israel, in collusion with the United States, went back on the warpath in a bid for control of the Kirkuk oil fields. Secretary of State Kissinger was believed to favor backing Kurdish activism as a means of diverting Iraq from providing military support to adversaries of Israel, like Syria during the Yom Kippur War.

In 1975, Barzani and Kissinger were simultaneously frustrated from an unexpected quarter. At an OPEC summit in Algiers, Saddam and the Shah of Iran buried their own hatchet. Iraq renounced its claims to Khuzistan (the Iranian area populated by people of Arab extraction) and ceded control of the Shatt al 'Arab (the channel where the twin rivers merge and flow into the Gulf). In return, the Shah closed the border, terminating the financial and logistic support the Barzanis had been receiving from Iran, Israel, and America. Baghdad took advantage of this situation to hit the Kurds with a major offensive. Mustafa Barzani fled to Iran and died in exile.

New York Times columnist William Safire viewed the Algiers transaction as Iranian betrayal of the Kurds in return for Iraqi participation in OPEC. British writer Patrick Seale reached a different conclusion: In collusion with Israel and the Shah, Kissinger had lured the Barzanis into a rebellion they were not intended to win, but which would prevent Iraq from aiding Syria against Israel, as it had in the 1973 war. Seale felt this cynical strategy had produced a backlash, in that one of Saddam's motives in invading Iran in 1980 was to tear up the 1975 Algiers Agreement.

In 1976 Barzani's ancient rival, Jalal Talabani, formed a second Kurdish party, the Patriotic Union of Kurdistan (PUK): Joost Hilterman, *Middle East Report,* Summer 2008. The Talabani Kurds enjoyed the political support of Iran and the Asad regime in Syria, but neither was of any utility in 1975, when Saddam instituted a cold-blooded expulsion of Kurdish, Turkmen, and Christian residents from the oil field area to southern Iraq, their replacement with Arabs from the south, and the execution of some Kurdish leaders. The United States sat silent through these events. 1978 witnessed another roundup of Kurdish opponents of the Saddam regime.

The Iraq-Iran war of 1980-88 afforded the Iraqi Kurds a new opportunity to pursue their campaign for self-rule. The KDP and the PUK papered over their differences and built up a formidable militia (*Pesh Merga*) with weapons from Iran. However, the Kurds continued to pay the price of their incorrigible tribalism. In 1983, Baghdad exploited the PUK's bid for negotiation by attacking the forces of the KDP and abducting several thousand males who were never seen again. In the ensuing years Baghdad punished the Kurds for their alliance with Iran by a brutal series of mass detentions, executions, and episodes of chemical warfare; it was characteristic of Iraqi politics that some Kurdish tribes still sided with Baghdad. During the war, some 3800 Kurdish villages were emptied, and upwards of 200,000 Kurds killed. (In the interest of balance, it should be noted that – as reported by Nicholas Kristof of the *Times* in 2003 – the Kurds of Turkey, who did not make common cause with any enemy state, have been treated even more brutally than the Kurds of Baathist Iraq.) The Iraqi Kurds have avoided conflict with Turkish forces, and have not interposed resistance to Turkey's periodic intrusions into northern Iraq in pursuit of rebel (PKK) Turkish Kurds.

1988 featured the infamous *Anfal* campaign by Baghdad against rebellious Kurds. In the village of Halabjah, suspected of having sided with Iran in the bitter border war that had been raging for eight years, hundreds of residents died from napalm and chemical-weapon attacks. Over 100,000 rebel Kurds lost their lives during Anfal from action by Iraqi forces and their Kurdish allies.

After Iraq's expulsion from Kuwait in 1991 and Bush 41's ill-considered call for an Iraqi uprising, the Kurds revolted in sync – but not in coordination – with the Shia in the south. Within weeks, they had captured three northern provinces. As in the south, the United States chose not to obstruct Baghdad's repression of the insurrection – until the plight of a million or two Kurds fleeing north from Iraqi attack, but blocked at the Turkish border, became so grave that Washington, London, and Paris felt compelled (in apparent violation of Iraqi sovereignty) to designate that part of Iraq north of the 36th parallel as a No-Fly Zone – off limits to Iraqi military air operations – and to enforce it by an Allied air umbrella based at Incirlik Air Base in Turkey. Washington even felt an obligation to set up a program to feed the 700,000 Iraqi Kurdish refugees in the Kurdish Autonomous Region (KAR) – but not the million who had taken refuge in Iran.

That fall Baghdad evacuated its forces and cut off all government services to the three Kurdish provinces. The Kurds set about establishing all the essential machinery of local government – army, police force, civil service, and a school system that teaches in Kurdish. In 1992 the KDP and the PUK collaborated in the election of a figurehead KAR parliament, although Kurdish leadership was still contested between the Barzanis, based in Irbil, and the Talabanis, based in Sulaymaniyyah. A meeting of Iraqi Kurdish dissidents, convened in Washington by the US Government in the interest of Kurdish reconciliation, was attended by Jalal Talabani, but Mas'ud Barzani declined.

All these events distressed Ankara. They reduced Turkish revenue from trade with Iraq, afforded sanctuary for the PKK, and had constituted the possible nucleus of Kurdish statehood. In their own parochial interest, the KDP and the PUK were collaborating with Turkey against the PKK, even to the point of taking military action against units that sought shelter in Iraq.

1994 witnessed another falling-out – this time over the distribution of customs revenue, notably from tolls paid by trucks carrying diesel fuel through Zakhu to Turkey. The route runs through KDP (Barzani) territory. In 1996, backed by its Iranian neighbors, the PUK was on the point of winning, when the battered KDP turned to Baghdad, whose ground forces reentered the Kurdish zone, drove PUK forces out of Irbil and Sulaymaniyyah, rolled up the CIA's assets in the area (Chapter 15), and reinstated KDP control of the disputed customs revenue. The PKK, stronger than the two Iraqi factions, but much weaker than Baghdad, was unable to intervene. Later in the year, the PUK retook Irbil and Sulaymaniyyah with help from Iranian Revolutionary Guards. In *The Nation* Dilip Hiro reported that the Zakhu customs arrangement was a breach of the UN sanctions on Iraq, but that Washington let it go, being averse to assuming responsibility for financing the Kurdish entity it had just created.

In the eyes of many Iraqi Kurds, the US had now betrayed their cause three times: 1975, 1991, and 1996. On the other hand, the Kurds continued to betray each other. In 1997, the KDP, in compact with Turkey, drove PUK forces out of Irbil and PKK forces out of the KAR. In 1998, the US mediated a truce between the KDP and the PUK, but the KAR remained split between them.

By the middle of 2004, the reconciled Kurds had taken advantage of America's preoccupation with Arab Iraq to come closer than ever before to an independent state. In a sector of the Zagros Mountains comprising 17,000 square miles and 3,500,000 people, an uneasy alliance of Barzanis (KDP) and Talabanis (PUK) was well along in the construction of a Kurdish Autonomous Region. In Baghdad's view, the KAR consists of three provinces (Dahuk, Irbil, and Sulaymaniyyah), but Kurdish pressure was concentrated on a fourth, Ta'mim, home of Kirkuk, the "Kurdish Jerusalem" (primarily because the KAR is indigent and the Kirkuk area produces a third of Iraq's petroleum output).

By 2009 the Kirkuk police force was largely staffed with Kurds, and the KAR was taking every opportunity to expel Arabs from Mawsil and other parts of northern Iraq with the same brutality the Arabs had once inflicted on the Kurds. So far, Kurdish expansionism had not been inhibited by warnings of American intervention, or by the more sobering threat of Turkish intervention. Claiming an obligation to protect the interests of the Turkmen minority, numerous in the Kirkuk area, the Turks are obsessed by the contingency that a Kurdish state in Iraq could galvanize Kurdish nationalism in southeastern Turkey.

No one knows how many Kurds are involved in these speculations. According to various estimates, their distribution is in the following ranges: Turkey- 10-15 million; Iraq- 4-8 million; Iran- 3-5 million; Syria- 1 million or more.

The UN Charter denies UN membership to stateless peoples. The Kurds are not even accorded the observer status held by the Palestine Liberation Organization. Nevertheless, under de facto American protectorate they have made impressive strides toward the acquisition of all the tangible institutions of a sovereign state. As for recognition, America, the adjoining states, and the UN are committed to the preservation of a sovereign Iraq within its present borders.

Iraq-Iran: Bad Fences Make Bad Neighbors

Emboldened, perhaps, by his role as an instrument of American policy, the Shah abrogated in 1969 an agreement of 1937 that specified the east bank of the Shatt al 'Arab as coincident with the Iraq-Iran frontier, and he took advantage of Baghdad's preoccupation with Kurdish insurrection to act in accordance with his claim that the dividing line should be the *thalweg* – the center of the river. In retaliation for Ayatallah al Hakim's refusal to condemn the Shah's position, the Baathist leadership expelled to Iran 20,000 Iraqi Shiites of alleged Persian origin.

The Algiers Accord of 1975 between Saddam and the Shah ostensibly resolved the dispute in Iran's favor, but it set the stage for a later explosion that no one foresaw: As a seemingly incidental consequence of the accord, Saddam in 1978 expelled Grand Ayatollah Ruhollah al Khomeini from Iraq, where he had been agitating against the regime of the Shah. Four months later, Khomeini burst on the international scene as the absolute ruler of Iran, and he lost little time before announcing that Iraq would be the next Shiite theocracy.

Both sides shared responsibility for the subsequent war. Khomeini fueled the initial hostility by public threats, border provocations, and deployment of the Iraqi exile faction, Al Da'wah al Islamiyyah, as an alternative to the secular regime in Baghdad. Saddam upped the ante on September 22, 1980, by launching a full-scale invasion. The result, unforeseen by any of the parties, direct or indirect, was eight years of carnage that involved most of the eastern Arab states and the United States (which may have been motivated by its feud with the Khomeini regime to encourage the invasion, and according to *The New York Times Magazine* of 7/11/04 supplied biological precursors anthrax and botulinum for use against Iran). As the war wore on, Iraq received valuable intelligence support from Washington and massive financial support from the oil states of the Arabian Peninsula. Among the diplomatic consequences of the war were the restoration of Iraqi-American relations, and the dissolution of the anti-Egyptian front precipitated by Egypt's betrayal of the Arab Nationalist cause at Camp David (Chapter 8).

The Arab oil states had their misgivings about Iraq's long-term designs on the peninsula, but their immediate concern was the new militance out of Iran, which had territorial claims along the western shore of the Gulf and was suspected of complicity in the bloody occupation of the Great Mosque in Mecca in November 1979 (Chapter 12).

Iran also had foreign backing – political support from Syria and Libya, and arms supplies from the Soviet Union, Libya, Israel, and the United States. (In secret collaboration with Israel, the National Security Council made an effort to effect the release of Americans held hostage in Lebanon by Hizballah, through the clandestine sale of arms to Hizballah's patron, Iran, and to use the proceeds against the rebels in Nicaragua. The "Iran-Contra Affair" contravened US policy – which enjoined bargaining with hostage-takers, and was backing Iraq versus Iran – and caused a furor in 1986 when it came to light.)

Saddam's invasion of Iran (like his subsequent invasion of Kuwait) was reckless and seriously miscalculated. He went in on the premise that the fall of the Iranian monarchy and the imprisonment or exile of the Shah's generals had nullified Iran's three-to-one population advantage. The early capture of the strategic river-port city of Khorramshahr encouraged this delusion. However, Iranian President Bani Sadr convinced Supreme Leader Khomeini to return some of the thousands of imprisoned officers to active duty, while the Iraqi offensive was impaired by the incompetence of officers selected for political reliability.

Since ground action was impeded on the central and northern fronts by the Zagros Mountains, and on the south central front by the riverine marshes, most of the fighting took place in the far south along the Shatt, where Iran had greater strategic depth. Iran's regular forces were significantly supported by devout teenagers who cleared minefields by the costly but effective method of simply running across them.

By 1982, Iran had retaken Khorramshahr and a chastened Saddam had proposed a truce, but Khomeini rejected the offer, promoted the formation of an Iraqi government-in-exile under Grand Ayatallah Muhammad Baqir al Hakim (SCIRI), and sent forces into southern Iraq. By resorting to chemical weapons, Iraq checked the Iranian advance, and by 1985 the conflict had bogged down in trench warfare.

In 1988, an Iranian airliner was shot down by a missile from an American cruiser. Disbelieving the American explanation that the missile had been fired in error, Khomeini seems to have concluded that Iran's military objectives were unattainable. He was also discouraged by successes scored by Iraq's better-armed Republican Guards, and by the panic sowed among the populace of Tehran and other cities by impacts of Scud surface-to-surface missiles.

In July 1988, Iran accepted a cease-fire resolution adopted by the UN Security Council in 1987. Iraq accepted it four weeks later. An eight-year war, costing hundreds of thousands of lives on both sides, ended in stalemate. Saddam had failed to extract Iranian acceptance of his unilateral abrogation of the 1975 Algiers Accord – let alone achieve his territorial ambitions in Khuzistan. Khomeini had failed to overthrow the "infidel" regime in Baghdad.

Despite the massive wartime subsidies from the Arab oil states, Iraq came out of the Iranian conflict deeply in debt, which was a prime motive for the subsequent invasion of Kuwait. In an effort to neutralize Iran during this new venture, Saddam capitulated on the Shatt boundary dispute, but

Iran was not to be appeased. It took advantage of Saddam's defeat in Kuwait to send in agents of SCIRI to back the 1991 Shiite rebellion. This initiative had a double backlash. In Iraq, it sobered moderate Shiites who had no interest in exchanging Sunni rule from Baghdad for theocratic rule from Tehran. In Washington, it set off alarm bells against the threat of Iranian expansionism.

Over the rest of the decade, there was some relaxation of tension between Baghdad and Tehran. In 1997, after 17 years, Iraq reopened the border and allowed the pilgrimage of Iranians to Iraqi shrines. In 1998 there was a major exchange of prisoners of war, but no return of the Iraqi aircraft that Saddam had sent to Iran on the eve of the first American invasion. By 1998 Clinton's eccentric policy of Dual Containment (simultaneously of Iraq and Iran) further narrowed the gap between Iraq and Iran.

However, there was always the danger that their subversive subsidiaries – Iran's SCIRI and Iraq's MEK – would get out of control. In 2000, there were reports of paramilitary operations in Tehran by elements of the MEK, and retaliatory attacks in Baghdad, presumably by elements of SCIRI's Badr Brigade. SCIRI was quick to capitalize on the American build-up for the invasion of Iraq, and was reportedly infiltrating activists in 2003, weeks before the Americans went in.

Kuwait: The Lost Province?

As long as Iraq exists, it will harbor the conviction that Kuwait is Iraqi territory. Oil makes Kuwait a widely coveted piece of real estate, but the Iraqi argument is stronger than that:

As noted by Geoffrey Kemp and Robert Harkavy, Iraq has always based its claim to Kuwait on the grounds that in Ottoman times Kuwait was part of the governorate of Basrah. From their occupation of Mesopotamia in the 1530's until the collapse of their empire in World War I, the Ottomans professed to rule the northeastern shore of the Arabian Peninsula. (The Kuwaiti counterargument rests on the European view that Kuwait was an autonomous shaykhdom from around 1756, and that its autonomy was reinforced in 1899 when Britain concluded with the Shaykh of Kuwait an agreement that placed Kuwait under British protection, in effect nullifying the Ottoman view that the Shaykh was the governor of an Ottoman district. According to Elaine Sciolino, the Ottomans never established complete sovereignty over Kuwait.)

The elaborate frontier separating Saudi Arabia, Kuwait, and Iraq was the cavalier concoction of Sir Percy Cox, who imposed it in 1922 with minimal consultation with Ibn Sa'ud and none at all with the Kuwaitis or the Iraqis.

In 1869-72, the new Ottoman Governor in Baghdad, Midhat Basha, was not only responsible for the administration of the area stretching from Mawsil in the north to Al Hasa in the Arabian Peninsula, he actually made an inspection tour to Kuwait and Al Hasa. In the last decades of Ottoman rule, this area was redivided into the three separate vilayets of Mawsil, Baghdad, and Basrah.

Cox's restriction of Iraq's coastline to a paltry 12 miles, solely for Britain's political convenience, was an intolerable derogation of Iraq's vital economic and strategic interests. As a matter of simple geometry, Kuwait sits between Iraq and the Gulf.

Iraq's earlier bids for control of Kuwait (1937 and 1961) were blocked by Britain (Chapter 7). In 1988, Saddam raised the issue again. Having failed to extend Iraq's frontier on the Iranian side, he turned his attention to the Kuwaiti side. Because of its dependence on oil exports, landlocked Iraq was obsessed with broadening its access to the sea. It was also driven by crushing postwar indebtedness, at a time when Kuwait and Saudi Arabia had refused to cancel Iraq's war debts, Kuwaiti over-production had helped drive the price of crude down to eleven dollars a barrel (Chapter 4), Iraq suspected Kuwait of slant drilling into rich Iraqi fields, and it coveted Kuwait's superior oil production system.

Saddam's own frame of mind was another central factor. Twenty years of absolute power is bound to corrupt a ruler's judgment – particularly one simultaneously embittered by assassination attempts and military frustration, and misled by Washington's knee-jerk favoritism for any antagonist of Iranian theocracy. On August 2, 1990, Iraqi forces took Kuwait in five hours, and Baghdad proclaimed Kuwait's annexation under a "Free Provisional Kuwaiti Government". The Kuwaiti army was brushed aside, but no Kuwaitis collaborated with the invaders, and there was an appreciable level of civil disobedience. By Resolution 662, the Security Council unanimously declared the annexation invalid. Resolution 678 authorized military action.

In 1991, soundly defeated by the American forces and their allies, bankrupt Iraq abrogated its claim of annexation, promised to pay compensation for damage done in Kuwait, suffered a small but painful alteration of its southern frontier, and accepted stiff UNSC terms for a cease-fire – including scrapping all weapons of mass destruction. In 1994, in an effort to escape UN sanctions, Iraq formally recognized the independence of Kuwait.

Turkey: Former Ruler, Future Threat?

Turkey is the Janus of the Middle East. Sitting at the gateway between Europe and Asia, it has always been pulled in opposite directions. Under Roman and Byzantine rule, it looked toward Europe. Under the Caliphs, it looked toward Asia. Under the Ottomans, it was a world power on both continents.

Mustafa Kemal wrestled Turkey onto a Western course. His military genius resuscitated the Turkish phoenix from the ashes of the Ottoman Empire. His political genius reshaped the country on the Western model. His military heirs made Turkey a mainstay of the Korean campaign, NATO (1952), The Baghdad Pact (1955), the OEEC, and The Council of Europe, and – aside from differences over Cyprus and Iraq – a key ally of the United States. Ankara's fondest hope has been to share in the financial and developmental benefits of membership in the European Union. Cultivation of close relations with its former Arab territories has been a secondary consideration. (Turkey entered a perfunctory claim to Mawsil after World War I.)

Ankara has profited from Middle Eastern disarray. The Iraq-Iran war was a financial windfall; Turkey boosted its shaky economy by trading with both sides. Otherwise, it concentrated on its own parochial concerns without visible concern for the interests of its neighbors.

When Syria gave refuge to PKK leader Abdallah Ocalan (in retaliation for Turkish diversion of the Euphrates), Turkey massed troops on the border, forcing Syria to expel Ocalan, who was eventually tracked down with CIA help and brought back to a Turkish prison. Turkish forces have made innumerable incursions into Iraqi Kurdistan in pursuit of PKK militia. The first visit of a Turkish President to Iraq in decades occurred in 1994, when agreement was reached on Turkish suppression of the MEK, and on Turkish and Iraqi suppression of the PKK. On occasion, Turkey has balanced Iranian support for the Talabanis' PUK by providing arms to the Barzanis' KDP.

As of 2005, Turkey shared one pressing interest with its three neighbors to the south: blocking the emergence of a state in Iraqi Kurdistan. It is also linked to Iraq as its most convenient source of oil. During the quietus of the PKK issue, Turkey had no political quarrel with Syria except the hardy perennial of Alexandretta (Iskenderun to the Turks), which France gave to Turkey as a bribe in 1939.

Looming over all these issues is the ecological specter of water shortage, as rising Turkish, Syrian, and Iraqi requirements approach the total flow of the Tigris and Euphrates rivers (Chapters 5 and 16).

The American Metamorphosis: From Friend to Enemy

Since America's entry into the Middle East maelstrom after World War II, its policy toward Iraq has been capricious, importunate, and increasingly destructive.

In the days of British supremacy, the American presence in Iraq was largely confined to two Jesuit schools, Baghdad College and Al Hikmah University. In 1959, the CIA adopted Saddam Husayn as a man of promise. Juan Cole's website cited Richard Sale's *UPI* report that the Agency subsidized Saddam in Baghdad, and in Cairo after his escape to Egypt.

In 1963 Iraqi dictator 'Abd al Karim Qasim showed up in Washington's sights because of his ties with the Communists. Those ties were probably less ideological than opportunistic – he needed their support for his land reform program, which was opposed by the Shiite merchant class – but, as reported by Hanna Batatu, and discussed in an article by retired FSO Jim Akins carried in *The Washington Report on Middle East Affairs,* OV, of January 2005, Washington authorized the CIA to subsidize the Baathist coup against Qasim, and to supply the new Baathist regime with the names of Communists (mostly Kurds) for elimination. Irony: In 1963, Washington paid Saddam to kill Kurds; in 2006 Washington hanged Saddam for killing Kurds.

In 1979, the Carter administration reportedly encouraged Iraq to attack America's new enemy, Iran. *The Washington Post* reported that Washington also had delusions of coopting Iraq into an Arab-Israeli peace settlement. In 1984, Donald Rumsfeld went to Baghdad to stress American support for the Iraqi war effort. Alexander Cockburn reported in *The Nation* that Rumsfeld said nothing about Saddam's use of mustard gas (imported from Western companies) against the Iranians and their Iraqi Kurdish and Shiite allies – despite the State Department's condemnation of the action. In 1988 the White House was still ascribing the notorious Halabjah gas attack to Iran, according to an analysis by Jon Anderson in *The New Yorker.*

In the Gulf, a pattern of aggressive Iranian tactics against Saudi and Kuwaiti tankers, Iraqi counterattacks against Iranian tankers, and trench warfare on the Faw Peninsula had evolved by 1986 into a war of attrition that drew in American forces – to the point of putting American flags on Arab tankers, seconding Air Force officers to Iraqi units, and destroying most of Iran's navy and offshore oilfields.

By 1988, Juan Cole reports, America was blinding Iranian radar, providing Iraq with valuable intelligence on Iranian deployments, and according Iraq billions of dollars in credits. According to *Middle East*

Report, in 1989 Bush 41 issued a secret national security directive authorizing the export of arms to Iraq.

On August 2, 1990, Saddam invaded Kuwait, and was reclassified in Washington from protégé to enemy. Just before the invasion, Ambassador April Glaspie had been called into an unexpected meeting with Saddam. She was an accomplished diplomat and a fluent Arabist, but on this tragic occasion two alien political systems were talking past each other. The public record does not suggest that the ambassador or her superiors in Washington appreciated that, once again, Saddam was going for broke.

When he complained that overproduction by the Gulf oil states was damaging Iraq's economy (already known to have been crippled by the war with Iran), the Americans seem to have inferred a possible intent to make a minor unilateral adjustment in Iraq's frontier with Kuwait. Preoccupied with their campaign to curb Islamist Iran, they apparently assumed that Saddam would continue to appreciate Washington's red lines. Saddam, after eight years of uncritical American support against Iran, seems to have misread the importance of tiny Kuwait in Washington's vision of the Middle East. According to one report, Saddam went so far as to tell Glaspie the United States could not risk the loss of 10,000 soldiers' lives in the Middle East.

Iraq took Kuwait in a few hours, and America – after a few days of indecision – initiated a highly successful campaign to form an international coalition to go to Kuwait's rescue. The risks of deeper involvement in the Middle Eastern morass were outweighed by counter-considerations: 1) Bush 41 feared that an Iraq-Kuwait state would join Saudi Arabia as a powerful swing producer of oil; Queen Noor of Jordan wrote in *Leap of Faith* that Bush told King Husayn he would not let a little dictator control a quarter of the world's oil. 2) Washington liked Middle Eastern frontiers the way they were, and particularly hated to see them altered by aggression.

By September of 1990, Washington had become so committed to armed intervention that, according to *The Christian Science Monitor,* it was issuing false allegations of Iraq's having massed troops on the Saudi border. Scott Silliman theorized that Washington saw to it that UNSC condemnations of the Iraqi invasion made no mention of Article 51 of the UN Charter in order to maximize American control of the countermeasures.

Under UN auspices, America amassed a force of 500,000 of its own troops and 200,000 from 36 other states, all covered by US aircraft from Incirlik, the Gulf shaykhdoms, and the Fifth Fleet. The expulsion of the Iraqi invaders was accomplished in four days of February 1991 at a cost of 147 American lives and 60 billion dollars – of which interested states like Kuwait, Saudi Arabia, and Japan paid some 80 percent. Washington's military performance suggested mixed motives: objectivity in its decision to preserve Iraq intact as a counterbalance to Iran, but – as noted by Bill Polk – vindictiveness in its disappointment at Iraq's acceptance of Security Council Resolution 660, which called for Iraqi withdrawal, and in its inflicting "near-apocalyptic" destruction on Iraq's infrastructure by attack from the air. Estimates of Iraqi deaths ranged from 30,000 to 100,000, most of them war-weary conscripts whose only objective was to get out of the line of fire.

In its resolve to restore the morale undermined in Vietnam, the US exceeded its strategic needs – notably by battering the Iraqi vehicles fleeing north on "the highway of death", an operation described in Rick Atkinson's history of the Gulf War, and – as reported in *Harper's* by James Bill – by carpeting Iraq with over a million tons of munitions, including uranium-tipped shells that later caused extensive birth defects. Among America's generally hawkish electorate, Bush 41's approval rating shot up to 83%.

This first American invasion of Iraq featured an ill-considered White-House call on the Iraqi people to oust Saddam, but there was no thought of going on to Baghdad – or even of shielding the post-invasion Shiite revolt from bloody Baathist retaliation. The coalition had no UN mandate to invade Iraq, its Arab participants opposed any action that could lead to a Shiite government in Iraq, and Washington was wary of creating opportunities for Iran.

In April 1991 the UN declared a cease-fire, in return for Iraqi acceptance of stiff terms for disarmament, including destruction of all WMD programs, and payment of reparations. By May, Iraqis were dying from collapse of the water, sewerage, and public health systems.

The Allied (not UN) proclamation of the Northern No-Fly Zone in October 1991, after Saddam had withdrawn his forces from the three Kurdish provinces, permitted the emergence of the KAR. The Southern No-Fly Zone, proclaimed in August 1992, had no overt political consequence, but it denied the sector to Iraqi aircraft. The Northern Zone was policed from Incirlik, the southern from Bahrain and later from the new airbase in Qatar. According to an officer of the National Lawyers Guild, the zones violated Iraqi sovereignty.

Vindictiveness was also suggested in the draconian implementation of Security Council Resolution 661 of August 6, 1990, which imposed on Iraq economic sanctions, including a worldwide trade ban, explicitly intended to disable Iraq's military establishment. Resolution 661 was enforced by a fifteen-member Sanctions Committee sitting in New York. Every member had veto power over any specific Iraqi request for an import license, and the American member often exercised it, citing possible dual use – military application of an ostensibly commercial product. Although the regime in Baghdad continued to prosper, primarily from proceeds of smuggling oil to neighboring states, the consequences of the sanctions for the Iraqi economy were ruinous, and for public health lethal. Hiro reports that in 1996 on "Sixty Minutes" Lesley Stahl asked Secretary of State Albright if the deaths of 500,000 Iraqi children were justified; Albright's reply: " … we think the price is worth it." Joy Gordon noted that the American member of the 661 Committee held up some import licenses for years – even on harmless items like vaccines and yogurt makers. In 1999 Washington relented, and the UN lifted the embargo on Iraqi oil sales, but specified that the proceeds would be collected in Paris under UN oversight.

For twelve years, America exacerbated Iraq's misery by a series of coup attempts and destructive air strikes: 1993 - Missile attack in retaliation for an alleged assassination plot against Bush 41 while he was on a visit to Kuwait; Randolph Ryan opined in *The Boston Globe* that Pentagon politics had violated the Constitutional requirement that Congress decide on acts of war; 1994 - Clinton's confirmation of earlier instructions to the CIA to arrange Saddam's ouster; 1996 - support for a coup effort by Iyad 'Allawi, which ended in fiasco; 1998 - A four-day wave of air strikes, which redounded to Washington's disadvantage, since the UN's prior withdrawal of its arms inspectors denied the Americans an illegal intelligence channel and enabled Saddam to discard his inspection agreement with Secretary General Annan on the grounds that the withdrawal of the inspectors showed their job was done.

In the early years of the sanctions, Washington regarded them as a means to hold Iraq to Security Council Resolutions 687 (no WMD's) and 688 (no repression of Kurds and Shiites). Later on, Washington began to look on them as devices for ousting Saddam. In 1998 Clinton signed the Iraq Liberation Act, which embodied that specific objective.

Chapter 10
The Cycle of Empire

The kaleidoscope of power in the Middle East is roughly encapsulated in Chapter 7. The challenge is to fit this fluctuating process into the matrix of geopolitical axiom – with particular reference to the rule that "a vacuum of power will inevitably be filled" (Chapter 1) and to the author's contention that the Middle East of today is such a vacuum. If these premises are correct, the instability of the region will subside as the number of contestants for regional hegemony is reduced.

Three possible routes to expansion for any contestant are <u>conquest</u>, <u>consensus</u>, and <u>settlement</u>. <u>Conquest</u> is the product of military action (although it may be facilitated by intergovernmental transaction, like the Louisiana and Alaska purchases). If the conquered and conquering entities remain segregated, the outcome is <u>imperialism</u> – the domination of one country by another. In the classic example, London ruled its far-flung dependencies through an imposed bureaucracy, supplemented by native collaborators. The personnel of the "Colonial Service" sent their children "home" to school, and went "home" themselves on retirement.

<u>Consensus</u>, an infrequent phenomenon, is exemplified by the merging of the Thirteen Colonies, by the European Union, and by Egyptian and Syrian participation in the short-lived United Arab Republic.

<u>Settlement</u> involves the mass transfer of population. The settlers may come from an imperial center (like British settlers in America), or they may bring that center along with them (as the Turks did in settling Anatolia), or they may come from the world at large (as in the idiosyncratic case of the Jewish settlement of Israel). <u>Settlement</u> may be officially sponsored, or it may be adventitious – like Jewish settlement in Palestine before World War I, or the Hispanic influx into the United States in present days.

In all three cases, the criterion of success is <u>assimilation</u> – the metamorphosis from <u>imperialism</u> to <u>unification</u>. <u>Imperialism</u> is ephemeral (Americans in the Philippines, whites in the Rhodesias, British in India). <u>Unification</u> endures (Saxons, Normans, Danes, et al. in England; countless lineages in America).

All these issues are confused by the conventional use of "colonialism" as a synonym for <u>imperialism</u>. This text will reserve the former term for <u>settlement</u>, like that conducted by the United States in its newly acquired territories, and by Israel in parts of occupied Palestine and Syria. In both cases, <u>settlement</u> was reinforced by ethnic cleansing – notably the American role in "the Trail of Tears" and the Israeli role in the mass expulsions of 1948 and 1967. Israeli hegemony over Arab communities in the West Bank, Gaza, and the Golan meets the criteria of <u>imperialism</u>.

<u>Assimilation</u> is the key to political survival. The American political system has enhanced its prospects for longevity by essentially depoliticizing ethnic diversity. Insofar as an empire blocks assimilation, it accelerates its own demise. (Alexander the Great made a dramatic start toward assimilation by marrying himself and 80 of his officers to Persian wives, and paying generous dowries for 10,000 of his soldiers who had taken native wives.)

Alien governors may be more efficient, but their different circumstances lead to different goals. Hence, every society detests alien rule, and empire, with its overtones of racism, is destined to decay. Decay was the fate of every empire that held sway in the Middle East. (Indications in 2010 were that Washington was moving toward writing off the American occupation of Iraq, as a temporary venture.)

Power struggles start small – tribe versus tribe, town versus town, or warlord versus warlord. At what stage does the victory of one adversary over another deserve to be classified as a case of imperialism?

This text draws the line between <u>region</u> and <u>sector</u>. The region under consideration here is the Middle East. The sectors that compose it are seven: Arabia (1,086,000 square miles); Egypt (384,000); Iran (632,000); Iraq (168,000); the Levant (120,000); the southern Caucasus (72,000); and Turkey, plus Cyprus (304,000).

In every one of these sectors, there has been an age-old struggle among its resident communities for hegemony. In most of them – notably the Levant and Iraq – the issue of hegemony is currently unresolved. However, it seems unlikely that any study of imperialism will produce useful conclusions unless the area of inquiry excludes such intramural conflict, and is confined to hegemonic change between two or more sectors. That definition of imperialism is the basis for the following tabulation of empires:

The Akkadian Empire (2370 – 2230 B.C.)

Sargon of Akkad, one of the giants of Middle Eastern history, united Mesopotamia, a segment of western Persia, a strip of southern Anatolia, and northern Syria to the Mediterranean, in what is the first known empire in history.

The Sumerian Empire (2100 – 2000 B.C.)

In one last eruption of militancy, the Sumerians brought Mesopotamia, southwestern Persia, and the eastern half of Syria under their sway.

Egyptian Expansion (1990 – 1780 B.C.)

A reunited Egypt dominated the Palestinian section of the Levant.

Amorite Expansion (1900 – 1600 B.C.)

Dominated Mesopotamia and Syria. Also known as the First Babylonian Empire. The lawgiver, Hammurabi of Babylon, was an Amorite.

Second Egyptian Expansion (1550 – 1175 B.C.)

Egypt extended its rule to most of the Levant, and on occasion exacted tribute from rulers in Mesopotamia.

First Assyrian Empire (1250 – 1100 B.C.)

From their base in northern Mesopotamia, the Assyrians took southern Anatolia and the northern Levant (Syria) to the Mediterranean. In Babylon, their rule was interrupted during the last quarter of the Twelfth Century by Nebuchadrezzar I, who was the conqueror of Elam (present-day Khuzistan) and should not be confused with Nebuchadrezzar II of the Second Babylonian Empire.

Second Assyrian Empire (911 – 824 B.C.)

Recovery of their former territories, plus western Persia.

Third Assyrian Empire (750 – 625 B.C.)

The Assyrians ruled Mesopotamia, Anatolia, western Persia, the southern Caucasus, Cyprus, and the Levant. Until 660 B.C., they held Egypt as well.

Second Babylonian Empire (625 – 561 B.C.)

Crushed the Assyrian Empire, briefly ruled Mesopotamia and the Levant. Although Nebuchadrezzar II conquered Jerusalem and sent its leaders into Babylonian exile (subject of Verdi's *Nabucco*), Jewish tradition viewed him as an instrument of God.

Third Egyptian Expansion (610 – 550 B.C.)

Retook the Levant from the Babylonians.

The Persian Empire (550 – 330 B.C.)

After taking control of Persia from the Medes, the Persians went on to establish the greatest and most enduring empire in the Middle East until the advent of Rome. At its zenith, the empire ruled Persia, Mesopotamia, Anatolia, the Levant, Egypt, Libya, Thrace, and large areas of central and south Asia. Its advance to the west was checked by the city-states of Greece.

The Alexandrine Empires (334 B.C. – c. 50 B.C.)

From his base in Macedonia, Alexander led an army, primarily composed of mercenaries, which conquered Greece and most of the lands held by the Persian Empire, which expired. When Alexander died, his empire was partitioned. The Ptolemies inherited Egypt, the southern Levant, and Cyprus. The Seleucids inherited Mesopotamia, most of Persia, the northern Levant, much of Anatolia, and the southern Caucasus. Macedonia reverted to General Antigonus and his heirs, whose periodic interventions in Anatolia were insufficient to qualify them as Middle Eastern emperors.

The Parthian Empire (200 B.C. – 224 A.D.)

Moving in from Central Asia, the Parthians took Persia, Mesopotamia, and Armenia, and held off the advance of the Romans.

The Roman/Byzantine Empire (133 B.C. – 638 A.D.)

Appearing in Anatolia in 133 B.C., the Romans gradually conquered Anatolia, the Levant, Egypt, and the southern Caucasus. The Seleucid and Ptolemaic dynasties expired. Roman expansion into Asia was facilitated by Asian disunity. It was easier to co-opt dynasties that needed help against their neighbors. In Mesopotamia, the Romans were stopped by the Parthians, who managed to capture and kill a Roman general in 53 B.C. To the west, Rome continued to advance. Egypt fell in 48 B.C., and Cleopatra, last of the Ptolemies, shared the Egyptian throne with Mark Antony, ruler of the west, until their suicides in 30 B.C. Antony was succeeded by Octavian, who became Augustus, the first Roman emperor.

At the beginning of the Christian era, the northern Middle East was divided between Rome and Parthia at the Euphrates: Parthia held Persia and Mesopotamia; Rome was dominant in Anatolia, the Levant, Egypt, and part of the southern Caucasus; western Arabia was ruled by an Arab dynasty, the Himyarites. William McNeill observed that, between latitudes 30° and 50° north, Eurasia was essentially ruled by four dynasties: Roman, Parthian, Kushan, and Chinese. Of these four, the Roman Empire was distinguished by its success in using the armed forces as a vehicle for the integration of its diverse peoples. Edward Gibbon considered the period from 96 to 180 the halcyon years in the history of the human race. Averil Cameron concurred that the Middle East prospered under Roman rule. In 212, citizenship was conferred on all free inhabitants of the Roman Empire.

In 224, the Parthian dynasty gave way to the Sasanian, but the succession did not materially alter the stand-off with Rome in Mesopotamia. By this time, as noted by Gibbon, the city of Nicomedia in Anatolia was functioning as a separate capital for the eastern half of the Roman Empire, which was divided de facto in 286.

In 330, Emperor Constantine made Byzantium, under the new name of Constantinople (City of Constantine), the capital of the whole empire. In 395, the empire was partitioned once and for all. The western half gradually succumbed to invasion by the tribes of northern Europe. Byzantium held on for another 1100 years, despite repeated challenges – notably an invasion of Anatolia by mounted Visigoth lancers in 378.

In 2005, the legacy of Rome was still with us – as symbolized in the nine countries (five in the Middle East) where the unit of currency was the dinar (*denarius*).

The Sasanian Empire (224 – 638)

From the decline of the Byzantine Empire in the 400's until the Islamic conquest in the 600's, dominion over the Middle East was contested among three primary poles of power – Persia, Anatolia, and Egypt. The unfortunates who lived in between were residents of a recurrent battlefield.

Under the Sasanians, the Persians were often on the offensive. In 531, they took the northern Levant. From 575 to 628, they ruled Yemen. In the early 600's, they held the Levant, Egypt, and most of Anatolia. In 627, a reformed Byzantium retook the Levant and Egypt, but the entire Middle East was on the verge of being overrun by a more invincible force:

The Caliphate of Islam (634 – 945)

In accounts by Max Rodenbeck and Hugh Kennedy, the aggressive energies of the tribes of Arabia surged at a point in history when the hegemonic powers of the Middle East (Byzantium and Sassanid Persia) had been debilitated by bubonic plague and internecine war. The only empire in history to have been based on religious faith, Islam swept Zoroastrianism, Buddhism, and Hinduism before it, and made Arabic, the vehicle of the Qur'an, a world language. Many Middle Eastern Christians, aggrieved by Byzantine absolutism, sided with the more tolerant Muslims. Having united Arabia by 634, the Arabians took the Levant and Mesopotamia in 638, Egypt and Persia in 642, and areas in Anatolia and the Caucasus thereafter. For a time, Asian Byzantium was reduced to an enclave along the south side of the Straits.

In the 700's, Byzantium regained most of Anatolia, but the reign of Harun al Rashid in Baghdad around 800 is regarded as the zenith of the Islamic Empire. In the 800's, Egypt became autonomous, with dominion over the Levant, under the nominal suzerainty of the Abbasid Caliph in Baghdad. In the 900's, Persia also acquired autonomous status, and Byzantium conquered the Levant and northern Mesopotamia.

The Buyid Empire (945 – 1055)

In 945, a Shiite dynasty, the Buyids, conquered Persia and Mesopotamia, but ruled under the nominal dominion of the Abbasid Caliph (who remained a Sunni).

The Fatimid Empire (967 – 1169)

The Fatimid emperors paid allegiance to the Isma'ili sect of the Shiite branch of Islam. They invaded Egypt from North Africa and went on to take the western coast of the Arabian Peninsula and parts of the Levant and Mesopotamia.

The Seljuq Empire (1037 – 1194)

Migrating from Central Asia, the Seljuq Turks took Persia, accepted Sunni Islam, deposed the Buyid (Shiite) rulers of Mesopotamia in 1055, and extended their rule (under a figurehead Abbasid Caliph) into Anatolia, northwestern Arabia, and the Levant, introducing 800 years of Turkish preeminence in the Middle East. Christian Byzantium was reduced to Constantinople, adjoining lands of Anatolia and Europe, and (briefly) Christian Armenia. At the Battle of Manzikert, in southeastern Turkey, the Seljuqs crushed a Byzantine army.

The Crusader Kingdoms (1098 – 1244)

The First and Second Crusades established four autonomous principalities that controlled the Mediterranean coast from Egypt to southwestern Anatolia. The Kingdom of Jerusalem dominated Palestine and Lebanon from 1099 to 1187. In 1191, British King Richard took Cyprus, which remained under European rule until 1571.

The Ayyubid Empire (1169 – 1260)

Salah al Din al Ayyubi, a Kurdish general in the service of the Seljuq ruler in Damascus, took Egypt from the Fatimids in 1169. From his Egyptian base, he defeated a Crusader army at Hattin in northern Palestine in 1187 and conquered Jerusalem and most of the territories taken by the Crusaders. The Ayyubid Dynasty went on to conquer most of Syria, much of Arabia, and southern Anatolia. In a final convulsion, Byzantium re-extended its sway over Anatolia proper.

The First Mongol Empire (1221 – 1335)

Fighting under the banner of Genghis Khan, creator of one of the most far-flung empires in history, an army of Mongols and Turks overran Persia, Mesopotamia, and southern Anatolia. The flood of nimble Asian horsemen, armed with powerful laminated crossbows, crushed the heavier cavalry of the Seljuqs, and transformed Islamic society. As their conquests multiplied, the Mongols assimilated Turks into their armies, until the cultural polarity reversed and the Mongols adopted Islam and the Turkish language. By devastating Persia and Mesopotamia, they did lasting harm to both sectors. Their advance into Syria, under the command of a Christian general, Kitbuga, was repelled by the crucial Egyptian victory at 'Ayn Jallut (1260), which saved Egypt and marks the turning point in the Mongol advance into the Middle East and Europe.

Through the 1200's, however, Mongol rule combined most of the Middle East and Central Asia into one empire – enabling Marco Polo to travel to China and back on one document (Frederick Starr, *Wilson*

Quarterly). The Abbasid Caliphate expired in 1258 (except in Egypt). A "Mongol" dynasty held on in Persia until 1335.

The Second Mongol Empire (1370 – 1506)

Timur Lenk, a Turkicized Mongol who claimed descent from Genghis Khan, established a Central Asian dynasty that also ruled Persia, Mesopotamia, the southern Caucasus, northeast Arabia, and parts of Anatolia and the Levant. Timur elevated his capital, Samarkand (in present-day Uzbekistan), to become the outstanding cultural and economic center in Central Asia.

The Mamluk Empire (1250 – 1517)

Turkish soldiers *(mamluk* means slave in Arabic) overthrew their Ayyubid masters and established a dynasty that ruled Egypt, the Levant, and the Hijaz (northwestern Arabia). It staged a brief resurgence from 1770 to 1830.

The Ottoman Empire (1400 – 1921)

Decades of battle between Seljuq and Ottoman Turks for control of Anatolia ended in Ottoman victory. As quoted by Perry Anderson in *The London Review of Books,* Caroline Finkel noted that the Ottoman Empire was founded on the idea of continuous warfare. Over the next 500 years, the Ottomans extended their empire to include, at its zenith, Anatolia, Cyprus, Constantinople (fell in 1453), Mesopotamia, the southern Caucasus, the Levant, Egypt, the western and northeastern coasts of Arabia (until the rise of Yemen's Zaydi-Shiite dynasty in 1597), the coast of North Africa, the Balkan sector of Europe, and the Black Sea coast of Russia. Two of the most dynamic states of the age, the Anatolian Ottomans and the Persian Safavids (most of whose soldiers were also Turkish), continued the age-old battling along their common frontier, which fluctuated wildly over the centuries. Their hostility was intensified by the sectarian rivalry between the Shiite Safavids and the Sunni Ottomans, who extracted from the Sharif of Mecca recognition of the Ottoman Sultan, and of the Ottoman nominee as Caliph of Islam. The empire owed its military success in large part to the fact that its army, composed of Christian boys converted to Islam (janissaries), was the first standing army in Europe.

The decline of the Ottoman Empire began in the 1600's, as a consequence of corruption, incompetent leadership, overextension, and the rise in the military power of the Europeans. By the late 1800's, the empire was deeply in debt, and it continued to function largely because the European powers were unable to agree on which of them should take control of the Turkish Straits. Meanwhile, the Europeans began the dismantling of the Ottoman domain by espousing a cluster of nationalisms in the Balkans. The Anglo-Ottoman Convention of 1838 required Constantinople to allow European merchants unrestricted operation, subject only to the jurisdiction of special non-Islamic courts. Civil war in Lebanon moved the Europeans to require the empire to set up a special regime in (Maronite Christian) Mount Lebanon. From 1854-56, to shore up the "sick man of Europe" and promote vague notions of national prestige, Britain and France invaded the Russian Crimea.

The state visit of Emperor Wilhelm II to Constantinople in 1889, a tactic in Germany's "Drive to the East", elicited Ottoman concurrence with a plan for German construction of a Baghdad Railway – Constantinople, Mawsil, Baghdad, Basrah – which the Sultan believed would be a valuable obstruction against the Arab liberation movement. The visit alarmed London, and foreshadowed World War I and a secret German-Ottoman treaty of alliance in 1914. Driven by hostility to Russia, the empire made the mistake of entering World War I on the side of the Central Powers. Despite significant loss of territory in the two Balkan wars, the Sultan still had an estimated 25,000,000 subjects (10,000,000 Turks, 6,000,000 Arabs,1,500,000 Kurds, 1,500,000 Greeks, and over a million Armenians), and his army made a significant contribution to the war effort in its resistance to the British advance from its southern territories.

The Covenant of the League of Nations, concluded in 1919, recognized in sanctimonious Article 22 the provisional independence of the Ottoman Empire's former Arab provinces, "subject to the assistance of a mandatory power." In 1920, by the Treaty of Sèvres, the empire was abolished, and four Arab territories were relegated to mandates: Syria and Lebanon went to France, Palestine (including Transjordan) and Mesopotamia to Britain. Kurdistan was to be autonomous, Armenia independent. Turkey was to be split into French and Italian spheres of interest.

Safavid Empire (1502 – 1736)

Isma'il I – descendant of a family that had converted from Sunni to Shia, and traced its ancestry to the Seventh Imam, Musa al Kazim – became Shah of Azerbaijan in 1501 and Shah of Iran a year later. The Safavids formed a warring triad, along with the Ottomans of Anatolia and the Mamluks of Egypt. (Note the analogous division of Middle Eastern hegemony among Persia, Anatolia, and Egypt before Islam united most of the region, a thousand years earlier.) Control of the lands between shifted from one to another. Under Shah Abbas I in the early 1600's, Iran became a great power, taking Mesopotamia from the Ottomans, and – with British help – the tiny Persian Gulf island of Hormuz from the Portuguese. Abbas's standing army benefited from reorganization by an Englishman, Sir Robert Sherley.

The Safavids were deposed by another Persian dynasty, the Afsharid Turkmens, who were followed by the Zands and the Qajars, who ruled an independent Persia – and Bahrain from 1602 to 1783, a fact that looms large in current Iranian policy toward Arabia. Elsewhere in Arabia, tribesmen from the Najd continued their sporadic forays into Mesopotamia and Syria, until the Egyptian Mamluks took the offensive again on behalf of their nominal Ottoman ruler, occupying Syria in 1771 and taking Hijaz from the Najdis in the early 1800's.

Europe and the Middle East

In the past 2400 years, there have been three great swings in the Eurasian pendulum of power:

I.   Toward Europe, during the Macedonian, post-Macedonian, and Roman eras.

II.   Toward Asia, with the Mongol invasions of eastern Europe, the Islamic occupation of southwestern Europe (exemplified by the plundering of the great Basilica of St. Peter in Rome in 846), and the Ottoman conquest of the Balkans. (In the broadest perspective, the Crusades were only a blip on history's radar screen.)

III.   Back toward the West, with the rise of Western imperialism, whose most notable practitioners have been Portugal, Britain, France, Russia, and the United States.

For contemporary students of Middle Eastern geopolitics, understanding Western imperialism is essential, because of the profound effects it has had, and is still having, on events in the region. In the global contest for survival, the Europeans suddenly took a commanding lead. If scholars continue to debate the causes, they must at least recognize the basics:

More Efficient Political and Economic Organization

The Magna Carta, the Renaissance, the Protestant Reformation, the Enlightenment, the French Revolution, the Industrial Revolution, the repression of slavery – all these were giant steps toward greater empowerment of the individual, and his or her enlistment in the national cause. Innovations like joint stock companies, standing armies and navies, and professional bureaucracies were effective tools in mobilizing the resources of that new political phenomenon, the state. By 1800, Europe was the center of a preeminent power system, and oriental appreciation of that reality was reflected in the employment of European experts in Middle Eastern civil services – even in states as isolated as Yemen.

Superior Technology

In *The Pursuit of Glory,* Tim Blanning reviews how the Europeans from the mid-1600's on boosted the economy with an agricultural revolution based on livestock enclosure, manuring, crop rotation, and development of better crops and blood lines. On its heels came the Industrial Revolution, which provided the tools to upgrade the infrastructure, improve the quality of life at home, and project national power abroad. Europe's unrivalled access to navigable rivers and the open sea contributed to the development of a maritime technology on which imperialism was heavily dependent. Ironically, in earlier centuries, European trade with the Middle East helped Europe catch up with the Asians, and the Muslim conquest then forced the Europeans to upgrade their maritime skills in order to exploit alternative routes to south and east Asia. Hence, the lethality of gunboat diplomacy – and of its modern equivalent, missile diplomacy. Also, the stormy seas of the north compelled the Europeans to build strong ships – which were superior gun platforms.

Self-Serving Policy

Technology still runs far ahead of ethics. As states accrued military and economic power, they continued to misuse it for their own aggrandizement. In the Westerners' ongoing contest for supremacy, they dealt with the less developed world out of shortsighted opportunism; the interests of subject peoples were inconsequential. As the side door to Europe, the Middle East has endured more than its share of imperialist exploitation.

In the geopolitical arena, the crucial action occurred in the 1830's. Egypt's dynamic new ruler, Muhammad 'Ali, put to work his new standing army, composed of Egyptian peasants conscripted on the French model. Occupying Syria, in 1839 the force defeated an Ottoman army at the Battle of Nizip, in southern Turkey north of Aleppo. The prospect of Egyptian conquest of the Ottoman Empire threatened the imperialist ambitions of Britain, Austria, Prussia, and Russia, which combined military and diplomatic action to compel withdrawal of Egyptian forces from the Levant, as specified in the Treaty of London of 1840. As a consolation prize, Muhammad 'Ali received hereditary rule of Egypt – which survived until the overthrow of King Faruq in 1953 (Chapter 11).

In the 1830's, Europe blocked Egypt's effort to develop a textile industry, in effect converting Egypt to a European cotton plantation. In the late 1800's, European intrusion into Egypt and Turkey began with imposition of dictatorial administrations to insure that foreign debts – incurred by local misrule – would be paid. In 1869, Empress Eugenie, Spanish wife of Emperor Napoleon III of France, presided over the opening of the Suez Canal – built on Egyptian land with Egyptian labor, but a European property. Britain had opposed the project at the outset, but by 1869 had switched to enthusiastic support. The debt Egypt incurred in its construction was to serve as a pretext for British military occupation in 1882.

In 1871, after Otto von Bismarck had led Prussia to victory in three wars, newly unified Germany became an empire, and the most powerful state in Europe. In 1878, Bismarck's Congress of Berlin resolved the anarchy ensuing from Russia's victory over the Ottomans, extracted British concurrence in French hegemony over Tunisia (to mitigate the loss of Alsace-Lorraine), and allowed Britain to take control of the Nile by establishing preeminence in East Africa, Sudan, and Egypt. In 1881 the Europeans took over control of most of the Ottoman Empire's revenues to ensure repayment of its debts.

The anguish of World War I drove Britain to extremes of hypocrisy: the secret Anglo-French Sykes-Picot land-grab deal of 1916, in blatant contradiction of McMahon's assurances to the Arabs in 1915; the false professions of the Balfour Declaration (Chapter 8); and the patronizing duplicity of the mandate system set up at Versailles in the Covenant of the League of Nations. This last performance has been described as "three ignorant and irresponsible men cutting Asia Minor to bits as if they were dividing a cake." In another view, "The old hag of colonialization put on a fig leaf and called itself a mandate." The bitter Iraqi resistance demolished Gertrude Bell's bizarre contention, cited by David Fromkin, that "no one in Baghdad or Basra could conceive of an independent Arab government." In prosecuting the standard imperialist strategy of divide-and-rule, the Versailles conferees cut up the Ottoman Empire into the jumble of heterogeneous states that obstructs the region's progress today.

Intermittent Altruism

Condemnation of imperialism should not extend to all its practitioners. For every case of flagrant racism (the Spanish expulsion of Muslims in

1609; the atrocities in King Leopold's private fiefdom, the Belgian Congo), there are a thousand colonial officers who dedicated their lives to elevating the quality of life in their areas of responsibility. The mandates were self-serving in intent, but they fortuitously extended many of Europe's advances in administration, judiciary, education, and public health to their subjects. India benefited immensely from the implantation of English as a lingua franca. The Europeans' profession of the humanitarian imperative was not always insincere.

Portugal Leads the Way

Having discovered the sea route to the east in 1498 (Chapter 2), the Portuguese defeated the Omanian navy, took control of the Arabian Sea and occupied major cities along the southern and eastern coasts of Arabia from 1507 to 1650 : *Middle East Policy,* Spring 2010, Jeffrey Lefebvre.

Britain Builds the Ultimate Empire (1600's – 1971)

History's vastest empire began in the 1600's with colonies on the Atlantic coast of North America and in the Caribbean. Over the next 300 years, it expanded to major positions on five continents. Following are key dates in the Middle Eastern chapter of the story:

1600 - Queen Elizabeth I chartered the East India Company.

1615 - Having ousted the Portuguese from India, as noted by Edwin Black, Britain took over Bombay (Mumbai). Since the rulers of the Mughal Empire favored Shiism, Britain took a similar line in the area, forming an alliance with Safavid Shah Abbas I of Persia.

1650's - Modernized by Oliver Cromwell, the British Navy replaced the Dutch Navy as the strongest in the world. As the fleet grew, so did Britain's revenue from commerce and shipping. Promoting British economic interests in the Middle East and South Asia were the Levant and the East India Companies. The prosperity of the empire depended on the importation of sugar, tea, and tobacco, whose economical production required slaves or subsistence workers. So Britain came to build, in the wording of Simon Schama, "an empire of soldiers and slaves." In Fernand Braudel's assessment, the European economy, unified by the time of the Reformation, was dominated by Britain from around 1700 until World War II. That preeminence was related to a succession of revolutions in technology and industrial enterprise. Some analysts ascribe great credit to the British invention of the steam engine, employed from the 1700's on to pump out the coal mines which were so central to the British economy.

1700's - As reported in *Saudi Aramco World,* the East India Company set up a depot in Jiddah, the only major port on the eastern shore of the Red Sea (thanks to conjunction of the Muslim pilgrimage and wind patterns; south of Jiddah, prevailing winds blew from the south; north of Jiddah, they came from the north).

1704 - Britain took Gibraltar as a crucial guard-post on the sea route to the east (the Lifeline).

c. 1750 - The East India Company helped Nader Shah build a fleet that extended Persian rule to Bahrain and parts of Oman.

1763 - The Treaty of Paris ended the Seven Years' War, fought among Britain, Spain, and Prussia for access to trade with Asia. The East India Company set up a Gulf headquarters in Basrah, on the London-Bombay mail route (by land to Basrah, by sea to Bombay).

1798 - Admiral Horatio Nelson secured the Mediterranean for Britain by sinking the French fleet off Alexandria at the Battle of Abu Qir, marooning Napoleon's ill-considered occupation of Egypt, and confirming Britain's dominance in the Middle East.

1798 - Omani ruler Sultan bin Ahmad signed a treaty of friendship with Britain.

1799 - In reaction to the French challenge, the British administration in Bombay set up a position in Aden, another link in the Lifeline to India. Britain had come to regard India as an indispensable source of British preeminence (compare America's current fixation on Middle East oil), and this obsession may have dictated Britain's policy toward the Middle East.

1800 - With French troops eliminated from the Middle East, Britain saw Russia as its chief competitor, and strengthened its ties with the Ottomans and Persia as natural allies against Russian expansionism. The Anglo-Persian treaty of alliance called, inter alia, for exclusion of France.

1814 - The second Treaty of Paris transferred Maltese sovereignty from the Knights of Malta to Great Britain, which made it another link in the Lifeline.

1815 - The Congress of Vienna patched up the hostility between Britain and France, who then formed a combine against Russia.

1827 - A British-French-Russian fleet crushed an Egyptian-Turkish fleet at Navarino, off the coast of Greece. The immediate result was Greek independence in 1832.

1839 - Troops sent north by Muhammad 'Ali, mutinous ruler of Egypt, defeated the Ottoman Turks in southern Anatolia. Opting, with its allies, to shore up the Ottomans as the safer barrier to Russian expansion, Britain used its navy to cut off the Egyptian troops from their home base, and in 1840 rammed through at the Conference of London a settlement requiring Muhammad 'Ali to give Syria back to the Sultan, but awarding Muhammad 'Ali a consolation prize – the position of hereditary Basha of Egypt. Meanwhile, Britain had intervened in Egypt to impose reduction of its army, termination of its economic monopolies, and acceptance of European exports. Egypt began to run into debt.

1853 - Britain signed a treaty of "maritime peace in perpetuity" with that part of eastern Arabia known as the Trucial Coast.

1853-56 - To suppress czarist ambitions in the Middle East, Britain, France, and the Ottomans ganged up on Russia in the Crimean War.

1857 - In reaction to the Persian invasion of western Afghanistan, Britain landed troops on the Persian coast and forced the Persians to withdraw.

1858 - As reported in *The London Review of Books* review of Anthony Pagden's *Edge of Empire,* the crown dissolved the East India Company in the process of creating the Empire of India.

1875 - Again thinking Lifeline, Prime Minister Disraeli made Britain the largest shareholder in the Suez Canal Company by buying the shares of the bankrupt Khedive. (A Frenchman, Ferdinand de Lesseps, had acquired the concession from Khedive Sa'id in 1854.)

1878 - By the Treaty of Berlin – as cited by Lenczowski – Britain, Austria, and France forced Russia to revoke some of its recent Balkan conquests from the Ottomans. In return for British protection against Russia, and the return of three Armenian provinces, the Ottoman Empire gave Britain control of Cyprus, another post on the Lifeline. (Cyprus was last used by Britain as the base for its abortive invasion of the Suez Canal Zone in 1956.)

1879 - By imposing financial controls to insure Egyptian debt repayment, Britain acquired supremacy in Egypt, under nominal Ottoman rule.

1882 - An Egyptian nationalist revolt, led by Ahmad 'Urabi, provoked the ruler (Khedive Tawfiq) to betray his country by inviting in British troops. Britain took advantage of the opportunity to insure its control of the Suez Canal by taking de facto mastery of Egypt. As Michael Doyle has stressed, the occupation was facilitated by the fact that the Egyptian landowners were as dismayed by the specter of agrarian revolution as the British were.

1883 - Evelyn Baring, a military officer who knew six languages – but never Arabic – became "Consul General" in Egypt, which he ruled as a latter-day pharaoh until 1907. He retired as the Earl of Cromer. Under his administration, Egypt rose from bankruptcy to the most developed country in the Middle East. However, the cost of the occupying army came out of the Egyptian budget, and Rashid Khalidi contends that Baring reduced the educational budget in order to inhibit the emergence of Egyptians indoctrinated in dangerous Western ideas of democracy.

1888 - In Constantinople, nine powers concluded a convention declaring the Suez Canal open to all ships in peace and war, subject to legitimate actions for the self-defense of Egypt and the Ottoman Empire. (Britain took the questionable action of closing the canal to its enemies' shipping in both World Wars, and Egypt closed it to enemy shipping in the 1948, 1956, 1967, 1970, and 1973 wars with Israel.)

1889 - Persia granted financial concessions to the two rival powers, Britain and Russia.

1891 - According to a recent article in *Middle East Report,* the Sultan of Oman had become a vassal of the British crown.

1892 - The tribes on the Trucial Coast signed over to Britain the management of their foreign relations. They had concluded Britain was less of a threat than the Ottomans to their autonomy.

1897 - Kaiser Wilhelm set out to challenge British dominion of the seas, precipitating a naval race, which was to focus European attention on oil – and thence on the Middle East.

1899 - Having ousted the Mahdi, protagonist of Sudanese nationalism, Britain set up the Anglo-Egyptian Condominium over the Sudan.

1899 - Kuwait ceded control over its foreign affairs to Britain, which accorded Kuwait protectorate status; the British umbrella enabled Kuwait in effect to terminate its status as part of the Ottoman vilayet of Basrah, and dispelled the risk of invasion by tribal armies from central Arabia. The British had been galvanized by the recent discovery of oil, and concerned by German designs on the Middle East.

Circa 1900 - A prevailing modern view is that maintenance of the empire had become an enormous drain on the British treasury. (Compare America's current expenditures in Iraq and Afghanistan.) Although India was Britain's largest market, its cost was believed to exceed its benefits. Rudyard Kipling, gifted writer and profoundly perceptive observer of Indian society, coined the phrases "white man's burden" and "half devil and half child", but exposed the flaws of imperial authority in *Kim* (1901), and concluded that imperialism was a failed system.

1901 - In the Arabian power struggle, Britain was backing the Saudis, Germany backing the Rashidis.

1902 - Germany acquired an Ottoman concession to build a railroad from Constantinople to Baghdad.

1904 - An Anglo-French declaration of French preeminence in Morocco and British preeminence in Egypt.

1906 - A clash between Egyptian villagers and British security personnel led to death sentences for four peasants. The British felt they were setting an example for "xenophobes" and "religious fanatics". For Egyptians, "Din Shuway" still symbolizes foreign oppression.

1906-11 - As a constitutional revolution shook Persia's Qajar Dynasty, which had sold out to British oil and tobacco interests, Britain and Russia intervened against the revolutionary parliament, and resolved their power struggle in the Afghan-Persian sector: Britain was to prevail in Afghanistan and southern Persia, Russia in northern Persia. Central Persia was to be neutral territory. The Anglo-Russian Convention of 1907 was an operative event in these transactions.

1913 - Kuwait, which had subsisted on the proceeds of smuggling, diving for low-grade pearls, and the slave trade, entered an era of affluence when the Amir gave Britain a blanket oil concession.

1914 - War loomed in Europe. Urged on by Winston Churchill, Britain bought control of the Anglo-Persian Oil Company. In Arabia, Britain dropped the Saudis in favor of Sharif Husayn, who enjoyed preeminence as custodian of the Holy Places, and whose army was in contact with Ottoman forces.

1914 - In the early days of World War I, to preempt intrusion by Germany, British troops from India took Basrah, critical to the defense of oil production in Kuwait and Persia. Sir Percy Cox assured the Arabs the British came as liberators.

1914 - Britain annexed Cyprus.

1914 - Britain deposed the Egyptian Khedive, ending the myth of Ottoman sovereignty, and assumed direct administration of Egypt as its base for conquest of the Ottoman Empire.

1914 - In Arabia, Britain brushed Ottoman "sovereignty" aside, consolidated its ties with the various tribes on the southern and eastern coasts, wooed Sharif Husayn with the honeyed McMahon letters, and unwittingly opened the door for the Saudis to build their kingdom. The Saudis' enemies, the Rashidis, stayed loyal to the Ottoman Empire, which entered the war on the German side.

1914-18 - Romanticized by Lowell Thomas, T. S. Lawrence led Arabian troops against the Turks. James Barr asserts in *Setting the Desert on Fire* that Lawrence sold London a bill of goods about a massive Arab nationalist movement – that the real Arab contribution to the war was negligible.

1915 - The British Navy made its transition from coal to oil. The strategic significance of the Middle East took a quantum leap.

1915 - Acting for the Government of India, Sir Percy Cox signed with Ibn Sa'ud a treaty of friendship that accorded him protection, a subsidy, and recognition as the ruler of Najd.

1917 - Over stiff Turkish resistance, but with the help of former Iraqi officers in the Ottoman service, British forces (largely Indian) took Baghdad.

1917 - British forces from Egypt took 'Aqabah.

1917 - The Balfour Declaration (Chapter 8) was a direct consequence of the war. London wanted a guaranteed base in Palestine to defend the Lifeline, and also sought Jewish support for American entry into the war. Britain managed to convince Sharif Husayn that the Zionists would be valuable allies against the Turks.

1918 - Britain and its Arab allies took Syria.

1918 - To maximize its control of Mesopotamian oil, Britain prevailed on France to revise the Sykes-Picot agreement: The Mawsil area would go to Britain, and France would have primacy in Syria and a share of Mawsil oil.

1919 - Britain bribed the Shah to agree to Persia's becoming a client state, supervised from London (later from Washington), although Persian nationalism forced Britain to withdraw its troops in 1921.

1919 - British deportation of Egyptian nationalist Sa'd Zaghlul precipitated a revolt that compelled Britain to rush troops in from Syria and let Zaghlul go to the peace conference at Versailles.

1920 - At San Remo, the Allies agreed to impose a British mandate on Iraq and Palestine, in contravention of wartime promises and the League Covenant's provisions for deferring to local wishes in the assignment of mandates.

1920 - Winston Churchill, Secretary of State for Colonies, convened in Cairo a conference of British officials who converted Mesopotamia to the Kingdom of Iraq, under the rule of Hashemite Prince Faysal, who was to take orders from London. A revolt by the Iraqi tribes was put down, largely by air power, with heavy casualties on both sides.

1921 - Faysal ascended the Iraqi throne, and was endorsed by a rigged plebiscite. Dissidents were exiled. London proposed to control Iraq by a network of RAF airfields. It overruled the provision in the Treaty of Sèvres (1920) that the area primarily populated by Kurds should be granted autonomy.

1921 - Churchill, characterized much later in *The Journal of Palestine Studies* as a strong Zionist, promised the Arabs the Jewish National Home would not result in their subjugation to a Jewish government.

1921 - Britain allowed Hashemite Prince 'Abdallah to invest himself as Amir of Transjordan (with a stipend from London).

1921 - Backed by Britain, Reza Khan led a Cossack unit to Tehran and took power as Commander-in-Chief of the armed forces of Persia. (The country had been known as Persia, or Iran, since ancient times. In 1935, Tehran chose Iran as the official designation.)

1922 - Britain imposed on the Middle East partition of the Ottoman Empire. Implementation of mendacious wartime promises would have produced a settlement at odds with Britain's acquisitive policies. Instead, London divided the Palestinian Mandate into two countries – Palestine and Transjordan; the latter was exempted from the provision for a Jewish National Home. All high positions in Palestine were assigned to Britons on the grounds that the Arabs and Jews could not reach agreement. The Allenby Declaration proclaimed Egypt an "independent" kingdom; the King never recognized the British claim of responsibility for Egypt's defense. The Iraq Mandate was supplanted by an Anglo-Iraqi treaty of alliance which gave Britain full control. British High Commissioner Sir Percy Cox imposed on Iraq, Kuwait, and Prince 'Abd al 'Aziz Al Sa'ud arbitrary boundary lines that were delineated on a map but never clearly marked on the ground. Autonomous Kurdistan disappeared from the British agenda.

1920's - Late in the decade, Faysal signed an oil concession agreement with IPC on terms favorable to Britain, but not to Iraq: *Middle East Report,* Summer 2007.

1923 - The Treaty of Lausanne replaced the Treaty of Sèvres, affirmed the end of the Ottoman Empire, and established the boundaries of Ataturk's new state of Turkey. Britain kept Cyprus. The Province of Mawsil went to Iraq to bolster Sunni demographics vis-à-vis the Shia, and to insure British access to its oil.

1924 - London made Cyprus a crown colony.

1924 - After the assassination of its military commander in Egypt, Britain stiffened its control of the country.

1927 - Ibn Sa'ud recognized Britain's special position in the principalities along the Gulf.

1928 - Britain and Iran resolved issues that had divided them. Bolstered by its control of the Anglo-Iranian Oil Company (AIOC), Britain was the most influential foreign power in Iran.

1930 - Britain and Iraq signed a new treaty under which "independent" Iraq was to remain a de facto protectorate. Britain retained military bases and control of the railroads and the port at Basrah.

1932 - British aircraft bombed dissident Kurdish villages in Iraq. Like the US in the next century, Britain was slow to learn that air power is not the answer to rebellion. According to Rashid Khalidi, the Council of the League of Nations discounted Iran's position that the AIOC concession, having been imposed by a foreign power, was invalid.

1932 - Iraq became the first Arab member of the League of Nations, even as Britain retained air bases there, and British personnel were exempt from Iraqi laws and taxes.

1936 - Britain and Egypt signed a treaty on the pattern of the Anglo-Iraqi treaty of 1930. Britain retained its major military position in the Canal Zone. Termination of British appointments to Egyptian army and police was a conciliatory gesture motivated by Italian expansionism in Africa.

1937 - Aden became a crown colony.

1939 - World War II broke out in September. Although Egypt did not declare war against Germany and Japan until 1945, Egypt was from the outset Britain's main base in the Middle East – notably as the site of the Middle East Supply Center.

1939 - Lenczowski reported that Germany had gained considerable influence over Iran, and had become its main trading partner.

1939 - Britain and France signed with Turkey a treaty of alliance which exempted Turkey from having to go to war against the Soviet Union, or anywhere outside the Mediterranean area. However, by 1941 the series of German victories in Europe had compelled Turkey to sign with Germany a nonaggression treaty that facilitated the German invasion of Russia, and the exchange of Turkish chrome for German arms.

1941 - After the defeat of France, Germany cultivated Iraqi nationalists, who briefly ousted pro-British Prime Minister Nuri al Sa'id, but British forces from India dispersed the rebels, reinstated Nuri, and backed the monarchy in the execution of some coup leaders and the purging of 3000 nationalist officers.

1941 - Reza Shah's policy of playing off Britain and the Soviets against each other collapsed with their alliance against Germany. Reza abdicated in favor of his son Mohammed. The Allies occupied Iran.

1941 - British forces took full control of Egypt, Palestine, Syria/Lebanon (under nominal Free French authority), and Iraq as a centralized area of operations against the Axis. A road they built from Haifa to Baghdad had great military value. According to a report in *The Journal of Palestine Studies,* Britain orchestrated secret collaboration between Zionist leaders in Palestine and Nuri al Sa'id's government in Baghdad.

1942 - To insure the support of Egypt's nationalist Wafd Party during World War II, British forces ringed King Faruq's palace with tanks and forced him to name a Wafdist prime minister.

1943 - Iraqi Prime Minister Nuri al Sa'id proclaimed Iraq at war with Germany, Italy, and Japan.

1945 - Labor won a surprise election in Britain. Attlee replaced Churchill as Prime Minister, and set out to dismantle the empire Churchill had striven to preserve. The British had never mastered the art of deimperialization. Labor's Palestine policy was undermined at the outset by Attlee's campaign effort to outbid the Tories for Jewish support.

1946 - London concluded a treaty with Transjordan, modeled on the Anglo-Iraqi Treaty of 1930. 'Abdallah was elevated from prince to king.

1947 - The British Empire began to crumble, starting with the partition of South Asia between India and Pakistan – an action variously condemned as: "the final botched job of an inattentive and insensitive ruling power"; a monumental betrayal of the South Asians by Nehru, Jinnah, and the British; and an atrocity imposed on the subcontinent by the British Labor government. London also gave Burma its independence, turned over the defense of Greece and Turkey to the United States, and signaled its intention to walk away from the mess in Palestine. British forces evacuated Iraq, except for two RAF bases.

1948 - A revision of the 1946 treaty between Britain and Jordan reduced the British military presence, but Britain retained two air bases, and a British officer (John Glubb) remained as commandant of the armed forces.

1948 - A British attempt to update the Anglo-Iraqi Treaty of 1930 precipitated nationalist/Communist demonstrations, which were repressed with heavy casualties. Three Communist leaders were hanged.

1948 - The "mischievous incompetence" of Britain's abandonment of Palestine led to the first round in the Arab-Israeli war. In George Lenczowski's assessment, British policy supported the Jordanian position, but contributed to the Egyptian defeat.

1951 - Libya, occupied by the British (and French) since expulsion of Axis forces, was granted its independence.

1952 - Calling for abrogation of the Anglo-Egyptian Treaty of 1936, the eviction of British troops from the Canal Zone, and the reunification of the Sudan with Egypt, Prime Minister Nahhas created a contentious political climate in which activists harassed the British forces. The British threw a cordon around the Canal Zone and occupied the town of Isma'iliyyah, precipitating on January 26, 1952, a nationalist/Communist riot in Cairo in which hundreds of enterprises were burned and 26 people killed, including several British civilians. On July 23, a group of officers formed under the leadership of Jamal 'Abd al Nasir overthrew the monarchy and exiled Faruq.

1953 - In collaboration with their Iranian agent, Shah Mohammed, Britain and the US promoted a coup which led to the overthrow of Prime Minister Mohammed Mossadeq, who had led Parliament's 1951 attempt to nationalize the oil industry, including the exploitive AIOC.

1954 - Britain capitulated to the demands of the military regime in Cairo, concluding a treaty that provided for withdrawal of British forces by mid-1956. The headquarters of the British Middle East Command was transferred from the Canal Zone to Cyprus.

1954 - Alarmed by Soviet machinations in the Arab East, Washington and London tried to swim against the political tide by mobilizing an anti-Soviet coalition, popularly known as the Baghdad Pact. The nucleus was a mutual assistance pact between Turkey and Pakistan – expanded in 1955 by the adherence of Iran, Britain, and Iraq.

1955 - British resolution of a dispute between coastal tribes and Saudi Arabia over the Buraymi Oasis was achieved by British expulsion of Saudi forces. For some observers, the incident was a victory for British oil companies over American.

1955 - Five signatories of the Baghdad Pact set up a permanent secretariat in Baghdad. Pressure on Jordan to adhere to the Pact precipitated a crisis, which King Husayn resolved by replacing Lt. General John Glubb with an Arab as commander of the Arab Legion. The action won Husayn immense popularity at home and credit in the Arab World. The Anglo-Jordanian alliance, cum subsidy, survived.

1955 - As reported in 2008 in *The London Review of Books,* Britain attempted to block *Enosis* (union of Cyprus and Greece) by promoting Greek-Turkish partition of Cyprus – an opportunity on which Turkey was quick to act.

1956 - Britain and France adamantly rejected Nasir's nationalization of the Suez Canal (Chapter 8). Secretary of State Dulles seemed to endorse the bizarre Anglo-French argument that the Suez Canal Company's "international character" took precedence over Egyptian sovereignty, but America was opposed to the use of force. After diplomacy of desperation failed, Britain, France, and Israel invaded, but Eisenhower quashed the invasion, unceremoniously demonstrating that Britain was no longer a great power – a reality Prime Minister Anthony Eden couldn't grasp. The episode led to Syrian sabotage of IPC's pipeline to the Mediterranean, damage to Anglo-Jordanian relations, enhancement of Soviet influence in the Arab World, and a boom in Nasir's prestige.

1956 - Jordan abrogated the 1948 treaty with Britain, which withdrew most of its military personnel.

1958 - Arab resentment of Western support for Israel had made the Baghdad Pact a non-starter. Nuri al Sa'id's political acrobatics (banning political parties, rigging elections, breaking relations with Moscow) were nullified by the overthrow of the Iraqi monarchy. The Pact had served no purpose except to nourish the anti-Soviet proclivities of Secretary of State Dulles and the neo-imperialist delusions of Prime Minister Eden.

1960 - Cyprus became an independent republic. Britain retained base rights, and the US established a major communications intelligence base.

1961 - Britain and Kuwait annulled the Treaty of 1899. Iraq threatened to invade Kuwait; Britain dispelled the threat by sending in troops. Saudi Arabia, Egypt, Jordan, and Sudan sent in token contingents.

1966 - Britain orchestrated the replacement of the reactionary ruler of Abu Dhabi (the most substantial of seven shaykhdoms on the Trucial Coast) with a more amenable Amir.

1968 - Britain announced that a crisis in its financial situation required it to terminate its military presence in the Persian Gulf area and the Indian Ocean. The Gulf rulers urged reconsideration of the decision.

1971 - Britain completed its disengagement from its historic commitments to the Arab states on the western shore of the Persian Gulf.

1971 - Writing in *Middle East Policy* in 2006, Thomas Mattair took the position that the Iranian occupation of the Tunbs and Abu Musa (inhabited by Arabs) was an offshoot of Britain's creation of the UAE.

French Imperialism in the Middle East (1920 - 1945)

In the 1100's, the arrival of the Crusaders generated collaboration between the Papacy and the Maronite Christian community in Lebanon. Since Spain was focusing on its own political evolution, and later on the New World, France was the only Catholic power with an interest in following up the Maronite connection.

In 1536, French King Francis I and Ottoman Sultan Suleiman I concluded an alliance against the Hapsburgs. The treaty accorded France special privileges (Capitulations), which, inter alia, implied French protection for Christians of the Latin rite who lived in Ottoman territory. The Franco-Ottoman collaboration was to endure for three centuries. A treaty of 1740, reaffirming the association, was confirmed by the Sultan and Napoleon in 1802, despite the brief interlude of Franco-Ottoman hostilities during Napoleon's abortive foray into Egypt and Syria.

In 1798, Napoleon invaded Egypt. His motive, as assessed in *Napoleon's Egypt* (Juan Cole), was to cripple the British Empire. The naval defeat of Abu Qir left France unable even to rule Egypt. Napoleon went home, but his army invaded Palestine and Syria, until the British ground forces in Egypt forced its surrender in 1801. Any French ambitions of unilateral empire in the Middle East were crushed in 1812 with the Russian victory over invading French forces. From then on, France turned its attention to

North Africa, whereas its operations in the Middle East were ancillary to those of the British.

In 1860, anti-Christian rioting in Lebanon brought British and French fleet units to the Levantine coast. France landed troops in Lebanon, and in 1864 exacted from the Sultan an agreement to grant the Sanjaq of Lebanon autonomy under a Christian governor. The eventual result was the transfer of political preeminence in Lebanon from the Druze to the Maronites.

The decisive Prussian victory over France in 1870 reduced French influence in the Middle East, but the loss of Alsace and Lorraine had a paradoxical effect of whetting the French appetite for empire. France came back to the region after World War I as the mandatory power in Syria and Lebanon – but only on sufferance from the British, who swallowed France's expulsion of their candidate for King of Syria, Hashemite Prince Faysal. French imperialism in the Middle East took a more activist form than that practiced by the British. The mandatory authorities gerrymandered Syria into four autonomous provinces, notably including an oversize Lebanon with Maronite leadership but a Muslim population, which soon became a majority – an embarrassment which the French and their Maronite allies concealed by not conducting a census. The French also made a futile effort to promote French language and culture at the expense of Arabic and Arab culture.

In 1924, France formed La Compagnie Francaise des Pétroles (CFP) to assume the French 25% share of the Turkish Petroleum Company, in accordance with the agreement at San Remo. The French government owned one-fourth of the CFP's shares.

In the mid-Twenties, French troops put down a major Syrian insurrection in which Druze tribes played a central role. In 1939, as war threatened in Europe, France reimposed its direct rule over Syria and Lebanon, and sought to ingratiate itself with Turkey by awarding it a piece of Syria – Alexandretta. In 1941, under the aegis of Britain, the local commander of the Free French conducted himself as the ruler of Syria and Lebanon. French efforts to retain control sputtered out in 1943 (except for a lethal shelling of Damascus in 1945), and Syria and Lebanon acquired full independence in 1945.

Russian Imperialism in the Middle East (1800's – 1991)

Russia has always had a compelling interest in acquiring assured access to southern waters. The prospect of hegemony over Iran, always remote, became academic in 1990 after the termination of Russian dominion over Central Asia. Russia and Turkey were always natural rivals for control of the straits – aside from their long history of conflict in the southern Caucasus and the Balkans.

In the 1800's, Russia asserted its military superiority over the Ottomans in the Balkans, and gradually conquered the southern Caucasus (Chapter 7) – only to lose it in 1991 with the breakup of the Soviet Union. The high-water mark of Russian influence in the Middle East came in 1833 with a Russian-Ottoman Treaty in which the Ottomans accepted Russian protection and agreed to close the Dardanelles to all warships "in case of need."

The Anglo-Russian Convention of 1907 divided Iran into spheres of influence. In 1911, in concert with Britain, Russia moved troops toward Tehran, forcing the collapse of the revolutionary movement (Chapter 11) – and the dismissal of American adviser Morgan Shuster, who was making great strides in reorganizing the Iranian financial system. Donald Wilber evaluated Shuster's *The Strangling of Persia* as a classic.

The Soviet Revolution of 1917-18 led to the embarrassing publication of the secret Allied agreements of World War I (notably the Sykes-Picot monstrosity), to the conversion of Russia to an ally of Turkey, and to the extinction of the Armenian Republic. The Turkish-Soviet Treaty of 1921 awarded the Soviets a piece of Georgia, including Batum. The Iranian-Soviet Treaty of 1921 gave the Soviets the right to intervene against any anti-Soviet operations based in Iran, but marked the abandonment of Russian expansionist designs on that country. (In 1920-21, the new Soviet regime had sponsored the short-lived "Soviet Republic of Gilan" in northwest Iran.)

In 1921, for protection against Britain, new governments in Persia, Turkey, and Afghanistan signed treaties with Moscow. In 1925, the day after the Council of the League of Nations awarded the Province of Mawsil to the British Mandate of Iraq, an aggrieved Turkey signed a ten-year treaty of alliance with the USSR.

The Soviet-German nonaggression pact of 1939 came as a great shock to Turkey, in its efforts to stay neutral in the Europeans' most ominous confrontation yet. Istanbul was presumably unaware of the secret German-Soviet talks of 1940, in which Moscow had specified its plans for expansion toward the Persian Gulf.

In 1941, Britain and Russia occupied the respective segments of Iran that the two powers had delineated in 1907. The objective was to defend the Middle East oil fields, the oil refinery at Abadan (Iran), and the supply line to the Soviet Union. In 1945, Truman, Attlee, and Stalin met at Potsdam to resolve various postwar issues. America and Britain resisted the Soviet demand for a role in defending the Dardanelles. Once the Axis threat had been dispelled, America and the USSR were released to pursue their rival recipes for global organization. Among the pernicious consequences were American overreach and forty-five years of Cold War – punctuated by hot wars between American proxies (such as South Vietnam and South Korea) and Soviet proxies.

In 1945, the Soviets moved to expand the Azerbaijan Soviet Socialist Republic into northwestern Iran, but with Allied support Iran succeeded in blocking their initiative. In 1946, the Soviets sponsored another secession in northwestern Iran – the Kurdish "Republic of Mahabad". The insurgents received military training and equipment from the Soviets, and according to some reports Soviet tanks crossed into Iran, but American intervention, including sending a carrier force to the Dardanelles, enabled Iranian forces to crush the initiative.

In 1947, the Soviet Union followed a denunciation of Zionism as an instrument of British imperialism by voting for partition of Palestine. In 1948, the Soviets recognized Israel. Although Zionism contravened the principles of Communism, Moscow was pragmatic enough to accept a Western initiative that was bound to unsettle the Western position in the Middle East. The Soviets reflexively condemned every Western effort to unite Middle Eastern states in alliance against outside (read Soviet) intrusion. They took advantage of Western commitment to Israel's military preeminence by selling arms to Egypt in 1955, and subsequently to Syria, Yemen, and Iraq. They backed Nasir's nationalization of the Suez Canal politically and logistically (by sending "volunteer" canal pilots).

The Soviets' influence with the Arabs was further enhanced by Israel's crushing defeat of Egypt, Syria, and Jordan in 1967. Beset at home by race riots and demonstrations against the war in Vietnam, Lyndon Johnson had antagonized the Arabs by embracing Israel in an effort to reinforce his political position in the United States. However, the Soviets had their own sources of embarrassment in the victory of Israel, armed by America, over the Arabs, armed by the Soviet Bloc, and by America's naval preeminence in the Mediterranean.

To counter the Sixth Fleet, Moscow obtained base rights for aircraft and missile forces in three Egyptian ports, built up its own Mediterranean fleet, and promised Egypt help in eliminating the consequences of aggression. In 1970, to oppose Israel's deep-penetration raids, Soviet pilots began flying operational missions over the Canal Zone (Chapter 8). Israel abandoned the deep-penetration strategy, but met the Soviets head-on over the Canal. The day of decision was June 30, 1970, when Israeli pilots shot down 5 MIG's flown by Soviet pilots, while newly arrived Soviet SAM-3's downed three Israeli jets. These events seem to have sobered the policymakers in Washington and Moscow. In July, after Israel had lost seven more planes, Nasir announced acceptance of a cease-fire. The Soviet Union had redeemed itself in Arab eyes by stalemating the War of Attrition – and by enabling Egypt to emplace on the west bank of the canal the missiles it would require in 1973 to attack the Israeli forces in Sinai.

In 1971, to keep Egypt in the Soviet camp, Moscow signed with Anwar Sadat the first-ever Soviet defense commitment to a non-Communist country. (The Soviets had long since left Arab Communist parties to their own devices.) Moscow later signed a treaty of friendship with Iraq and an economic cooperation agreement with Syria, while America was consolidating its ties with Iran and Saudi Arabia. By the 1970's, the USSR had acquired important air and naval facilities in Egypt, Syria, Iraq, and the two Yemens. 1973 was the high point of Soviet-Egyptian cooperation. Having provided arms and military advice, Moscow conducted a huge postwar resupply operation for Egypt and Syria, and undertook to resupply the Egyptian Third Army (trapped behind Israeli lines) by air, if that became necessary. (It didn't; Washington forced Israel to open its cordon.) However, the Soviets' objectives were regional, whereas Sadat's were strictly Egyptian. Recognizing that his only hope of recovering Sinai lay in Washington, he abruptly changed horses (see below).

In 1979, the Soviet Union undertook its first exercise in pure imperialism since the conquest of Central Asia. To bail out a Marxist regime in Kabul, it invaded Afghanistan and by 1980 had occupied all major cities. Bogged down in bitter fighting with Afghan tribesmen increasingly well armed by the West, the Soviets withdrew their troops in 1989.

In the 1980's, the Soviets provided military assistance to Iraq, and Soviet naval craft began to appear in the Persian Gulf, but the scene in Russia itself was beginning to shift. In 1987, new Secretary General Gorbachev introduced *glasnost* (openness) and *perestroika* (restructuring), promoting consequences he had not anticipated. The Berlin Wall fell in 1989, and by 1991 the Soviet Union was history.

As a country with 17,000,000 Muslim residents, and as a close neighbor, the new Russia still has a built-in interest in the Middle East. In 1995, it infuriated Turkey by hosting the third meeting of the Kurdish "Parliament in Exile". Nevertheless, Russia and Turkey are active trading partners, Russia sells high-tech arms to Iran, and it is keenly interested in reestablishing a major trade and arms link with Iraq – and in recovering some eight billion dollars of Iraqi debt.

Russia considered the American bombing of Iraqi targets in 1998 a violation of international law, and presumably has similar views about the Anglo-American invasion, but it was lately inhibited from condemning the invasion by economic weakness. With a budget just over $150 billion (compared to an American budget of $2.7 trillion), Russia was heavily dependent on loans from the IMF, whose policies are strongly influenced by Washington. Russia has to be frustrated by recent American infiltration of former Soviet territories in the Caucasus and Central Asia, but has faced major sedition in its own sector of the Caucasus – notably the district of Chechnya. It has recognized the Georgian secessionist enclaves of Abkhazia and South Ossetia (Chapter 11).

The United States: From Distant Observer to Nationmaker/breaker

Since early colonial times, the Americans have adhered to a policy of militant expansionism. At first, its imperialist aspects were mitigated – except in the unfortunate case of the natives – by full assimilation, political and cultural. As analyzed by Stephen Kinzer in *Overthrow,* that changed in 1897 with imperialist President McKinley's foray into Cuba. After World War I, Wilson's high-sounding mantra of "open covenants, openly arrived at" was brushed aside by the unregenerate imperialism of the Europeans. His acceptance of the Allies' offer of a mandate over Armenia was rejected by Congress.

The Tripartite Pact of 1940, the Axis powers' analogue to the Sikes-Picot agreement, proposed to divide Europe between Germany and Italy, and assign East Asia to Japan. It also guaranteed joint action against any new combatant on the Allied side. With the Soviets (temporarily) sidelined by treaties, the Tripartite Pact was obviously aimed at the US, so it was helpful to Roosevelt's campaign to bring America into the war while there was still time to save Britain.

As comprehensively discussed by Lenczowski, World War II transformed the American presence in the Middle East. Before the war, Washington was content to leave the security of the region to Britain and France. During the war, America provided lend-lease aid to several states in the region – notably Turkey, marooned between Axis and Allied armies. In Iran Washington built an airbase at Abadan. In Saudi Arabia, it built a more permanent air base at Dhahran, and opened a legation in Jiddah. In North Africa, as reported in Gerhard Weinberg's *A World at Arms,* Roosevelt's rush shipment of Sherman tanks enabled the British Eighth Army to defeat Rommel's Afrika Corps at Al 'Alamayn in 1942.

After the war, America was drawn in to the Middle East by an electrifying constellation of events:

– The Palestinian Mandate became the home of a Jewish state.

- Middle East oil became a global preoccupation.
- Britain shed its empire.
- Soviet-American alliance degenerated into forty years of Cold War.

It is apparent from the chronology of American action that Washington began to exert its influence on the region before the Cold War was over. At what time and place did influence become hegemony? If Israel meets the specifications of an American colony (Chapter 8), the question is easily answered: May 14, 1948, in Palestine. Otherwise, there is a wide range of plausible answers, culminating in May 1, 2003 – the date when President Bush proclaimed the conquest of Iraq:

1943 - Roosevelt found Saudi Arabia eligible for financial assistance under the Lend-Lease Act of 1941. Payments were made throughout World War II, partly as a lever for access to Saudi oil.

1945 - Roosevelt guaranteed Saudi Arabia's security in return for privileged access to Saudi oil.

1947 - Under the Truman Doctrine, the United States assumed responsibility for the security of Turkey, as the front line of defense against Soviet expansion into the Middle East. Under an agreement with Iran, America was to provide military training.

1947 - The Palestine Partition Resolution was a blatant case of the West's disregard for the rights or the interests of its territorial possessions.

1948 - The founding of Israel.

1948 - America initiated a permanent naval presence in the Persian Gulf.

1948 - Jordan reached a secret understanding with Israel on terms tantamount to making it an Israeli protectorate. Washington subsequently reinforced the relationship by annual subsidies to Jordan and a secret stipend to its ruler.

1949 - As a precaution against any Soviet designs on oil fields around the Persian Gulf, Truman authorized pre-positioning of ordnance near the fields. The directive was implemented in the 1950's.

1949 - Seeing Israel (backed by its patron, the United States) as a potential ally versus the USSR, Turkey recognized Israel.

1950's - While Washington continued to rely on Britain to oversee the security of the Arab principalities along the Gulf, it promoted the expansion of American oil companies' activities in Saudi Arabia and Kuwait, and it established a number of military bases and installations in Turkey – which was a valued participant in the Korean War.

1951 - America and Saudi Arabia signed a five-year mutual defense agreement, under which Washington was to provide arms sales and military training in return for American use of the airfield at Dhahran.

1951 - In concert with Britain, France, and Turkey, America proposed a Middle East Command. The stated objective was to settle the Anglo-Egyptian dispute over control of the Canal Zone. The proposal was protested by Moscow and rejected by Egypt.

1952 - Turkey joined NATO (as its only Muslim member).

1953 - To preserve the Anglo-Iranian Oil Company's venal concession, and keep quisling Shah Mohammed on the throne, Eisenhower authorized the CIA to collude with the UK in orchestrating a coup against Prime Minister Mossadeq, who had won great popularity for trying to nationalize the company. At one point in the confusion, the enterprise seemed to have failed, and the Shah fled the country. With the help of hired rioters and corrupt police, Kermit Roosevelt's cabal salvaged the operation, the Shah returned, and America was rewarded by a 40 percent share in the company. In *All the Shah's Men,* Stephen Kinzer reports how America suffered the delayed consequences when Ayatollah Khomeini took the country over in 1979.

1954 - Turkey allowed the US to build an airbase at Incirlik.

1955 - Operating behind the scenes, Secretary of State Dulles took another stab at mobilizing Middle Eastern regimes against Soviet infiltration, and preserving an inside track to Middle East oil. Turkey, Iran, Iraq, Pakistan, and Britain adhered to the "Baghdad Pact". The US confined its participation to the role of "observer", to allay Israeli fears of isolation, and to protect American oil interests in Saudi Arabia. Egypt condemned the Pact, and Jordanians rioted against it. The enterprise was one of many examples of the futile predilection of the West for trying to recruit Middle Easterners in support of alien interests. Under Nuri al Sa'id, Iraq was envisioned as the vanguard of pro-Western forces in the Arab World.

1956 - By nullifying the tripartite invasion of Egypt (Chapter 8), Eisenhower administered the coup de grace to European imperialism in the Middle East.

1957 - Britain gave up its two air bases in Iraq and withdrew the forces it had sent to Jordan during the disturbances of 1955. Secretary Dulles declared Jordanian independence vital to the United States. King Husayn went onto the CIA payroll.

1957 - The one gain from the 1956 Suez fiasco was America's success in securing passage for Israeli shipping through the Strait of Tiran.

1957 - Recognizing the power vacuum left in the Middle East by the dissipation of the French and British presence, and seeking to ensure access to Persian Gulf oil, Washington came up with a clumsy alternative – the Eisenhower Doctrine, which matched the Truman Doctrine's offer of financial and material assistance to contracting states, but ostensibly went it one better by providing for the use of force. Egypt denounced it as imperialist meddling. The only Arab state to join was Lebanon.

1957 - The Saudi-American defense agreement was renewed and expanded.

1957 - America financed the rigging of Lebanese elections on behalf of Camille Sham'un. Result: a brief civil war. Washington financed an unsuccessful attempt to overthrow the government of Syria.

1958 - In reaction to the union of Egypt and Syria in the United Arab Republic (UAR), Jordan and Iraq announced their federation, and America sent troops to Lebanon.

1958 - The Iraqi monarchy was overthrown (Chapter 9).

1959 - Regretting America's failure to join the Baghdad Pact, Iran obtained an American security guarantee, which the Soviets denounced.

1959 - Under a Turkish-American treaty, Washington gave Turkey a promise of support against any Soviet aggression, and Ankara gave America missile bases. The missiles were secretly negotiated away to resolve the 1962 crisis over Soviet missiles in Cuba, in a triumph of statesmanship on the part of John Kennedy.

1959 - The revolutionary regime in Iraq withdrew from the Baghdad Pact. Washington tried to repair the damage by forming a new regional security organization: CENTO.

1963 - In reaction to hostilities along the Saudi-Yemeni border, America conducted supportive military flights over Saudi Arabia for several months.

1964 - Washington averted Turkish intervention in Cyprus by an implicit threat to waive the American treaty commitment to help defend Turkey against Soviet intervention.

1967 - Recognizing that Lyndon Johnson and Congress were united in their desire to reduce the Egyptian threat to Israel by undermining Nasir – notably by terminating sales of American wheat for Egyptian currency under Public Law 480 – Nasir preempted them by terminating the program himself.

1969 - Mu'ammar Qadhafi carried out a military coup against the pro-Western regime in Libya, and then proposed union with Egypt. The British air base at Tubruq and the American air base near Tripoli were nationalized.

1970 - Nasir died of a heart attack. His Vice President, Anwar Sadat, succeeded him. Although Kissinger had told the press (for background) the United States wanted Egypt to expel the Soviet combat forces, Nixon rejected conciliatory overtures from Sadat.

1972 - In Moscow, Nixon and Kissinger consolidated Soviet-American détente. On their return trip, they went via Tehran and guaranteed the Shah major arms assistance in return for Iranian support in filling the power vacuum left by the dissipation of the British Empire, and promised to join Iran in providing financial aid to anti-Baghdad Kurds in Iraq.

1972 - Iraq signed a treaty of friendship with the Soviet Union.

1973 - In reaction to the Israeli advance against Egyptian forces in Sinai and along the canal, Brezhnev threatened unilateral action if Israel did not accept a cease-fire. Nixon and Kissinger wanted a decisive Israeli victory, but the Soviet threat compelled them to order Israel to leave an escape route for Egyptian forces trapped in Sinai. On October 24, Kissinger chaired a rump meeting of the National Security Council, which ordered a global military alert (Defense Condition Three). The ostensible reason was the Soviet threat; the real reason – revealed in *In Confidence,* by Soviet Ambassador Anatoly Dobrynin – was the administration's desire to divert the attention of the American public from the Watergate scandal.

1974 - Turkey occupied the Turkish sector in northern Cyprus. Over administration opposition, the Greek lobby forced Congress to cut off arms supply to Turkey, which retaliated by abrogating most of its military cooperation with the United States, including key facilities for surveillance of Soviet activities. (The arms embargo was lifted in 1977; military cooperation resumed in 1980.)

1974 - Saudi Arabia and the United States announced agreement on economic and arms cooperation. (America was to modernize the Saudi National Guard. Its security guarantee was implicitly reaffirmed.)

1975 - The Algiers Agreement between the Shah and Saddam (Chapter 9) led to termination of Iranian and American support of Iraqi Kurds, who felt they had been betrayed.

1975 - Sultan Qabus of Oman initiated the purchase of TOW missiles from the United States, a step in the development of closer military cooperation.

1975 - Having decided to work for détente with Washington, Sadat officially reopened the Suez Canal.

1979 - With the overthrow of the Shah by Ayatollah Khomeini, America lost its major ally in the Middle East. It looked to Turkey and the states of the Arabian Peninsula to help fill the gap.

1979 - After the signature of an Egyptian-Israeli peace treaty, Israeli naval units were allowed to transit the Suez Canal.

1979 - Iran, Pakistan, and Turkey withdrew from the Central Treaty Organization (CENTO), which expired.

1979 - Since a succession of Presidents had relied on America's alliance with the Shah (for Carter in 1977, Iran was "an island of stability"), and America and Israel had supported the repressive operations of Savak (the secret police), the Khomeini regime and a majority of Iranians were hostile toward America. Carter's decision to let the ousted Shah enter the United States for medical treatment (reportedly after David Rockefeller and Kissinger had threatened to denounce him if he denied the Shah entry) precipitated the seizure of Embassy Tehran and the holding of the staff hostage for over a year. The seizure probably contributed to Carter's electoral defeat in 1980.

1979 - Soviet troops invaded Afghanistan and set up a puppet regime. The Carter and Reagan administrations poured arms and money into the resistance campaign, primarily via Pakistan's Inter-Services Intelligence agency (ISI). (After the Soviet withdrawal in 1989, the Afghan, Pakistani, and Arab fighters [mujahideen] turned their weapons on the Americans and their Afghan allies.)

1980 - Carter's State of the Union address, January 23, 1980: Although Carter had been advised that control of the Gulf was vital to Europe but not to the United States, he was sufficiently concerned by the fall of the Shah, the Soviet invasion of Afghanistan, and an Islamist insurrection in Mecca to proclaim the Carter Doctrine: Any move by a hostile power to gain control of the Gulf would be regarded by Washington as "an assault on the vital interests of the United States" (access to oil), and would be resisted if necessary by military force. For this contingency, Carter set up the Rapid Deployment Force, which was later incorporated in the Central Command, which conducts all major American military operations in the Middle East.

1980 - America signed a defense treaty with Turkey.

1980 - Washington revealed it had conducted joint air exercises with Egypt from bases near Luxor. Since Camp David (Chapter 8) had eventuated in an Israeli-Egyptian peace treaty, Egypt had become a key ally and recipient of a handsome annual subsidy. (Biannual war games, involving troops from Egypt, America, and nine other states, have been regularly conducted.)

1981 - In return for a defense guarantee and a subsidy, America obtained agreement from Oman for access to base facilities, which proved valuable during Gulf War I.

1981 - Reagan announced America would not allow Saudi Arabia to fall into the hands of any external or internal forces that threatened to embargo oil sales to the West. The Carter Doctrine had been directed against outsiders; Reagan was understood to have expanded the doctrine to oppose any anti-American Saudi regime. Saudi Arabia looked to Washington for support against the hostile theocracy in Iran, unrest in Yemen and South Yemen, a coup attempt in Bahrain, the Soviet invasion of Afghanistan, and radical Islamist pressures in Saudi Arabia.

1981 - To help Iran versus Iraq, and insure the safety of Jewish residents of Iran, Israel was sending arms to Iran – a strategy which grew into the Iran-Contra affair.

1981 - Fifteen minutes after Reagan was sworn in, Iran put the Embassy hostages on a plane for home. Critics of the Reagan administration alleged an "October surprise" – a secret deal by the Republicans to sell arms to Iran if it would delay release of the hostages, and if the Republicans won the election.

1983 - In return for an American subsidy, Turkey was allowing American intelligence to monitor Soviet submarine traffic through the straits.

1983 - Reagan created CENTCOM to guard Persian Gulf oil.

1984 - In reaction to Iranian threats to close the Strait of Hormuz to foreign shipping, Reagan announced America would not permit closure of the Strait.

1985 - A "confederation of outlaw states" cited by Reagan included three in the Middle East: Iran, Iraq, and Syria.

1986 - Reagan named sixteen maritime "choke points" which the USSR had contingency plans to block. The list included the Suez Canal, the Bab al Mandab, and the Strait of Hormuz.

1986 - To provoke Libyan ruler Qadhafi into providing America a pretext for attack, Washington sent naval units into waters claimed by Libya. Libya obliged by firing missiles at US planes. America then bombed Tripoli.

1987 - At Kuwait's request, the US Navy provided escort (against the threat of Iranian attack) to eleven tankers that had been reflagged as American.

1987 - To reduce the risk of an Iranian victory over Iraq, and gratify defense contractors, Washington was providing Iraq with military material and satellite intelligence on Iranian deployments.

1988 - Saudi Arabia PNG'ed the American Ambassador for protesting (under instruction) the Saudi purchase of medium-range missiles from China (after Congress had blocked the sale of American missiles).

1990 - The United States assumed primary responsibility for expelling Iraqi forces from Kuwait, and for building a coalition to this end. Bush froze Iraqi and Kuwaiti assets in America and banned most imports from Iraq. Saudi Arabia, its pride in Arab independence of action set aside by the Iraqi threat, invited American troops into its territory, under the misimpression that they would leave as soon as Kuwait had been liberated. Jordan, Algeria, Tunisia, Yemen, and the PLO were among the states that opposed American military action.

1990 - Bush I authorized the CIA to bring about the covert overthrow of President Saddam Husayn: Robert Woodward, *The Commanders.*

1991 - The US-led coalition liberated Kuwait, operating from Prince Sultan Air Base in Saudi Arabia and seven seaports: four on the Gulf and three on the Red Sea. Kuwait agreed to allow the US Navy access to Kuwaiti ports. America guaranteed the defense of Kuwait.

1991 - Turkey's support for the Allied coalition was a radical departure from its previous policy of neutrality in inter-Arab conflicts. Its motives were to be on the winning side, to obtain American and Arab subsidies, and to advance its campaign for membership in the European Union. Despite areas of friction (Turkish use of American helicopters against Kurdish villages; Cyprus; American unilateralism; American protection of Iraqi Kurds), Turkey closed the pipeline from Iraq, allowed US planes to stage attacks on Iraq from Incirlik, and participated in the postwar sanctions regime. The United States was cited in *Middle East Policy* as Turkey's closest ally. Washington relied on Turkey as a regional power, a market for arms, and an ally of Israel. President Ozal imposed the pro-Western policy over substantial opposition in Turkey; Gulf War I and its aftermath had cost Turkey some 20 billion dollars by 1994, but Ankara's greater concerns were membership in the EU, and the threat of an autonomous Kurdish entity in northern Iraq.

1991 - Turkey upgraded its ties with Israel by sending an ambassador. Israel was a source of arms denied by the Europeans on the grounds that Turkish policy toward its Kurds violated their human rights.

1992 - Turkey was the cornerstone of the American security structure in the Gulf, particularly as a base against Arab radicalism and Iranian theocracy.

1992 - Qatar signed a defense agreement with the United States.

1992? - Bahrain allowed the United States to establish a naval base at Al Manamah, which became the headquarters of the Fifth Fleet.

1993 - Turkey denied America the use of Incirlik Air Base for attacks on Iraq, and was unsympathetic with its use for patrolling the Northern No-Fly Zone.

1993 - Mubarak was allowing the CIA to base its Middle East operations in Cairo.

1994 - As Saudi Arabia's main source of arms, and with the help of Export-Import Bank financing, America beat out Europe's Airbus for a six-billion-dollar upgrade of the Saudi commercial fleet.

1994 - America had pre-positioned, in both Kuwait and Qatar, material to equip one brigade, but Islamist pressure had blocked a similar arrangement with Saudi Arabia. Kuwait also let America station an air squadron on its territory.

1995 - American sanctions against Iran were now "watertight".

1995 - The United States maintained some 20,000 military personnel in the Gulf area, many of them on the 20 ships now designated as the Fifth Fleet, which reported to Central Command Headquarters in Tampa. The United States had secret defense agreements with Kuwait, Bahrain, Qatar, the UAE, and Oman, and a verbal agreement with Saudi Arabia. With the two strongest Gulf states (Iran and Iraq), it had no formal relations at all. The American military presence was incurring great Arab resentment.

1996 - Annoyed by Syrian sheltering of Kurdish dissident Ocalan, by Syrian and Iraqi complaints about Turkish diversion of water from the Euphrates and the Tigris (Chapter 5), and by reported Syrian clearance for use of its air bases by Greek planes in the event of war between Greece and Turkey, Ankara signed a landmark defense agreement with Israel. Obstructed by the Greek lobby from access to American arms, Ankara saw Israel as an alternative source. Israel needed more scope for jet training, and more regional allies.

1996 - American and British overflights of the Northern No-Fly Zone from Incirlik were under stricter restraint from Ankara. France dropped out. (American flights from Incirlik were supervised by the European Command, those from Arabia by the Central Command.) America began to fly some of its patrols over the Southern No-Fly Zone from a base in eastern Jordan (entering Iraqi air space via Saudi Arabia).

1996 - Shaken by the bombing of American residential quarters at Khawbar Towers, Saudi Arabia denied US planes the right to fly air raids against Iraq from its territory.

1996 - In recognition of the strategic significance of the Strait of Hormuz, Iran had posted troops on the islands of Abu Musa and the Tunbs (sovereignty contested). The tanker lane through the Strait was carrying twenty percent of the world's oil production. Iran was stationing naval units and missiles along the Strait. America had concluded with Oman an "access agreement" so discreetly consummated that most Omanis were unaware of it.

1996 - Congress adopted in secret an appropriation of funds for covert action to change the government in Iran – plus the Iran-Libya Sanctions Act (ILSA), which authorized the executive to impose sanctions on third-country firms that invested more than 40 million dollars in Iran or Libya. The bill lost contracts for American bidders and was ignored by the foreigners it was meant to intimidate. Iran read the bill as Clinton support for regime change in Tehran.

1997 - Fixated on the strategic importance of the Turkish Straits, and gratified by Turkey's participation in Gulf War I and its alliance with Israel, Washington was pursuing close association with Ankara despite resistance from the Greek, Armenian, and human rights (pro-Kurd) lobbies. Ankara welcomed the association as a source of arms, financing, support for EU membership, and a buffer against Turkish Islamism. Ankara was troubled, however, by Israel's preference for an independent Kurdistan in Iraq, and by America's punitive policy toward Iraq, which ran counter to Turkey's ties of trade and propinquity. Even though many observers doubted that Turkey would ever gain admission to the EU, Washington had been putting great pressure on the EU in Turkey's favor.

1998 - With American participation, Turkey and Israel held their first joint naval exercises. Jordan sent an observer.

1998 - The White House relaxed sanctions on Iran by allowing importation of food and medicine.

1999 - The new Amir of Bahrain was a strong proponent of close partnership with the United States. Site of the headquarters of the Fifth Fleet, Bahrain received military aid from America – plus financial aid from Saudi Arabia. Saudi Arabia and Kuwait were reimbursing the US for the cost of water and fuel consumed by its forces stationed in the Gulf.

1999 - Qatar was the first Gulf state to establish overt trade relations with Israel.

1999 - The key new phenomenon in the Middle East was the American-Israeli-Turkish alliance. Israel processed Turkish products for resale to America (duty-free all the way), backed Turkey on Cyprus, and helped in the upgrading of Turkey's infrastructure. The United States supported pipeline routes via Turkey, closed its eyes to Turkish violation of its Kurds' human rights, and allowed Turkey to get around the restrictions on the purchase of Iraqi oil. Washington defined the PKK as a terrorist organization and helped trap Kurdish dissident Ocalan, but Turkey was immensely disturbed by the Kurdish safe haven in north Iraq. Late in the year, Israeli Prime Minister Barak visited Ankara, the first such example of cooperation since a secret visit by Ben-Gurion in 1958. The Department of State told Congress alliance with Turkey was vital, because it was a democratic secular state at the nexus of Europe, the Middle East, and Central Asia. According to William Safire, the natural rivals of the American-Israeli-Turkish alliance were Iran, Iraq, Syria/Lebanon, and the Palestinians.

1999 - Iran strongly opposed the American military presence in the Gulf; Washington continued to maintain sanctions against Iran.

2000 - Clinton's long-standing policy of "Dual Containment" of Iraq and Iran ran counter to Turkey's economic interests in those two states. There were signs of Turkish restlessness over America's Iraq policy. (However, American support in 2001 for a major loan to Turkey by the IMF was a pointed example of Washington's economic influence over Ankara.) As the largest debtor to the IMF, Turkey hoped its alliance with the United States and Israel would induce Washington to support rescheduling Turkey's repayments to the IMF.

2000 - Because of Russian construction of a nuclear power plant at Bushehr in Iran, Congress had cut American aid to Russia in half.

2001 - Turkey looked to its Israeli allies to mobilize American Jewish support against the creation of a Kurdish state, and shield Turkey against American reprisal for any Turkish opposition to American initiatives in Iraq.

2001 - A representative of the European Union stated that the secondary sanctions called for in America's Iran-Libya Sanctions Act had no basis in international law.

2002 - Turkey received a twelve-billion-dollar loan from the IMF.

2002 - Vice President Cheney, in Ankara, tried with little success to enlist Turkey in the peacekeeping effort in Afghanistan, and to sell Turkey on possible American invasion of Iraq.

2002 - Turkish Prime Minister Ecevit issued an unprecedented condemnation of the "genocide" practiced by Israel against the Palestinians in the Occupied Territories. His remarks won broad public support.

2002 - In recognition of Jordanian cooperation, Washington was paying it 450 million dollars a year in financial aid.

2002 - Oman granted the United States access to military facilities on Masirah Island. Washington awarded Oman 50 million dollars in military assistance.

2002 - The State Department and the Voice of America were calling on the people of Iran to abandon theocracy.

2002 - Disinvited by Saudi Arabia from basing its Middle Eastern air operations at Prince Sultan Air Base, Washington concluded a secret agreement to set up an alternative headquarters at al 'Udayd in Qatar.

2003 - Cheney, Secretary of Defense Rumsfeld, and Joint Chiefs Chairman Myers briefed Saudi Ambassador Bandar Al Sa'ud on the

American plan for invading Iraq. Saudi Arabia would permit the American forces restricted access to the air control center at Prince Sultan, and the right to overfly Saudi territory.

2003 - Hard bargaining between Washington and Ankara. America wanted to stage ground attacks into Iraq from Turkey. The Turkish National Security Council wanted a large low-interest American loan, EU membership, permission for Turkish troops to follow American troops into Iraq, a share of Iraqi oil, and a guarantee against the creation of a Kurdish state. The negotiations collapsed when the Turkish Parliament rejected American transit in a close vote, and the military failed to intervene – in contrast with its activism against the civilian government during four previous disputes.

2003 - On the eve of invading Iraq, Washington had arranged for stationing troops in Qatar, and for staging the invasion from Kuwait, with ancillary operations in Jordan, Saudi Arabia, Oman, and the UAE.

March 19, 2003 - Thousands of American Special Operations forces poured into Iraq from Saudi Arabia and Jordan.

March 20, 2003 - Invasion of Iraq.

April 2003 - Washington initiated the transfer of its Middle Eastern air force headquarters from Prince Sultan to al 'Udayd.

May 1, 2003 - Outfitted in combat gear, Bush landed on the carrier Abraham Lincoln and declared that the American military mission in Iraq had been accomplished. The aircraft, a four-seater, carried the legends "Navy One" and "George W. Bush, Commander-in-Chief". Also on the plane were two US Navy pilots and a Secret Service agent.

2003 - The neoconservative bloc in Washington was agitating for deployment of the MEK (Chapter 9) against Iran.

December 2003 - The US Department of Defense had barred French, German, and Russian companies from bidding on reconstruction contracts in Iraq.

December 12, 2003 - Bush 43 signed the Syrian Accountability and Lebanese Sovereignty Restoration Act, which prohibited the export of dual-use products to Syria and called on it to cut ties with the Palestinian resistance organizations, withdraw its troops from Lebanon, stop developing long-range missiles, and stop aiding "terrorism" in Iraq.

June 28, 2004 - Washington transferred nominal control of Iraq to a handpicked regime headed by Iyad 'Allawi, a one-time Baathist and longtime recipient of a stipend from the CIA.

June 28, 2004 - *The New Yorker* (Seymour Hersh) reported that Israel had sent intelligence and military operatives into Iraqi Kurdistan to expand its presence as a precaution against anarchy in Iraq, despite the risk to its new alliance with Turkey.

2007 - Kuwait detached its dinar from the US dollar.

2007 - *The Washington Post Weekly* reported that for the past seven years the CIA had been secretly holding "terrorists" in Jordanian Intelligence headquarters in Amman, where torture was routinely inflicted.

11/17/08 - US Ambassador Crocker and Iraqi Foreign Minister Zebari signed a status-of-forces agreement (SOFA) effective for three years, subject to one year's notice of cancellation. US forces – excluding trainers and support teams – would leave most Iraqi cities by 6/30/09 and the country by 12/31/11. The Iraqi Islamic Party, a member of Tawafuq (a Sunni bloc), demanded that the agreement be subjected to a referendum.

1/1/09 - The SOFA replaced the UN mandate for foreign military operations in Iraq. The US transferred to Iraq responsibility for security in all 18 provinces, including the Green Zone.

Recap

Over the past seven millennia, hegemony over the Middle East has been contested among its inhabitants, and between them and invaders. The usual bases of indigenous power have been the four most populous sectors: Anatolia, Persia, Mesopotamia, and Egypt.

Unity Versus Division - In its past 4300 years, the Middle East has seen at least thirty-five empires come, and thirty-four go; the Americans are joined at the hip with Israel, and still occupy Iraq. Twenty-eight were indigenous or transplants. At least eight conquerors were based outside the region: Macedonians, Romans, Ethiopians, Portuguese, British, French, Russians, and Americans.

Over the past 2500 years, the Middle East in whole or in part has suffered some 500 years of foreign-based domination (Hellenic - 10; Roman - 350; European - 100; American - 50). Persia survived 850 years of non-Persian rule (640-1502) – mitigated by Buyid autonomy, 945 to 1055.

Overall, the region has been the site of one or more empires for some 3600 years. Only three empires managed to unite essentially the whole region: the Persian for a century, the Macedonian for a decade, and the Islamic for two centuries.

If these phenomena lead to any conclusion at all, it is that there has been a constant impulse toward unification – rarely achieved, but repeatedly attempted. The corollary is that the present fragmentation of the region into twenty-six entities (Table A) is impermanent and inherently unstable. Over the last 100 years, the region has generated at least twenty wars and insurrections. Failing a greater degree of political unification, the new century's prospect is for more of the same.

Western Imperialism is Exploitive - The Hellenic and Roman periods, for all their militance, provided the Middle East some degree of assimilation, acculturation, and stability. No such mitigation can be credited to the imperialism practiced by the Europeans or the Americans. On the record (Chapters 7, 8, 10, and 15), the incidental benefits of their interventions are far outweighed by the damage inflicted. Separately or collectively, Britain, France, and America have colluded with self-serving Middle East regimes to betray the long-term interests of the general population.

Europe's imperial possessions were organized to maximize the profits of the rulers. Boundaries were juggled for the imperialists' convenience. Inequitable land tenure patterns were favored – as noted by Michael Hudson and Jeffrey Sommers.

There were no British atrocities in the Middle East to match those in India. To put down and avenge the "Indian Mutiny" of 1857, Britain lined a main road with the corpses of hanged Indian soldiers, and devastated the city of Delhi (an action made known belatedly, to most Americans at least, by *The New York Review of Books* in 2007). The "jewel in the crown" began the imperialist era with per capita incomes comparable to those in Britain, and ended the era poverty-stricken and brutally divided. Imperialism created the Atlantic slave trade. (See *Colossus,* Niall Ferguson.)

However, the record in the Middle East is not much better. British rule left Egyptians impoverished and badly served. In Jaffa (Palestine), Napoleon shocked his own officers by slaughtering 3800 Arab prisoners of war: This episode is featured in Samia Serageldin's historical novel, *The Naqib's Daughter.* Western imperialism exacerbated instability across the region, but most egregiously in Palestine.

As Washington began to focus on the Middle East, it betrayed a visceral predilection for backing compliant autocrats, most of whom placed more importance on their own survival than on the welfare of their subjects. In the late 1900's, Washington concentrated on tactics of indirection – public support for meaningless initiatives like the Tripartite Declaration and the Oslo Agreement, blundering involvement in coup attempts (Iran in 1953, Lebanon and Syria in 1957, Iraq in 1963 and the 1990's), and assassination attempts (against Fadlallah of *Hizballah* in 1985). In 2003 Washington graduated to full-blown imperialism, whose results as of this writing have not been as advertised. As noted by Amy Chua in *Day of Empire,* intolerance is a sign of imperial decay.

Western Imperialism is on the Decline - The French Empire ended with de Gaulle's proclamation of Algerian independence in 1962. The

British Empire sputtered out about 1970. The Russian Empire collapsed in 1990. After having controlled 84 percent of the land surface of the globe in 1914 (Paul Kennedy's reckoning), the Europeans have shifted their attention to building unity at home. A sign of the times was the 1960 UNGA Declaration on the Granting of Independence to Colonial Territories.

World Domination is an Illusion - In 1450, the Islamic civilization – reinvigorated by the assimilation of the Turks – seemed on its way to Mediterranean domination. From 1500 to 1800, two world powers – Spain and the Ottomans – fought for preeminence. At the time of World War II, the world was divided into four spheres of interest: American, Soviet, German, and Japanese. At the moment, Russia, Germany, Japan, and China are in the second tier. America stands alone.

History offers no reason to assume permanent preeminence for America or any other contestant. China is on the rise, and Europe has made astounding progress from civil war to continental comity. Washington's recent obsession with building a chain of strategic positions across Asia was worse than importunate – it was delusional.

As for the Middle East, the tides of foreign intervention have always receded, and home rule has repeatedly bobbed back up to the surface.

Cultural expansion resists reversal – as the global spread of the English language has demonstrated. The American experience suggests that continental colonialism succeeds. However, political subjugation is ephemeral – a failed offshoot of the evolutionary tree of political organization.

Chapter 11
Stages of Government

For the first six thousand years of history, government was tribal, communal, monarchial, or imperial. The advent of democracy – government by all the governed – had to await the evolution of the complex political machinery on which it depends. As David Fromkin has noted, it took post-Roman Europe 1500 years to develop the nation-state system. As late as the 1900's, fascism prevailed in Germany, Italy, and Spain, and Communism in Russia. The Nineteenth and Twentieth Centuries may come to be exalted as the era when democracy took its first faltering steps – originally in Europe and North America, later in Latin America.

The Middle East is behind the curve. It has no democracies. Up until the present day, it has known nothing but autocracy, whose capacity for atrocity – monstrously exemplified by Nazi Germany – has been demonstrated over and over again in the Middle East. Robert Fisk cites the example of Agha Mohammed Khan, the shah of 18th century Persia who retaliated against an offending village (It had sheltered his predecessor) by exterminating its adults and blinding its children. Only three years ago *Vanity Fair* cited four Arabian states for condemning foreign workers to forced labor. All governments, democratic or not, practice thought control, but in the Arab world information is so trammeled that the Saudi regime was able to keep the Iraqi invasion of Kuwait a secret from the Saudi public for four days.

Aside from the Israelis, the people of the Middle East have a love-hate relationship with the West. They appreciate its achievements, but loathe its foreign policies. However, the persistence of autocracy has a more fundamental cause: In the process of political evolution, the region is two or three centuries behind the West. Its political, electoral, and judicial systems are still in the embryonic phase. Future historians may look back

279

to discern a prevailing pattern: Stage one - traditionalist autocracy; stage two - military coup (as in Iran in 1921, Iraq in 1936, Syria in 1949, Egypt in 1952, and Iraq again in 1963); stage three - partisan dictatorship (as in Syria from 1961, and Iraq from 1968 to 2003); stage four - social revolution, introduced by France in 1789, and now seething just below the political surface of the Middle East.

Autocracy comes in several forms. Although every state is *sui generis*, as of 2009 all but two of the nineteen states of the Middle East fell into five categories: tribal autocracies (7), military autocracies (3), partisan autocracies (lately reduced to one), ethnocracies (5), and one theocracy. Lebanon and Iraq were in political limbo.

Tribal Autocracies

The Arabian Peninsula may be the last bastion of tribal government in the world. In the assessment of Kristian Ulrichsen (*Middle East Policy*), as population rises and oil production falls, the peninsula's welfare systems are nearing expiration.

The five emirates along the Gulf – lately characterized in *The London Review of Books* as not so much countries as petrol stations – have evolved in parallel, but not in synchrony. Many cabinet ministers are appointed for life. Each of the five has a *majlis al shura*. Otherwise, they differ.

Bahrain - On this tiny island, a Shiite majority is ruled by a Sunni Amir, who chooses a son as his successor under the Constitution of 1973. Amir Shaykh Hamad bin 'Isa al Khalifah, who became ruler in 1999, governs by decree – subject to initiatives allowed the bicameral legislature. Decisions of the lower house, where the elections of 2006 combated gerrymandering sufficiently to put 40 percent of the seats in the hands of the pro-Shiite *Wifaq* Party, can be overruled by the upper house, whose members are appointed by the Amir. His government is trying to raise the Sunni percentage of the population by such devices as naturalizing Saudis. The *Times* of 4/6/09 stated that Shiites are barred from almost all positions in the military and security services.

Women have been allowed to vote and hold office, but few if any women have been elected. Internet chat rooms and TV broadcasts by Al Jazeera (see below) are banned, but in 2008 the Amir signaled his close ties with the US by sending a lady from Bahrain's tiny Jewish community to Washington as the Bahraini ambassador.

In March 2009, following the detention of 23 leaders of the Shiite community, Bahrain was experiencing nightly demonstrations in support of their release, and in protest of alleged governmental discrimination against the Shia. Neha Vora wrote in *Middle East Report* of Fall 2009 that Al Wifaq was losing its role as spokesman of the Shiite community to the more confrontational Al Haqq.

Jordan - Although this relic of British imperialism has had a stormy history, the Hashemite monarchy has preserved its rule over a state with a Palestinian majority, thanks to British, American, and Israeli support (Chapter 8), and the ingenuity and resolve of Western-educated Kings Husayn and 'Abdallah II. In 1991, the regime survived the economic shock of the unexpected return of hundreds of thousands of citizens who lost lucrative jobs in Kuwait after the expulsion of the Iraqi invaders.

'Abdallah, who succeeded his father in 1999, has confronted the opposition head-on, repressing Hamas and other Palestinian factions, while subsidizing his power base, the Jordanian tribes. In 2002, he dissolved the powerless Parliament and banned unions and professional associations in order to control reverberations from Intifadah II next door. Despite the public uproar against the American invasion of Iraq, he managed in that same year to engineer the election of a 110-seat Parliament dominated by pro-government forces (against 24 Islamists). He also appointed a 40-man Senate.

In 2001, as a reward for the regime's determined loyalty to US policy, notably its collaboration with Israel, Washington had made Jordan the first Arab state to have duty-free access for its exports to the US. *The Nation* reported in 2006 that the unemployment rate of 30 percent had not been markedly alleviated by the establishment of a free-trade zone, since guest workers from South Asia and China had taken low-wage jobs Jordanians declined.

In 2007, selection of mayors and councils for cities outside 'Amman was determined by election. However, the Islamic Action Front, the political wing of the Muslim Brotherhood in Jordan, refused to participate, alleging that the elections were rigged.

Jordan had to accept hundreds of thousands of Iraqi refugees from the sectarian bloodshed of 2006-07. Explosion of the ambiguous situation in Iraq could have severe consequences for Jordan, which has close economic ties with Iraq, and sensitive political ties with Iraq's Sunni community.

Kuwait - The Emirate of Kuwait is essentially a family-run corporation – the family being the hereditary rulers, the Sabahs. At this writing the ruler was Shaykh Sabah al Ahmad al Sabah. Political parties are banned, but Islamists constitute an unofficial opposition. In earlier years, of some 900,000 people who were classed as permanent residents, only males had full citizenship, although women had a much freer role in business and government than women in Saudi Arabia. The National Assembly (*Majlis* *al Ummah*) elected in 2003 was controlled by loyalists, but Islamists won over a third of the seats. It is the only parliament in the Gulf to have real legislative power: *Middle East Report.*

In 2005 women gained the vote. In June 2006, 345,000 Kuwaitis (including 200,000 women) elected a new National Assembly of fifty members (no women). In 2008 the *Times* discerned widespread frustration at the government's resistance to economic and political reform. Elections of May 2009 seated four women in a National Assembly of fifty. Analysts were detecting growing polarization between urbanites and Bedouin – many of whom had been naturalized.

Oman - In the 1600's, the rulers of Oman expelled the Portuguese (Chapter 10) and took over from them the island of Zanzibar (later taken by the UK). In 1737, Persia took advantage of civil war in Oman to invade, but four years later Ahmad bin Sa'id Al Bu Sa'id expelled the Persians, was subsequently elected 'Ibadi Imam (Chapter 6), and established the dynasty that rules Oman today. The US established official ties with Oman in 1840.

In 1920 the Treaty of Sib temporarily divided Oman into an imamate, based in the interior, and the Sultanate of Muscat under Sultan Taymur. By 1959, with the help of British forces, the Sultanate had terminated a Saudi foray into the Buraymi oasis, jointly administered by Oman and Abu Dhabi, and suppressed the rebellious tribes in the interior. In 1970 the British deposed reactionary Sultan Sa'id in favor of his reformist son, Qabus. In 1971 Oman joined the UN and the Arab League.

Ten years later, as reported by Chas Freeman in *Middle East Policy*, the failed American operation to rescue American hostages held in Iran was staged in Oman, to the temporary displeasure of Sultan Qabus.

Educated in England, Qabus has liberalized Omani society, instituted universal education in Arabic and English, and awarded women the right to vote, sit in the Majlis, and hold senior government positions. Sultan Qabus University opened in 1986.

In 1990, Qabus established an appointive Consultative Council (*Majlis al Shura*). In 1996, Qabus decreed a Basic Law, which, inter alia, provided for a bicameral legislature and an independent judiciary, and assigned hereditary rule to the male descendants of Ahmad bin Sa'id. In 1997, Qabus set up a *Majlis 'Uman* (Council of Oman), which incorporated an upper house, the Council of State (*Majlis al Dawlah*). As of 2009, political parties were still banned. Four-fifths of Oman's labor force are guest workers.

The traditional center of agitation for reconversion of Oman to an 'Ibadi imamate is Nazwa, in the mountains seventy miles southwest of

Musqat, the capital. In 2005 Qabus commuted the sentences of 31 Omanis condemned of plotting a sectarian takeover.

Four-fifths of Oman's labor force are guest workers. 79% of government revenues come from oil and gas although Oman does not belong to OPEC.

Qatar - This tiny projection of the Arabian Peninsula into the Persian Gulf has more petroleum than water. Settlement was initiated in the 1800's by Arabian tribes, ruled ever since by the Al Thani family, whose independence from Bahrain and Saudi Arabia was assured by the British Navy. International importance was won by the discovery of oil, now largely depleted, and the gigantic North Dome Field of natural gas under the Gulf. As reported by Louay Bahri and Phoebe Marr, the discovery of oil in the 1930's enabled Qatar to offer schooling to all, women included. Qatar University, including female students and teachers, was inaugurated in 1977.

In a bloodless coup, *Amir* Hamad bin Khalifah Al Thani took over from his father in 1995, and restricted the succession to male descendants of Hamad bin Khalifah Al Thani. Prince Hamad and Crown Prince Jasim (a son by his third wife) are both graduates of Sandhurst. One of Hamad's wives, Shaykhah Mozah bint Nasser al Misnad, makes effective public appearances.

Revenues from oil and gas have enabled the regime to maintain a quintessential welfare state for its citizens, including negligible taxes, subsidized usage of utilities, civil service jobs for high school graduates, a free plot of land with a tax-free loan to develop it, and free education through college at one of the campuses maintained by several American universities, among them Cornell's Weill Medical College: Mehran Kamrava, *Middle East Journal,* Summer 2009. Political parties are illegal, but Hamad has made some noteworthy changes. He has abolished censorship and allowed the establishment of Al Jazeera (The Peninsula), a TV station which practices judicious self-censorship while articulating the regime's disagreements with Saudi Arabia and reporting boldly on Arab Nationalist themes. It has acquired a broad and devoted Arab audience.

In 1999, Qatar became the first Gulf emirate to let women vote and run for an elective body (municipal council). The constitution of 2003 provides for a Parliament of 60 members – 15 appointed by the Amir, 45 elected. Meanwhile, there is a Consultative Council whose 35 members are appointed by the ruler.

Of Qatar's 900,000 (?) residents, perhaps a fourth are citizens – most of them Sunni. The rest are guest workers, a plurality of them from Pakistan.

The establishment are Wahhabis, but more liberal in their politics than their coreligionists in Saudi Arabia.

Saudi Arabia - Tom Barger recalls that, when he arrived in Saudi Arabia as an Aramco geologist in 1937, "nearly everybody was hungry most of the time." In the subsequent seventy years, the country has had to adapt to the stresses of modernity at a breakneck pace.

The Economist has noted that Saudi Arabia is one of the four Muslim states never conquered by Europeans, and the only one never invaded by Europeans. The royal family is shored up, and constrained, by the alliance concluded in 1744 between an ancestor and Shaykh Muhammad ibn 'Abd al Wahhab, founder of the Wahhabi branch of Sunni Islam. Recovering from the exile of the Saudi leadership to Kuwait by the pro-Ottoman Rashidis in the late 1800's, the alliance resiled in the 1900's to conquer all of Arabia except Yemen and the five emirates on the Gulf. The founder of the resurgent kingdom, Shaykh 'Abd al 'Aziz Al Sa'ud (Ibn Sa'ud) consolidated his ties with other tribes by taking over 200 wives, seriatim, and siring 44 sons, five of whom have been rulers since his death. Ibn Sa'ud's compact with Standard Oil of California in 1933 initiated the momentous alliance with America, based on exchange of diplomatic relations in 1940, the meeting between FDR and Ibn Sa'ud in the Suez Canal in 1945 (Chapter 4), and the symbiosis between the monarchy and the American-built colossus, Aramco. The Americans struck oil in 1938, and the kingdom rapidly lurched from poverty to opulence. Since 1980, Saudi Arabia has owned Aramco, which became Saudi Aramco in 1988.

The legal system is based on the Sharia. Trials are normally conducted privately. Modern temptations like liquor and movies are illegal. Slavery was outlawed in 1962. Up to that date, some affluent pilgrims to Mecca were said to have brought along a slave or two as a convenient equivalent of a traveler's check. Women are still forbidden to drive cars; conservatives have pointed out that building parallel roads for the two genders (to prevent men from seeing the faces of unveiled women) would be prohibitively expensive. Islam is the only religion allowed; conversion of a Muslim to another faith is a capital crime. In *The Shia Revival,* Vali Nasr writes that Shiites have been excluded from the cabinet and from influential positions in government service.

The 30,000-strong royal family includes 7,000 princes, who receive handsome stipends, and are exempt from prosecution. Dissidents are jailed, tortured, exiled, or executed, depending on the magnitude of the offense. After the 1979 Islamist attack on the Great Mosque (Chapter 12), the regime moved even farther to the right in its religious conservatism. Political parties are banned, as is criticism of the royal family. The press is controlled, and radio and TV stations are owned by the state. Under a Basic Law issued in 1992, the King has the right to designate his successor. Also in 1992, King Fahd formed a Consultative Council, noting that "elections are not part of Islamic ideology." In 2005, male citizens were allowed to vote in elections for half the members of 178 municipal councils. The other half were appointed by the monarchy.

King 'Abdallah is an absolute monarch, but he has to juggle the competing interests of the tribes, the clerics, and the burgeoning population. In the assessment of Gregory Gauze, he is the ranking member of a guardian council of senior sons of Ibn Sa'ud. So far, they have suppressed a number of challenges: 1987 - formation of the Saudi Hizballah, which was suspect in the 1996 bombing of Khawbar Towers; 1993 - brief emergence of a Committee for the Defense of Legitimate Rights, during a period of mismanagement by then-King Fahd; 1993 - pressure from the non-violent Shiite Organization of the Islamic Revolution; 2003 - bombings in Riyadh (Shiite and Iranian complicity suspected); 2003 - amnesty for Shiite Shaykh Hasan al Saffar, who while in Kuwait had formed The Islamic Reform Movement; 2004 - rise of a group advocating constitutional monarchy (leaders were jailed).

As Islamist violence has escalated around the world, the regime has promoted Islamist teachings in the schools, kept the veiling of women compulsory, maintained the ban on contact between Saudi males and Saudi females who are not their relatives, and built up the National Guard as a homeland security force and as a check on any untoward initiatives from the army. This schizoid arrangement presents the insuperable problem of building forces strong enough to defend the country, but too weak to threaten the regime. In 2007, Anthony Cordesman wrote in the *Middle East Journal* that Saudi Arabia could not sustain military combat without American technical assistance.

The historic power base of the regime is the alliance between the Saudi family and the Shaykh family (descendants of Shaykh Muhammad ibn 'Abd al Wahhab). Under pressure from rising unemployment, falling prices of oil, Islamist violence, Al Qa'idah's denunciations, exiles' criticism – notably *Cities of Salt* by the late 'Abd al Rahman Munif – and reformist agitation, the regime has made hesitant gestures toward liberalism, such as allowing a radio talk show that takes complaints about official actions, and setting up a Council of Ministers, chaired by the Crown Prince, but composed of twenty-four commoners. Disaffection continues to grow, exacerbated by the institutionalization of nepotism (subsidization of princes and many tribal shaykhs, favoritism for enterprises sponsored by princes, and reservation of government jobs for members of the religious hierarchy), at the expense of citizens who are out of the loop – like the fifteen Saudis who took part in the attacks of 9/11. (According to *The Nation,* they were non-Wahhabi residents of 'Asir, a district where women are allowed to drive and the monarchy is unpopular.)

In 2003, eyewitnesses were horrified when morals police sent female students back into a burning school – some to their deaths – so they would not appear in public without their *abayah*'s. In 2004, with oil prices ranging from 40 to 50 dollars a barrel, Saudi Arabia instituted a crash program to combat unemployment and disaffection by instilling in young Saudi males the novel idea that they might take over some of the jobs traditionally done for them by guest workers – and acquire some of the unfamiliar skills they would need if they did go to work (Chapter 3). Of the 8.8 million foreign workers, the government reportedly (*The Washington Post Weekly*) hopes eventually to send 6 or 7 million home. Meanwhile, the regime has had some success in rounding up Islamist activists, raising an existential question: Could the Saudi monarchy survive the repression of Wahhabiism?

Saudi Arabia's two million Shiite citizens, most of whom live along the Persian Gulf, pose a special problem. Their bid for full acceptance by the Sunni majority is inhibited by the invective of hard-line Sunni clerics, but King 'Abdallah is taking small steps on the Shiites' behalf – allowing the construction of Shiite mosques and the distribution of Shiite literature. Demonstrations in support of Lebanon's Hizballah in 2006 (Chapter 8) went too far, however, and the leaders were arrested.

The reconciliation of hidebound tradition with accelerating globalization is becoming increasingly difficult. Conservative mores (gender separation, arranged marriage, ban on movie theaters, religious fundamentalism) confront a mounting barrage from radio, satellite television, and the Internet – with its elusive Facebook. *The Guardian Weekly* has recounted how the infiltration of private homes by addictive Turkish soap operas elicited a cautionary fatwa from the ranking Saudi cleric. The Bush 43 speech of 2003 suddenly advocating democracy in the Middle East was not welcomed by America's autocratic clients.

In times of falling oil prices, world trade takes on political importance. In the opinion of Jean-Francois Seznec, Saudi Arabia's adherence to the World Trade Organization in 2006 will require the sidelining of the *Salafi* (fundamentalist) elements of its society. Charles Kestenbaum also infers incompatibility between WTO regulations and Saudi Arabia's sectarian restraints. King 'Abdallah has attacked the cultural divide by contracting with Saudi Aramco to establish the (nonsectarian) King 'Abdallah University of Science and Technology near Jiddah, and planning the establishment of six industrial cities on the Red Sea coast. In 2007, General Electric sold its plastic division to The Saudi Basic Industries Corporation (SABIC), the country's largest public corporation.

One member of the royal family is so liberal that he is a longtime exile in France. He is Prince Talal bin 'Abd al 'Aziz, father of financier Walid Talal, and sponsor of the Saudi Democratic Opposition Front, which advocates a constitutional monarchy with an elected parliament.

In February 2009, as reported by *Newsweek* and *The Financial Times,* King 'Abdallah continued his campaign of liberalization by assigning moderates to head the religious police and the judiciary, and appointing a woman (Nura al Fa'iz) as a Deputy Minister responsible for girls' education. She has converted the first three grades to coeducation. (Patrick Seale, *WRMEA,* May 2010.)

UAE - Activated by Britain's decision to pull its forces out of the erstwhile Trucial Coast (Chapter 10), the tribes in the area – already loosely affiliated – initiated discussions that led in 1971 to the formation of the United Arab Emirates, which is a loose federation of seven principalities (Abu Dhabi, Dubai, 'Ajman, Sharjah (*Al Shariqah*), Umm al Qaywayn, Ra's al Khaymah, and Fujayrah. Abu Dhabi is by far the biggest and richest of the seven. Bahrain and Qatar declined the opportunity to join. The Sultanate of Oman previously considered the seven emirates part of its territory.

The UAE has a constitution (1996) and several Federal organs – notably the Supreme Federal Council, composed of the seven rulers, who elect the UAE's President and Vice President from among their membership. All citizens of the UAE receive low-cost education and medical services. 80 percent of UAE residents are foreign workers (largely South Asian) who leave when their jobs terminate. Educational opportunity is gender-equal. The American University of Sharjah is the flagship institution of Sharjah's University City.

Abu Dhabi is the permanent capital, and its ruler the logical President of the federation. The present incumbent, and Commander-in-Chief of the Union Defense Force, is Amir Khalifah bin Zayid Al Nahyan. The Minister of Economy and Planning, Shaykhah Lubna al Qasimi, niece of the ruler of Sharja, studied computer engineering in California. NYU/Abu Dhabi was due to open in 2010.

The stability of the UAE hinges on the longevity of the ties between Abu Dhabi and Dubai. Abu Dhabi has huge oil and gas reserves and the biggest sovereign wealth fund in the world. Christopher Davidson reported its estimated value at over a trillion dollars: *Middle East Policy,* Summer 2009. Dubai has little oil left, but a dynamic ruler (Shaykh Muhammad bin

Rashid Al Maktum), a graduate of Cambridge. For deep-pocket tourists, he has been trying to create a desert Shangri-la of skyscrapers, resorts, an inside ski run, and artificial fairyland resort islands. For entrepreneurs, there is a business-friendly economy, with a modern banking system, a free-trade zone, the world's largest excavated dry docks, the world's largest Internet-protocol telephony system, a legal code that favors property and ownership, and no tariffs or taxes.

All this has been financed by judicious foreign investment, largess from the ruler of Abu Dhabi, high-end tourism, and entrepot proceeds. In the last department, Dubai has profited from political unrest in rival Beirut, and from proximity to Iran, whose entrepreneurs desperately need an escape hatch from theocracy's onerous constraints – and from Washington's embargo on sales to Iran. Dubai's economic miracle depends on a liberal culture, the Jabal 'Ali Free Zone, permission for foreigners to own property, and the services of foreign workers, who greatly outnumber citizens. The foreign workers run the gamut from lawyers of the criminal court to laborers – who stay out of sight in ethnic clubs and restaurants, and sleep in secluded camps. Most Dubai employers follow the illegal practice of holding the passports of their foreign workers: *Middle East Report.* According to *The National Geographic,* Dubai sees more tourists than India and more ships than Singapore. Robin Wright reports that many of Dubai's elite are of Iranian descent, and thousands of Iranian companies have offices in Dubai. Its foreign residents are said to include 400,000 Iranians. The Dubai airport is one of the world's busiest.

Abu Dhabi and Dubai have followed the lead of Saudi Arabia and Kuwait in investing widely in Europe, India, Japan, and the United States. In early 2009, American media reported that Dubai's "moonbase" economy, in free fall from the global downturn, had obtained an Abu Dhabi bailout, at the heavy cost of surrendering to direct Abu Dhabi oversight.

Military Autocracies

Egypt - The steady degeneration of the Albanian Dynasty culminated in mid-1952 in the exile of King Faruq, who was replaced by a group of midlevel army officers who styled themselves the Revolutionary Command Council. In the next year or so, Jamal (Gamal in the Egyptian vernacular) 'Abd al Nasir emerged as their leader, and in 1954 as President of the Egyptian Republic. Although Nasir and his successors (Anwar Sadat and Husni Mubarak) have cultivated the trappings of representative government, they all came from the military. Sadat and Mubarak were chosen by their predecessors, and Mubarak is grooming his son Jamal (a civilian) to succeed him.

Nasir made a commendable effort to modernize Egypt's fossilized social structure and revive its traditional leadership role in the Arab World, but Western machinations (Chapters 8, 10, and 13) and Egyptian inertia were too much for him. He presided over the collapse of the UAR (Chapter 14) in 1961 and the Israeli conquests of 1967. Sadat engineered the minor military triumph of 1973, and then fell back on the strategy of if-you-can't-lick-'em, join-'em. In 1978, at Camp David, he washed his hands of Palestine and Arab Nationalism, in return for the recovery of Sinai and an annual American subsidy of some two billion dollars which, so far, has been enough to counteract the Egyptians' growing poverty, and their rising resentment of the peace treaty with Israel.

Mubarak has followed in Sadat's footsteps, practicing a stubborn despotism that allegedly allows room for corruption. According to Milton Viorst, Mubarak has joined other Arab rulers in accommodating the contemporary surge in Islamism by seeking political alliance with the clerics, while continuing to jail hard-line Islamists and reformers. In the 1990's, after two decades of violent dissidence, including the assassination of Sadat, the Muslim Brotherhood renounced violence. Since then it has maintained an uneasy truce with the military regime.

The maintenance of law and order in Egypt is confounded by the constant rise in the number of its inhabitants, and decline in the area of arable land. In 1997 *The National Geographic* deplored the plight of 60,000,000 Egyptians trying to live off farmland then estimated at 7.5 million acres, but suffering constant reduction from urban expansion, pollution, coastal sinking, erosion, salination, conversion of topsoil to bricks, and the loss of riparian sediment since the construction of the High Dam at Aswan. The only alleviation was expensive irrigation projects in the desert. In these circumstances, rejection of America's annual Camp David subsidy (Chapter 8), or of the financial assistance occasionally provided by the pro-American oil states, would be traumatic. In 2007, *The Middle East Journal* reported that by 2000 the rising use of contraception had reduced Egypt's fertility rate to 3.5%, but the population continued to increase, and unemployment along with it.

By 2000, the level of dissent threatened anti-regime protest. Egypt was still an unalloyed police state, with press and broadcast media controlled, and some 10,000 Islamists in jail – although Hala Mustafa and Augustus Norton have concluded that ever since the time of Sadat the regime has been even harder on liberals than on Islamists. The American invasion of Iraq in March 2003, coming on top of rising inflation, unemployment, the inefficiency of state-owned industries, and strains on Egypt's dilapidated infrastructure, sparked a huge demonstration in Cairo. Islamist, Marxist, and liberal marchers chanted slogans against Mubarak, and called for jihad against America. Police arrested 800 and tortured suspected ringleaders.

By late 2004, Mubarak and son had liberalized the Egyptian autocracy sufficiently to license 17 political parties. Reformists across the spectrum were testing the limits of repression. As reported by *Current History*, liberals had founded a new activist organization, *Kifayah* (Enough). The Muslim Brotherhood was still banned, but it was still the leading opposition faction. Activists who crossed the line were in jail, in some cases to be tortured. They claimed that the real offense of Ashraf Ibrahim, jailed in late 2003 on a charge of plotting against the regime, was the size of the demonstrations he had organized against the American invasion of Iraq (and by implication against the regime's subservience to Washington).

In the fall of 2005, Mubarak staged fraudulent elections to reelect himself as President – for the first time by direct ballot – and reconfirm his National Democratic Party (NDP) as the dominant force in Parliament. Secular parties were banned from the Parliamentary elections. Ayman Nur, the leader of the liberal democratic *Al Ghad* (Tomorrow), won half a million votes in the Presidential election, but lost his seat in Parliament and was jailed for five years on trumped-up charges. Earlier in the year, the conviction of an alleged agent of the Brotherhood, Sa'd al Din Ibrahim, had been overturned by Mubarak under a threat from Bush 43 to reduce the annual subsidy.

On the grounds of its status as a religious organization and its record of violence, the Muslim Brotherhood was disallowed from running a Presidential candidate, but bloody intervention by regimist mercenaries did not prevent Islamist "independents" from winning 88 seats in Parliament, making the Muslim Brotherhood the first opposition party of Egypt's modern era. The reformist wing of the Brotherhood had Kifayah support.

In May 2006, the prospect of governmental reprisal against judges who charged fraud in the 2005 Parliamentary elections sparked the reappearance of protesters, who were clubbed into submission by riot police. In August, Hizballah's stand against Israel enhanced public support for the Brotherhood. Opposition weekly *Al Dustur* contrasted the contributions of Hasan Nasrallah's son, who died in 1997 fighting the Israel occupation, with those of Jamal Mubarak.

In 2007 the Brotherhood ran candidates for 19 seats in Egypt's upper house, but lost all 19 in another rigged election. In fraudulent municipal elections of 2008, all Brotherhood candidates were disqualified or jailed. *Middle East Report* of Spring 2009 reported that the organization, under a new generation of more liberal leaders, had formed a Guidance Office under Secretary General Mahmud 'Izzat; there was a widespread conviction that the government of Egypt had been hopelessly compromised by its dependence on Washington. However, reformist groups like The April 6 Group were learning that Internet sites like Facebook were immune to being shut down because of their broad popularity.

In late 2008, Samir Shehata diagnosed a deteriorating economy, record inflation, and 40 percent of the population kept alive by subsidized bread. Mubarak, now in power for 27 years, had moved his son up the government ladder to the position of Chairman of the Policies Secretariat of the secularist National Democratic Party. (Jamal Mubarak, born in 1963, had received an MBA from the American University of Cairo and worked for the Bank of America in Cairo and London before transferring to the government in the 1990's. He has appeared effectively on US television.)

With 18,000 political prisoners under the State of Emergency Law, the polity calcified, and the economy stultified – as described in *Current History,* Egypt was no longer competitive in world markets, and no longer the political/cultural leader of the Arab world. Foreign observers found the class gap widening, the population distraught, rightists and leftists making common cause, and the regime consumed with protecting itself. To this inglorious end, as reported by *The Washington Post Weekly,* Mubarak had forbidden workers from going on strike, and required the military to replace the subsidized bread being diverted to the black market, while relying on an internal security force twice the size of the army as the last bulwark against revolution.

In July 2009, *The Economist* reported that Mubarak was said to be ailing; his likeliest successors were his son Jamal or longtime Intelligence head General 'Umar Sulayman, reputed CIA henchman for rendition jobs : Adam Shatz, *London Review of Books,* 5/27/10. Of Egypt's 384,000 square miles, perhaps 12,000 were arable – sustaining a population per arable square mile approaching 7,000. Egypt has been an extreme example of the Malthusian vicious circle: Poverty begets overpopulation. Overpopulation begets poverty.

According to the *Guardian Weekly* Egyptian crowds responded to the Gaza flotilla incident by chanting that Mubarak was a Zionist.

Turkey - This is the only post-Ottoman country to have been gifted with brilliant leadership. Mustafa Kemal demonstrated his military genius by liberating Turkey from foreign occupation, and his political genius by putting the country on the fast track to modernity. The Middle East has had many coups d'etat, but only three revolutions – two in Iran, and the

Kemalist in Turkey. (A coup is the product of a cabal. A revolution is a mass movement.)

As reported by Perry Anderson in the 9/15/08 *London Review of Books,* circumstance favored Kemal from the outset. World War I ended with him in command of an Ottoman army on the Black Sea coast, out of reach of Allied troops; the leader of the Young Turks' Committee for Union and Progress (CUP) was assassinated by an Armenian, allowing Kemal to take over that organization; his troops were keenly motivated by hatred for their principal adversary, the Greek occupiers. (To lure King Constantine away from Germany, the busybody Allies had promised him Smyrna: *Middle East Policy,* Winter 2009, Arthur Bonner.) Kemal was supported by Russia's new leader, Lenin, who shared his interest in combating Allied influence.

An early military initiative was a lethal attack on Soviet Armenia. In 1923, the Grand National Assembly elected Kemal President of the new Republic of Turkey. He instituted social changes much more comprehensive than those of Shah Reza in Iran, and a constitution based on Western models. However, Turkey was no readier for the practice of democracy than was Iraq in 2003. Until Kemal's death in 1938, he ruled as an autocrat who was just as insensitive to Kurdish rights as any of his successors. In the late 1800's, says *Foreign Affairs,* the military had been the first Turkish institution to modernize. By selecting and training officer candidates from their early teens, the Kemalist military made itself into a self-perpetuating institution which enjoyed preferential pay and perks, and intervened as necessary to keep Turkey on the autocratic path it favored. That path included eclipse of the Caliphate, Arabic script, Islamist education, and Islam as the state religion. The only approved language is Turkish, even in the call to prayer.

As a nonbeliever, Kemal concentrated on the consolidation of Turkish nationalism – even an effort to purge Turkish of Persian and Arabic terms. While Kemal invented a history in which Turks had "descended from Hittites and Trojans," the basic Islamic culture pattern continued to evolve at its traditional glacial pace. As the power structure rocketed ahead, it left behind a general public deeply committed to the mystique of an Islamism strongly imbued with Sufiism.

In 1934, The Grand National Assembly decreed that all Turks adopt surnames, and assigned Kemal the surname of Ataturk, "Father of the Turks". That was the year he gave women the right to vote. Turkey's first free elections (1950) ushered in a predemocratic period of instability, which was summarily put back on the autocratic track in 1960 by the military, which jailed the President, hanged Prime Minister Menderes, and "to restore democracy" made General Cemal Gursel de facto Prime Minister and Chief of State. In 1961, a free referendum established a new constitution, and a National Security Council (NSC) as the primary instrument in the military's campaign to secularize Turkey.

By 1970, Turkey's ancient permeation in Islamic culture had begun to reassert itself, and in 1971 the military carried out its second intervention in politics – deposing Prime Minister Demirel. In 1980 came the third intervention, which dissolved the National Assembly, political parties, and trade unions, imposed martial law, and jailed and tortured thousands of dissidents. In 1982 came the promulgation of a new constitution, which legitimated the all-powerful NSC, but introduced a hint of democracy by assigning the Council a membership of five officers and five docile civilians.

In 1983, the ban on political parties was lifted. As Prime Minister, later as President, Turgut Ozal (of mixed Turkish-Kurdish origin) did his best to stand up to the military. After his death in 1993, the NSC resumed its bloody repression of minority dissidence – Islamist, Alevi, and Kurdish. Whenever the military relaxed its grip on Turkish politics, pro-Islamic leaders emerged – first Necmettin Erbakan, later Recep Tayyip Erdogan. In 1995, when Erbakan was elected Prime Minister, he proposed a startling return to Islamic basics. In 1997, after a year in office, he was ousted by military intervention number four, in favor of Mesut Yilmaz. At the time, an estimated 100 Turkish journalists were in jail for "subversive" writings. In 1998, Turkey's highest court banned the perennial Islamicist party (which underwent periodic name changes) in order to "preserve the world's only Muslim democracy," disregarding the fact that the Islamicists generally won free elections. The court expelled Erbekan from Parliament and prosecuted him for sedition.

His successor as leader of the Islamicist faction was Erdogan, founder of the Justice and Development Party (AKP), which spoke for the peasants, the slum dwellers, and the new entrepreneurial class. The NSC presumed to ban Erdogan from politics for life. During this period, scores of Turks were being jailed as "terrorists" for criticizing the NSC's interventions and its repression of Kurds, who occupied some 25 percent of seats in Parliament. Political prisoners were routinely tortured. Criticism of the death sentence for Kurdish rebel Abdallah Ocalan came from several European governments (but not from Washington, which had helped Turkey catch him).

In 1999, Turkey was confronted with an economic crisis. The US set up an IMF loan, which averted melt-down.

As of 2001, Turkey was being governed by an NSC composed of President Ahmet Sezer, four cabinet ministers, and five top generals. Turkish secularism was contradicted by a requirement that official ID cards indicate the bearers' religious affiliation. The state owned 50 percent of the land and 60 percent of industry, in a society in which corruption was endemic, the economy was in crisis, and the gap between rich and poor was cavernous. The regime ruled by martial law.

In 2002, Erdogan (despite the ban) led the Islamicists to a smashing victory in the Parliamentary elections. The new Parliament abrogated the ban. He entered Parliament in 2003, and was almost immediately designated Prime Minister. Erdogan was cautious about pursuing his Islamic agenda, but criticism of the NSC became bolder. (Example: "Most states have an army, but in Turkey, the army has a state.") Parliament reduced the NSC's executive powers, but did not reduce the government's control of every mosque in Turkey.

With "a burning sense of his own authority," the charismatic Erdogan took full command of the regime, with remarkable success – according to *The London Review of Books* – in lowering Turkey's sky-high inflation rate, privatizing industry, improving social services, working for greater separation of mosque and state, and promoting the rights of Kurds and non-Muslims in line with European norms. In 2003, civilians acquired a majority on the NSC. Parliament's startling rejection of Washington's request for land access to Iraq in 2003 (Chapter 15) may prove to be a historic turning point in Turkey's evolution from military autocracy to democracy.

By late 2004, Turkey had brought its fiscal house into some semblance of order, reduced unemployment to 20 percent, enshrined political dissent and religious pluralism, relaxed repression of the Kurds, and amended the Constitution to allow a civilian to chair the NSC. Turkey had a working parliamentary system of government, favoring a two-party system, with a largely ceremonial President elected by Parliament. In 2005, with IMF help, Erdogan worked to reduce the role of state-owned companies, which were losing money. The economy was in its fourth year of expansion.

The military had not capitulated. In 2005 and later the convictions of soldiers who bombed a Kurdish bookstore were overturned, a new penal code spoke ominously of (factual) references to the genocide inflicted by the Young Turks and Kurdish allies on the pro-Russian Armenians in 1915, Orhan Pamuk – who was to win a Nobel prize for literature in 2006 – was saved by international protest from conviction for speaking about that atrocity to a foreign magazine, and a Turkish journalist was assassinated for raising the genocide issue. Omer Taspinay wrote in *The Middle East*

Journal that Turkish Christians were still denied positions in the military or the foreign service.

The Observer saw the secularists in control of the military, the judiciary, and the civil service, but challenged by the rising poor and a new middle class largely composed of devout Muslims of rural origin. In the Parliamentary elections of July 2007, these elements, backed by most of Turkey's fifteen million Kurds, gave Erdogan's AKP a decisive victory over the military's secularist Republican People's Party (which according to Sinan Ciddi's *Kemalism in Turkish Politics,* reviewed in *Middle East Policy,* had reluctant Alevi support) and the rightist Nationalist Action Party. Jenny White saw this election as a historic step toward democracy. In August the top generals stayed away from the Presidential inauguration of Abdullah Gul, devout Muslim and first incumbent who was not from the military or the bureaucracy. In the words of *The New York Review,* the moderate Islamists had conquered Ataturk's castle. They had ushered in an era of greater gender equality and more freedom of expression for the Kurds. They had stabilized the currency, brought inflation down to 10 percent, and elevated the annual GNP to 400 billion dollars.

By 2008, in the assessment of Sabrina Tavernise, the economic gap between the cosmopolites and the underprivileged masses had been significantly narrowed. By bringing suit against the Islamicists, the secularist party came close to toppling the Erdogan Government and shutting down his party. As of 2009, Turkey was still polarized between the secularists and the Islamicists – whose faith was still gentled by the pervasive influence of Sufiism. (Former Prime Minister Erbekan was a Naqshabandi Sufi.) The Kurds' political organization, the Democratic Society Party, continued to dominate in the Diyarbakir area.

The *Wall Street Journal* of 7/20/09 reported that, with the apparent approval of Chief of Staff General Ilker Basbug, a would-be junta headed by two retired generals was to go on trial on a charge of plotting a coup against the AKP government. On the other hand, in December 2009 the Constitutional Court disbanded the Democratic Society Party, the only legal Kurdish party, on a charge of undermining national unity by cooperating with the PKK. In February 2010, 52 ranking military officers were detained on coup charges.

Yemen - In 1955, the Hamid al Din family defeated its rivals and regained the throne of north Yemen, which has a Zaydi majority and a Sunni (Shafi'i) minority. In 1978, years of civil war ended when a military regime, backed by Egypt (Chapter 14), took power. South Yemen (Britain's South Arabian Federation), populated by Sunnis, harried the British out in 1967. In 1990, the two Yemens ostensibly merged under a regime which was military in character, but strongly affected by the balance of power in Yemen's tribalized society, and destabilized by social inequities (including an underclass of over a million impoverished Yemenis of presumed African origin who are disparaged as *al Akhdam*: the Servants), and by cultural incompatibility between the north, which had enjoyed autonomy since Ottoman times, and the south, which had been semi-Westernized by a hundred years of British rule.

North-south friction over oil revenues and the regional division of power erupted in 1994 into military combat. According to Fred Halliday, the South Yemeni Abyan Army and Mujahidin back from Afghanistan provided crucial support to the North in its stamping out of the effort of the south to secede. Since that episode, the Zaydis and Sunnis have had their own political parties, but the 1997 elections were not notably chaotic. Women were allowed to vote and run for office. Under the rule of 'Ali 'Abdallah Salih, President since 1978, Yemen has enjoyed relative stability and until recently seemed to have made more progress on the road to democracy than any other state in Arabia. Backed by his own Zaydi tribe (the Hashid), Salih was skillfully managing the natural discord between the tribes and the central government. Some observers suspect he had hidden contacts with Al Qa'idah, while cooperating with Washington's efforts to obliterate that organization.

The President had initiated a campaign against the national addiction to chewing *qat (Catha edulis)*, a plant classified as a mild stimulant, but inducive of indolence.

By 2009, the situation in Yemen had sharply deteriorated. Ulrichsen reported that growing population was outstripping dwindling oil and water reserves, and unemployment had climbed to 40 percent. *Foreign Policy* noted that the crisis had been exacerbated by a flood of refugees from war-torn Somalia. Increasing lawlessness in Yemen raised the question whether the country had entered the military-government stage too soon. In the Summer 2008 issue of *The Middle East Journal*, Stephen Day reported that major cities of Yemen had been witnessing large, sometimes violent, demonstrations to protest north-south issues, corruption (Hashid-slanted), and escalating economic distress. The San'a' regime was using lethal force against activists of the Yemen Socialist Party in the south and rebellious Zaydis of the Huthi tribe in the north. The *Times* of 6/12/09 reported that militants had taken control of large areas outside the capital. *Newsweek*'s report from Guantanamo may have been a relevant indicator: Of the remaining 240 detainees, nearly half were Yemenis.

In the *Washington Report on Middle East Affairs* of November 2009, Patrick Seale reported that the regime faced unprecedented violence from the Huthis in the north, Shafi'i tribes in the south, and Al Qa'idah in the Arabian Peninsula (AQAP), which claimed responsibility for the 2008 bombing of Embassy San'a'. Saudi Arabia, which shared Yemen's suspicion of Iranian arms smuggling, had sent in forces to repel the Huthi tribes it had once supported.

Partisan Autocracy

Syria - As discussed in Chapter 14, the regimes of Saddam Husayn in Iraq (Chapter 9) and Hafiz al Asad in Syria were offshoots of the Baath Party, which is secularist and, in principle, anti-Islamist. In both cases, ultimate power seems to have resided in the party structure. Saddam did not come out of the military. Asad did, but his successor (his son Bashar) did not. Like the tribal autocrats, the party leaderships in Iraq and Syria guarded against the constant threat of military takeover by handpicking loyalists for high command, and setting up various counterbalancing military and security organizations. Saddam shared power in Iraq from 1968 until 1979, when he had himself declared President. Asad, who had already managed to pack the Syrian officer corps with high-ranking Alawites, became President in 1971.

As a country with not much oil, a primitive financial system, an inefficient state-owned business sector, a corrupt bureaucracy, and a deep ethnic divide between Sunnis and Alawites, Syria is difficult to govern. Flint Leverett noted that the stabilization of Syria was Hafiz al Asad's primary accomplishment – bolstered by land reform, which appealed to rural Sunnis, and secularization, which appealed to Christians and Druze, but not to Kurds.

Once Asad had disposed of the Islamist opposition (Chapter 12), he had two major preoccupations: Israel and Lebanon. The watchword vis-à-vis Israel was caution, since Israel has given no quarter in military confrontation, and no hint of any inclination to return the Golan, conquered in 1967 (Chapter 8). Lebanon offers much more scope for Syrian initiative, but it is a constant challenge. The two states are geographically, economically, and culturally indistinguishable, but Lebanon was excised from Syria by French intervention – originally by pressure on the Ottomans, later by machinations during the Mandate. The Lebanese became attached to the attractions of autonomy, and for many, Syrian dominion is unacceptable.

The opportunity for Damascus to close the artificial gap was afforded by the gory Lebanese civil war of 1975-90. With cold-blooded pragmatism, Asad outlasted the Israeli (and American) invasion of the 1980's, and orchestrated Syrian army and intelligence to preserve an approximate balance of power between the pro-Western (largely Christian and Sunni) and pro-Arab (largely Shiite) factions, and ultimately to win authentication from the Arabs (excluding his bitter enemy, Saddam) and the West of Syria's role as peacekeeper in a Lebanon which had demonstrated no ability to keep the peace on its own. Tempering his dictatorial instincts with broad consultation among the embittered parties, and trading on Washington's eagerness to enlist Syria in the 1991 coalition to expel Iraq from Kuwait, Asad achieved a signal political victory in Lebanon. Foreshadowed by the Ta'if Accord of October 1989, the dual regime was sealed by the military defeat inflicted on the separatists in 1990 by a Syrian-Lebanese force commanded by Lebanese Colonel Amil Lahhud.

To assure Syrian control, Asad stationed a large garrison in Lebanon, worked through like-minded Lebanese (notably Lahhud, who became President of Lebanon in 1998), and concluded a series of bilateral agreements. A 1991 Treaty of Coordination was followed up by an agreement recognizing Syria's right to a voice in the internal affairs of the Lebanese "region" (*qutr*). However, the two systems had evolved so differently that Asad excluded any hint of annexation from the discussions.

As Asad's health declined, the Damascus regime adhered to standard dynastic practice (not unknown even in Western democracies). Asad's older son, groomed for succession, had died in a traffic accident, so the mantle fell on second son Bashar, who was studying ophthalmology in London, and had shown no interest in politics. Called back from England, Bashar was given a crash course in dictatorship, notably including the formidable assignment of running Lebanon. As President of the Syrian Computer Society, Bashar opened Syria to cell phones and the Internet. After the death of Hafiz in 2000, the Syrian Baath power structure (nominally operating through the National Progressive Front) moved rapidly to qualify Bashar for the Presidency by appointing him Secretary General of the Baath National Command and Commander-in-Chief of the Armed Forces, and by lowering the Presidential age minimum in the Syrian Constitution. On June 27, 2000, the Syrian Parliament unanimously elected Bashar al Asad President of Syria. 'Abd al Halim Khaddam (Sunni) stayed on as Vice President. An orderly transition had been accomplished. In 2001, Bashar symbolized the ongoing process of Alawite-Sunni assimilation by marrying Asma Akhras, a Londoner of Sunni Syrian origin who had been employed by J.P. Morgan.

Having risen to power almost by accident (Chapter 6), the Alawite leadership seemed to have consolidated its position by co-opting key Sunni officers and concluding a political alliance with the Syrian business community, who were mostly Sunnis. Hafiz also relied heavily on the advice and support of Syria's other influential minority, the Christians. It was Hafiz al Asad's Old Guard who supervised Bashar's expeditious assumption of the Presidency. They may have been taken aback by Bashar's reformist impulses. Early in his administration, Bashar released some of Syria's 1500-3000 political prisoners (mostly Islamists), banned display of photographs of himself and his father except in government offices, proclaimed wage increases, legalized satellite dishes, and began the liberalization of the statist economy by introducing private banks: *Current History*, December 2009, Lindsay Gifford. As of late 2002, martial law was still in effect, and torture was still an interrogation tactic.

By 2004, problems had arisen in the other half of Bashar's hermaphroditic realm. As Lebanese never tire of recounting, their society had been cosmopolitan since the Phoenicians first colonized Mediterranean shores and sailed out into the Atlantic (although the term "Phoenician" has lately become politically incorrect, having been appropriated as a code word for "Christian"). As memories of the savage civil war faded, Lebanese grew impatient of Syrian domination. When the pro-West faction swept the Lebanese Parliamentary elections of 2000, activists began to agitate for reduction of the Syrian presence. Syria's staunch ally, Hizballah, counterdemonstrated, and the agitation subsided.

However, as Israel's most intransigent neighbor, Syria has had to contend with automatic hostility from the US. As a refuge of Palestinian resistance leaders, it has long been on Washington's list of "terrorist" states. In 2003, Bush signed the Syrian Accountability and Lebanese Sovereignty Restoration Act, which would impose minor economic sanctions against Syria until it terminated its support for Hizballah and the Palestinian resistance, closed the border with Iraq, and withdrew its troops from Lebanon. In 2004, Washington managed to extract from the UN Security Council Resolution 1559, which mentioned neither sanctions nor Syria, but called for the dismantling of all militias in Lebanon and the withdrawal of all foreign forces. (Russia and China abstained.)

By these two initiatives, Washington posed a threat to vital Syrian interests. Lebanon employs hundreds of thousands of Syrian workers, its free-enterprise economy is Syria's main source of hard currency, and Beirut is Damascus' natural entrepot (as Latakia is for Aleppo – now that Alexandretta is lost to Turkey). More crucially, Lebanon's southern border, so staunchly defended by Hizballah (not by the separatists), is a major sector in Syria's natural line of defense against any Israeli encroachment.

Bashar met the separatist challenge head-on in September 2004 by persuading the Lebanese Parliament to revise the Constitution and extend the tenure of President Lahhud for another three years. Under the Ta'if

Accord, Syrian troops were to have evacuated Lebanon by September 1992, but 20,000 Syrian troops were still there. In 2005 international pressure forced them out. The marginalization of Syrian influence and the rise of the Lebanese Hizballah had set Lebanon off on an independent course – discussed below.

In Syria, the loss of Lebanon, high unemployment, depletion of oil reserves, and the elimination of the Old Guard – notably 'Abd al Halim Khaddam – had weakened Bashar's position. By 2006, Syria was under fire from all sides: the UNSC calling for normalization of relations with Lebanon (Russia and China abstaining); exiles 'Abd al Halim Khaddam (on stipend from Saudi Arabia in Paris) and Muslim Brother 'Ali al Bayanuni (London) teaming up in a National Salvation Front; a million-plus refugees streaming in from tortured Iraq (The Baathist constitution allows any Arab to settle in Syria, "part of the Arab nation," but the Iraqis are denied the right to work); and Washington still excluding Syria from the WTO. *Middle East Policy* noted speculation that Syria's primary motivation in acceding to withdrawal from Lebanon was fear that it was next on Washington's hit list.

According to Seymour Hersh in *The New Yorker,* the National Salvation Front had CIA support. The Syrian branch of the Brotherhood favored Hizballah, but seemed ready to collaborate with Washington versus Syria, where over a thousand Islamists were in prison and membership in the Brotherhood was a capital offense.

In March 2009, *AP* reported that Bashar seemed to have a surer grip on power. The Syrian-Iranian alliance had gotten a big political boost from the anti-Israel furor spreading across the Arab World since the bloody attack on Gaza in the winter of 2008-09. It was the third time in three years that Sunni rulers like Mubarak and King 'Abdallah of Saudi Arabia had been compelled to make up with the Shiite rivals they preferred to disparage.

The opening of a Damascus stock market in April 2009 reflected Bashar's campaign to privatize Syria's cumbersome economic system: Shana Marshall, *Middle East Policy.* Internet cafes were numerous but closely monitored. Progress was obstructed by US sanctions, dearth of foreign investment, a forbidding legal code, prolonged imprisonment of thousands of dissidents, and a climate of corruption favoring cronies like Bashar's brother-in-law, Rami Makhluf.

Ethnocracies

Five Middle Eastern states are based on ethnic communities. The special situation of Israel is reviewed in Chapter 8. The unique case of

Cyprus is discussed below. The other three, briefly freed from Russian rule after World War I, were reborn in 1991, and are deeply engrossed in consolidating internal security and international acceptance.

Armenia - In 1987, Mikhail Gorbachev unwittingly won an honored place in history by initiating a program of transparency (*glasnost*) and reorganization (*perestroika*), which took the world by surprise when it precipitated the collapse of the Soviet Union. In 1991, the Soviet Union broke up. Its Middle Eastern territories – the southern Caucasus – were reincarnated as three independent states. Armenia became independent under an anti-Communist movement that held orderly elections. By 1998, however, war with Azerbaijan (see below) had caused economic disruption. Svante Cornell wrote in *Current History* that during the 1990's half the population of Armenia emigrated.

After the war, democracy gave way to despotism, under the leadership of Armenians who had been resident in Azerbaijan's Nagorno-Karabakh. In late 1999 the Prime Minister was assassinated. The border with Turkey, which had been closed by pro-Azeri Ankara, was guarded on the Armenian side by Russian troops. By 2004, economic blockade imposed on Armenia by Azerbaijan and Turkey had crippled its economy and left it heavily dependent on remittances from the Armenian diaspora. In October 2009 Turkey signed with Armenia protocols envisioning restoration of diplomatic relations and reopening the border: *Washington Report on Middle East Affairs,* January 2010, Patrick Seale.

Azerbaijan - This country has had difficulty in building an effective government. In 1988, three years before the end of the Soviet era, Nagorno-Karabakh, an Armenian-populated enclave of 1700 square miles, declared its independence of the Azerbaijani Soviet Socialist Republic. Over the next five years, Azerbaijan's energies were squandered in a ruthless conflict with Armenia. The war was suspended in 1993 with Armenia in control of the disputed territory, and Azerbaijan's elected President, disgraced by defeat, ousted by Heidar Aliyev, a survivor from the Soviet era. Under Aliyev's despotic rule, corruption was pandemic.

Although Azerbaijan had a clear population advantage over Armenia (Table A), and Armenia and the disputed enclave were not contiguous until Armenian forces cleared a short, narrow corridor, Armenia had the advantages of political dissension in the Azerbaijani capital (Baku, population two million) and crucial support from Russia and Iran. At last report, Armenia's border with Azerbaijan was closed, and a million Azerbaijani refugees from Armenian occupation were confined to miserable camps in Azerbaijan.

Ilham Aliyev replaced his father as President in 2003, and was reelected in 2008 – when the truncated country was prospering from oil revenues and Iranian tourism, drawn by Azerbaijan's more lenient moral code: *Atlantic*, December 2009.

Cyprus - With Britain and the Turkish minority opposed to the Greek majority's plan for *Enosis* (union with Greece), Britain, Greece, Turkey, and Cypriot leaders approved a plan under which, in 1960, the British Crown Colony was proclaimed an independent republic. According to *The London Review of Books,* British support for partition was warmly seconded by Turkey. (One justification for the hanging of Prime Minister Menderes was his promotion of a pogrom against the Greek community.)

By 1974, communal strife led to a Greek coup, immediately followed by Turkish invasion of the northern sector of the island, and heavy casualties. Suspicion that Washington had consented to the invasion precipitated Greek Cypriot violence, including an attack on the American Embassy in which Ambassador Rodger P. Davies died. De facto partition led in 1975 to the proclamation of a Turkish state in the north, but it has not received international recognition. Cyprus was admitted to membership in the EU in 2004. In 2008, its new President became the first Communist leader of an EU member state.

The *Middle East Report* of Summer 2009 observed that negotiations for federation of Cyprus's two sectors had repeatedly broken down in a welter of lawsuits over disputed properties. Whereas European courts had held that the laws of the Greek sector were valid throughout the island, including "the area not controlled by the Government of Cyprus," the 180,000 Turks in the northern sector resisted. According to *The Economist* of 7/25/09, the European Union had given Turkey until December 2009 to reopen its ports, air and sea, to Greek Cypriot traffic.

Georgia - The diverse communities of Switzerland have benefited from a "straddle culture", which enabled them to establish a nationalism that overrode their towering topographical divisions. In the southern Caucasus, no such unity has been achieved. Its three states are afflicted by political fragmentation – Georgia worst of all. Here, the advantages of a humid subtropical climate (in the shelter of the high Caucasus) and access to the Black Sea have been largely nullified by ethnic violence, which Russia has long exacerbated. Three small enclaves – Adjaria, Abkhazia, and south Ossetia – have resisted Georgian authority, even under Soviet rule. Since the shocking disintegration of the Soviet Union in 1991, each of the three has had its own history.

Georgia is an important pawn in the global power equation. Geography places it in the Russian sphere of interest; Peter Savodnik reports that many Russians consider Georgia part of their country.

The case of Muslim Adjaria, centered on Batumi, Georgia's major seaport, was resolved in Georgia's favor by President Mikhail Saakashvili in 2004. The disposition of south Ossetia and Abkhazia is greatly complicated by their location between Georgia and Russia – the only state that ever managed to project its hegemony across the Caucasus Range. Catherine the Great had sent troops into south Ossetia. Two hundred years later the Soviet Union subdued the whole south Caucasus sector.

In 1990-91, the collapse of Soviet dominion led to unrest in the two border enclaves. The failure of the forces of Georgian President Zviad Gamsakhurdia to subdue it precipitated in 1995 his replacement by former Soviet Foreign Minister Eduard Shevardnadze. With the help of a peacekeeper force from Russia, Shevardnadze had some success in reconciling ethnic conflicts, but he was unable to control corruption – for which Georgia is legendary: William Langewiesche in the *Atlantic.* Two attempts on Shevardnadze's life were viewed by Georgians as evidence that Russia resented his part in the break-up of the Soviet Union, and was maneuvering to keep Georgia in its orbit. Russia was exercized by the escape of Chechen rebels into Georgia. Shevardnadze was inhibited by Georgian dependence on such military help as Russia was prepared to give, and on the remittances from half a million Georgians employed in Russia.

In the fall of 2003, crisis struck again, when anti-corruption rioting, the breakdown of government services, and economic collapse forced Shevardnadze to resign the Presidency. Abkhazia and south Ossetia, recipients of Russian arms, autonomous for a decade, had declared independence. Their unit of currency was the ruble, and many of their citizens held Russian passports. *The Washington Post* described Georgia as a failed state. In the "Rose Revolution" of January 2004, the exuberant Mikhail Saakashvili was elected President. Fluent in English (and Russian), strongly pro-American, he set out to bring Georgia into NATO.

He failed to appreciate the strategic advantage enjoyed by Russia, newly ruled by Vladimir Putin, who was focusing on the reassertion of Russian preeminence in its onetime socialist republics: Svante Cornell, *Current History.* South Ossetia – population 70,000 – was to be Saakashvili's comedown. Ossetians are distinguished from Georgians by their language, an Indo-European tongue descended from Scythian, an ancient dialect of Persian. For years, their main livelihood had been smuggling contraband through the Roki Tunnel, the main route between south Ossetia and Russia

– via Russia's district of north Ossetia. Saakashvili's efforts to stop the smuggling had left them dependent on Russian subsidy. In 2006, Putin communicated to Saakashvili a warning – possible suspension of energy supplies to Georgia and of importation of Georgian wine.

Concurrently with an April 2008 NATO summit, which gave favorable attention to the prospect of membership of Ukraine and Georgia, outgoing Russian President Putin issued a decree that Moscow would treat the two border enclaves as parts of the Russian Federation. In the opinion of Marshall Goldman, Russia would also like to put Georgia's pipelines out of business.

In the importunate approach taken by the administration of Bush 43, which proposed to dominate events all the way to the Russian frontier, and deploy defensive missiles in Poland, Georgia would be a member of NATO. Washington has special strategic interest in the country as a link in its favored pipeline route from the Caspian to the West – bypassing Russia and Iran (Chapter 4). Jonathan Steele has noted the widespread belief that Saakashvili was elected with clandestine American support. However, Washington's disapproval of Russian intervention in south Ossetia and Abkhazia was nullified by its own capricious invasion of Iraq, and its promotion of the separation of Kosovo from Serbia. Also, in its overenthusiastic support for Saakashvili, Washington seemed to have forgotten its need for Russian cooperation in dealing with the nuclear threat from Iran.

Saakashvili, head of a one-party regime, seemed inclined to act on impulse. It was revealed on August 7, 2008, when he ordered Georgian troops to invade the south Ossetian capital, Tskhinvali, affording Putin an ideal pretext to launch an instantaneous response, dispose of the invading force, occupy south Ossetia and adjoining areas of Georgia, capture 65 tanks equipped with the latest American and Israeli technology, enhance the Russian position in the south Caucasus, and dash Western hopes for Georgian membership in NATO.

In May 2009 south Ossetians elected a parliament loyal to Moscow-backed "President" Eduard Kokoity.

Abkhazia, whose natives are Muslims or Greek Orthodox (and who speak a pre-Indo-European language with few if any vowels: *Atlas of Languages*), was inevitably drawn into the altercation. With a near-tropical climate, a long frontier with Russia, and a residual population of perhaps a quarter of a million – most of them Russian citizens – it has strategic interest for Moscow. Its capital, Sukhumi, was a resort favored by Soviet officials. In the early 1990's, during its battle for autonomy, which had support from Russian volunteers, it expelled three hundred thousand Georgians. In 2009 the *Times* reported that the number of Abkhazis resident in Turkey far exceeded those still living in Abkhazia.

In 2004, Abkhazia held an election for a "President". Georgia pronounced the election illegal. According to Neal Ascherson, Abkhazia had become a Russian protectorate, but not a puppet. On August 15, 2008, with Washington's acquiescence, Saakashvili agreed to a truce that broadened the mandate of the Russian peacekeepers in south Ossetia and Abkhazia. Two weeks later, Georgia and Russia broke diplomatic relations. In September, Russian President Medvedev granted the two enclaves security guarantees in return for base rights. Russia, Nicaragua, Venezuela, and Hamas have recognized them as independent states.

Washington has promised Georgia a billion dollars in aid, but the events of 2008 dampened Western enthusiasm for Georgia as a major pipeline bypass of Russia.

Theocracy in Iran

In the long history of Iran, Sandra Mackey discerned one crucial date – 680, when Husayn died at Karbala'. Out of the ashes of that defeat was to rise the Shiite mystique, which has condemned Iranian society to an existential conflict, still unresolved, between the secular and the spiritual. Like every Middle Eastern state, Iran is beset by communalism. Half of its subjects pay allegiance to minority groups. One-fourth of its population are Azeris, who inhabit the northwest and in many families speak their own language instead of Persian.

The Middle East has arguably witnessed only three social revolutions: Turkey's Kemalist revolution of 1923 and two in Iran – the constitutional revolution of 1905-11, and the theocratic revolution of 1979. The Turkish and first Iranian revolutions looked to the future. The following chronology is submitted to support the thesis that Iran's theocratic revolution looked to the past, and this anomaly has haunted every subsequent government of Iran.

1736 - Nader Shah, who began his career as the leader of a band of Sunni Turkic robbers, assumed the Iranian throne. An indifferent statesman, he failed to convert the Iranians to Sunniism, but he excelled at war, routing the Turks from Iran, conquering Bahrain and Oman, and occupying the Mughal capital of Delhi.

1905-11 - The constitutional revolution affirmed the supremacy of the Sharia, but operating through the monarchy. A century later, *The Nation* looked back on it as the first democratic revolution in the Middle East. In the analysis of Yitzhaq Nakash, it provided the Shiite clerics a vision of what an Islamic government should be.

1911 - Russian troops imposed a coup that aborted the constitutional revolution.

1918-19 - Flare-up of an ongoing Azeri insurgency.

1926-41 - With British backing, Reza Khan ousted the Qajar dynasty, founded the Pahlavi dynasty, secularized law and education, and integrated women and minorities into civil society, but alienated the clerics by favoring secularization and reducing their powers.

1941 - British and Soviet troops forced pro-Axis Shah Reza to abdicate in favor of his son, Mohammed.

1945-46 - Another Azeri flare-up.

1951 - Mohammed Mossadeq, alumnus of the constitutional revolution, became prime minister, nationalized the Anglo-Iranian Oil Company, and subsequently broke relations with Britain.

1953 - Britain and the US staged a coup (Chapter 4) that ousted Mossadeq and reinstated the Shah, who arrested Mossadeq, executed several dozen rebel officers and student leaders, and imposed a despotic regime, as narrated in Kinzer's *All the Shah's Men*. The coup created a political vacuum that was filled by the clerics – although Vali Nasr writes they were reluctant to back the Pahlavis.

1957 - With help from America and Israel, as reported in *The National Geographic*, the Shah established a new intelligence organization, Savak.

1960's - *Middle East Report* and *The Nation* have written that the Shah's White Revolution, aimed at enfranchising women, breaking up estates, and cementing ties with Washington, enraged the newly empowered clerics.

1963 - Pro-Mossadeq students founded *Mujahedeen-e Khalq* (People's Freedom Fighters: MEK, discussed in Chapter 9).

1964 - The Shah banished *Ayatollah* Rohallah Khomeini, who moved to Najaf in Iraq, and there evolved the doctrine of *velayet-e faqih* (rule of the jurisprudent cleric).

1970's - Ali Shariati, Shiite cleric who died in 1977 shortly after two years of imprisonment at the order of the Shah, adapted Marxism (collective ownership and class war) and anti-imperialism to Islam in a doctrinal system that was to have profound influence on future Iranian leaders, including President Mahmoud Ahmadinejad: Jon Lee Anderson, writing in *The New Yorker* of 4/13/09. Vali Nasir cites a debate between two grand ayatollahs, Ruhollah Khomeini and quietist Abol-Qassem al Khoi, over Khomeini's advocacy of the *velayat-e faqih*. According to Nasr, Khomeini borrowed from Shariati.

1977 - On a visit to Tehran, Carter described the Iranian monarchy as an "island of stability."

1977 - According to Robert Fisk, the Red Cross discovered 3000 Iranian political prisoners who had been severely tortured.

1979 - Resentment of the Shah's misrule (tens of thousands of demonstrators killed) and his subservience to Washington had reached the explosion point. On January 16, under rising pressure from hostile demonstrations, the Shah fled the country again (Chapter 10). This time his Western patrons were unable to save him. Savak had crushed the leftist opposition, and the Shah had exiled Ayatollah Rohallah Khomeini, but in devout Iran the monarchy could hardly eliminate the Shiite clerics. The only faction well enough organized to take over, they brought Khomeini back from Europe to be the Chief of State. He appropriated the honorific of *Imam*. Nasr notes that other Shiite leaders (Musa Sadr and Muqtada Sadr, who named his army Jaysh al Mahdi) have stressed this concept, but Khomeini seemed to apply it to himself. Dilip Hiro asserts that during the takeover the army killed at least 10,000 civilians.

Abbas Amanat's *Apocalyptic Islam and Iranian Shiism* (reviewed by Malise Ruthven in *The New York Review of Books* of 7/2/09) concludes that Khomeini, a reactionary and a consummate political operator, sold Iran on a radical break with its tradition of de facto separation of religion and state, and as Imam stressed the dualistic Zoroastrian (pre-Islamic) doctrine of a world eternally divided between pure believers and polluting infidels – a doctrine that had long been incorporated into Shiite theology.

Citing Ray Takeyh's *Guardians of the Revolution,* Ruthven describes Khomeini as "a relentless ideologue willing to sacrifice his nation for the sake of his religious speculations."

On April 1, after a landslide victory in open referendum, Khomeini proclaimed Iran an Islamic Republic. (According to Juan Cole, he was a pan-Islamist – reason enough to espouse the Palestinian cause and despise America.) A new constitution, based on the Koranic pronouncement of an absolute God, called for the elimination of poverty and illiteracy and proclaimed the laws of Islam as the base of a regime to be headed by an unelected Supreme Leader (known as *Rahbar-I-Muazam* or *Vali-e Faqih*). After 500 years of rule by Shiite dynasties (Chapter 7), the clerics had assumed direct rule, and Iran became the world's only enduring theocracy (Chapter 12). According to R. K. Ramazani, the Supreme Leader is regarded as deriving his authority from the word of God, as handed down by the Prophet Mohammad and the Imams. The Leader holds temporal and spiritual authority pending the return of the Twelfth Imam, the *Mahdi*. As a means of reinforcing clerical authority, Khomeini and his successor

(1989), Ali Khamenei (of Azeri descent, like Khoi), reinstituted compulsory veiling and child marriage; targeted leftists, feminists, gays, Kurds, and minorities but favored Azeris, whose native language is Turkic, but who are predominantly Shiites. Khomeini and Khamenei were responsible for the execution of thousands of monarchists and dissidents (notably members of the MEK) at home and abroad.

However, by trying to infuse their regime with democratic institutions, the theocrats created a Mobius-strip form of government: The Assembly of Religious Experts appoints the Supreme Leader, whose guidance is presumably divine, but the people elect the Assembly of Religious Experts, whose guidance is presumably democratic. The resultant contradictions have produced an ongoing battle for the soul of Iran. Distrusting the officers of the armed forces as holdovers from the era of the Shah, Khomeini created his own security force, The Revolutionary Guard Corps (*Pasdaran*): Fareed Zakaria, writing in *Newsweek* of 8/3/09. In the views of Khomeini and his successor, Khamenei, opposition to the regime was blasphemy. In the ensuing thirty years, reformist (not secularist) officials have responded to the call of educated Iranian youth by working to reduce the absolutism of the Supreme Leader and his hard-line supporters.

1980-88 - Against secularist Iraq, the Iranian theocracy fought its first war – which in Hiro's view reinforced Khomeini's sectarianism. Ramazani concluded that the brunt of the fighting was born by the Pasdaran and their affiliate, the Basij, a volunteer militia, who participated with the consummate courage of the devout, and were further inspirited by eery government horsemen, shrouded in white, posing as other-worldly emissaries: Vali Nasr. The Iranians were fought to a standstill by Iraq's professional units, supplied by Washington with crucial weapons and intelligence, and making decisive use of chemical and biological weapons obtained from Europe, Russia, China, and the United States. The MEK fought on the Iraqi side.

1980's - Desperate for arms, Khomeini went along with the Israeli promotion of clandestine American arms sales to Iran (the "Iran-Contra Affair"). Israel was prepared to deal with its Iranian enemies for the sake of blocking a military victory by its Iraqi enemies: Roger Cohen, *Times* of 4/08/09.

1982 - The Pasdaran found time to help found Hizballah (Chapter 12).

1988 - Iran executed thousands of political prisoners.

1989 - Khomeini died. President Rafsanjani arranged the succession of Ali Khamenei (expecting to control him) and amended the Iranian constitution to eliminate the position of Prime Minister. (Then Prime

Minister Mir Hussein Moussavi was to be a major candidate in the 2009 election for President.)

1994 - Iran was flying arms into Zagreb for the Bosnians.

1995 - Washington believed Iran was supplying money and operational advice to Hizballah, Hamas, and Islamic militants in Cuba, Iraq, Libya, North Korea, Sudan, and Syria.

1997 - Opposed by Khamenei and Ali Akbar Hashemi Rafsanjani, but bolstered by the 1992 Berlin affair (Chapter 16), reformist Mohammed Khatami won a landslide victory for the Presidency. Iran was being swept by profound cultural and political changes. Khatami promoted greater freedom of speech (not of the media). The Internet was flourishing; Bill Berkeley reported that, after English and Chinese, Persian was the most-used language in the global blogosphere. In sharp contrast with Saudi Arabia, Iranian women could drive cars, hold jobs, vote, and occupy government jobs and seats in Parliament. They were required to cover their hair in public, but not their faces. Reform was still not moving fast enough for the students, who were gaining political impact. Over half the population of Iran was under age 20, and the minimum voting age was 16. The schizoid constitution left open the basic question: Where did ultimate power rest – with the electorate, or with the Supreme Leader, who in the conservative view was divinely inspired? The political controversy was intensified by economic distress, which the statist system seemed unable to alleviate.

1998 - More student demonstrations in support of democracy and the rule of law. They were attacked by the Basij, a thousand were jailed, and two leaders were killed. Tensions were raised by economic consequences of soaring population, government mismanagement, and a sharp decline in the global price of oil.

1999 - Student leaders called on the Supreme Leader to leave government operations to elected officials. The response was a violent attack by vigilantes. Several days of clashes ended in capitulation by the students, but no resolution of the issues. Many of the demonstrators were jailed, and four were condemned to death.

2000 - The reformists won a majority in Parliament, which chose moderate theocrats for its three top positions, but Khamenei blocked reformist legislation, closed many reformist publications, and jailed the more troublesome dissidents. Khamenei and Khatami were maintaining a precarious coexistence. The reformists controlled elective offices (Presidency, Parliament, municipal councils) and the ministries of Interior and Intelligence. The conservative Supreme Leader appointed the commanders of the armed forces, six of the twelve members of the Guardian

Council (which can veto parliamentary bills and electoral candidates), the directors of the national radio and TV networks, prayer leaders, the heads of the major religious foundations, the members of the national security councils, the chief prosecutor, and the chief judge. Khamenei's preeminence seemed to give the conservatives a slight edge.

2001 - President Khatami was reelected – according to Hiro, by a 5-1 margin.

2001 - Robin Wright detected progress in the grueling effort to moderate the Iranian political system in the direction of separation of mosque and state. A major bone of contention was the conservatives' interest in preserving the state's giant religious foundations.

2002 - There were more indications of subtle advance toward cultural and political liberalization, but neither of the two major warring camps advocated secularism, whose supporters were confined to a minority of clerics and students. In the words of Jahangir Amuzegar, Iran was "...a closed-circuit theocratic oligarchy masquerading under a democratic façade," with a bloated bureaucracy and chronic budget deficits. Its popular support was declining in favor of a vibrant subculture which violated Islamic strictures and watched impious satellite TV on hidden dishes.

2003 - More clashes between demonstrators and vigilantes. Zahra Kazemi, Iranian-American photojournalist, was one of the thousands in Iranian prisons, and one of the many who died there, probably of torture: Jon Lee Anderson, *The New Yorker,* 4/13/09. In the light of day, the authorities were now allowing satellite dishes to proliferate. They were illegal, but enforcement of the ban would have been too disruptive: *Times,* 6/29/09.

2004 - The conservatives managed to rig the elections of 2004 to produce a Parliament with a strong conservative bias.

2005 - Organized violence, jailing of reformist activists, and the rigged election had put the conservatives in the driver's seat. Backed by the 150,000-man Pasdaran and by the merchant class, the conservatives controlled the police, radio and TV, the ministries of Interior and Defense, the Shahab missile program, and the lucrative black market. However, as recapped by Pollack and Takeyh in *Foreign Affairs,* the clerisy was corrupt, the country was suffering from double-digit rates of inflation and unemployment, private enterprise and educational opportunity were stifled, and the oil infrastructure needed an estimated 70 billion dollars for modernization. A quarter of the labor force worked for the state. The regime had presumably concluded from the contrasting experience of Iraq and North Korea that a nuclear-weapon capability would be the best insurance against American invasion, but it was under heavy Western pressure to prove it had no such intention.

2005 - Khamenei staged a coup (*The Economist*'s reading) by orchestrating the election of former Basiji Mahmoud Ahmadinejad as President of Iran. A little-known religious conservative, disciple of Ayatollah Mohammed Taqi Mesbah-Yazdi (who opposed elections in principle), Ahmadinejad benefited from exclusion of leading reformist candidates by The Guardian Council, illegal campaigning by the Basij, and his image as a devout Shiite of modest means and a man of the people, as distinguished from his affluent rival, Rafsanjani. The election was dominated by veterans of the Iraq war. According to *The Nation,* 20 million reformists boycotted it. Hiro noted that the new President resegregated university classes by gender and reinforced the ban on satellite dishes.

2005 - By assigning the Expediency Council nominal supervision over the President's staff and the Parliament, Khamenei awarded Ali Rafsanjani, its head, what *The New Yorker* described as sweeping new powers – possibly at the expense of Mahmoud Ahmadinejad, whose policies as seen by the *Times* had taken Iran back to 1979.

2006 - Pressures were mounting on President Ahmadinejad. Azeri and Kurdish dissidence in the northwest, Baluchi dissidence in the southeast, and Ahwazi dissidence in the southwest had been met with public hangings. Two-thirds of the economy, in the estimate of Christopher de Bellaigue, was encumbered by state ownership. In nationwide city-council elections, moderate conservatives and reformists outperformed Ahmadinejad's hardline conservatives: *Middle East Policy,* Summer 2007.

2007 - UNSC Resolution 1747 banned further financial aid to the government of Iran. Unemployment exceeded 11 percent. Ten million Iranians lived below the poverty line. Reformists were banned from holding meetings, public or private. Hundreds were in jail, pending trial in revolutionary courts. Cataloguing the elected authorities (President, Assembly of Religious Experts, Parliament) and the unelected (Supreme Leader, Guardian Council, senior clerics, judiciary, armed forces, Pasdaran), *The Economist* characterized Iran as a quasi-democracy – which was executing more people than any other country but China.

2007 - The Assembly of Religious Experts chose as its chairman Ali Rafsanjani, runner-up to Ahmadinejad in the Presidential election of 2005.

2007 - In *The Shia Revival,* Vali Nasr seemed to anticipate the uprising of the moderate theocrats in 2009. He characterized the Islamic revolution as a spent force, and assessed the Ahmadinejad faction as anti-Sunni rather than pan-Islamic. They were out of step with the dynamic culture of Iran, "the modern face of Islam".

2008 - Following up their victories in the Parliamentary elections of 2004 and the Presidential election of 2005, the conservatives won the Parliamentary elections of 2008, gaining control of all three branches of government: Presidency, judiciary (directly controlled by the Supreme Leader), and the Parliament. Their victory had been insured by the Council of Guardians, which had disqualified 70 percent of the reformist candidates, thereby driving most urbanites away from the polls. Gradualist Mohammed Khatami blamed Bush's anti-Iran campaign for the hard-liners' victory. However, the election of moderate Ali Larijani as Speaker was a sign of protest against the dismal economy. Another possible harbinger of liberalization was the election for the members of the Assembly of Religious Experts that produced a centrist body.

2008 - According to Michael Klare, the regime's campaign against reformism was being implemented by agents of the Pasdaran, who threw student "conspirators" out of windows and hacked Darioush Forouhar and his wife to death. In 2009, the *Times* noted that Iranian culture still discriminated harshly against women.

2008 - Akbar Ganji assessed the Iranian theocracy as repressive, but not totalitarian. Brutal in its treatment of dissidents, it allowed expression of differing opinions. According to Ervand Abrahamian, Khamenei had less power than Khomeini had, and took advice from hard-liner Ahmadinejad, moderate Khatami, and pragmatist Rafsanjani (who as the chairman of the Assembly of Religious Experts and the Expediency Council was the second most powerful figure in Iran – but too old to run for President).

2008 - *The Washington Post Weekly*: Inflation in Iran had risen to 25 percent, because of state monopoly of the economy, and American sanctions, which had forced Iran to turn to China for spare parts. Barbara Baktiari noted in *Middle East Policy* that Iran was self-sufficient in neither gasoline nor food. Analysis in *The New Yorker* by Laura Secor credited President Ahmadinejad's economic populism with keeping inflation from rising even higher, by holding down interest rates, but at the cost of reducing the availability of credit. Joseph Cirincione wrote in *Current History* that Ahmadinejad had skillfully diverted attention from his failed economic policies by posing as the defender of Iran, notably by foiling foreign efforts to deny Iran its right to nuclear technology. Mahmoud Sariolghalam advanced the view that Iran could never liberalize its political system until it reduced the near monopoly (85 percent) of the state over the economy.

2008 - *Middle East Report* of Summer 2008 reported that, thanks to concessions made under Presidents Rafsanjani (1989-97) and Khatami (1997-2004), Kurdish districts now had considerable local autonomy.

2008 - The regime was downplaying its Shiite identity in favor of support for pan-Islamism.

11/6/2008 - Writing in *The London Review of Books,* Abrahamian discerned a power struggle between Maximalists and Minimalists. The Maximalists, who had been helped by Bush 43's obstreperous criticism of the Iranian leadership, sought to consolidate Iran as a clerical autocracy. The Minimalists, led by Khatami and mentored by Abdulkarim Soroush, anticipated liberalization on the road to ultimate democracy.

2009 - Reviewing the Iranian situation, Abrahamian stated that the theocratic revolution had survived on a populist surge against the stark imbalance in Iran between the upper and lower classes, and in the world between East and West. The regime had made progress toward the promise of a welfare state by putting social expenditure ahead of military. The vision of Ali Shariati still lived.

6/12/09 - With unemployment at 17 percent and inflation at 24 percent, Iran held a Presidential election – perhaps the most polarizing election in the history of the Islamic Republic: PBS, Lehrer Report, Afshin Molavi. The two principal candidates were Maximalist incumbent Ahmadinejad and Minimalist challenger Mir Hussein Moussavi. Two hours after the polls closed, the government proclaimed a huge Ahmadinejad victory.

6/13/09 - The government had cut off cell-phone service and blocked Facebook. (Access to the Internet had long been restricted.) By July it was confiscating satellite dishes.

6/15/09 - After two days of violent clashes between anti-Ahmadinejad students and pro-Ahmadinejad security forces, the opposition staged in Tehran a silent march of between one and three million people – the largest demonstration in Iran since the 1979 revolution. Smaller protest marches were to take place in subsequent days.

6/13-23/09 - Massive evidence of ballot-rigging was accumulating: the premature announcement of an Ahmadinejad victory; large majorities for Ahmadinejad even in the home towns of his opponents; participation in Ahmadinejad's campaign by some members of the Guardian Council, which rules on elections; alleged vote counts exceeding the numbers of eligible voters; unexplained police movements on election day. Opposition candidates rejected the government's offer of a partial recount.

6/22/09 - Joe Klein of *Newsweek* reported on CNN that the 86 members of The Assembly of Religious Experts, which technically has the power to remove Khamenei from office, were split three ways among pro-Ahmadinejad, pro-Moussavi, and undecided.

6/24/09 - In *The Wall Street Journal,* Edward Luttwak commented that, after years of humiliating social repression and gross mismanagement of the economy, the better educated, more productive Iranians had turned their backs on the regime. Predicting national paralysis until Khamenei and Ahmadinejad left office, Luttwak made a bold comparison between Iran and the USSR in the time of Gorbachev. The *Times* explained the effectiveness of Ahmadinejad's crackdown by his success in having packed the security forces with hardline allies. His past service with the Pasdaran was critical.

6/30/09 - With some 20 demonstrators dead, hundreds injured, and hundreds jailed, The Guardian Council certified the reelection of Ahmadinejad for four more years. Although not all ranking clerics had chosen sides, the Khamenei regime seemed to have suppressed the opposition for the time being.

7/17/09 - In a direct challenge to Khamenei, Rafsanjani (his onetime sponsor) publicly demanded restoration of the people's trust in the government.

7/21/09 - According to the *Times,* the intervention of the security forces was widely seen as the beginning of the conversion of the Iranian regime from theocracy to a military junta with a clerical façade.

7/23/09 - Abrahamian wrote in *The London Review of Books* that, since Iran had no deep-rooted political parties, the peoples' major medium of expression was the mass demonstration, while the major defenses of the regime were armed repression and rigged trials.

7/29/09 - Amid stories of brutality and death among the 2500 (?) citizens arrested for demonstrating against the Ahmadinejad regime, all but 150 had reportedly been released, but public rage seemed to be escalating.

7/31/09 - The ostensible lineup of political forces was as follows:

For Ahmadinejad: Supreme Leader Khamenei, operating through one of his sons, Mujtaba (Roger Cohen, *The New York Review,* 6/15/09); Saeed Jalili, head of The National Security Council; Ayatollah Ahmad Janati, Secretary-General of the Guardian Council and a leader of the campaign to indict Britain for inciting the demonstrations; Mohammad Mesbah-Yazdi, Amadinejad's spiritual mentor; The Revolutionary Guard Corps (Pasdaran), which had gigantic economic interests and a force of 130,000 with its own ground, sea, and air forces (separate from the much larger regular army of conscripts who were generally assigned to the frontier); two Pasdaran affiliates, the Quds Force and the Basij (three million vigilantes who often moved by motorcycle and had conducted violent post-election attacks on opposition personnel and their property); the police; a majority of the cabinet; The Guardian Council; the governors of the thirty provinces, all Ahmadinejad appointees; the rural poor, who had benefited under Ahmadinejad's Presidency.

For Moussavi: Rafsanjani, former right-hand man to Khomeini, former President and *Rahbar*-maker, current head of the Assembly of Religious Experts and The Expediency Council, who had split with Khamenei and was thought to be the opposition leader behind the scenes, and whose daughter Faezeh, former MP, had marched with the protestors; Mahdi Karroubi; Mohammed Khatami; Ayatollah Seyyed Hussein Tabrizi; Iranian youth and members of the middle class.

8/5/2009 - Ahmadinejad was sworn in for a second term.

10/18/2009 - On the border with Baluchistan, a suicide bomber from the Baluchi separatists' Jondallah killed 42 members of the Pasdaran.

12/8/09 - *Times*: Anti-regime demonstrations began to feature a more revolutionary note – denunciation of Khomeini and theocracy.

3/20/10 – *Times*: Rafsanjani was wavering.

Outlook: The opposition was crippled by the absence of any organization to focus its energies. Moussavi's Green Wave, which included a cadre of fervent young secularists (*The Nation*, 7/13/09), was probably ahead of its time. Supreme Leader Khamenei presumably had the power to hold a new election, but the recent one, rigged or not, had been conducted so clumsily that he would risk sharing Ahmadinejad's humiliation in the event of an unfavorable outcome. More likely, the two hardliners would try to stand firm behind the powerful security apparatus – the latterday palace guard which could emerge as the ultimate beneficiary of the theocracy's travail, in replication of ancient oriental precedent. (See the Mamluk takeover of Egypt's Ayyubid Sultanate in 1250.)

Since the dawn of the Age of Reason, societies have been polarized between the dogmatists and the questioners. The questioners may have taken the initiative in the West, but they are still subordinate in Twenty-first Century Iran.

States in Limbo

America's implantation of a client state in the center of the Middle East, and the attendant Israeli-American intrusion into the politics of the region, have exacerbated gravitational stresses affecting every one of its nineteen sovereign states. In the cases of Iraq and Lebanon, those stresses threaten to tear them apart.

Iraq - Once a partisan autocracy, dominated for the past six years by an American expeditionary force, it is now challenged to fill the awesome vacuum the Americans are leaving behind. Its murky future is discussed in Chapter 15.

Lebanon - In schizoid Lebanon, power is shared between a civilian government and a dominant sectarian militia. During the Middle Ages, two tenacious minority sects, harassed by the Sunni majority, sought refuge in the mountains of Lebanon – the Maronite Christians in the north, the Druze in the south. In the 1800's, Ottoman reliance on the standard imperial practice of divide-and-conquer led them to incite the Druze against the Maronites, producing a massacre of Maronites in 1860. As a result of this atrocity, the Maronites won formal autonomy, which was consolidated under French protection after the collapse of the Ottoman Empire in 1920.

France went on to exploit its postwar mandate by separating "Christian" Lebanon from Muslim Syria – even though the two territories were politically and culturally identical, and the artificial frontier between them left Lebanon with almost as many Muslims as Christians. In 1943, the advent of independence confronted the country with a constitutional dilemma. It was resolved, without benefit of sectarian census, by the Lebanese Compromise: The Presidency would be reserved for a Maronite, the Premiership for a Sunni, and the speakership for a Shiite. As Michael Young recently wrote, the Christians promised not to look to join the West, and the Muslims promised not to join an Arab nation.

In the sage words of George Nakkash, two negations do not make a nation. The Lebanese Compromise was a recipe for civil conflict, which has been the country's fate for over sixty years, and has been exacerbated by the presence of three or four hundred thousand refugees from Palestine. The inevitable civil war of 1975-90, which by Michael Neumann's estimate cost 175,000 Lebanese and Palestinian lives, was ended by Syrian occupation, endorsed by the Western powers and most of the Arab states. Saudi Arabia sponsored the Ta'if Accord, which as reported by Robert Betts changed the ratio in the Lebanese Parliament from six to five (54 Christians, 45 Muslims) to all even (64 Christians, 64 Muslims) – even though by this time Christian emigration and a higher Muslim birth rate had probably produced a large Muslim majority.

Syrian hegemony was institutionalized in 1991 by two bilateral agreements: The Treaty of Brotherhood and The Defense and Security Agreement. All militias were to be demobilized except Hizballah, which had been founded with Iranian help in 1982 and in subsequent clashes with Amal had established itself as the dominant Shiite organization in Lebanon.

For the pro-Western faction, Syrian rule was intolerable. For the Israeli-American diarchy, it was a geopolitical threat. Augustus Richard Norton pointed out that Lebanon's Shia have had ties with Iran since the time of the Safavids (Chapter 10). Control of Lebanon by pro-Iranian Syria facilitated the supply of Iranian arms to Iran's protégé, and Israel's nemesis, Hizballah. In the 1990's, Israel managed to kill two successive Hizballah leaders.

In 2000, *Sayyid* Hasan Nasrallah, the newest leader of Hizballah, concluded an incongruous alliance with Presidential hopeful Michel 'Awn, leader of a major Maronite faction. During this period, Syria was controlling Lebanese affairs through a succession of proconsuls, the last of whom was Syrian President Bashar al Asad himself. Syria's primary asset in Lebanon was Hizballah, but that organization paid greater allegiance to the Supreme Leader in Iran, and sent many of its soldiers to Iran for religious instruction and military training. Since the expulsion of the Palestinian forces from Lebanon to Tunisia and elsewhere in 1982 (Chapter 8), Hizballah had been the mainstay of the Lebanese opposition to Israel. Instead of making the PLO's mistake of trying to build a conventional army, it was training, arming, and fortifying a highly effective guerrilla force well adapted to operations in the mountainous terrain of Lebanon.

In September 2004, the US and France sponsored UNSC 1559, which called for the withdrawal from Lebanon of "foreign" (Syrian) forces, and the disbandment of all Lebanese militias. With Iranian support, Syria countered by announcing the extension of the term of President Amil Lahhud by three years, to 2007.

In February 2005, pro-Saudi and pro-Western ex-Prime Minister Rafiq al Hariri was killed by a gigantic truck bomb in central Beirut. Weeks later, the UN set up an investigatory commission which, as reported by Joshua Hammer in the December 2008 *Atlantic,* was still at work in total secrecy under a Canadian prosecutor. A predecessor, who had overseen the arrest of four Lebanese generals, had gone home to Germany after he had implicated Syrian officials and was subsequently told that his life was in danger. The four generals were released in April 2009 on grounds of insufficient evidence.

Most of the assassinations of anti-Syrian journalists and politicians in Lebanon in recent years have been routinely ascribed to Damascus.

In March 2005 a huge rally by adherents of Hizballah was topped within days by an even bigger rally of Christian, Sunni, and Druze supporters of the pro-West "Cedar Revolution". By the end of April, under strong pressure from Crown Prince 'Abdallah of Saudi Arabia (per *Middle East Report),* and the dread contingency of American invasion, Syria had withdrawn its troops from Lebanon, but was still counting on President Lahhud. David Hirst concluded that the Lebanese were not so much opposed to the idea of Syrian rule as to the corrupt and repressive character of Syria's Baathist regime.

A pro-Syrian alliance of Shiite Hizballah, Shiite Amal, and the secularist Syrian Social Nationalist Party participated in the Parliamentary elections of May and June, 2005, winning 35 of the 128 seats, effecting the reelection of Amal leader Nabih Barri as Speaker, and producing a partisan stalemate. The pro-West forces were led by Sa'd Hariri, son of the murdered Rafiq. They later elected a member of the Hariri faction, Fu'ad Sinyurah, as Prime Minister, but his government endorsed Hizballah as a defender of Lebanon, exempt from the requirement in the 1989 Ta'if Accord and UNSC 1559 that Lebanese militias should be disbanded. Hizballah entered a Lebanese Government for the first time.

Hizballah's impressive defense against the Israeli invasion of 2006 (Chapter 8) elicited admiration across the Middle East. Lebanese from both factions had to recognize the systemic inability of the army of their sectarianist country to come to its defense. After the fighting was over, army units complied with the UNSC's call to deploy to the south in support of an enlarged UNIFIL. Meanwhile, as noted by Juan Cole, the thousands of Lebanese unhoused by Israel's bombing of Shiite neighborhoods in Beirut benefited from competition for their political support between Sinyurah's government, funded by Kuwait and Saudi Arabia, and Hizballah, funded by Iran. According to Augustus Richard Norton, Hizballah was distinct from rival factions, including the Shiite Amal, in not being corrupt.

In early 2007 Lebanese politics took another step toward chaos when Fath al Islam, a small *takfiri* (virulently anti-Shiite) organization with links to Al Qa'idah chose the Al Nahr al Baridah Palestinian refugee camp near Tripoli as a base for banditry in northern Lebanon. Against this group, which – like the Palestinian refugees – had few friends in Lebanon, the sectarian army had no compunctions about taking violent counteraction, ravaging the camp and callously precipitating the flight of most of its 31,000 registered refugees, but eventually killing or dispelling the offenders. Seymour Hersh advanced the opinion that Fath al Islam, which had a large Saudi component, was one of several bands formed to implement the master plan of Cheney and Abrams in Washington and Bandar in Saudi Arabia to mobilize Sunni Jihadists against Hizballah, Syria, and Iran.

In August, the surprise bye-election victory of Michel 'Awn's candidate was a defeat for the Sinyurah faction and for Washington, which had been slipping Sinyurah cash – and political support, like denying pro-Syrian functionaries entry to the US. *The New York Times* cited the rule of thumb that American backing for a Lebanese politician was generally a handicap.

In November 2007, the expiration of Amil Lahhud's term left Lebanon without a President, pending resolution of the factional deadlock. It was resolved in May 2008, when Hizballah forces reacted to a jurisdictional challenge from Sinyurah by staging – against negligible opposition – a symbolic occupation of West Beirut and adjacent areas of the mountains. The army wisely maintained its customary neutrality in factional disputes, since in the opinion of Bilal Saab, writing in *Middle East Policy,* Hizballah's militia was better armed than the army, and much more cohesive. Hizballah's demand for veto power in Parliament was satisfied, and Washington and Tehran acceded in Lebanon's standard resolution of political deadlocks: the May 25 swearing in of the Commander-in-Chief of the army, Maronite General Michel Sulayman, as President of Lebanon. The thirty portfolios in the cabinet were divided equally between Christians and Muslims, with eleven reserved for Hizballah. Damascus responded to this turn of Lebanese events by finally recognizing the state of Lebanon.

The parliamentary election of June 7, 2009, was an elemental power struggle between the pro-American March 14 Group (Sunnis, Druze, and most Christians – also known as the Cedar Revolution) and the anti-American March 8 Group (Shia, some Sunnis and Druze, and Christians affiliated with the Free Patriotic Movement led by a Presidential hopeful, retired General Michel 'Awn). Under the new rules of apportionment, Parliament's 128 seats are reserved as follows: <u>Christian</u>, 64 - Maronite 34; Greek Orthodox 14; Greek Catholic 8; Armenian Orthodox 5; others 3; <u>Muslim</u>, 64 - Sunni 27; Shia 27; Druze 8; Alawite 2.

The outcome was variously influenced: by tradition – notably vote-buying and the deeply embedded feudal system; by circumstance – particularly the calming effect of Obama's tactful repudiation of the contentious tactics of the Bush administration, including Obama's abandonment of the campaign to disarm Hizballah; and by the artificial distribution of Parliamentary seats; a census would probably reveal that Shiites outnumber Sunnis and Druze, and that Muslims far outnumber Christians.

In any case, the surprise victory of the March 14 Group, 70 seats to 58, was painted over by the formation of a unity government, and the opposition's retention of veto power. Political stalemate produced an artificial balance of portfolios: March 14 Group - 15; Hizballah - 10; President Sulayman - 5. At this writing, the Lebanese economy – unlike that of its archrival, Dubai – was holding up well in a time of global economic crisis, Damascus was maintaining a low profile, Hizballah was enjoying cautious and effective leadership from moderate Islamists Hasan Nasrallah and his deputy, Na'im Qasim, and schizoid Lebanon was stalemated between a pro-

Western civilian government and an anti-Western paramilitary hegemon with a social-service net relied on by underprivileged Shia and stateless Palestinians.

Arab Spring

2011 was a landmark year for the Middle East. By April, reformists in five Arab Middle East states (Egypt, Bahrain, Jordan, Syria, and Yemen) had followed the Tunisian lead by mounting demonstrations that – at high cost in lives – had boldly challenged their autocratic regimes. In the March 18 *Guardian*, John Vidal had suggested that these uprisings had been triggered by intolerable social pressures of declining water supply, rising food costs, and massive unemployment: in short, by overpopulation.

So far, these events are revolutions in embryo. The paradigm is Egypt, where belated intervention by the army was the reformists' only salvation from brutal suppression by Mubarak's "security forces". In effect, the protesters carried out a coup d'état against President Mubarak on behalf of his High Command.

The reformists' bid for secular democracy was blocked by the army-sponsored referendum of March 19, which merely amended the Constitution of 1971, thereby favoring the two undemocratic political organizations already in being – The Muslim Brotherhood and Mubarak's National Democratic Party. The reformists are forced to look to the example of Turkey's AKP, which has evolved from Islamicism to professed renunciation of any discriminatory link between mosque and state: *Financial Times*, March 22, 2011.

Chapter 12
Islamic Fundamentalism

In the parochial power struggles reviewed in Chapters 7 and 11, pragmatism often overrode theology. Conversion of convenience was a common phenomenon – pagans to Judaism, Jews to Christianity, Christians, pagans, and Zoroastrians to Islam, Sunnis to Shiism, Druze to Maronite Christianity, and so on.

Beneath the umbrellas of the five major linguistic communities (Chapter 6), these sectarian vicissitudes took place in an environment of immense doctrinal diversity. Middle Easterners had long been divided among three camps – Marxist, secularist, and sectarian – but the stresses of survival in a bewildering new era of Euro-American intrusion and whirlwind globalization seem to have kindled a latter-day resurgence of religious faith. Communists once mounted a significant challenge in Iran, Iraq, and the Levant, but they never managed to form a government. The secularist regimes in Iraq (Baath), Syria (Baath), Occupied Palestine (PLO), Iran (Pahlevis), and Turkey (military) have been generally marginalized if not brushed aside, leaving faith as the prevailing medium of political opinion.

Arab autocracies have traditionally sought to mute political opposition by professing and promoting dedication to the spiritual preoccupations of their Faith. Islamic dynasties relied on the clerics to appease unfortunates with the homily that the privations of this world were the price they had to pay for the raptures of the next. As secularist Saddam Husayn's grip on power grew shakier, he stepped up his recourse to religious imagery, like adding *Allahu Akbar* to the Iraqi flag. During the Israeli attack on Gaza in 2008-09, when the collaborationist Cairo regime was being besieged with demands to help the beleaguered Gazans, a government-appointed preacher provided emotional catharsis for his exasperated audience at Al Azhar by belittling Jews as "monkeys and pigs." Christian communities in the Levant and the Caucasus instinctively reach out to coreligionists in the West. The champions of secularism in Kemalist Turkey have lost ground of late to Islamicism. Even agnostic leaders of the Israeli ethnocracy ritually cite dedication to Judaism as a rationale for Jewish statehood.

In the violent scenario now playing out in the region, the ascendant theology is Islam. Contrary to the Western misconception that all Muslims are zealots, Islam encompasses the same spectrum of belief – from conjecture to certainty – as the other world religions, and the same tendency to ramify into a myriad of variant creeds. For articulation of early Muslim agnosticism, consider these two quatrains, composed in Persian by Omar al Khayyam around 1100 (Fitzgerald translation, Doubleday/ Doran, 1933):

LVII

Oh, Thou, who didst with Pitfall and with Gin
Beset the Road I was to wander in,
Thou wilt not with Predestination round
Enmesh me, and impute my Fall to Sin?

LII

And that inverted Bowl we call The Sky
Whereunder crawling coop't we live and die,
Lift not thy hands to *It* for help – for It
Rolls impotently on as Thou or I.

Of the 360 million inhabitants of the Middle East, estimates classify 300 million (85 percent) as Muslims. Some 200 million profess affiliation with Sunni Islam, 100 million with Shiite Islam, and half a million Omanis with the 'Ibadi sect of Islam. (The two million Alawites of Syria are commonly regarded as Shiites.)

An unknown fraction of Middle Eastern Muslims are fundamentalists, who believe that the Qur'an, as the inerrant word of God, should govern the actions of society. A still smaller fraction are committed to activism, including violence, in promoting their ideology; herein, Muslim activists are termed Islamists.

From the geopolitical perspective, two generalities have compelling relevance:

The Developmental Gap

While the Islamic world has not yet mastered the practice of democracy or the skills of modern technology, it is painfully aware of the social, economic, and political price it pays for having fallen behind in the evolutionary race. In 2007, *Middle East Policy* cited Islamists' skillful exploitation of the yawning gap in the Third World between rich and poor. For Anoushiravan Ehteshami, writing in the *Middle East Journal,* Islamism is a direct response to the cultural effects of economic globalization. Evolution toward the Western way of life may occur over the centuries, but in contemporary lifetimes the challenge is to upgrade Middle Eastern society – theology and all – to the Western level of efficiency.

As the region painfully sloughs off the residue of Western imperialism, it seems condemned to revert to the time-honored sway of dynasticism (Chapter 11). Fifty years of conditional independence have been too brief to demonstrate that autocracy is not the answer. As the seminal UNDP study of 2002 elucidated, the secular regimes have failed the developmental challenge. Repressed by the autocrats, deprived of their Soviet patrons, the left collapsed. In 2005, Egyptian reformer Sa'd al Din Ibrahim pointed out that, under the region's endemic autocracy, the mosque was the last sanctuary of free speech; the result was the emergence of Islamism as the spearhead of Middle East reform. Islamists are the only leaders left to meet the demand that Middle Eastern society catch up in the technological race.

Western Imperialism

The Middle Easterners emerged from the mandatory period with an understandably jaundiced view of Western policies, and some optimism that they were now on the track to peace, prosperity, and self-determination. This optimism was shattered by the neoimperialism practiced briefly by the Soviets, and currently by the United States. There were several crucial irritants:

1948 - The creation of Israel. Joel Kovel identified the US-Israel axis as the major indirect cause for the rise of Islamism.

1953 - The Western coup that put the Shah back on his throne.

1967 - The Six-Day War. The crushing Israeli victory energized the Islamists, and convinced them that the secular Arab regimes had to be replaced.

1979 - The Egyptian-Israeli peace treaty sparked Islamist violence against the West and its Middle Eastern allies.

1979-92 - The Soviet occupation of Afghanistan brought about the destruction of its tribal elites. The arming of the Islamists by Pakistan, Saudi Arabia, and the United States promoted the takeover by the Islamist Taliban.

1982 - The Israeli invasion of Lebanon, with subsequent American participation.

1991 - The American expulsion of Iraq from Kuwait. Although Islamists detested Saddam's secular policies, most of them opposed the American intervention, and particularly the concomitant expansion of the American military presence in Saudi Arabia, guardian of Islam's holiest places.

2003 - The blatant grab of Iraq by the United States and token European ancillaries further enraged Islamists and, by eliminating a secularist regime, broadened their scope of operations. Robert Pape's *Dying to Win* finds a high correlation between American invasion and Islamist suicide terrorism.

Islamism in History

Soon after the death of the Prophet Muhammad in 632, the record of Allah's revelations to him was collected in the Qur'an. Recollections on his life were collected in the *Hadith*. Between 632 and the Mongol invasion of 1258, the Islamic Caliphate conquered a significant area on three continents (Chapter 10). Its Islamist approach to conquest and conversion was epitomized by its vision of a world divided into *Dar al Ummah* (Realm of the Nation) and *Dar al Harb* (Realm of War). As the balance of power shifted to the Europeans and the Central Asians, the stress on conquest dissipated, but conversion to Islam has continued, notably in Africa, and devotion to the faith resists secular pressures.

Muslim clerics seem to infer three gradations of offense against the faith: 1) heresy (*ilhad, bid'ah, hartaqah*) - deviation from true understanding of all-encompassing Allah; 2) apostasy (*riddah, irtidad*) - conversion from Islam, which is forbidden by Islamic law, although according to Cyril Glasse (*The Concise Encyclopedia of Islam,* 1989), punishment is extremely rare; 3) association with false beliefs (*shirk*) - exemplified by paganism or agnosticism. Glasse cites the Muslim conviction that *shirk* is the one sin Allah cannot forgive.

The Caliphate survived a series of challenges:

632-661 - Qurayshi Dynasty (Arabian). The Muslim Arabs defeated Persian adherents of the much more ancient Zoroastrian faith in the Battle of Qadisiyyah in 637.

661-750 - Umayyad Dynasty (subject to the Shiite defection).

750-945 - Abbasid Dynasty.

945-1171 - Several Persian dynasties.

1171-1258 - Return of the Abbasids under Seljuq protection.

1200's-1517 - Puppet dynasty in Egypt.

In 1780, the Ottoman Sultan made the groundless claim that the Caliphate had been transferred from the Abbasids to the Ottomans in 1517. Most Middle Eastern Sunnis and a few Shia gave it credence. Even in 1922, after Turkey had abolished the Sultanate, its Grand National Assembly elected the former Ottoman Crown Prince as Caliph. Two years later, the Assembly dissolved the office of Caliph; Islamists still hope to restore it.

Four schools of Sunni Islam prevail today: *Hanbali* - The most restrictive, it is official in Saudi Arabia; *Maliki; Shafi'i* - widespread in Yemen; *Zahiri*. Islamic theology remains the subject of vehement debate and the periodic cause of lethal violence. One of the fastest-growing Islamist movements is the Salafis, who according to Mary Anne Weaver originated in Egypt around 1900, and seek to pattern their lives on those of the companions of the Prophet. Their teachings have influenced militants in Egypt, Algeria, Afghanistan, Saudi Arabia, the Balkans, and the Russian Caucasus (notably Chechnya).

Many Muslim communities cling to customs, Islamic or pre-Islamic, that range from quaint to horrific in Western eyes. They include: prohibition against charging interest, which leads to intricately evasive procedures; prohibition against insurance, as being equivalent to betting on the changeless word of God; genital mutilation of women; "honor killings" of women for drifting toward Western social customs. *Times* columnist Nicholas Kristof deplored a statement by a member of the current Pakistani cabinet defending the burial alive of three women for presuming to choose their own husbands, and of two others who came to their defense.

Shiism

Shiism has added its own features to Islamic practice and doctrine. As elucidated in Vali Nasr's *The Shia Revival* and Juan Cole's invaluable blog, devout Shiites differ basically from Sunnis in their conviction that the first three Caliphs (Abu Bakr, 'Umar, and 'Uthman) were illegitimate. The Prophet should have been succeeded by his direct descendants, starting with his son-in-law 'Ali and culminating in the Twelfth Imam, who went into hiding (was occulted) as a child in 874. Some day he will return as the Mahdi to rule the earth until the return of Jesus, which will coincide with the Day of Judgment. To the Sunni *shahadah,* "There is no God but God; Muhammad is the Prophet of God," Shiites add " 'Ali, Muhammad's companion, is the vicar of God." For Shiites, an Imam is infallible. (Sunnis do not hold this belief in the case of the Caliphs. Sudan's Mahdi was a reviver of the Sunni faith.)

Shia accord special veneration to 'Ali's son Husayn, who died for their faith, to 'Ali's daughter Zaynab, who saved the life of the Fourth Imam, to Husayn's son 'Ali, and to Fatimah, daughter of the Prophet and mother of Husayn and Zaynab. Shiites who trace their lineage to the Imams, like Khomeini and Sistani, wear black turbans, and carry the title of Sayyid (Arabic), Seyyed (Persian), or Mir (Azeri).

'Ashurah, the annual commemoration of Husayn's death, is exclusively Shiite, with no foundation in the Qur'an.

Whereas Sunnis regard the primary responsibility of the Caliph as preservation of an orderly community, Shiites – perhaps in analogy to Catholics – feel a need for inspired intermediaries between the worshippers and God. The Shiite hierarchy is self-generating. Any aspirant can study with an established scholar to become a *mujtahid* (jurisprudent), worthy of emulation. As such, he is an independent authority, subject to no outside discipline. By further study and teaching, he can rise to the rank of *hujjat al Islam* (authority on Islam), and ultimately, with the support of *ayatallah*'s (exemplars of Islam), he can become an *ayatallah* himself. Grand *Ayatallah* is a title awarded by popular acclamation. In 2007, according to 'Abd al Sattar Jawad, there were five in Iraq – all of Iranian birth – and several in Iran. The world's most highly respected Shiite cleric is thought to be 'Ali al Sistani of Iraq.

Two major schools of Shiism are the *Usuli* (empirical), which looks to the clerics for any innovation in Shiite law, and the *Akhbari* (traditional), which restricts the clerics' role to expounding existing law. Nasr views the Islamic revolution in Iran as a victory for the Usuli school.

Even the rituals of prayer for Sunnis and Shiites differ. Sunni fundamentalists – Wahhabis and Salafis – disparage a Shiite as a dissenter, infidel (*kafir, mulhid*), or even an apostate (*rafidi* in the Shiite case), and consider their veneration for the family of the Prophet idolatrous. However, the 57 member states of the Organization of the Islamic Conference (*Munazzamat al Mu'tamar al Islami*), established in Saudi Arabia in 1971, include Shiite Iran and 'Ibadi Oman. Vali Nasr notes that a rector of Al Azhar has issued a fatwa recognizing Shia law as a fifth school of Islamic law.

Sufiism

As early as the Umayyad Caliphate, pious Sunnis, disturbed by the worldliness of the period, evolved a movement that revered the *Shari'ah* but diverged sharply from mainstream Islam in its search for direct personal experience of God through asceticism and mysticism. The Arabic for mystic is *sufi*. The golden age of Sufiism was the 1200's, when Jalal al Din al Rumi, the greatest mystical poet in the Persian language (in the evaluation of the *Britannica*), and the founder of the *Mevleviyah* fraternity, composed lyrics for his mystical beloved. In the 1300's, Persian Sunni Shaykh Safi al Din founded the Safavid order of mystics to cleanse Islam of the "Mongol strain". Over the centuries, Sufi poets made important contributions to Arabic, Persian, Turkish, and Urdu literature. Sufi disciples evolved Qur'anic mantras (*dhikr*) and whirling dances designed to transport the worshipper into a hypnotic state closer to God.

Sufiism links Sunnis and Shiites, in that it has won devotees from both sects. Shiites and Sufis share devotion to certain shrines, belief in the clerisy's role of intermediation, and veneration of the Prophet's family.

At this writing, Sufiism is widely practiced in the northern regions of the Arab and Kurdish East. Theoretically banned in Turkey in 1925, Sufiism – notably the *Mevleviyah* fraternity – is still active there and elsewhere, including the United States. There are some 200 Sufi fraternities in Aleppo, Syria. There is little literature to suggest that the practitioners of Sufiism have tried to move from the religious realm to the political, although they have established militias for self-defense. Wahhabis and Salafis regard Sufis as apostates, and condemn many of their beliefs and practices, such as prayer at the graves of relatives, as blasphemous.

According to the *Times* of 6/12/09, Shiite governments in Iran have disdained Sufiism, but some Sufi orders have associated themselves closely with Shiism.

Theocracy

For many Islamists, the only acceptable form of government is theocracy, wherein the state is directly governed by the clerics – leaders of the dominant sect. So far, at least, Islamic theocracy seems to be losing.

Iran - Nasr traces the link between Iran and Shiism to the marriage of the daughter of the last Sasanid king to the Imam Husayn. Although Shiism became the state religion in 1501, no Iranians recognized their government as divinely inspired until 1979, when Ayatollah Khomeini ousted the Shah and proclaimed the doctrine of *velayat-e faqih*. He foresaw Iraq as the next Shiite theocracy. Even so, the Iranian clerical establishment has had great difficulty in repressing liberal currents, particularly among the students, and theocracy seems to be a minority cause among Iraqi Shiites.

Afghanistan - The Russian withdrawal in 1992 opened the way for the establishment of a Sunni theocracy by the Taliban in 1996. It was recognized by only three states (Pakistan, Saudi Arabia, and the UAE), and the Taliban were overthrown in 2001 by the Americans, who enjoyed the significant advantage that the Taliban's repression of poppy cultivation (now flourishing) was widely unpopular in Afghanistan. Based on the Pashtun community, which constitutes a plurality in Afghanistan, the Taliban remain a significant force in the continuing Afghan power struggle.

Sudan - Islamists formed a government in the 1990's. Sudanese luminary Hasan al Turabi sponsored a series of Islamist conferences, which decried American policies. In 1999, Turabi was jailed, but Sudan retained the rubric of Islamic Republic.

Azerbaijan - According to *Middle East Policy,* Iran has been financing pro-Iranian mosques, but has not made much headway against a strong current of secularism (instilled by Soviet rule: Nasr).

Middle Eastern Islamism: 2009

In reflection of the political fragmentation of the Middle East, Islamism has tended to evolve differently from country to country. Following are some of its noteworthy variants:

Egypt - In 1871, Jamal al Din al Afghani, a Persian Shiite who had established a following in Afghanistan and Anatolia, moved to Egypt, where he inspired young Egyptians including Wafdist Sa'd Zaghlul and Islamic reformer Muhammad 'Abduh. Both Afghani and 'Abduh sought the restoration of the golden age of the Caliphate, but a Caliphate compatible with modernism. In 1879 Khedive Tawfiq deported Afghani as a suspected republican. In Paris, Afghani and 'Abduh published a newspaper, *Al 'Urwah al Wuthqah* (The Indissoluble Bond), which focused on condemning British imperialism in the Middle East. Back in Iran, Afghani clashed with Qajar Shah Naser od-Din, who deported him in 1892. Four years later, Afghani instigated Naser od-Din's assassination. Afghani's mausoleum is in Kabul.

In 1928, in reaction to the dissolution of the Caliphate, the breakup of the Ottoman Empire, and the secularist movement of Mustafa Kemal in Turkey, Hasan al Banna founded *Al Ikhwan al Muslimun* (The Muslim Brotherhood). His mantra was: "God is our objective; the *Qur'an* is our constitution; the prophet is our leader; struggle is our way; and death for the sake of God is the highest of our aspirations." Although his organization may have received secret support from King Faruq as a counterweight to the *Wafd* Party, it was banned by the British rulers of Egypt, as was the *Wafd*.

By World War II the Brotherhood had half a million supporters across the eastern Arab world, and had developed a militant wing. In 1948, a member assassinated Egyptian Prime Minister Nuqrashi for ordering the Brotherhood's dissolution. The Egyptian secret police retaliated by killing Banna. He was succeeded by Sayyid Qutb, whose sojourn in the United States had convinced him of the decadence of Western society, and who regarded the military regime in Egypt as infidels. In *The Looming Tower*, Lawrence Wright writes that Qutb reintroduced the ancient concept of *takfir*, the condemnation of a Muslim as an apostate, thus getting around the prohibition against the killing of one Muslim by another.

In 1954, a member made an unsuccessful attempt to kill Nasir, probably on the grounds that the evacuation agreement he had concluded with Britain was too lax. Nasir retaliated by having six conspirators executed, torturing Sayyid Qutb (who wrote the Brotherhood's basic text, *Milestones*, in prison), and breaking the power of the organization in Egypt for twenty-five years. The Brotherhood went underground, and set up branches in Jordan, Syria, Lebanon, and Saudi Arabia. In 1966, Nasir had Qutb hanged. In the 1970's, new Egyptian President Anwar Sadat relaxed the restrictions on the Egyptian branch of the Brotherhood as a counterforce to the Nasirists and the leftists. He even tolerated the Brotherhood's more activist offshoot, The Islamic League, and he used Islamist slogans in official statements during the 1973 war.

In 1981, the League orchestrated the assassination of Sadat for concluding the 1979 treaty with Israel. Many members were jailed, including Ayman al Zawahiri, an associate of Sayyid Qutb in the 1960's, who served three years, and was radicalized by torture. At that time, the spiritual mentor of the Egyptian Islamists was Shaykh 'Umar 'Abd al Rahman, resident in New York City. In 1991, the League launched a terrorist campaign against the regime of Egyptian President Husni Mubarak, who arrested 20,000 suspects. The League was reportedly receiving contributions from residents of the Arabian Peninsula, and possibly from Iran. As the battle between the Islamists and the regime intensified, the state took over administration of mosques. As Islamists began to win elections in professional associations, the regime countered by such measures as dissolution of the Engineer's Union. In 1994, the Brotherhood was considered by some the strongest party in Egypt; the government neutralized its power by rigging every election.

In the meantime, Ayman al Zawahiri had left the League to found The Islamic *Jihad* (Holy War), which bombed the Egyptian Embassy in

Pakistan. An Egyptian analyst concluded that the Islamists were gaining recruits because of the failure of the Mubarak regime to raise the standard of living and to accord Egyptians a greater voice in government. In 1996, Shaykh 'Umar 'Abd al Rahman was jailed in New York City on a charge of terrorism. Zawahiri conducted an unsuccessful attempt to kill Mubarak in Ethiopia, and was expelled from his refuge in the Sudan. Egyptian imprisonment and torture of Islamist suspects continued. In 1996-97, Islamist influence in professional associations remained strong, while the League adopted a scorched-earth strategy culminating in a campaign to kill officials, and to undermine the lucrative tourist industry by, inter alia, attacking a party of tourists near the Pyramids (18 dead) and another in Luxor (62 dead). Egyptian Coptic Christians also fell victim to the most lethal Islamist violence in decades.

The brutality of these attacks alienated many Egyptian moderate Muslims, while the severity of government security operations was taking effect. In 1997, four months before the Luxor killings, both the League and Jihad renounced violence in Egypt. The Islamists had achieved part of their program, in that the Egyptian legal system had taken a more conservative approach; for example, one court ruled that if a man's writings on the *Qur'an* were adjudged to resemble atheism, he must divorce his wife. In 1999 – after the loss of 1200 lives on both sides – the confrontation between the Islamists and the Mubarak regime came to an end with the release of 12,500 long-time prisoners. In 2001 the League denounced the Al Qa'idah attacks of September 11 (as did Hizballah's spiritual mentor, Ayatallah Muhammad Fadlallah, in Lebanon). In 2002 the League disbanded its armed wings.

The Muslim Brotherhood is still illegal in Egypt, but in its less violent incarnation, candidates it supported won 17 of 454 seats in the 2000 parliamentary elections, and it has been allowed to maintain its network of social-welfare centers. Islamists remain influential in Egyptian professional associations.

Analysts speculate that Mubarak's release of selected Islamist prisoners in 2002-03 was a response to a message on the worldwide web, attributed to Zawahiri, that Egypt should be exempted from Al Qa'idah's campaign against Americans and pro-American regimes. However, Mubarak has suppressed a moderate offshoot of the Muslim Brotherhood, *Al Wasat,* which advocates democracy. To reduce the Islamist threat, Egypt has given the *'ulama'* (government-appointed clerics) greater latitude, but the Islamists still command great support from the general public, who consider the regime corrupt and brutal.

In 2005, under US pressure (*London Review of Books*, 5/27/10, Adam Shatz), Mubarak let the brothers run in elections for the lower house of Parliament (444 seats). To the horror of Mubarak and Washington, they won 88 of the 160 contended seats. More recently, *Current History* concluded that the regimes of Sadat and Mubarak (1970 to date) have coincided with the steady Islamization of Egypt, exemplified by an amendment to the constitution proclaiming the Shariah the main source of the law. Benefiting from political pressure from Saudi Arabia, Islamist parties had won more privileges than the liberals in Egypt's political system – in which the regime derives immense powers from the emergency law that has been in force since 1981.

In 2007, the Egyptian constitution was amended to ban all political activity based on religion. *Newsweek* identified the leader of the Egyptian branch of the Muslim Brotherhood as Muhammad Mahdi 'Akif. In the Spring 2009 issue of *Middle East Policy,* Joshua Stacher reported vehement parliamentary debates between Brotherhood and NDP MP's over Egyptian linkage with the US, and over Egyptian closure of the border with the Gaza Strip.

In February 2010, outgoing IAEA chief Muhammad El Baradei (al Barad'i), returning to a hero's welcome in Egypt, advocated that the Muslim Brotherhood form a political party.

Al Qa'idah - According to *The Bin Ladins* (Steve Coll), Usamah bin Ladin was born in 1958 to a Syrian wife of Muhammad bin Ladin, who had risen from penniless laborer in the Yemeni Hadramawt to wealthy builder and confidant of the Saudi royal family. At his death in 1967, his wealth was distributed among his numerous heirs – some 28 million dollars of it, per Robert Vitalis, to Usamah. In subsequent years Usamah was profoundly influenced by Palestinian Islamist 'Abdallah 'Azzam.

About 1980, the head of Saudi intelligence operations sent Usamah to the Pak-Afghan border to organize and help finance the CIA-backed resistance to the Soviet invasion. There he met Egyptian fellow-resistant Ayman al Zawahiri. They had both been deeply affected by the 1978 sell-out of the Palestinians at Camp David, and by three events of 1979 – a watershed year for Islamists: the Khomeini revolution in Iran, the Soviet invasion of Afghanistan, and the Israeli-Egyptian peace treaty. Bin Ladin's long-term objectives (expulsion of American troops from the Middle East, termination of American military operations in the region, and an end to American support for Israel and the regimes in Egypt and Saudi Arabia) were consistent with those of Zawahiri. Peter Bergen reports Zawahiri merged his *Al Jihad* into bin Ladin's Al Qa'idah in 1988.

The Soviet withdrawal from Afghanistan in 1989 presented Al Qaʻidah with a formidable force of battle-hardened devotees. Christiane Amanpur reported that a battle won by Arab volunteers over the Soviets had made Usamah a *mujahid,* but his offers of their services against Communists in south Yemen, and against the Iraqis in Kuwait, were rejected by the Yemenis and the Saudis. In Usamah's view, the Saudi acceptance of American support against Iraq was an intolerable violation of the traditional injunction: "Let there be no two religions in Arabia."

After Gulf War I, the royal family allowed American forces to stay in Saudi Arabia as extra insurance against Islamist insurrection. Under restraint by Saudi security for smuggling arms from Yemen to Saudi Arabia, bin Ladin took refuge in Sudan, where he set up training camps. Frustrated in his attempt to reform the "near enemy", the Saudi regime, he set out to attack the "far enemy", its American protectors. In 1992, in league with Zawahiri, bin Ladin issued his first call for jihad against the American military presence in Saudi Arabia and East Africa. His pronouncements have had great impact on the Muslim world, mainly for their content, but also for his command of classical Arabic. Jane Mayer reports that Al Qaʻidah's Khalid Shaykh Muhammad (KSM, Baluchi) funded Ramzi Yusuf's attempt to blow up the World Trade Center in New York City in 1993. (KSM was apprehended by American operatives in Rawalpindi after the 9/11 attacks, and in 2009 was at Guantanamo, presumably awaiting trial in a civil court.) Al Qaʻidah also supported the anti-American operations of Mohamed Aideed in Somalia.

In 1994, in reaction to bin Ladin's 1993 condemnation of the Saudi regime and his support for the north in the Yemeni civil war, Saudi Arabia (which had supported the failed secession of the south) stripped him of his Saudi nationality. According to *The New York Review,* Al Qaʻidah's first major operation was the 1995 bombing of a National Guard compound in Riyadh, in which five Americans died, and for which four Saudis were beheaded.

In 1996, under pressure from Washington, Sudan expelled bin Ladin, who went back to Afghanistan, where the Taliban had captured Kabul and imposed an Islamist society. Here bin Ladin told Robert Fisk the Khawbar Towers bombing had been an Al Qaʻidah operation, and he issued his second call to jihad in the form of a "Declaration of War against the United States". Couched in Salafi phraseology, it rejected the legitimacy of the Saudi monarchy and – in the opinion of British historian Bernard Lewis – licensed his followers to kill Americans. In February 1998, in association with Zawahiri and other Islamist leaders, bin Ladin issued a *"fatwa"* (he is not an *imam)* condemning American "occupation" and "plundering" of

Islamic lands, and proclaiming the formation of the World Islamic Front for Holy War Against the Jews and the Crusaders. Operating from an unknown Afghan base, bin Ladin urged Muslims to kill Americans. The manifesto cost Al Qa'idah some of its members – those opposed to killing civilians.

In August 1998, Al Qa'idah's suicide bombings of the American embassies in Kenya and Tanzania killed a total of 223 people, probably in retaliation for American "extraordinary rendition" of Egyptian Islamists to Egypt. Clinton's retaliatory missile attacks against targets in Sudan and Afghanistan seemed to have no consequence except more publicity for bin Ladin, who was reported to be receiving financial and political support from sympathetic officials in Pakistan, Qatar, the UAE, Yemen, and Saudi Arabia, whose government was apprehensive of revelations about his ties with members of the royal family. He had consolidated his alliance with the Taliban by marrying a daughter of Taliban leader Mullah Omar. On October 23, 2000, Al Qa'idah operatives carried out a bombing of the American guided-missile destroyer, the USS Cole, that killed 17 sailors. By this time, bin Ladin was a hero in the Muslim world, and Washington had placed a price of five million dollars on his head.

By 2001, Al Qa'idah's sanctuaries had been reduced to two: Afghanistan and Iran. On September 11, 2001, 19 operatives (fifteen from Saudi Arabia, the others from the UAE, Lebanon, and Egypt) carried out the meticulous hijacking of four American jetliners, and flew three of them into the World Trade Center in New York and the Pentagon in Washington, killing 3000 Americans. In the view of Lawrence Wright, the main objective of Al Qa'idah's attacks on American targets, culminating in 9/11, was to punish the US for its overseas military commitments. The operation was reportedly staged in Germany and America, <u>not</u> in Afghanistan.

According to the *Times* of 10/31/09, the early financing came from Sa'id Bahaji, a German member of an Al Qa'idah cell in Hamburg headed by 9/11 leader Muhammad 'Atta.

Newsweek analysts noted the disturbing fact that both the planners and the operatives of 9/11 came from states whose governments were allied with the United States. In Afghanistan, the Taliban regime rejected the Bush 43 demand that it deliver bin Ladin and company. On October 7, a new bin Ladin manifesto focussed for the first time on the plight of the Palestinians (occupation) and the Iraqis (sanctions).

After 9/11, Pakistani leader Musharraf made a difficult decision to give American forces access to Afghanistan via Pakistan. Until he was ousted in 2008, he seemed to be groping for a paradoxical policy of desperation: shelter the Taliban and Al Qa'idah leaderships in Pakistan as allies against India, but tolerate American efforts to destroy the Afghan wings of those two organizations. The Pakistani entryway seemed crucial to American victory over the Taliban – a victory that, as of this writing, was still out of sight.

In April 2002, Al Qaʻidah admitted its responsibility for 9/11, and rationalized the operation as an obligatory response to American support for apostate regimes in Saudi Arabia and other Muslim states. By this time, Al Qaʻidah had operatives in 65 countries, headed by Afghanistan, Pakistan, Iran, Syria, Yemen, and Saudi Arabia, and possible sleeper cells in the United States. Under relentless pursuit by Washington, it had transferred much of its recruiting and publicity efforts to the Internet. The capture of major figures like Khalid Shaykh Muhammad, reputed organizer of 9/11, had been undercut by evidence of continuing recruitment, and the fact that bin Ladin and Zawahiri were still at large.

From 2003 to 2007, a number of bombings in several Western countries, plus Turkey, bore the fingerprints of Al Qaʻidah – notably the Madrid train attacks that led to the withdrawal of the Spanish contingent in Iraq. Just before Secretary of State Powell visited Saudi Arabia in May 2003, 20 people – eight of them American civilians – died in suicide bombings of four compounds in Saudi Arabia. The subsequent bombing of a residential area for foreign residents (mainly Arab) in Riyadh killed seventeen.

The theology of Al Qaʻidah and kindred Islamist organizations (Ansar al Sunna, Zarqawi's Tawhid wal Jihad) is a combination of the Salafi school and latter-day Islamist activism. Ansar al Sunna, once active in Iraq, condemned democracy as apostasy because it places the caprice of the people above the will of God. Ahmad Hashem and Lawrence Wright have reported on a letter of July 2005 from Zawahiri to Abu Musʻab al Zarqawi, then leader of "Al Qaʻidah in Iraq", citing Al Qaʻidah's objectives: Expel the Americans from Iraq, win over the Shia, reestablish the Caliphate in Baghdad, and pursue operations against Israel. (Given Zarqawi's antipathy toward Shiites, and bin Ladin's reportedly low regard for Zarqawi, the US forces may have done Al Qaʻidah a favor by eliminating him.)

In 2006, the Internet carried a video in which Zawahiri denounced the leaders of Egypt, Iraq, Jordan, and Saudi Arabia as traitors. According to Robert Leiken and Steven Brooke, his faction also despised moderate Islamists like Hamas and some Muslim Brothers for embracing elections, even those in occupied Iraq, instead of violence.

As far as Western media were aware, the Al Qaʻidah leadership and its surviving operatives – Arab, Pak, and Afghan – were hiding in North Waziristan. In September 2007, when bin Ladin made his first video for TV in three years, the media reported that Al Qaʻidah's rebuilt organization in the Peshawar area was dominated by former members of Zawahiri's Islamic

Jihad and directed by a council that reports to bin Ladin. A *Times* article of May 2008 featured Abu Yahya al Libi, an Islamic scholar who escaped from an American prison in Afghanistan in 2005, as a new member of the high command. The Summer 2008 issue of *Middle East Policy* carried a report by Abdullah Ansary that the Saudi regime had had some success in reeducating Islamist dissidents through use of the school system and the Internet, and close control of the clerical hierarchy. In 2009, however, AQAP bands hiding out among Yemeni tribes had reportedly committed several recent attacks, including an assault on the American Embassy (Chapter 11).

In 2009, the *Times* reported the CIA was having success in taking out Al Qaʻidah leaders in Pakistan with its Predator drones, but that vacancies were being filled by volunteers from across the Muslim World, and the Taliban continued to derive guidance and inspiration from the organization. *Middle East Policy* identified Al Qaʻidah's new spokesman on the Internet as an American convert to Islam, Adam Gadahn.

Syria and Lebanon - When Syria emerged from French domination after World War II, the new government was controlled by Sunnis – in keeping with the ethnic composition of the country. Soon after World War II, however, the country entered its military-government phase (Chapter 11), and a series of coups depleted Sunni officer ranks. As each new faction took over, it killed, jailed, or exiled its predecessors, until the disdained Alawites fortuitously rose to the top, and Syria awoke one day in 1966 to realize that it had an Alawite dictator: Salah Jadid. Out of the crucible of the 1967 humiliation by Israel, Hafiz al Asad concocted in 1970 the overthrow of Jadid and the establishment of an Alawite dynasty that survived his death in 2000, and the succession of his second son, Bashar.

In the pathologically communalist Middle East, Syria's Sunni majority was bound to chafe under Alawite rule. The faction best organized to lead the resistance was the Syrian branch of the Muslim Brotherhood, for whom Shiites were infidels, and Alawites weren't even Shiites. Although Asad paraded his loyalty to Islam by amending the Constitution of 1973 to restrict the Presidency to a Muslim, the unmollified Brotherhood launched a bloody campaign of subversion. In 1980, activists killed two of the several thousand Soviet military advisors in Syria. In 1981, a series of car bombs inflicted heavy casualties in Damascus, and according to *The New Yorker* an Iraqi power struggle produced the first modern suicide bombing in the Middle East – an attack on the Iraqi Embassy in Beirut.

In 1982, Asad launched a massive artillery attack on the city of Hamah, center of Muslim Brotherhood activity in Syria. The city center was devastated, many thousands of civilians were killed, and the Brotherhood's leadership was liquidated. Since that object lesson, Islamism has not posed any serious challenge to the regime, although it has enjoyed some degree of resurgence in the wake of the milquetoast response of Arab regimes to the American invasion of Iraq.

The eclipse of the Muslim Brotherhood (Sunni) in Syria coincided with the rise of Hizballah in Lebanon. The traditional champion of the Shiite community in Lebanon had been *Amal* (Hope). Its Arabic name is an acronym for *Afwaj al Muqawamah al Lubnaniyyah* (Lebanese Resistance Battalions). Founded by the charismatic *Imam* Musa al Sadr in 1974, it proclaimed Iran's Ayatollah Khomeini as the Imam of all Muslims. However, Amal's strategy was too moderate for the Khomeini faction – the only outright anti-American regime in the Middle East. Some days after the 1982 Israeli invasion of Lebanon, Iran sent in via Syria a team of its Revolutionary Guards to train a paramilitary force of Lebanese Shia.

The product of Iranian and Syrian backing and Lebanese Shiite fervor was Hizballah (The Party of God). Since the Shia had traditionally been excluded from the Lebanese power structure (except for the figurehead post of Speaker of Parliament), their original reaction to the Israeli invasion – like that of the Iraqi Shia to the American invasion – was muted. However, the highhanded behavior of the Israeli forces, including the gratuitous devastation of Shiite villages, rapidly enraged and energized the ranks of Hizballah. The longer the Israelis held out in Lebanon, the more they tipped the political scale against Amal, in favor of Hizballah.

Hizballah's resistance took two parallel tracks. Against the Israelis and the Americans in Lebanon, it introduced the vehicle-bomb – notably to kill 63 people (17 Americans, including the CIA's top Middle East expert, Bob Ames) at the Beirut Embassy in April 1983, and 241 at the Marine barracks in October 1983. (The reputed planner of these two operations, 'Imad Mughniyah, had an American price on his head, and was killed, presumably by Israeli intelligence, in 2008.) Subsequent operations were the hijacking of a TWA plane in 1985, the abduction, torture, and killing of Embassy Beirut station chief William Buckley in 1985, the abduction and hanging of Lt. Colonel William Higgins in 1988, and the kidnapping and sometime killing of American civilians in the 1990's.

Outside Lebanon, Hizballah operatives have been suspected of involvement in a broad spectrum of anti-Western actions, including the 1992 bombing of the Israeli Embassy in Buenos Aires, the 1994 bombing of the Jewish Community Center in Buenos Aires, the 1996 bombing of the Khawbar Towers in Saudi Arabia, collaboration with Hamas and Islamic Jihad in the Occupied Palestinian Territories, and possibly with Al Qa'idah. The two bombings in Buenos Aires have been seen as retaliation for Israel's assassination in 1992 of Hizballah leader 'Abbas al Musawi, whose successor, *Hujjat al Islam* and *Sayyid* (descendant of the Prophet) Hasan Nasrallah, according to Turkish official of the UN Timur Goksel, has enhanced the reputation of the organization for efficient social services, incorruptibility, and staunch resistance to Israel expansionism. *Newsweek* assessed him as a spellbinding speaker. Charles Glass believes that, after Hizballah took over south Lebanon, Nasrallah displayed statesmanship in preventing reprisals against the Lebanese who had collaborated with the previous Israeli regime.

In its early years, Hizballah was distrusted in Lebanon and repressed in Syria, which according to Augustus Richard Norton executed some of its members in 1987. However, Israel's evacuation of its forces in 2000 (Chapter 8) was credited to constant Hizballah harassment, and won the organization wide popularity and respectability in Lebanon. It became the only Lebanese faction whose militia carried weapons openly. In 2000, it had 13 of the 27 Shiite seats in the Lebanese Parliament. (Amal had 8, and its leader, Nabih Barri, was the Speaker.) Hizballah had a social-service net, a TV station (*Al Manar*), a training program for its own version of Boy Scouts, an army of several thousand, satellite cells in Arabia and elsewhere, and a one hundred million dollar budget, financed by Iran, by private donations from around the world, and – per a Khomeini directive – by tithes of Lebanese Shiites.

In 2006, Juan Cole reported close ties between Hizballah and Iraqi principals Muqtada al Sadr and Prime Minister Maliki. In 2007, according to Seymour Hersh, Shaykh Hasan Nasrallah was under death sentence from Jordan, Israel, and Al Qa'idah (although Zawahiri reportedly praised the prowess of "our brothers" during the Hizballah War of 2006).

In early 2009, Hizballah regarded Iran's Supreme Leader, Ali Khamenei, as its own leader, but in Lebanon it was headed by Nasrallah. Its unofficial spiritual mentor, Ayatallah Muhammad Husayn Fadlallah (who escaped a bloody CIA-Saudi assassination attempt in 1985) has condemned suicide bombing and Al Qa'idah's attacks of 9/11, and taken the position that no Shia leader has a monopoly on truth. Augustus Richard Norton considers him the second most respected cleric in the Shiite world (Sistani being the first). Vali Nasr classifies him with the moderates.

Syria's inclusion on Washington's list of states sponsoring terrorism is charged to Syrian support of Hizballah and tolerance of Hamas and Islamic Jihad offices – even though all three organizations are independent of Syrian control, participate in elections, do not call for restoration of the Caliphate, and are not known to have carried out operations in the US: *Current History*, Emile Nakhlah. The Hamas office in Damascus has long been headed by "political" leader Khalid Mish'al (Chapter 8). According to Flint Leverett, Syrian Grand Mufti Ahmad Kaftaru has been directing an effort to coopt moderate members of the Syrian Muslim Brothers, which is a Salafist movement modeled on its Egyptian analogue.

Alawite rule is unlikely to be the end of the Syrian story, given the reputed distribution of its population: Of 19 million Syrians, there are 12 million Sunnis, two million Alawite Shiites, and smaller communities of Christians, Kurds, and mainstream Shiites (*Mutawali*, plural *Matawilah*).

Palestinian Territories - Before the formation of Fatah and the PLO in 1964, the nearest thing the Palestinians had to political leadership was their Sunni religious hierarchy, headed by the Mufti of Jerusalem, Hajj Amin al Husayni. In 1921, the British leadership of the new Palestinian Mandate appointed him permanent President of the newly created Supreme Muslim Council. In 1936, the rivals for Palestinian political leadership created a permanent executive organ, the Arab High Committee, under the chairmanship of Hajj Amin, who had won a dynastic battle with the Nashashibi clan. In 1937, when a general strike developed into an anti-British rebellion, the British removed him as President of the Supreme Council and declared the High Committee illegal. He fled to Lebanon.

Hajj Amin's allegedly misguided rejection of a British compromise in 1939 led to the Palestinian civil war between Arabs and Jews in 1947, and the first Arab-Israeli war in 1948 (Chapter 8). In 1951, Jordanian King Husayn dismantled the Supreme Muslim Council and assigned its sectarian responsibilities to his own government. Rejecting this decision, Palestinian Islamists formed the Islamic Liberation Party.

By the 1970's, Israel had begun to encourage the activities of Palestinian Islamists as a counterweight to the growing influence of the PLO. In 1973, *The New Yorker* reports, Israel was happy to support Shaykh Ahmad Yasin's Islamic Center. Ariel Sharon, Military Governor of the Gaza Strip, and his colleagues on the West Bank were impressed by the Islamists' preoccupation with the seemingly innocuous erection of a social safety net.

Reports by Mouin Rabbani (*Journal of Palestine Studies,* Spring 2008) and Adam Shatz *(London Review of Books,* 5/4/09) indicate that Palestinian Islamist leaders took a militantly nationalist direction at an organizational meeting in Jordan in 1983. The outbreak of Intifadah I in 1987 coincided with Shaykh Ahmad Yasin's issuance of the first communiqué from the *Harakat al Muqawamah al Islamiyyah* (The Islamic Resistance Movement), whose Arabic acronym, *Hamas,* means fervor. As reported in Glenn Robinson's *The Palestinian Hamas,* its charter condemned any politician who made peace with Israel, as a violator of the perpetual *waqf* of Palestine. Hamas's leadership came from the Muslim Brotherhood. Its armed wing was named in honor of 'Izz al Din al Qassam, a Syrian religious shaykh.

Concurrently, Fathi Shiqaqi, a Palestinian physician resident in Egypt, founded *Al Jihad al Islami* (Islamic Holy War).

In 1989, Israel outlawed Hamas and arrested Yasin, who pled guilty of planning the death of four Palestinian suspects of collaboration, and received a life sentence. Hamas continued to operate underground, publishing a covenant calling for jihad to liberate all of Palestine. This action committed Hamas to breaking with the PLO and its ward, the Palestine Authority, after they became bound by the 1993 Oslo Agreement to the unpromising two-state solution (Chapter 8). As Israel continued to expand its presence on the West Bank in violation of the spirit of Oslo, Hamas and Islamic Jihad (equally totalitarian in its territorial objectives) began to gain adherents at the PLO's expense. Armed clashes between Hamas and the PLO had already occurred in 1988. Hamas was further radicalized by direct confrontation with Israel. In Egypt, agents of Islamic Jihad (Egyptian branch?) killed a professor (Faraj Fawdah) for his relentless critiques of Islamic fundamentalism.

In 1993, after a wave of kidnapping of Israeli soldiers and suicide bombings (including an operation in Tel Aviv that killed 22 Israelis, the deadliest so far in Israeli history), Israel dumped 413 members of Hamas in a desolate area of Lebanon, where they made camp – and picked up expertise in the use of explosives from members of Hizballah. (They were allowed back some years later.) It was reported that Hamas had adopted the suicide-bomb strategy in retaliation for a suicide attack on Arabs by Israeli Baruch Goldstein. One analyst suggested that the Palestinian Islamists' strategy was to torpedo Palestinian peace talks, leaving the ultimate demise of Israel as the only outcome of the battle for Palestine.

Through the 1990's, the popularity of Hamas fluctuated – sometimes reduced by Israeli closures of the border to day-workers, sometimes elevated by Israeli brutality. In 1995, Fathi Shiqaqi, who had been resident in Damascus, was assassinated, and Ramadan Shallah left a professional post in Florida to replace him in Damascus as leader of Islamic Jihad in the Territories. Damascus was also the base of the leader of Hamas, which had continued to expand its network of mosques, schools, orphanages, clinics, and hospitals in the Territories.

By 1996, Israel had adopted assassination ("targeted killings") as a standard weapon against Islamist activists. One of the first victims was Yahya 'Ayyash, "the Engineer", who was reputedly Hamas's top explosives expert. According to the media, his elimination was a subtle operation in which a double agent inveigled him into using a cell phone that was rigged to explode by radio signal. In retaliation, Hamas staged a series of suicide bombings, which were credited for the election of arch-Likudist Benjamin Netanyahu as Prime Minister. In 1997, the Khalid Mish'al affair (Chapter 8) forced Israel to release Ahmad Yasin, who was regarded as a moderate, to the extent that he seemed open to the strategy of temporary toleration of the existence of Israel. At this stage, Israel still accepted Hamas's distinction between its "political" and "military" wings. The popularity of the Islamists in the territories was in decline, and hundreds had been jailed by the Palestine Authority.

The power equation was disrupted again in the fall of 2000 when Ariel Sharon made his provocative visit to the Temple Mount. The outbreak of Intifadah II torpedoed Oslo and generated support for the radical strategy advocated by the Islamists. Nevertheless, a broad spectrum of Arab Islamist organizations condemned Al Qa'idah's attacks of 9/11/01. Ahmad Yasin did so on behalf of Hamas, which had habitually eschewed the anti-American focus of Al Qa'idah and, in the 1980's, of Hizballah. In fact, as noted by Michael Scott Doran, the strain of Palestinian nationalism in the pronouncements of Hamas left it open, under strict Salafi doctrine, to a charge of idolatry. Islamic Jihad should also have been suspect in Al Qa'idah eyes for its alliance with Shiite Hizballah and its Iranian patrons.

In 2004, Israel assassinated Hamas leader Ahmad Yasin and, a few weeks later, his successor, 'Abd al 'Aziz al Rantisi.

In 2006, Hamas made its first foray into the Palestinian electoral arena (Chapter 8), and scored an upset victory. The presence of six women in its delegation of 74 was an indication of the faction's liberal strain among Islamist organizations.

In 2008, 47 of Hamas's 50 MP's from the West Bank were in Israeli prison as representatives of an illegal organization. *The Link* noted that the Bush administration endorsed their sentences.

Jordan - In the civil war of 1970 between the monarchy and the PLO, the Muslim Brotherhood sided with the monarchy, and according to Nir Rosen was rewarded with jobs in the Ministry of Education. In the 1980's, the Islamists were the best organized opposition faction in Jordan. After they had won 40 percent of the seats in the elections of 1989, King Husayn revised the elections law.

Some 300,000 Palestinians were expelled from Kuwait in 1991 for having welcomed the invasion by their patron, Saddam. Nir Rosen reports that most of the expellees settled northeast of Amman in al Zarqa, which became a Salafist center for Jordan and Iraq. In al Zarqa, Ahmad al Khalaylah (nom de guerre: Abu Mus'ab al Zarqawi), said to be a Jordanian *takfiri* from the Bani Hasan tribe, was an organizer for those Islamists who questioned the legitimacy of the monarchy. (The Jordanian Brotherhood did not.) In Afghanistan, Zarqawi had been the reputed founder of *Al Tawhid wal Jihad* (Monotheism and Holy War) as a rival to Al Qa'idah.

In 1995, Jordan expelled a Hamas leader, Musa Muhammad Abu Marzuq, who was subsequently taken into Federal detention in the United States. In 1997, the Islamic Action Front (IAF, political wing of the Brotherhood) boycotted the elections. Jordan was a major conduit for contributions to Hamas, which had been a beneficiary of the termination of the cash flow from Arabian shaykhdoms to the PLO.

King 'Abdallah II broke with his father's policy of tolerating Hamas as a counterbalance to the PLO. Possibly acting in concert with Israel, Jordan's de facto protector (Chapter 14), Jordanian security arrested four Hamas principals and closed their office in Amman. Later the four were released and transferred to Qatar. In 2000, a number of Islamists were rounded up, Islamist imams were replaced, and a Jordanian military court sentenced six Islamists to hang for conspiring to attack American and Israeli targets in Jordan. In late 2002, there were armed clashes between security forces and Islamists in Ma'n, and Laurence Foley, an AID official at Embassy Amman was murdered, reportedly by Islamists affiliated with Zarqawi (who had been released in 1999 from his second stretch of torture in Jordanian prison) and Shakir al 'Absi, leader of Fath al Islam (see Lebanon).

Nine/eleven and the American invasion of Iraq were particularly stressful for schizoid Jordan. The IAF condemned 9/11, and won – directly and indirectly – 22 of 110 seats in the 2003 Parliamentary elections. The 2005 bombing of three tourist hotels in Amman was attributed to Zarqawi's Salafists. The shock of the Hamas victory in the Palestinian elections of January 2006 led King 'Abdallah II to further intensify restrictions on the Islamists. He faced the additional challenge of dealing with hundreds of thousands of refugees from the sectarian civil war in Iraq. Residency permits were readily available to Iraqis who could put $150,000 in an Amman bank, but the impoverished – especially Shiites – were viewed with suspicion. In 2006 Shiite prayer halls (*husayniyyat*) were banned.

On 1/5/10, in their determination to locate Al Qa'idah's leadership, a CIA station in Afghanistan gave a Jordanian source with a high-level Jordanian recommendation unprecedented access. The source carried a concealed bomb that killed himself, his Jordanian sponsor, and seven CIA veterans.

Iraq - In 1958, Muhammad Baqir al Sadr founded *Al Da'wah al Islamiyyah,* dedicated to the struggle to establish an Islamic regime (not a theocracy). He was Shiite, but his manifesto, *Al Usus,* was pan-Islamic. In the ensuing fifty years, his party fragmented. The Al Da'wah of current Iraqi Prime Minister Maliki is a much smaller organization.

By continuing the tradition of Sunni rule over the valley of the Tigris and Euphrates, Saddam Husayn fostered among the Sunni community a sense of solidarity with the regime. His major domestic problems came from the Kurds and the Shiites, and he dealt with them ruthlessly (Chapter 9).

Although the Iraqi Baath was perhaps the most secularist regime in the Arab World – tolerant of Christians and advanced in the area of women's rights – the conservatism of Saddam's Muslim subjects impelled him to make gestures in their direction. Back in 1976, he presented Saudi King Fahd with an ornate text of the Qur'an. During the Iraq-Iran war (fought largely by Shiites on both sides), he stressed Islamic themes, sponsored Islamic conferences, nationalized all 3200 Muslim mosques and shrines, claimed direct descent from the Imam 'Ali, and added the Muslim Brotherhood's slogan, *Allahu Akbar* (God is Great), to the Iraqi flag. During the war, veiling became more prevalent among female students.

According to Faleh Jabbar, Ayatallah Muhammad Baqir al Hakim, leader of SCIRI (Chapter 9), came back from Iran to Iraq after Gulf War I and advised the armed forces to follow SCIRI's dictates – an action that alienated many Iraqis, particularly Kurds. However, he was on good terms with his spiritual superior, 'Ali al Sistani, who according to *Middle East Policy* became head of the Najaf *hawzah* (Chapter 9) in 1992 and is today the most revered ayatallah in the world.

In 2001, Kurdish Sunni Islamists, under the leadership of "Mullah Krekor" (Najm al Din Faraj Ahmad) founded *Ansar al Islam* (Champions of Islam), according to Juan Cole with support from Abu Mus'ab al Zarqawi, now moved from Jordan via Afghanistan to Iraq. Just before the American invasion, the Ansar established a base in Iraqi Kurdistan along the Iranian border. After the invasion, Zarqawi reportedly activated Monotheism and Holy War as an instrument for suicide bombings. In the early months of the invasion, this group was implicated in the bombings of the Jordanian Embassy, UN headquarters in Baghdad, and the Shrine of the Imam 'Ali, where Muhammad Baqir al Hakim was killed.

In 2004 Zarqawi renamed his group "Al Qa'idah in Mesopotamia" (AQI) and swore fealty to Usamah bin Ladin. Ansar and Zarqawi were suspected of complicity in the March railroad bombings in Madrid, which reportedly convinced the Spanish government to withdraw its troops from Iraq. In August, Islamists led by Zarqawi, operating under the title of Monotheism and Holy War, and flying a black and yellow flag, were said to have seized control of Anbar Province (from Baghdad to the Syrian border) in alliance with Al Qaʻidah. Islamists had killed several former Baathists who had entered into negotiations with the ʻAllawi regime. A recording attributed to bin Ladin proclaimed Zarqawi the leader of Al Qaʻidah forces in Iraq.

In 2005 the group warned Sunnis that voting in the October referendum on the constitution would be tantamount to rejecting Islam.

In 2006, according to Mark Danner, an intercepted letter to bin Ladin and Zawahiri outlined Zarqawi's plan to "awaken the sleeping Sunnis" by precipitating sectarian civil war – in direct opposition to Zawahiri's advice to conciliate the Shia. Zarqawi got his civil war by destroying one of the Shiites' most sacred shrines, the "Golden Dome" – al ʻAskariyyah Mosque in al Samarra' (Chapter 15). By this time, Mullah Krekor had moved to Norway as a political refugee.

Muqtada Sadr is reportedly a devout Jaʻfari who believes that the return of the Mahdi is near, and that the Americans invaded Iraq in an effort to defer the Mahdi's return.

Iran - In 1906 the Iranian Assembly declared the *Jaʻfari* (Twelver) branch of Shiism the state religion. Under the monarchy, the Shiite clerics enjoyed a fair degree of independence as long as they stayed out of politics. Grand Ayatollah Rohallah Khomeini did not meet this requirement, and he was exiled in 1964. He lived in Najaf (as did his former classmate, Muhammad Sadiq al Sadr, father of Muqtada), until Saddam expelled him from Iraq.

In 1979 Khomeini took power in Iran, which was declared an Islamic Republic. According to Abbas Amanat's *Apocalyptic Islam and Iranian Shiism,* reviewed by Malise Ruthven in the 7/2/09 *New York Review of Books,* Khomeini suspended the Iranian tradition of de facto separation of mosque and state by imposing a "guardian jurist" (himself, with the title of Imam) to exercize power on behalf of the Hidden Imam until his return. Khomeini adopted a vehemently anti-American posture – closing a radar station used by Americans to monitor Soviet performance under the SALT accord, thanking the PLO for its financial and military support during his exile, giving them control of the Israeli Embassy, promising to lend reciprocal support for the elimination of Israel, and allowing student vigilantes to overrun the American Embassy compound and hold most of its personnel hostage for over a year.

The students had three possible motives: 1) to retaliate for Washington's admission of the Shah for medical treatment; Curtis Wilkie of *The Boston Globe* suggested that Carter and Secretary of State Vance had given in to the Shah after Henry Kissinger threatened to brand Vance for cowardice if the Shah died elsewhere; 2) to hold hostages against any American inclination to attempt another imperialist coup; 3) to act on behalf of hardliners who wanted to undermine any effort by interim Prime Minister Mehdi Bazargan to arrange détente with Washington.

Amanat argues that Khomeini's malice toward America was not simply resentment of the blatant intervention in Iranian politics in 1953 (Chapter 10), or the marriage of convenience between Washington and the Shah (and between the CIA and the infamous Savak), or the built-in animus of every Islamist toward Jewish occupation of the Dome of the Rock: Khomeini's denunciation of "the Great Satan" reflected Iranian Shiism's incorporation of Zoroastrianism's eternal conflict between pure believers and polluting infidels.

In 1980, Iran's pragmatic President, Ali Rafsanjani, released the American hostages to the incoming Republican administration. In 1981, Tehran's desperate need for arms induced it to deal with the US and Israel in what snowballed into the Iran-Contra Affair. In 1982, Iran sent agents of the Pasdaran to help Lebanese Shiites organize Hizballah.

On 7/3/88 the USS Vincennes mistakenly shot down Iranian Air Flight 655 over the Gulf. Two instances of possible Iranian retaliation have appeared in the media: 1) an attack in the US on the wife of the Captain of the Vincennes; 2) the destruction of Pan-American Flight 103 over Scotland on 12/21/88. With Qadhafi's concurrence a Scottish court imprisoned Libyan operative 'Abd al Basit al Megrahi (Miqrahi) for complicity in the Pan-Am bombing, but Alexander Cockburn supports a different hypothesis: The operation was carried out by the Palestinian PFLP/GC on behalf of Iran: *Counterpunch*, 9/1/09; *London Review of Books*, 9/24/09, Gareth Pierce. Cockburn suggested that Bush 41 and Margaret Thatcher, needing Iran's help in expelling Iraqi forces from Kuwait, pinned culpability on Libya.

In the 1990's, Islamist organizations across the Middle East cultivated closer ties with the Iranian theocracy. Iran subsidized the Palestinian Hamas, and provided arms and military trainers to Sudan, whose dictator, Lt. General 'Umar al Bashir, was allied with Islamist Shaykh Hasan al Turabi. The schism between Iran's hard-liners and moderates, personified by new Supreme Leader Khamenei and new President Khatami, respectively, resulted in a two-track foreign policy. On the moderate side, Iran cultivated good relations with neighboring states. On the radical side, it opposed Oslo, supported Islamists, issued a death threat against "blasphemous" author Salman Rushdie, and assassinated Iranian dissidents overseas. In 1996, the Saudi Government claimed to have proof that the Khawbar bombing had been carried out, with Iranian support, by a Saudi branch of Hizballah. There were more recent indications that Iran was leaning toward promoting Shia-Sunni détente under Iranian leadership.

In his will, Khomeini denounced the Arabian monarchies as illegal, and called for the Saudi family to be publicly cursed for treachery to *Dar al Islam*. His successor, Ali al Khamenei, was another hardliner. Nevertheless, as long as he was in office, President Khatami continued the onerous campaign to moderate the Iranian theocracy, and Iran continued to cultivate amicable relations with its neighbors and the states of Europe and Asia, although its failure to comply with the 1948 Universal Declaration of Human Rights (signed by, of all people, the Shah) had prevented the European Union from concluding a comprehensive treaty of trade and cooperation with Iran.

Toward Afghanistan, Iran had maintained a cautious stance complicated by support for the anti-Taliban Shiites. In 1998, the Taliban's execution of eleven Iranian diplomats almost precipitated Iranian invasion, but Iran adopted a conciliatory posture toward the subsequent Karzai regime, and promised financial aid to upgrade the Afghan educational system. As of mid-2003, Iran still sheltered over two million refugees from the Afghan wars, and had won high marks from the UN for the facilities it was providing refugees from southern Iraq.

For the United States, the overriding issues with Iran are its opposition to an Arab-Israeli settlement, and its nuclear ambitions. Even the moderate faction in Tehran favors continuation of support for Hizballah, Hamas, and Islamic Jihad. In 2002, Israel intercepted in the Red Sea a ship carrying arms from Iran meant for Hizballah or the Palestine Authority.

It is inconceivable that Iran is not closely involved in Shiite politics in post-invasion Iraq. However, few specifics on such activity have filtered into the media. The invasion elicited a knee-jerk condemnation from Tehran, but the Iranians must have welcomed the overthrow of secularist Saddam, and they maintained correct relations with the Iraqi authorities appointed by the Coalition Provisional Authority. The unanswered question is whether either or both factions in the Tehran regime have formed alliances with one or more Shiite groups in Iraq (Chapter 15).

The putative reelection of Ahmadinejad in June 2009 left the Presidency in the hands of a foreign-policy hardliner and a devout Ja'fari who prayed at the UN that Allah bring back the Mahdi soon.

According to press reports, American agents had been conducting secret operations in Iran. Thomas Mattair reported (*Middle East Policy,* Summer 2009) that the Kurdish PEJAK was on the State Department's list of terrorist organizations, but the Baluchi Jondallah was not.

Saudi Arabia - The founder of Wahhabiism accepted only the Qur'an and the Traditions, condemning all borrowed practices. The worship of saints and shrines was polytheism. Not even the Prophet was to be venerated.

The government of Saudi Arabia is still constrained by the ancient alliance between the royal family and the Wahhabi sect. In 1801, Saudi tribesmen sacked the Shiites' holy city of Karbala'. In 1806 they smashed "idolatrous" tombs in Mecca and Medina. However, for some zealots, the Wahhabi position is not conservative enough. In 1979, the regime was traumatized by a Sunni reaction to the Shiite revolution in Iran – armed seizure of the Great Mosque in Mecca by a group led by Juhayman al 'Utaybi. After the rebellion was put down with considerable bloodshed, the regime made concessions to the archconservatives by awarding the Sunni imams control over the schools, the courts, and cultural affairs, but Nasr notes that Khomeini misjudged his ability to coopt the Saudi clerisy, and his call for supranational control of Mecca and Medina fell flat.

Also in 1979, Saudi Arabia and America concluded a secret accord to collaborate in sending mujahidin to expel the Russians from Afghanistan. The Soviet withdrawal in 1989 was a signal victory for Islamism.

Saudi Arabia still has one of the most culturally repressive societies in the world. Morals police (*Mutawwi'in*) patrol the cities against music, immodest dress, and women at the wheel. There have been no female broadcasters on TV, and stores are closed at prayer times. The first Gulf War incensed Islamists against the American presence in the Peninsula, even though the regime had cleared the invitation with the ranking clerics (*'ulama'*).

Islam is the state religion of most Arab states, but as of 1999, Saudi Arabia and Sudan were the only two to have designated the Islamic *Shari'ah* as the law of the land. Kuwait and Yemen had allowed Islamists to run for, and serve in, parliament, whereas Bahrain had not. Bahrain's situation in this regard is particularly sensitive, since it has a Shiite plurality, and Iran has traditionally claimed sovereignty. In 1981, the Khomeini regime backed a Shiite coup there. At last report, an organization calling itself the Islamic Front for the Liberation of Bahrain was based in Damascus, while Bahrain's Parliament was dominated by Islamists.

In 1998, Saudi Arabia was subsidizing Islamist movements in Afghanistan (Taliban), Palestine (Hamas), Sudan, Russia, and the Balkans, and financing Islamic schools from Kano to Jakarta: Nasr. Nasr also writes that Pakistan named the city of Faysalabad in King Faysal's honor, but the King never got his wish to pray at Al Aqsa Mosque in Jerusalem.

In more recent years, the Saudi regime became increasingly preoccupied with rebel movements at home. In *Saudi Arabia and the Politics of Dissent* Mamoun Fandy catalogued the leaders of Islamist groups advocating the monarchy's reform or, at least on the part of Usamah bin Ladin, its elimination. According to Rashid Khalidi, Saudi Islamists dislike the term *Wahhabiyyin* and prefer to be called *Muwahhidun* (monotheists).

By 2003, economic strains, cultural repression, and America's aggressive foreign policy had disaffected Saudi public opinion to the advantage of the Islamists, although it is unlikely that the sequence of car bombs against foreign residents had broad support. In 2006 *The Washington Post Weekly* reported that Saudi Islamists looked for guidance to a Jordanian cleric, Abu Muhammad al Maqdisi (birth name: 'Isam al 'Utaybi al Burqawi). Maqdisi, now in prison, is a takfiri who considers democracy heresy, mentored Zarqawi, and endorsed Zarqawi's suicide operations, beheadings, and body burnings. He has issued a fatwa excommunicating the "sacrilegious" Saudi royal family. Juan Cole called attention to a shift in basic Saudi policy – the milestone Mecca Declaration that the Sunni and Shia faiths are not inimical to each other, that their differences are matters of personal interpretation, not of principle. The *Economist* assessed the Saudi educational curriculum as stultified by rote and religious dogma. Science and secularism were vilified.

In 2007, it was estimated that 45 percent of the foreign militants in Iraq were Saudis. The regime has had some success in jailing or eliminating ringleaders. The largest cadre of detainees transferred from Afghanistan to Guantanamo were Saudis. The regime has lately dismissed some 1300 radical Islamist teachers.

Yemen - Although the abortive attempt by the South Yemenis to secede from the union in 1994 was essentially a Sunni operation, it appears that their motivation was political rather than theological. According to Vali Nasr, the Zaydi branch of Shiism recognizes only five early Imams, and does not share the Ja'fari belief in a hidden Imam.

After nine/eleven, 'Ali 'Abdallah Salih felt compelled to maintain a balance between pro-Islamist tribes and anti-Islamist Washington. On the pro-Islamist side there were mysterious "escapes" from Yemeni jails. On the anti-Islamist side, a CIA Predator was allowed to take out a carload of militants in the desert, and in raids of 12/24/09 and January 2010 Yemeni planes killed a number of ranking AQAP operatives.

A clash between the Zaydi-dominated government of unified Yemen and a dissident Zaydi faction in 2004 ended with the death of the dissidents' leader. An uprising in favor of reinstating the Zaydi Imamate (overthrown by the military in 1962) was subdued in 2007.

By this time Islamists hunted in Saudi Arabia had taken refuge with sympathetic tribes in Yemen, and Saudi and Yemeni affiliates of Al Qa'idah had united as Al Qa'idah in the Arabian Peninsula (AQAP). Under the leadership of Nasir al Wuhayshi, they carried out attacks, notably the September 2008 bombing of the American Embassy in Sana'a' by a suicide squad reportedly trained in the Hadramawt, the easternmost province of Yemen.

AQAP connections were ascribed to American Major Nidal Hasan, who fired on US personnel at Fort Hood, Texas, in the fall of 2009, and to a Nigerian Islamist who tried to blow up an airliner over Detroit on 12/25/09.

UAE - The Federation arrests Islamists and turns them over to American or Pakistani authorities. However, business is business. The *AP* reported in 2006 that Al Qa'idah had been able to make financial transfers via UAE banks.

Turkey - As discussed by Perry Anderson in the 9/11/08 *London Review of Books,* the Ottoman Empire preserved the ancient Islamic legislation that discriminated against non-Muslims – including special taxes and prohibition against bearing arms or marrying Muslim wives. However the Empire did not proselytize or expel them.

By the advent of World War I, the Islamic Caliphate was a historical relic. The Ottoman Sultan's call, in his purported role as Caliph, for jihad against Britain elicited no response from his Arab subjects. In 1923, General Mustafa Kemal, a confirmed secularist, was elected President of the new Republic of Turkey; the Republic jettisoned Islam as the state religion in 1928, and abandoned the Arabic script (the alphabet of the Qur'an) in favor of a Latinate alphabet. Over the ensuing eighty years, the Turkish military has done its best to erase religious influence over politics. Its failure is one more example of the glacial pace of social change, particularly in a country whose people are "saturated with religion."

Kemal put mosques under state control, and outlawed Sufi brotherhoods. Result? The brotherhoods survived, and in 1996 Necmettin Erbakan became the first openly Islamicist Prime Minister of Turkey. He was not an Islamist, although many of his constituents were. One reason for their persistence had been a wave of Marxist activity in the 1960's and 1970's, and a consequent relaxation of the regime's restraints on Islamists, and on the assemblies of Sufi *tekke*'s (lodges). At this writing, both Islam and Islamism were active in Turkey. Instances of violent Islamism included suicide truck bombings of two synagogues, a British bank, and the British Consulate General in Istanbul in November 2003, with some fifty fatalities and many more wounded. Suspect organizations included the Kurdish Hizballah (Chapter 6).

In 2004, Islamic Justice and Development, the party headed by Prime Minister Recep Tayyip Erdogan, controlled 367 of the 550 seats in Parliament – the body which had denied American ground troops access to Iraq in 2003. The Erdogan government had reformed the judicial system, moderated the restrictions on Kurdish freedom of expression, and on the evidence reined in the generals. The Islamicist movement carried considerable cultural weight by virtue of a newspaper, a magazine, two radio stations, and a TV station.

The United States Against Islamism

In *The Nation* of 9/14/09, Christopher Hayes cited two controls on covert action: 1) In 1976 Gerald Ford decreed by Executive Order 11905: "No employee of the US Government shall engage in . . . political assassination." 2) In 1978 Carter signed the Foreign Intelligence Surveillance Act (FISA) which required that US officials acquire a warrant before wiretapping an American citizen. (This requirement was bypassed by Bush 43.)

In 1979, Carter added Afghanistan to the list of countries (Somalia, Ethiopia, Angola) where the United States was engaged in proxy wars against the Soviet Union. Washington authorized 500 million dollars for nonlethal aid to the mujahidin fighting the puppet regime in Kabul. Carter saw the Soviet intervention in Afghanistan as a bid for hegemony over the Persian Gulf. His successor shared that concern. Reagan's Secretary of State, Alexander Haig, optimistically perceived "strategic consensus" linking Egypt, Israel, Turkey, Pakistan, and China in an anti-Soviet belt. During the Reagan administration, the CIA supplied funds, and possibly training, to bin Ladin's forces in Afghanistan via Pakistani Intelligence. CIA director Casey built up the station in Islamabad to become the biggest in the world. Saudi Arabia participated in the mujahidin program, primarily as a means of opposing the Shiite theocracy in Iran. For Washington, the Iranian regime was a supporter of terrorism, because of the aid it provided to Hizballah in Lebanon, and to Hamas and Islamic Jihad in the Palestinian Territories.

In 1985, according to Mike Davis, Casey and Saudi Prince Bandar collaborated in backing an attempt by Lebanese agents to kill Hizballah leader Muhammad Fadlallah by a bomb that missed him but killed 75 passers-by.

The linkage between the CIA and Sunni Islamists was snapped in 1993 by Al Qa'idah's first attack on the World Trade Center. In 1995, 'Umar 'Abd al Rahman was convicted of complicity in that attack and others that were contemplated. In 1996, Clinton signed a law banning financial transactions between American companies and countries believed to be supporting terrorism: Cuba, North Korea, and five Muslim states (Iran, Libya, Iraq,

Syria, and Sudan). Sudan was later taken off the list because of the special interest of Occidental Oil in the country, as was Syria to pave the way for peace talks with Israel.

In 1996, Kabul fell to the Taliban, and its relations with Washington began to deteriorate. In 1998, after the bombings of American embassies in Kenya and Tanzania, the Clinton administration lobbed missiles against presumed Al Qa'idah targets in Sudan and Afghanistan, and provided for economic sanctions against pro-Islamist regimes under the United States Freedom from Religious Persecution Act. Egyptian officials, Muslim and Christian, condemned the act as a device to demonize Islam and damage Christian-Muslim relations.

The enormity of Al Qa'idah's operations of September 11, 2001, instantaneously thrust the United States into open confrontation with Al Qa'idah and its patron, the Taliban regime. Congress voted Bush broad powers to confront terrorism. Pronouncing the Geneva Conventions inapplicable in the global war on terrorism, Bush signed a directive to the CIA to kill Usamah bin Ladin and destroy his organization. On September 17, according to Lisa Hajjar (*Middle East Report,* Summer 2009), he authorized the CIA to carry out secret detentions and interrogations of terrorist suspects in foreign countries. In Hajjar's words, the renditions of the Clinton era (abduction of suspects to the US for trial on criminal charges, as in the case of Adolph Eichman to Israel) were ramped up to extraordinary renditions (as described by Scott Horton in *Harper's,* illegal detention and torture in secret prisons of CIA or allied regimes). "Black sites" were set up in countries known to use torture. Bush told Congress on September 20: "Our war on terror ... will not end until every terrorist group of global reach has been ... defeated." Secretary of State Powell asked Saudi Arabia and the UAE to break relations with the Taliban regime. On September 28, Washington issued a declaration that the Taliban did not represent the Afghan people, and Security Council Resolution 1373 condemned terrorism.

Western military action against the Taliban regime began on October 7, 2001, with American and British air attacks. On December 7 the Taliban lost their last major foothold in Afghanistan with the fall of Kandahar to the Northern Alliance, which was funded by the CIA. On December 5, four opposition factions concluded an agreement naming Hamid Karzai, a Pashtun tribal leader of the Sunni faith, as President of a new Afghan government. American forces continue to support Karzai, under a UN resolution of December 20 for a multinational security force, but in 2010 the effort to unite the country's many warlords and eliminate Taliban resistance was looking increasingly doubtful.

On the clandestine front, Washington has conducted a worldwide sweep of militants, imprisoning thousands at Guantanamo and in Iraq, Afghanistan, and elsewhere, and transferring others to the custody of anti-Islamist regimes that can interrogate suspects more imaginatively, with fewer legal complications for the United States.

As of 2009, the US was moving painfully to phase out Guantanamo, and Obama had stated that US use of torture had sullied the national image without achieving demonstrable results. However, he was still prosecuting a two-front war against Islamism: In Afghanistan, he had mapped out an intensified effort to help the Karzai regime unify the country. In Iraq (Chapter 15), Washington looked forward to steady reduction of the American presence, subject to the buildup of the Iraqi security forces and the upshot of the 2008 Status of Forces Agreement, whose schedule for the drawdown of the American occupation force was still slated to be submitted to Iraqi referendum.

Concurrently, Washington was providing financial assistance to anti-Islamist regimes (Egypt, Jordan, Yemen, Armenia, Azerbaijan). According to Seymour Hersh, DOD's Special Operations Forces, in cooperation with the CIA, had been conducting highly secret operations against selected targets in Pakistani Waziristan and elsewhere (in technical violation of international law).

December 2009 press reports (*The Nation*, Jeremy Scahill; *Times*) stated that the CIA, US Special Forces, and Blackwater units were conducting abductions and assassinations of Islamists in Afghanistan, Pakistan, Yemen, and Somalia. In 2010 an American helicopter crew assassinated an Al Qa'idah trainer in Somalia, and (per *Times* report of May 7), the US Government set a precedent by authorizing the killing of Anwar al 'Awlaqi, a naturalized American (!) who at this writing, from hiding in Yemen, was advocating anti-US jihad.

In a letter carried by *The New York Review* of 5/27/10, David Cole asserted that certain memos from the Justice Department of the Administration of Bush 43 were violations of the contemporary American statutes and international conventions prohibiting torture. A UN report questioned the legality of US use of attack drones for assassination: *Times*, 6/3/10.

Evaluating the American Response

The "global war on terrorism" is a triple misnomer:
1. There are countless agents of anti-Americanism, but they are largely autonomous, and none of them is global.

2. Hostile action from a nongovernmental entity may be serious enough to engage Washington, but as elucidated by British analyst Michael Howard in *Foreign Affairs* the response should be police action and/or policy adjustment – not military engagement. James Bamford's *The Shadow Factory* cites evidence that the American intelligence community mishandled crucial intercepts before nine-eleven. Tim Weiner (*Legacy of Ashes*) notes that the missiles Clinton launched in reprisal for the bombings of our two African embassies were either ineffective (Afghanistan) or lethally misdirected (Sudan). Elimination of the anti-Islamist Saddam regime strengthened the Islamist position. Washington's post-invasion strategy was also self-defeating: Ruling out Islamic regimes in the Middle East supports bin Ladin's contention that America is an enemy of Islam. There is growing recognition that any benefits derived from invading Iraq were infinitely exceeded by the damage done to Arab and American interests (budget-busting, casualties, devastation, refugees, burnishing the image of Al Qaʻidah). The same diagnosis of imperial overstretch is likely to be made for the invasion of Afghanistan, which Lawrence Wright describes as stepping into bin Ladin's trap. Andrew Bacevich wrote in the 3/26/09 *London Review of Books* that if Obama followed Neocon advice to prosecute the Long War, his presidency would fail. In the 7/9/09 *London Review of Books,* Rory Stewart took the position that Western creation of an Afghan state was an impossibility, and that in the Twenty-first Century governmental support is not essential to conducting subversive operations against a state.

3. Terrorism is most usefully defined as the resort to illegal violence for political purposes. As conventionally used in the American media, it is hypocritical, because it is automatically reserved for anti-American operations. When American agencies retaliate outside international law, their actions are euphemized as "special operations", "counterterrorism", "shock and awe", etc. The best way to avoid this loaded dichotomy is to eschew the term "terrorism" altogether. The American violators of international law are in no position to denounce the Middle Eastern violators.

The formulation of America's anti-Islamist strategy has been vitiated by the propagation of misinformation about Islamist hostility toward the United States. Some egregious examples:

The Bush/Rumsfeld thesis that "the US is at war with Islamic fascism."

"To suppress Islamism, kill off its leaders."

"Islamists are reacting to a perceived Judeo-Christian conspiracy to annihilate Islam." Amanat says Khomeini harbored this prejudice, but there is much less evidence of it among his successors, let alone Sunni Islamists.

"The Islamist resistance against Israeli occupation and Al Qaʻidah's operations against the United States are two aspects of a single conspiracy." In fact, the issues in each case are totally different: for the Palestinians, land; for Al Qaʻidah, hegemony. The Organization of the Islamic Conference (established in 1971), which has endorsed the Palestinian resistance, condemns suicide attacks on civilians. Hamas and Hizballah currently oppose operations outside occupied territory.

"Young Muslims have been brainwashed to see a duty to fight modernism".

"Islamism will not survive because there is no Islamic way to fix a car."

"Revising policy in the wake of an act of terrorism is inexcusable."

"Never negotiate with terrorists."

In the words of Bush 43, speaking nine days after 9/11: "Islamists hate us for our freedoms."

That Muslims and Christians see the world differently is not grounds for war; everyone sees the world differently. That Muslim texts can be biased and bigoted is not news; every society has its own examples of bias and bigotry. Islamism may be one symptom of "social dislocation" – of the Middle East's having missed out on the benefits of modernization. However, the reality on which American policymakers should focus is that their Middle East policy is exploitive (Chapter 10). Anti-Americanism is the inevitable consequence. Its Islamist cast is a transient circumstance of Middle Eastern political evolution; at this stage in the history of the region, Islamists are in the ascendancy.

September eleven demonstrated the criticality of the Islamist threat. Subversion is cheap: That whole operation may have cost Al Qaʻidah $500,000 – supremely economical in comparison with the two or three trillion dollars the United States have spent on the wars in Iraq and Afghanistan and on long-term treatment of the wounded. America's open society is highly vulnerable, even to a tiny coterie of psychopaths, let alone to a well-organized apparatus like Al Qaʻidah. In 2004 *The Washington Post Weekly* reported that, despite Herculean efforts, the Department of Homeland Security had devised no effective defense against a truck-bomb.

In linking its policies with those of Israel, Washington has also drifted toward emulation of Israeli strategy. Israel has chosen to take on the Islamists in their own realm of clandestine reprisal. This may be the inevitable recourse of a state at perpetual war. The worldwide interests of a superpower are too vulnerable for it to take this route. The downing of a Pan-Am plane was an indefensible price to pay for Reagan's capricious bombing of Libya, (or, if Iran and the PFLP/GC were the culprits, for the downing of an Iranian airliner). Likewise, the death of hijacked sailor Stethem would not have been worth the assassination of Fadlallah.

In October 2009, a talk by Charles Freeman reminded us of Washington's disingenuous suppression of Al Qa'idah's real motive – ascribing actions like nine-eleven to "Islamic savagery", instead of facing up to the reality that American bias inevitably provokes retaliation. Political problems require political solutions. However effective our security measures may be, we must start thinking the unthinkable: excision of some of the more abrasive aspects of our foreign policy. We have already capitulated on various secondary issues: withdrawal of forces from Lebanon after the bombing of the Marine barracks; negotiation with Libya after the destruction of the Pan-American airliner. Washington should jettison the vainglorious rhetoric about never surrendering to terrorism, and base its foreign policy less on domestic politics and more on the national interest.

In the short term, Washington may have to face up to the "nightmare scenario" of an Islamist state in Iraq. The Bush administration preached democracy, but its officials sought to exclude Islamists from power in Iraq, the Palestinian territories, and elsewhere, regardless of the results of free elections. Iran has been an Islamic theocracy for 30 years, and America has survived the shock. In fact, Iran's so-called terrorism has not been directed at the United States (with the possible exceptions of an attack on the wife of the commander of the USS Vincennes, or the destruction of the Pan-American airliner).

As for Al Qa'idah, one objective of 9/11 – perhaps the central objective – was to goad America into a disproportionate response. Brian Urquhart has written that, by invading Iraq, America fell into bin Ladin's trap. For all its crimes, the Saddam regime was a stronger barrier to Islamism than the American occupation. If Iraq takes the Islamist route, Washington can blame itself.

Chapter 13
The Rise of The Israeli-American Diarchy

Since World War II, the history of the Middle East has been dominated by the Arab-Israeli conflict. The succession of events catalogued in previous chapters reveals that over the past sixty-four years (1945-2009) the power of the United States and that of its inseparable associate, Israel, have escalated in tandem: The United States is the strongest power in the world; Israel is the strongest power in the Middle East. The record further reveals that the benefits of their association are not reciprocal. Alliance with Israel confers no appreciable strategic advantage on the United States, whereas alliance with the United States is the main source of Israel's power. The expansion of Israeli hegemony (currently Palestine and the Golan) was in large measure a product of American support for Israel, and American confrontation with Israel's adversaries.

Given the immense complexity of events in the period under review, comparison of America's support for Israel with its support for Israel's opponents is a subjective endeavor. In the interest of presenting the sharpest possible picture, American policy has been reduced herein to a series of major actions, classified as <u>political</u>, <u>economic</u>, <u>military assistance</u>, or <u>intervention</u>, and divided between those that are judged to have advanced the Israeli cause (<u>Pro-Israel</u>) and those that are judged to have advanced the cause of one or more Arab regimes (<u>Pro-Arab</u>) or the cause of Iran. This analysis makes no attempt to factor in the dichotomy between Arab regimes (all of which are more or less responsive to American leverage) and Arab populations (which are generally adversarial to Israeli and American policy).

The Unintended Consequence

Like the man who came to dinner, the United States made an unobtrusive entry into the Middle East. Until 1945, its attention to the region was largely confined to the wellbeing of a network of Protestant and Catholic missionary schools and colleges, whose significant contribution to Arab and Turkish education – and indirectly to government – was widely appreciated. Even Washington's endorsement of the baleful Balfour Declaration (Chapter 8) was neutralized by Woodrow Wilson's phantasmal call for the self-determination of subject peoples. In the heady days that followed World War I, few if any observers – Middle Eastern or American – anticipated that the region would be plunged into a century of bloodshed.

As for Palestine, there seemed to be a general assumption that the Americans would not allow their arbitrary interest in the implantation of a Jewish homeland to override their pragmatic interest in good relations with the region at large. Presumably, any inconsistency between the two would be ironed out by responsible diplomacy.

Who could have predicted that the adventitious emergence of a Jewish entity in Palestine, propelled by the domestic politics of a distant superpower, was to pyramid into a binational colossus that would bestride the region in ways reminiscent of the British Empire?

Pro-Arab Actions by the United States

Political

1945 - In his meeting with Ibn Sa'ud, Roosevelt accorded Saudi Arabia a tacit security guarantee, which has been honored by every one of Roosevelt's successors. (His secret promise not to favor Israel over the Arab states was scrapped by Truman, who promised in 1948 to ward off aggression against Saudi Arabia, in return for Ibn Sa'ud's promise never to join any Arab war against America over the Palestine issue.)

1953 - To force Israel to suspend diversion of Jordan water to the Negev (at Syrian and Jordanian expense), Eisenhower threatened to cancel the IRS exemption on private American donations to the United Jewish Appeal (which gave substantial financial support to Israel).

1957 - To consolidate ties with Jordan, and reinforce Hashemite rule there, the CIA put King Husayn on its payroll. (This action, ostensibly pro-Arab, was effectively pro-Israel, since Jordan was the one Arab state that had cooperated with Israel.) The CIA's arrangement with the King was subsequently disclosed.

1958 - Washington secretly backed the Iraqi Baath Party (to which Saddam Husayn belonged) against Dictator 'Abd al Karim Qasim, who as a land reformer had formed an alliance with the Iraqi Communist Party.

1961 - Kennedy, the first President to acknowledge the phenomenon of Arab Nationalism, made an effort to reach an understanding with Nasir.

1975 - Under American political pressure, Israel finally accepted the Sinai II Disengagement Agreement, whereby in the words of George Ball, Washington bought back a slice of Egyptian real estate from Israel and paid Egypt for accepting it. Syria later recovered most of the territory Israel had occupied in 1973.

1976 - The United States and Israel acquiesced in the entry of Syrian troops into central Lebanon.

1978 - At Camp David, Carter arranged for Egypt to recover all of Sinai. (The only beneficiary on the Arab side was Egypt. The principal victims were the Palestinians.) (See below.)

2009 - Speaking in Cairo, Obama made a vague and perfunctory statement of US refusal to accept the "legitimacy of continuing settlements." New Prime Minister Netanyahu rejected Obama's position.

Economic

1943 - Roosevelt found Saudi Arabia eligible for assistance under the Lend-Lease Act of 1941.

1951 - Saudi Arabia accepted American aid under Point Four.

1955 - Egypt was offered American and British grant aid, plus a World Bank loan, to finance construction of the Aswan High Dam. (The offer was withdrawn in 1956, as reported below.)

1956 - Secretary Dulles declared the integrity of Jordan a vital American interest, and instituted an annual subsidy.

1961 - Kennedy approved the sale of American wheat to Egypt for local currency under Public Law 480.

1978 - At Camp David, in return for Egypt's acceptance of peace with Israel, Carter initiated the payment to Egypt of an annual subsidy in the range of two billion dollars.

1982 - In support of the Iraqi war effort against Iran, Reagan removed Iraq from the list of countries sponsoring "terrorism", making it eligible for various forms of agricultural and commercial aid.

1992 - Bush 41 protested the expansion of Jewish settlements in the Occupied Territories by holding up a loan guarantee of ten billion dollars to Israel, but only for several months.

1996 - Food rations to the Iraqis rose as a result of the UN's institution of an Oil-for-Food program.

1998 - While continuing its harassment of Iran's economic development, the United States lifted its restrictions on the sale of food and medicine to Iran – perhaps in reaction to the election of moderate President Khatami.

1999 - In appreciation for Jordan's conclusion of a peace treaty with Israel, the United States had increased its aid to Jordan from $125,000,000 in 1996 to $325,000,000 in 1999.

2000 - The Palestine Authority (which came into being under the PLO-Israel Oslo Agreement) had been receiving subsidies from many foreign governments and UN agencies since 1993. Total foreign aid in the first half of 2000 was $183,000,000 – of which approximately $37,500,000 had come from the United States. (As the channel for transmission of foreign aid to the Authority, the Israeli Government had considerable control over its allocation.)

2001 - Although the federal government had been barred by Congress from providing financial aid to the Palestine Authority, Congress had awarded some $75,000,000 to NGO's for Palestinian social programs since 1994. (In tacit recognition of its primary responsibility for the 1947 Partition Resolution, which gave rise to the creation of Israel and the corollary Palestinian refugee problem, the United States continued to pay a modest and declining share of the expenses of the UN Relief and Works Agency (UNRWA) which fed, housed, and educated millions of refugees and descendants.)

2002 - American economic aid to Jordan since 1952 had reached a total of over $2,000,000,000.

2002 - The United States doubled the annual financial subsidy to Jordan, to approximately $450,000,000.

2004 - The United States concluded a free-trade agreement with Bahrain, the third with a Middle East state. (The others were Israel and Jordan.)

2005 - Bush promised the Palestine Authority 50 million dollars in aid – the third such contribution in ten years.

Military Assistance

1948 - The United States established a permanent naval presence in the Gulf.

1949 - Truman ordered DOD to cooperate with the British in storing ordnance near oil fields in the Gulf.

1951 - Under a Saudi-American mutual defense agreement, Saudi Arabia leased America an airfield (not to be designated as a base) at Dhahran, and America would sell the Saudis arms and train their armed forces.

1953 - Eisenhower found Saudi Arabia eligible for military assistance under the Mutual Defense Assistance Act of 1951.

1957 - In return for Saudi extension of the 1951 Dhahran airfield agreement, Eisenhower stepped up American military grant aid, training, maintenance, and arms sales.

1962 - Kennedy agreed to provide training to Saudi air pilots. Saudi Arabia would abolish slavery.

1963 - During the Saudi-Yemeni War, America showed its support for the Saudis by demonstration flights over Saudi cities.

1963 - After a Baathist coup in Iraq, Saddam returned from Egypt, and acquired from the CIA the names of Iraqi Communist activists – many of whom were then killed by the Baath.

1973 - Having provided Israel the emergency equipment needed to turn the tide of battle in the Yom Kippur War (by which Egypt and Syria hoped to recover the territory Israel had taken from them in 1967), Kissinger (under Soviet pressure) introduced a belated note of objectivity into the American position by pressuring Israel to allow Egypt to resupply its Third Army, which had been trapped in Sinai.

1974 - Announcement of a Saudi-American agreement to escalate American military assistance, including modernization of the Saudi National Guard (which the royal family prized as a counterbalance to the Saudi Army).

1978 - At great subsequent electoral cost, Carter (and Senator George McGovern) won a bitter fight for congressional agreement to sell F-15 jets to Saudi Arabia.

1978 - America made its first unconditional offer to sell jet fighters to Egypt.

1980 - The United States and Oman signed an agreement whereby America would accord Oman a security guarantee, and a grant of 260 million dollars to modernize four Omani military bases. Oman endorsed the provisions of the Camp David Agreement.

1980 - America met an urgent Saudi request by deploying four AWACS planes to defend Saudi Arabia against any Iranian reprisal for Iraqi use of Saudi airfields.

1981 - Reagan forced through Congress agreement to sell AWACS planes to Saudi Arabia (but at the cost of reinforcing the political influence of the Israel lobby).

1982 - Concerned by Iraq's reverses in its war with the Khomeini regime in Iran, Washington began to supply Iraq with photographic intelligence on the deployment of Iranian forces, and to approve Iraqi purchase of military equipment from Arab states and Western companies.

1983 - Reagan's Special Envoy, Donald Rumsfeld, met with Saddam in Baghdad and concluded an agreement to normalize Iraqi-American relations, share intelligence, and provide American arms – including cluster bombs and precursors for chemical and biological weapons.

1991 - Washington concluded a secret agreement reaffirming arms sales to Saudi Arabia and providing for the construction of a huge Saudi-American air base (Prince Sultan?).

1991 - The United States and Kuwait signed a ten-year treaty providing for joint military training, pre-positioning of military equipment, and access for the US Navy to Kuwaiti ports.

1991 - The US and Egypt had a close arrangement for sharing intelligence.

1992 - In the aftermath of Gulf War I, Kuwait and Qatar signed defense agreements with the United States.

1994 - The United States negotiated expanded access rights in the Gulf: stationing of an air squadron in Kuwait; pre-positioning of equipment in Qatar; military cooperation with the UAE. By 1996, by official account, there were 5,000 American troops in Saudi Arabia and 4,000 in Kuwait, Bahrain, and the UAE. Those in Saudi Arabia were primarily engaged in policing the Southern No-Fly Zone (Iraq south of the 32nd parallel) and manning a Patriot missile battery at the Saudi air base at Dhahran. According to an unofficial report, the number of American military personnel in Saudi Arabia was closer to 20,000, and their primary mission was to guard the Saudi regime against a coup attempt.

1997 - America was maintaining enough tanks and armored personnel carriers in Kuwait and Qatar to equip three brigades, plus standing forces of combat aircraft in Saudi Arabia, the UAE, and Turkey. (Deployment of all these forces was subject to the consent of the host government.)

1997 - Shocked by the Saudis' inability to match Iraq's military power in 1990-1, Bahrain had allowed America to establish a naval base at Manamah. It had become the homeport for the US Fifth Fleet. America was providing Bahrain with military assistance.

2001 - US Marines, Arab troops, and European troops totaling 70,000 carried out a military exercise in Egypt.

2001 - Under a new Kuwaiti-American defense agreement, US troops and British air units would stay in Kuwait another ten years, largely at Kuwaiti expense.

2002 - Because of the growing hostility of the Saudi people to the American military presence, the United States was building a giant air base at al 'Udayd, in Qatar, to replace its regional headquarters at Prince Sultan Air Base in Saudi Arabia. The United States and Qatar signed a secret agreement for construction at al 'Udayd.

2002 - America had formal defense cooperation agreements with the five Gulf Shaykhdoms, but not with Saudi Arabia.

2008 - Over the next ten years, annual economic aid to Egypt would fall to 500 million dollars a year, while annual military aid would be 1.3 billion dollars a year.

Intervention

1956-57 - In an eye-opening display of American economic power, Eisenhower torpedoed the tripartite invasion of Egypt and forced Israel to evacuate the territories (Sinai and the Gaza Strip) it had occupied in the Suez War.

1982 - At the request of PLO leader Yasir 'Arafat, and in accordance with an agreement for the withdrawal of PLO forces from Lebanon (orchestrated by American mediator Philip Habib), Reagan sent a small force of Marines to Lebanon. Withdrawn after two weeks, they returned after Israeli invasion forces had betrayed Washington by tolerating – if not abetting – a massacre of a thousand or more Palestinian and Lebanese noncombatants by Maronite militiamen.

1986-87 - In retaliation for Iraqi attacks on the Iranian oil terminal on Khark Island, Iranian planes and missiles began to attack the ships of Iraq's Arab allies. The United States responded by putting the American flag on some Kuwaiti tankers, and joining the UK and France in increasing its naval force in the Gulf. American naval units provided escort to Kuwaiti tankers and in 1987 destroyed three Iranian patrol boats and two Iranian offshore oil platforms.

1987 - To protect Kuwaiti shipping from Iranian attack during the Iran-Iraq War, America put its flag on eleven Kuwaiti tankers and provided US Navy escort. Washington felt the need to rebuild Arab confidence in America's constancy, after it had arranged a secret arms deal with Iran (see below). According to one report, Reagan was solicitous of Chevron's interests in Kuwaiti oil because it had been one of his major campaign contributors.

1988 - Iran mined the lower Gulf, damaging an American ship. American naval units sank six Iranian patrol boats, killing several hundred Iranians.

1990 - At the request of the Saudis, alarmed by the Iraqi takeover of Kuwait, Bush sent American troops to Saudi Arabia, on the understanding that they would be withdrawn "when the job is done." For King Fahd, the job was to oust Iraq from Kuwait. For some American officials, the job was to overthrow Saddam Husayn.

1991 - An international coalition, spearheaded by American forces, expelled the Iraqi forces from Kuwait. The principal beneficiaries were Kuwait, Saudi Arabia – and Israel.

1996 - Clinton expanded the American military presence in Saudi Arabia, Kuwait, Bahrain, Qatar, and perhaps the UAE. American naval units in the Gulf were now designated the Fifth Fleet.

2003 - American military personnel in Qatar, mostly Air Force, now numbered 3300. Their presence was widely resented by Qataris.

Pro-Israeli Actions by the United States

Political

1945 - In a meeting with Ibn Sa'ud, Roosevelt said America favored a Jewish homeland in Palestine. (Ibn Sa'ud rejected the idea, but did not make an issue of it.)

1947 - The United States deployed all its political and economic leverage to bulldoze an unbalanced resolution for the partition of Palestine through the UN General Assembly. The Soviets also supported it. America's motives were a combination of altruism and political opportunism. The Soviet motive was wholly opportunistic; they hoped to exploit the inevitable Arab resentment of the American action.

1948 - The May 14 proclamation of the establishment of the State of Israel by Jewish leaders in Tel Aviv was communicated by the Washington representative of the Jewish Agency to Truman, who – over Secretary George Marshall's opposition – immediately authorized announcement of America's de facto recognition. The Soviets recognized Israel de jure May 17, 1948. The United States accorded de jure recognition in 1949. Moscow vetoed the Israeli application for UN membership in December 1948, but relented in 1949.

1957 - CIA funds helped reelect Lebanese President Camille Sham'un (serving Israel's security interest). He had been the only Arab leader to accept the Eisenhower Doctrine.

1957 - Senator Lyndon Johnson blocked an initiative to terminate the United Jewish Appeal's tax exemption.

1966 - Title I food sales to Egypt lapsed.

1967 - On June 7, in the midst of the Six-Day War, Israeli planes and torpedo boats attacked an American surveillance ship, the USS Liberty, killing 34 Americans and nearly sinking the ship with all hands. Overwhelming circumstantial evidence has convinced most well placed American observers that some Israeli commander gave an explicit order to obliterate ship and crew. The motive remains a mystery. The Israeli claim that the Liberty had been mistaken for an Egyptian freighter has been rejected by everyone who is not a partisan of Israel. Johnson issued a blanket injunction against discussion of the attack by American personnel. According to a report in *The Washington Report on Middle East Affairs* of July 2008, Secretary of Defense McNamara recalled the rescue aircraft sent from Naples by Rear Admiral Larry Geis, Commander of the carrier units of the Sixth Fleet. Geis demanded confirmation of the recall. When Johnson came on the phone, Geis protested that Americans were being killed. According to Geis, Johnson said, "I don't want to embarrass one of our allies." Forty-two years later, a campaign for a full inquiry was still blocked, apparently out of deference to the Israel lobby.

1967 - With firm participation by the United States, the Security Council blocked an Arab campaign for an explicit call for Israeli withdrawal from all territory occupied during the Six-Day War. Resolution 242 contained ambiguous language about withdrawal from unspecified territories. America became Israel's preeminent international supporter.

1967 - Washington took no steps toward enforcement of UNSC resolutions disallowing Israel's alleged annexation of East Jerusalem.

1967-70 - Shortly after the June War, Jewish settlers were allowed to infiltrate the West Bank (*The New York Review*, 7/15/04; *Arab and Jew*, David Shipler, page 144). There were no reports of American resistance to this activity, which violated the Geneva Conventions and would ultimately constitute an insuperable obstacle to the partition, which Washington still professed to anticipate in 2009.

1967 - Johnson secretly promised Israel he would use the American veto in the Security Council on its behalf, in return for the Israeli Embassy's lobbying among American Jews for his (flawed) Vietnam policy.

1969 - As noted by Norman Finkelstein, Nixon and Kissinger realigned US policy to correspond with the Israeli contention that it was entitled to keep its territorial conquests.

1970 - In an effort to overthrow the pro-Israel monarchy in Jordan, the PFLP (Popular Front for the Liberation of Palestine) precipitated a civil war between the Palestinian Resistance forces and King Husayn's tribal army by hijacking four civilian airliners to Jordan and holding hundreds of hostages, including Americans and Israelis. Husayn attacked the Palestinian refugee camps. In response to an urgent Palestinian request, Syrian dictator Hafiz al Asad sent an armored force into north Jordan, reportedly to help the Palestinians set up a safe haven. Nixon and Kissinger approved Husayn's request for intervention on his behalf by the Israeli Air Force. Sobered by Israel's announcement of a military alert, Asad withheld his air force from the intervention, and soon withdrew his ground forces, which had taken punishment from Husayn's ground and air forces. The episode further damaged relations between Asad and Yasir 'Arafat, and branded Husayn as having betrayed the Arab cause against Israel.

1971 - Nixon and Prime Minister Golda Meir agreed to set up, via Kissinger, a communications back-channel that would bypass the Department of State (whose Secretary was William Rogers), and to abandon the effort to achieve a comprehensive Arab-Israeli settlement. Soon after, Nixon agreed to consult with Israel before initiating any Arab-Israeli settlement talks with any Arab state.

1972 - The Nixon Doctrine was based on the fallacious premise that Israel was a strategic asset versus Soviet infiltration of the Middle East. National Security Adviser Kissinger overruled the State Department's recommendation for withholding arms from Israel until it moderated its posture vis-à-vis the Arabs. Kissinger favored Israel's policy of diplomatic stalemate (while consolidating its control of the Occupied Territories).

1972 - Nixon secretly arranged for large-scale emigration of Soviet Jews to Israel.

1973 - On October 10, with Egyptian forces on the east bank of the Suez Canal, Moscow indicated support for a cease-fire in place – a victory, in Washington's eyes, for the Soviets and Egypt. To frustrate such an outcome, Kissinger urged Israel to "make the maximum military effort in the next forty-eight hours." Israel complied by attacking the Syrian forces, already driven back behind the post-1967 lines.

1973 - On October 22, with Israeli forces established on the west bank of the Suez Canal, the Security Council adopted cease-fire Resolution 338, which favored Israel by rejecting the Arab claim for prior implementation of 1967 Resolution 242, and by requiring the Arab parties to enter into direct talks with Israel. Resolution 338 was defective in that it did not specify the cease-fire lines and it included no arrangements for its enforcement.

1973-78 - Although the Arab parties were the ostensible beneficiaries of the postwar disengagement agreements, in that they recovered some territory, the greater advantage accrued to Israel: In return for giving Egypt and Syria pieces of their own territory, Israel received from Washington stepped-up supply of jet fighters and financial aid, a promise to meet any shortfall in its oil imports, a guarantee to veto any Security Council condemnation of Israeli action against terrorism from Syria, and a guarantee not to recognize or deal with the PLO until it recognized Israel's right to exist and accepted Resolutions 242 and 338. In the analysis of Donald Neff, American orchestration of the disengagement process amounted to the conclusion of a de facto Israeli-American military alliance that set the stage for invasion of Lebanon in 1982.

1975 - Washington promised Israel it would oppose any adverse change in Resolutions 242 and 338, and it would consult with Israel if it were threatened by a world power.

1975 - On December 8, Washington vetoed a Security Council draft to condemn Israel for a "preventative" raid on Palestinian refugee camps in Lebanon that killed 92.

1976 - Washington vetoed a Security Council draft to call for Israeli withdrawal from lands taken in 1967, and to endorse the Palestinians' right to a state.

1977 - Moshe Dayan divulged a secret Israeli-American working paper on the Palestine problem in which neither the PLO nor a Palestinian entity was mentioned.

1978 - The Camp David Summit accorded Israel passage through the Suez Canal and the Strait of Tiran, and a freer hand in the Occupied Territories. Sadat sacrificed any linkage between Arab-Israeli peace and self-rule for the Palestinians in the Occupied Territories. The summit laid the groundwork for the 1979 Israeli-Egyptian peace treaty, and set up handsome annual subsidies for Israel and Egypt. The Palestinians were left out; Carter subsequently caved on the issue of Begin's continued expansion of Jewish settlements.

1978 - Although Carter prevailed on Israel to withdraw the forces it had sent into south Lebanon, the pro-Israeli force commanded by Lebanese renegade Major Sa'd Haddad retained control of the border area, denying access to the personnel of UNIFIL (the UN force in south Lebanon). Israel continued military attacks on PLO posts in south Lebanon, driving 200,000 Lebanese toward Beirut. Its possible motives were to crush the PLO, or to depopulate south Lebanon, or to break up Lebanon, or to prevent détente between the PLO and Washington.

1980 - Carter repudiated an American vote for a March 1 Security Council resolution calling on Israel to dismantle Jewish settlements in the Occupied Territories.

1981 - Reagan came into office with a proactive approach to foreign policy and an anti-Soviet focus that gratified Prime Minister Begin. Reagan regarded Israel as a strategic asset to the United States, and its settlements in the Occupied Territories as "non-illegal".

1981 - However, he authorized his representative, Philip Habib, to negotiate a Palestinian-Lebanese-Israeli cease-fire, which was honored by the two Arab parties but shattered by Israel in 1982.

1982 - Vice President Bush told a meeting of the United Jewish Appeal the American commitment to Israel was "nothing less than sacred."

1982 - America and Israel were the only states to vote against General Assembly affirmation of the Palestinians' right of self-determination (August 19).

1983 - America vetoed a Security Council call on Israel to stop setting up Jewish settlements (which were in violation of the Fourth Geneva Convention).

1984 - Reagan took the Israeli-American alliance to a new level by announcing on March 13 a "formal strategic arrangement". King Husayn told the press the United States had lost its credibility as a mediator in the Arab-Israeli conflict. Washington vetoed a Security Council draft that would have condemned the settlements in the Occupied Territories as illegal.

1984 - Washington vetoed a Security Council call on Israel to end its restriction on south Lebanon.

1985 - Another American veto on this issue.

1985 - Jonathan Pollard, a US Government employee who sold secrets to Israel, was sentenced to life in prison. According to Joel Kovel, citing a Seymour Hersh article in *The New Yorker,* the material Pollard transmitted included the names of American agents, some of whom were revealed to the USSR and were killed. Washington desisted from pressing Israel for an investigation of Pollard's defection, possibly inhibited by an Israeli threat to release information on CIA spying on Israel.

1987 - Rabbi Jacob Neusner wrote that Israel, having priced itself out of independence, had become a client state.

1987 - The Tower Commission on illegal Israeli and American sales of arms to Iran noted Israel's effort to be considered America's only strategic partner in the Middle East.

1988 - Washington vetoed a Security Council call on Israel to repatriate Palestinians it had deported from the Territories to Lebanon.

1989 - Bush I continued the policy of strong support for Israel, including blocking entry of Soviet emigrants to the United States, in the interest of diverting them to Israel.

1991 - The only states to oppose a December 19 General Assembly call on Israel to stop settlement construction in the Territories were Israel and the United States.

1995 - Clinton endorsed a secret allocation by Congress of 18 million dollars to finance the overthrow of the government of Iran.

1996 - In retaliation for Hizballah rocket attacks, including one that wounded 36 residents of Kiryat Shemona, Israel launched disproportionate retaliation in the form of Operation Grapes of Wrath, a seventeen-day air and artillery assault that caused major damage in south Lebanon, Beirut, and the Biqa' Valley, inflicted many deaths – including 102 victims of the inexplicable shelling of a UN base in Qana, and reduced nearly 400,000 Lebanese to refugee status. In the analysis of Avi Shlaim, the Israeli objective was to pressure Syria into suppressing Hizballah and giving Israel free run of south Lebanon. The effort failed. The General Assembly condemned the operation 64-2(US and Israel)-65. The United States had no military role, but as noted by commentator William Pfaff, Washington was diminished by its failure to moderate or even condemn the "irrational brutality" of the assault, or its violation of the American-brokered cease-fire of July 1993.

1996 - In the assessment of *Yedioth Ahronoth,* Clinton was the most pro-Israel President yet.

1996 - Under AIPAC pressure, Congress adopted the Iran-Libya Sanctions Act (ILSA), providing for the United States to impose sanctions on third parties that invested substantially in the oil or gas industries of either country. The bill was not only unenforceable, it was counterproductive, in that it motivated Iran and Libya to favor foreign companies over American; it became dormant by 2000.

1998 - Clinton concluded with Prime Minister Barak the Wye Plantation Agreement, which "[crossed] the threshold from partnership to strategic alliance" (*The Boston Globe*). Subsequent discussions pursuant to the Agreement focussed on the defense of Israel against the threat of Iranian acquisition of nuclear weapons.

1998 - In a patent campaign to overthrow the Saddam regime in Iraq, Clinton signed the Iraq Liberation Act, which allocated 97 million dollars to support Iraqi exile groups.

1999 - America exploited personnel in UNSCOM (UN inspection unit in Iraq) to plant electronic eavesdropping devices to accelerate the ouster of Saddam. By perverting UNSCOM's purpose, for the sake of Israel, Washington had destroyed the valuable precedent UNSCOM represented.

1999 - A Kurdish and a Shiite dissident Iraqi faction accepted American financing.

2000 - In *Dishonest Broker,* Naseer Aruri opined that Israel had been virtually integrated into the American union.

2000 - Since 1997, the FBI had been investigating a "radioactive" report that Israeli intelligence had tapped White House, State Department, and FBI phone lines. The mainstream media buried it.

2000 - The UN humanitarian coordinator for Iraq advised that the sanctions imposed on Iraq violated the Universal Declaration of Human Rights.

2001 - Sandra Mackey speculated that the administration of Bush 43 had avoided dealing with the Palestine problem because key elements of its power base (Jewish Zionists, Christian fundamentalists, and hawks) seemed to place the interests of Israel above those of the United States.

2001 - Under AIPAC pressure, Congress extended the (ineffective) Iran-Libya Sanctions Act of 1997 for another five years.

2001 - The Departments of Defense and State sent "observers" to a London conference of Iraqi exile groups.

2002 - Congress proposed the Syrian Accountability Act, calling for additional economic sanctions against Syria if it did not cease alleged support for terrorism, development of WMD's, and military occupation of Lebanon. Congress wanted Syria to stop its program to develop surface-to-surface missiles inferior to those already deployed by Israel.

2002 - Millions in Iranian assets in America were still frozen. The 1996 act against Iran and Libya (ILSA) was still in force.

2002 - The United States vetoed a Security Council draft condemning Israel's destruction of a World Food Program warehouse in Gaza and the killing of a British official of UNRWA.

2002 - After 9/11, Bush 43 endorsed Sharon's plan for a massive military strike in the Occupied Territories. According to Finkelstein, the operation committed multiple war crimes against the people of the Territories.

2003 - Under pressure from the neoconservative bloc in Washington, the United States broke off talks with Iran. Reza Pahlavi, son of the late Shah, had cultivated officials in the Sharon government and its neoconservative allies in the United States. American officials accused Iran of sheltering members of Al Qa'idah and supporting Hizballah in Lebanon.

2003 - Rachel Corrie, American member of the International Solidarity Movement (ISM), participating in a peaceful effort to discourage the Israeli destruction of homes in the Gaza Strip, was plowed under by an Israeli bulldozer. According to ISM witnesses, the circumstances of her death could be explained only by reckless intent on the part of the operator of the machine. There is no report that Washington conducted the standard inquiry into the death of an American citizen overseas – to determine why the demonstrators were not removed from the scene (as Jewish settlers were before the withdrawal from the Gaza Strip), and whether someone in authority chose a strategy of ruthless intimidation.

2003 - Prime Minister Sharon pursued construction of an anti-infiltration barrier, which amounted to a major land-grab of Occupied Territory. Bush posed no significant objection.

2003 - America vetoed a UNSC draft calling on Israel to dismantle the Security Barrier. The General Assembly sent the issue to the World Court. (Over the previous 35 years, Washington had cast 80 vetoes in the Security Council – half of them against condemnations of alleged Israeli violations of international law.)

2004 - The Security Council condemned an Israeli military foray into Gaza. Washington abstained – its first failure to veto an anti-Israeli resolution since September 2002.

2004 - The UNGA adopted 150-6 a resolution calling on Israel to dismantle the Security Barrier. Washington voted against the resolution.

2004 - The World Court ruled that Israel's Security Barrier is illegal, 14-1(US). Congress condemned the verdict by huge majorities in both houses.

2006 - According to *Current History,* Washington reacted to Hamas's victory in the February parliamentary elections by collaborating with Egypt and Jordan in arming and training on behalf of the Fatah faction of the Palestine Authority a Presidential Guard to oust Hamas.

2007 - *The New York Times* reported that Israel's arms sales to China and its use of American-made antipersonnel weapons in Lebanon in 2006 had violated its commitments to DOD. No protest recorded.

2009 - Prime Minister Netanyahu largely ignored Obama's request that Israel suspend construction in the settlements.

Economic

1949 - The Export-Import Bank granted Israel a $100,000,000 loan – more direct American financial aid than any Arab state had ever received from the Bank.

1949 - Setting a precedent for common subsequent practice, the White House overruled a State Department recommendation for putting economic pressure on Israel to comply with its political obligations.

1963 - IRS Ruling 63-252 authorized the Secretary of the Treasury to declare the deductibility of private contributions to specified charitable organizations, including those that transmit their proceeds to foreign charitable organizations. This provision has been broadly applied to the benefit of official Israeli charities.

1974 - Nixon ruled that all but $700,000,000 of a 2.2 billion dollar postwar loan to Israel would be grant aid.

1975 - The United States doubled aid to Israel as a reward for its withdrawal from some of the land it had taken from Egypt and Syria in 1973.

1978 - In consequence of the Camp David Summit, the United States committed to annual awards to Israel of approximately three billion dollars, and to Egypt and Jordan (essentially for accepting the Camp David accord) awards of approximately two billion dollars and a few hundred million dollars respectively.

1979 - The United States paid almost 100 million dollars to compensate Jewish settlers forced out of Sinai.

1984 - Under Public Law 98-473 ("the Cranston Amendment"), "...the funds provided... Israel shall not be less than the annual debt repayment from Israel to the United States." In short, Israel would never have to make a net repayment of the massive loans it had already received from Washington.

1985 - The United States signed a free-trade agreement with Israel.

1987 - Israel had a constant balance-of-payments deficit; "the engine that has run the Israeli economy has been American aid."

1990 - In reaction to Iraq's occupation of Kuwait, Security Council Resolutions 661 and 663 imposed economic sanctions on Iraq under Chapter VII of the UN Charter. Security Council Resolution 661 ordered all UN members to impose a commercial and financial boycott on Iraq.

1990 - Bush 41 imposed a unilateral naval blockade on all trade with Iraq except medicine, under Article 51 of the UN Charter. The Security Council quickly endorsed it. It was the most stringent peacetime blockade in modern history.

1991 - Security Council Resolution 687 imposed economic sanctions on Iraq for failure to cooperate with WMD inspections. They prohibited all trade with Iraq except for "essential human needs".

1990-2003 - Although Israel was not mentioned in Resolutions 661 or 687, it was their primary beneficiary. Washington's alleged objective in supporting the resolutions was to block Iraqi development of weapons of mass destruction and the missiles to deliver them. Subsequent events, culminating in the invasion of 2003, indicate that the real objective was to eliminate Iraq as a military power. Contrary to assertions by the administration of George W. Bush, Iraq posed no security threat to the United States. However, as a state that was still at war with Israel, that had fired Scuds into Israel (in 1991), and regularly compensated the families of Palestinian suicide bombers, Iraq was Israel's Public Enemy Number

One. The people of Iraq were subjected to twelve years of a kind of Chinese water torture. The Sanctions Committee, set up under Security Council Resolution 661, essentially under American control, implemented its functions so brutally that it devastated Iraq's educational, social-welfare, and public health systems, and did grave damage to its economy. In 1998, Denis Halliday, UN Humanitarian Coordinator for Iraq (until he resigned in protest), said, "we are ... destroying an entire society." Several UN agencies estimated that twelve years of sanctions had increased infant mortality in Iraq by 500,000.

1995 - Security Council Resolution 986 ("Oil-for-Food") had the effect of giving the United States access to Iraqi oil and the option to veto Iraqi imports of food and medicine.

1995 - For Clinton, Bush 41's concentration on Iraq was not enough. He added Israel's Public Enemy Number Two, Iran, to the list of economic targets, and called his new strategy Dual Containment – which made no sense except as national-security insurance for Israel. A central feature was a campaign to block construction of an Iranian pipeline to serve new Central Asian oil fields, in favor of more extensive, less secure lines across the southern Caucasus to Turkey.

1996 - The main recipient of American grant aid was Israel (1.8 billion dollars a year of military financing, 1.2 billion dollars of economic financing). The main recipient of assistance under the American AID program was Egypt (1.3 billion dollars in annual military aid, .8 billion dollars in economic aid); this program was a blatant reward for Egypt's collaboration with Israeli-American policy.

1996 - To alleviate infant mortality caused by the damage done by the UN sanctions to Iraq's public health system, UNICEF and the World Food Program established twenty Nutritional Rehabilitation Centers in Iraq. (The sanctions invited examination as possible violation of the human-rights provisions of the United Nations Charter).

2000 - Allocations from revenues collected under Security Council Resolution 986 (Oil-for-Food) had significantly benefited the economy of Iraq's Kurdish enclave (whose leaders were collaborating with America and Israel).

2000 - Jordan (the second Arab state to sign a peace treaty with Israel) became the fourth country to conclude a free-trade agreement with the United States (following Canada, Mexico, and Israel).

2000 - The United States contributed 300 million dollars to help Israel finance its withdrawal from south Lebanon.

2001 - The United States blocked Iran's application to join the World Trade Organization.

371

2001 - Congress adopted the conference report for the annual foreign aid bill. It earmarked $2,724,000,000 for Israel (plus $60,000,000 for refugee resettlement and $214,500,000 for arms purchases), $1,955,000,000 for Egypt, $225,000,000 for Jordan. Iraq, Iran, and Syria were among the states declared ineligible for American aid.

2001 - AIPAC outmaneuvered the White House in Congress on the issue of easing sanctions on Iran.

2002 - The Pentagon concluded Iraq's crude production capacity had been reduced 25 percent by ten years of sanctions. (After the invasion, DOD shifted its rationale for the reduction, from sanctions to Saddam's alleged mismanagement.)

2003 - Bush signed H.R. 1828, The Syrian Accountability and Lebanese Sovereignty Restoration Act, which prohibited the export of dual-use products to Syria, and called on Syria to cut its ties with the Palestinian resistance movement, withdraw its troops from Lebanon, cease development of long-range missiles and WMD's, and stop aiding terrorism in Iraq.

2003 - Congress authorized loan guarantees to Israel totaling $9,000,000,000 over the next three years, proceeds to be spent on a variety of development projects and military needs.

2004 - Egypt, Israel, and the United States signed an agreement exempting specified Egyptian goods from American import tariff provided they contain at least 11.7 percent of Israeli content.

2006 - *The Washington Report on Middle East Affairs* calculated that US grant aid to Israel from 1949 to 2006 had totaled 108 billion dollars.

2006 - With only eight noes, the House endorsed the Israeli assault on Lebanon.

2009 - The *Times* of July 29 reported that H.R. 1828 of 2003 had been enforced to exclude export to Syria of all but food and medicine, but the Obama administration had stated the sanctions would be eased.

Military Assistance

In its battle for Arab acceptance, Israel had an uncritical champion in Harry Truman. He strongly supported the creation of the Jewish State, and he interposed no opposition to its expansion beyond the lines laid out in the 1947 Partition Resolution. In 1952 Truman authorized a Mutual Defense Assistance Agreement with Israel. Subsequently Washington approved French and Canadian arms supply to Israel.

Eisenhower tried to inject more balance into the American position. He made repeated efforts to reduce Arab-Israeli tension. The Arabs – sobered by their humiliation in 1948 – were receptive. Israel was not. In the battle between Israeli moderates and expansionists, the expansionists usually prevailed.

1955 - So it was in the seventh year of Israel's existence. In February 1955, Defense Minister Ben-Gurion and Chief of Staff Dayan, ignoring the moderate counsels of Prime Minister Sharett, ordered a gratuitous attack that killed thirty-nine Egyptian troops at Egypt's army headquarters in Gaza. Egyptian leader 'Abd al Nasir had hoped to concentrate on domestic affairs, but Israel's activism subjected him to intolerable pressure to upgrade his armed forces. Aware that Israel was receiving secret arms shipments from France, he turned to Washington, but the Americans would not supply any arms for use against Israel. In September 1955, Nasir announced that Egypt had contracted for arms from "Czechoslovakia" (the USSR). For Moscow, this transaction was to be the Soviets' nose in the Arab tent. It set the scene for the supply of Russian arms to Yemen, Syria, and Iraq, it boosted Soviet trade with the Middle East, and it undercut the Western position. All this for a price Khrushchev was willing to pay – disavowal of Arab Communist parties.

1956 - For Eisenhower and Dulles, Soviet intrusion into the region was intolerable, but they continued to trudge along the path of conciliation until May 1956, when once again the Arab-Israeli conflict flew out of control. The cycle of retaliation began with an Israeli-Canadian arms deal. Nasir countered by recognizing Communist China. Washington's response to this enormity was an insulting release cancelling financing for the High Dam. Nasir nationalized the Suez Canal. France withdrew its canal pilots. With Soviet help, Egypt immediately punctured the conventional wisdom that it lacked the technical expertise to operate the canal. Washington and London spent the summer of 1956 in a Keystone-Kops effort to put the toothpaste back into the tube. In October (Chapter 8), England, France, and Israel made the monumental misjudgment of going to war. An infuriated Eisenhower brought all three to heel, and in so doing became the last President to check Israeli expansionism.

1961 - Arlene Lazarowitz observed that Kennedy's decision to sell Hawk missiles to Israel was a radical departure from previous Middle East arms policy.

1963-69 - Under Johnson, who saw Israel as an asset in his effort to contain the Soviet Bloc, the United States tilted sharply toward Israel. His sale of jet fighters to Jordan, ostensibly a pro-Arab action, was in fact pro-Israeli. By abandoning the previous policy of withholding American offensive weapons from either side in the Arab-Israeli conflict, Johnson opened the door to his real objective: supplying Israel.

1964 - Prime Minister Eshkol briefed the Knesset on an LBJ commitment to defend Israel from Arab aggression.

1965-75 - To tie down Iraqi troops in Kurdistan, in agreement with Iran (Israel's principal oil supplier), Israel supplied the Kurdish tribes in north Iraq with arms and money.

1967 - Washington agreed to sell tanks and jets to Israel.

1967 - Eshkol told *US News* Washington had advised Israel to rely on the Sixth Fleet.

1967 - On June 3, Mossad (Israeli intelligence organization) told the Cabinet that Defense Secretary McNamara had given Israel the green light to go to war.

1968 - Johnson ordered the CIA to keep Israeli acquisition of a nuclear weapon secret, even from Rusk and McNamara.

1968 - Johnson authorized the supply of Phantom jet fighters to Israel.

1970 - The United States sent another shipment of jet fighters (Phantoms and Skyhawks) to Israel.

1970 - The United States signed with Israel a landmark agreement for regular exchange of military intelligence.

1970 - In Jordan's civil war between the monarchy and the PLO, Washington took a pro-Israel position by asking Israel to respond to Husayn's request for American or Israeli support versus the Syrian intervention. Israel's mobilization of its air force sufficed.

1970-86 - A succession of Israeli-American agreements on military cooperation in effect merged their military-industrial complexes and insured for Israel vast military superiority over its neighbors. Nixon sent Israel top-of-the-line jet fighters needed in Vietnam. Nixon's National Security Adviser, Henry Kissinger, spoke so warmly of the Israeli-American alliance to Israeli Ambassador (later Prime Minister) Yitzhak Rabin, that Rabin described the remarks as the most far-reaching endorsement ever from an American President. Under the Nixon Doctrine, Washington regarded Israel as a strategic asset. This gratified Kissinger's innate sympathy for the Israeli side. He was to be granted a rare opportunity to follow his instincts during the Yom Kippur War (see below), when – as described by Walter Isaacson – Nixon was incapacitated by despair over Watergate and the foreign-born Kissinger was the de facto President of the United States.

1971 - Nixon promised Israel more arms.

1972 - Nixon authorized Kissinger to accept the Shah's proposal that the United States follow Israel's lead in giving arms and money to the Iraqi Kurds for use against the Iraqi armed forces (as revealed by the Pike Committee in 1976).

1972 - After a Syrian-Israeli air battle, in which Syria lost three planes, the United States vetoed a Security Council draft condemning Israel for indiscriminate attacks on Lebanon and Syria. Washington defended its veto on the grounds that the draft did not condemn Arab terrorism against Israel.

1973 - Driven back by the shocking effectiveness of the Egyptian and Syrian attack, Israel was bailed out by an emergency airlift of state-of-the-art American arms, first from Europe, later from the United States. Apparently in order to allow Israel to improve its military position on the west side of the Suez Canal, Kissinger allowed it to ignore the Security Council's cease-fire resolution 338 for three days. By October 21, American arms and money and Israeli valor had turned the tide of battle. In Moscow, Kissinger negotiated a cease-fire plan that did not require Israel to withdraw from areas it had occupied in Egypt and Syria beyond the lines established in 1967. These terms were incorporated in Security Council Resolution 338 of October 22.

1975 - Washington announced a decision to sell Israel the Lance missile, capable of carrying a nuclear warhead.

1975 - After Iran had closed the border with Iraq (Chapter 9), Washington hoped the cessation of arms supply to the Iraqi Kurds would induce Iraq, relieved of attacks on the Kurdish front, to step up pressure on its Baathist rivals in Syria, which might then become more receptive to Washington's campaign for a Syrian-Israeli disengagement agreement.

1978 - Announcing in May that in the 1979 budget almost half the military loans and grants would go to Israel, Carter stressed America's commitment to the survival of Israel.

1979 - In Israel, Carter stated Israel was a strategic asset to the United States (a proposition he didn't believe). This was one of the few times of divergence between the policy of the US (which as John Cooley has noted was on good terms with Saddam) and that of Israel, which distrusted him.

1979 - The Israeli-Egyptian peace treaty of March 26 contained an annex that committed the United States to consider urgent action against any violation of the treaty, to be responsive to Israeli economic and military needs, and to guarantee Israel's oil supply for fifteen years.

1979 - On September 2, according to reports assembled by Joel Kovel, Israel and South Africa exploded an atomic device in the South Atlantic. In return for technical expertise, Israel received enriched uranium. There was no public reaction from Washington.

1981 - In violation of American law, Israel was reportedly shipping American arms to Iran.

6/81 - Under a strategy of preemption against any possible Arab attempt to acquire nuclear weapons, Prime Minister Begin sent planes to destroy the French-built Osirak reactor near Baghdad. The American vote for Security Council Resolution 487, which condemned the Osirak attack, was a pro forma action, which concealed the more relevant fact that the satellite photography that insured the effectiveness of the air raid had been supplied by the CIA.

1981 - America and Israel signed a Memorandum of Understanding on Strategic Cooperation. It provided for joint naval exercises, pre-positioning of American military materiel in Israel, and cooperation in military research and development. Suspended to protest Israel's annexation of the Golan, it was reinstated in 1983.

1981 - Washington stated August 24 the administration was committed to maintain Israel's "substantial military advantage over potential adversaries."

1982 - Opting to help the lesser of two evils, Israel supplied Iran arms that contributed to Iran's recovery of some of the territory lost to Iraq in 1980-81. The Israeli Ambassador to Washington told *The Boston Globe* that Israel had been sending arms to Iran, in coordination with the United States, to bolster pro-Western Iranians.

1982 - Secretary of State Haig gave tacit endorsement to Sharon's plan to invade Lebanon, destroy the PLO, and set up an amenable government in Beirut. Haig instructed Ambassador to the UN Jeanne Kirkpatrick to veto any Security Council attempt to impose sanctions on Israel, which she did. The Israeli invasion took advantage of American surveillance aircraft, missiles, cluster bombs, and electronic countermeasures, and was supported by air cover from the Sixth Fleet.

1982 - At the request of (pro-Israel) President Amin Jumayyil, U.S. Marines began to train Lebanese soldiers.

1982 - America did not participate in the Security Council vote (14-0) for Israel to lift its food blockade of west Beirut.

1983 - Reagan issued National Security Decision Directive III, which further expanded the scope of Israeli-American cooperation, converted the annual military subsidy from a loan to a grant, and accorded Israel access to financing and technology for construction of its jet fighter, the Lavi. (The Lavi project was abandoned years later.) According to former Deputy Secretary of State George Ball, Directive III made the United States and Israel cobelligerents.

1985 - Over the opposition of Secretaries of State Shultz and Defense Weinberger, the National Security Staff of the White House became involved in the arms supply to Iran that Israel had initiated in 1980. An

Israeli aim was to prolong the Iran-Iraq War. A White House aim was to negotiate the release of Americans taken hostage by Hizballah (Iranian-backed) in Lebanon; another was to generate secret funding for the Contra forces in Nicaragua. The sales to Iran violated acts of Congress.

1985 - Washington condoned an Israeli air raid on PLO facilities in Tunis, allegedly using American satellite imagery stolen by U.S. Navy employee Jonathan Pollard (subsequently jailed), killing 71 Palestinians and Tunisians. The Security Council condemned it.

1986 - The Pentagon's Center for Low Intensity Warfare, headed by (Zionist) Richard Perle, would be structured to carry out joint secret operations with Israel.

1987 - Israel admitted it had violated the Security Council embargo on arms sales to South Africa.

1987 - Reagan had signed with Israel an agreement putting Israel on a par with NATO states in access to military contracts.

1989 - America and Israel conducted their first joint maneuvers at battalion level.

1991 - Under strong American pressure, Prime Minister Shamir stayed out of Gulf War I, despite Israeli military doctrine that Israel has primary responsibility for its own defense. The US-manned Patriot batteries that Washington provided Israel for defense against Iraqi Scuds were not very effective, but neither were the Scuds (one Israeli death). Israel's primary objective in the war was the devastation of Iraq, and this America accomplished.

1991 - Possibly influenced by Iran, Hizballah released the last American hostage in Lebanon – Terry Anderson.

1991 - Bush allocated funds to the CIA to work for the ouster of Saddam.

1992 - Washington took no corrective action against illegal Israeli arms sales to China.

1992 - In a policy reversal congenial to Israel, the United States began to organize Iraqi exile groups in the interest of overthrowing the regime of Saddam Husayn.

1996 - A CIA plan for anti-Saddam elements to mount a coup from the Kurdish enclave ended in fiasco when the ancient Barzani-Talabani feud led the Barzanis to collude in an Iraqi foray which repelled the Talabani advance and rolled up a four-year CIA operation.

1998 - Arabs speculated that the joint Israeli-Turkish-American military exercise of January was a warning to Syria to participate in the Arab-Israeli peace process.

1998 - Congress appropriated $5,000,000 to fund "Radio Free Iraq". Washington made a major effort to reconcile the rival Kurds and build an anti-Saddam exile coalition.

1998 - Scott Ritter (American), long-time head of the UN's WMD inspection team in Iraq, resigned to protest American penetration of the inspections process for military intelligence, which the CIA shared with Israel.

1998 - Clinton signed the Iraq Liberation Act, and allocated 97 million dollars to finance the training and equipping of an Iraqi opposition army by the Department of Defense. Regime change in Baghdad was now official policy.

1998 - American and Israeli officials met in Washington to plan closer defense cooperation, "crossing the threshold from partnership to strategic alliance."

1999 - Washington made progress in unifying the diverse anti-Saddam exile factions.

1999 - Ignoring American protests, Israel was mounting AWACS-quality radar on Russian-made planes for sale to China. In 2000 Israel cancelled the project under Washington pressure.

2001 - Attacks by American jets from airfields in Kuwait and carriers in the Gulf destroyed key nodes of a fiber-optic communications system built in Iraq by China.

2001 - Israeli aircraft were flying recon along the Turk-Iraqi frontier.

2001 - *Middle East Policy* carried an independent assessment that illegal American air strikes on Iraq harmed the population they were meant to protect.

2001 - Three days after the attacks of 9/11, Congress authorized Bush to use "all necessary and appropriate force" to respond to terrorist attacks on the United States. Senate: 98-0; House: 420-1. The authorization did not supersede the War Powers Resolution of 1973 (which requires Congressional approval for extended combat).

2002 - Bush 43 directed the Departments of State and Defense to spend up to $92,000,000 for arms and training for six specified Iraqi exile factions.

2004 - The Department of Defense was paying a stipend of $340,000 per month to the Iraqi National Congress through its leader, Ahmad Chalabi, under the Iraq Liberation Act of 1998.

2004 - Since the Security Council first called on Israel to place its nuclear program under the trusteeship of the IAEA (Resolution 487), Israel had never complied, and neither the White House nor Congress had ever made an issue of that noncompliance.

2007 - Washington announced that over the next ten years, US military aid to Israel would be increased from 2.4 to 3 billion dollars a year. Seventy-four percent of the funds would be spent in the US, the balance in Israel.

Intervention

1956 - Inter-Arab friction over the Baghdad Pact led Washington to send units of the Sixth Fleet (based in Naples) to the eastern Mediterranean (as it had in 1946 in reaction to Soviet pressure on Turkey).

1958 - Alarmed by the surge of Arab Nationalism sparked by Nasir's political victory of 1956-7 – as manifested by unrest in Lebanon and the fall of the monarchy in Iraq – Eisenhower responded to a request from the pro-Israel Maronite (Christian) President of Lebanon by deploying small contingents of Marine and army troops to Beirut. They left after three months, having conducted no combat operations, and had no visible repercussions on the balance of power in the region.

1967 - The Six-Day War brought the Sixth Fleet back to the eastern Mediterranean.

1970 - During the war of attrition between Israel and Egypt, the United States flew reconnaissance flights over the Suez Canal, over Egyptian protests.

1979 - To demonstrate support for Saudi Arabia, and concern over an incursion into Yemen by South Yemeni forces that had Soviet support, Carter ordered a carrier task force into the Arabian Sea.

1980 - The United States acquired from Oman access to the port of Muscat and the air strip on Masirah Island, in return for economic and military assistance.

1982-85 - In May 1982, Secretary of State Haig told the media the ongoing civil war in Lebanon required a radical solution. Israel took this, and/or other signals, as a green light to invade. Using an attack on its Ambassador in London as a pretext, Israel sent in troops in June. Washington voted for Security Council Resolution 509 calling for withdrawal, but various sources reported that Haig favored Israeli intervention to knock out the Soviets' Palestinian and Syrian "proxies". Allegedly, the Israeli leadership intended to confine the operation to South Lebanon, but it took Defense Minister Sharon only three days to advance the troops north to the outskirts of Beirut. After a Soviet warning of "global consequences", Reagan ordered Israel not to block Syrian access along the road from Damascus to Beirut. However, Haig voided Philip Habib's cease-fire accord of June 11 by persuading Reagan not to demand Israeli withdrawal. On June 25, Reagan came into focus, replaced Haig with George Shultz, and required Israel to accept a cease-fire with the PLO, but Washington vetoed a Security Council call for limited withdrawal of Israeli and PLO forces.

On August 12, Habib prevailed on the White House to order a stop to saturation bombing of the Palestinian sector of Beirut; Michael Deaver had reportedly threatened to resign if Reagan didn't intervene. On September 1, under an agreement negotiated by Habib, the PLO evacuated its forces from Beirut, on the strength of Habib's guarantee that Israeli forces would stay out of Beirut and Palestinian noncombatants would not be harmed. Announcing that a contingent of Marines landed in August to help restore order had accomplished its mission, Reagan announced its withdrawal. Sharon had lied to Habib. After the departure of the Marines and the PLO forces, Israeli troops entered the city and allowed pro-Israeli Phalangist militiamen to carry out the massacre of a thousand or more civilians in two refugee camps. Recognizing its share of guilt (failure to keep a leash on Sharon), the White House sent 1500 Marines back in, less than two weeks after their premature departure. According to Reagan, the Marines were there to help the Lebanese Government restore order, not to engage in combat.

In September 1983, with Israeli-Arab hostilities still underway, and American Marine positions in Beirut coming under Arab fire, White House aide Robert McFarlane – in violation of mission directives, and over the objection of the Marine commander on the scene – ordered Marine and Sixth Fleet artillery to target Arab positions in the hills above Beirut. On October 12, the Shiite militia organization Hizballah carried out simultaneous suicide truck bombings of the Marine compound and that of a French component of the international force in the area, killing 58 French and 241 Americans. Reagan immediately proclaimed that American policy would not be swayed by terrorism, but in February 1984 discretion prevailed and the Marines were withdrawn.

Through 1984 and 1985, Washington continued to support Israel at the United Nations, vetoing a 1984 draft calling on Israel to respect international law in Lebanon and a 1985 draft condemning Israeli killings of civilians in South Lebanon.

1990 - A breakdown in communication between the United States and Saddam Husayn led him to suspect that, after years of American support against Iran, he could get away with the annexation of Kuwait. On August 2, Iraqi forces occupied Kuwait in five hours. After a few days of reflection, Bush 41 decided on military action, if diplomacy failed. Secretary of State Baker expended major effort and considerable financial incentive to build a coalition of Western powers and Arab states. To obtain Syrian participation in the coalition, Baker agreed to Syria's wiping out all anti-Syrian resistance in Lebanon. Security Council Resolution 678 authorized all necessary means to restore peace and security in the region. Washington was to cite Resolution 678 often in future years, but its actions often exceeded the terms of the Resolution – such as setting up two No-Fly Zones. To justify the initial intervention (which passed in Congress by a close vote), Washington tried several rationales before settling on "elimination of Iraq's nuclear threat".

1991 - The allied air war against Iraq began January 16. Iraqi Scuds began landing in Israel, but the Iraqi Air Force did not engage the Coalition, and Saddam sent many of his fighter planes to safety in Iran – no longer the principal enemy. Coalition air strikes ravaged Iraq's infrastructure, particularly in the oil industry. The only conceivable beneficiary of the "near apocalyptic" damage done to Iraq was Israel.

On February 24, the Coalition launched a ground war – after Iraq had agreed to withdraw from Kuwait. Four days later, the United States declared victory. The Coalition force of 500,000 Americans and 200,000 allies had routed the Iraqi conscript units, killing them in the thousands, along with many thousand civilians. The United States lost 266 lives from all causes. Some 3500 Kuwaitis had died.

As the hostilities ended, Bush issued an impulsive suggestion that the Iraqi people oust Saddam – not realizing that there is no "Iraqi people". Many Iraqi Shia and Kurds revolted en masse, killing any Baathist official they could get their hands on. Bush belatedly realized that Saddam's ouster could lead to a Shiite theocracy in Baghdad, and/or civil war, and/or partition of Iraq – contingencies which alarmed Washington and appalled its Arab allies. By concluding a cease-fire with Saddam, Washington enabled his elite Republican Guard, most of which had been held back from the front, to put down the Shia and Kurds with the same brutality they had inflicted on the Baathists. The best Washington could do for the Kurds, now feeling betrayed again, was in 1991 to declare northern Iraq above the 36th parallel off-limits to the Iraqi Air Force. In 1992, for the Shia, Washington set up a second No-Fly Zone below the 32nd parallel. Britain and France helped patrol the two zones.

In April 1991, America began to withdraw its troops from their salient in southern Iraq, but units were sent into northern Iraq to relieve the pressure imposed on Turkey by 700,000 Kurdish refugees from Iraqi retribution. There was no UN authorization for this program, or for the No-Fly Zones. Security Council Resolution 687 conditioned the Iraq-coalition cease-fire on Iraq's elimination of any program to develop nuclear weapons, dismantling of long-range missiles, acceptance of UN demarcation of the Iraq-Kuwait border, payment of compensation for war damages, and the return of Kuwaiti property and POW's. It contained no enforcement mechanisms.

Security Council Resolution 688 of April 1991, calling on Iraq to cease repression of the two rebellions, set up a "safe haven zone" for Iraqi Kurds. The United States and the United Kingdom have cited it as their authorization for setting up the No-Fly Zones. Dilip Hiro argued that Washington's citation of Security Council Resolution 688 was groundless because 688 did not cite Chapter VII of the UN Charter.

1992 - Under British and American protection, the Kurdish Autonomous Region held elections for a legislative council in which the KDP (Barzanis) and PUK (Talabanis) shared power. It didn't last.

1993 - Clinton ordered spasmodic American aircraft and missile attacks that took a number of civilian lives in southern and central Iraq. The most extensive operation, in June, was retaliation for a thinly documented claim that Saddam had tried to have ex-President Bush killed while he was visiting Kuwait.

1996 - The Southern No-Fly Zone was extended north from the 32nd parallel to the 33rd. France withdrew from patrolling the Northern No-Fly Zone. Citing Resolution 688, America bombarded Iraqi air defenses with cruise missiles in reprisal for Iraq's sending troops into the Northern Zone in support of the anti-Turk Kurdish faction, the PKK. The Senate endorsed the attack with only one opposing vote.

1997 - After the 1996 debacle in the Kurdish zone (see above under *Military Assistance*), the United States reduced its presence there.

1998 - In December, Clinton notified the UN to withdraw its weapons inspectors from Iraq. Within hours, the United States and the UK subjected Iraqi targets to three days of heavy air strikes. The rationale was Saddam's noncooperation with the inspectors. The real objective was to reduce Saddam's security structure, and if possible to kill him. Critics described the enterprise as disarmament by tantrum, and questioned its justification under the UN Charter. Its only significant consequence was Saddam's formal exclusion of the inspections regime. It also damaged American relations with the Arab states and Turkey. Clinton did not obtain congressional clearance for the operation under the War Powers Act.

1998 - Analysts noted the Arab view that America and Israel cannot abide an Arab challenge to their joint primacy in the region.

1998 - In protest against the air attacks on Iraq, France withdrew from patrolling the Southern No-Fly Zone.

2000 - Two years of American military action against Iraq had killed about 300 Iraqis.

2002 - The protection afforded Iraqi Kurds, notably by British and American patrolling of the Northern No-Fly Zone, had enabled them to organize some 17,000 square miles of Iraq into a de facto state with a population of some 3,500,000, its own parliament, army, constitution, currency, and passports, and designs on Kirkuk, which sits on Iraq's northern oil fields. Iraqi Kurds regarded Kirkuk as their Jerusalem, but its majority community were Turkmens, who enjoyed Turkish protection, reinforced by the deep-seated Turkish opposition to any expression of Kurdish identity in Turkey or nationalism in Iraq. The de facto state of Kurdistan had an income from tariffs on trade between Iraq and Turkey, plus a guaranteed 13 percent of Iraq's receipts under the Oil-for-Food Program, plus subsidies from the CIA. The power structure was an uneasy combination of the Barzanis' KDP and the Talabanis' PUK. (The Savichi Kurds were still close to the Saddam regime.)

2002 - UNSC Resolution 1441 (US initiative?): Failing WMD disarmament, Iraq would face "serious consequences".

2003-04 - <u>Invasion</u>: In February 2003, Bush 43 took the American presence in the Middle East to a whole new level by invading a major Arab state, replacing its leadership with an American military regime, and embarking on a breathtakingly revolutionary program to convert Iraq from a communalist dictatorship to a neoconservative "democracy". Most specialists on the Middle East dismissed the endeavor as sheer fantasy. As of late 2004, the only positive achievement had been the elimination of a brutal dictator – to the clear benefit of Israel, and the potential benefit of the Iraqi people. The consequences for the invading power were adverse. The consequences for the Middle East were impossible to predict.

2003 - Most Arabs regarded America as Israel's proxy in the Middle East, notably in invading Iraq.

2008-09 - After the failure of two prime ministers, Washington settled on a third, Nuri al Maliki, as its protégé in Iraq. Maliki was torn between his dependence on the support of the American occupation forces, and Iraqi expectations that the post-occupation government would demonstrate freedom from foreign influence – particularly on the Palestine issue.

Wrap-up

Since 1947, America's Middle East policy has orbited around Israel. There was one major spasm of objectivity under Eisenhower, and a stab at "even-handedness" under Kennedy. Over all, there has been inexorable advance toward today's posture of across-the-board favoritism for Israel, coddling regimes that tolerate Israel, and harassing those that do not. In all four geopolitical arenas – political, economic, cultural, and military – Israel has received special treatment:

Political favoritism was exemplified by the all-out support for partition in 1947, by Israel's preeminent access to IRS exemption, by the succession of lonely pro-Israel votes in UN forums, by 32 US pro-Israel vetoes in the UNSC since 1982, by American frustration of Arab attempts to put Israel's nuclear arms on the IAEA agenda, by the improbable cover-up of the attack on the USS Liberty, by tolerance for Israeli expansionism, by Washington's slavish deference to Israel's lead on the Palestine issue, and by its active support for Israel's nuclear monopoly in the Middle East. Even US aid to Arab states, ostensibly favorable to Arab interests, was more advantageous to Israel, because the recipients were status-quo governments. Revolutionary regimes, Arab or Iranian, were off Washington's gift list. Washington has rarely taken a pro-Arab position that conflicts with Israeli policy; the most recent case may have been the 1982 Habib attempt to guarantee the safety of Palestinians in Lebanon (an initiative that Israel scotched).

Economic favoritism is self-evident: Israel and compliant Arab regimes are the leading beneficiaries of American financial assistance. The top four recipients of US grant aid in 2008 were: Israel (2.4 billion dollars), Egypt (1.7 billion), Pakistan (.8 billion), and Jordan (.7 billion).

Culturally, Israel and America are intimately intertwined in innumerable ways – although not in the fundamental matter of political philosophy (Chapter 16).

Militarily, they are inseparable allies – despite the fact that US support for Israel is a primary cause of Arab and Islamist subversion of American interests. When overmatched Arabs fell back on guerrilla warfare, Washington penalized them for practicing the same "terrorism" to which Israel and the US have repeatedly resorted. Except for the brief 1983 aberration in Lebanon, the Israelis and the Americans have managed to avoid fighting side by side – but they haven't needed to. Washington has proved its loyalty during every Arab-Israeli conflict. In 2003 it went the last mile, at tragic cost, by disposing of Israel's deadliest enemy. In the view of an anonymous former official of the Bush 43 administration, the most enthusiastic advocates of invading Iraq were those most dedicated to the welfare of Israel. Those who questioned the wisdom of invasion were suspected of opposition to the Israeli position.

Chapter 14
The Wraith of Arab Nationalism

In the continuum between unity and anarchy, the Middle East has experienced long eras of relative centralization, under the hegemony of two or three rival powers, and shorter periods of chaotic splintering (Chapter 10). Century after century, the region has been whipsawed by the dichotomy between geographic proximity and dynastic antagonism. Under the Ottomans in the west and the Safavids in the east, geography produced comparative unity. With the decline of those two empires and the intrusion of the Europeans, the region disintegrated into the present miscellany of nineteen states and various disputed territories (Table A). This interregnum of fragmentation suits Washington's momentary preoccupations. It is a commentary on mankind's power of adaptability to the caprice of circumstance that Washington, swayed by its pro-Zionist mindset, is content to regard this situation – subject to a little tweaking here and there – as the closest the world can get to the long-term norm for the Middle East.

The Price of Disunity

After World War II, a European was asked how America could help Europe. The reply: "It's very simple. Put barriers between the 50 states, use different currencies, and speak different languages." The people of the Middle East have complied with that accommodating practice. In so doing, they converted their region into an island of backwardness. The plethora of rival regimes eats up revenue and undermines rational coordination of economic enterprise and political leverage. Turning "in unity is strength" (Chapter 1) on its head, they present a diorama of disarray. The haphazard development of the Tigris-Euphrates watershed epitomizes the region-wide predicament: Iraq owes its existence to those two rivers, but it has little voice in Turkey's plans for diversion of their headwaters.

Consider the adventitious separation of oil fields and people. Most of the oil lies in the east; most of the people live in the north and west. Parochial politics has induced oil states to bypass Arab and Turkish labor pools in favor of compliant temporary workers from South Asia.

Lebanon's Elysian setting makes it the ideal center for tourism, but civil war and Israeli-American invasion made it unlivable for fifteen years.

Iran, Iraq, and the six peninsular oil states are neighbors, with a vital interest in close cooperation. Instead, they have fought wars against each other, and are amassing arms in readiness for the next one. Of the top ten arms purchasers during the period from 2000 to 2003, five were countries in the Middle East: UAE, Egypt, Israel, Saudi Arabia, and Kuwait. Economic logic would dictate a Middle East in which Gulf oil was produced by indigenous labor, shipped via Syrian, Israeli-Palestinian, and Turkish pipelines and the Egyptian canal, and its proceeds ploughed back into region-wide consumption and development. Instead, the perversity of parochial politics has closed pipelines, repeatedly shut down the canal, and left millions out of work. Economic integration was a basic recommendation of the first Arab Human Development Report, written in 2002 by Arab experts for the UN Development Program.

Divide and Rule

At the start of World War II, as detailed in Chapter 10, most of the eastern Arab world was in a state of abject vassalage to the Western powers. France ruled Syria and Lebanon (and North Africa from Morocco to the Fezzan in Libya). Britain dominated Egypt, Palestine, Iraq, Jordan, and the shores of the Arabian Peninsula (and Sudan and, later in the war, coastal Libya). European control was based on military occupation, reinforced after the war by an American military presence in Saudi Arabia and the Persian Gulf (and Libya).

In the shortsighted imperialist view, the European occupations were strategically advantageous and economically profitable. Dividends flowed in from controlling interest in Arab and Iranian oil, Egyptian cotton, the Suez Canal, and the Aden entrepot, from tuition paid by the thousands of Middle Easterners who attended English and French-language schools in the region and the West, and from promiscuous arms sales.

As the British and French presences eroded, America began to show an interest in replacing them, less exploitively at first but more intrusively: It introduced an element the Europeans had never accomplished – a Western affiliate:

The Arab-Israeli Divide

Although Israel speaks an Asian language and sits on Asian terrain, it is in essence a salient of Western technology and American political influence. As long as the United States is the preeminent world power, and its basic Middle East policy is dictated by a Zionist state, Israel will be safe from invasion, but an obstacle to regional advancement, and as such inimical to the vital interests of all Middle Easterners, including the Israelis themselves.

In their myopic preoccupation with their own survival, Arab leaders have missed every opportunity to mitigate the Israeli challenge. During World War I, the Hashemites swallowed the incoherence of the Balfour Declaration. After the war, they failed to grasp the blatant fact that "mandate" was a euphemism for dependency, or that General Gouraud's separation of an expanded Lebanon from Syria would provide an opening for Zionist manipulation. Arab leaders missed the opportunity to make the best of a bad bargain by accepting the UNGA's Partition Resolution of 1947. They denounced the founding of Israel in 1948, but probably failed to appreciate the geopolitical significance of the first territorial barrier between Arab Africa and Arab Asia since the Crusades.

Israeli foreign policy underwent several shifts. In May 1950, Prime Minister Ben-Gurion affirmed Israeli neutrality in great-power disputes. After the Jewish trials in Moscow in 1953, the Soviet Union briefly broke relations with Israel, which moved closer to the United States. The outbreak of the Algerian rebellion in 1955 brought Israel a sharp increase in the supply of French arms, while Israel waved off an American proposal for a bilateral security pact based on existing frontiers – a concept which informed American policy in 1957 when President Eisenhower became the only President ever to impose an ultimatum on Israel (Chapter 8).

The Suez War of 1956 cemented a friendship between France and Israel, which lasted until 1967, when Israeli conquests of Palestinian and Syrian territory led de Gaulle – who had advised Israel not to attack – to cut off the arms supply. Concurrently, crucial American military aid to Israel from Lyndon Johnson – who had already shown favoritism for Israel over Egypt (Chapter 8) – solidified an association that was to evolve into something even closer than a military alliance (Chapter 13), despite the evolution of Germany as Israel's second-ranking partner in trade.

In 1961, the mere location of Israel between Egypt and Syria was probably the decisive reason why Nasir refrained from taking military action against Syrian secession. By 2002-3, when both parties in Israel called on the United States to invade Iraq, and George W. Bush complied (?), the Israeli-American association appeared to have reached its culmination.

All the well-intended initiatives to reconcile the Arabs and Israel have foundered on the rocks of geopolitical reality: Their conflict is a zero-sum game. Israel is the quintessential communalist state. The Arabs' best – perhaps only – hope of progress lies in submerging every ethnic community in the area, including Jews, in a secular union.

The Battle for Independence from the West

Segmental in its contemporary make-up, the Middle East has been segmental in its achievement of self-determination. Turkey expelled foreign forces in the 1920's (Chapter 7), and has angled for incorporation in the European Union. Geopolitics says Turkey belongs in the Middle East, but many influential Turks seem bent on divorce from their region. Iran achieved full autonomy with the theocratic revolution of 1979. After centuries of political separation, it is unlikely to engage in any early supranational associations with its Arab neighbors – even with a Shiite-dominated Iraq.

The situation of the Arab "Shatterbelt" (Chapter 1) is generically different. Over half the people of the Middle East speak dialects of Arabic. Most Arab regimes pay lip service to the concept of Arab unity. There have been some abortive moves toward this objective (including the United Arab Republic of Egypt and Syria, 1958-61, and the Iraqi "annexation" of Kuwait, 1990), and two existing linkages (Syrian pressure for hegemony over Lebanon; nominal unification of Yemen and South Yemen). The logical nucleus of an Arab union is Egypt, but in the 1800's the expansionist efforts of Muhammad 'Ali were checked by the Europeans, and in the 1900's the unionist concepts of 'Abd Al Nasir in Egypt and the Baath in Syria and Iraq were frustrated by Arab dynastic rivalries and the Israeli-American diarchy.

The following chronology of intraregional alignments contains persistent evidence of Israeli-American success in promoting the unique interests of each Arab country (as they would state it), or in exploiting the venality of self-serving regimes (as Arab Nationalists and Islamists would put it).

Political Alignment: Nothing is Permanent But Change

As far back as history carries us, four population centers (Mesopotamia, Egypt, Anatolia, and Persia) have contested control of the Middle East, and formed alliances with each other to that end. In 1260 B.C., the Egyptians were allied with the Hittites (Anatolian) against the Assyrians (Mesopotamian). In 600 B.C., the Kingdom of Judah (Levantine) was caught up in conflict between the Egyptians and the Babylonians (Mesopotamian).

Since World War II, Anatolia and Persia have been largely engrossed in their own affairs, but the four Arab sectors have been caught up in a chaotic game of musical chairs, as revealed in a radically abbreviated compilation of events:

1744-1818 - First appearance of Saudi Arabia, ended when Egyptian troops captured 'Abdallah Al Sa'ud and sent him to Istanbul, where the Sultan had him beheaded.

1800's - Sunni nomads settled in southern Mesopotamia and converted to Shiism, making the Shia the largest community in that sector.

1800's - Syrians staged repeated revolts against Ottoman rule.

Late 1800's - France, Britain, Russia, and American Presbyterians were active in Syria/Lebanon, the first three cultivating ethnic favorites, the Americans staying out of politics.

1843-91 - Second Saudi emergence, expunged by the Rashidis.

1914 - In reaction to the proclamation of jihad by the Ottoman Sultan/ Caliph, Britain dazzled the Sharif Husayn of the Hijaz with the mirage of Arab Nationalism, offering to make him the first ruler of the Arab nation.

1915-16 - In Damascus, secret Arab societies conspired on behalf of Arab independence, until the Ottomans dispersed them and hanged some of their leaders.

1916 - Sharif Husayn proclaimed himself King of the Arabs.

1917 - In calling on Congress for war against Germany, Woodrow Wilson made passing allusion to the "concert of free peoples".

1918 - The twelfth of Wilson's Fourteen Points was "autonomous development" for the non-Turkish portions of the Ottoman Empire.

1918 - The Ottomans signed the Armistice of Mudros, ending their opposition to the British-orchestrated Arab Revolt.

1919 - Arab Nationalist ferment in Damascus. A "General Syrian Congress" called for a state of Greater Syria (Syria, Lebanon, Palestine, and Jordan).

1921 - Adeed Dawisha noted in *The Middle East Journal* of Spring 2008 that King Faysal I (1921-33) brought Syrian Sati' al Husri into the Iraqi government as Minister of Education. Husri considered Shiites heretics (*Foreign Affairs,* 2006), but he shared Faysal's enthusiasm for pan-Arabism.

1932 - Third Saudi appearance – the Kingdom of Saudi Arabia.

1934 - Iraq opened its military college to male applicants from all ethnic communities. Shiite officers tended to favor Iraqi nationalism, Sunnis Arab nationalism.

1936 - Michel 'Aflaq, studying in Paris, was disillusioned with Communism by the failure of the French administration formed by Leon Blum's Popular Front to work for divestiture of the colonies. 'Aflaq began to devise a program for secular Arab Nationalism with fascist overtones.

1937 - Having settled border disputes with Syria and Iran, Iraq signed the Saadabad nonaggression pact with Turkey, Iran, and Afghanistan: *Middle East Policy,* Summer 2008.

1939 - German invasion of Poland ignited World War II. Under British direction, Egypt broke relations with Germany and became the main Middle Eastern base for the Allies during the war. Britain set up the Middle East Supply Center to allocate scarce resources and make the region more self-supporting. (After the war, Egypt kept the Center in being for a time in an effort to promote regional cooperation.)

1940 - Germany defeated France, but allowed it to set up a captive regime in the southern 40 percent of the country, and retain control of its possessions. Relations between the Vichy Government and the neutral United States enabled American infiltration of North Africa. French officials in Syria/Lebanon stayed loyal to Vichy, out of resentment of British operations in the region.

1940 - By executive action, Roosevelt trespassed on America's pose of neutrality by providing 50 destroyers to Britain in return for 99-year leases on various British sites in the Western Hemisphere.

1941 - British forces reentered Iraq, executed the leaders of the pro-German regime (Chapter 9), and expelled 3000 army officers, many of them Arab Nationalists.

1941 - Italy entered the war on the side of Germany, partly because of Mussolini's resentment of British control of the Mediterranean (Gibraltar, Malta, Cyprus, Suez). Germany invaded the Soviet Union. Pearl Harbor brought Japan and the United States into the war.

1943 - The Soviets repelled the Germans at Stalingrad. Italy surrendered, later declared war on Germany.

1943 - Syrians Michel 'Aflaq (Greek Orthodox) and Salah al Din al Baytar (Sunni Muslim) founded the Arab Socialist Renaissance Party (ASRP or Baath, from *Ba'th*) in Damascus.

1943 - As reported in Hart's *Saudi Arabia and the United States,* Prince Faysal came to Washington to discuss Ibn Sa'ud's concern that the Hashemites were promoting an anti-Saudi union of Syria, Jordan, Palestine, and Iraq. He was told that the US favored no postwar territorial changes that did not accord with the wishes of the people concerned, as prescribed in The Atlantic Charter.

1945 - Representatives of seven Arab states (Egypt, Iraq, Lebanon, Saudi Arabia, Syria, Transjordan, Yemen), meeting in Cairo, founded the Arab League. Anglophile Nuri al Sa'id from Iraq was a prime mover. As of 2009, the League was still in existence, but it had never made significant progress in transmuting Arab disarray into concrete achievement. The basic rationale for the League was common defense against Zionism.

1945 - Saudi Arabia declared war on Germany, thereby acquiring a seat at the San Francisco meeting that created the United Nations.

1946-48 - British efforts to build a congenial alliance of Arab states resulted in the emergence of a pro-British bloc of Iraq and Transjordan (ruled by Hashemites since Britain had enthroned them after World War I) and an independent bloc of Egypt, Syria, and Saudi Arabia. The Hashemite bloc was riven by strategic differences: Jordan's King 'Abdallah favored the Greater Syria state (see 1919 entry), but under his rule; Iraqi Regent 'Abd al Ilah favored a joint invasion of Syria. Frustrated by failure of its plans for the Arab East, London was animated by an element of spite in its tolerance of Zionist activism.

1948 - Founding of Israel, which routed the forces of Syria, Iraq, and Egypt from three-fourths of Palestine (Chapter 8). At Soviet direction, all Arab Communist parties except that in Iraq supported the creation of Israel.

1949 - The Arab League condemned Transjordan's (prearranged) annexation of the Palestinian West Bank. Egypt took no comparable action in the Gaza Strip. The Israel-Lebanon Armistice guaranteed the Maronite Order of Monks continued access to churches and monasteries in Israel – thus facilitating future initiatives for alliance between Israel and the Maronites.

1949 - Syrian Colonel Adib al Shishakli carried out a bloodless coup d'etat in Damascus.

1950 - The Arab League rejected Israel's request for peace negotiations with each of its seven members, and ruled that Transjordan's annexation of the West Bank had violated that policy, but it took no punitive action against

Amman. King 'Abdallah declined to attend the meeting, but delegated his ambassador to Egypt in his place.

1950's - As a counterweight to British influence in the Peninsula, Yemen cultivated ties with Egypt and the USSR.

1951 - The Arab League concluded a Collective Security Pact, which provided for expulsion of any member that signed a separate peace treaty with Israel. Jordan signed, but was excluded from the League's military system.

1951 - A Palestinian nationalist assassinated Jordan's King 'Abdallah for accepting partition of Palestine, and/or for annexing the West Bank, and/or for conspiring with Israel.

1952 - The military's overthrow of the Egyptian monarchy had repercussions across the Arab world. In reaction to Arab Nationalist rioting in Iraq, Nuri al Sa'id imposed martial law.

1953 - Libya joined The Arab League.

1954 - Akram al Hawrani merged his Arab Socialist Party with the ASRP, which soon became the dominant faction in the Syrian government.

1955 - In Baghdad, Nuri al Sa'id presided over the first meeting of the Baghdad Pact. Britain, Turkey, and Iran sent representatives.

1955 - With France secretly violating the British-French-American Tripartite Accord (Chapter 8) by selling arms to Israel, and the United States – under British and Israeli pressure – dragging its feet on complying with Egyptian arms requests, Nasir shocked Washington by announcing an agreement to buy arms from the Soviet Bloc.

1955 - Egypt concluded agreements with Syria and Saudi Arabia to set up a joint military command under an Egyptian commander.

1955 - A Jordanian plan to join the Baghdad Pact organization (Chapter 10) provoked a Cairo radio campaign for the ouster of King Husayn, and anti-regime demonstrations in Jordan. Husayn dissolved Parliament but abandoned the plan.

1955 - Sudan declared independence, recognized by Britain, America, and Egypt. Egypt had expected Sudan to opt for Egyptian-Sudanese union.

1956 - Egypt, Saudi Arabia, and Yemen signed a five-year military alliance aimed at ousting Britain from the Arabian Peninsula.

1956 - Egypt angered Eisenhower and Dulles by recognizing the People's Republic of China (PRC). Syria followed suit in recognizing China and concluding an arms deal with the USSR.

1956 - After Egypt, Syria, and Saudi Arabia offered to replace the British subsidy of Jordan's Arab Legion, King Husayn ousted its British commander. Later in the year, Husayn agreed to coordinated defense planning with Egypt, Syria, and Lebanon in the event of war with Israel, ended the alliance with Britain, broke relations with France, and recognized the USSR and China. Syria and Saudi Arabia sent troops to Jordan.

1956 - The members of the Baghdad Pact, including Iraq, supported the Tripartite Invasion of Egypt (Chapter 8).

1957 - The rise of Soviet and Communist influence in the eastern Arab World as a result of Soviet support for Egypt in the Suez War led Washington to proclaim the Eisenhower Doctrine (Chapter 10), which – on the model of the Truman Doctrine of 1947 – offered support to Middle East states threatened by Communist aggression. In application, the Doctrine was directed against Arab Nationalism. For the Arabs, most of whom were concerned with the threat of Israeli aggression, the Doctrine was irrelevant. Lebanon was the only state to officially accept. Nasir's political victory over the West bolstered Arab radicals and weakened Arab accomodationists.

1957 - Alarmed by the surge in Nasir's popularity across the Arab World after the US-engineered collapse of the Tripartite invasion, King Sa'ud made a state visit to Washington, initiated cooperation with America against Egypt, and in a meeting with Regent 'Abd al Ilah, set the stage for rapprochement with Iraq. Washington negotiated extension of the Saudi-American airfield agreement.

1957 - Egypt launched a massive propaganda campaign for Arab union, and late in the year called on Jordanians to oust King Husayn, then age 22.

1957 - Saudi Arabia, Iraq, and Jordan consulted on joint resistance to the Egyptian campaign.

1957 - Secretary of State Dulles announced that the independence of Jordan was vital to American interests. Husayn went onto the CIA payroll – at least until 1977, when the arrangement was publicized in the American press. Egypt, Syria, and Saudi Arabia terminated subsidies to Jordan.

1958 - Fearing a Communist victory in upcoming Syrian elections, Baytar and 'Aflaq went to see Nasir and proposed Syrian-Egyptian union. Nasir proclaimed the formation of the United Arab Republic (UAR) under his Presidency. Sensibly advised by Charles Yost, Ambassador to Syria, Washington accorded recognition.

1958 - To counter the UAR, Iraq and Jordan proclaimed a loose federation under King Faysal of Iraq. Nuri al Sa'id became Prime Minister.

1958 - To obtain military assistance against British forces in South Yemen and/or to buy protection against Arab Nationalism in Yemen, the regime in Yemen concluded a nominal confederation with the UAR, to be known as the United Arab States.

1958 - Syria blocked transport of fuel to Jordan, Cairo's "Voice of the Arabs" called for Husayn's death, and the UAR smuggled arms to Arab Nationalists in Jordan and allegedly tried to kidnap or assassinate Husayn.

1958 - With Nasir's endorsement, "Free Officers" overthrew the Iraqi monarchy and declared a republic. Nuri al Sa'id, King Faysal, and the former Regent were killed. Arab Nationalism rode high in Baghdad, but Nasir failed to exploit that advantage. Iraq's new leader, 'Abd al Qarim Qasim, cultivated Iraqi nationalists and Communists to check Egyptian influence. Nasir and the Baath were hostile to Arab Communism for having deferred to Soviet policy to the point of suspending opposition to British and French occupation during World War II and – except the Iraqi faction – endorsing the creation of Israel.

1958 - In immediate reaction to the coup in Iraq, and per an earlier request from Lebanese President Sham'un, US Marines made an inconsequential landing in Beirut. A brief Lebanese civil war was resolved in favor of a faction which ousted Sham'un but managed to maintain neutrality between Egypt and the West. Iraq had sent troops to shore up the Sham'un regime.

1958 - Qasim won a power struggle with Iraqi Arab Nationalists and became more dependent on the Iraqi Communists, who were mainly Kurds and Shiites. A radio war ensued between Baghdad and Cairo.

1958 - Morocco and Tunisia joined the Arab League. In Cairo, Algerian rebels against French rule proclaimed a provisional government. Egypt controlled the League (Egyptian Secretary General, headquarters in Cairo, budget largely financed by Egypt).

1959 - Soviet leader Khrushchev warned the UAR against persecuting Arab Communists, but Soviet arms shipments to the UAR continued. This strategy enabled the USSR to win access to former British bases in Egypt and French bases in Syria.

1961 - Yugoslavia, India, and Egypt sponsored, in Belgrade, a follow-up to the "Positive Neutrality" conference of 1955 in Bandung, Indonesia. Egyptian strategy was to undermine Western imperialism without falling under Soviet domination.

1961 - Britain and Kuwait revoked their protectorate pact of 1899, but Britain still recognized an obligation to defend Kuwait against attack. Qasim reacted by declaring the Anglo-Kuwaiti treaties of 1899 and 1961 invalid, on the grounds that Kuwait was an indivisible part of Iraq. Britain and Saudi Arabia sent troops to defend Kuwait if required. Nasir, allowing his animus against Qasim to override his commitment to the principle of

Arab Nationalism, approved the British troop movement, and endorsed Arab League recognition of Kuwait's independence.

1961 - Various Syrian factions, disillusioned with union with Egypt (the military by Egyptian arrogance, the Baath for having been shut down, the mercantile community by Nasir's program of nationalization) welcomed a military coup that took Syria out of the UAR. Jordan and Saudi Arabia backed the secession. However, many rank-and-file Arab Nationalists lamented the action, and signatories of the secessionist document, including Baytar and Hawrani, were forever discredited.

1962 - The Imamate of Yemen, already unsettled by attacks by Cairo's Voice of the Arabs, was overthrown by a pro-Egyptian faction of the military. The ousted Imam escaped and organized a tribal resistance which received ground support from Saudi Arabia and air support from Jordan. Egypt sent a large force to defend the revolutionary regime. Yemen became the major arena for the ongoing conflict between Arab Nationalism and Arab traditionalism. The Saudi monarchy viewed Yemen as its major rival for domination of Arabia. Jordan's Husayn concluded a treaty of alliance with Saudi Arabia.

1962 - After the falling-out between China and the USSR, both competed for influence in Yemen by major development projects. In Washington, Faysal Al Sa'ud obtained from Kennedy reaffirmation of Truman's pledge of 1950 that the United States would regard any threat to the independence of Saudi Arabia as a matter of deep concern.

1963 - After air attacks on Saudi towns by Egyptian forces in Yemen, Faysal asked for American air cover. Washington demurred unless Saudi Arabia would cease military support for the Yemeni royalists. The Department of State said Kennedy's assurances to Saudi Arabia implied no military commitment.

1963 - Iraqi Baathists who had been in contact with the CIA staged a coup in Baghdad, killed Qasim, and set up an Arab Nationalist regime which carried out widespread killings of Communists in retaliation for a Communist massacre of Baathists in Mawsil in 1959. The CIA provided names of Communists.

1963 - King Husayn met secretly in London with a representative of Israeli Prime Minister Eshkol. It was the first of many clandestine meetings between Husayn and Israeli leaders.

1964 - King Sa'ud mended fences with Nasir in Cairo, where they participated in the first Arab Summit, a reaction to Israel's project to pipe water from the upper Jordan to the Negev, and to attendant border clashes between Israel and Syria. The Summit set up a joint Arab Command and a Palestine Liberation Organization under Egyptian direction, and agreed to a plan for counterdiversion of Jordan River water into Jordan.

1964 - Impelled by Nasir's call for Arab solidarity, the Libyan Prime Minister announced his government had asked Britain and America to negotiate the liquidation of their bases in Libya.

1964 - While the Syrian Baath had abrogated the treaty of military union with Iraq, 'Aflaq was promoting a new Baathist leadership in Baghdad, including Saddam Husayn, but they lost control to 'Abd al Salam 'Arif, who was promoting union with Nasir's Egypt.

1964 - Yemen and Egypt agreed to coordinate policy, but Egyptian forces in Yemen were bogged down by the unfamiliarity of mountain warfare and the intricacies of Yemeni tribal politics.

1964 - Lyndon Johnson allowed the lapse of American sales of wheat to Egypt for local currency under Public Law 480, using Egyptian involvement in Yemen and the Congo as pretexts. Protesters burned the USIS library in Cairo, and Nasir took a defiant stance, condemning Iran under the Shah as "an American and Zionist colony."

1965 - Nasir and Saudi King Faysal signed an agreement, which purported to end the war in Yemen. According to Vali Nasr (*The Shia Revival*), Faysal opposed Arab Nationalism as an atheistic doctrine.

1966 - The Syrian Baath purged 'Aflaq, who was given haven by the Iraqi Baath, which was falling under the control of Saddam, who favored an Iraqi brand of Arab Nationalism.

1966 - Egypt and Syria resumed diplomatic relations (broken in 1961), and concluded a pro forma defense treaty.

1966 - Israel carried out (under Ariel Sharon) one of its cross-border raids in retaliation for small-scale operations by Palestinian infiltrators into Israel. The target was the Jordanian village of Sammu', which took heavy casualties. Jordan accused Syria of supporting the infiltrators. Syria called on the Jordanians to overthrow King Husayn. The Arab League Defense Committee voted to send Iraqi and Saudi troops to Jordan's defense.

1967 - Egypt's failure to come to the assistance of Jordan (after Sammu') or of Syria (engaged in costly air battles with Israel over the Golan) intensified inter-Arab recrimination.

1967 - As expectation of Arab-Israeli Round Three mounted, Egypt and Syria jointly accused America of deploying the Sixth Fleet to protect Israel, Saudi Arabia put its forces on alert, Iraq announced the transfer of aircraft to the "Israeli front", and King Idris of Libya ordered Libyan units to join Egyptian forces along the Israeli border. To avert civil war in Jordan, Husayn concluded an alliance with his recent adversary, Nasir. Iraq joined their alliance.

1967 - Israel launched the "June War" (or "Six-Day War") with a shattering air and ground attack on Egypt (Chapter 8), which still maintained 50,000 troops in Yemen. (Why Nasir provoked Israeli attack before repatriating his forces has not been explained.) Iraq, Kuwait, and Saudi Arabia declared war on Israel. In Baghdad, Arab oil ministers resolved to embargo oil sales to any state condoning aggression against an Arab state. Iraq broke diplomatic relations with the United States. Saudi Arabia cut off oil shipments to the United States and some European countries. Following up the abrupt victory over Egypt, Israel invaded Syria. During the Israeli conquest of the West Bank, the Jordanian army was largely destroyed.

1967 - Discredited by Israel's humiliation of Nasirism in Egypt and Baathism in Syria, Arab Nationalism went into eclipse. Leadership of Middle East resistance to Western imperialism was to be assumed by the gradual rise of Islamism (Chapter 12).

1967 - After the cease-fire, Syria called on the Arabs to uproot the presence of America, Britain, and all other states that had supported Israel in the Six-Day War. No actual retaliation was noted except a momentary decline in American trade with the Arab World.

1967 - In October, after Saudi-Egyptian mediation of a cease-fire, Egypt completed withdrawal of its forces from Yemen.

1967 - As reported in *The Middle East Journal* in 2006, an Arab meeting in Khartoum officially ended the undeclared cold war between the radical states, led by Egypt, and the conservative states, led by Saudi Arabia.

1968 - In July, the Iraqi Baath took power in Baghdad.

1969 - Mu'ammar Qadhafi, a devotee of Nasirism, led a military coup that toppled the Libyan monarchy, and instructed America and Britain to stop training flights (from Tripoli and Tubruq, respectively). Later in the year, Libyan, Egyptian, and Syrian conferees agreed on promoting commando action throughout the Arab homeland, and Libyan, Egyptian, and Sudanese chiefs of state agreed in Tripoli to coordinate operations versus Israel. (There were none.)

1969 - Ashraf Marwan, Nasir's son-in-law, allegedly went on the payroll of Israeli intelligence (Mossad). (Years later, some reports suggested that he had been a mole for Egypt.)

1969 - Saddam Husayn acquired a seat on the Iraqi Revolutionary Command Council (RCC), with responsibility for organizing the security and intelligence agencies. (In his earlier years of command, he effected major improvements in education, housing, and public health.)

1970 - The USSR received authorization to use specified ground and naval bases in Egypt, in return for providing air defense against Israeli attack (Chapter 8). Kuwaiti ground units along the Canal took casualties. Algerian forces also participated.

1970 - The Arab League adopted a plan for a Supreme Command under an Egyptian general, but it was not implemented.

1970 - For help in repelling the Syrian intrusion into Jordan (Chapter 8), King Husayn asked the Israeli Air Force (via London and Washington) to attack the Syrians. Noting Israeli preparation for air action, Asad withheld Syrian aircraft, leaving his ground forces vulnerable to Jordan's small air force; they withdrew.

1970 - Asad took power in Damascus, ousting his former Baathist colleagues, reversing most of the Syrian Baath's economic decisions, and sentencing 'Aflaq and Baytar in absentia for treason. 'Aflaq was in Baghdad. Syria broke relations with Iraq. The split between Asad's Syria and Saddam's Iraq was both dynastic and strategic: Syria's enemy was Israel; Iraq's was Iran.

1970 - After Nasir's death, Anwar Sadat succeeded to the rule of an Egypt crippled by economic distress and military losses. In a bid for financial assistance from Saudi Arabia, he moderated the revolutionary policies pursued by his predecessor.

1971 - Granted independence by Britain, Qatar established a special relationship with France.

1971 - An Egyptian general announced that twelve Arab states had drawn up plans for military and financial cooperation against Israel.

1972 - In Algiers, Sadat, Qadhafi, and Boumedienne of the new state of Algeria proclaimed that a battle with Israel was inevitable and should be waged by a coordinated Arab alliance.

1972 - Sadat, dissatisfied with the level of Soviet support, expelled most of Egypt's resident Soviet advisers.

1973 - Syria, Jordan, and Egypt appointed an Egyptian commander-in-chief for the Israeli front. Iraq unilaterally declared resumption of diplomatic ties with Iran, in order to free its troops for participation in the anticipated hostilities against Israel. Iraqi troops fought on the Golan front.

1973 - King Faysal made a state visit to Cairo.

1973 - Yasir 'Arafat, who as founder of Fatah had taken control of the PLO (see the 1964 entry), made an official visit to Riyadh and made amends for the PLO's killing of three Western diplomats, including Americans George Curtis Moore and Cleo A. Noel, Jr., in the Saudi embassy in Khartoum.

1973 - Although Egypt and Syria had achieved détente with Jordan, King Husayn allegedly made a secret trip to warn Israeli Prime Minister

Golda Meir that Egypt and Syria were planning a surprise attack. Husayn and the Israeli military had a practice of exchanging sensitive confidences, but according to the report the Israelis discounted the warning. Husayn denied the allegation in an interview with an Israeli historian.

1973 - On October 5, the Soviet Union flew the families of its official personnel out of Egypt and Syria. The Soviets' information was better than that of the Israelis or the Americans. The Egyptians and Syrians launched a coordinated attack October 6. Four days later, as Israeli reserves finally reached the front lines, Iraq committed forces to the conflict, and Sudanese units reached the front. By October 14, Iraqi and Jordanian forces had been deployed in Syria, plus token forces from Saudi Arabia and Morocco. On October 17, Kuwait reinstated its previous small annual subsidy to Jordan. In November Moroccan troops arrived in Egypt, but by October 26 the Israeli forces, bolstered by Nixon's emergency airlift of state-of-the-art technology, had taken the initiative on both fronts. By establishing a bridgehead on the western bank of the Canal, Israel had trapped Egypt's Third Army in Sinai. In reaction to a Soviet threat to assume responsibility for supplying the Third Army, Kissinger met with Sadat in Cairo November 3, reactivated Egyptian-American diplomatic relations, and set the stage for the eventual disengagement of Israeli troops from Egypt, the conclusion of an Egyptian-Israeli peace treaty, and the incorporation of Egypt into the American sphere of influence (Chapter 8). In consonance with Sadat's détente with the United States, he consolidated reconciliation with Saudi Arabia.

1973 - Kissinger also negotiated the withdrawal of Israeli forces from the approaches to Damascus, but Israel razed the city of Al Qunaytirah before giving it back, and kept the Golan.

1973 - Qadhafi sparked the 1973-74 Arab oil embargo (Chapter 4) by doubling the price of crude.

1973 - As Daniel Yergin noted in *The Prize,* in its first major foreign-policy split with the United States since World War II, Japan endorsed the Arab position in the Arab-Israeli dispute.

1973 - Whereas Arab support for the Egyptian and Syrian campaigns in the June War of 1967 had been unfocussed and largely irrelevant (including anti-Jewish riots in North Africa and anti-British riots in Aden), nine Arab armies saw combat against Israel in 1973. Nevertheless, after heavy initial losses from the Arab advantage of surprise and the ingenuity of Egypt's crossing of the Canal, Israel had ridden incomplete Egyptian-Syrian coordination, American emergency aid, and its own basic military superiority to a decisive victory.

1974 - In Lebanon, Shiite cleric Musa al Sadr (a relative of the Iraqi Sadr's) founded *Amal* to promote Shiite Islamism. The PLO provided training of an Amal militia. (Sadr later mysteriously disappeared while on a visit to Libya.)

1975 - After the Soviets failed to satisfy Egyptian requests for arms and rescheduling of Egypt's debt, Sadat told Arab media he would seek economic aid from the United States. The Israeli-Egyptian Disengagement Agreement of September reinforced America's tacit commitment to the security of Israel, and entailed its promise not to recognize or deal with the PLO until the PLO accepted UN Security Council Resolutions 242 and 338 (Chapter 8). The Agreement foreshadowed Egyptian withdrawal from the Arab front against Israel.

1976 - Reportedly because of the USSR's having forbidden India to sell Egypt parts for Soviet-built planes, Sadat had the Egyptian People's Assembly abrogate the Soviet-Egyptian Friendship Treaty of 1971, and he cancelled Soviet naval access to Egyptian ports.

1976 - In Lebanon, Amal joined Syrian forces fighting the PLO, in the interest of prevailing on the PLO to cease military operations against Israel.

1976 - Egypt and Sudan signed a joint defense pact.

1977 - Sadat made a dramatic visit to Israel. Most other Arab states reacted in shock and condemnation. Algeria, Libya, South Yemen, Syria, and the PLO formed a front aimed at blocking the "high treason" of Sadat's unilateral peace initiative. Iraq, now under the control of Saddam (who was outmaneuvering President Bakr), stayed out because the other participants refused to reject UN Resolutions 242 and 338.

1977 - Egypt closed a number of Soviet Bloc consulates and cultural centers.

1978 - A bloody war of assassination and bombing between the PLO and Iraq for control of the Palestinian resistance was resolved when Saddam and 'Arafat made common cause against the Israeli-Egyptian compact at Camp David.

1978 - At Camp David, Carter hammered out an Egyptian-Israeli agreement, which was to lead to a peace treaty, while leaving Syria, Jordan, and the Palestinians out in the cold (Chapter 8). Egypt got Sinai, a big American subsidy, and the hope of no more humiliating defeats by Israel. Israel got passage through the Suez Canal and the Strait of Tiran, recognition by the major Arab state, a bigger American subsidy, and a free hand in the Occupied Territories.

1978 - Alarmed by Sadat's détente with Israel, Syria shifted its support from the Christian side to the Muslim/PLO side in Lebanon.

1978 - King Husayn felt Washington had betrayed him. Asad buried the hatchet with the PLO and Iraq. Saddam convened an Arab Summit (still minus Asad), which restored cooperation between Iraq and Jordan and imposed various penalties on Egypt, including suspension from the Arab League.

1979 - In reaction to the signature of an Israeli-Egyptian peace treaty on March 26, 1979, nineteen of the twenty-two members of the Arab League, meeting in Baghdad, resolved to terminate diplomatic and economic relations with Egypt, and to transfer League headquarters from Cairo. The only non-participants were Egypt, Oman, and Sudan. Islamist Iran also condemned the treaty.

1979 - The outbreak of fighting between Yemen and South Yemen led Saudi Arabia to withdraw its component of an Arab peacekeeping force in Lebanon. Sadat accused the Saudis of engineering the Arab League's break with Egypt, but some analysts suspected the Khomeini takeover in Iran had inclined the Saudis to favor the Israeli-Egyptian peace treaty for having freed up Egypt's forces for possible defense of Saudi Arabia against Iranian radicalism.

1979 - Saddam exploited a secret overture from Bakr to Asad (in behalf of Iraqi-Syrian union) to force Bakr's resignation from the Presidency. Saddam followed up this advantage by staging a chilling party meeting from which some twenty associates were led out to be killed on a charge of conspiracy. Saddam had consolidated his one-man rule by building a Baathist security force organized into secret cells. The efficiency of his rule was vitiated by his belief that he had been anointed by Allah and by the recklessness that was to result in the costly stalemate with Iran, the disastrous expulsion from Kuwait, and the enmity of the United States.

1979 - Qadhafi broke relations with the PLO for not being bold enough in its conflict with Israel – for example, not sinking a ship in the Suez Canal. The PLO lost the Libyan subsidy, but was receiving a larger one from Saudi Arabia. Qadhafi channeled Libyan subsidies to radical Palestinian organizations.

1980 - Salah al Din al Baytar was killed in Paris, seemingly by agents of Hafiz al Asad.

1980 - Iraq invaded Iran, igniting an eight-year war in which Jordan, Saudi Arabia, Kuwait, Yemen, Egypt, Sudan, and the United States backed Iraq, while Syria, Libya, Algeria, South Yemen, and the Lebanese Shia backed Iran. The Arab Gulf states backed Iraq, with the exception of Oman and the UAE (which, torn between Abu Dhabi's preference for Iraq and Dubai's preference for Iran, claimed neutrality.) The PLO tried to ride both horses at once.

1980 - Asad, wedged between Israel and Saddam's Iraq, signed a twenty-year treaty of friendship with the USSR.

1981 - Saudi Arabia, Kuwait, Bahrain, Qatar, the UAE, and Oman – perceiving a threat from revolutionary Iran – founded the Gulf Cooperation Council (GCC), which up to the present writing has never demonstrated any political efficacy. (As of 1991, Iran was reserving two seats in Parliament for Bahrain.)

1981 - In return for stepped-up oil supply from the UAE, Portugal announced that the Azores would not be available as a refueling base for the United States Air Force in any future Middle East conflict.

1981 - Saudi Arabia and Bahrain signed a security agreement. (Bahrain is linked to the mainland by a causeway.)

1981 - Egypt sent the United States an item of great intelligence value – a Soviet-made SAM-6 missile battery.

1982 - The one accomplishment of the Israeli invasion of Lebanon (Chapter 8) was the expulsion of the PLO forces from Lebanon to Tunisia. 'Arafat got no backing from the Arabs. Even the Lebanese Sunnis wanted the Palestinians out of Lebanon.

1982 - The Kuwait Parliament voted to end payments to the Syrian peacekeeping force in Lebanon, because of Syria's (temporary) support for the Maronite side in Lebanon, and for Iran versus Iraq.

1982 - A Syrian official called on the Iraqis to oust the Saddam regime.

1982 - In Lebanon, Iran mobilized Shiite rage at the Israeli occupation, and enthusiasm for the new regime in Tehran, to form *Hizballah* (the Party of God), which was to become the most successful paramilitary organization in history.

1984 - Gradual reconciliation between Egypt and Arab governments: visit by a Saudi prince, readmission to the Islamic Conference, resumption of diplomatic relations with Oman, Sudan, Jordan, and the PLO – all over opposition from Syria, Libya, and Iran.

1985 - Hizballah began its metamorphosis from an undercover organization to a political party by issuing a critique of Western policy. However, a TWA hijacking may have been a Hizballah ploy to overshadow its tamer Shiite rival, Amal.

1985 - Qadhafi, again subsidizing the PLO, expelled many Syrian workers from Libya in retaliation for Syrian support for Lebanese Shia in their attacks on Palestinian refugee camps in Lebanon.

1985 - King Husayn visited Hafiz al Asad, their first meeting in six years.

1986 - Syrian TV accused Saddam of directing lethal bombings by the Muslim Brotherhood in Syria.

1986 - Moroccan King Hassan II (Hasan al thani) entertained Israeli Prime Minister Peres. Syria broke relations with Morocco. Under a barrage of Arab criticism, Hassan resigned as chairman of Arab Summit meetings, which had been postponed by Arab disarray, and cancelled Morocco's pro forma treaty of union with Libya.

1987 - The first Arab Summit meeting since 1982. Asad of Syria and Mubarak of Egypt face to face for the first time. By attending, Asad served notice on Iran of Syrian disapproval of the Iranian counterinvasion of Iraq.

1987 - The second Arab Summit of the year authorized resumption of diplomatic relations with Egypt. All League members complied except Syria, Algeria, and Libya. (Oman, Sudan, and Somalia had never broken with Egypt.) The Summit demanded Iranian cease-fire and withdrawal from Iraqi territory. Syria had been sobered by loss of Kuwaiti, Qatari, and UAE financing, and feared losing the Saudi subsidy as well.

1987 - By requesting Soviet protection against Iranian attack on its tankers, Kuwait managed to achieve what Saddam never did: to induce Washington to provide its tankers the protection of the Fifth Fleet (based in Bahrain). The United States had the ancillary objective of reassuring the Arab states after reports of its arms sales to Iran had leaked.

1988 - With heavy reliance on chemical weaponry (some components supplied by American companies), Saddam managed to extract a cease-fire from Iran.

1988 - Syrian troops (already in eastern Lebanon) occupied southern Beirut to end fighting between Amal and Hizballah. Syrian relations with its longtime ally, Iran, were strained because Hizballah, with Iranian backing, was challenging the Shiite primacy of Syria's protégé of the moment, Amal.

1989 - Reconciliation of Syria and Egypt shocked Saddam, who consolidated his alliance with Jordan.

1990 - Yemen and South Yemen proclaimed political union.

1990 - Under economic pressure, and misreading ambiguous signals from Washington, Saddam decided to resolve an oil field dispute with Kuwait and Iraq's historic sense of claustrophobia by annexing Kuwait, and in so doing grasp the standard of Arab Nationalism. Within hours of the invasion, Secretary of State Baker obtained from his Soviet opposite, Shevardnadze, a joint condemnation of the Iraqi action. At the time, Russia was in dire need of American economic support.

1990 - The UNSC voted against the annexation, 15-0 (including Yemen).

1990 - Saddam's offer to withdraw from Kuwait if Syria withdrew from Lebanon, and Israel from the Occupied Territories, was an imaginative concept, but a nonstarter.

1990 - For parochial reasons, most members of the Arab League rallied behind Baker's anti-Iraq coalition, or abstained. Mubarak was particularly effective. Even though Syria did not fire a shot, it was the major beneficiary of the bandwagon (resumption of expanded Arabian subsidies, free hand in Lebanon). Half of Egypt's foreign debt was cancelled. Opposition to the coalition came from Iraq, Yemen, Libya, Tunisia, Algeria, the PLO, and (agonizingly) Jordan – which lost financial aid from America and the oil states and had to absorb hundreds of thousands of Palestinians expelled from the Gulf. Tunisia had been embittered by America's tolerance of the violent Israeli air raid on the PLO headquarters in Tunis in 1985. When Yemen voted against the coalition, Secretary Baker told the Yemeni Representative to the UN "That's the most expensive no-vote you ever cast." US aid to Yemen was cancelled three days later. After the war, Saudi Arabia and the Gulf states expelled up to a million Yemeni workers in retaliation for Yemen's "neutrality", causing Yemen major economic distress. All the Arab Gulf states had security agreements with Saudi Arabia; Iraq had been a more formidable ally versus Iran, but the Gulf states had been alienated from Iraq by its invasion of Kuwait. Hamas opposed both the Iraqi invasion of Kuwait and the American expulsion of the Iraqi forces: *Journal of Palestine Studies,* Spring 2008.

1990 - The Arab League transferred its headquarters from Tunis back to Cairo.

1990 - According to an analysis in *The Nation,* several major powers backed Baker's anti-Iraq coalition out of pragmatism rather than principle. France and Britain feared Washington might retaliate by promoting Germany and Japan as replacements for them on the Security Council. India needed American support for its request for IMF credits. Russia suffered enormous trade losses from the ostracism of Iraq, but it was compensated by six billion dollars in subsidies from the Gulf states, and its ultimate economic dependence was on the US-dominated IMF. Turkey also received financial compensation.

1991 - In reaction to the Iraqi invasion of Kuwait, Iran and Saudi Arabia resumed diplomatic relations.

1991 - In February, American troops expelled the Iraqis from Kuwait, inflicting heavy casualties, and occupied southern Iraq. Arab coalition forces entered Kuwait.

1991 - Fearful of Iran, and now of Iraq as well, the states of the GCC concluded bilateral defense treaties with the United States. The states of the Arabian fringe, which had emerged under British protection (Chapter 10), were now wards of America. A special relationship was developing between the UAE and Oman.

1991 - Under the Damascus Agreement of March 1991, Egyptian and Syrian troops were to have served in the peninsular states as permanent defense forces, but negotiations with Saudi Arabia and Kuwait over financial compensation broke down, and all Egyptian and Syrian troops in the Peninsula were withdrawn.

1991 - Despite the Reagan-Gorbachev détente, the USSR had remained a rival in the Middle East, and posed some inhibition to American freedom of action. This factor in the power equation was largely dissipated in December when the USSR disintegrated.

1992 - After Gulf War I, Jordan became Iraq's window on the world, and a channel for Iraqi evasion of UN sanctions (Chapter 9).

1992 - Saddam renewed the Iraqi claim to Kuwait, "the nineteenth province", and called on larger Arabian states to divide up the other four Gulf states.

1993 - An American air strike on Iraqi missile batteries in southern Iraq drew widespread Arab criticism, even from Syria and Egypt.

1993 - As cited by Adam Shatz in *The London Review of Books,* Paul McGeough's study noted that, by adhering to the Oslo Agreement, 'Arafat had in effect signed on as Israel's policeman in the West Bank.

1994 - War broke out between the armies of Yemen and South Yemen, which had never actually implemented the unity proclamation of 1990. South Yemen, emboldened by subsidies from GCC states (which feared the demographic weight of a united Yemen), declared secession. However, the Yemeni forces of President 'Ali 'Abdallah Salih, reinforced by mujahidin back from the war in Afghanistan, easily put down the rebellion. Reaffirmation of union was a major strategic blow to Saudi Arabia and the other GCC states except maverick Qatar, which had sided with the north.

1994 - In keeping with its policy of staying as close to the United States as possible for a country with compelling ties to Palestine, Jordan became the second Arab state to sign a peace treaty with Israel.

1995(?) - After Qatar had accused Saudi Arabia of supporting a failed coup attempt in Doha, the Amir promoted the founding of Al Jazeera, outspoken TV station.

1996 - The Middle East was in greater disarray than usual. Bahrain, Qatar, the UAE, and Oman favored relaxation of Western sanctions against Iraq, but Kuwait, Saudi Arabia, and Jordan backed a failed BritishAmerican coup attempt against Saddam. There was friction between Syria and Turkey, the Arabian Peninsula and Iran, Egypt and Sudan, Syria and Jordan, Kuwait and Jordan, Syria and the Palestine Authority, and Qatar and Bahrain. However, Syria brokered reconciliation between Amal and Hizballah, which had been at war from 1987 to 1990 and political adversaries thereafter.

1996 - Qatar allowed Israel to open a trade office.

1997 - Allergic to the idea of elections, Saudi Arabia tried to dissuade Yemen from its plan to elect a parliament.

1997 - Syria stopped anti-Saddam broadcasts, reopened the border with Iraq, and signed with Iraq an agreement that helped it evade the UNSC oil embargo.

1997 - Although the GCC states had not established any common currency or joint military force, and its members were caught up in several bilateral disputes, they all favored détente with Iran and Iraq and opposed America's policy of "Dual Containment" of those two states. Qatar had full diplomatic ties with Iraq.

1997 - Syria, Egypt, and Saudi Arabia were losing interest in the American campaign to unseat Saddam.

1997 - The US Navy decided to start refueling some of its ships at Aden (Chapter 12, re USS Cole).

1998 - Overtaking Amal, Hizballah had become the most effective political party in Lebanon.

1998 - America's Operation Desert Fox (four days of bombing targets in Iraq) provoked sharp Arab criticism and international disapproval.

1999 - Media war between Saddam and his Arab adversaries (Saudi Arabia, Egypt, Kuwait). However, since the reopening of the border between Iraq and Syria in 1997, their bilateral relations had warmed. Syrian trucks were bringing Iraqi oil to Damascus, in contravention of UN sanctions.

1999 - Jordan continued its delicate balancing act between the Arabian oil states and Iraq, its natural trading partner and its oil supplier.

1999 - Bashar al Asad had established warm ties with Saudi Arabia and a close relationship with Jordan's King 'Abdallah II.

1999 - Overshadowed by its three big neighbors (Iran, Iraq, and Saudi Arabia), the UAE was building a closer relationship with Oman although, of the two, the UAE was more supportive of Saddam. The UAE was heavily invested in Oman, and Oman had accorded UAE citizens the right to own Omani property. Thousands of Omanis were living in the UAE, many serving in its United Defense Force.

2000 - Credit for harrying Israeli forces out of Lebanon was widely accorded to Hizballah, which had built an impressive network of schools, clinics, hospitals, and rehab centers for war wounded. It had its own TV station and significant representation in Parliament (as did Amal), and it had become the most influential faction among the Shia, who numbered 40 percent of the population of Lebanon. Hizballah's current leader, *Shaykh* Hasan Nasrallah, kept a low profile; Israel had assassinated his two predecessors. Hizballah's main backer, Iran, had provided it up to two billion dollars over the previous twenty years, but Hizballah was thought to oppose conversion of Lebanon to an Islamic republic on the Iranian model. It was cultivating closer ties with the two Palestinian Sunni Islamist organizations, Hamas and Islamic Jihad. Estimates of the size of Hizballah's militia ranged from one to five thousand – much smaller than Lebanon's regular army of 60,000 – but the army, fractured along sectarian lines, was in no position to challenge Hizballah's dominance of south Lebanon. Hizballah's fighters were the only militia not disarmed by the Syrian occupation force.

2000 - Saudi Arabia and Iran signed a security agreement and concerted an OPEC production cut to raise prices.

2000 - Hizballah staged huge demonstrations in support of Intifadah II. According to Egypt's Ahram Center for Political and Strategic Studies, Hizballah had been training Hamas militants for years.

2000 - The October arrival in Baghdad of a high-level Syrian delegation symbolized the rising tide of Arab opposition to Western sanctions on Iraq. Syria reopened the rail line and pipeline to Iraq, which began pumping oil to Syria. Several Arab states resumed commercial flights to Baghdad. Saudi Arabia reopened the border to truck traffic. Bahrain, Oman, Qatar, and the UAE now had diplomatic relations with Iraq. Egypt hosted an Arab Summit, the first that Iraq had attended since the Gulf War. Bahrain, Qatar, and the UAE called for an end to sanctions.

2001 - After the IMF agreed to a request from the Palestine Authority to monitor its revenues and expenditures, Saudi Arabia, Kuwait, the UAE, and other Gulf states began to release funds in accordance with a promised aid package from the Islamic Development Bank. The donor governments' resentment of Palestinian support for Iraq during Gulf War I had been overridden by their constituents' concern for the increasingly desperate plight of the residents of the Occupied Territories. Israel was still withholding $180 million in taxes collected from the territories.

2001 - Egypt, Iraq, Libya, and Syria signed a free trade agreement. The exchange of Iraqi oil for Syrian consumer goods was flourishing. Syria authorized direct flights to Baghdad, in violation of UNSC resolutions.

2001 - The GCC had assembled a joint Peninsula Shield Force, but it still had no common defense strategy.

2001 - On the eve of anticipated American military action against Iraq, Arab regimes were torn between the pragmatic advantages of cooperating with the superpower, and the domestic problem of managing public resentment of Western domination and Arab impotence. Jordan's King 'Abdallah, abandoning the pro-Iraqi tilt adopted by his father in Gulf War I, came down closer to the position of the United States, from which Jordan was receiving $400 million a year. Kuwait was the least anti-American of the Arab countries. Oman was the only Arab state to allow construction of an American base. In a last-ditch effort to avert American invasion, Saudi Arabia promoted a Beirut summit which extracted ostensible recognition of Kuwait by Iraq, on condition of Arab support against American attack. The conferees called for an end to the sanctions, and Saudi Arabia pledged to oppose any American effort to topple the regime in Baghdad. By fall, conciliation had dissipated. Saudi Arabia offered the use of its bases by any assault authorized by the UN, and according to one report, it began to let the United States stage bombing runs against Iraq from Saudi bases. Syria was committed to supporting Hizballah, which Washington regarded as a "terrorist" organization, but Damascus hoped that its valuable cooperation in the campaign against Al Qa'idah would earn it removal from Washington's black-list of "terrorist" states. Yemen was suspected of playing both sides – of signing on to the anti-terrorist campaign and letting the United States use Predator drones to eliminate Al Qa'idah operatives hiding out in Yemen, but taking no anti-Qa'idah actions of its own, and also of buying Scud missiles from North Korea.

2003 - Saddam was reported to have stated that he sought to turn Iraq into a superpower that would liberate Jerusalem, expel the United States, and rule the Middle East.

2003 - The invasion of Iraq in March (Chapter 15) received reluctant but broad Arab regime support: from Egypt, passage for American air and naval units; from Saudi Arabia, no objection to overflight of American missiles; from the Gulf states, full use of Arab bases; from Jordan, staging rights for American Special Forces. Even Iran, hostile to Al Qa'idah, was collaborating with the CIA. The Arab League issued a ritual condemnation of the invasion, but a preinvasion Summit convened by Egypt broke up in the usual inter-Arab recrimination. Bahrain, Kuwait, and the UAE advised Saddam to defuse the crisis by stepping down; Syria/Lebanon and Yemen wanted the Arab League to rally behind Saddam; most members wanted Saddam to meet IAEA demands.

2003 - Gulf War II was costly for Syria, which lost its supply of low-cost oil when Defense Secretary Rumsfeld ordered closure of the Iraq-Syria pipeline – even though Syria was providing valuable intelligence on the operations of Al Qaʻidah and had offered to close the Damascus offices of Hamas and Islamic Jihad.

5/03 - Iranian President Mohammed Khatami received a hero's welcome in Lebanon, where he had close ties with the Shiite leadership.

2003 - The foreign ministers of the 22 members of the Arab League voted unanimously to accord provisional recognition to the US-picked interim government of Iraq, the Iraq Governing Council. Iraq's Interim Foreign Minister Hoshyar Zebari (Kurd) took his seat for a period of one year.

2004 - Although Saudi Arabia was still assuring Washington of its readiness to raise oil production to keep prices in line, the price of crude was fluctuating around 50 dollars a barrel. The transfer of CENTCOM Air Force headquarters from Saudi Arabia's Prince Sultan base to Qatar's Al ʻUdayd base consummated the status of the United States as the primary guarantor of the security of the five Arab gulf states.

2004 - Rich Arab summer-vacationers, put off from travel to the West by intensified security restrictions, were flocking to Lebanon, sparking an economic boom. To insure its continued control, Syria arranged for the Lebanese Parliament to extend the constitutional term of the pro-Syrian President of Lebanon, Amil Lahhud. The United States promoted passage of UNSC Resolution 1559, calling on Syria to withdraw from Lebanon, and on Hizballah (in effect) to disarm. France, the GCC states, and Jordan supported the resolution. China did not favor it, but did not use its veto.

2005 - In March, jubilant demonstrations in Beirut for the withdrawal of Syrian forces and replacement of pro-Syrian Amil Lahhud with a separatist President countered Hizballah's earlier organization of a pro-Syrian demonstration of up to half a million Lebanese. Washington and its Lebanese allies accomplished withdrawal of Syria's garrison from Lebanon, although Syria was still the power behind the scenes.

2005 - Hizballah (unlike Amal) esteemed Khamenei as its *marjiʻ al taqlid* (Chapter 12), but opposed theocracy and favored Arab unity.

2006 - July: In its war with Israel, Hizballah had the immediate endorsement of the governments of Iran, Syria, Lebanon, and Algeria, and the Palestinian organizations in Gaza. At the July 17 Arab League summit (in Cairo), Egypt, Saudi Arabia, Jordan, and some Gulf states chided Hizballah for irresponsibility. Concurrently, Egyptians who protested their government's failure to take a position in support of Hizballah received the usual rough treatment by the police. Once it became clear that Hizballah was holding its own, formerly critical governments scrambled to distance themselves from Washington, and the Arab world was swept by a wave of fervor for Hasan Nasrallah and Hizballah (the first Arab force to have acted expressly on the Palestinians' behalf as well as its own since 1948).

According to Shibley Telhami, Hizballah's performance had sparked a "new Arabism".

2006 - The missiles launched against Israel by Hizballah included a few Fajr-3 (range 30 miles) and Fajr-5 (45 miles) and one C-802, which with the aid of Lebanese Army radar damaged an Israeli warship. They were provided by Syria and Iran. Iranian Revolutionary Guardsmen provided technical guidance.

2006 - According to Juan Cole, the Iraqi Baath had announced a new Secretary General, Dr. Khadir Wahid al Murshidi, but many analysts suspected the real leader was 'Izzat Ibrahim al Duri.

2006 - Saudi King 'Abdallah felt insulted by Bashar al Asad on three counts: the killing of his friend Rafiq al Hariri in 2005, support for Lebanese Shia versus Sunnis, and a reference to Arab leaders who failed to stand up for Hizballah in 2006 as "half men".

2006 - Syria and Iraq resumed diplomatic relations, broken in 1982. (Iraqi Prime Minister al Maliki had spent years in Damascus as head of the Al Da'wah office there.)

2006 - Haaretz.com noted Egypt's failure to stop smuggling of arms into the Gaza Strip, and speculated that Egypt intended to let the Jews and the Palestinians bleed together. Egypt was acquiring impressive military superiority over the other Arab states (with US-supplied arms?).

2006 - Writing in *Foreign Affairs,* Prem Kumar reported that Syria and Iran had formalized their strategic alliance by concluding a mutual defense pact. As the Alawite ruler of a Sunni country, Bashar needed all the backup he could find.

2007 - Qatar invited Ahmadinejad to a GCC summit in Doha.

2007 - *Middle East Policy* reported that, as a counter to Iranian aid to Hizballah, the US, Europe, and the GCC had pledged billions in aid to the government of Lebanon.

2007 - According to *Mother Jones,* Saudi Arabia was fencing its border with Iraq to keep out refugees from the civil war.

2007 - An article in *Middle East Policy* by Kessler and Kattouf reported that Syria had integrated Palestinian refugees into its society to the extent that the Yarmuk refugee camp was more like a neighborhood of Damascus.

2007 - Iraqi DP's in the Arab World were unwelcome unless they were rich. In Lebanon, illegal immigrants had a choice between repatriation and jail.

2008 - Khalid Mish'al of Hamas was backing the Sunni resistance in Iraq, had cordial relations with Qatar, Saudi Arabia, and Turkey, had forged close alliances with Syria and Iran, and supported King 'Abdallah's Palestine peace plan: Adam Shatz, *The London Review of Books.*

2008 - Saudi Arabia sent an ambassador to Qatar, the first in six years. Under orders from the Amir, Al Jazeera had toned down its criticism of the Saudi regime and of the "insurgency" in Iraq, possibly in reaction to the rise of the Shiites.

2008 - Bahrain yielded to American urging by reopening its embassy in Baghdad.

2008 - Under international pressure, Syria finally recognized the Lebanese zone (*qutr*) as an independent state. It also sent an ambassador to Iraq – the first Syrian ambassador in Baghdad in over 20 years.

2008 - King 'Abdallah of Jordan made the first visit by an Arab head of state to post-invasion Baghdad.

2008 - Round Two between Israel and Hamas initially split the Arab League again, until a tide of public exasperation forced holdouts Saudi Arabia, Jordan, and Egypt to change their tune, as they had in 2006 vis-à-vis Hizballah. Egypt had incurred sharp criticism from Arab media for its failure to open the border with Gaza to relieve the supply crisis precipitated by the Israeli blockade. Syria's Bashar al Asad called for the closure of every Israeli embassy in the Arab World. Qatar and Mauretania cut diplomatic and economic ties with Israel. Iranian officials condemned Egypt's refusal to open the border.

2009 - In March, press photos featured Saudi King 'Abdallah's warm welcome for his recent antagonist, Bashar al Asad, beneficiary of mass approbation for standing by beleaguered Hamas. Oman and Qatar further defied Egypt and Saudi Arabia by participating in a pro-Hamas conference in Qatar.

2009 - In *The Middle East Journal* of Spring 2009, Lawrence Pintak cited Al Jazeera (Qatar) and Al 'Arabia (controlled by Saudi interests but broadcast from Dubai) as the two most influential satellite channels in the Arab World.

2009 - In response to an Egyptian accusation that Hizballah had sent agents to smuggle arms into Gaza, attack Israeli tourist sites (Sharm al Shaykh?), and fire on ships in the Suez Canal, Hasan Nasrallah responded that he had sent an agent to Egypt to organize help for the Gazans, not to commit attacks on Egyptian soil, even though the Egyptian authorities were agents of Israel and America: *Times,* 4/14/09.

2009 - John Newhouse wrote in the May *Foreign Affairs* that Saudi King 'Abdallah regarded Iraqi Prime Minister Maliki as an Iranian agent.

2009 - The *Times* of May 16 reported that Iran's size and proximity required Sultan Qabus of Oman to maintain close ties with Tehran. The Omani Governorate of Musandam, at the tip of the rugged Musandam Peninsula, one hour from Iran by speedboat, was a valuable source of products banned under Western sanctions. The boatmen paid taxes and tariffs to Oman, but not to Iran.

2009 - In a July meeting of the Middle East Policy Conference, Helena Cobban said Qatar was bringing in Iraqi technocrats (many of them Baathists from the Saddam era) to replace departing Egyptians.

2009 - Saudi Arabia was sending aid to Yemen at a rate of two billion dollars a year.

2009 - After several days of heavy fighting between Saudi forces and Yemeni Huthis, Saudi Arabia imposed a coastal blockade against smuggling of arms, which, according to Saudi Arabia and Yemen, were coming from Iran.

2009 - The UAE had invested 31 billion dollars in Iraq, more than any other country: *Times*, 11/13/09. Turkey and Iraq had become major trading partners. Since the Shiite takeover in Baghdad, trade with Iran and Syria had increased at the expense of trade with Jordan: *Middle East Report*, Fall 2009.

2009 - Egypt had had no embassy in Iran since 1979. In the Palestinian power struggle, Egypt backed Fatah. Iran backed Hamas: *Middle East Policy*, Winter 2009, Gawdat Bahgat.

4/29/10 – The *Times* reported that Hasan Nasrallah had accused Egypt (meaning Mubarak) of shirking its Arab obligation to help Gaza against Israeli attack in 2008.

Overview

The foregoing tabulation of inter-Arab relations records a hundred years of failure to implement the common interest in Arab comity. Fifty years ago, three unionist movements were on the march: The Arab Nationalist Movement (ANM), the Baath, and Nasirism. The ANM never took power in any state; it survives in the vestigial form of the late George Habash's Popular Front for the Liberation of Palestine (PFLP). Nasirism was consumed in the flames of the 1967 war with Israel. Baathism disintegrated into Syrian and Iraqi parochialism.

Several conclusions emerge:

The Arab League has never played a decisive role in Middle East affairs.

The GCC is equally ineffective. A striking example is the UAE's announcement of its award to an international consortium of a contract to build four nuclear reactors to provide the electric power now fuelled by imported natural gas – even though its next-door neighbor, Qatar, reportedly sits on the world's biggest field of natural gas.

In 2003, American influence over Arab governments was sufficient to nullify the trend toward rehabilitation of the Saddam regime.

Aside from efforts at unification of Syria and Lebanon, and Yemen and South Yemen, the only contemporary manifestation of Arab Nationalism is the proliferation of newspapers and broadcasts with region-wide appeal – notably Al Jazeera satellite television.

Western imperialism had contributed massively to the unionist debacle. The historical record contains numerous instances of opportunistic collusion with Western imperialism.

Recognition of the validity of the unity principle persists – in the lip service paid to it by Arab regimes, in the veneration accorded the memory of Jamal 'Abd al Nasir, in the flag of Baathist Iraq (whose three stars represent the failed union of Egypt, Syria, and Iraq of the 1950's), in the impressive tomb of Syrian Michel 'Aflaq in Baghdad, in the visceral empathy for the Palestinians, and in the obdurate loom of Islamism.

Britain, America, and Israel have no overarching vision for the Middle East – least of all, appreciation of the pressing need for greater regional cooperation. Their policies have been generally myopic, capricious, opportunistic, and inconsistent. As of 2009, the United States supported autonomy for the Kurds in Iraq, but not in Turkey. It cultivated the Shiite leadership in Iraq, but not in Iran or Lebanon. It advocated modernization of Arab society, but clung to alliances of convenience with archaic regimes. It preached democracy, but tried to rig Iraqi elections against a Baathist resurgence or an Islamist victory, and opposed electoral heavyweights in Lebanon and Palestine – Hizballah and Hamas. It tolerated brutal Israeli repression of stateless Palestinians, and then condemned the handcuffed Palestinian Authority for not subduing the inevitable armed resistance. It paid lip service to the "road map" for a two-state solution, but interposed no effective opposition to Israeli colonization of the West Bank, annexation of an inflated Jerusalem and the Golan, cordon around the Palestinian entities envisaged in Prime Minister Barak's "generous offer" of 2000, confiscation of West Bank land west of the Security Barrier, or keeping 1.5 million "liberated" Gazans on lockdown – a situation that presumably gratified the Mubarak government, which already had too many people to feed and police.

If unity works for America (Chapter 1), it should work anywhere else. In the Middle East, American policy has two opportunistic themes: support for Israel, and opposition to Arab unification. It has been arbitrarily grounded on the premise – never questioned, never even examined by policymakers – that unity is forever excluded by irresoluble ethnic and dynastic divisions. In this hidebound spirit, Americans in government and the media seek a security framework that will assure each Arab state of its "territorial integrity" (the sanctimonious term of choice in a 2004 article by two members of The Council on Foreign Relations). For Washington, any challenge to such a framework is unacceptable: In 1990, Iraqi occupation of Kuwait; in 2005, Syrian hegemony over Lebanon; in 200?, universal Arab rapprochement.

Chapter 15
Occupation: American Aims Versus Iraqi Reality

The American occupation of Iraq in 2003 was a clear case of direct imperialism (Chapter 10). It was a quantum leap from the indirect imperialism the United States had previously pursued via its protectorates over several Arab monarchies – notably Kuwait – and its diarchy with Israel.

Motivation

Government habitually relies on pretext to hide its real motives – from the electorate, and sometimes from itself. The professed rationale for the invasion of Iraq was particularly implausible:

"WMD's" - In late 2002, Bush told Americans that Iraq, having expelled the IAEA inspectors, would soon have nuclear weapons that it might well pass on to its Islamist allies in Al Qaʻidah. He was wrong on three counts: 1) The inspectors had been pulled out in 1998 because Clinton was about to bomb targets in Iraq; 2) Iraq had suspended its nuclear-weapons program after Gulf War I. Saddam declined to let the IAEA in on the secret because he wanted Iran to think Iraq was about to become a nuclear power (Duelfer Report of 2004). Bush may have known his accusation was unwarranted; some analysts have cited persuasive evidence that Bush pressured the CIA to produce alarmist intelligence. 3) There was no alliance between secularist Iraq and Islamist Al Qaʻidah, although Washington persuaded many Americans to the contrary. The absence of confirmation of any Saddam-bin Ladin tie was reported to Congress by CIA Director George Tenet and to the NSC by Richard Clarke.

Bush also cited alleged Iraqi possession of biological weapons. He did not mention that the United States had authorized sales of biological precursors to Iraq in the 1980's – in violation of an international convention ratified by Washington in 1972.

"Democratization" - After the American forces failed to find the hypothetical WMD's, Washington switched signals – asserting that its basic motive was to liberate Iraq. Saddam's tyranny was not in question, but the liberation claim was:

1) Sacrificing American lives for good government overseas is not in the President's job description. 2) Washington reportedly rejected an opportunity to support a palace coup against Saddam. 3) Washington's preference for dealing with complaisant autocracies rather than capricious democracies is a matter of public record. America financed the overthrow of an elected Iranian Prime Minister in 1953 (Chapter 4). Deputy Defense Secretary Wolfowitz faulted the Turkish military in 2003 for not intervening to overrule the Parliament's refusal to allow the passage of American ground troops for deployment in Iraq.

What were the Bush Administration's real motives? Copious evidence supports the following elements:

Supremacism - "The National Security Strategy of the United States" (Chapter 1) heralded the towering ambition that imbued Bush 43 foreign policy. It may have reflected a sense that America was emasculated by its failure to oust Saddam in 1991. This attitude was crudely expressed by a neoconservative in 2003: "Every ten years or so, the United States needs to pick up some crappy little country and throw it against the wall, just to show the world we mean business." There was an ancillary intent, in both Gulf wars, to rekindle the morale of the armed forces.

Domestication of the Iraqi Government - A sign in a CPA office in Baghdad listed three objectives: durable peace, representative government, and an Iraq that no longer poses a threat to its neighbors. According to Naomi Klein, American objectives were even more ambitious, in that they envisaged Iraq as a showroom for laissez-faire economics.

Oil - Recent American administrations have been uncomfortable with the conventional strategy of relying on the process of supply and demand. Roosevelt set the precedent of the special relationship – assurance of American access to Saudi oil in return for a guarantee of Saudi security (Chapter 4). In the opinion of several analysts, America invaded Iraq, inter alia, to establish physical control of Iraqi oil fields. (In early 2005,

American troops in Iraq were consuming an average of 1.7 million gallons of fuel per day.)

Military Base - Iraq's central location made it (in the view of many commentators) a base from which the Bush administration intended to control events in the region. The most sardonic expression of this thesis came from novelist John le Carré: "... an old colonial war launched by a clique of war-hungry Judeo-Christian geopolitical fantasists ... who exploited America's post-9/11 psychopathy."

Israel - For the United States, Saddam Husayn posed no serious threat, even as ruler of Iraq and Kuwait combined. For Israel, he was Public Enemy number one: paymaster for the families of Palestinian suicide bombers; the only Arab ruler to have exploded missiles on Israeli soil.

For Israel, the results of Gulf War I were incomplete. In the prosecution of Gulf War II, to minimize domestic opposition, Washington had to avoid any suggestion of joint planning with Israel. However, as noted later by Colin Powell, Anthony Zinni, and professors Mearsheimer and Walt, the circumstantial evidence was formidable:

1. Israel's people and government had long favored the ouster of Saddam.
2. The Bush administration was simultaneously driven by strategic reliance on Israel (Chapter 13), by pressure from the Israeli Government, by pressure from major American Jewish organizations, by the expectation that the pacification of Iraq would open the way to Arab-Israeli peace on Israel's terms, by its hope of reducing the Democrats' traditional lock on a big majority of the Jewish vote, and by the ostensible conviction of Bush 43 and many of his fundamentalist Christian supporters that, since a resurgent Israel would be the precursor of Judgment Day, striking down Israel's enemies was God's work.
3. Many well-known advocates, planners, and principals of the invasion were reported believers that the national interest of the United States and that of Israel are identical. Prominent in their ranks were Undersecretary of State for Arms Control John Bolton, Vice President Cheney, evangelist Jerry Falwell, Undersecretary of Defense for Policy Douglas Feith, David Frum, ORHA Chief Jay Garner, *Weekly Standard* Editor William Kristol, columnist Charles Krauthammer, Richard Perle, former *Commentary* editor Norman Podhoretz, evangelist Pat Robertson, Defense Secretary Donald Rumsfeld, and Deputy Secretary of Defense Paul Wolfowitz. In December 2007 the Krauthammer column made the extravagant

claim that, by deposing Saddam, the US had elimated the risk that his dynasty would "rearm and threaten the world."

Reelection - For every regime, Middle Eastern or American, the primary motivation behind policy is the compulsion to stay in power. This rule is uppermost in the case of initiatives, like the invasion of Iraq, that raise supersensitive issues: military casualties, conscription, and the humiliation of defeat. In this respect, the ultimate architect of American policy in Iraq was Karl Rove. He is credited with the impressive Republican victory in the election of 2004, and his shrewd guidance is widely inferred in the sequential attenuation of the Administration's goals in Iraq, as they were increasingly impeded by Sunni resistance and Shiite recalcitrance.

Chaos? - Maureen Dowd suggested that the leaders of Israel and their closest allies in America (notably Paul Wolfowitz, who for Israeli dove Uri Avnery was "the father of the Iraq war") had so sophisticated an understanding of the Arab World that they could not possibly have swallowed the Bush Administration's democratization fantasy – that they must have anticipated chaos and hoped Israel would profit from it. Potential benefits would be the neutralization of Arab military effectiveness such as two Arab states had mustered in the 1973 war, or the emergence of a de facto state of Iraqi Kurdistan, or better cover for more ethnic cleansing of the West Bank. This hypothesis is plausible, but in the absence of corroborative data, it fails the test of Ockham's razor. The 1982 invasion of Lebanon demonstrated that Israeli readings of Arab politics are not infallible.

Timeline For Occupation

George Bush seems to have come into office resolved to overthrow Saddam Husayn, if only to dispose of the man who allegedly schemed to assassinate Bush the father. The chronology was abrupt:

1/20/01 - Bush was sworn in as the 43rd President. According to former Treasury Secretary Paul O'Neill, the decision to invade Iraq was made at Bush's first cabinet meeting.

2/01 - The media reported that the Bush administration had approved a plan, drafted by the Clinton administration, to fund Iraqi dissident organizations to collect evidence that Saddam was a war criminal.

5/01 - The White House released a report from the Vice President that the invasion of Iraq was essential to insure access to Middle East oil and block the threat of WMD's.

9/11/01 - The Islamist attack on New York and Washington had no known Iraqi participation, but it created a climate of outrage that enabled the Administration to convince most Americans, including irresolute Democratic leaders who should have known better, that the regimes in Kabul and Baghdad should be eliminated.

9/20/01 - Bush reportedly told British Prime Minister Blair that he intended to invade Iraq.

11/01 - American media reported that, under pressure from Cheney, Bush had ordered Rumsfeld to prepare for war with Iraq, and the administration was drawing up plans to privatize Iraqi industry.

Late 2001 - Bush had Defense Secretary Rumsfeld update the standing plan for invasion of Iraq. By yearend, the Administration was drawing up occupation plans. According to a later report by Stephen Walt and John Mearsheimer, the Israeli Government was playing a key role in advocating invasion.

1/29/02 - State of the Union address: Bush warned of an "axis of evil" – North Korea, Iran, and Iraq.

2/02 - General Tommy Franks reportedly told Senator Bob Graham military resources needed in Afghanistan were being shifted for use in invading Iraq.

6/02 - Cheney spoke to the Veterans of Foreign Wars about the benefits that would accrue from the ouster of Saddam.

7/02 - According to Jonathan Freedland, National Security Adviser Rice told the State Department's Richard Haass "The President has made up his mind."

7/02 - In July 2003, the *Times* reported that the US Air Force was using alleged Iraqi violations of the No-Fly Zones as a pretext for conducting attacks on Iraqi defenses.

2002 - Kurdish leaders Mas'ud Barzani and Jalal Talabani were brought to Washington to plan military training of Kurds in the KAR.

7/23/02 - At a meeting of British officials in London (summarized in "the Downing Street Memo"), the head of British intelligence said US intelligence on Iraqi intentions was being "fixed around" Bush 43's decision to oust Saddam: *Vanity Fair,* February 2009.

8/02 - Douglas Feith of DOD, close to Israel's Likud, set up an office to look for anti-Saddam intelligence the Intelligence Community might have missed.

9/12/02 - Bush alerted the UN Security Council to Washington's intention to act alone if the Council did not move to insure Iraq had no WMD's.

10/10-11/02 - Congress authorized Bush to attack Iraq (by 77 votes in the Senate, 296 in the House). The vote was predicated on erroneous intelligence reporting on the status of Iraq's WMD program.

11/8/02 - UNSC Resolution 1441 declared Iraq in material breach of the Council's prior resolutions, set up a new WMD inspection regime, and warned of "serious consequences" if Iraq did not prove it had disarmed. By authorizing UNMOVIC (UN Monitoring, Verification, and Inspection Commission) (for chemical and biological inspections), and the IAEA (for nuclear inspections) to establish zones off limits to Iraqi military action, the Council took a step toward legalizing the two No-Fly Zones imposed by America and Britain (Chapter 9). Bush interpreted 1441 as an authorization to go to war.

11/13/02 - Iraq agreed to comply with Resolution 1441, and denied it had WMD's.

1/20/03 - Bush signed National Security Presidential Directive 24 setting up the Office of Reconstruction and Humanitarian Assistance (ORHA) in the Department of Defense to run post-invasion Iraq, under the direction of retired Lieutenant General Jay Garner.

1/31/03 - Bush and Blair agreed on March 10 as the date to initiate the attack: *Vanity Fair.*

2/26/03 - Washington sponsored the first meeting of Iraqi dissidents on Iraqi soil (the KAR) in nearly ten years.

3/19/03 - **Invasion:** The United States launched Operation Freedom with air attacks on Baghdad.

3/21/03 - American ground troops invaded Iraq from Kuwait.

3/03 - Kurdish militia (Pesh Merga) rose in the north, and in combination with US Special Forces overran villages controlled by Ansar al Islam (Chapter 12) along the Iranian border. According to Vali Nasr, Grand Ayatallah 'Ali al Sistani instructed his following not to resist the American invasion. His farseeing goal was to seize the opportunity for a historic transfer of power from the Sunnis to the Shia – making Iraq the first Arab state in modern times to be under mainstream Shiite rule. During the occupation, he never met with the Americans, leaving that function to his son.

3/28/03 - The UNSC authorized the UN Secretary General to take over the management of the Oil-for-Food Program.

4/9/03 - The fall of Baghdad precipitated two months of unrestrained looting, arson, and theft of irreplaceable antiquities, undermining the Iraqis' confidence in the competence of the occupation forces. (In 2007, *The Nation* cited Ambassador Barbara Bodine as its source for the report that the American forces in Iraq were instructed by Washington not to interfere with the looters.) The turmoil may have been exacerbated by a highly organized resistance operation to seize especially valuable equipment.

4/03 - American forces blew up the pipeline linking northern Iraqi oilfields to Syrian ports.

4/03 - Ayatallah 'Abd al Majid al Khu'i, flown into Iraq by the Americans, was hacked to death in Najaf.

4/10/03 - The US Army and the Pesh Merga captured Kirkuk. Arabs fled, as Kurds looted.

4/13/03 - Washington announced that retired Lieutenant General Jay Garner was the head of ORHA, whose mission was to guide Iraq to self-rule.

4/14/03 - Coalition Forces declared victory, after 26 days of combat.

4/16/03 - General Franks outlawed the Baath Party of Iraq (BPI).

4/20/03 - Despite the widespread Iraqi desire for early withdrawal of the Coalition Forces, Washington was planning to establish four permanent military bases.

4/21/03 - Press report: Garner was to be replaced by L. Paul Bremer, who would head a Coalition Provisional Authority (CPA) – the interim government of Iraq. Washington did not explain the abrupt shift, but observers considered it a tacit admission that the situation in Iraq had already gotten out of American control.

4/27/03 - Skirmishes in Mawsil between Arabs and Kurds. US forces disarming Turkmen militia in Kirkuk.

4/28-30 - US troops fired on demonstrators in Fallujah, killing thirteen.

4/03 - Mass flight of Iraqi refugees to Jordan.

5/1/03 - Bush announced the end of major combat in Iraq, "one victory in a war on terrorism." The armor of the Republican Guard had been largely destroyed. Most Iraqi soldiers had deserted. The White House picture of the President, having just landed in pilot gear on the deck of the USS Abraham Lincoln, conveyed the image of a man who, despite his never having seen combat, took pride in his role as a war president.

5/6/03 - Bush designated Bremer a Presidential Envoy. As a retired Foreign Service Officer, he would be a civilian administrator, but he would supervise ORHA Chief Garner (sic) and report to the Secretary of Defense. Bremer had been a consultant to Kissinger Associates, which continued to exert great influence on the foreign policy establishment from behind the scenes. He was close to Rumsfeld, Wolfowitz, and other neoconservatives.

5/8/03 - The criminal courts in Baghdad resumed operation.

5/11/03 - American-sponsored exiles organized an Interim Iraqi National Assembly.

5/13/03 - Bremer arrived in Iraq. Garner and the ORHA team prepared to leave. The impromptu transfer of authority was tacit recognition of the Coalition's failure to replace the defunct Saddam regime with an effective civil administration; public services were shattered; security was breaking down. The Bremer appointment had been the compromise product of bitter infighting between the Departments of State and Defense.

5/16/03 - A Bremer directive banned higher-level members of the BPI from positions in the new Iraqi government.

5/16/03 - Bremer had ordered that a pro-Iranian Shiite militia force, the Badr Brigade, be disarmed. (The directive was not implemented.) The Kurdish militia were not to be disarmed.

5/22/03 - UNSC Resolution 1483 lifted the sanctions on Iraq and assigned the United States and Britain responsibility for running Iraqi affairs, subject to consultation with the Secretary General's Special Representative (Algerian diplomat Lakhdar Brahimi). The Oil-for-Food Program was to be phased out over six months. Iraq's foreign debt was to be rescheduled. The British-American "Occupying Authority" was to administer oil revenues for the benefit of the people of Iraq. Resolution 1483 empowered the CPA to disburse Iraqi oil revenues, subject to international audit (which was never conducted).

5/22/03 - Bremer informed Bush he planned to dissolve Saddam's military and intelligence structures.

5/23/03 - In consultation with Wolfowitz and Feith, but against Garner's recommendation, Bremer disbanded the Iraqi army and cancelled its pensions, throwing hundreds of thousands of soldiers out of work. He also expelled the top four levels of BPI membership from government service, and dissolved the Republican Guard and the Ministries of Information and Defense.

5/24/03 - The Iraqi oil infrastructure had been so badly damaged that production was down from the prewar two million barrels a day to 300,000. The American military was trucking product from Kuwait.

5/29/03 - The Coalition Forces had held municipal elections in a few Iraqi cities. The result in the disputed city of Kirkuk was a Kurdish mayor and a city council with a Kurdish majority.

6/1/03 - In the seven weeks since the capture of Baghdad, Iraq had become a free-trade zone, with immediate termination of the protective tariffs on which Iraqi industry had depended.

6/03 - Mass Shiite protests foiled a British effort to set up an interim governing council in southern Iraq. SCIRI (Chapter 9) promised to boycott any council appointed by Bremer. Sistani and Mas'ud Barzani (Kurd) called for the election of a constituent assembly.

6/03 - General John Abizaid took over command of CENTCOM.

6/24/03 - Recognizing that disbandment of the army had been a costly error, the CPA offered to resume paying 370,000 conscripts and 250,000 officers. Not all those eligible accepted the offer.

6/26/03 - Sistani issued a fatwa demanding general elections for a constituent assembly and a referendum on the draft constitution.

7/13/03 - Bremer and Sistani having finally reached an accord, the Iraq Governing Council (IGC) held its inaugural meeting. Of its 25 members, 13 were Shia, representing all the major Shiite factions except that of Muqtada al Sadr. All had been handpicked by the CPA. In *The Middle East Journal* of Spring 2008, Adeed Dawisha noted that, up until the first American invasion in 1991, most Iraqi political parties had taken an Iraqi nationalist stance, but the anti-Baath uprising incited by Bush 41 in 1991 had compelled Saddam to enhance the Sunni character of his regime, and in 2003 the Coalition Authority had exacerbated the sectarian switch by its ethnic assignments of slots in the IGC. Of the 275 seats in the National Assembly filled by the election of December 2005, 250 were on the basis of community.

7/22/03 - US forces killed Saddam's sons, Uday and Qusay.

7/03 - Although the CPA had included the leader of SCIRI in the IGC, they feared that SCIRI was too close to the government of Iran. They cancelled plans for an election in Najaf for fear SCIRI would win, and they raided SCIRI headquarters and carted off its files.

7/30/03 - The IGC agreed to rotate its presidency monthly among its 25 members.

8/03 - Bremer undertook to create a National Defense Force, a Civil Defense Corps, and ancillary security services, and to reactivate the Iraqi police force.

8/7/03 - Jordan Embassy in Baghdad bombed (by Zarqawi?).

8/14/03 - UNSC Resolution 1500 welcomed the formation of the IGC.

8/18/03 - UN Headquarters in Baghdad bombed (Zarqawi?). Vieira De Mello killed.

8/29/03 - Ayatallah Muhammad Baqir al Hakim, like Sistani a supporter of the IGC and an advocate of staying out of the battle between the resistance and the CPA, died in a bombing (Zarqawi?) near the Shrine of Imam 'Ali, one of the two holiest sites in Shiite Islam. In 2003, *Middle East Policy* reported that Khomeini had designated Muhammad Baqir al Hakim as the future leader of the Islamic republic of Iraq. Christopher de Bellaigue cited Muhammad Baqir's faction (SCIRI) as the CPA's principal interlocutor in Iraq. He was succeeded by his brother, 'Abd al 'Aziz al Hakim, a member of the IGC.

9/1/03 - The IGC appointed an interim cabinet of 25, whose ethnic distribution matched that of the IGC.

9/19/03 - The CPA privatized 200 state companies. Foreign firms began moving into Iraq.

9/21/03 - The Iraqi Interim Minister of Finance announced a law (drafted by the CPA) allowing foreign investors to own up to 100 percent of any asset except oil enterprises and real estate. (The law would threaten some Iraqi industries.)

10/16/03 - UNSC Resolution 1511 conferred a mandate on the CPA to rule Iraq until an indigenous government was formed, but no later than December 31, 2005. It set a December 15, 2003, deadline for the IGC to lay out a timetable for drafting a constitution and setting up a democratic government in Iraq.

Fall 2003 - Although the CPA was constrained by Washington's quixotic promise to democratize Iraq, reaffirmed by Resolution 1511, its more pragmatic concern was to block a Shiite theocracy. To this end, it announced a plan to select the members of an interim government via regional caucuses (an American contrivance never tried in the Middle East). Sistani rejected the scheme.

11/15/03 - As reported by Thomas Ricks, after consultations in Washington with Rumsfeld, Rice, and Bush, Bremer announced that the US would hand over power to the Iraqi authorities by the end of June 2004. (The elaborate plans for an American occupation of several years had been abandoned. Apparently Washington had realized that, since the ideologues were losing control in Iraq, the time had come for radical lowering of the American profile, to avoid adverse consequences for the Republican ticket in November 2004.)

11/29/03 - The CPA had set up 88 neighborhood councils, nine district councils, and one city council, whose members were modestly compensated by the CPA but had no authority and no budgets.

12/13/03 - US forces captured Saddam near his hometown of Tikrit.

12/29/03 - The IGC replaced the Baathist civil code with one based on Islamic law, to be administered by Shia and Sunni clerics. Women's rights were attenuated.

1/04 - By staging huge Shiite demonstrations, Sistani intimidated the CPA into accepting his fatwa blocking plans for CPA appointment of an interim government.

2/04 - The Association of Muslim Clerics (Sunni) came out against the proposed election.

3/8/04 - The IGC endorsed the Transitional Administrative Law (TAL), an interim constitution drafted by the CPA. It guarded Kurdish autonomy and restricted Shite ambitions, by setting up a Presidential Council of three (one Kurd) and stipulating that any three provinces (the KAR encompassed three of Iraq's eighteen) could veto a final constitution by two-thirds majority of the popular vote. The Shia delegates to the IGC signed under protest. Bremer tried to get around the Geneva-Convention prohibition against changing the law of an occupied territory by inserting into the TAL Article 26, which stated that the CPA's edicts would remain in force after the transfer of authority. The TAL provided for the general election of a constituent assembly by January 31, 2005. Sistani had compromised on the postponement of the general elections, for fear of a civil war.

3/24/04 - US Marines took over control of the Fallujah area from the 82nd Airborne.

3/26/04 - Bremer had issued an executive order specifying that, after the transfer of sovereignty, operational control of the Iraqi armed forces would rest with the American Commander in Iraq, Lt. General Ricardo Sanchez, in accordance with UNSC Resolution 1511. Bremer granted Americans on duty for private contractors immunity from Iraqi law: *Times*, 11/11/09. (Blackwater personnel on trial for the Nisur Square shooting of 9/16/07 cited this exemption.)

3/26/04 - Armed resistance erupted in Al Fallujah. On 3/31, four Blackwater contractors were killed.

3-4/04 - By ordering the closure of *Al Hawzah*, the newspaper of Muqtada al Sadr (who had been agitating behind the scenes, possibly with Iranian encouragement), and the arrest of several of his aides, the CPA precipitated a Shiite resistance effort by Sadr's JAM. Under American attack, Sadr's forces took cover in the holy cities of Najaf and Karbala'. After heavy fighting and considerable damage to the neighborhoods of the shrines, Sistani arranged mutual withdrawal of the two opposing forces – the JAM still carrying its weapons. Sistani had reaffirmed his status as the leader of the Shiite sect. Sadr had burnished his image as the warrior who had challenged the occupiers and condemned their Iraqi representatives, the CPA-appointed government.

4/5/04 - Marines launched an attack on Fallujah, but aborted it on 4/28 after allied Iraqi forces had disengaged.

4/16/04 - Bush and Blair accepted the plan of Secretary General Annan's Representative, Lakhdar Brahimi, for the transfer of sovereignty to an Iraqi caretaker government on June 30. The Sistani faction was looking to the general election of January 2005 to defeat the Kurds' campaign for autonomy.

5/04 - Zarqawi's AQI beheaded Nicholas Berg, abducted American contractor.

5/2/04 - The Interim President of the new Iraq was to be Ghazi al Yawar, Sunni, a member of the influential Shammar tribe. Sistani had blocked Bremer's unimaginative choice, 'Adnan Pachachi, whose last official position had been with the British-backed monarchy in 1958.

5/04 - Robert Woodward's *Plan of Attack* (2008) revealed that American foreign policy was being directed by Cheney, Wolfowitz, and Feith.

5/24/04 - The CPA had introduced a flat income tax.

5/28/04 - The Interim Prime Minister would be Iyad 'Allawi, Shiite, one-time associate of Saddam, later head of the Iraqi National Accord, a secularist Arab exile group long financed by the CIA.

6/1/04 - The CPA and the IGC announced the composition of the upcoming interim government. It would include President Yawar, two Deputy Presidents (one Shiite, one Kurd), Prime Minister 'Allawi, five ministers of state, and twenty-six ministers of portfolio. The IGC was to expire at time of transfer of authority.

6/8/04 - UNSC Resolution 1546 authorized the transfer of "full sovereignty" by June 30. 1546 had been meticulously drafted to downplay two awkward facts: 1) The invasion of Iraq had been an unauthorized, unilateral American action. Two months had elapsed before Washington had brought the conflicted Security Council on board (its Resolution 1483 of May 22, 2003). 2) The "sovereign Interim Government of Iraq" was to be the creature of the CPA. Responsibility for the physical security of its Prime Minister was to be assigned to American bodyguards, and its survival was to depend on American military suppression of the resistance. Under 1546, the UNSC agreed that the UN Assistance Mission for Iraq (established August 14, 2003; cut back sharply after the bombing of UN headquarters in Baghdad August 18, 2003) would play a leading role in facilitating the emergence of "a federal, democratic, pluralist and unified Iraq." Under pressure from Sistani, Washington had drafted 1546 to omit any mention of the TAL. To mollify the Kurds, 'Allawi agreed to keep the TAL in force, pending a ruling by the government to be elected in 2005. The Coalition Forces, identified in 1546 as the "multinational force", were to remain in Iraq (under American command) for an unspecified time.

6/27/04 - Bremer's Executive Order Number 9 authorized the Coalition Forces to appropriate property as needed, notably for American headquarters and embassy in Baghdad's "Green Zone".

6/28/04 - Two days ahead of the Resolution 1546 deadline (a security precaution), the CPA transferred pro forma sovereignty to the Interim Government, and then dissolved itself. Bremer left Iraq. Saddam's former

"Republican Palace" was to become the American Embassy. Bremer had prevailed on 'Allawi to honor CPA edicts favoring foreign investment, but the concession was academic: The resistance had destroyed the investment climate.

6/04 - Muqtada al Sadr arranged a prisoner exchange with 'Allawi's security forces and ordered his militia to go home. They remained the de facto government and police force in Sadr City. Sadr adopted a more conciliatory tone vis-à-vis the Interim Government.

6/29/04 - Ambassador John Negroponte presented his credentials to the leaders of the Interim Government (Yawar and 'Allawi).

7/1/04 - General George Casey replaced Lt. General Ricardo Sanchez as commander of the Coalition Forces. By this time, the American effort to stabilize, pacify, and democratize Iraq had been blocked by the automatic resentment that all people feel for alien rule, exacerbated by the innate perversity of the country's demographic make-up: In the center, the occupiers were wrestling with a recalcitrant Sunni-Shia mix; in the south, the British were trying to keep the lid on Shiite factionalism; in the north, the Kurds were moving fast to exploit their sudden autonomy.

7/6/04 - 'Allawi signed the National Security Law, which gave him emergency powers.

7/04 - The CPA was setting up an Iraqi Special Tribunal under the direction of a nephew of Ahmad Chalabi.

8/04 - There was a second clash in Najaf between US and Sadrist forces.

8/04 - With CPA help, the Interim Government convened a National Conference of 100 and a Consultative Conference of 1000. Neither produced operational results.

10/04 - General David Petraeus published an op-ed claiming that "tangible progress" had been made in Iraq. Paul Krugman suggested it was timed to help the administration in the November election.

11/22/04 - Industrial states cancelled 80 percent of the 39 billion dollars they were owed by Iraq. Debts totaling over 100 billion dollars to Middle East states were still outstanding.

11/8-18/04 - Concluding that Fallujah was the nerve center of the resistance, the Coalition Forces (American with some help from Kurd and Shiite forces of the Interim Government) conducted a massive offensive against the city, leaving it a shambles, depopulated except for a few hundred resisters hiding out in the rubble. Sistani stood aside (as if defense of Sunnis is not a Shiite concern). Naomi Klein has noted that the Fallujah operation contributed to the alienation of the Sunni community, whose general abstention from the January 2005 election was to leave the Transitional Government under the control of the Shia and the Kurds.

12/14/04 - Bush awarded the nation's highest civilian decoration, the Medal of Freedom, to three dubious recipients: Paul Bremer, Tommy Franks, and George Tenet.

1/30/05 - Per Resolution 1546, the election for a 275-member Transitional National Assembly (TNA) was held, under extreme security. In the words of Mark Danner, it was an "ethnic census", not a democratic procedure. The results were unrepresentative, because most Sunnis and many Sadrists had boycotted it, allowing SCIRI to win forty percent of the vote in Baghdad and take control of six of the eight Shia-majority provinces in the south.

2/05 - The first of a wave of Shiite revenge killings of BPI leaders.

4/05 - The CPA abandoned its campaign to privatize Iraqi industry.

4/7-8/05 - After two months of altercation, the TNA elected – per the TAL of March 8, 2004 – the leaders of the Transitional Government: Prime Minister Ibrahim al Ja'fari (Shiite Arab), President Jalal Talabani (Sunni Kurd), Vice President Ghazi al Yawar (Sunni Arab), Vice President 'Adil 'Abd al Mahdi (Shiite Arab), and Speaker Hajim al Hasani (Sunni Turkmen). The TNA took no action on basic constitutional issues. Election of a permanent government was scheduled by December 31, 2005.

4/05 - The designation of Bayan Sulagh (Bayan Jabr), Shiite Turkmen, former officer of the Badr Brigade, as Minister of the Interior coincided with the emergence of anti-Sunni death squads: Ken Silverstein.

5/05 - The Transitional Government of Prime Minister Ibrahim al Ja'fari was sworn in. Basic constitutional issues continued to divide the three main ethnic factions.

5/05 - In an unsuccessful attempt to end the Iraqi resistance, the American occupation forces instituted the Israeli practice of targeted assassination of resistance leaders: *Newsweek,* Michael Hirsch and John Barry, 5/14/05, cited in *Middle East Policy* of Fall 2008.

6/13/05 - The Kurdish "National Assembly" elected Mas'ud Barzani President of Kurdistan and Commander in Chief of its armed forces.

7/05 - In Tehran, Ja'fari signed an agreement for major Iranian military and economic aid.

8/05 - The new Iraqi army was being organized by sect: 60 Shiite battalions, 50 Sunni, 10 Kurd (in addition to the Pesh Merga?).

8/05 - US prisons in Iraq were holding 40,000 Islamist, Sunni, and Sadrist militants.

8/05 - The media began to report on a draft constitution. It reportedly required a two-thirds vote in Parliament to form a government. According to *The Middle East Report* of Winter 2005, most Sunni factions, including the Iraqi Islamic Party and the Association of Muslim Scholars, were distressed that the draft called for de-Baathification and federalism, and omitted reference to non-Arab Iraqis in the specification that "the Arab people of Iraq are part of the Arab nation." Defenders of the draft said it protected Sunni interests by providing for per-capita division of oil revenues. In *The New York Review of Books* of 10/6/05, Peter Galbraith reported that Condoleeza Rice had required the Shia and Kurds to accept Sunnis in the drafting process, but the views of the Sunni team, dominated by Baathists chosen by Salih al Mutlaq, had been overruled in favor of a draft slanted to produce three autonomous entities – one Sunni, one Kurdish, and one Shia under Iranian influence. A federal regime would control foreign affairs, defense, and economic affairs other than taxation, but other matters, including newly discovered oil, would be reserved for the regional governments. According to the *Times* of 12/29/05, the draft constitution provided for a referendum on whether Kirkuk's province should come under the administration of Baghdad or the KRG. The May 2007 *Atlantic* reported that, if ten percent of residents of any of the three provinces adjoining the KAR (Ninawah, Ta'mim, Diyala) should petition to join the KAR, a referendum would be held to decide the issue.

10/15/05 - In *Current History* of January 2006, Phoebe Marr reported that the TNA had ratified the draft constitution. Formation of a government would require a two-thirds majority vote in Parliament. Vali Nasr detected the influence of Sistani in the provision that no law should contradict the tenets of Islamic jurisprudence, although in Nasr's view the Shia revival was open to democratic change. According to Joost Hilterman, Article 140 set a deadline of 12/31/07 for a plebiscite on the future disposition of Kirkuk. (As of mid-2010, no plebiscite had been held.) In Hilterman's opinion, the constitution gutted the power of the central government.

9/05 - Zarqawi "declared war" against "collaborators," meaning Shiites, excepting Sadrists.

10/05 - Peter Galbraith: A war between Sunni and Shiite death squads was breaking out in Baghdad. Mark Danner: The Sunni Islamist aim was to spark sectarian war that would draw in Sunni forces from neighboring countries. Killings were also reported in Basrah.

11/8/05 - At the request of Prime Minister Ja'fari, the UNSC extended the mandate of the multilateral force until 12/31/06.

12/15/05 - The United Iraqi Alliance (SCIRI, Al Da'wah, Sadrists) won a near majority of the 275 seats in the new Parliament. Peter Galbraith reported in *The New Yorker* that the Kurds had won the right to their own oil, their own army, and their own law. Muqtada Sadr failed to win Sunnis over to an anti-American Shia-Sunni bloc: Juan Cole. According to Nasr,

American Ambassador Khalilzad warned the Alliance that exclusion of Sunnis from the next government could mean loss of American financial aid.

1/06 - Clashes in northern Iraq between Kurds and a combine of Arab and Turkmen forces.

1/7/06 - The *Times* reported clashes between AQI and Sunni resisters, alienated by AQI's strategy of ethnic cleansing of Shiites.

2/16/06 - Parliament confirmed Ibrahim al Ja'fari as Prime Minister after he promised Sadr he would oppose a federal system and Kurdish takeover of Kirkuk, and support a timetable for the withdrawal of American troops.

2/22/06 - By destroying the Golden Dome of Samarra's 'Askariyyah Mosque, site of the tombs of the tenth and eleventh Imams, AQI finally achieved its objective of sectarian civil war. In the ensuing religious frenzy, Sadr lost control of many of his Shite militants, who revere their shrines as devoutly as Salafists hate them.

4/6/06 - Patrick Cockburn reported in *The London Review of Books* that Article 140 of the new Iraqi constitution provided for returning Kirkuk to its demographic status before Saddam's expulsion of over 100,000 Kurds and their replacement with Arab settlers from south Iraq.

4/06 - Thousands of Iraqis were fleeing from homes in ethnically mixed neighborhoods.

5/06 - Nuri al Maliki replaced Ja'fari as Prime Minister. Maliki had spent most of his exile, not in Iran, but as director of the SCIRI office in Damascus. He was a follower of Lebanese cleric Muhammad Husayn Fadlallah (not Ayatallah Sistani who, according to Juan Cole, was closer to the tamer Amal). At Sunni insistence, Bayan Sulagh lost the ministry of interior and went to the ministry of finance.

5/20/06 - Swearing in of a new cabinet of 37: 20 Shiites, 8 Sunni Arabs, 8 Kurds, 1 Christian. Three of the 37 were women.

6/8/06 - The US military killed Zarqawi and some of his aides.

6/06 - Sectarian violence still escalating. Sabotage of the oil pipelines from Iraq to Turkey came to a stop.

7/11/06 - Militiamen in black were roaming some Baghdad neighborhoods, killing Sunnis on the spot.

8/11/06 - Juan Cole Blog: Clashes in Basrah between followers of Ayatallah Mustafa al Ya'qubi of Najaf and those of Sayyid Mahmud al Sarkhi of Karbala'. The pro-Sarkhi faction reacted to criticism of their leader in the Iranian press by burning the Iranian consulate.

8/19/06 - The Jordanian ambassador, first Arab envoy to post-invasion Iraq, presented his credentials, but no embassy was opened (?). An Egyptian ambassador was abducted and killed a month after his arrival: *Middle East Policy*, Winter 2009, Gawdat Bahgat.

8/06 - To reduce the risk of confrontation with Turkey over Kurdish autonomy, the State Department appointed General Joseph Ralston as a special envoy to assist Iraq and Turkey in suppressing PKK activity in the KAR.

Summer 2006 - The non-Iraqi Arabs leading AQI, which had been in league with the Mashhadani tribe, made a fatal error of trying to impose a reign of terror, marked by torture, imprisonment, summary executions, beheadings, and fanatic Islamism (veils, no smoking) in viscerally tribal Anbar Province. As reported by Patrick Cockburn in *Muqtada*, by Ahmad Hashim in *Current History*, and by Pepe Escobar in *Asia Times Online*, AQI's proclamation of an "Islamic State of Iraq" was the last straw. Caught between the Shia and AQI, Sunni tribes joined in formation of the Anbar Sovereignty Council (later called *Al Sahwah*, The Awakening, by the Anbaris; "Concerned Local Citizens" by the Americans). The organization's aim was to shut down AQI (and later to deal with the Shia leadership in Baghdad).

Summer 2006 - The sectarian battle of Baghdad ended with three-fourths of the city under Shiite control.

9/06 - Looking for financial and military help against the AQI and the Shia, the tribal leaders of the resistance approached Marine officers in Anbar Province, and offered to change sides. Petraeus followed the previous examples of the British and Saddam in putting tribal militants, both Sunnis and Shiites, on salary (approximately 300 dollars a month).

9/1/06 - KAR President Mas'ud Barzani ordered that the Kurdish flag be flown in place of the Iraqi flag. New international airports in Irbil and Sulaymaniyyah offered direct flights to foreign destinations. KAR society was more liberal than the rest of Iraq. It was enjoying a building boom.

9/9/06 - First audio message from Abu Hamzah al Muhajir (Abu Ayyub al Masri), reputed successor to Zarqawi as head of AQI. Thought to be an Egyptian explosives expert trained by Al Qa'idah in Afghanistan.

10/11/06 - Over the objections of Sunnis and some Shiites, Parliament adopted a law providing for each of Iraq's provinces to hold a referendum offering two choices: a unified state or a federation of autonomous regions.

10/16/06 - Report that the US military was building two bases in the KAR.

10/18/06 - *Reuters:* Iraq had an unemployment rate of 60% and inflation of 70%.

11/06 - Suspecting that Prime Minister Maliki had become an American puppet, thirty Sadrist MP's walked out, leaving Parliament unable to muster a quorum. (They were back by June 2007.)

11/06 - The administration's failure to pacify Iraq produced a Democratic victory in the congressional elections. Bush replaced Rumsfeld with Robert Gates.

12/06 - The US had hoped to keep the trial of Saddam under strict control – in part to exclude any mention of Washington's authorization of the sale of anthrax and botulinum to Iraq for use against Iran in the 1980's: *The New York Times Magazine* – but Saddam was hanged by the embittered Shiite government in a manner more like a revenge killing than a judicial procedure.

12/6/06 - The Iraq Study Group (Baker and Hamilton) issued a gloomy estimate of the prospects of the US occupation of Iraq, which was in the throes of intense sectarian warfare, with some neighborhoods of Baghdad, per Juan Cole's blog, already depopulated of Sunnis. The ISG report was a thinly veiled indictment of Bush's foreign policy.

2007 - The Spring issue of *Middle East Report* stated that the Transitional Administrative Law promoted by the occupation authority enshrined ethnic divisions, including a "Shiastan" of the nine southern provinces.

1/10/07 - Surprise announcement by Bush that he would send 20,000 reinforcements to Iraq (characterized in the media as "the surge").

2/07 - Two Sadrists, former officials of the Ministry of Health, were arrested on charges of organizing the murders of hundreds of Sunni staff, patients, and visiting relatives in Baghdad hospitals.

2/14/07 - US officials and the Maliki Government instituted the Baghdad Security Plan.

3/28/07 - At the 19th Arab League summit, King 'Abdallah of Saudi Arabia pronounced the occupation of Iraq illegal.

4/07 - Over 200 Sunni tribal leaders in Anbar Province agreed to form the Iraqi Awakening (Sahwah) Party to oppose the "insurgency". Also known as The Anbar Sovereignty Council (ASC).

4/16/07 - Sadr withdrew his six ministers from the government in protest against Maliki's failure to set a date for withdrawal of the American troops.

5/07 - According to Pepe Escobar, control of Anbar Province was split between the ASC, headed by Shaykh 'Abd al Sattar Abu Rishah, and AQI, headed by Abu 'Umar al Baghdadi and Abu Hamzah al Muhajir.

5/07 - Amid emerging confrontation between Iraqi unionists and federalists, Muqtada appealed for a united Shia-Sunni front.

5/07 - The oil pipelines from Kirkuk to the Mediterranean were inoperative (sabotaged by the resistance).

6/07 - SCIRI changed its name to the Islamic Supreme Iraqi Council (ISCI).

6-9/07 - During this four-month period, four associates of Sistani were shot.

7/07 - In a video appearance, Zawahiri (Al Qa'idah) warned AQI to work for Sunni unity.

7/10/07 - The Green Zone, hideout of the American leadership and the Iraqi Government, was hit by projectiles – probably fired from Sadr City – that killed three, including one American and one member of Parliament, and wounded 22 MP's: *Times,* 2/26/09.

8/07 - Tawafuq, the main Sunni bloc in Parliament, withdrew its fifteen ministers from the Maliki Government. (*Tawafuq* is variously translated in the media as Accord, Consensus, or Dialogue.)

8/07 - The KRG Parliament enacted an oil law.

8/20/07 - Clashes between Sadr's JAM and the Badr Force led to 51 deaths in Karbala'. Two ISCI provincial governors had also been killed.

8/28/07 - Maliki announced agreement to the reinstatement of all but senior Baathists in jobs they had held in the Saddam Government.

8/29/07 - Sadr ordered his JAM to freeze its activities for six months. Outside observers inferred that casualties inflicted on JAM by ISCI's Badr Force, and/or by Maliki's "governmental" forces, with American air support, had decided Sadr to wait out the anticipated departure of the American forces. The freeze had the added advantage of dissociating JAM from the expulsion of Sunnis from most of Baghdad.

9/13/07 - Shaykh 'Abd al Sattar Abu Risha, leader of the Awakening forces in Anbar Province, was killed – presumably by AQI.

9/16/07 - In Baghdad's Nisur Square 17 civilians died when Blackwater contractors guarding an American convoy opened fire, which was defended by Blackwater as an appropriate response to the circumstances, but denounced by Iraqi officials as lethal irresponsibility. The occurrence cost Blackwater its license to operate in Iraq. An article in the 2/1/09 *Times* suggested that this tragedy was the tipping point between acceptance and rejection of the American military presence.

10/07 - Nir Rosen concluded that Iraq had broken up into city-states, loosely associated in sectarian cantons.

10/6/07 - Nechirvan Barzani, KRG Prime Minister, wrote in *The Wall Street Journal* that the KRG's oil law followed the central government's formula for division of oil revenues: 83 percent for Baghdad, 17 percent for the KRG. So far the KRG had signed eight production-sharing contracts. It hoped for continuation of the American presence.

10/13/07 - British forces in Iraq were transferred from Basrah to a nearby air base.

10/29/07 - The Americans' impending transfer of authority in Karbala' Province would bring the number of provinces under direct Iraqi control to 8 of 18.

11/12/07 - Near the Basrah oil terminal, the US Navy was building a military installation as a link in America's defense structure in the Gulf.

11/07 - A dramatic drop in bombings and murders in Iraq, especially Baghdad, was due to the 2006-07 "surge" in the number of American forces, to ethnic cleansing – including the Shiites' concurrent expulsion of nearly a million Sunnis from Baghdad (reported by Juan Cole in *The Nation* of 1/12/09), to compartmentalization of major cities by checkpoints and blast walls, to American recruitment of the Awakening forces, to tighter Syrian and Saudi restrictions on entry of foreign militants into Iraq, and to JAM's stand-down.

11/07 - Tawafuq was boycotting Parliament in protest against the alleged arrest of its leader, 'Adnan al Dulaymi.

12/17/07 - Report that the UK had transferred control of Basrah to the Maliki Government.

12/19/07 - Report that the UNSC had extended the Multinational Force's mandate to 12/31/08.

1/08 - Parliament ruled that all but the most senior members of Saddam's BPI could return to their previous positions in the Iraqi Government (see 8/28/07 entry).

2/08 - Since the evacuation of British forces from Basrah, the city had become the arena of a Shiite power struggle.

3/08 - The Sunni resistance to the Baghdad regime was intensifying in Mawsil, whose leadership was primarily Kurdish, but whose 1.8 million residents were mostly Arab.

3-6/08 - Three major Shiite factions maintained militias in Iraq: ISCI (Badr Brigade), the Sadrists (JAM), and Fadilah. Maliki deployed the new Iraqi army against restive JAM forces in Baghdad, Basrah, and Maysan provinces (presumably hoping to consolidate his regime's position while the American forces were still around to help). In reaction to initial JAM successes (*Times* of April 7), US air units, Special Forces, and Awakening allies intervened in decisive force (*Times* of June 21), and sealed off Sadr City. Muqtada shut down JAM's military operations, even those in Sadr City, and called on his forces to cooperate with the regime.

4/10/08 - The *Monitor Online* reported that AQI, defeated in Anbar, had moved north to Diyala, Salah al Din, and Ninawah Provinces.

5/08 - Since January, the pro-Baghdad authorities in Mawsil had arrested 1100 Sunni militants, most of them former Baathists.

6/08 - AQI was blamed for several bombings in Anbar, Baghdad, and Ninawah Provinces, killing many Iraqis and several American soldiers.

7/19/08 - Tawafuq cancelled its walkout of almost a year after Sunnis were guaranteed five ministries and one deputy premiership. The Sadrist bloc was still boycotting.

7/22/08 - According to Robert Dreyfuss, writing in *The Nation* of 3/9/09, twelve Iraqi nationalist (unionist) factions had founded the "7/22 Gathering" to denounce the assignment of political position by ethnic community. They blamed the Coalition, in its emphasis on ethnicity (as exemplified in the language of the Constitution and in the election of 2005), for Iraq's having set up a government that was unrepresentative and incompetent.

7/28/08 - Clashes between Kurds and Turkmens in Kirkuk.

7/30/08 - *AP* reported that over the preceding year nearly 40 Sadrist leaders had been killed and over 60 detained by Maliki's forces. Muqtada was studying Islamic theology in Qom, Iran.

8/08 - Patrick Cockburn commented that the Americans had gotten themselves into the position of subsidizing two rival factions (Sunnis and Shia), but the only pro-American community in Iraq was the Kurds. According to *The Washington Post Weekly,* the US was practicing "Saddam-style politics".

8/08 - Kurdish forces under the command of Masrur Mas'ud Barzani controlled the key city of Kirkuk (population 900,000).

8/22/08 - Pro-Baghdad authorities were arresting Awakening leaders in Diyala Province.

8/25/08 - *The Washington Post Weekly* reported that many units of the Iraqi army were unisectarian.

8/08 - The Awakening was challenging the traditional dominance of the Iraqi Islamic Party in Anbar Province.

8/08 - Kristian Ulrichsen: Iran had taken an active role in the construction of a new international airport for the Shiite pilgrimage center of Najaf.

10/23/08 - Peter Galbraith wrote that the Kurds, alienated from their former Iraqi allies, were striking out on their own. Kurdish officials affirmed their intention to retain control of the government of Ninawah Province and restated their claim to its eastern districts.

10/28/08 - Baathist and nationalist Sunnis in Ninawah, resentful of the Kurdish presence and of the support given it by the Americans, had formed *Al Hadbah* (The Mountain?) to contest the upcoming provincial elections.

11/08 - The Maliki Government took over responsibility for paying Awakening's militants.

11/27/08 - Parliament adopted a **Status of Forces Agreement** (SOFA) 149-35(including 30 Sadrists); of 275 MP's, 198 were present. Either signatory wanting to disengage from the SOFA had to give one year's notice. US forces would withdraw from urban areas by 6/30/09, from Iraq by 12/31/11. As of 1/1/09, the government of Iraq would take military responsibility for the Green Zone, the US would conduct no military operations in Iraq without Baghdad's consent, and its civilian security contractors would be subject to Iraqi law. Maliki said America's 58 bases in Iraq would revert to Iraq. The agreement fell far short of Washington's invasion objective of making Iraq America's primary military base in the Arab World: Michael Schwartz, *TomDispatch*. According to Patrick Cockburn (*The London Review of Books*), the agreement had rendered the invasion a failure. Juan Cole reported in *The Nation* that the Shiite opposition (Sadrists and Virtue Party) opposed the agreement as too liberal; its endorsement by the national referendum scheduled for July 2009 was not assured.

12/08 - The Kuwaiti Ambassador had presented his credentials. Kuwait was holding out for payment of Iraq's war debt.

12/4/08 - The Presidential Council of three approved the SOFA, subject to referenda on it and on other key political issues.

12/23/08 - Parliament extended until 12/31/09 Iraq's exemption from civil suits for damages inflicted by the Saddam Government.

12/24/08 - Parliament approved the stay of non-American foreign troops beyond 12/31/08.

1/1/09 - The US transferred to Iraq responsibility for The Green Zone and all 18 provinces. Britain turned over control of the Basrah airport.

1/31/09 - Iraq held elections for the provincial councils of 14 provinces, deferring the process in the three provinces that comprise the KAR and in a fourth province (Ta'mim) claimed by the KAR. Religious symbols were banned. Turnout was low, partly because ethnic cleansing had converted millions of eligible voters to DP's; those abroad had lost eligibility, and those in Iraq were separated from their precincts. Parliamentary elections were to be held by 1/30/10 (per schedule change of May 2009).

In the analysis of Robert Dreyfuss, writing in *The Nation* of 3/9/09, the election was a decisive victory for nationalism and secularism, and a defeat for separatism. ISCI and Al Da'wah were crippled, their coalition (the UIA) was defunct, and the Sunni Arabs, who had boycotted the election of 1/31/05, had taken control of four provinces, and crushed the Kurds in those provinces where Kurds still held positions of leadership. The Maliki Bloc, benefiting from its position of power, American support, and Maliki's success in projecting an image of nationalism that overshadowed his affiliation with Shiite Al Da'wah, won a plurality in Baghdad, Basrah, and several other provinces. Opposition parties cried fraud. The Awakening captured Anbar Province from the Iraqi Islamic Party (a component of Tawafuq). The Sunnis' Al Hadbah won big in Mawsil. An Awakening/Tawafuq/'Allawi alliance carried Salah al Din Province – a Baathist stronghold in the Saddam era.

2/9/09 - In the costliest incident for Americans since 5/2/08, four soldiers were killed in Mawsil by a suicide bomber – presumably sent by AQI, whose forces had been driven north by Awakening forces.

2/10/09 - French President Nicolas Sarkozy made a state visit to Iraq. It was seen as an early move by Maliki to end his government's client status – something of a challenge while that government was still heavily dependent on the support of the American forces. Dead set against arming an anti-Israeli regime, Washington had resisted Baghdad's requests for modern weapons.

3/13/09 - Iraqi Government forces surrounded Camp Ashraf, detention point for the MEK.

3/24/09 - The *Times* reported that, of 94,000 Awakening Council militants (stipend 300 dollars a month), 84,000 had been transferred to Iraqi control, but only 5,000 had gotten appointments to the army (750 dollars a month) or the police (600 dollars a month). According to a later *AP* report, none of the transferees were being paid. Iraq's unemployed/underemployed rate was 38 percent.

3/30/09 - *Times:* The members of the Maliki Government had voted themselves enormous pay raises.

4/7/09 - On the anniversary of the founding of the Baath Party, "The National Islamist Pan-Arab Front" sent the *Times* the text of an audiotape message from 'Izzat Ibrahim al Duri, who had been Deputy Chairman of Saddam's Revolutionary Command Council. The message called on Iraqis to topple Maliki's "puppet regime".

April 2009 - The new Iraq was still in a state of confusion. The provinces were just beginning to form the councils provided for by the January elections. Parliament had finally elected a speaker – Iyad al Samarra'i, head of the Iraqi Islamic Party. While the Kurds were besting the Sunni Arabs in a contest for control of the northern oil fields, the

Shiites held the huge Rumaylah field in the south. April was punctuated by a rash of deadly bombings, some claimed by the "Islamic State of Iraq", a Sunni organization that included AQI, now said to be led by Abu 'Umar al Baghdadi.

5/25/09 - American media carried an *AP* report that funds allocated by Washington for the reconstruction of Iraq now totaled 50 billion dollars, but there was no accurate accounting of how they had been spent.

5/27/09 - The KRG had begun exporting crude to Turkey. Baghdad planned to apportion the revenue from KRG shipments among Iraqi provinces and "regions".

6/10/09 - Further to the Parliamentary decision of 11/27/08, Baghdad and Washington agreed on the terms of a Status of Forces Agreement (SOFA), subject to a subsequent Iraqi referendum. If the SOFA should be voted down, the American forces would have to complete withdrawal from Iraq within a year from the date the referendum had been held.

6/12/09 - Tawafuq leader Harith al 'Ubaydi was shot dead at Friday prayers in Baghdad.

6/22/09 - A new Iraqi contingent, the Special Operations Forces, had been conducting attacks on insurgents in the Baghdad area. They reported to Prime Minister Maliki, but were in effect a branch of the American armed forces.

6/24/09 - The third massive bombing of Shiite crowds in two weeks. Presumed objectives: to discredit the Maliki government, possibly to reignite sectarian war. At least some of the violence was claimed by the AQI and two new groups using the titles The Mujahidin Army and The Islamic Army of Iraq.

6/26/09 - *Times,* quoting an Iraqi official: Most of the 130,000 American troops in Iraq had evacuated the cities, with the exception of huge Camp Victory on the western edge of Baghdad, in anticipation of the June 30 deadline specified in the SOFA. After the total withdrawal deadline of 12/31/11, the US was expected to leave 35-50,000 trainers/advisers. Those already in country were living in compounds fortified against the risk of fragging by infiltrators into the Iraqi forces under training.

6/30/09 - Iraqis celebrated the Americans' evacuation from the cities.

June 2009 - The *Times* of 7/10/09 reported the KAR Parliament's approval of a new constitution that accorded the KAR President extraordinary powers and endorsed Kurdish claims to a large segment of northern Iraq and to the oil and gas beneath it. This language was condemned by the Maliki Government, the KRG opposition (*Gorran*), and Vice President Biden (on a visit to Iraq).

7/1/09 - 'Izzat al Duri and The Association of Muslim Scholars hailed the withdrawal of American forces from urban areas, and adjured Iraqis to fight Americans, not other Iraqis. Muqtada al Sadr (studying in Iran?) condemned the withdrawal as insufficient.

7/3/09 - The February visit by French President Sarkozy and the July visit by Prime Minister Fillon helped Baghdad reestablish the close political and economic ties that linked Iraq and France in the Saddam era.

7/25/09 - An election in the KAR reelected Mas'ud Barzani as President and chose the members of a 111-seat parliament. Gorran was believed to have won at least 25 seats.

July 2009 - The relative quiet in Iraq was still being interrupted by sporadic but lethal snipings, bombings, and assassinations of factional leaders and civilian and security officials of the Maliki Government. The *McClatchy* news agency reported that agricultural production had been crippled by drought, decline in river flow, three wars since 1980, UN sanctions, and official incompetence and corruption. The primary subject of debate was whether US adherence to the SOFA schedule would jeopardize the rebirth of an independent Iraq. No referendum on the SOFA had been held.

8/16/09 - Report that AQI and the Islamic State of Iraq, having joined forces, were responsible for much of the violence in northern Iraq, including two gigantic bombings.

8/25/09 - Juan Cole Blog: *Al Zaman* had reported that Sadrists, ISCI, Fadilah, and Ibrahim al Ja'fari's Islah Party, in association with some Sunnis, had formed The Iraqi National Alliance (INA). INA and Maliki's State of Law Party were the two main electoral blocs in Iraq: *Times*; *New York Review*, Joost Hilterman.

10/09 - Reports that Baghdad, not recognizing the KRG's oil contracts, had closed the pipelines to Turkey, forcing the KRG to stop pumping. With the infrastructure devastated, the economy hostage to local warlords, and no functioning banking system, Iraq's oil production was stalled out at 2.5 million barrels per day, versus 2.8 million before the American invasion: *Times*; *Middle East Report*, Pete Moore.

11/09 - *Intervest*, Reidar Visser: Vice President Tariq al Hashimi had left Tawafuq to form his own party.

1/10 - Plans to hold Parliamentary elections in March had been blasted by an unexpected Parliamentary decision to ban over 500 candidates, most of them Sunnis, including Salih al Mutlaq and Dhafir al 'Ani, allies of Iyad al 'Allawi and Tariq al Hashimi (*'Iraqiyyah* Party).

2/1/10 - Times: Baghdad had blacklisted the oil companies operating in the KAR.

2/26/10 - A pre-election maneuver by the Maliki government was the reinstatement of 20,000 officers who had been dismissed from the army after the invasion.

3/7/10 - Under heavy American and Iraqi security, and despite continued bombings (Al Qaʻidah?), Iraqis turned out in good numbers to elect an Iraqi Parliament of 325.

3/26/10 - Announcement of results of March 7 election: Former Prime Minister Iyad ʻAllawi's 'Iraqiyyah coalition (with large Sunni support) – 91 seats; sitting Prime Minister Nuri al Maliki's State of Law coalition – 89 seats; United Iraqi Alliance of Sadrists, ISCI, and other Shiite groups (all close to Iran) – 70 seats; Kurdish coalition – 43 seats; Kurdish opposition (Gorran) – 8 seats.

4/19/10 – Two AQI leaders were reported dead: Abu ʻUmar al Baghdadi (Hamid al Zawi) and Abu Hamza al Muhajir.

The Anatomy of the Opposition to the Occupation

In their patriotic habit of following Washington's lead, the American media referred to Iraq's armed opposition as the insurgency, which carries the connotation of illegal violence against constituted authority. However, as UN Secretary General Kofi Annan publicly stated, the American invasion of Iraq, as a violation of the UN Charter, was itself illegal. Therefore, any Iraqi counteraction to it – at least at the outset – deserved the appellation of resistance (an "organization engaged in a struggle for national liberation in a country under military ... occupation").

Some lawyers will take the position that Security Council Resolution 1483 of May 22, 2003, put to rest the legality issue. Others will dismiss 1483 as the "fruit of a poisoned tree." As of this writing, the juridical jury was still out.

Since the Baathist regime of Saddam Husayn was rooted in the Sunni community, the invasion was tacitly welcomed by mainstream Shiites and Kurds, and the resistance was largely based on the "Sunni Triangle", which roughly corresponds to the territory between the Tigris and the Euphrates, from the Baghdad area to the Syrian border. It included the Sunni segment of Baghdad, Al Mawsil (Iraq's third largest city), and several other populous cities along the two rivers. Greatly outnumbered by the quiescent Shia, the Sunnis fought an uphill battle against American armor, planes, and artillery. They had no allies of note in the Kurdish community except Ansar al Islam, an Islamist splinter group. In the Shia community, Muqtada al Sadr condemned the American invasion of Fallujah, but his spasmodic resistance efforts were not coordinated with the Sunnis; they were a backhanded challenge to Sistani's leadership of the Shia. In 2009, after the Americans inflicted heavy casualties on JAM forces in Najaf, Sadr joined Sistani in the background and suspended his paramilitary campaign.

Like the other communities, the Sunni resistance was fragmented, with no overall leader. However, there were factors operating in its favor:

Early Start - American officials concluded that, by staffing his administration with officials who had served his father in Gulf War I, Bush 43 alerted Saddam to make preinvasion arrangements for himself and his sons to go into hiding (those arrangements failed), and to set up the machinery for an underground resistance. The postinvasion orgy of looting may have been intentionally abetted by resistance strategy.

The BPI wing of the resistance was believed to be well financed by party funds banked in Syria. American intelligence initially estimated its numbers at over 2000 hard-core Baathists, plus several thousand part-time operatives motivated less by party discipline than by financial compensation. In early 2005, the Sunni resistance was estimated to be half BPI, a quarter Iraqi Islamists under the leadership of Jordanian Abu Mus'ab al Zarqawi (Chapter 12), and a quarter foreign Islamists – for a total of 40,000, plus 160,000 part-time auxiliaries. The BPI wing seemed to have an intelligence net deep inside the interim government. The violent campaign to undermine law, public services, and Coalition authority, not visibly set back by the capture of Saddam, was holding its own in the Sunni Triangle and adjoining areas.

Coalition intelligence suspected that the BPI was running its operation from Aleppo, which was conveniently situated and politically congenial – since Syria, despite its Alawite leadership, is a Sunni country. The resistance was "a monster with its head in Syria and its body in Iraq". The role of voice of the resistance had been appropriated by The Association of Muslim Scholars, an ad hoc organization which claimed to represent 3000 Sunni mosques, and condemned Interim Prime Minister Iyad 'Allawi as an "American lackey".

Foreign Islamists - Although prewar accusations of collaboration between Baathists and Islamists have never been verified, the invasion converted canard to reality. Sunni volunteers from Syria, Lebanon, Saudi Arabia, Turkey, Yemen, Tunisia, and Morocco entered Iraq via Syria in numbers sufficient to play a significant role. For six months in 2004, Fallujah was under the control of a combine of Iraqi and foreign Islamists. In December 2004, some diehard defenders were still hanging on in the rubble, despite the American assault's having demolished many of its buildings, devastated its public services, emptied the city of its 250,000 residents, and converted it to a ghost town.

'Abdallah II, less solicitous of Jordan's neutrality than his father had been in Gulf War I, had angered the Iraqi resistance by letting American units deploy along the Iraqi border, but he may have hedged his bets by providing clandestine assistance to his Sunni coreligionists in Iraq.

BPI-Islamist Coordination - Whereas the Baathist wing of the resistance relied on conventional ambushes, furtive use of artillery, and the placement of camouflaged remote-control explosives (IED's) along roadsides, the Islamist factions were considered responsible for introduction of the suicide car bomb. In mid-2003 infiltrators carried out three devastating bombings (the Jordanian Embassy, UN headquarters, and the Shiite shrine of Imam 'Ali). In 2004, there were over 450 suicide bombings against the interim regime.

UN Special Representative Sergio Vieira De Mello died in the bombing of his office. By choosing to operate outside the Green Zone, he had facilitated contact with Iraqis; Shiites who shunned Bremer would see Vieira De Mello. However, his neutrality was suspect in the eyes of the resistance. The UN had been the vehicle for America's harrowing interwar sanctions, and Vieira De Mello himself had become Bremer's invaluable adviser. He had been the only non-Iraqi to speak at the inauguration of the IGC, which he had helped the Americans concoct, and – as noted by Phyllis Bennis of the Institute for Policy Studies – his mission was deemed to operate under the auspices of the CPA.

The nom de guerre, Abu Mus'ab al Zarqawi, surfaced in 2004. A tape recording attributed to Usamah bin Ladin described Zarqawi as Al Qa'idah's leader in Iraq. The Zarqawi group and another calling itself Ansar al Sunna were held responsible for 2004's wave of abductions and occasional beheadings of foreigners, and of suicide bombings, possibly including a particularly lethal attack on an American mess tent near Mawsil in December 2004. The Islamist wing of the resistance was believed to be receiving subsidies from sympathizers in the Middle East and beyond.

Suspicion Between Kurds and Shia - Viewed as a voting bloc, Shia and Kurds far outnumbered their Sunni rivals, and they were united by their resolve to terminate 450 years of Sunni Arab rule of Mesopotamia/ Iraq. However, as the haggling over the interim constitution revealed, they had incompatible agendas: The Shia favored early general elections as a crude means of establishing Shiite rule over an integrated Iraq. The Kurds wanted a high degree of autonomy – if not outright independence.

Occupation: 2006-09

By early 2006, the American attempt to pacify Iraq by conventional patrols, vehicle or foot, had been frustrated by a stubborn guerrilla resistance whose most lethal weapon was the IED. In the mystifying environment of Iraq, incidental expenditure on upgrading the school system, the CIA's takeover of Iraqi intelligence, and the construction of an immense network of military bases, was irrelevant. On February 22, 2006, the bombing of the Golden Dome threw the Americans into the middle of a sectarian civil conflict, with the Shiites resisting Ambassador Khalilzad's futile efforts to bring Sunnis into the government, and the Sunnis raging at the Americans for failing to protect them from Shiite death squads.

According to Michael Schwartz, by August 2006 the sectarian fighting had spiraled out of control. The American forces, which had entered that conflict in Baghdad in May, with heavy ground and air shelling, had done serious damage to buildings and public services, and by enclosing neighborhoods with concrete blast walls had ghettoized the city, from which 800,000 had taken flight.

By the end of the year, American forces and those of the Maliki regime were under attack by Sunni mujahideen and Muqtada's Shiite nationalists – who were probably responsible for most of the shells falling on the Green Zone, sanctuary of the American command and Maliki's government. America's Provincial Reconstruction Teams were blocked from pursuing their designated mission by their restriction to base, or to armored convoys. Baghdad had disintegrated into sectarian fragments, and countrywide sabotage of the infrastructure was making normal life an impossibility. Suicide bombings, new to Iraq, from 2003 to the end of 2007 exceeded 750. Nir Rosen cited castration and torture by electric drills as signature practices of the Shiite militias.

In early 2007, American forces (140,000, backed by 160,000 civilian contractors, including 25,000 armed guards, mostly Americans) were taking casualties from more sophisticated IED's – Explosively Formed Projectiles (EFP), which in the view of US Intelligence were being made in Iran, and supplied to Shiite militants by the Quds Force of the Iranian Revolutionary Guard. In the cynical words of an American soldier, "Our basic mission is to drive around until we get blown up." In Basrah Province, the British occupiers were under constant fire, whether on base or out on patrol. Retired General Barry McCaffrey came back in April from a visit to Iraq with an estimate that, despite having killed 20,000 militants and imprisoned another 27,000 (exclusive of 37,000 in GOI custody), the

Americans and their poorly equipped Iraqi allies were confronted by 100,000 Sunni and Shia militants.

May 2007 was the third deadliest month to that time for American soldiers. The first battle of Fallujah had brought deaths in April 2004 to 147. The second battle of Fallujah brought the total in November 2004 to 140. Deaths in May 2007 were 120. However, the overall situation was about to change. First, in February 2007, against the advice of his military chiefs, Bush instituted the "surge", which raised the force in Iraq from 140,000 to 160,000. Second, Muqtada ordered JAM to stand down – presumably with the intent of waiting until he could take on his Iraqi enemies after they had lost their American air support. Third, the Shiites had expelled Sunni residents from large areas of Baghdad, deescalating the sectarian conflict. Fourth, the American command had recruited thousands of Awakening militants, many of whom had been active in the resistance; new American commander Petraeus had switched the emphasis from killing to conciliating. The strategy was simple but expensive: pay both sides in the sectarian confrontation.

In February 2008, when the American force in Iraq was back up to 157,000, Thomas Ricks wrote that the US was fighting three wars in Iraq: The war against AQI was going fairly well (thanks to the rift between AQI and The Awakening); the war against the mainstream Sunnis was dormant (by virtue of the new strategy of cooptation); the heaviest American casualties (down to 36 in February) were coming from the war with the Shiite militants, who were believed to be receiving arms, training, and funding from Iran. Lt. General Raymond Odierno told the *Times* US casualties were coming half from AQI, half from the Shiites. According to *The Nation*, the American forces were still relying on massive air attacks.

In April 2008, US and GOI forces occupied the southern quarter of Sadr City to inhibit the firing of rockets into the Green Zone. In June, the US command was recruiting Sadr City Shiites as "neighborhood guards".

In January 2009, with the new administration in Washington committed to early withdrawal of "combat" troops, troop strength in Iraq was 145,000; Iraqis in American custody numbered 16,000 (plus 24,000 held by the Maliki regime). The fortress/embassy, sitting on 104 acres, had a staff of a thousand plus a maintenance staff of several thousand, and was self-sufficient in water and electric power. The few thousand remaining Brits would be gone by the end of the year.

The resistance had not conceded. The January 26 crash of two helicopters, killing four soldiers, was claimed by 'Izzat al Duri's Naqshabandi Army (Baathist). Iraq had a sovereign government, but no heavy weapons, no air force, and no navy, and its constitution had been honored mainly in the breach. By June 2009 the American casualty rate had diminished, but military and civilian Iraqis were taking fairly steady casualties from vehicle and suicide bombing. *The Christian Science Monitor*'s report that "low-level insurgency is expected to continue for years" contradicted the American presumption that the Maliki regime was the established government of Iraq, rather than one of several competing factions – the one that happened to enjoy US support at the moment (cf. South Vietnam).

The Shiite Campaign to Make History

If the Shiites' dream is realized, Iraq will become the first-ever mainstream Shiite Arab state. (The Egyptian Fatimids, Yemeni Zaydis, and Syrian Alawites – as outlined in Chapter 6 – paid allegiance to heterodox branches of Shiism.) Under Shiite rule, Kurds and Arab Sunnis could become disempowered minorities, like the Azeris in Iran, the Kurds in Turkey, the Copts in Egypt, and the Arabs in Israel.

However, as pointed out by Christopher de Bellaigue, the Iraqi Shiites are no less fractionated than their rivals. In 2003, he discerned three main factions: the Sadrists, led by Muqtada al Sadr; SCIRI (The Supreme Council of the Islamic Revolution in Iraq) led by the Sadrs' ancient enemies, the Hakims; and Al Da'wah (The Call), relic of the group assembled in Saddam's time by the revered Muhammad al Sadr, Muqtada's father. Above their worldly altercations sat Ayatallah 'Ali al Sistani, primary cleric in the Shiite world.

The Quietism of 'Ali Sistani - Cosmopolites like Iyad 'Allawi and Ahmad Chalabi functioned effectively in international milieus like the corridors of power in Washington and the Green Zone in Baghdad, but they did not produce evidence of significant following in Iraq. The Shiite masses looked to their sectarian leaders – the five surviving Grand Ayatallahs, headed by the reclusive 'Ali Sistani.

As a "quietist" (an opponent of direct clerical participation in politics), Sistani escaped elimination by Saddam, and he took no positions in the IGC, the Interim Government, or any Shiite political party. From behind the scenes, he aimed at neutrality in factional disputes, but exerted decisive influence in the wrangling between the Americans and their Iraqi proteges.

In principle, Sistani opposed American Middle East policy, particularly Bush's inclusion of Iran in the "Axis of Evil", and the American occupation. Within days of the invasion, he issued a fatwa calling on Muslims to defend Iraq. He avoided meeting with CPA authorities, but he took no part in the armed resistance. His apparent strategy was to hang back while the Americans whittled down the Sunnis and the activist Shiites.

On the political front, however, Sistani exerted constant pressure on the CPA and the Interim Government for holding a nationwide election, on a proportional basis, for a transitional government and a constituent assembly. Impressed by early indications of Sistani's power to mobilize the Shiite street, the Americans tended to comply; hence UNSC Resolution 1546, and the election held in January 2005 – although analysts concluded that the Americans had managed to block outright Shiite control of the Transitional National Assembly by imposing the requirement for a two-thirds majority, and by assuring the Kurds a disproportionate number of seats.

The Challenger - To the surprise of the neophyte Americans, and perhaps even Sistani, the occupation activated a new contender for power – Muqtada al Sadr. Young and unschooled, he held the modest rank of *Hujjat al Islam*, far below an *ayatallah* in Shiite hierarchy. However, he derived vicarious charisma from his late father and uncle, both ayatallahs, and both presumed victims of Saddamist police. Martyrdom is a central theme in Shiite tradition. Muqtada also received a valuable endorsement from Grand *Ayatollah* (Persian spelling) Kazim al Ha'iri, resident in Qom, Iran.

In April 2003, the American invaders returned an exiled cleric, 'Abd al Majid al Khu'i, to Najaf, where he was murdered. The motivation (antioccupation? anti-Sistani?) has not been established, but the four suspects picked up by the Americans were followers of Sadr. From then on, relations between Sadr and the occupiers deteriorated. The absence of any member of the Sadr faction from the IGC was consistent with Sadr's demand in July 2003 for the Americans' withdrawal, his condemnation of anyone (Sistani?) who tolerated their presence, and his recruitment of an untrained but large and impassioned militia, the *Jaysh al Mahdi* (The Army of the Rightly Guided One, JAM). In August 2003, his militia went underground to evade an American order that all militias disband. In September 2003, a police station in "Sadr City" (the sprawling Shiite section of Baghdad) was the target of a suicide bombing, two Americans died in a clash there, and a Sadrist imam preached an anti-occupation sermon. More violent clashes followed.

In March 2004, the CPA closed Sadr's newspaper, *Al Hawzah,* on a charge of inciting violence, and arrested a Sadr associate for suspected complicity in the Khu'i killing. Sadr unleashed his militia. Under American attack, the JAM took refuge in the holy sites of Najaf and Karbala', cities in which Sadr had a large following. As the Americans began to take casualties, their solicitude for the sanctity of Shiite shrines dissipated, and some 1500 of Sadr's soldiers were killed.

Although Sadr was maintaining a façade of solidarity with Sistani, the ayatallah had to be hugely embarrassed by the Najaf resistance, which complicated his strategy of extracting American agreement for a general election, posed a sharp contrast to the quietists' inaction, and reminded the faithful which Shiite faction had stood up to Saddam. The CPA wanted Sadr in prison and his soldiers disarmed, but Sistani demurred. Wary of alienating the Shiites as well as the Sunnis, the CPA capitulated. JAM evacuated the holy cities with its weapons, the Americans withdrew, and Najaf and Karbala' reverted to Iraqi control. Sistani got credit for defusing the crisis. Sadr emerged chastened, but with his prestige as defender of the faith enhanced.

The next four years were beset by intermittent violence between the occupiers and JAM, even after Muqtada made the strategic decision to stand his forces down, while he reportedly moved to Qom to pursue clerical studies aimed at achieving elevation to ayatallah. In the summer of 2008 he reportedly split JAM into a social service wing, the *Muhammadun,* and an elite militia, *Al Yawm al Maw'ud* (The Promised Day). Many Shiites believe the return of the Hidden Imam is near.

The Ancient Rivalry - When the Americans arrived, the Sadrs and the Hakims were separated by an ancient Shiite feud. During the occupation, Muqtada joined the resistance, and the Hakims sat it out. In 2009, as the Americans began to leave, there were reports that Muqtada al Sadr and 'Abd al 'Aziz al Hakim had found the rise of the latest American protégé, Nuri al Maliki, ominous enough for them to set their historic enmity aside.

Kurdistan: District or State?

The Kurdish Autonomous Region (KAR) was an unplanned consequence of America's anti-Saddam policy. Incorporating the Iraqi provinces of Dahuk, Irbil, and Sulaymaniyyah, it has taken shape with about 17,000 square miles, 3,500,000 residents, a "capital" (Irbil), a constitution, a government, a flag, a police force that maintains a respectable level of law and order, an airport at Dahuk, a school system, and the most formidable indigenous militia in Iraq, the Pesh Merga. The KAR has held no recent elections, but its structure seems to have submerged the ancient Barzani-Talabani feud (Chapter 9). It has all the attributes of sovereignty except international recognition and a delineated frontier. It pays no Iraqi taxes, and has adopted legislation claiming control of all oil produced within its territory.

Two central issues remained to be resolved:

Autonomy - Ayatallah Sistani is thought to have engineered the omission from UNSC Resolution 1546 of any mention of the interim constitution (TAL), which at Kurdish insistence had codified language protecting minority rights. Most Iraqi Kurds want an independent Kurdistan. If the government of the new Iraq fails to meet minimum Kurdish demands for autonomy, Kirkuk, and a share of oil revenues, the KAR might opt for secession. It is difficult to conceive how the new government in Baghdad could block it. As for Washington, it may have let the Kurds down in the past, but it could not in good conscience take military action against an entity it was instrumental in creating – even though the Kurds have no strong American lobby.

However, an independent Kurdistan could expect opposition from Turkey and Iran. The Iraqi Kurds have traditionally been on guard against antagonizing their powerful neighbor. In 1998, the Barzani and Talabani factions joined in signing in Washington an agreement to cooperate in Turkey's campaign to suppress its own Kurdish resistance, the PKK.

The viability of a Kurdish entity in Iraq would be enhanced by control of the Kirkuk oil basin, and by alliance with an outside power. The Iraqi Kurds' only steadfast friend is Israel, which has been providing them financial and military assistance for over forty years. Israel has always been on the lookout for allies in the region. Its alliance with the Lebanese Maronites collapsed after the Syrians occupied Lebanon. Its alliance with Turkey is still operative, but it was shaken in 2003 by the Turkish Parliament's opposition to the invasion of Iraq, and in 2009 by Turkish outrage at the intensity of the Israeli assault on the Gaza Strip.

In June 2004, Seymour Hersh cited unconfirmed reports that Israel, unconvinced of the American ability to co-opt Iraq, had initiated a fall-back strategy of setting up a Kurdish island of stability in the Middle Eastern sea of turmoil. To this end, Israeli teams were said to be training KAR commando units and running covert operations into Iran and Syria, with the possible objective of developing the KAR into a base for Israeli-Kurdish operations against common adversaries. Israel has special access by virtue of 150,000 Kurdish-Israelis of Iraqi origin.

After 150 years of persecution, the Kurds of Iraq like those of Turkey are widely dispersed. Eight hundred thousand lived in Baghdad before the invasion. The KAR's priorities were to unify its residents, bring back emigrants, and move its western frontier to the Tigris. By 2006, its Parliament (based in Irbil) had combined the administrations of the KDP and the PUK, trenched its southern boundary, posted Pesh Merga units to guard it, prohibited the entry of forces of the Government of Iraq, installed a "President of the Kurdistan Region" (Mas'ud Barzani), hoisted its own flags in place of Iraqi flags, and concluded oil agreements with several foreign companies. It had not yet corrected the communications problem caused by inheritance of two incompatible cell phone systems – one based in Irbil (former KDP territory), the other in Sulaymaniyah (PUK).

In early 2006, most of the PKK's 5,000 militants, according to Stephen Kinzer, were hiding out in the KAR, protected from Turkish attack by the American occupation of Iraq. The militants' leader was Murat Karayilan.

In 2007, as reported by Tom Friedman, the KAR initiated the establishment of an American University of Iraq in Sulaymaniyyah. The regional economy was booming, with investment flowing in from Turkey and the US. On 8/6/2007 the Kurdish Parliament adopted a KAR oil law that endorses the formula for the division of oil revenues (17% for Kurdistan) laid down in the Iraqi Constitution. *The Wall Street Journal* reported that, since the KAR law had not been recognized by the regime in Baghdad, the major companies had stayed away from the KAR. Hunt Oil had signed a contract, and shipments to Turkey began in June 2009.

By 2008, the KAR was requiring all immigrants from other parts of Iraq to carry ID cards that had to be renewed every three months.

The Boundary Dispute - The western frontier of the KAR adjoins the Iraqi provinces of Ninawah, Ta'mim, and Diyala. It maintains claims on parts of all three. Article 140 of the Iraqi Constitution called for a referendum to determine the future of disputed territories by the end of 2007, but Baghdad let this deadline slip because the Kurds have been so successful in establishing, as they say in occupied Palestine, "facts on the ground".

In Ninawah Province, the pre-election mayor of Mawsil deferred to his Kurdish deputy and relied on Kurdish guards to protect him from the resistance, even though the city is largely inhabited by Arabs west of the Tigris and by Turkmens and Christians east of the Tigris. KAR forces dominated the eastern section. By 2008 law and order had given way to Arab-Kurd clashes and assassinations. Pepe Escobar described Mawsil public services as a shambles. The provincial election of January 2009 empowered the Arab community to wrest control of Ninawah from the Kurds.

In Ta'mim Province, where no election was held, Kurdish officials include the Governor and most members of the Provincial Council. Kirkuk, which sits on one of Iraq's two richest oil fields (the other is in the Basrah area), was victimized by population transfers imposed by Saddam; Kurds were dispossessed, and Arabs (mainly Shia) were brought in from southern Iraq. Within weeks of the American invasion, the Kurds' irredentist campaign, undeterred by Coalition disapproval, was well underway. By late May 2003, the Kirkuk police force was largely manned by Kurds.

Prospect - From the Arab point of view, the Kurds have never been good citizens of Iraq. They fought on the Ottoman side in World War I, the Iranian side in the 1980's, the Coalition side in 1991, and the American side in 2003-04. Their only ally is Israel. CPA efforts to divert the KAR from its insistence on autonomy were unsuccessful. Kurdish nationalism promises to be an issue of mounting international concern, inasmuch as it impinges on the status of Kurds in Turkey, control of Iraq's northern oil fields, allocation of the flow of the Tigris and Euphrates, boundary disputes, the Arab-Israeli conflict, and nuclear proliferation. A base in Kurdistan might facilitate Israel's campaign to preserve its nuclear-arms monopoly in the Middle East.

The Kurds were enraged by the CPA's support for Sistani's exclusion of endorsement of the TAL from UNSC Resolution 1546, but they temporized on the issue to gain time for the assimilation of Kirkuk. In the long run, the KAR will have to tread a cautious path among its three adversaries: Iraq, Iran, and Turkey.

The main issues with Baghdad are frontiers and oil. If past history is any guide, the ultimate frontiers will be imposed by the winners of a paramilitary power struggle (see below). In the realm of oil, the KRG has challenged draft legislation that would set up an Iraqi National Oil Company (INOC).

KAR relations with Iran and Turkey will be clouded by the reliance of the PKK and its Iranian affiliate, PEJAK, on hideouts in the KAR's Kandil Mountains.

The Iranian Factor

The ruinous eight-year war (Chapter 9) underscored Iran's interest in maximizing its influence in Iraq. The Shiite accession to power, after the fall of bitter enemy Saddam, rendered Iran a major foreign beneficiary of the invasion – perhaps the only one. The post-invasion leadership in Iraq included SCIRI, Al Da'wah, and Jalal Talabani – all long-time allies of Iran. As Mohsen Milani noted in *Foreign Affairs* of July 2009, Iran was the first country to recognize the new government in Baghdad.

However, the long-standing feud between the Baathist regimes in Baghdad and Damascus showed that, in the Middle East at least, appearances can be deceiving. There is no guarantee that the men and money Iran has been infiltrating into Iraq will translate into Iranian control, particularly since, as elucidated by Faleh Jabar, Iraqi and Iranian Shiites tend to belong to two different schools – *Akhbari* and *Usuli* – and speak different languages. In appreciation of the unpredictability of Iraqi politics, Iran has reportedly been subsidizing all factions except the fanatically anti-Shiite AQI.

The outcome is doubly convoluted by the arcana of Iranian politics. Schizoid Iran could well have two contradictory policies: one reflecting an effort by the hard-line theocrats under Supreme Leader Khamenei to promote theocracy in Iraq; the other by the moderate theocrats to settle for a secularist regime in Baghdad.

At this delicate stage in the history of Iraq, it seems unlikely that either faction in Tehran would assert new territorial claims against Iraq, where the Iranians have to pick their steps carefully among the jumble of Shiite factions. In 1991, when the battle for Kuwait had sparked SCIRI demonstrations for an Iraqi Islamic Republic, Iraqi Sunnis and many Shia had recoiled. In 1998, Clinton's equal-opportunity policy of "dual containment" had the effect – perhaps its only one – of driving Iraq and Iran closer together. That was the first year of major exchanges of prisoners from the 1980-88 war. There has been no report of Iran's returning any of the aircraft Saddam parked there in 1991.

Just before the American invasion of Iraq, Iran admitted several Iraqi exile leaders to consult with SCIRI leader Muhammad Baqir al Hakim on how to exploit the opportunity. In April 2003, US intelligence initiated cooperation with agents that Iran had sent into Iraq, including members of SCIRI's Badr Brigade.

In 2005, the *Times* reported that members of the Badr Brigade had preempted top positions in Basrah Province. By 2006, the Quds Force of the Iranian Revolutionary Guard – possibly acting independently of top Iranian leadership – was reportedly supporting the Shiite wing of the Iraqi resistance (primarily JAM) with money, training, and arms, including rockets and increasingly lethal IED's. In August, American Ambassador Khalilzad blamed Iranian incitation for the increase in shelling of the Green Zone.

In January 2007, Patrick Cockburn reported that during a failed attempt to seize two high-ranking Iranian guests of Talabani in Irbil, US forces had clumsily grabbed five Iranian officials of the Iran-KAR liaison office. Iran and KAR President Barzani had vehemently protested the action.

According to David Ignatius, Iran's ranking foreign-policy strategist has been Brigadier General Qassem Soleimani, commander of the Quds Force. Under his shrewd direction, Iran has practiced extreme caution toward the imponderable situation in Iraq, allowing for the Iraqis' opposition to theocracy and their wariness of growing Iranian power, and hedging its bets by collaborating with all major Shiite factions, and even on occasion with Sunni factions. Iran's vision of Iraq is a state that is orderly and unified (to block the emergence of a Kurdish state) but not so strong as to challenge the new Iranian leadership in the Gulf area. Press reports of 2008 suggested that Iran would favor ISCI's reputed plan for a federalized Iraq in which the nine southern provinces would be a semi-autonomous unit.

In March 2008, when bloody clashes between JAM and the Badr Brigade in Karbala' during pilgrimage season were a collective Shiite embarrassment, Soleimani upstaged Iraqi Prime Minister Maliki by brokering a truce. Although Iran has maintained its ties with Muqtada, who at this writing was studying in Qom, it presumably places more trust in the organization it created – ISCI. Iran is believed to have subsidized preferred candidates in the Iraqi provincial elections of January 2009.

Tehran, Baghdad, and Ankara will continue to collaborate in opposing Kurdish autonomy and the operations of the PKK, and of PEJAK, which continues to mount sporadic attacks in northwestern Iran.

The *Times* reported in March 2007 that the economies of Iraq and Iran were becoming closely integrated. Iraq's ravaged infrastructure desperately needs help. Many Iraqis go to Iran for medical treatment. Iran is to build two small power plants in Iraq. President Ahmadinejad visited Baghdad in March 2008.

The Mujahedeen-e Khalq - For years, Iraq and Iran subsidized militias composed of each other's exiles. Iran sponsored the Badr Brigade, the military wing of SCIRI. Saddam sponsored the MEK – People's Freedom Fighters (*Mujahedeen-e Khalq* in Persian), a well-armed celibate force, or cult, of 30,000 (as many women as men), plus 7000 dependents, which was founded in Iran in the 1960's by Iranian Massoud Rajavi, occupied two bases in Iraq, and had a long record of subversion in Iran under the monarchy and the theocracy, including a bombing on June 28, 1981, that killed 73, and another on June 2, 1998, that killed three. In April 2003, Sulaymaniyyah was the scene of clashes between, it seems, affiliates of Badr and the MEK.

MEK put the American occupiers in a quandary: Should they suppress it as a Saddamist creation, or exploit it against the forces of evil in Iran? They ended up by doing some of both. In April 2003, they bombed its bases. Two weeks later, they relented and authorized it to keep its weapons. In September 2004, an Iranian official reported the arrest of MEK members on a charge (probably valid) of spying on Iran's nuclear program. The *Times* of 3/28/09 reported that in 2002 the MEK had provided intelligence on the program.

Since late 2004, some members have reportedly been refugees, or detainees, in France (where Rajavi's widow, Maryam Rajavi, the only known exception to the celibacy rule, used to operate Persian-language radio and TV stations). The bulk of the surviving membership were under American custody at Camp Ashraf, in Diyala Province. Washington had disregarded an Iranian request for their extradition.

In January 2009, *The Guardian Weekly* reported Iraqi plans to respond to Iranian protests by closing Camp Ashraf and requiring its inmates to leave Iraq. In July 2009 they were under pressure from surrounding forces of the Maliki regime.

The Turkish Factor

Aside from concessions to the European Union, Turkey's foreign policy has been dominated by its tradition of fierce loyalty to the borders established by Ataturk in the 1920's, and of intolerance of any hint of political or even cultural autonomy for ethnic minorities. In 1925, the Kemalist government stripped the Kurds of any legal identity. Their first uprising was crushed, and 47 "bandit" leaders were executed. In the 1930's, Turkish law required Kurdish dispersal, to insure that no district had a Kurdish population exceeding five percent. By 2000, the insurgency conducted by Abdullah Ocalan's PKK (founded in 1978) had cost the razing of thousands of Kurdish villages and the loss of 30,000 Kurdish and Turkish lives. Atrocities had been committed on both sides. In the 1990's as many as 5000 Kurdish activists disappeared – probably eliminated by police death squads. Upwards of 2,000,000 Kurds left southeastern Turkey for refuge in the cities.

On the Iraqi front, the 1990's were marked by annual spring forays of Turkish troops in search of PKK units in the Kurdish north. Neither Baghdad nor the two Iraqi Kurdish factions interposed any resistance.

Despite Ankara's scorched-earth strategy, its conscription of a Kurdish force that fought for the regime, the proscription of the PKK, the ban on Kurds' return to their ancestral home unless they signed a document that blamed the PKK for the destruction of Kurdish villages, and the consequent assimilation of millions of Kurds into Turkish society, the PKK had managed by 1996 to nullify government control of ten southeastern provinces.

In 1999, the capture of Abdullah Ocalan brought a lull in the Kurdish resistance, and Turkey lifted a State of Emergency that had been in effect for fifteen years. As a gesture to the European Union, Ankara announced that the state broadcasting authority would allow limited programs in Kurdish.

In their common antipathy to Kurdish nationalism, Turkey and Iraq were natural allies, and their concord was reinforced by Turkish reliance on Iraqi oil and the revenues from pipeline transit (Chapter 4). Interruption of these revenues by Gulf War I cost Turkey billions. In 1998, John Tirman perceived a de facto alliance of Turkey, Iraq, and the Barzani Kurds (whose territory was transited by the pipeline) against the Talabani Kurds (who were closer to the PKK and Iran). Turkey was also suffering financial losses from UN sanctions against Iraq. By 2002, trade between Turkey and Iraq was back up to a billion dollars a year.

When the Americans invaded Iraq, the Turkish Parliament went along with public opinion, rather than the military, by blocking access to American ground troops. Since the invasion, Turkey has been preoccupied with keeping Kirkuk out of the Kurdish sphere of influence. To this end, it has stressed its support for the Turkmen minority, which has been receiving Turkish arms and military training against Kurdish encroachment in the neighborhoods of Kirkuk and Tall 'Afar (population: mostly Sunni Turkmens).

American forces have seized arms meant for Turkmens, expelled squads of Turkish commandos on suspicion of anti-Kurdish activity, and reported an attempt on the life of the Kurdish Governor of Kirkuk. The Iraqi IGC vetoed a Turkish proposal to send a peacekeeping force to Iraq.

In December 2004, five Turks died in the ambush of a Turkish military convoy in Mawsil (outside Iraqi Kurdistan). Meanwhile, the PKK had launched a new campaign against Turkish forces. As Turkish Kurds, PKK personnel spoke either Turkish or their own dialect of Kurdish, but enjoyed strong sympathy from their Iraqi cousins. By 2006, the new power structure in the KAR was offering more latitude for PKK operations and less cooperation from Washington. Iraq's Kurdish President Talabani was infuriated by the 2006 visit to Turkey by Prime Minister Ja'fari, and according to de Bellaigue, Bush was still stewing about Turkey's denial of transit rights for US invasion troops. Some Turks theorized that Washington was more tolerant toward Kurdish nationalism in hopes that PEJAK could divert Iran from its campaign to undermine the American occupation of Iraq. Under the rubric of The Party for Free Life in Kurdistan, PEJAK was running operations into Iran from Talabani country in the KAR. In late 2006, according to Seymour Hersh, the US and Israel were jointly supporting PEJAK's intelligence penetration of Iran.

In 2006 Turkey initiated F-16 strikes on PKK sites in the KAR, at a time when Ankara was refusing to deal with Talabani or with KRG President Mas'ud Barzani.

In 2007, Peter Galbraith noted that Erdogan had switched to a more pragmatic posture. Ankara was supporting Turkish investment in the KAR (80 percent of total foreign investment there), had reopened the consulate in Mawsil, and was allowing charter flights between Turkey and the KAR. The Turkish military, which had maintained a force of 1500 in the KAR since the conclusion of a KDP-Turkish alliance against the PKK in the mid-nineties, was opposed to the détente with the KAR. In December 2007, frustrated in its demand for Iraqi extradition of PKK leaders, Turkey mounted the heaviest air strikes on PKK targets in the mountains of Iraq since the American invasion. Although the US military disclaimed any role in the tripartite dispute, a Turkish official alleged that the strikes had benefited from American intelligence. The heavy dependence of the American occupation force on supply lines from Turkey may have been an element in the political equation.

In February 2008, Turkey carried out a ground incursion, insubstantial but the first one since the American invasion. In March Talabani went to Turkey for meetings with President Gul and Prime Minister Erdogan, and in July Erdogan made the first Turkish state visit to Iraq in eighteen years.

The Saudi-Jordanian Factor

True to their Wahhabi origins, conservative Saudis refer to Shiites as apostates (*rawafid*), and Riyadh shared the dismay of the Bush administration at the sudden materialization of a Shiite cordon from Hizballah-dominated Lebanon through Alawite-dominated Syria and newly Shiite Iraq to Iran. Saudi Arabia maintains close ties with Iraq's Sunni tribes, and Saudi citizens and/or officials have been financing Sunni elements of the resistance. More anti-Shiite, anti-American mujahidin have come from Saudi Arabia than from any other country.

Jordan is not in a position to finance any faction, but it is a Sunni state, close to Saudi Arabia, and in Saddam's time close to Iraq. When Iraq loses access to the Gulf, as periodically happens, its primary seaport is Jordan's Al 'Aqabah.

Washington on the Tigris: A Tragedy of Errors

The invasion was the Bush administration's original sin in Iraq. There is broad agreement that it was compounded in the subsequent six years by multiple errors of execution.

Illegality - Belated UNSC Resolution 1483 did not whitewash America's initial violation of the UN Charter, or its cutting legal corners at Abu Ghurayb Prison, or its effort to contravene the Geneva Convention by altering Iraqi laws. According to Samantha Power, 1483 was the first time the Council had ever upheld the occupation of one UN member by another. America's performance hardly qualified it to "bring ... Iraq into the community of law-abiding nations." For the ultraliberals like Noam Chomsky, the invasion of Iraq was "the kind of crime for which Nazis were hanged at Nuremberg."

Hubris - In Washington, as in Baghdad, pietistic exuberance overwhelmed logic. Policy seemed to be guided by a sublime conviction that, when the cause is righteous, means are secondary. In the rush to war, expertise was brushed aside, world opinion was disregarded, and reality was denied. Garner's urgent request for at least two of the State Department's experts on Iraq was rejected by Cheney. In June 2003, just as the resistance was beginning to gain momentum, Bush issued a gratuitous taunt: "... some ... feel ... conditions are such that they can attack us ..." "My answer is, bring them on." Years later, he had the grace to apologize for that braggadocio.

Hubris damaged America's image. More seriously, it inhibited America's capacity to admit mistakes. In the administration of Bush 43, as in the Johnson administration in the late sixties, humiliating disengagement from a failed initiative seemed not to be an option. Even many Democrats bought in to the fantasy that, now America was in Iraq, it had to stay until "the job was done."

Driven by ideological fervor – allegedly for Arab democracy, more likely for American supremacism – the White House dismissed "negativists" and went into Iraq with visions of being met by dancing in the streets. Bush assigned reconstruction to the warmakers (DOD) instead of the people in departments who derived no career advantage from combat (*Newsweek*, 6/9/08) and had spent their lives trying to understand Iraq. In the absence of advance planning, the Pentagon disregarded basic responsibilities of an occupying power like control of looters, sometimes resorted to irresponsible improvisation (disbanding the Iraqi army and the Baathist civil service), and then put lipstick on the pig by setting up an Arabic-language TV program to broadcast propagandistic versions of reality.

Neoconservative Dogma - George Soros noted that Neocon foreign policy, having dreamed up a "universal adversary", stressed international rivalry instead of international cooperation. Washington's blanket condemnation of Islamists and Saddam as agents of Satan shut out rational analysis. The first rule of conflict is Know the Enemy. The distorted perspective of the Bush Administration not only misread existing enemies, it created new ones. William Boykin, the latter-day crusader who belittled the God of Islam as inferior to Christianity's, was still a Deputy Undersecretary of Defense a year later. As documented by Peter Galbraith and Naomi Klein, the CPA was staffed with knee-jerk ideologues who pursued a bizarre scheme to convert Iraq overnight from state socialism to a supply-side economy, even to the point of decreeing a flat tax on personal and corporate income. Deputy Defense Secretary Wolfowitz predicted that Iraqi oil would finance the invasion and the reconstruction.

Ineptitude - The invasion and occupation of Iraq were distinguished by disregard for the elementary principles of governance. American troops were sent into Iraq by an innately incurious Chief Executive who was reported to be unaware that Iraqi Muslims were split between Sunnis and Shiites, and who, according to an assessment by Lawrence Freedman in *Foreign Affairs,* ceded full control over operations in Iraq to the zealotry of his Vice President. Three years after the invasion, Bush still seemed perplexed that the Iraqi Shia were siding with the Lebanese Hizballah against Israel and the US. British Ambassador to the UN Greenstock was *Vanity Fair*'s source for the report that responsibility for the witless disbandment of the Iraqi armed forces had not been established.

Thomas Ricks diagnosed in *The Gamble* Rumsfeld's inability to change course after making a mistake. Ricks's *Fiasco* documented errors of the military leadership in Iraq, where the Air Force destroyed the electric power system, and the ground forces bungled their responsibility as occupiers to maintain order. Bremer's transfer of Iraq's over 200 state companies to "free enterprise" imposed mass lay-offs on workers, who were replaced in many cases by employees of foreign firms.

Samantha Power reported that the occupation leadership, having stayed close to UN representative Vieira de Mello when they needed him as an intermediary, kept him at arms' length once they saw no more need of his services. Criticism in his press releases of the deaths of Iraqi civilians in Coalition actions may have had some relation to the absence of American military security around UN Headquarters when it was blown up and Vieira de Mello was killed.

In 2006, *The London Review of Books* reported that American entrepreneurs had exploited Washington's failure to maintain accountability over its 20 billion dollar Iraq Development Fund.

In Over Their Heads - Bewilderment at the alien culture of Iraq has long haunted American Middle East policy. Clumsy attempts to play ethnic politics included CIA dalliance with the Baath in the 1960's, the unconscionable support for Iraq versus Iran in the 1980's, and the bizarre rivalry in Washington for the favor of Iraqi exiles in the 1990's. The contest between DOD backing for wily Ahmad Chalabi and CIA backing for onetime Baathist Iyad 'Allawi persisted for years – undimmed by the bombing of Chalabi's headquarters by agents of 'Allawi in 1995. The Chalabi contact did US interests greater damage. The Iraq Study Group, headed by Howard Baker and Lee Hamilton, concluded that Chalabi provided (invented?) information that Saddam had WMD's – information seized on by Cheney and Wolfowitz, who were not troubled by reports of Chalabi ties with Iranian intelligence.

In the early days of the invasion, Washington flew Shiite cleric al Khu'i in to his death in Najaf. Ahmad Chalabi underwent a startling transformation from westernized Pentagon protégé to tribalized ally of Muqtada al Sadr. The huge Dulaymi tribe (Sunni) was temporarily alienated by the inadvertent killing of one of its leaders and his family.

Resourceful American officers on the ground did their best to come to terms with local concerns, but the cultural gap was too wide and the language barrier impervious – especially after the resistance began to kill the translators. The failed attempt in August 2004 (Patrick Cockburn) on the life of Muqtada al Sadr, and the pointless killing of one of Muqtada's aides, alienated a formidable Iraqi leader and helped provoke the JAM insurrection. Muslims will not forget desecration of Shiite mosques in Najaf and Sunni mosques in Fallujah, nor countless domestic humiliations. Also in 2004, the media cited Petraeus's alleged pacification of Mawsil as a textbook case of effective counterinsurgency; four months later, according to Frank Rich, Petraeus's choice for Chief of Police defected to the resistance.

According to Lawrence Korb, the pragmatic strategy of coopting mainstream Sunni resisters was delayed by the misconceived insistence of the occupation authorities that all participants sign a loyalty oath to the (Shiite) regime in Baghdad.

Mismatch of Strategy and Objective - As a response to 9/11, the invasion of Iraq was worse than irrelevant – in at least four respects, it was counterproductive: 1) It diverted resources needed in South Asia. 2) It mobilized more Muslims to the anti-American cause. 3) It set a precedent that future adversaries might exploit. 4) It mired the core of the American military in a domestic conflict foreigners could never win.

Washington drew a false analogy between the occupation of Iraq and those of Germany and Japan. Millions of Americans fell for the myth that the invasion of Iraq was a legitimate part of the "war on terror", but common sense told them Iraq is no case for conscription or another Marshall Plan, and the proof came in Bush's ultimate acceptance of a status-of-forces agreement that incorporated a deadline for American withdrawal unconnected to resolution of Iraq's caustic issues. The longer the Iraqis resisted American domination, the less persuasive was the mantra dreamed up by some Washington sloganeer that "It's better to fight terrorism over there than over here." As stated in *Middle East Policy* in 2006, US policy errors had contributed to the rise of a resistance powered by twenty anti-American factions. Two years later, that publication carried the common-sense observation of Douglas Macgregor that, by being "over there," our forces were at much greater risk than if they had stayed "over here."

Experienced campaigners have learned that civil unrest and subversion are political problems irresoluble by military action – least of all dropping bombs. After the "safer-America" argument lost traction, Washington began to mouth expressions of benevolence toward ravaged Iraq – as if Iraqis weren't aware that responsibility for their plight lay on Washington as much as on Saddam. After the invasion of 1991, in which US forces killed unknown numbers of Iraqi soldiers, some buried alive by the bulldozing of trench parapets, some finished off from the air while trying to escape along the "Highway of Death" – followed by twelve years of vindictive sanctions, the gratuitous invasion of 2003, the killing of 1500 Iraqis in Najaf, and the razing of Fallujah, how could Americans pose as the liberators of Iraq? In Washington's cowboy-and-Indian rhetoric, "bad guys" were being killed to protect "good guys." The iniquity of the occupation was best encapsulated in a Beattie cartoon: "Whoever we don't kill, we register to vote."

In plain logic, America was cultivating whoever hoped to profit from the occupation, and repressing whoever didn't. "Liberation" meant installation of a regime that was docile and non-Islamist. For an appropriate analogy to the American occupation of Iraq, we need go back only eighty years. British imperialism had more favorable circumstances; 1) Just emerging from Ottoman rule, the Iraqis (like the Palestinians) had no national leadership. 2) There was no regional Islamist movement. 3) There were no real-time satellite broadcasts by Al Jazeera and Al 'Arabia. Even so, Britain held out in Iraq only thirty-eight years (Chapter 10). America's actuarial prospects are much less promising.

The Bush administration drew a false dichotomy between "Iraqis" and "terrorists" by equating the former category with America's collaborators and the latter with its adversaries. It seemed to be operating on a premise that terrorists were a finite number, whose elimination would bring Iraq under American discipline. In fact, the Americans' heavy reliance on air strikes – in Iraq as in south Asia – was creating enemies faster than the bombs eliminated them.

In 2008, Peter Galbraith examined Bush's meretricious definition of victory as a unified, stable, democratic Iraq. If that Utopian future was indeed the goal, Washington should have set about it in a peaceful, deliberate way. Instead, it exacerbated instability by mindlessly inserting the biggest militia of all (Nir Rosen's trope) into the country's explosive mix. Backed by Iraqi analysts from institutions as prestigious as Brookings, Washington elevated Maliki's organization to the status of a "government", oblivious that it was just one more contender in an ongoing power struggle. In fact, the Americans' commitment to that one faction reduced them to the same lowly role, leaving their overstretched forces no option except to buy off Maliki's adversaries. America dismantled the old army, only to find that it had to pay for a new one. In America's current economic circumstances, the cooptation option can be nothing but a stop-gap.

In *Muqtada,* Patrick Cockburn noted a central irony of the American enterprise in Iraq: Intended to put the country on an anti-Iranian track, it brought Baghdad and Tehran closer together than they had been in five hundred years.

Exploitation - There is no hope of convincing the world that the motivation of the invasion was benign – because it wasn't. Washington's fallback pretense that it went to war for the sake of the Iraqi people was exploded in numerous ways. It tolerated disdain for Iraqis among the soldiery. (Example: *Times* report of a proposed T-shirt: "Kilo Company: Killed more people than cancer.") It entertained suggestions from the media that Israel could live with an Iraq split three ways. It packed the IGC with unpopular exiles. It tried to reconfigure the Iraqi economy for the benefit of American corporations. It diverted Iraqi oil revenues, while pinching the allocation of Congressional appropriations, or diverting them to unaudited American contractors. Some contractors were not paid from American government funds, as prescribed, but from Iraqi oil revenues put under CPA control by Security Council Resolution 1483. In 2004 Washington manipulated the trial of Saddam Husayn to avoid American embarrassment (as by revelation of American sale of biological contaminants during the Iraq-Iran War: *The New York Times Magazine,* 7/11/04).

Although in 2007 Washington pledged 30 million (sic) dollars toward the education of Iraqi refugees living abroad, there was no explicit expression of concern for the wretched plight of over four million displaced Iraqis – let alone any hint of America's primary responsibility for their misfortune (Julie Peteet in *Middle East Report* and Nir Rosen in *The New York Times Magazine*). Retired ambassador Barbara Bodine explained that, if Washington conceded there was a refugee crisis, it would have to admit that its forces, surge and all, had lost control of the security situation; the results of America's twenty-year record of breaking the back of Iraq's middle class (Patrick Cockburn, as reviewed by Charles Tripp in *The London Review of Books*), and destroying what had been a modern country, had to be blamed on Saddam, or bin Ladin, or general Arab beastliness. The Blackwater guards and helicopter pilots who gunned down seventeen Iraqi civilians on September 16, 2007, have not yet been called to account.

Having obligated trillions of dollars and sacrificed thousands of American lives and hundreds of thousands of Iraqi lives in trying to convert the country into the garrison for a Middle Eastern Pax Americana (*TomDispatch*), Washington now seems resigned to packing in the whole sorry enterprise, with short shrift for the indispensable Iraqis who risked taking jobs with the occupiers. Noting America's reception of only 1600 of them between October 2006 and 2007, *The Washington Post Weekly* cited the contrast with the one million loyalists admitted from Vietnam.

Neither the administration nor the media reminded the American electorate that American reconstruction aid to any country in the Middle East is subject to an unwritten but ironclad restriction: As long as American policy is premised on the survival of Zionist Israel, no other state in the region can be upgraded to the point of challenging Israel's economic, technological, or military supremacy (Washington stalled Iyad 'Allawi on his request for two mechanized divisions) – or of setting a democratic example that would highlight the undemocratic aspects of Zionism.

Cost-Benefit Analysis of the Invasion and the Occupation: 2009

Everyone agreed that Saddamist Iraq needed reform – notably, replacement of the tyrant, and moderation of Sunni domination. The challenge, as flagged by former CENTCOM commander General Anthony Zinni, was to accomplish these objectives without leaving the country worse off than before. As America apprehensively begins to draw down its forces, retrospect strongly suggests that its intervention in Iraq was mishandled in three irredeemable respects: 1) it was implemented by meat-axe tactics; 2) reforming Iraq is a job for the Iraqis; America had no business getting involved. 3) Iraq is not ready for democracy, least of all at the barrel of a gun.

If bin Ladin was shrewd enough to orchestrate 9/11 as a means of provoking American overreaction, the Bush administration was eager to accommodate him.

Benefits

Saddam Ousted - Saddam gave the country basic services (the most efficient food-distribution system in the Middle East), secularism, women's rights, economic development, and the Middle Eastern version of law and order. He cannot be faulted for having been a widely hated dictator – ethnicity-ridden Iraq can expect nothing else – but he exacerbated the hatred by brutality, extortion, barbarity (uncaring ruination of ecology in Kuwait and the Iraqi marshes), and recklessness (three disastrous wars – although Washington took his side in the first one). On balance, he was a bad dictator, but the case for condemning Iraq to the horror of war to get rid of him is demolished in advance by America's inability to insure that his replacement is any better.

Reconstruction - After the devastation America inflicted on Iraq by Gulf War I, sanctions, intermittent air attack, Gulf War II, and the anarchy that followed, it was only fitting that the CPA help Iraq recover. The bright spot was the renovation and resupply of many schools, and pay raises for teachers.

Costs

It seems self-evident that the incidental benefits of the invasion were overwhelmingly outweighed by its appalling costs. The ouster of Saddam gratified Iran (the end of Sunni dominance) and Israel (elimination of an enemy regime), but its clumsy means did grave disservice to the national interests of Iraq and the United States. No American can plausibly defend going to war just to replace one foreign dictator with another.

For many observers, the language of the Status of Forces Agreement, by providing no authorization for a permanent American military presence in Iraq, marks the failure of the invasion. An "advisory" contingent of twenty or thirty thousand American troops would be too many for normal relations and too few for self-defense in the event of a shootout. Washington will do well to extricate all its armed forces – plus their 130,000 private contractors (Jeremy Scahill; "Bill Moyers Journal" of 6/5/09) – from Iraq as soon as that is politically possible. After fifty years of floundering, the Middle East needs to get back on its own feet. If the Americans' invasion should prove to be the catalyst, perhaps they would have some feeble claim to credit.

Casualties - Over 4000 American soldiers and 1100 auxiliaries have lost their lives in Iraq. According to *Foreign Policy* of March 2008 and *The Nation* of 5/12/08, 31 percent of the 1.6 million American personnel deployed to Iraq and Afghanistan have returned with physical and/or psychological injury. Washington kept no records on Iraqi deaths (an insensitive omission for avowed liberators), but the *Times* reported 1/10/08 that WHO and Government of Iraq estimates indicated that 151,000 Iraqis had died, most of them violently, between March 2003 and July 2006. *The Nation* of 2/16/09 carried an estimate that 100,000 Iraqi civilians had died since 2006.

Expenditure - The *Times* of 3/1/09 carried an estimate that the Iraq War had cost the American budget 860 billion dollars. American contribution to reconstruction had been minuscule – that amount of Congressional allocations of some 50 billion dollars not squandered by overhead or by profligate American contractors. No system of accountability had been set up. In September 2008 Joseph Stiglitz said the Iraq War, fought on credit, was the central cause of America's three trillion-dollar deficit.

As cited in *The Nation* of 7/7/08, the invasion of Iraq exacerbated America's financial stresses by spiking the price of oil in a combination of ways: reducing Iraqi production, conjuring the specter of terrorism, and empowering Iran as a threat to Arabian oil supply.

Infrastructure Devastated - War with Iran, sanctions, invasion, and occupation inflicted massive damage on Iraq's power, water, and sewerage systems. Until 2006, resistance sabotage of oil pipelines was ongoing. A public-health system that had been one of the best in the Middle East is currently unable to meet demands – least of all in Fallujah. As of July 2004, the Tigris was an "open sewer." As of November, mortality rates were still rising because of insufficient drinking water. As of January 2005, provision of electric power in Baghdad and Basrah had fallen to a new low.

By 2009, Iraqi annual production of electricity was reportedly up to 6000 megawatts *(Times,* 6/18/09), 150 percent of the prewar level, but *Newsweek* of 6/12/09 reported that in Al Mahmudiyyah, 40 miles south of Baghdad, public services were almost nonexistent.

Breakdown of Iraqi Society - In the words of Bill Polk, America shredded the social fabric of Iraq. The educational and healthcare systems had been devastated by mass exodus of professionals. Ten percent of the population had fled the country for their lives, most of them to Syria and Jordan, where they were trying to survive with no ration cards, and no prospect of return to Iraq: The sectarian menace still existed, and their homes had been usurped.

Iraq's Shiite clerics were no longer inhibited by a secular power structure. Indulged by a deferential CPA, they set out to reverse liberal trends (women's rights) promoted by Baathist ideology. Policewomen who had been on street patrols were reassigned to desk jobs. Tribalism was reinvigorated by Petraeus's strategy of recruiting tribal levies, 20 percent of whose salaries went direct to the tribal leaders. Pepe Escobar reported that the killing or flight of most Western-educated professors had crippled the University of Baghdad and even the Mustansiriyyah, founded as a school of Islamic law in 1233 by al Mustansir, Caliph under the Seljuqs (Glasse: *Encyclopedia of Islam*), restored in modern times as a museum and a university.

Economy Shattered - Insecurity, power shortages, smuggling, and neocon revisions of Iraqi law had combined to hobble industry, cripple authority, and deny employment to half the adult population. State-owned companies were working at half capacity. Many factories were in shambles. Finance was stagnant. In 1996, under pressure from American-imposed sanctions, Saddam had established a state system for monthly distribution of rations. That system had broken down, especially for DP's. In 2007 Oxfam diagnosed a humanitarian crisis: four million Iraqi refugees in dire need of food assistance; two million of them still in Iraq, but driven from their homes, ignored by the "government", the occupation authorities, and the UN; seventy percent of Iraqis denied access to adequate water supply; most hospitals lacking basic medical necessities.

Security Vacuum - Even before the invasion, Bush's "war on terror" had been widely interpreted as an assault, on Israel's behalf, on the Arab and Islamic worlds. Washington represented the invasion as having made Iraqis and Americans safer. This was a minority view – overseas, and from 2005 on even in the United States. Anti-Americanism had risen, and American relations with traditional allies had been shaken.

As of 2009, Iraq was the latest candidate for the mournful category of failed states. Six blood-soaked years of confrontation between the occupation, relying on its domination of the air, and the resistance, relying on its familiarity with the land, had denied a decisive victory to either side, but it had made Iraq "the most dangerous place in the world" (*London Review of Books,* November 2008). Across wide areas of the country, responsibility for law and order had increasingly fallen on local militias.

Inhabitants of Iraq were compelled to adapt to a whole new environment – riven by ethnic cleansing, ghettoized in urban areas by the blast walls set up by a desperate occupation force. As of June 2007, Juan Cole noted that tens of thousands of former residents of devastated Fallujah were living in tent cities in the desert. In February 2008 Michael Schwartz reported that most of the 200 Baghdad neighborhoods that had been ethnically mixed were now homogeneous. According to The UN High Commissioner for Refugees, in April 2008 there were nearly 2.5 million displaced Iraqis in-country. Few had received financial aid from the Maliki regime. According to *The Nation,* Syria, Jordan, and even eleven of Iraq's eighteen governorates had closed their borders to Iraqi DP's.

In 1990, according to *The Washington Post Weekly* of 4/28/08, northern Iraq was the home of 1.35 million Christians (most of them Chaldean

Catholics, affiliated with the Church of Rome). By 2008 their archbishop, based in Mawsil, had been killed, and their community had been reduced by death and flight to 5-600,000. Their nemesis, according to the *Times,* was AQI. Driven out of Fallujah by US Marines, AQI had moved to Ninawah Province and attacked the Christians as American allies. The American forces were unwilling to come to their defense, for fear of adverse propaganda. The Pesh Merga welcomed the pretext to take over the five districts of Ninawah claimed by the KAR.

In 2009, the occupation forces were collaborating with an organization which was styled the Iraqi Army, but which might turn out to be the private militia of current Prime Minister Nuri al Maliki. In 2008 Washington had taken comfort in the subsidence of ethnic warfare, but the sporadic but persistent bombings of 2009-10 suggested that the Iraqi power struggle was yet to be resolved.

Democratic Claims Compromised - There was no evidence that democracy was the objective of the invasion of Iraq. By invading without due cause, condemning an anti-invasion decision by the Turkish Parliament, trespassing on the Geneva Conventions, maneuvering to prevent Iraq from electing a theocracy, and setting up a hand-picked interim government, Washington projected an image of classic imperialist opportunism.

In 2005, Washington had presumed to impose three prohibitions on the next Iraqi government: 1) It should not be under Iranian influence; 2) It should not set a date for American withdrawal; 3) It should not set up an Islamic state. In 2009 it appeared that Washington had struck out on all three demands.

Civil War? - No state could have expected to invade Iraq without inflaming its endemic communalism (Chapters 6 and 9). The mayhem was widely predicted. Political rivalry was backed by standing militias: Maliki's "Iraqi Armed Forces", Kurdistan's Pesh Merga, SCIRI's Badr Brigade, Sadr's JAM, the Baathist resistance's Army of Muhammad, the Iraqi Hizballah, and others.

Warnings of civil war began to circulate in 2004. By December, Muslim attacks on Christians had mounted, and the violence was beginning to take on the shape of an ethnic war. Sunnis were manning the resistance, and Shia and Kurds were doing the fighting for the 'Allawi Government – except in Najaf and the north, where Kurds and Shia sometimes fought each other. The Kirkuk/Mawsil area was the arena of a four-way dispute among Sunni Arabs, Shia Arabs, Kurds, and Turkmens. Most of the Arab beneficiaries of Saddam's ethnic transfers in Kirkuk had been Shiites, some of whom (followers of Muqtada al Sadr) condemn the secularist-minded Kurds as Muslim apostates. Whereas Saddam had forbidden Kurds to buy or build in Kirkuk, the postinvasion provincial governor and police chief were Kurds. In 2005, the Mayor of Mawsil was guarded by Kurdish militia who were fired with anti-Arab hostility. Most Iraqi victims of resistance killings had been Shia.

In 2007 there was heavy fighting between JAM and Maliki's forces (backed by the British) in Nasiriyyah. In 2008, according to Patrick Cockburn in *The Independent,* many of Baghdad's ghettoes were flying one of three flags: Sunnis displayed the old three-star flag, Shia a new Iraqi flag, Kurds the KRG flag. In February 2009 American media reported "ferocious enmity" between Baghdad's Nuri al Maliki and the KRG's Mas'ud Barzani. In the summer of 2008, there had been a face-off between their forces at Khanaqin, a town on the Iranian border in Diyala Province, at the outer edge of the KRG's area of control. Reports suggest that a clash was averted only by the intervention of American soldiers.

American Leadership Discredited - American occupation specialized in panicky expedience: frequent shifts in occupation leadership, both military and civilian; disbanding the Iraqi armed forces, then offering to rehire them; attacking Fallujah, pulling back, and then destroying the city months later; adoption, then abandonment, of a plan to introduce the caucus to Iraq – it might have worked in the Caucasus; spasmodic efforts to convert the economy to free enterprise; chasing Muqtada Sadr, and then leaving him for 'Allawi to worry about; switching from complacent unilateralism in 2003 to an appeal for UN Secretariat help in getting unstuck from the Iraqi tarbaby in 2004. Added to all this were unseemly dissension among State, Defense, and CIA, and the Administration's staunch position that its intervention in Iraq was blameless – but if blame was indicated, it should fall on the CIA.

Of all the traumatic consequences of the invasion, the worst was the infliction on the Middle East of another gigantic flood of refugees (*The Iraqi Refugees,* Joseph Sassoun, reviewed in *The Middle East Journal*) – compounded by Washington's reprehensible failure to face up to the problem, let alone to assume responsibility.

Iraq's Murky Future

UNSC Resolution 1546 of June 8, 2004, produced the national election of January 31, 2005, for a Transitional National Assembly charged with forming a Transitional Government and drafting a permanent constitution, "leading to a constitutionally elected government by 31 December 2005." In a note of realism, 1546 welcomed efforts to develop indigenous forces that would ultimately "assume full responsibility for the maintenance of security and stability in Iraq."

As of early 2010, that responsibility was being gingerly shed by the country that boldly appropriated it in 2003. The excruciating pressure on Washington to rescue the American economy, plus Obama's inexplicable commitment to step up American operations in Afghanistan, seemed to reduce Washington to one option in Iraq: the rapid reduction of its forces. The disadvantage to leaving advisers and trainers behind in sovereign Iraq will be their necessary collaboration with whichever faction happens to control Baghdad, however unsavory it may be, and the requirement to back them up with an American contingent capable of protecting them from attack by hostile factions in or out of government.

Whatever happens, Washington will profess to have set up the scaffolding of representative government. Iraq may keep up the Potemkin image for a time, with the simulation of a parliament and the pretense of a prime minister, but there is no enduring precedent for democracy in the history of the Middle East. Iraq's elected authorities have stayed in office by leaning on the American forces, and deferring action on the big issues: control of the oil fields, division of oil revenues, union versus federation, ethnic reconciliation, the role of Islam in government, and the division of power.

If the recent experience catalogued in previous chapters is any guide, Muslim states are destined to follow a turbulent sequence from tribalism to autocracy – military, partisan, or theocratic – long before they have built the political infrastructure of democracy. In the meantime, factional disputes are generally settled by coup d'etat or civil war.

If the Israeli-American diarchy has had enough of Iraq, the likely power struggle to determine its next dictator could be complicated by partition and/or by intervention by one or more adjoining states. The prospects of a negotiated settlement are undermined by ongoing power struggles in eight countries in the neighborhood: Iraq, Iran, Jordan, Kuwait, Lebanon, Saudi Arabia, Syria, and Turkey.

Outlook: 2010

In the volatile politics of Iraq, a situation report is hardly more enlightening than a snapshot taken during a football game, but the results of the reputedly orderly parliamentary election of March 2010 gave grounds for hope that a slender plurality of voters had taken to heart the recent grim lesson of ethnic fanaticism, and were in an unprecedented mood to reject sectarianism in favor of Iraqi nationalism.

Up until the election, Iraq has had an extra-constitutional Presidential Council (President Talabani and two Vice Presidents). The constitution provides for the President of Iraq to ask the leader whose faction commands the most parliamentary seats to form a government. The outcome depends upon the intricate post-electoral interaction of four major political factions:

'Iraqiyyah (91 seats) – Former Prime Minister Iyad al 'Allawi, a Shiite secularist, is closer to the Arab World than to Iran, and the champion of Sunnis, including Vice President Tariq al Hashimi, and pragmatic Shiites. 'Allawi's public image (like that of the Taliban's Mullah Omar) benefits from a reputation for personal courage, enhanced by his survival from an attack by two of Saddam's axe murderers.

State of Law (89 seats) – Shiite Nuri al Maliki, who rejected the results of the election, had clout as the sitting Prime Minister – able to call on American military support in his campaigns to repress his rivals, notably Kurdish expansionists and Muqtada Sadr. Maliki ran as a secularist; his bloc included Sunni Hajim al Hasani, former Speaker of the National Assembly.

Iraqi National Alliance (70 seats) – INA, the unlikely Shiite alliance of former adversaries Muqtada al Sadr and 'Ammar al Hakim (ISCI), along with former Prime Minister Ibrahim al Ja'fari, Ahmad al Chalabi, and Vice President 'Adil 'Abd al Mahdi, is reportedly the faction closest to Iran.

Kurdistan Alliance (53 seats) – The KDP and the PUK campaigned separately, but ran as a bloc. It did not include Gorran (8 seats), a reform group that broke off from the PUK: *Times*, 3/6/10.

On May 5, 2010, the *Times* reported a new alliance between Maliki's State of Law and the Iraqi National Alliance. Failing emergence of a coalition with a parliamentary majority (at least 163 of the 325 members), the inevitable power struggle is likely to lapse from the unfamiliar arena of debate to the traditional arena of coercion and violence—subject to the possible reemergence of Ayatallah 'Ali al Sistani. According to an *AP* report of 5/6/10, the major Shiite factions had agreed to accord the ultimate decision to the M*arji'iyyah*, which Sistani presumably still controls.

Chapter 16
Through a Glass Darkly:
A Policy Prescription

Middle Eastern Alignments

As the would-be arbiter of Middle Eastern affairs, Washington has been groping for a strategy that will bring the region under American discipline. This unrealistic effort has been blocked by a phalanx of insuperable obstacles:

- Trying to reconcile the rival communities and states is like herding cats.
- Most of the states are internally beset by a disconnect between disaffected populaces and repressive regimes. As Charles Freeman stated 10/23/09, the Arab monarchies collude with elements that attack the Muslim community. (However, at the present stage of political evolution in the Middle East, repression may be essential to functioning government.)
- The illusionary convenience of Washington's unilateral approach has been nullified by huge socioeconomic problems that require multilateral attention.
- American objectives – an inside track to oil, preferential status for Israel, preservation of the geopolitical status quo – are contrary to the interests of the region.
- American strategy has been naive: reward compliance, punish opposition. Worse, it is predicated on fallacy: that the national

interests of Israel and the United States are identical; that the segmentation of the Middle East into ministates is permanent.

The contemporary result is the following lineup of regimes (not populaces):

Pro-American (11)	Anti-American (2)	Unresolved (6)
Azerbaijan*	Iran	Armenia*
Egypt	Syria	Cyprus
Gulf States (5)		Georgia *
Israel		Iraq
Jordan		Lebanon
Saudi Arabia		Yemen
Turkey		

* Maintained token contingents in Iraq during the American occupation, but were also members of the Russian-led Commonwealth of Independent States (*The World Almanac*, 2009).

Pro-American

Azerbaijan - Situated in a traditional battleground between Turkey and Iran, Azerbaijan is a natural ally of Turkey and adversary of Iran. Although both Azerbaijan and Iran have Shiite majorities, they are separated by language family (Altaic versus Indo-European) and ideology (secularist versus theocratic). Azerbaijan has harbored the South Azerbaijan National Liberation Committee, which has irredentist designs on northwestern Iran, home of the 7,000,000 Iranians whose first language is Azeri.

Azerbaijan's oil wealth has created a long-term symbiosis with the West on two counts – market and development expertise – but it lost the bitter war with Armenia (see below) in part because it couldn't compete with the Armenians' American lobby, on whose behalf Congress in 1992 restricted aid to Azerbaijan (*The Middle East Journal*, Spring 2009). Clashes with Russian troops in Baku in 1990 left a legacy of hostility between Russia and Azerbaijan, whereas Russia provided Armenia the arms and financing it needed to conquer the Armenian-peopled enclave of Nagorno-Karabakh and a diminutive connecting corridor.

Azerbaijan has been aiming for a strategic position midway between Russia and the US. It has allowed US military aircraft to refuel, but has not broached membership in NATO.

Egypt - A majority of the population is critical of American policy for Palestine and infuriated by the invasion of Iraq, but President Mubarak has kept the country in the American camp, even to the point of joint military exercises, and follows Washington's lead in return for arms and money.

Gulf States - The five countries along the eastern coast of the Arabian Peninsula continue to follow their traditional strategy of affiliation with a great power (earlier Britain, now America) as insurance against conquest by one of their bigger neighbors.

Kuwait - barred civilians from 60 percent of its territory, for American staging of the 2003 invasion of Iraq.

In 2001, Rumsfeld personally arranged with Sultan Qabus American base rights in **Oman.** Washington concluded a free-trade agreement with Oman in 2006. Qabus kept Oman neutral in the Iran-Iraq war, backed Kuwait in 1991, but opposed the invasion of Iraq. A US-Oman agreement (arms and a small subsidy for US access to Masirah), signed in 1980, is still in effect : Lefebvre, *Middle East Policy,* Spring 2010.

Qatar - was settled from Arabia, and followed the Saudi lead until 1995, when its new leadership (Chapter 11) struck out on a more independent course, allowing Al Jazeera to air criticism of the Saudi regime, and cultivating Iran as a counterweight. The spread of a gigantic gas field across the Iran-Qatar border in the Gulf imposes the need for close cooperation.

To insure American support for an independent Qatar, its ruler has hosted America's biggest pre-positioning base (Al Sayliyyah) in the Gulf and CENTCOM's headquarters at Al 'Udayd air base, and in 1996 he allowed Israel to open a trade office in Doha: Uzi Rabi, *Middle East Journal,* Summer 2009. He closed it in 2009 in concert with the general Arab condemnation of the Israeli foray into Gaza (Chapter 8), and suspended all diplomatic and economic ties with Israel (*Middle East Policy,* Spring 2009). The Qatari representative on the UN Security Council has consistently voted for Arab and Iranian positions.

Bahrain - is the headquarters of the Fifth Fleet; it may also have been the first Arab state to have sent a Jewish (lady) ambassador to Washington.

The **UAE** was particularly exercised by Iran's 1972 occupation of three strategic islets in the southern Gulf (the Tunbs and Abu Musa); nevertheless, Dubai is Iran's major foreign entrepot, and Iranian leaders rely on Dubai as a safe place to bank their money (*Middle East Policy,* Summer 2008). The UAE has collaborated with the US in several ways (handing over Islamist activists, allowing visits of US fleet units, according base facilities to US recon and refueling aircraft), but it has not participated in Washington's economic sanctions against Iran, it adamantly opposes Western military action against Iran, and its banks have handled financial transfers for Al Qa'idah.

Israel - After sixty years of independence, Israel has achieved a peace treaty with only two of its Arab neighbors – Egypt and Jordan. Several others, including some in the Pro-American column, still consider themselves in a state of war with the country that continues to "persecute their Palestinian brothers." Israel has provided military support to the Iraqi Kurds since 1965. The 1996 treaty of alliance with Turkey may have been undermined by Israel's reported infiltration of Iraqi Kurdistan in 2004, and by widespread Turkish resentment of Israel's large-scale use of force against Lebanon in 2006 and the Gaza Strip in 2006 and 2008. Israel supported Azerbaijan against Armenia in the 1990's. It bases air and naval units in Turkey.

Jordan - King 'Abdallah II has steered a more pro-American course in Gulf War II than his father did in Gulf War I – probably allowing the CIA to maintain black sites for the interrogation of suspects (*Times*, 4/10/09) – but he may have felt compelled by domestic pressures to allow some support for the Iraqi resistance against the Americans.

Saudi Arabia - Since 1945, Riyadh and Washington have had an understanding based on Saudi attention to America's oil and financial needs, and America's guarantee of Saudi security from outside attack. The Saudi military is dependent on technical support from private American companies. Although there is no known contractual basis for the stationing of American forces in Saudi Arabia, the American air command still has access to refueling and command and control facilities on Saudi territory.

The relationship was shaken by the attack of 9/11, in which a number of Saudis participated, and by growing Saudi frustration with Washington's Middle East policy, as manifested by Saudi signature of a joint security pact with Iran in 2003. Foreign Minister Sa'ud Al Sa'ud had said in 2002 that his government opposed any attack on Iraq, and would bar air strikes against Iraq from Saudi territory. The people of Saudi Arabia were almost unanimous in their opposition to the invasion, and their government was distressed by the subsequent emergence of Shiite hegemony in Baghdad.

David Ottaway reported in *Foreign Affairs* of May 2009 that Saudi Arabia was still cooperating with Washington against Al Qa'idah, and in the establishment of King 'Abdallah University, planned as a major coeducational institution, but had rejected joint action against the new Shiite cordon across the center of the region, and opposed military action against Iran.

Turkey - In World War I, Turkey made the big mistake of taking the side of Germany. In World War II, it remained neutral until 1945, when it declared war on Germany in order to get a seat at the founding of the UN in San Francisco. In 1951, under the Truman Doctrine, Turkey and Greece joined NATO. In the 1990's, Turkey sided with Azerbaijan and closed its border with Armenia.

In 1996, Turkey entered into military alliance with Israel – the only Muslim state to take this step. Turkey has been counting on American and Israeli help in its campaign to join the European Union. It initiated joint naval exercises with those two allies in the late 1990's. The alliance with Israel afforded Turkey military technology, in return for letting the Israeli Air Force train and do recon in Turkish air space. American aircraft still have access to the Incirlik airfield near Adana. Incirlik was a headquarters for American air operations during Gulf War I and the sanctions period. Washington compensates Turkey with arms and financial aid. The opening to Israel aggravated the perennial power struggle between Turkey's generals, who have been dedicated to the defense of secularism and Turkish nationalism, and its politicians, many of whom reflect the popular consensus for preservation of Islamic values and honoring the human rights of the Palestinians – and even those of the Kurds. In the last century, the insistence of the generals' National Security Council on expunging Kurdish ethnicity imposed an immense budgetary burden on a government grappling with inflation approaching 100 percent, and damaged Turkey's relations with neighboring states and the European Union.

By 2000, Turkey had normal relations with Greece (reestablished in 1930), and was attempting to downplay the Cyprus dispute, in the interest of closer ties with the EU. (Many observers thought the EU had erred in accepting a divided Cyprus as a member.) Looking forward to EU membership, President Ozal had relaxed restrictions on the Kurds and overruled the military by giving full support to the American expulsion of Iraq from Kuwait in 1991. In 1999, a Cyprus plan to deploy Russian anti-aircraft missiles had been averted by a Turkish threat to bomb them.

2003 was the notable year when Parliament stood up against the American invasion of Iraq. Turkey's reception of Hamas leader Khalid Mish'al in 2006 was consistent with Prime Minister Erdogan's charge that Israeli military operations versus the Palestinians in the Occupied Territories constitute state terrorism. In 2009 Erdogan gave expression to this resentment at the economic summit at Davos by telling Israeli delegate Peres "You know well how to kill," and walking out of the meeting (*Washington Report on Middle East Affairs*). Turkish relations with Israel and America could be further eroded by conflict of interest in northern Iraq – highlighted by reports of clandestine Israeli collaboration with the armed forces of the KAR.

By May 2009 Turkey had moved into close cooperation with Syria (*Foreign Policy*, citing Yigal Schliefer of *The Monitor*), and according to *The Washington Report on Middle East Affairs* had opened to Palestinian plaintiffs Ottoman files that revealed that some Zionist documentation on land ownership had been forged. In September Turkey and Syria lifted restrictions on each other's citizens.

The *InterPress Service* of 10/13/09 cited a report in Turkish daily *Hurriyet* that, as an expression of disapproval of Israel's 2008-09 attack on the Gaza Strip, Turkey had excluded Israel from its NATO war games for an unspecified period: *Washington Report on Middle East Affairs*, December 2009. Erdogan's newly independent policy might be termed "Middle East for the Middle Easterners": Saban Kardas, *Middle East Policy*, Spring 2010.

The *Guardian Weekly* of 6/11/10 reported agreement on visa-free travel between Turkey and Syria, Lebanon, Jordan, and Libya.

Anti-American

Iran - Vali Nasr explains how the only Shia power in a region dominated by Sunnis has to pursue contradictory objectives. Suspicious of Shiite Azerbaijan's designs on Iran's Azeri districts, it prefers an Azerbaijan that is weak and unstable: *Middle East Policy*, 2007. It shares with Israel an elemental apprehension of Sunni coalescence – whether by restoration of the Caliphate or by Arab unity – but it needs to reduce the relentless hostility among the sects of Islam.

In 1979, pan-Islamist Khomeini cancelled all agreements with the United States, broke diplomatic and commercial relations with Israel, turned the Israeli Embassy over to the PLO, declared his support for the people of Occupied Palestine, and took Iran out of the Central Treaty Organization. Thereafter, Iran has made belligerent common cause with the Arabs against Israel and its allies – although for a time Khomeini orchestrated a war of words against the tribal regimes in the Arabian Peninsula: Ulrichsen.

For Carter's presidency, the Iranian revolution was terminal. Under pressure from friends of the Shah, including Kissinger, Carter allowed the Shah to enter the US for medical treatment. As Embassy Tehran had warned, Iranians retaliated. Student volunteers overran the compound and took American personnel hostage; according to Sheikh Ali, their motivation was to insure against a repeat of the British-American coup against Prime Minister Mossadeq in 1953. Khomeini – locked in a three-way power struggle among Islamists, nationalists, and communists – chose not to intervene. The foreign minister explored a settlement with Washington, and was executed for his trouble. A daring American effort to rescue the hostages by helicopter failed. They were mysteriously released in 1981, hours after the inauguration of President Reagan.

During the administrations of Reagan and Bush 41, relations with Iran were rancorous, particularly during the Iran-Iraq war of 1980-88. As another flare-up of the ancient power struggle between Shiites and Sunnis, the war should have been a strictly Middle Eastern matter, but the wanton interventionism of latterday American foreign policy converted the US into a participant. Washington was superficially annoyed by Iran's venture into theocracy, but driven up the wall by its sudden hostility toward Israel. In 1988, a series of clashes between Iranian and American naval units resulted in the destruction of half the Iranian navy. Three years later, Iraq drifted into Washington's sights, setting off a concatenation of events that switched Iraq from the Sunni to the Shiite side. In their devious ineptitude, the American policymakers had managed to do their Iranian adversaries a huge favor.

The foreign policy of the Iranian theocracy has not been much cleverer. In 1992, four Kurdish leaders from Iran were assassinated in Berlin. A German court implicated new supreme leader Khamenei, President Ali Rafsanjani, and Foreign Minister Ali Velayati. The US and Saudi Arabia believed that the Quds Force, covert army of the Pasdaran, had carried out the 1996 bombing of the Khawbar Towers apartment building in which 19 US military personnel died.

As reported by John Duke Anthony, in 1995 Clinton responded to Zionist pressure by issuing an executive order cancelling Conoco's concession to develop the South Pars offshore oil field, and another purporting to restrict foreign investment in Iran. Clinton's underlying objective was to undermine the Iranian regime. The bizarre Iran-Libya Sanctions Act of 1996 allegedly disallowed foreign states from investing more than 40 million dollars in either target country. The European Union ignored it.

The election of reformist President Mohammed Khatami in 1997 ushered in a conciliatory phase in Tehran. Bolstered by the Berlin atrocity, Khatami won in a landslide, and as reported by *Middle East Policy* set out to moderate Iranian policy toward Saudi Arabia and the West – although he was inhibited by Khamenei and, as noted by Zbigniew Brzezinski, by the anti-Clinton Congress, which blocked dialogue with Iran. Iran has been a bitter opponent of the hardline Sunni Taliban. After the Al Qaʻidah attacks of 9/11, Khatami cooperated with Washington in support of the Karzai regime in Afghanistan.

In so doing, as Gary Sick observed in his review of Ray Takeyh's *Hidden Iran,* Khatami put aside Bush 43's irresponsible denunciation of an illusory Iranian-Iraqi-North Korean Axis of Evil. In *Treacherous Alliance,* Trita Parsi noted that Bush's formulation had contributed to the fall of the Iranian liberals, which was the theme of de Bellaigue's *The Struggle for Iran.*

Iran saw the invasion of Iraq as an ominous precedent. Iraq's President Talabani and Prime Minister Maliki have had close ties with Tehran, while the Pasdaran have reportedly provided sanctuary to Al Qa'idah fugitives from American pursuit.

By 2006, Iran's primary agency for foreign affairs (as seen by Flint Leverett), the Supreme National Security Council (members appointed by the Supreme Leader, chaired by the President), was preoccupied with countering pressures from the US – even though Washington had done Iran three inadvertent favors by ousting the Taliban from Afghanistan, the Iraqi Baath from Baghdad, and Syrian forces from Beirut. Even the US-sponsored UN sanctions on Iran were useful to the Iranian hardliners: All the experts note that Ahmadinejad has thrived on crisis.

So far, the UNSC has imposed on Iran three rounds of sanctions: Resolution 1737 of December 2006 banned trade that could advance Iran's nuclear program; 1747 of March 2007 banned Iranian exportation of arms; 1803 of March 2008 banned exportation of dual-use merchandise to Iran. According to *The Wall Street Journal,* insofar as American-sponsored sanctions were applied by European companies, they expanded business opportunities for the Pasdaran and their commercial rivals, the shrines, which had magnified their pilgrimage industry into clusters of *bonyad*'s, crowding out private enterprise.

At a more ominous level, Bush's Iran Freedom Support Act, assessed in *The Middle East Journal,* hinted at regime change in Tehran. Also among Washington's quiver of harassments, Robin Wright cited the blacklisting of Iranian banks and the prevention of foreign oil companies from providing the developmental assistance Iran desperately needs. The sanctions had exacerbated Iran's economic strains by raising the prices of staple foods. Ahmadinejad was taking the heat for stagflation, budget deficit, and a painful shortage of gasoline. Over a fourth of the GDP had been diverted to subsidies for basics like food and energy.

In 2007, Washington imposed the toughest sanctions yet. They included a ban on financing for the Pasdaran's Quds Force, whose exportation of ballistic missiles was condemned as terrorism. According to *The Wall Street Journal,* the Pasdaran were exporting revolution by providing arms and money to Hamas and branches of Hizballah in many countries. The

UNSC had frozen Iranian assets thought to be linked to its missile and nuclear programs, and The World Bank had suspended allocations for Iran, but Iran had preemptively switched its oil pricing from dollars to the Euro and the yen, and was finding ways to evade the American sanctions – notably by reverting to the primitive *hawalah* system of promissory notes, and by trading through Dubai.

In *Middle East Policy* of Spring 2008, Ray Takeyh stressed that the Islamic Republic, rejecting the Sunni effort to relegate it to secondary status in the Islamic spectrum, has always sought recognition as a generic Muslim state – and one qualified to reprimand Sunni regimes. The authoritative right-wing daily *Al Kayhan* has condemned Saudi King 'Abdallah as a puppet, and accused Egypt's Mubarak of subservience to Zionism.

Laura Secor (*The New Yorker*) and Ervand Abrahamian (*Middle East Report*) agreed that Iran would not be able to attract the capital needed to exploit its oil and gas resources until the American embargo was lifted. *Middle East Policy* carried Jean-Francois Seznec's judgment that Iran would not be able to build a significant industrial capacity until it joined the WTO. The European Union has favored Iranian membership, but so far Washington has blocked it.

William Blum's blog of 2/3/09 condemned Washington's Iranian policy. In his view Iran had as much right to arm Hamas as the US had to arm Israel; boarding Iranian freighters in search of arms was an indefensible act of war. In the *Times* of 9/2/09, Jerry Giro assessed America's sanctions on Iran as ineffective and in some cases counterproductive. In 2010 (*Times*, May 31) US officials accused Iran of providing Afghan insurgents with arms and training.

Syria - Bashar al Asad has continued his father's cautious leadership (with the possible exception of even deeper involvement in Lebanon's lethal politics). Before the invasion of Iraq, Syria was a useful source of intelligence on the activities of Al Qa'idah. Since Syria's condemnation of the invasion, hostility toward Syria has been building in Washington, which accuses Damascus of abetting the Iraqi resistance. In 2003, the Syrian Accountability Act of 2002 had evolved into the more severe Syria Accountability and Lebanon Sovereignty Restoration Act, adopted by an overwhelming majority in Congress. Under the new act, Bush 43 banned exports to and investment in Syria (penalizing American firms to the benefit of their European competitors). The Bush administration made no secret of its interest in Syrian regime change: *Middle East Policy*, Summer 2009.

Unresolved

Lebanon - In October 2004, Security Council Resolution 1559 called for the evacuation of all foreign (Syrian) troops from Lebanon, disarming of militias (Hizballah), and – in effect – cancellation of changes Damascus had made in the Lebanese constitution. In 2005, Lebanese separatists demonstrated for withdrawal of the small Syrian garrison, and ultimately for termination of Syrian hegemony. Pro-Syrians, mobilized by Hizballah, demonstrated in Syria's favor. Under broad international pressure, Syria completed the evacuation of its forces on April 26, 2005, but pro-Syrian elements still held key positions in the Lebanese power structure. As of early 2009, the strongest military force was the pro-Iranian, pro-Syrian Hizballah.

The solid victory of the pro-American faction in the election of June 2009 would appear to bring Lebanon back into the American camp, except for the elephant in the room – Hizballah, which in 2008 used its preeminent military power to stage a brief but sobering takeover in Beirut, thereby insuring its veto power over the pro-American government.

Armenia - With a strong lobby in Washington, Armenia should be squarely in the American camp, but it is painfully conflicted by its military and economic dependence on Russia. Its solid victory in 1992 over Azerbaijan (see above) was facilitated by Congressional restriction of American aid to Azerbaijan (*Middle East Journal,* Spring 2009), but it was primarily due to arms supplied by Moscow (*Middle East Policy*, October 1999). Its hold on 20 percent of Azerbaijani territory has been frozen since the cease-fire of 1994. A million Armenians work in Russia, while the influence of Armenia's American lobby is increasingly countered by the oil lobby, which is focused on the oil of Azerbaijan.

Cyprus - As a member of the European Union, the Greek segment of Cyprus is able to keep some distance from Middle Eastern turmoil, but the partition of the island has been recognized only by Turkey.

Georgia - Georgia would like to disengage from its giant neighbor and one-time hegemon. Circumstances have intervened. Until mid-2005, Russian troops were based there, on the strength of a Russian threat to cut off vital supply of oil and natural gas. In 2008 additional pressure was exerted in the form of Russian intervention to guarantee the de facto secession of Abkhazia and South Ossetia (Chapter 11). According to Robert English, the intervention was a reaction to Russia's perception of a campaign by Bush 43 to isolate and encircle it.

In 2005, Bush made history by visiting Georgia. In keeping with his forward foreign policy, Washington was providing Georgia with military training and financial aid (over 100,000,000 dollars a year). The Americans see Georgia as their preferred exit route for Caspian oil, but Russian companies are buying into Georgian energy enterprises.

In 2008 an Israeli website noted friendly Israeli-Georgian ties, and reported that Israel was selling Georgia as many high-tech arms as Russia would tolerate.

Iraq - The inflammatory situation in Iraq is discussed in Chapter 15. Postoccupation Iraq can be expected to move closer to Iran, reassert hostility to Israel, and renew the claim to Kuwait.

Yemen - Opposed to the invasion of Iraq, but sobered by the long reach of the American superpower, Yemen has tried to stay out of the line of fire. Its handling of the bombing of the USS Cole in Aden did not meet all Washington's expectations, but Yemen did not make an issue of the assassination of Al Qa'idah activists in Yemen by drone aircraft deployed by American Special Forces sitting in Nevada. As of this writing, the centralist regime of 'Ali 'Abdallah Salih was under severe pressure from rightist dissidents in the north, leftist dissidents in the south, and Al Qa'idah affiliates in Yemen.

The Turkish Obsession with Membership in the EU

All Middle Eastern states are under domestic pressure to modernize and prosper. One possible route is to join the European Union. Cyprus (minus the Turkish segment) has taken that route. Ankara would like to. The United States supports the effort, but has negligible influence over the outcome. Turkey made formal application for membership in 1987. In its favor, it has membership in NATO (1951), associate membership in the European Economic Community (1963), and a Turkish-EU customs union (1995). In 1999, the EU accepted Turkey as a <u>candidate</u> for membership. In 2004, the EU's Executive Committee voted to approve Turkey as an <u>applicant</u> for membership, subject to the endorsement of at least 25 EU Chiefs of State. In October 2005, the EU voted to initiate accession talks with Turkey.

In 2005, the AKP – and the Turkish Kurds – welcomed the opening of accession talks. By 2006, however, basic disagreements had soured the relationship. The EU requested that Turkey open its ports to Cypriot ships and aircraft; Ankara countered with a demand that Cyprus lift its embargo on the Turkish enclave. The Turkish electorate was resentful of European prejudice against Turkish guest workers, enraged by America's senseless invasion of Iraq, and suspicious that the resurgence of the PKK reflected Washington's resentment of the Turkish position on Iraq. *Foreign Affairs* reported that Turkey had been rebuilding ties with Iran, Syria, and the Arab world. On the other side of the argument, Israel and its allies were appalled by Turkey's overtures to the new Hamas regime in Gaza – including the 2006 reception of Khalid Mish'al – and by a big anti-Israeli demonstration in Istanbul. Since 2003, there had been a decline in the magnitude of joint Turk-Israeli defense projects.

In 2007, de Bellaigue noted that enthusiasm for Turkish accession to the EU was waning in Europe and even in Turkey.

In 2008, the AKP did some fence-mending. The Greek prime minister made the first high-level formal visit to Turkey in 50 years. According to *The London Review of Books,* Erdogan had purged his party of opponents of the invasion of Iraq. For Washington, Turkish cooperation was critical. Of the masses of supplies it was shipping to Iraq, three-fourths went via Incirlik. Also, in return for intelligence on the operations of the PKK, Washington reportedly hoped Turkey would reinforce those elements of its million-man army already serving in Afghanistan.

Membership in the EU, if it materializes, is still a long way off. The obstacles are formidable:

Economic Distress - The Turkish economy still falls short of EU requirements. In 2001, Turkey devalued its currency to stave off financial collapse. The IMF helped out with a 17,000,000 dollar loan. By 2009, Prime Minister Erdogan had achieved noteworthy progress in alleviating Turkey's economic difficulties.

Islam - Against the background of France's problems with its North African minority, the EU is concerned about the slow rate of assimilation of its Turkish workers, including two million in Germany alone. Traditional Muslim practices like "honor killings" of shamed female relatives clash with European mores. The French rejection of the draft EU constitution in 2005 has been interpreted in part as implicit rejection of Turkey's application for membership.

Issues with Greece and Cyprus - Turkey has yet to iron out disputes over hegemony in Cyprus and smaller islands in the Aegean. Turkish ports are still closed to ships of Cyprus registry.

Human Rights - By EU standards, Turkey's political system is profoundly corrupt, and the Kurdish minority is victimized.

Geopolitics - There has been no public evidence that the EU has appreciated the extent to which Turkish membership would reengage it in thorny Middle Eastern issues that the Europeans shrugged off in the aftermath of World War II. The Turks have preferred to look to the north, but their more basic foreign policy problems are to the south: allocation of the waters of the Tigris and the Euphrates; resolution of Kurdish demands; factionalism in the world of Islam; and now the future of Iraq.

In June 2009, *Agence Globale* carried a report by Patrick Seale (cited by *The Washington Report on Middle East Affairs*) that recent indicators suggest the formation of a new entente among Turkey, Syria, Iraq, and Iran. Washington should frame its policies to allow for the contingency that Turkey will conclude that its geopolitical destiny is not as a labor source for Europe, but as an engine of stability and development for the Middle East. Of the nineteen states in the region, Turkey is the closest to democracy. In a European role, it would be a follower; in a Middle Eastern role, it would resume its ancient tradition of leadership.

The Alternative to Washington

All three superpowers – America, China, and Russia – are dependent on the uninterrupted flow of Middle Eastern oil and gas, and on access to the revenue it generates. They are linked by a vital interest in regional stability and the prevention of disruptive military action, such as an attack on Iran.

Otherwise, they are competitors. China is handicapped by the stresses of autocracy, exemplified by Uighur dissidence in Sinkiang Province. Russia is handicapped by economic underdevelopment. Dependence on Western financial aid reduced Moscow's ability to save Iraq from American invasion. In 2009, an op-ed in the *Times* cited the judgment of former Soviet official Yegor Gaidar that a decision on September 13, 1985, by Saudi oil minister Ahmad Yamani to alter Saudi oil production policy precipitated the collapse of the Soviet Union six years later. The US is handicapped by its linkage with Israel, and by its consequent penchant for interventionism, which Russia and China have effectively exploited.

China has long figured in the international relations of Egypt, Syria, Iraq, and Yemen, but it was not fully represented in the Persian Gulf until 1990, when it established diplomatic ties with Saudi Arabia.

In 1995, Dilip Hiro spotted the emergence of a French-Russian-Chinese axis which suspected that one reason America favored sanctions on Iraq was to keep oil prices high, so oil states could afford to buy American arms. He credited a Yeltsin intervention with averting American-Iraqi crisis over weapons inspection in 1997 – the year Iraq announced the signing of a major contract for Russian development of the West Qurna oil field. In 1999 Russia contracted to upgrade Iraq's air force and air defenses; Russia looked to Saddam for eventual payment of Iraq's eight billion dollar debt.

Also in 1999, on a visit to Saudi Arabia, President Jiang Zemin announced a strategic partnership with that country.

In 2000, Iranian President Khatami made a historic trip to China, which has become one of Iran's principal sources of nuclear technology.

Iraq's major trading partners in 2002 were France, Italy, Russia, and Egypt. Saddam regarded Russia as his chief ally against new UN sanctions or American invasion.

In reaction to the Primakov Doctrine (Russian-Chinese-Indian projection of strategic balance against the United States), Washington took precautions, including blacklisting Russian firms that sold missile or nuclear technology to Iran. In 2001, Russian President Putin authorized resumption of arms and nuclear technology sales to Iran. In 2005, the EU favored Iranian entry into the World Trade Organization, but Washington was blocking it.

In 2006, China was the destination of Saudi King 'Abdallah's first foreign trip as ruler.

By 2007, Iran was expanding consular, defense, and nuclear technology contacts with India, and work had begun on construction of a gas pipeline between the two countries. In 2008 *Middle East Policy* cited Charles Freeman's report that China was building a huge automotive industry in Iran.

By 2009, Saudi Arabia, Iran, and Oman were China's major suppliers of oil. China had sold intermediate-range ballistic missiles to Saudi Arabia, and anti-ship cruise missiles to Iran – one of which may have been the projectile that damaged an Israel naval ship in the Hizballah War (Chapter 8). The Kuwait Petroleum Corporation had agreed to build an entire petrochemical industry in China.

In *Middle East Policy* of Summer 2009, Mahmoud Ghaffour reported that Russia and China saw Iran as a quasi-ally against the American effort to maintain a military presence in the Middle East and Central Asia; American sanctions on Iran had opened up "tremendous opportunities" for China. In the fall issue of *Middle East Policy*, Mark Katz wrote that, despite Russian reliance on Israel for cutting-edge military technology, Russia had acquired exclusive cargo-flight rights from Iraq: *Times*, 11/13/09. Brzezinski pointed out in *Foreign Affairs* of January 2010 that Russia would be the only one of the three great powers to benefit from a spike in the price of oil.

March 2010 featured the first visit by units of the modern Chinese navy to a Middle East port (Abu Dhabi).

American Policy for the Region: Time to Reevaluate

In a few hours' time on September 11, 2001, an anonymous band of Islamist subversives carried out an action that has engulfed the forces of the United States in two agonizing wars, for which Washington has never succeeded in framing a plausible rationale. American leadership has committed the country to victory in Iraq and Afghanistan, without providing a straight answer on what "victory" means. The 428 pages of *The 9/11 Commission Report* (publication date unspecified) are expended on an exhaustive review of security procedure, a few pages of platitudes about moral leadership and a better future, and some stern condemnation of reactionary Arab regimes, misdirected Muslim charity, intolerant elements in Islam, and terrorists who have nothing to offer but "visions of violence and death".

The report implies failure by Washington to communicate the virtues of American policy, but evades a net assessment. Neither government nor mainstream media have floated the presumptuous suggestion that maybe the policy is defective. Page 362 of the report is categorical on this point: The allegation that America is the font of all evil "is not a position with which Americans can bargain or negotiate."

It is essential to eliminate subversive gangs, but not by going to war against the countries where they happen to operate. The orientation of the future governments of Afghanistan and Iraq is a mystery, but the enormity of American policy for the Middle East is a known. It is misdirected, incoherent, and unrealistic: misdirected in trying to wage "war" against a strategy – "terrorism" – and killing innocent civilians wholesale in the process; incoherent in that it is pursuing alliance with states on both sides of the elemental conflict of interest in Palestine – a policy that, as Britain demonstrated during World War I, requires regular resort to hypocrisy; unrealistic because Washington is clinging to the status quo in a region where the status quo is doomed.

Andrew Bacevich has precisely diagnosed America's hypertrophied military structure in the Middle East as the proximate cause of the 9/11 tragedy. He cites one of Rumsfeld's fallacies (changing the way Americans live is unacceptable, so Americans will change the way Muslims live) to explain why the "global war on terrorism" is a failure. Individuals can be eliminated, but not mass movements. Middle Eastern dictators have tried to consolidate their autocracies by jumping on America's jerry-built bandwagon. The policy that conceived it derived from the worst possible provenance – a combine of abysmal ignorance, venal opportunism, and supreme self-assurance. Current example: Washington has seemed oblivious to the fact that its support for the moldering Fatah wing of the Palestine Authority is the political kiss of death.

Washington's certitude rings false in a region whose future is obscure. Middle Eastern society is dysfunctional. Its public opinion is anti-American. The Arab-Israeli confrontation is deadlocked. The only escape lies in according the Middle Easterners the same hazardous right of self-determination the Americans assumed in 1776. Brian Urquhart nailed America's mistake: It doesn't need a bigger army; it needs a smaller foreign policy.

Militarization of Political Issues

Over the past fifty years, American foreign policy has shifted from conciliation toward coercion. This trend was accelerated in 1990 when the Soviet Union collapsed, leaving the United States as the lone superstate, vulnerable to the corruptive influence of too much power. Washington has applied force to problems not susceptible to a military solution (notably anti-Americanism), and the Department of Defense has usurped the normal responsibilities of the Department of State.

Under the Eisenhower Doctrine of 1957, Washington tried and failed to exclude Soviet influence from the region by feeble military gestures (Chapter 8). By the 1970's, American forces had access to the Incirlik air base in Turkey, a naval base in Bahrain, and air bases in Oman.

It had also acquired from the UK proprietary rights to the central feature of the British Indian Ocean Territory, the atoll of Diego Garcia, conveniently located in the Indian Ocean 2000 miles south of the Arabian Peninsula – out of the path of monsoons, remote enough from Asia and Africa to allow unchallenged exploitation, but close enough for basing air and naval units for emergency deployment in the Middle East and South Asia. David Vine's *Island of Shame* (reviewed by Jonathan Freedland in the 5/28/09 *New York Review of Books*) deplores the unceremonious expulsion of the natives to Mauritius in the purported interests of military security. The US has converted the ten-square-mile atoll to an air base from which bombing raids have been staged against targets in Iraq and Afghanistan.

In the late 1970's, America created the Rapid Deployment Force (RDF). In 1980, the RDF was assigned a specific task by the Carter Doctrine: Any attempt by any hostile power to cut off the flow of oil from the Persian Gulf would be repelled by any means necessary. Some years later, Washington divided the planet into five military commands: NORTHCOM, SOUTHCOM, PACOM, EUCOM, and CENTCOM. CENTCOM, successor to the RDF, was assigned responsibility for security in Egypt, Sudan, and southwest Asia (except Turkey, Israel, and the three states of the south

Caucasus, which fell under EUCOM). Its commander had become the most powerful American official abroad. It had two headquarters, one in Tampa, one in Qatar.

Kemp and Harkavi report that American operations against Iraq in 1991 depended heavily on GCC ports, on eleven air bases built in the Arabian Peninsula by the US, on the airports of Dhahran and Riyadh, and on two pre-position bases in Oman. After Gulf War I, Washington took steps to integrate Saudi Arabia and the five Gulf states into its Middle East security structure. Arms were pre-positioned in Qatar and Kuwait. American naval units in Middle Eastern waters were designated the Fifth Fleet, based in Bahrain. By 2004, America had 480,000 soldiers on active duty, of whom 250,000 were sited overseas on 702 bases in 130 countries. 180,000 were deployed in and around Iraq, including a small mission to Georgia. America operated bases in eight Middle Eastern states, two east African states, two Central Asian states, and Diego Garcia. It had conducted operations in those states, as well as Egypt, Georgia, Azerbaijan, Tajikistan, and Kyrgyzstan. The world's leading maritime power had now become the leading land power in the center of the "world island".

America's and Israel's burgeoning militance had manifested itself in myriad ways:

1. Exploitation of UN sanctions and inspection regimes in Iraq, of the No-Fly Zones, and of the two Gulf wars for parochial intelligence acquisition and to wreak devastation that would snuff out Iraq as a modern state and leave it dependent on foreign aid for years to come.

2. Exploitation of Al Qa'idah's attacks of September 11, 2001, for partisan political advantage, particularly by whipping up the American reaction from shock to bellicosity ("Bring 'em on").

3. Expansion of the Pentagon's authority to conduct clandestine operations abroad, via the secret Strategic Support Branch in DIA (the Defense Intelligence Agency) and the Special Operations Command (SOCOM) in Tampa, which directed the supersecret Joint Special Operations Command at Fort Bragg, North Carolina, a combined operation of army, navy, and air force. SOCOM's commander, a four-star general, was commander-in-chief of the war on terrorism. By one account, the Special Forces had become the President's "private army".

4. Unprecedented (short of World War II) expenditures on the armed forces. In 2008, per *TomDispatch,* the United States (with 30 percent of the world's GDP) had an annual military budget approximating 540 billion dollars, plus an additional 170 billion

dollars to finance the wars in Afghanistan and Iraq. US military expenditures came to over half the global total, which approached a trillion dollars a year. In 2009 Secretary of Defense Gates wrote that the US Navy was bigger than the thirteen next biggest navies combined. The US budget was running a staggering deficit, but its military component was sacrosanct.

5. Resort to discretionary war in Iraq, for mysterious motives, and prosecution of that war in Fallujah and elsewhere by scorched-earth strategy inimical to the professed objective of winning over the Iraqi people. Once Washington had fixed on liberation as its objective in Iraq, occupation became indefensible; one is the antithesis of the other. If the American forces stay on, the liberation argument is exploded. If the forces leave, the justification for the invasion will stand or fall on subsequent events beyond Washington's control.

6. Detention and manhandling of "terrorist" suspects in ways foreign to The Hague and Geneva Conventions, supplemented by "extraordinary rendition" of special cases for interrogation by allied regimes that are even less inhibited by international law. Disinterest in counting casualties inflicted on Afghans and Iraqis.

7. Absence of any measured comparison of the relative cost in money and lives between trying to assure access to oil by force, and relying on the world market – as other states do.

8. Deployment of Iraqi Shiites and Kurds against Sunni resisters – exacerbating the risk of civil war. In 2005 the Interim Government sent hundreds of Kurdish militiamen into Mawsil to enforce election security.

9. Resort to lethal new weapons: cluster bombs, "smart bombs", "bunkerbusters", depleted uranium shells, DIME, white phosphorus, and hunter-killer drone aircraft, the ultimate in riskless killing. The 5/10/09 broadcast of CBS's "Sixty Minutes" featured declassified data and pictures on a Nevada air base that controls the operations of Reaper and Predator drones against targets in Iraq and Afghanistan. This conversion of the United States to a theater in these two Asian wars might in the minds of some adversaries legitimate retaliatory action against sites in the United States.

10. Visiting military destruction on countries in dire need of economic, social, and ecological therapy.

11. Reported provision of funds for construction of an Azerbaijani navy on the Caspian Sea.

12. According to the *Times* of 10/28/08, the US and other governments are developing a legal doctrine – cited by Israel for its anti-hijacking operation at Entebbe in 1976 – that Article 51 of the UN Charter justifies acts of self-defense in countries with which the active party is not at war.
13. Conducting abductions and assassinations in neutral countries: *The Nation*, 12/21/09, Jeremy Scahill.
14. Enlisting the services of private "contractors" in sensitive military operations: NPR, 12/15/09, "Fresh Air", Jeremy Scahill.
15. America's "informal national security elite", founded by Paul Nitze and James Forrestal, had fostered an atmosphere of permanent crisis, and weakened the role of Congress in declarations of war: *New York Review of Books*, 12/17/09, Brian Urquhart; *The Limits of Power*, Andrew Bacevich.

Unilateralism

Washington has periodically arrogated to itself the right to act without consultation with the international community, or consideration of the legitimate interests of affected states. American troops were deployed to Saudi Arabia in 1990 reportedly without UN authorization. America's "strategic presence" in the Middle East was established in consultation with no one but Downing Street. America and Britain set up the No-Fly Zones, and bombed Iraqi targets in and around them, without UN concurrence.

Initiatives of the Bush 43 administration revealed an abiding suspicion of international organization (including the United Nations, a triumph of American diplomacy). Washington's blanket denunciation of Iraq, Iran, and North Korea, in the absence of evidence of collusion among them, closed the door to diplomacy, affronted European allies, and exacerbated anti-Americanism. America invaded Iraq in violation of the UN Charter, which bans resort to arms except in self-defense or with Security Council authorization. Once there, it issued a flurry of decrees that violated "occupation law" prescribed by The Hague and Geneva Conventions. *Times* columnist Paul Krugman concluded that, in the absence of any relevant congressional law or Presidential directive setting up the Coalition Provisional Authority in Iraq, that country had become the President's personal fiefdom (like the Belgian Congo for King Leopold?). Washington seemed to visualize itself as the sole guarantor of Gulf security.

All these postures reflected America's unique relationship with Israel, generally in isolation from America's other allies – as exemplified time after time when those two states voted virtually alone in UN councils (Chapter 13), in 1973 when Portugal was the only European state to provide landing rights for America's emergency airlift, and in 2004 when the ICJ voted 14-1(US) that the Security Barrier Israel was building in Occupied Palestine was illegal.

Consolidation of American hegemony in Iraq, wrote Jonathan Schell, would be the start of a "planetary coup d'etat."

In *The New York Review* of 7/16/09, Robert Skidelsky's review of Martin Wolf's *Fixing Global Finance* pointed out that the linkage of East Asian currencies to the dollar had avoided global deflation and enabled the US to finance deployment of its forces overseas by the simple device of printing money, but had created macroeconomic imbalances that could be corrected only by American renunciation of its exclusive "mission" to insure global security, in favor of sharing that responsibility with other powers.

Taking Sides

In dealing with the protean Middle East, America has persisted in the amateurish approach of classifying regimes and factions as friends or enemies, and then plunging into the fray on the side of the "friends". In arranging support for Saudi security, Roosevelt foreshadowed the special relationship with Israel. Truman established it. Since then it has dictated the overall policy of every administration but Eisenhower's. For every other President, Israeli interests have been identified with American interests – if not given precedence. The consequences have been costly to the national interest of the US. They are a standing threat to the interests of the people of Israel.

Even Eisenhower ousted an elected Iranian Prime Minister, and backed a failed coup in Syria. Johnson supported Israeli expansionism and tried to oust Nasir. Nixon gave free rein to Kissinger, who used it to Israel's advantage against Egypt. Carter stood ready to defend the Gulf states against all comers, and served Israel's interests in occupied Palestine. Reagan presumed to defend the Saudi regime even against domestic opposition, sided with Israel against Lebanon and Syria, and backed Iraq against Iran. Bush 41 expelled Iraq from Kuwait and ignited an ethnic brush fire in Iraq. Clinton proposed to "contain" Iraq and Iran simultaneously.

Bush 43 proclaimed "with us or against us," maintained diplomatic and economic sanctions against recalcitrant regimes, favored regime change in Iraq, Iran, and Syria, and introduced a faith-based note that indulged Israel and undermined America's hallowed separation of church and state. The allusion in his "National Security Strategy" to "a battle for the future of the Muslim World" implied overweening American intent to determine the outcome of said battle. After the Turkish Parliament denied permission for American troops to transit Turkish territory, his administration withdrew a pending aid offer.

Even levelheaded Obama gave free rein to pro-Israel Vice President Biden (who warned the Lebanese that, if the anti-West faction won the June 2009 election, they would take a cut in US aid), and embraced Bush 43's problematic war in Afghanistan. Obama's initiatives have been obfuscated by an inclination for ambivalence: In Afghanistan, he opted for an increase in the troop level, but appeared to nullify that decision by setting an arbitrary date for withdrawal; on Iranian sanctions, he simultaneously warned China of the risk of preemptive attack by Israel, and allowed mention of his reliance on his own ability to dissuade Israel from attacking: *Times*, 2/11/10.

Taking sides in foreign conflicts is a treacherous practice:

1. Economic sanctions against a country are more likely to punish its hapless citizens than the regime that dictates their circumstances.
2. Contrivances like Dual Containment and third-party embargoes (ILSA) invite exploitation by foreign companies at the expense of American competitors.
3. Hostile rhetoric and policy reinforce hard-line factions in the target country, at the expense of moderates.
4. Taking sides in internal conflicts is particularly risky. The intervention in Lebanon in 1983 took American lives to no purpose.
5. American opposition to nuclear proliferation sounds reasonable enough, but it ignores the inevitability of technological advance, and it sidesteps the ethical sword of Damocles – the responsibility on America, as the abettor and guarantor of Israel's nuclear monopoly, to insure that it is never implemented. More immediately, Washington should stiffen its opposition toward the possibility of Israeli preemption against nuclear installations in Iran – or Iranian preemption against Israel.
6. Washington likes to rest on the laurels of its policy of reward: security guarantees for Iraq, Jordan, Saudi Arabia, and the Gulf states; financial subsidies for Jordan, Egypt, Turkey, Georgia, and the tamer wing of the Palestine Authority. The arrangement with Saudi Arabia entails the added benefit of massive Saudi investment in American banks and stocks. In the perspective of history,

however, all contemporary regimes and some of the countries they govern are ephemeral artifacts of recent circumstance. American policies were undone by the unexpected switches of Iran and Iraq from ally to enemy.

Washington would better serve the national interest if it took a longer view, reduced its involvement in the minutiae of Middle Eastern rivalries, and recognized that resistance to American policies is not automatically reprehensible. The surest ally is the regime loyal to the legitimate interests of its own country, not those of the superpower.

Pontification

The yawning gap between American preachment and American performance in Iraq was blatantly apparent to most Arabs, if not most Americans. Cynicalized by their experience with British imperialism, few Iraqis swallowed the gushing of American neoconservatives that the invasion was motivated by "enlightened altruism". No amount of saccharine propaganda will advance the American cause. The best hope of propagating American values is by putting them into practice – an innovation not lately tried in the Middle East:

Misrepresentation - Early in the Iraqi campaign, Bush stated that the weapons of mass destruction had been found. That allegation was exploded by the admission of Deputy Secretary of Defense Wolfowitz that "we settled on [WMD's] as the one issue that everyone could agree on…" Bush's prediction that "a free and self-governing Iraq [would] deny terrorism a base…" clashed with evidence that the invasion had sparked Islamist recruitment, and with Iraq's failure to date to attain self-government.

Cheney proclaimed alliance between Al Qaʻidah and the Saddam regime – a myth exposed by the report of the 9/11 Commission.

Double Standard - American Middle East policies often fail the test of consistency:

- Condemnation of factional "terrorism", while practicing state "terrorism", notably by the practice of rendition.
- Sponsorship of a Kurdish entity in Iraq, but tolerance of repression of Kurds in Turkey.
- Condemnation of Iraqi, Syrian, and Palestinian violations of UN resolutions, but acquiescence in Israeli violations.
- Advocacy of restraint in the Arab-Israeli conflict, but provision of arms to both sides (in accordance with a ratio that preserves Israel's military preeminence).

- Disregard for Israeli rejection of UN authority over Occupied Palestine (on the dubious grounds that The Hague and Geneva Conventions do not apply because the issue of post-mandate sovereignty was never resolved, and consequently that the territories are not "occupied"), even though the legitimacy of the Israeli state is based on the UNGA's Partition Resolution of 1947.
- Transparent switch from support for the Iranian claim to the three islets in the Strait of Hormuz, to support for the UAE claim after the fall of the Shah.
- As Stephen Zunes has pointed out, switch from support for the Iranian monarchy's nuclear program, to opposition to the nuclear program of the Islamic Republic.
- Pressure on Syria to forego development of missiles of a category already in the arsenals of Turkey and Israel.
- Condemnation of Syria's semi-consensual influence in Lebanon, but acquiescence in Israel's forty-year occupation of Syrian and Palestinian territory.
- Holding out against an ICJ majority of 14-1 condemning the punitive and expansionist route of Israel's Security Barrier.
- Speaking for the country that had just conquered Iraq, Secretary of State Powell condemned the Iraqi opposition as thugs "who respect only force."
- Acquiescence in Israeli use of force to take over Palestine, but condemnation of Palestinian use of force to recover Palestine.
- Endorsing Israel's right to acquire arms, but collaborating with Israel's arms blockades against Gaza, which under international law is an independent entity with the same right as Israel to act in its own defense, and against Hizballah, which is a de facto arm of the sovereign state of Lebanon.

"Democratization" - After the WMD justification for invasion had lost traction, Washington fixed on democracy as its guiding star – despite Bush 43's faith-based approach to policy, Washington's habitual preference for pliable autocracies, the imperious management style of its representatives in Iraq, and its phobia against any agency, democratic or not, that threatens Israel:

- Closure of contentious Iraqi newspapers.
- Cancellation of an election in Najaf for fear of a SCIRI victory.
- Effort, frustrated by Sistani, to select a national assembly by appointment, rather than election.
- Manipulation of the Iraqi electoral structure to inhibit the emergence of a Shiite theocracy.

- Trying to sell the theses that Iraq was the site of the "first democracy-building project" in the Arab World, that this success would energize reformers across the region, and that its (American-picked) interim prime minister had taken the "constitutional road to power."
- Authorizing Iraq's electoral commission to disqualify uncongenial parties.
- Granting foreign contractors immunity from Iraqi law.
- Labeling as "democratic" Iraq's January 2005 elections, which had been impaired by the security requirement to withhold the names of the several thousand candidates until three days before the voting, which were dominated by two ethnic groups – Shia and Kurds, and which allegedly awarded the Kurds a disproportionate share of seats. Arab Human Development Report Number Three charged that America and Israel have impeded progress toward democracy in Occupied Palestine and Iraq.
- Rejecting the unwelcome results of the Palestinian elections of 2006.

Unification Versus Segmentation

On the road to economic development and civil order, the Middle East has fallen far behind. The historical record affirms that the primary obstacle to progress is factionalism. The indicated therapy is unification. This approach is condemned by a powerful array of vested interests – residuals of Western imperialism: archaic regimes, absorbed in insuring their own survival; fossilized ethnicities, desperately resisting inundation by the tides of social evolution; oil states intent on channeling their adventitious bounty into incongruous skyscrapers and artificial tourist attractions – instead of the economic development of the region.

Factionalism has been relentlessly promoted by Western powers for opportunistic reasons: competition for economic monopoly or strategic advantage; shameless bidding for the Zionist vote. Result: a heavy toll of backwardness, impoverishment, humiliation, and conflict on the helpless residents of the Middle East.

The United States has taken up where the Europeans left off. However diverse its policies, they have converged in their commitment to segmentation: patronizing ministates; denying Israeli racism; condoning Israeli exclusion of non-Jews from its power structure; opposing Arab Nationalism; opposing Islamism; expelling Iraq from Kuwait; obliterating central government in Iraq; supporting Kurdish autonomy in Iraq; colluding with Sunnis against Shiites; opposing reunification of Syria and Lebanon; promoting the factional division of Lebanon; compounding the British partition of its Palestine mandate (into Palestine and Jordan) by promoting further partition of the Palestinian remnant into two ethnic states.

The Americans' dedication to regional disunity is imposed by their commitment to the survival of a Jewish state, but it affords them the side benefit of perpetuating the market for arms sales to the farrago of rival regimes. In effect, America is conspiring against the people of the Middle East.

Since this reality is indefensible, Washington is reduced to peddling the lame surmise that the Middle East is different, that it is somehow unqualified to enjoy the benefits of regional coordination, that fragmentation is its destiny. This argument leads to the arbitrary classification of separatist elements as good, unionist as bad. Once the bad are eliminated, we are told, peace and prosperity will prevail. American media have signed on to the project by dismissing Arab union as a "leftist ideology".

Cowed by the abject collapses of Baathism and Nasirism in the 1960's (Chapter 14), most Middle Eastern regimes are opportunistically aligned with American neoimperialism in their opposition to Arab union – and to each other. As a non-Arab contestant for a place in the Arab World, Israel has three automatic strategies: 1) fostering Arab division, such as the split between Syria and Lebanon, and the campaign for the tripartition of Iraq; 2) exploiting Arab division, as by Israel's unwritten security guarantee to the Hashemite monarchy in Jordan; 3) alliance with the strongest possible combination of non-Arab neighbors (monarchist Iran, Turkey, the Kurds). America has automatically espoused this same divisive strategy, as exemplified by the Security Council's call of September 2004 for withdrawal of Syrian troops from Lebanon.

Separatism is a prescription for continued war. The people of the Middle East are still too disunited and disempowered to redirect their leaders, but millions of them sense that the present configuration of the Middle East is a dysfunctional aberration. They pay covert allegiance to the reformists or revolutionists of their choice. In the new century, the unionist threat comes from the Islamists, who rule Iran, have scored significant electoral gains in Turkey, Iraq, and Occupied Palestine, are on the rise in Syria and Egypt, and are fighting the Americans in Afghanistan.

Islamism and Arab Nationalism are ideological opposites, but they share a common dedication to union and contempt for the status quo. In this regard, they both have history on their side. In 1981, when Israel took out Iraq's nuclear reactor, Saudi Arabia reportedly derived secret satisfaction. In 2006, traditionalist Arab regimes were quick to condemn a Hamas operation against Israel, but equally quick to change their opportunistic tune under public pressure. Likewise in 2006, as cited by Charles Glass, these same regimes set out to criticize Shiite Hizballah for fracturing Middle East peace, until Arab public opinion forced them to join the pro-Hizballah chorus.

Regional consolidation is currently impeded by Western opportunism and Middle Eastern impotence. The region's traditional power centers are handcuffed by internal conflict: in Egypt, between the dictatorship and the reformers; in Iran, between hardline and moderate theocrats, and possibly between theocrats and the Revolutionary Guard; in Iraq, among a medley of rival factions; in Saudi Arabia, between the dynasty and reformers; in Syria, between the Alawite regime and the Sunni populace; in Turkey, between the secularist military and the ethnic parties.

The logic of operating the Middle East as an economic unit was demonstrated in World War II, when the Allies did just that from The Middle East Supply Center in Cairo. The United States, avatar of unity, cannot in fairness deny it to any other region.

The Betrayal of American Values

Linkage with Israel has inflicted material damage on American interests, like the anti-American oil embargo of 1973-74, but it has had graver consequences for American traditions of conciliation and democracy.

Lebanon, 1982-84 - Washington let Israel try to set up a puppet regime in Beirut, and then compounded the error by joining the conflict on the Israeli side.

Iraq, 1991 - But for Israeli encouragement, America would probably have dealt with the Iraqi occupation of Kuwait in more collegial fashion – possibly without resort to military action. Reportedly Saddam had agreed to withdraw before the allied attack.

Dual Containment, 1990's - This strategy served no demonstrable interests except those of Israel.

Iraq, 2003-? - According to former CENTCOM Commander Anthony Zinni, the role of the neoconservatives in pressing for war with Iraq for the benefit of Israel was "the worst-kept secret in Washington." The American invasion did terrible damage to the national interests of Iraq and America. The only beneficiaries were Iran and Israel. Both welcomed the demise of Saddam, but geopolitics will dictate the national interests of Iraq, whatever government emerges. In January 2009 Fareed Zakaria called attention to a reference to Israel, by America's latest Iraqi protégé, Nuri al Maliki, as a "murderous regime".

Iran - One by one, the Israeli-American diarchy has eliminated Israel's most dangerous adversaries: Egypt by the peace treaty of 1979, Baathist Iraq by the invasion of 2003. Israeli Prime Minister Sharon told *The New York Times* he hoped Iran would be America's next target (in view of Iran's emergence as a major contender for regional domination). In 2008 Bush 43 reportedly denied Israel permission to send planes over Iraq to attack Iran's nuclear installations. This welcome epiphany dramatized the guilty secret that the basic interests of Israel and the US are not identical. The US harasses Iran for Israel's benefit, not its own. Israel aside, Washington and Tehran would have important common interests: opposition to the Taliban in Afghanistan; finding the cheapest pipeline route from the Caspian Sea to the Indian Ocean; averting a nuclear exchange in the Middle East.

Palestine, 1945-? - The Europeans are distressed to see Americans making the same mistakes they once made themselves. Britain created the Palestinian imbroglio (Chapter 8), but the United States has perpetuated it by letting Israel call the exclusivist tune. Under Washington's patronage, Labor, Likud, and now Kadima have pursued expansionist policies at the expense of Palestinian rights and Arab-American comity. Most recently, Washington has allowed Israel to conduct another land-grab via the erection of the Security Barrier, and it has bought into the specious claim that Palestinian violence was the product of 'Arafat's vicious leadership, rather than Palestinian desperation.

Hard-line Islamists reject democracy as an affront to God, because it purports to subordinate His will to the caprice of the multitude. Zionism takes a parallel position, insofar as it resorts to the theology that the Zionist State of Israel is beyond debate because it was ordained by God.

Bush was not prepared to cite Israel, or theology, as justification for the invasion of Iraq. Casting around for a plausible rationale, he settled on democracy – apparently not realizing that when democracy does germinate in the Arab World, it will not only confront Israel, it will expose the truth about Israel. If the people of Iraq actually got good government, their neighbors would expect it too. Good government implies democracy and regional unification. Zionist Israel is the antithesis of both. Washington continues to close its eyes to the challenge of directing the people of Israel toward a more viable political system.

For sixty years, US policymakers have been asking the wrong question about events in the Middle East: Is it good for America and Israel? Before events reach critical geopolitical mass, they must ask; Is it good for America? If that question is asked about Israel, the honest answer is that, as long as it epitomizes communalism, it will be a focus of conflict. The only resolution will come from desegregation, hopefully by a peaceful process.

American militarism is being alleviated in one key respect: by private support for new universities in Bahrain, Kuwait, Oman, Qatar, the UAE, and Saudi Arabia (the majestic project for creation of the King 'Abdallah University of Science and Technology: *Wilson Quarterly*, Winter 2010, David Ottaway).

Israel in the Middle East Power Struggle

The unexamined commitment to Israeli security has drawn America into the unnatural role of a direct party to the regional power struggle, while allowing Israel to procrastinate on its geopolitical responsibility to establish a modus vivendi with its neighbors. The Zionists are devoted to their Palestinian home, but if they had the technology, they would tow it out of the Middle East. In the words of one of their officials, "We want to turn our backs on the Arabs." They can talk like this because they live in an American cocoon: Their financial and physical security – even their oil supply – are guaranteed by the United States. Locked in the straitjacket of Zionism, Israel has instinctively adopted policies that preclude integration into the region.

Their patron cannot be so irresponsible. As a superpower, it needs to maintain working relationships with the international community. As a multicultural democracy, it has to listen to its minorities – even to one that insists on a special tie with a far-off country that repudiates democracy. That special tie is reinforced by the fallacy that the interests of patron and protégé are identical – a claim given nationwide currency by the mainstream American press, and by craven politicians in both major American parties. To protect it, Lyndon Johnson covered up the Israeli attack of 1967 on the USS Liberty, the media downplayed the official Israeli role in the Pollard espionage case of 1987, and politicians and media combine to propagate the myth of Israel as "the only democracy in the Middle East."

Israel has long represented itself as America's bastion in the region. The reality is that Israel has been the insuperable obstacle to Arab-American understanding ever since 1945, when Roosevelt failed to convince Ibn Sa'ud to agree to the admission of more Jews to Palestine.

In the United States, the traditional WASP leadership is moving aside to make room for the growing influence of the communities of Hispanic and African origin. Instead of replacing Palestinians with migrant labor from abroad, Jewish Israelis should shed apartheid and gradually make room for the Arabs in their midst. They will have to abandon the false dichotomy between "legitimate" use of force by Israel and "terrorist" use of force by Arabs.

The Nuclear Sword of Damocles

A nuclear power is too dangerous to be invaded. The only state that can safely launch a nuclear strike is one that holds a nuclear monopoly, as the US did in 1945. The *Times* of 7/7/09 quoted Former Secretary McNamara that nuclear weapons have become useless except to deter their use by an enemy. As discussed by Max Rodenbeck in the 1/15/09 *New York Review of Books,* America's postwar adversaries had overriding interest in breaking the American monopoly. America exercized sensible restraint in not trying to preempt their nuclear programs – contrary to the triumphalist mentality that seems to imbue "The National Security Strategy of the United States of America" (Chapter 1).

In any power struggle, the participants are arguably better off with a balance of nuclear capability – nukes for none, or nukes for all. The American-Russian-Chinese precedent suggests that Obama's goal of a nuclear-disarmed world will be extraordinarily hard to achieve. Saudi Arabia was a major financier of the Pakistani nuclear-weapons program: Vali Nasr. On May 21, 2009, the US signed on to provide financing for US companies due to help the UAE develop a nuclear program (putatively minus reprocessing of uranium).

Israel would have been less likely to contemplate a nuclear strike against advancing Egyptian forces in 1973 (Stephen Green, *Living by the Sword*) if Egypt had had the same option. By analogy, the Israeli-Iranian confrontation is more dangerous now, with Israel as the only nuclear power in the region, than it will be if and when Iran becomes the next one.

That is Iran's presumed objective, as reported by Jon Lee Anderson in *The New Yorker* of 4/13/09. Iran has motive – a history of repeated foreign intrusion, Washington's reckless invasion of Iraq, and the American cordon of military installations across the Middle East and Central Asia: Mohsen Milani, *Foreign Affairs,* July 2009. America invaded nukeless Iraq; Israel took out suspected nuclear sites in nukeless Iraq and Syria; Tehran seems to have drawn a cynical conclusion from America's warier handling of nuke-empowered North Korea. Iran is acquiring the capability to build the weapon and the delivery vehicle, the solid-fuel Sajjil rocket: *AP,* 5/20/09. On April 9, 2009, Iran inaugurated at Isfahan its first plant for the manufacture of nuclear fuel. It seems unlikely to be dissuaded by economic sanction, or by the current deployment of anti-missile defenses on US ships and in four Gulf states – whose identities have not been released but, according to a report in the *Times*, are Kuwait, Bahrain, Qatar, and the UAE. Iran is emboldened by the negative attitudes of Russia and China toward sanctions: *TomDispatch*, Dilip Hiro, 1/12/10.

According to one school of thought, Israel and/or America should preempt an Iranian nuclear capability at all costs – even by a nuclear strike if necessary. Here, the analogy with 1945 falls down. Ethical, legal, and geopolitical considerations aside, the only victim of nuclear attack in 1945 was already prostrate from conventional military action. A nuclear attack on Iran would not only skyrocket the cost of oil, it would – as John Duke Anthony pointed out in *Middle East Policy* of Summer 2008 – threaten the existence of at least five states (the Arab shaykhdoms on the Gulf). It would also devastate America's relations with China, which looks to Iran as a major petroleum supplier, and with Russia, which maintains a protective policy toward Iran, as recognized by Steve Coll in the 4/20/09 *New Yorker*.

Most crucial of all, it would rock the geopolitical status of the American superpower as the primary guarantor of the international system (despite the inconsistency of its policies, such as endorsing the Shah's nuclear program [Nader Entessar, *Middle East Policy,* Summer 2009], and tolerating the nuclear capability of India, which has not signed the Nuclear Proliferation Treaty, but seeking to deny that capability to the theocratic regime in Iran, which has signed). In July 2008, Ray McGovern wrote in *Consortium News* (cited by *The Washington Report on Middle East Affairs*) that Admiral Mike Mullen, Chairman of the JCS, had carried a warning to Israel that the American military would not participate in any cover-up of Israeli provocation of war with Iran. In the spring of 2008, Bush 43 deflected an Israeli request for logistic support (bunkerbusters, refueling, right to overfly Iraq) for an air attack on the Iranian nuclear installations at Natanz: *Times,* 7/6/09. But the "Nuclear Posture Review", released by the Obama Administration 4/6/10, warns "outlier" states North Korea and Iran that the US might use the nuclear weapon against any effort to transfer nuclear technology to a "terrorist" organization. Does this warning revoke Washington's keystone commitment to "No First Use"?

In the *New Yorker* of 5/10/10, Connie Bruck suggests a pre-election contrast between Hillary Clinton and Barack Obama on the Iranian-nuclear issue: In reply to a question about the response of a Democratic administration to an Iranian nuclear attack on Israel, Clinton is quoted as proclaiming "We will obliterate them." Obama's answer seems to have been less bombastic—and more Presidential.

Conclusion: Conventional preemption against an Iranian nuclear capability would probably fail, while consolidating the position of the hardliners in Tehran. Israel might perceive advantage in widening the breach between Tehran and Washington, but the consequences of attack would be disastrous for the national interest of the United States.

Israel has the capability to deliver a nuclear weapon by plane (F-4, F-15), submarine, or missile (Jericho II - range 1000 miles; Shavit - range 5000 miles), but American participation in the rise of Israel conveys responsibility for Israel's actions. Humanity's interest in precluding the use of nuclear weapons for all time imposes on Washington a unique obligation to interdict a nuclear strike by Israel – or against Israel.

The Trajectory of Zionism

The Jewish seizure of Palestine from its Arab natives is the latest instance of a recurrent syndrome in Middle Eastern history. The Arab Muslims' conquest of Egypt from its Coptic Christian natives, like the Turkish Muslims' conquest of Anatolia from its Orthodox Christian natives, demonstrated that conquest can endure if it is consolidated by cultural assimilation.

In contrast, the Turkish conquest of the Arab East, never unified by a common language, dissolved in World War I.

In Palestine, Jewish military conquest is complete, but Jewish-Arab assimilation has been stalemated – even in Israel proper – by the ethnocentricity of Zionist doctrine. Loser in the demographic contest, Israel has had to be propped up by Britain and America. This arrangement offers no promise for the longevity of the Jewish state – as the Israeli leadership itself instinctively recognizes in its insistence on retaining ultimate responsibility for national security, and in its innate allergy to foreign security guarantees, such as the American garrison along the Jordan lately proposed by Zbigniew Brzezinski in *Foreign Affairs*.

Israel has been on the rise for sixty years, but in its present exclusivist configuration, it is approaching the peak of the bell curve. In the long term, it is not a viable state.

Belling the Cat

Given America's visceral commitment to the wellbeing of Israel, any direct action against perceived Israeli interests, or in support of regional unification, is inconceivable. In the 2004 Presidential elections, advocates of early withdrawal from Iraq – even after the capture of Israel's archenemy, Saddam – never got past the primaries. President Obama is classified as a liberal, but in foreign policy he has not diverged sharply from his predecessor. Most members of his foreign-policy team seem wedded to continuation of "war" against anti-Americanism, and to automatic support for the basic policies of Zionist Israel.

In current circumstances, pressure on Israel as intense as that imposed by Eisenhower in 1957 is impossible to visualize. However, even myopic politicians are swayed by grim reality. As geopolitical pressures mount, Israel will have to adapt. For some Israelis, adaptation would mean resuscitation of the threadbare two-state solution. It faces inexorable impediments:

- The territories contemplated for the Palestinian state have no geopolitical rationale. They are residues of historical accident.
- In the chaotic Middle East, governments are evanescent. A Zionist Israel could not risk the emergence of a non-Zionist sovereignty west of the Jordan River. Israeli elections never reflect the conciliatory tone of the polls. Even the "withdrawal" from the Gaza Strip was structured to leave Israeli forces in relentless control of its frontiers, its economy, its very existence. If Israel denies independence even to this tiny enclave, the chances of Israeli acceptance of an independent West Bank must be nil.
- Israel's system of proportional representation imposes immense complications on the formation of a government. The settler vote alone is probably enough to block a Palestinian state.
- Palestine is not large or rich enough to support two independent states; it is an economic and hydrologic entity, and should be a political entity.

The only viable solution is a unified Palestine. If unification cannot be promulgated in one fell swoop, it will have to come by infinitesimal degrees. The key is assimilation – political and social. Zionists decry it. Segregationists like Avigdor Lieberman have elaborate plans to block it. Ironically, the seizure of the Occupied Territories in 1967 may prove to have been a giant step toward the outcome segregationists abhor.

Only as Israel edges toward greater equality for its Arab citizens and greater opportunity for its stateless Arab subjects, will Washington be able to anticipate the ultimate pacification of the Middle East.

Meanwhile, Matthew Arnold's dirge for humanity's loss of faith will apply with equal force to the loss of purpose in the Middle East:

> And we are here as on a darkling plain...
> Where ignorant armies clash by night.

INDEX

C

Sultans, Ottoman (1703 – 1922)

1703-30 — Ahmed III

1730-54 — Mahmud I

1754-57 — Osman III

1757-74 — Mustafa III

1774-89 — Abdulhamid I

1789-1807 — Selim III

1807-08 — Mustafa IV

1808-39 — Mahmud II

1839-61 — Abdulmecid I

1861-76 — Abdulaziz I

1876-1909 — Abdulhamid II

1909-18 — Mehmed V

1918-22 — Mehmed VI

Shahs, Iranian (1779 – 1979)

1779-97 — Agha Muhammad

1797-1834 — Fath Ali

1834-48 — Muhammad

1848-96 — Naser od-Din

1896-1907 — Mozaffar od-Din

1907-09 — Mohammed Ali

1909-25 — Ahmad Mirza

1925-41 — Reza Pahlavi

1941-79 — Mohammed Reza Pahlavi

Rulers, Egypt (1798 – 2010)

(1798-1805 — French occupation)

1805-41 — Muhammad Ali Basha (by fiat of Ottoman Sultan Selim III)

1841-48 — Muhammad Ali Basha (now designated hereditary ruler)

1848 — Ibrahim Basha

1848-54 — Abbas I Basha

1854-63 — Sa'id Basha

1863-67 — Isma'il Basha

1867-79 — Khedive Isma'il (new designation by Sultan Abdulaziz I)

1879-92 — Khedive Muhammad Tawfiq_

(1892-1952 — British forces held de facto control)

1892-1914 — Khedive 'Abbas Hilmi II

(1914-1922 — UK declared Egypt a protectorate)

1922-36 — King Fu'ad I

1936-52 — King Farouk (Faruq)

1952-56 — RCC

1956-70 — President Jamal 'Abd al Nasir

1970-81 — President Anwar Sadat

1981-2011 — President Husni Mubarak

2011 — Supreme Council of the Armed Forces